# Spain

**Second edition 2008**

Guy Hobbs

Revised by Heleina Postings

## crimson

Published by Crimson Publishing, 2008
www.crimsonpublishing.com

4501 Forbes Blvd., Suite 200, Lanham MD 20706

Westminster House, Kew Road, Richmond, Surrey TW9 2ND

Distributed in North America by National Book Network
www.nbnbooks.com

Distributed in the UK by Portfolio Books
www.portfoliobooks.com

ISBN 978 1 85458 430 4
Printed and bound in China by Everbest Printing Co. Ltd

As the second edition of *Live and Work in Spain* goes to press, public interest in moving abroad remains at an all-time high. A recent BBC survey found that 50% more people are now considering moving abroad than ever before, and crucially, showed that emigration now holds a strong appeal for the young – 18–25-year-olds were the most likely to want to get out of the UK for good.

Is it surprising that it's not just retirees who are heading out in search of new lives? As the cost of living in Britain continues to rise compared with that of our continental counterparts, Europe provides the perfect alternative. Spain, in particular, promises a particularly hefty slice of the good life – property prices, though slowly rising, remain fairly low, the climate is hospitable all year round, and the pace of life outside the buzzing metropolises of Madrid and Barcelona is still refreshingly leisurely.

Add to this better health services and lower taxes, and it's no wonder that Spain is the top destination for UK émigrés. According to a recent survey, more than half a million people have bought a property abroad and 41% of those have chosen Spain as the site of their new life.

Long one of the UK's most popular holiday destinations, Spain offers something for everyone, and as Spanish tourism has evolved to meet the demands of savvy 21st-century travellers, a wider world of opportunities has been thrust into the limelight. Visitors to Spain are no longer simply lazing on the country's magnificent beaches; they are taking city breaks, spa breaks and walking holidays; they are visiting vineyards and art galleries and staying in mountain lodges, on working farms and in converted monasteries. Similarly, those settling in Spain are no longer looking for 'Blackpool with tapas', they are exploring new regions – living in tumbledown fincas and enjoying the breathtaking views of Spain's fabulously diverse countryside; or finding a studio in the electrically hip *Barri Gotic* in Barcelona and living the whirlwind existence of Spain's most vibrant and cosmopolitan city. Whatever you are looking for, you can find it somewhere among Spain's 17 uniquely different autonomous regions.

As Spain's popularity has increased, the dream of making a new life there has become a far more achievable proposition. This is partly due to the effects of the low-cost flight revolution. In 2003, Ryanair flew to Spain from the UK for the first time. By 2005 it was flying 5.5 million people to a range of new destinations, and since then it has added new low-cost routes to Seville and Murcia in the south. In 2008, it will expand its route further, making it possible to fly to Alicante and Girona from Liverpool, Birmingham and Durham. As a result, travelling back and forth to Spain can now often be quicker and cheaper than travelling between UK destinations. Some people are even choosing to spend their weekends in Spain and commute to work in the UK during the week. Any worries you may have had about losing touch with family and friends can be forgotten, in fact you can expect the opposite problem – when you're settled in your new villa, sipping Sangria while overlooking the sea, you may not be able to get rid of them!

Prohibitively high house prices in the UK have also made Spain a more practical country to live in and these days even first time buyers are turning their backs on the UK and getting on the first rung of the property ladder in Spain. The average cost of a property in Spain is just £185,000, and for the money that might buy you a cramped apartment in London or Manchester you can bag yourself a spacious villa on one of the costas or a large, centrally-located flat in a mid-size city. The area stretching from Denia to Murcia is a particular favourite, as are the Canary and Balearic islands. After 10 years of price rises, it seems that the market in these areas might be flattening out, and there are some real bargains to be found. See Chapter 3, *Setting up home,* for advice that will help you to navigate the many options available.

For some the prospect of a better lifestyle may be a sufficient attraction, and it is true that most people who relocate to Spain do not do so to further their careers. As a rule, people in Spain work to live, rather than the other way round. However, there are signs that this may be beginning to change, with a recent influx of immigrants and a hefty 3% drop in the unemployment rate, which had historically hovered at around the 11% mark. Spain's economy is growing by an impressive 3% each year, and the opportunities for work are definitely there if you know where to look. For example, there is an enormous demand for trained professionals in Spain. The pace of economic development has led to shortages of skills in many white-collar positions and Spanish universities can barely keep up with the country's demand for 21st-century professionals. There is also a dearth of 'international' business professionals in Spain, caused in part by the relative lack of high-level fluent English speakers. Those who learn Spanish to a good level should find a range of opportunities available to them. Salaries are at least 8% higher than they are in neighbouring France – and the gap grows as you climb the corporate ladder. Impressive benefits packages are less common in Spain than in other countries, so salaries are higher to compensate.

Those looking for casual employment possibilities will find that during the tourist season they exist in abundance, from bar and hotel work to crewing yachts and teaching English. Information and advice on finding a variety of jobs is given in Chapter 6, *Working in Spain.*

Once you have decided to make the move to Spain, this book will act as your reference manual, helping you steer a smoother and more informed path through the essential preparations. It provides information needed before, during and after the move – from taking your pets and obtaining a residence card, to understanding the education system and handling the routine matters of day-to-day existence.

The book is divided into two sections: Living in Spain and Working in Spain, which between them cover all areas of moving abroad, including Spanish banking, arranging a mortgage for Spanish property, employment regulations, information on retiring to Spain, and advice and ideas for setting up a small business. Social and cultural aspects are also covered, with sections on the aesthetics of Spanish social life, language, education and culture. A variety of people who have made the move to Spain have been canvassed in the researching of this book and their stories, good and bad, frustrating and inspiring, are interspersed with the text to give you a more personal view on starting a new life in the new Europe. All of them have at times been bewildered by their new life, but they all agree on one thing – they don't for a moment regret their decision to move to Spain. We hope that you will find this book an essential part of your preparations, and that it will help you get the most from the potentially enriching and rewarding experience of living and working in a foreign culture.

**Guy Hobbs and Heleina Postings**
June 2008

# Acknowledgements

The author would like to thank the following people and organisations, in no particular order, for their invaluable help in compiling this book: Anna Henri of www.spanishforum.org, The Labour and Social Affairs Office of the Spanish Embassy in London, Chantal Becker-Cid, a lawyer with offices in Madrid and Marbella, Pilar Solana Elorza, coordinator of the *Ventanilla Unica Empresarial* in Madrid, *TurEspaña* – the Spanish National Tourist Office, Colin Richardson of *The Spanish Bookshop*, *Invest In S*pain at the Spanish Embassy Office for Economic and Commercial Affairs in London, UK Trade and Investment in Madrid, Jos Arensen of Start With Us, and *Age Concern España*. Dan Boothby's *Buying a House in Spain* has proved an invaluable source for the chapter on setting up home.

Thank you also to all those who provided information and the fruits of their own experience of living, working and travelling in Spain, especially: Stuart Anderson, Liz Arthur, Peter Deth, Philippe Guémené, Michael and Vivian Harvey, Louis Henderson, Rita Hillen, Peter Lytton Cobbold, Joanna Mudie, Nancy Ryan, Hal Shaw, Peter Siderman, Graham Smith, Richard Spellman, Tim Stonebridge, Martine de Volder, Lindy Walsh, David Burton, Marina Smith, Dan Hancox, Kerry Hughes and Amishi Patel.

Thanks to all those who kindly allowed the use of their photographs in this book. For a fill list of photo credits, see page 466.

# Contents

## Daily Life 161

## Working in Spain 227

## Starting a business in Spain 299

## Running a business in Spain 349

# Contents

# How to use this book

## Telephone numbers:

Please note that the telephone numbers in this book are written as needed to call that number from inside the same country. To call these numbers from outside the country you will need to know the relevant international access code; these are currently 00 from the UK and Spain and Portugal and 011 from the USA.

Spanish area telephone codes are given on p178.

**To call Spain:** dial the international access code +34 and the number given in this book minus the first 0.

**To call the UK from Spain:** dial the international access code then +44 then the number minus the first 0.

**To call the USA from Spain:** dial the international access code +1 then the complete number as given in this book.

## Exchange rates:

| Euro € | British pound £ | US dollar $ | Australian dollar A$ |
|---|---|---|---|
| €1 | £0.79 | $1.55 | A$1.63 |
| €10 | £7.90 | $15.50 | A$16.25 |
| €20 | £15.80 | $31 | A$32.50 |
| €50 | £39.50 | $77.60 | A$81.30 |
| €100 | £79 | $155.30 | A$162.50 |
| €1,000 | £790 | $1,553 | A$1,625 |

At time of press

# Why Live & Work in Spain?

# ■ ABOUT SPAIN

**SPAIN FACTS**

| | |
|---|---|
| **Capital:** | Madrid |
| **Currency:** | Euro |
| **Population:** | 40.4 million |
| **Time zone:** | GMT +1 |
| **GDP:** | $1.109 trillion |

Spain (along with Portugal and the South of France) could now be thought of as the European equivalent of the American sun belt. It has been popular as a holiday destination for northern Europeans since the first charter flights of 1959 opened the floodgates to the Mediterranean Costas (from north to south: the Costa Brava; the Costa Dorada; the Costa del Azahar; the Costa Blanca; the Costa Cálida, the Costa de Almería, the Costa Tropical and the Costa del Sol). Every year, the Spanish tourist trade plays host to a staggering 60 million visitors, 20 million more than Spain's indigenous population. Annually Spain earns around €46 billion from tourism, which employs 1.5 million workers and contributes over 11% to the country's national income.

With this long history of welcoming British visitors, Spain has now become a prime destination for those wishing to start a new life outside the UK. Britons say they prefer the warm weather (which remains the principal attraction for many Britons in Spain). Many who come are nostalgic for holidays spent there, are looking for a change of lifestyle, or simply long for the sun.

For younger people, Spain is also considered a good starting point for those whose international career may subsequently take them further afield and who wish to gain a first experience of living and working abroad. Communications with the rest of the world are relatively straightforward, and Spanish is one of the 'world' languages: a passport to employment and a useful asset as Latin America is liberalised and opens up to trade, as well as being helpful in many other countries around the world.

Younger residents, working in English teaching or tourism – and other related areas where their language and other skills are in demand – cite the way of life and more relaxed social *mores* as their reason for choosing to live in Spain. Festivals and a laid-back enjoyment of life are part of the Spanish way of doing things. Cafés and restaurants are plentiful and cheap, and food and drink are instinctively enjoyed and understood in this country where rural and agricultural roots are still very much in evidence. Outside the cities, local traditions still play an important part in daily life. In both towns and villages, the evening starts with a leisurely stroll through the main streets, where the latest fashions are on display (as in Italy); many Spaniards take a *siesta,* and lunches, even at work, are long and languid.In the towns and cities, and along the coast, nightlife continues into the early hours, one attraction for younger visitors.

The onset of mass tourism inevitably led to the expatriate property-buying boom which began in the 1960s and has been continuing ever since. Places like

Jávea and Altea, whose climate was declared among the healthiest in the world, represent the extreme of expatriate saturation; at least a quarter of their residents are estimated to be British. Other areas are catching up fast and the Costa del Sol, roughly from Málaga to Gibraltar, has firmly established its reputation as a centre of expatriate life, while Marbella is only now beginning to lose its patina of exclusivity and is still popular with the European jet set.

In 2006, there were 274,000 Britons registered as living permanently in Spain, although it is estimated that around 750,000 Brits spend at least a portion of the year there. Of these, the majority live in Andalucía (on the Costas de Almería, Tropical, del Sol and de la Luz), closely followed by Valencia (mostly on the Costa Blanca), the Canaries, the Balearics, Catalonia (especially Barcelona), and Madrid. Alicante and Málaga alone account for 50% of British residents, but the fastest-growing area is Murcia, which opened its doors to 13,300 Britons in 2006. Many have set up businesses catering for their fellow countrymen and women, or have found employment in the tourist industry or with British, American and Spanish firms.

Tourists who visit may choose eventually to make Spain their home or to retire there. Then there is the 'halfway house' of timeshare accommodation, or the current vogue for elderly British tourists-cum-expatriates to spend the winter months in a Spanish resort and avoid the heating bills and cold weather back home. About 400,000 Britons spend the winter in Spain each year, during the so-called 'swallow season'. Over 200,000 of them own property there.

Ciudad de la Artes, Valencia

Away from the tourist areas, Spain's cities have a hip, multicultural vibe

There are social as well as economic consequences of this wave of emigration-cum-tourism, with some expatriates complaining of isolation, difficulties with bureaucracy and poorer quality hospital treatment and social services than they are used to back home. But the British Consulate-General in Madrid reports that there are relatively few problems considering the size of the community. The Spanish have a live-and-let-live attitude and no deep-seated antagonism towards Britons, and on the whole are accepting to expat communities.

More generally, however, Spain has been undergoing a series of radical reforms – both political and economic – bringing it from a dyed-in-the-wool 36-year-old dictatorship which lagged far behind the rest of western Europe (with the exception of neighbouring Portugal) to an increasingly liberal and open society where democracy is firmly established and young people look forward to the future with optimism. It was classed as a developing nation by the United Nations as recently as 1964, but today it is the world's eighth industrial power, and half the jobs created in the EU in the last five years were in Spain. Nowadays, Spain takes its modernity for granted. Government used to be highly centralised, but power has been devolved to the regions, most notably the Basque Country, Catalonia and the Canary Islands.

Spanish people are welcoming. Most have rejected the isolationist attitudes of the past and most young people have no sense of being 'second-best'. They speak more languages and drink more beer and less wine. This cosmopolitan outlook also comes from Spain's history as one of the world's great imperial powers (see below) and its present position within the EU (which it joined in 1986). Events like the 1992 Olympic Games held in Barcelona and Expo '92 in Seville brought Spain to international attention, as have cultural figures such as director Pedro Almodóvar and author Carlos Ruiz Zafón; these are some of the cultural reasons which may also prompt Britons and others to consider moving there.

Other recent economic developments, such as European Monetary Union, followed by the adoption of the Euro currency in 2002 and the ongoing programme of privatisation, have brought a new wave of workers in areas like finance, consultancy, electronics, information technology and industrial design, which have little to do with the service sector and tourism. These are some of the reasons for Spain's booming economy, low inflation and low public sector deficit.

As Spain changes, the kinds of workers and expatriates who move there are changing too. In winter and high summer, expatriates and shorter-term residents continue to be a familiar feature of life along the stretch of the Mediterranean coast from the Costa del Sol to the Costa Brava and the Balearic Islands (Mallorca, Menorca and Ibiza). Elsewhere, Madrid boasts a large expatriate population, as do Barcelona and, to a lesser extent, Valencia and Seville. Students and young people flock to laid-back Santander in the north, and many find themselves staying longer than anticipated. There is a continuing interest in living and working in a country that has much to offer to older and younger residents alike. In the following pages

FACT

■ As Spain changes, the kinds of workers and expatriates who move there are changing too.

you will find an overview of life in Spain, and information about the key issues to be considered when planning a move there.

# ◼ REASONS TO LIVE IN SPAIN

Research commissioned by Parador Properties in 2004 attempted to unravel the mystery of why Britons are escaping to Spain in record numbers. Of those who have bought homes in Spain, the research shows that 65% said that they were attracted by the climate, 45% wanted to spend more time outdoors and 40% were lured by the cheaper cost of living. Overwhelmingly, then, people are seeking a better quality of life from their move to Spain, rather than career advancement or financial gain. But while these may be the factors that lure people to Spain, it is the more subtle elements of the Spanish way of life and culture that prevent them from returning home.

## Climate and health

Spain's climate is certainly a draw, especially for those coming from the dreary and drizzly climes of northern Europe. Spain's climate varies dramatically, but it is possible to enjoy sunshine all year round, especially on the southern Mediterranean coast and in the Canary Islands. The Costa del Sol offers expatriates 3,000 sun hours each year, an enormous benefit for those who enjoy being able to spend time outside. Retirees cite the health advantages of living in Spain, which come from the mild climate and the ability to spend more time being active. This is not just a myth: the Spanish have one of the highest life expectancies in Europe. The World Health Organization recently claimed that the Valencian coastline is one of the healthiest places to live on earth due to its climate, recreational facilities and relaxed way of life.

**FACT**

◼ The Costa del Sol offers expatriates 3,000 sun hours each year, an enormous benefit for those who enjoy being able to spend time outside.

## Lower cost of living

The lower cost of living is also important. Crucially, it is the things that make life more enjoyable that are considerably cheaper: wine, beer, cigarettes, eating out, leisure activities. However, many of life's necessities are not that much cheaper and prices are certainly catching up. For example, house prices in Spain have been rising steadily for years now, becoming restrictively expensive in the bigger cities, although in the past two years prices on the coasts have begun to stagnate or even fall. Estimates suggest that overall the cost of living is around 26% lower than in the UK, but this is set against the fact that salaries are also considerably lower. But as more expats move into the big cities and on to the coasts, inflation is becoming a problem for many locals, some of whom have seen the cost of living rise by 10% per annum in recent years.

Soaking up the sun in Cantabria

## Cheap and plentiful flights

Spain has always been sunnier and cheaper than Britain or USA, so why is it that so many more of us are moving to Spain now? Clearly the country's increasing accessibility is a major factor. Getting to and from Spain has never been easier (see page 466 How to get there), with an increasing number of no-frills carriers offering more regular flights to numerous destinations in Spain. Those who live in Spain or have a second home there travel back and forth from the UK an average of six times a year, something that has only been made possible for the majority by the cheap flight revolution.

## Reduction of red tape for EU members

Equally important is the abolition of a great deal of bureaucratic red tape for those who wish to live and work there. Visitors from Britain and other EU countries do not need a work permit to work in Spain and, under recent regulations, as long as they intend to work or become self-employed. Nor do they need a residence permit (*tarjeta de residencia*), although they must have a valid passport. North Americans considering moving there will have to satisfy a wide range of criteria, which means in practice that getting a job will be much more difficult for them. However, there are still many rules and regulations that British workers need to be aware of, covering everything from equivalence of qualifications and setting up a business to tax and other requirements that are different to those in the UK.

## Enjoy unemployment in the sun

One advantage of the EU for those who may at present be unemployed is that there are provisions for transferring your Jobseeker's Allowance (unemployment benefit) to a specific destination in Spain for up to three months if you are going to look for work there. Low-price winter packages mean that this is a reasonable option (if you have paid your national insurance contributions: this is for 'contribution-based' Jobseeker's Allowance only). A winter spent job-seeking on the Costa del Sol may seem a more attractive option than the same thing in Britain. Some advice: take enough money with you to tide you over if there are problems, and visit your local employment office to make your preparations well in advance. This is a period of jobseeking, not a holiday, and the authorities do not look kindly on those who they feel are abusing the system.

## Easier to buy and sell property

Another distinct advantage of moving to Spain is that over the last few decades the procedures involved in buying and selling property have become better documented, and there are many agencies in the UK that specialise in removals and conveyancing. Nowadays it is probably best to avoid some of the pitfalls simply by consulting one of the reputable relocation agencies or specialists. There are also a number of useful books dealing with the subject, such as the newly updated *Buying a House in Spain* (Crimson Publishing, 2008) by Stuart Anderson and Leaonne Hall. Still, despite the simplification of the procedures, the most common problems are associated with 'the language barrier and property purchases', according to the honorary British Consul in Benidorm, John Seth-Smith.

Another increasingly popular and often very useful option is to consult a *gestor*, a professional consultant who bridges the gap between a layman and a lawyer and who has in-depth knowledge of the country's bureaucracy surrounding issues such as property, mortgages and tax. A gestor's job is basically to fill in forms correctly, and for a relatively reasonable fee he or she will handle all your paperwork for you.

## Strong expatriate community

Other advantages of Spain often cited by emigrants include the fact that there is already an enormous community of foreigners of which they can become a part. On a basic level, the presence of so many expats makes it far easier to adapt, with English-speaking friends, neighbours, clubs and societies all abundant in most areas. This is a particular advantage for retirees with time on their hands, but it is also beneficial for those looking to start a business or become self-employed. You only have to glance at the classifieds of an English language newspaper such as *Sur* or *The Costa Blanca News* to see the plethora of English-speaking plumbers, electricians, translators, hairdressers, satellite television engineers, dog groomers and every other imaginable service. The number of English people emigrating to Spain shows no sign of diminishing so, for the foreseeable future, there will always be a demand for those offering, in English, the kinds of services to be found at home.

## Unspoilt traditional areas

For others the presence of so many British, Dutch and German communities represents a corruption of the uniquely Spanish way of life that they have come to enjoy. Fortunately Spain is two and a half times the size of the UK and has only two-thirds of the population, so there are vast areas of unspoilt beauty away from

**TIP**

■ Consult a *gestor*, a professional consultant who bridges the gap between a layman and a lawyer and who has in-depth knowledge of the country's bureaucracy surrounding issues such as property, mortgages and tax.

the noisy and hectic coastal resorts. Many people consider the attraction of Spain to lie in its more traditional way of life. Emigrants rave about Spanish characteristics such as the lack of violent crime, feeling safe in the streets, the respect that young people show for the elderly, the love of children that the Spanish display, the sense of community and a slower pace of life. Spain has modernised incredibly quickly over the last few decades, yet somehow much of the country has retained strong rural and agricultural roots and the air of a simpler, more relaxed way of life still lingers here. Those with children may relish the chance to bring them up bilingual, and to raise them in a healthier, safer environment where children are made to feel far more welcome and enjoy greater freedom than in northern Europe.

# ■ WORKING IN SPAIN

Most people who relocate to Spain do not do so to further their careers. People in Spain as a rule work to live rather than the other way round, and while career opportunities do exist, they are not as numerous as in Britain or the USA. Unemployment is higher in Spain than in most other EU countries, (currently estimated at around 8.3%). While it is difficult to find a downside to living in Spain in terms of the lifestyle it offers, there are more 'cons' when it comes to working.

## Challenging employment market

Employees who have a specific skill that is not locally available are favoured in the job market. Non-EU job applicants have to be 'very qualified' according to one agency. Despite the increasing presence of American, international and UK-based companies and the burgeoning demand for English language teachers and academic staff, the prospects are not quite so encouraging in skills-oriented fields which will bring you into direct competition with Spanish workers. However, as the Spanish economy expands, demand for skilled professionals is increasing, and there is also a growing need for bilingual businessmen or women as Spanish companies expand into the rest of Europe.

High unemployment means that most general vacancies are likely to be taken by Spaniards. However, even this major disadvantage can be mitigated by the possession of certain skills and qualifications likely to impress potential employers or which enable one to be self-employed.

**FACT**

■ Demand for skilled professionals is increasing, and there is also a growing need for bilingual businessmen or women as Spanish companies expand into the rest of Europe.

## Spanish language skills necessary

A working knowledge of the Spanish language is also essential. One advantage of Spanish is that it is considered one of the easier languages for English speakers to learn. Some knowledge of other Romance languages, French and Italian for example, or Latin, will also help you to recognise many Spanish words. A word of warning, however: many people find that the Spanish they have acquired in a classroom setting needs a lot of polish and practice before it can be truly useful, both because of the raft of vernacular terms in use in everyday Spain, and also the sheer speed at which locals talk here.

Those looking only for casual employment in tourism or in related fields can probably get by without Spanish, as the clientele is likely to be largely British or

English-speaking, although this is more likely to be the case in resorts than in cities – in the latter, employers will often require a good level of spoken Spanish even for relatively simple jobs such as bar or hotel work. English is more widely spoken in Spain than neighbouring Mediterranean countries nowadays, especially in the resorts and among the young (older people are more likely to speak French); but there is still a 'language deficit' which is also one of the principal assets of English-speaking staff seeking employment there. There is also a geographical variation here; it's relatively easy to find an English speaker in the north, and the chances decline as you move south, until you get to Andalucía where English speakers are still something of a rarity among those who are middle-aged or over.

## Casual employment opportunities

There are normally plenty of more 'casual' employment possibilities, from bar work to crewing yachts to selling timeshares, where speaking English may be one of the advantages. Even without a residence or work permit some non-EU jobseekers already living there can find this kind of work. At present, the relatively high pound, and the strength of the UK economy, is favouring the tourist trade with Britain.

## Long working hours

One of the disadvantages of working in Spain is likely to be the relatively long hours, probably far longer than would be considered tolerable in Britain or the USA. This is particularly true of seasonal work, for those running bars or restaurants, or working as employees in them. Those working for Spanish companies may be pleasantly surprised by the long lunch break, although times are changing, and in the last year or so stories have abounded of companies in Madrid and Barcelona abandoning the *siesta* altogether. But in many companies a longer and slower afternoon break lingers on. Remember that Spanish nightlife begins late and usually ends in the small hours in the cities and resorts; days off for seasonal and tourism workers may prove impossible in high season.

# ■ PROS AND CONS OF LIVING IN SPAIN

**Pros:**

- Residence and work procedures are straightforward for EU citizens.
- There are well-established procedures for buying and selling property.
- Property prices are generally lower than in the UK or USA except in the most popular areas, e.g. the Costa del Sol and Madrid and Barcelona.
- Spain is an interesting country with a fascinating history and a vibrant culture.
- The large expatriate population offers employment opportunities for British qualified staff, eg medical or in hospitality, to set up facilities to cater for them.
- Good employment prospects exist for those with the right qualifications in other specialised fields.
- There are plenty of casual jobs in tourism and there is a need for English language teachers.
- The major cities and the most popular resorts aside, you can still live relatively cheaply in Spain (as many retired Britons and 'part-time' residents have found).
- Communications are good and air travel is inexpensive.
- The culture is welcoming to foreign visitors and residents.
- The economy is booming and prospects for the future are good.

**Cons:**

- Spanish and Spanish-speaking applicants will be favoured for most jobs.
- Unemployment is still relatively high compared to the rest of Europe.
- Some property may not be up to UK or US standards.
- Property prices are high in the major cities.
- Older residents in particular may find it difficult to adapt.
- Social services may not be up to British or American standards.
- There is strong competition for jobs at the unskilled level.
- It may be difficult to find long-term work outside tourism.
- Crime rates are quite high on the costas and in some major cities like Barcelona, Seville and Madrid.
- Language can be a barrier in dealing with officialdom and finding work.
- Tax rates at the top level are high.

# ◤ PERSONAL CASE HISTORIES

## *Michael Harvey*

Michael Harvey was a wheat farmer in England for many years before he and his wife, Vivian, decided to move the business out to Spain. In 1981 they bought a farm in rural Andalucía and they have been living there ever since. The uninhabitable farmhouse, or *cortijo* as they are known in Andalucía, and the 70 acres of surrounding farmland were purchased for around £80,000. Nowadays, with a shortage of land in the area, the property is worth about £40,000 an acre. Originally they intended to grow avocadoes, but they have diversified into other areas of farming, as well as running a garden centre, a landscape gardening business and a B&B (www.andalucia.com/gardens/papudo/home.htm). We asked Michael:

### Why did you decide to relocate to Spain?

In 1981 farming in England was going through a bad spell and the government was telling people to diversify. So we did. We diversified out here in Spain. We had visited a cousin in Portugal who had set up a citrus farm – he had some avocado trees, which were huge and falling off with fruit and I was very envious, but land in Portugal was very expensive. My half-sister was working in Sotogrande, so we came out to Spain for a holiday and looked around. I wanted to buy a farm on a hill with lots of water. An English lady showed us lots of farms where plenty of water meant enough for one cow to drink, but then we found this place, which is perfect. There's an underground lake supplied by the river and it's very clean. That is why we bought the farm, we didn't really look in the house – it was uninhabitable.

### How did you finance the move and the renovation of the farm?

When we arrived we had no money, so we had to get a loan and the only way we could get a loan was to form a Spanish company. So we formed an SA (*Sociedad Anónima* – a limited company) and that has been going ever since we started. We secured a Spanish agricultural loan and were able to pay it back over five years. The SA owns everything here and we don't – we are just shareholders, unpaid directors of the company. We are taxed in England on our personal income because we still have a farm there, but here the company puts the tax returns in. This creates a clear distinction between our personal finances and the company's finances.

We have had very little luck with grants. The town council offered us a grant to renovate the house but we never received it. Then, when we started putting in the transformers, water pipes, pumps, greenhouses, etc., we were accepted for an EEC farm improvement grant. But after we had done all of the work they decided that we couldn't have it after all. In Spain they like to tell you what you want to hear and even when something has been agreed, they often go back on it.

### What has been your experience of farming in Spain?

It all started off with a contract to grow camellias for a New Zealand firm who came out to Spain and showed us what to do, but it was a bit of a disaster and the company stopped paying us the rent after six months. So we started selling the camellias and I brought some other plants in from New Zealand. We also bought some babacoas (a type of fruit) and put about 50 plants in. We used to go to the markets selling babacoas and camellias and a few other plants. We went to various local markets on different days of the week. We had to have a plate full of babacoa for them to taste – because they didn't know what it was. At most of these markets you needed a licence to sell, which we didn't have. We asked for a licence, but they said there was no space, so we continued going illegally. There were gypsies who were doing the same thing and they would whistle when the police were coming, giving us warning to follow them around the corner!

### What about the other businesses?

The sales in the nursery soon built up because there was only one other nursery in the area. When we did our own garden we realised how well things grow here and immediately spotted a gap in the market. We were getting seeds and cuttings and introducing new plants that weren't already here. Mostly we grow plants that aren't native, plants that people can't get anywhere else. People tend to come here from all over the Costa del Sol to look for specific plants.

There was a market in Sotogrande on Saturdays and I would take a lot of plants over there, and that was quite good advertising that we are here. The market itself didn't actually pay our time, but it did in terms of the amount of work that it brought in. The B&B is also a good advert for the other side of the business. People come here and they are either looking for a house, or they know someone who is buying a house with a garden that needs work.

We only really get one or two customers a day in the nursery, but they spend around €100 each when they come, which is better for us. Everybody who comes here loves it and it's nice to have people around.

Landscape gardening jobs bring in quite a lot of money as well. It's very efficient for me being a farmer, I don't have to go out and buy plants, and I can just go around the nursery and find everything I need. Most of our customers are people who have just bought new houses and they want the garden prettying up. We have a few Spanish customers, but the majority are English, Dutch, German and Swiss.

### Any regrets about leaving the UK?

Not at all. The place is a paradise now, as a result of lots of hard work. But I enjoy working hard – I couldn't come out to Spain and do nothing. Also, I was fairly bored in England growing wheat and just looking at it all winter. The decision to move out here was not affected by a romantic dream of living abroad, it was a practical business decision and it has been very successful.

# Graham Smith

Graham Smith retired from farming in Scotland at the age of 62 and went in search of warmer climes. He and his wife had travelled frequently to the coastal resort of Benalmádena for the previous 16 years and loved the town and its people, so they decided to move there permanently. But the lifestyle of a retired expat did not live up to Graham's expectations – 'after six months I was bored to tears' – so he decided to buy his own bar. Toni-Lee's Bar and Bistro is now a thriving business catering mainly to the huge community of British expatriates on the Costa del Sol. We asked Graham:

## How did you go about buying your own bar?

Well, this place was advertised in the local paper, so I rang up and came to see the owner. I liked what I saw, came back again and made him an offer, and two days later he accepted. Simple as that. I knew the guy who owned the place, but we still got the *gestoría* to check that everything was OK. The offer was accepted, we paid 10% and when the legal work was all done we paid the rest. You would be a foolish man to buy a bar without having your *gestor* check that all the bills are paid. If you took something on where the bills haven't been paid, then you would be liable for them.

I bought a *traspaso* (leasehold) – I tried to get the freehold, but the guy who owns this place wouldn't sell it. Freeholds are difficult to come by because the landlords aren't keen to sell. They like the bars to change hands every three months or so because they get around 15% of the leasehold money. So if it changes hands three or four times a year, they get a nice quarterly income. The fact that so many people come over here and open up bars without knowing the first thing about running one means that they are on to a nice little earner as the majority will fail very quickly.

## How is the business going and what difficulties have you run into?

I am delighted with they way it is going but we have only been going for a short time. We are now coming to the time of year when it is definitely quieter. One problem with running a bar or hotel in a tourist area is that it is a very seasonal business. November through to February is very quiet, but then it builds up again and takes off until the end of September.

It is also hard to deal with the amount of competition here. Some businesses are killing each other by continually undercutting until they're selling at prices on which they can't make a profit. I would never do that, but what I have got is a beautiful place here, good food and very clean premises. And to be honest we are not struggling. It is difficult to get customers, but once we get them here we keep them. We talk to the residents, we get to know them and we now have a good clientele who will be here all year round.

I believe it takes around two or three years to establish a bar properly. Next year we'll have people who came here this year coming back and so the business will grow that way.

### What advice would you give someone thinking of opening a similar business in Spain?

I think my story is completely different from 90% of people here. Most people come over with anything between £15,000–£25,000, with which you can buy a poorly positioned bar, and they don't have any reserves. What they don't cater for are taxes and the slower months. There are so many things on top. The transfer of the licence is about €600. People don't take all of these things into consideration. Then you've got your stock to buy. It's not cheap to stock a bar, although it's cheaper over here than in the UK. You really do have to consider all of these things.

I also think it is essential for people to learn Spanish before coming over here to start a business. All of our suppliers are Spanish and I find that the Spanish are much easier to deal with and more honest than the British out here. The Spanish will work twice as hard, twice as long for less money – but then again because I have lots of friends here, I have always been directed to the right people.

# Dan Hancox

Dan Hancox, 26, a freelance journalist and writer, moved to southern Spain with his girlfriend in 2006: 'We just got sick of England,' he explains. He got by financially by combining freelance work from home with casual work.

## Did you find enough work to get by?

In the end it worked out fine, but it was nerve-wracking at first, because my Spanish isn't that great. I managed to find work in an Irish pub, though, so I could practice my language while working predominantly with English speakers. I also had some savings to fall back on if things got tough. I think if I was doing it again, I would try to set up something more long-term, or try to find work before I headed over. Having said that, the spontaneity was all part of the adventure, and I don't regret a second of it! In fact, I wish I'd put myself 'out there' a bit more and applied for a job in a Spanish restaurant or bar: I know people who did, and made a lot of Spanish friends that way. Moving abroad is a once-in-a-lifetime experience and you owe it to yourself to take some risks and really make the most of it.

## Were you able to live comfortably in Spain on your wages?

Yes, but I was also lucky in that I had freelance writing work in Britain that I could continue with while I was in Spain, and that, together with my bar job, easily paid the rent, with some money left over for eating out and socialising. When you're earning in pounds and spending in euros things are easy, but we made the decision to live very centrally and we wouldn't have been able to do that on just what I was earning in the bar. Most of the people I met lived out in the suburbs, although Spain is a lot cheaper than Britain for food and drink and no one I worked with ever said they felt really poor, even though we were earning a very low wage by British standards.

## What differences did you find between working casually in Spain and in the UK?

Working in a bar is completely different. In bars or pubs in the UK, you work with set measures, and every drink you sell is logged on the system. In Spain it's much more of a free-for-all, and you can serve customers any way you like. It feels a bit like a constant party at times, and you get very close to the people you work with, although it is very tiring because Spanish licensing laws are more relaxed than ours and at the weekends bars stay open until three or four in the morning; some places only close when the last customer leaves. It's a different experience, and you come back to the UK with fresh eyes. In fact, I can't wait to go back, and I'm currently looking into buying an apartment in Spain!

# David Burton

**David Burton, 33, from Black Mountain, North Carolina, lived in Seville during 2006 with his wife, who is British. Having never visited mainland Europe before, he found himself immersed in an unfamiliar culture.**

### What were the most prominent differences you noticed between Spain and North America?

The pace of life is completely different in Spain. It's much slower, much more relaxed, and people seem to live their lives around what's pleasurable much more. You see crowds of office workers drinking on the street during lunchtimes on weekdays; you hardly ever see that in the States. But although people seem to drink a lot more here, you don't see people getting really drunk that often. Spanish people just seem to enjoy life a lot, and there doesn't seem to be the same kind of work culture that there is in America.

In terms of the landscape, I was overwhelmed by the sense of space you get as soon as you leave the cities. The countryside around Seville reminded me a lot of Arizona: I hadn't expected to find anywhere that wild in Europe, which seems very densely populated.

### How did you tackle the cultural differences?

Spain's the sort of place where it's fairly easy to fit in if you just make the effort, so I tried as hard as I could to get talking to people in bars and cafés. I also did my best to speak a little Spanish when possible. I didn't feel any of the hostility towards Americans that I'd been warned about and people seemed very open and welcoming as soon as they realised that you were trying to understand their culture. Also, when I started feeling culture-shocked, there was an American bar that I would go to, just to feel at home for a few hours and be able to speak English without confusing anyone. Most of the time, though, I preferred to try out the local Spanish bars and restaurants.

### Are there any practical factors that foreigners should be prepared for?

Spain doesn't seem as commerce-driven as America or the UK, and it's not the kind of culture where you can buy anything you want at any time of night or day. Lots of the shops still shut on Sundays so you need to buy groceries ahead of time, and there are a lot of public holidays where everything shuts down, including services like pharmacies.

There were also fewer English speakers than I'd expected, and although the Spanish people I met were very friendly and go out of their way to accommodate you, it's easy to feel lost if you don't know the language.

## What advice would you give to Americans coming to live in Spain?

I think the best advice is to learn as much Spanish as you can before you come. It is possible to get by in English, but speaking Spanish makes things much, much easier, and more than that, you will feel a lot less like a foreigner and be less isolated as a result. I'd also advise anyone coming here to plan ahead as much as possible: my wife speaks Spanish, but if she didn't I think things like finding accommodation would have been a nightmare. If you don't speak the language very well, it may be easier to do as many of the administrative things as you can from home.

## Peter Deth

**Peter Deth was working as an agricultural engineer in Germany until a diving trip to the Red Sea nine years ago inspired him to open his own scuba diving centre. He moved to Spain where he identified both year round opportunities and an untapped market. Scuba (self-contained underwater breathing apparatus) diving has been a real growth industry in Spain in the last 20 years and one that has been tapped by enthusiasts up and down Spain's costas. Peter opened The Happy Divers Club (www. happy-divers-marbella.com), situated on the seafront in Marbella, and the business is going from strength to strength. We asked him:**

### Why did you decide to give up your job and relocate to Spain?

Basically I was looking for a career change and this opportunity arose, so I though 'why not?' The idea first came up over a beer with my own diving instructor in Egypt. I asked him if he knew anywhere to open a dive centre and he recommended Spain and put me in touch with some people who could help. Within a couple of months of coming home I had reached an agreement with a hotel here in Marbella and we went ahead.

Scuba diving is booming in Spain – the industry is still developing and more and more people want to dive. At the start of the nineties there was 10% growth every year throughout the industry. I found a gap in the market and that was an important factor for success. Scuba diving was big on the Costa Brava and in the Canary Islands, but very few people offered diving on the Costa del Sol, which is incredible because diving here is great!

### How did you go about setting up the business?

I started everything from scratch. I formed an SL (limited company). It was quite complicated because I did not speak much Spanish at that time and I couldn't find any professional advice back home. In the end I found a *gestor* here to help me. I let the professionals do a lot for me. It is an expense, but without it I couldn't exist. My time is too expensive. Lawyers, *gestores* and accountants know exactly what they have to do, whereas I would waste a lot of time and money finding out. It took about a year to formalise all the paperwork here.

The first year was horrible. We had weeks where nothing was happening, nobody knew me, and I didn't really know what I was doing. I had to learn everything by experience and I didn't make any money. When you start a business you need money to live on at least for the first year because any money you make must be reinvested in the business.

### How have you attracted customers to your centre?

Most of my clients are foreigners, although in August there are a lot more Spanish people. It has taken us a long time to build up a client base, but now we have customers who come back every year. Treat the customers that you have well and they will come back again and again. But we have not become complacent. We don't wait for the customers to find us, we go out to different hotels promoting the business, offering try-dives. We also advertise in dive magazines, visit exhibitions all over Europe and have our own website.

In the low season there are far fewer tourists, which causes some businesses to run into problems. However, we have come up with a solution: we run instructor courses in the months when there are less tourists. We are able to train novice divers up to instructor level and that is my niche here on the Costa del Sol.

## How has the business grown and changed over the years?

When I started the business consisted of one divemaster and me. Now I employ eight people. It is very easy to find staff but it is harder to find qualified staff. We have to train them ourselves, to our own requirements. It takes six weeks before they can start working for us. For a long time we had a very high employee turnover and we are still in the process of finding stable staff.

The equipment for scuba diving is expensive, so we operated on the philosophy – start slow and let it grow. There is no need to start a massive operation. I started with very little and gradually brought in more and more equipment. It was a constant growth as the business built up.

Things have changed tremendously. When I started, the dive association PADI (the Professional Association of Diving Instructors) didn't exist in Spain. Now it has 150 affiliated dive centres and there is much more competition. I am very happy that other serious dive centres have opened here because we cannot serve everyone. Tourism has exploded in recent years. In the last five years, there has been a massive increase in the number of tourists in the area, which is great for business but it does mean that our costs have gone up – which can be quite difficult.

## Any regrets about leaving Germany?

No, certainly not. These last nine years have been full of lots of very rich experiences and I hope it will continue. The experience has been far better than I ever expected. I am enjoying what I am doing and I would do it all again the same way.

# *Hal Shaw*

Hal Shaw, 25, from Greenville, South Carolina spent much of 2004 living in Madrid and doing an internship for a large entertainment company. Hal's interest in Hispanic culture and the Spanish language stemmed from the growth in the prevalence of Spanish-speaking people in the United States. This interest led him to Ecuador where he completed a Spanish immersion course, then to Mexico City where he worked for a large construction company, and finally to Madrid. Although he has now returned to the US he regards his Madrid experience as one of the most enjoyable times of his life. We asked him:

### What were your first impressions of Spain?

My first impressions of Spain revolved around the social environment and all of the cultural things to do. Madrid was smaller than I imagined and I could walk everywhere. The walking aspect is great because it helps you to burn off all of the extra calories you consume while enjoying Spanish cuisine and the nightlife. I was immediately impressed at the large amount of cultural venues, dining establishments, friendly people and nightlife.

I was impressed at how easy it is to travel around the country by train. Each region of Spain offered a completely different feel, due to the country's dynamic history.

### Where in Spain did you live and why?

I lived in an apartment about three blocks from Atocha train station, where the March 11 bombings occurred. With the exception of the bombings, the location was outstanding. I was 10 minutes from the centre of the city and five minutes from the Prado, Reina Sofia, and the Museo Thyssen. When I first arrived in Spain, I was attending a language school, which placed me in an apartment about 30 minutes outside the city. I quickly decided that if I was going to be living in Spain, I wanted to live in the centre of the action. I ended up paying quite a bit more for my apartment, but it was well worth it.

### How did you go about finding work?

I began networking for my job well before my arrival in Spain and actually had three rounds of interview for it in the United States. I had my fourth round in Spain, but I moved over there on a leap of faith that I would land the job. Just in case I did not get the job, I enrolled in a language immersion school to fill my time. For my American friends who thought they would be lucky and find a job, their job hunts proved very difficult and fruitless. I would highly recommend that Americans do their employment legwork before they leave the US.

## What about red tape – any problems?

Obtaining a work visa in Spain is a difficult process for Americans. In fact I never managed to get one! In truth I believe that I could have obtained one had I decided that I wanted to stay in Spain, but I was ready to return to the United States and my travel visa was set to expire. For Americans to obtain a visa, they either have to know the correct people in Spain, or have their visa application well organised through their company. The most important aspect to obtaining a visa as an American is proving oneself to be uniquely suitable for a job, and that a Spaniard could not fill the position effectively.

## How did you find working there compared with home?

I found working in Spain to be very different from working in the US, although very enjoyable. In the US, work is much more intense than in Spain and lunch is eaten quickly (although exceptions are made for business lunches). Furthermore, Americans arrive at work early and leave around 6pm. However, in Spain, work began around 9am, usually with a strong coffee and things didn't start moving until 9.30am or 10am. Around 1.30pm we would take lunch for an hour to an hour and a half. Wine was also part of the meal, which is unusual in the US. Smoking is also permitted in most places in Spain, rarely the case in the US. Finally we would not leave the office until around 7pm or 8pm in the evening. While roughly the same amount of work is accomplished in Spain, I found the work day to be more drawn out and much less stressful.

## How does the quality of life compare with other countries you have lived in?

The quality of life, in terms of food, entertainment and culture, has very few rivals in the world. Spain is a melting pot of cultures with a fascinating history and energetic citizens. I love travelling and every place I visit offers unique attractions, but, all in all, Spain is one of my favourites. With the exception of pickpockets in crowded tourist areas, I found the city to be very safe, and there was always something going on. Furthermore I found the emphasis Spaniards put on finding a healthy work–play balance, with the emphasis on playing to be definitely up my alley. Although due to my poor timing I got hammered by the exchange rate (the dollar was very weak during my time there), as long as you avoid the tourist traps, the country is relatively affordable. Even in Madrid.

# Lindy Walsh

Lindy and her husband Bill were approaching 50. Free of debt, they were bored with their jobs and their children had left home. Bill also had a bad back and wanted to escape the English winters. They had inherited a house in London and worked out that with the income from the rental of the London house, plus working during the summer months in the UK, they could afford about six months a year living in a small house abroad that they would gradually renovate themselves (having had experience of such a project in the UK). They were planning to look for a property in Italy, Portugal, Spain or southern France. In the autumn of 1987 they explored France and Spain, discovered Almería and found 'The House'. This was a massive *cortijo* with 250 acres of land and it was for sale for far more than they were looking to pay. However, with the sale of the London house they were able to afford the *cortijo* and moved to Spain permanently in the autumn of 1988.

## What were the factors that influenced you on your choice of location?

We chose this area firstly because it has the most beautiful scenery of anywhere I've ever been, and secondly, because the people here are so friendly. Let's be honest, the climate is pretty good, but that's a definite third in importance.

Location was certainly the most important factor. We didn't want to be on the coast in an English ghetto. We needed minimal support from other English speakers while we learned Spanish. There were a few (very few) English and Dutch living nearby on whom we could call. The property is 10 minutes' drive from the town, which has a police station, a petrol station and mechanic, a 24-hour health centre, a bank and shops. It covers our basic needs.

## How difficult was the process of renovating the cortijo and how did you find local builders?

The house, the equivalent of a manor house in the UK, was abandoned and falling into ruin. There was another, larger and even more ruinous farmhouse 100 metres or so up the hill. We decided to convert this into youth hostel type accommodation for 40 people. The manor house (*cortijo*) was finally completed at the end of 2002 (12 years after we first bought the property). If I had known how long a project it would be I would never have begun it, although now it is completed I love the house and wouldn't change a thing, except perhaps the standard of workmanship.

Our first builder was excellent. He retired before we'd finished phase one. Our second builder was good himself, but most of his team were poor. I've had a problem with a drain for nine years because it was put in without the correct 'fall'. My third builder was a criminal who may or may not have been any good as a builder but took my 25% deposit and vanished. My fourth builder was a very poor builder with a very poor team. My fifth builder is a good builder and totally reliable. Most other (Spanish) tradesmen: electricians, plumbers, carpenters, decorators etc., seem very reliable in their standard of work as well as actually turning up to work when they should. Most British tradesmen in this area seem no better and most, I gather, are working illegally.

## How traumatic or otherwise is dealing with bureaucracy in Spain?

We used an *abogado* for the purchase, but it was still fairly traumatic as he was a city lawyer (there weren't any local *gestor*s who spoke English) and didn't know much about laws affecting property such as ours and what licences we needed. For example we got 'denounced' (the Spanish word is *denuncia* and refers to being reported to the police by a neighbour for – generally – a minor infraction such as having a dog that barks all night long, or putting up an unsightly satellite dish that 'lowers the tone' of a neighbourhood) to the river police for having a well dug without their permission. We'd got four licences (local town hall, local ministry of the environment, mines, water authority) and he didn't know that within half a kilometre of a dried-up riverbed we needed another permit too. He got the hunting laws wrong which led to lots of trouble and he didn't bother to find out about the Andalucían tourist laws, which affected us greatly, telling us we only had to keep inside the building regulations. For nearly 10 years our business was 'illegal' and I am still unable to develop certain aspects that we had planned for back in 1988 and which he had told us would be 'no problem'.

## How traumatic or otherwise was the process of moving your life to Spain?

Moving our lives to Spain wasn't traumatic at all. It was exciting and lots of fun. We started out camping in a ruin with rats, and I didn't like that, but we quickly made at least one rat-proof room. We shipped our stuff very gradually over 12 years, using family and friends to bring over a bit at a time as we had space for it. Some things we had crated up in 1988 intending to bring over 'one day' got irrelevant as time passed and got given away or just abandoned.

## What advice would you give to someone looking to buy a property and settle in Spain?

Buying 'inland' is totally different from buying on the coast. Buying rural is as different again from buying inside a town or village boundary. Don't take anything for granted. I know awful cases of people buying land with water running through it, but not being allowed to use one drop; of buying land with trees and finding out too late that they hadn't bought the trees (or their harvest); of buying a 'house' (it looked like a house) and finding that it was registered as a chicken shed and not able to be registered as habitable because it didn't conform to the newest building standards. Check and check again and don't part with any money until you have a copy of a registered *escritura* that has been looked over by a local (but perhaps not too local as he may be the vendor's brother) *gestor* or *abogado*. Better a local *gestor* who doesn't speak English, and pay the extra to a translator, than an English speaker who doesn't know the area.

# Martine de Volder

Martine de Volder, 50, moved away from her home country of Belgium, where she was working as a nurse in the emergency and operation ward of a Belgian hospital, to Las Galletas in Tenerife 25 years ago. She became enchanted by what she considers the most important facets of the country, 'the spirit of Spain, their art of living, and the warmth of their human relations' and has never looked back. She is now married to a Spanish banana farmer, is self-employed as a private nurse and says that the only thing she misses about Belgium is the food! We asked her:

### Did it take you long to acclimatise to life in Spain?

Not at all, but then I already spoke Spanish before I moved here and that made it much easier. If you want to live here and build up solid social relationships, you have to learn Spanish. Tourists come and go so you cannot rely entirely on them for your social life. Spanish people are very warm and friendly if you make an effort with the language. Many foreigners have entirely the wrong attitude and treat the Spanish as though they are superior to them. That is not the way to establish friendships.

### How did you go about finding work?

I was lucky in that I already had a contract from Belgium. However I did have to have my qualifications recognised in Spain. There are many different nursing degrees in Europe, all of differing levels. It is necessary to ask for recognition from Madrid. In Spain there are two levels of nurse. Those with the *diplomada universitaria,* a bachelor degree, are fully qualified nurses who have taken nursing at university. Anyone with an inferior degree is classed as a carer. Carers are very competent and work with a great deal of responsibility. They are superior to the average level of nurse in Europe and in my opinion superior to many of the British, French and German nurses I have seen here in Tenerife.

### What is your opinion of the Spanish public healthcare system?

The fact that free healthcare is available to all in Spain is a real advantage compared to most EU countries, where the patient always has to pay at least a proportion of the costs of medical attention. However, there are certain disadvantages. For example: long waiting lists; having to go to the doctor at a specific time; having to visit special national health service centres *(consulta de seguridad social),* which are not necessarily available in smaller towns; the fact that you cannot see a specialist without first visiting your GP. Another disadvantage, especially for the elderly and infirm, is that home visits are very rare and only made in exceptional circumstances.

In general the quality of state care is very good, I would say excellent. The system can be a pain and home care is virtually non-existent, but the quality of the doctors, nurses and hospitals is very high.

## How do you find working in Spain, compared with home?

The attitude to work in Spain is far more relaxed, and I am far less stressed than I was working in the hospital in Belgium. The relaxed attitude doesn't come naturally to me, I still have more get up and go than many Spanish. They call me a workaholic!

## What advice would you give someone thinking of coming to live and work in Spain?

As long as you make an effort to adapt to the epicurean style of living, learn the language and do not look down on the Spanish, you will soon become immersed in the Spanish way of life.

# Before You Go

# ■ THE PAPERWORK

For EU nationals, moving to Spain can be accomplished with a minimum of hassle and paperwork. However, for non-Europeans, the process is far more complex and time-consuming. This chapter gives guidance on the administrative procedures that need to be undertaken when moving to Spain, and provides help with practical matters such as opening a bank account. Other useful sources of advice include the websites of the Department of Work and Pensions (www.dwp.gov.uk), the Spanish immigration ministry (www.mir.es) and Spanish embassies; these are listed in the Appendix at the back of this book.

## Numero de Identificación de Extranjeros (NIE)

The first step for anyone moving to Spain is to apply for a foreigner's identification number. If you reside in Spain, or if you own a property and are non-resident, then you need an NIE. This is a tax identification number and allows you to undertake any form of work or business activity, file tax returns, vote in local elections, and open a bank account. The NIE is obtainable from the *oficina de extranjeros* (foreigners office) or police station. An application form can also be downloaded from www.mir.es. The completed form and a passport are usually sufficient to obtain the NIE, which will be sent to you by post as soon as it has been processed.

The application process is the same for both EU and non-EU citizens, although non-EU citizens must have entered the country with the correct visa. Once this number has been received then you can begin applying for a residence card, if you require one. The NIE does not need to be presented as a document, simply memorised or copied onto a slip of paper, which you can carry around with you.

## Gestores

Many administrative matters, including applying for residence and work permits may be more conveniently tackled by a *gestor* the peculiar Spanish love of bureaucracy has created the need for an equally peculiar and quintessentially Spanish institution known as the *gestor*. Spanish bureaucracy is so labyrinthine that ordinary people need to be guided through it by a special official. Admittedly this profession dates back to the time of mass illiteracy, when ordinary folk needed help with official paper work. However, the need still exists in Spain as even straightforward procedures can require three or four different pieces of paper, all with small print and fees that have to be paid at different counters, probably in different towns. If you have fluent Spanish, limitless patience and no time restrictions then you may save some money by wading through the quagmire of red tape yourself. Otherwise, it is recommended that you consult your local *gestoría* (the office of *gestores*). The *gestor* is less qualified than a full lawyer but also far less expensive. *Gestorías* are listed in the Yellow Pages (*Páginas Amarillas*).

## Residence cards for citizens of the EU

British and other EU citizens (as well as nationals of Norway, Iceland, Liechtenstein and Switzerland) intending to remain in Spain for a continuous period of more than

**FACT**

■ The peculiar Spanish love of bureaucracy has created the need for an equally peculiar and quintessentially Spanish institution known as the *gestor*. Spanish bureaucracy is so labyrinthine that ordinary people need to be guided through it by a special official.

90 days will no longer be issued with a residence card and may reside in Spain with a valid passport, as long as they are:

- employed workers;
- self-employed;
- students; or
- retired persons who have contributed to the Spanish Social Security scheme.

A valid passport is theoretically sufficient for these groups to purchase property, make simple bank transactions, obtain a driving licence and even be included on the electoral roll and participate in municipal and European elections.

However, immediate family members of an European Economic Area (EEA) national who are not EEA nationals themselves do need to apply for a residence card. According to the Spanish Interior Ministry, these relaxed regulations also do not apply to 'inactive' citizens, i.e. EU citizens who have retired to Spain and those of independent means, who are still required by law to carry a residence card.

However, even if you don't need a residence card, it is important to remember that the law in Spain states that everybody must carry some form of identification, which is all very well for Spanish citizens who carry a *Documento Nacional de Identidad* (ID card), but for foreign citizens can mean carrying around a passport, which does not fit in your wallet, and is expensive to replace if lost.

Although EU citizens in Spain will no longer be issued with residence cards, a forthcoming directive will make it compulsory for them to register as foreigners at their local *ayuntamiento* (town hall). Being included on the *padrón*, the list of inhabitants in the municipality, will allow you to be included on the electoral roll and will offer proof that you are in fact a resident. To register you need to bring along proof of your residence, such as a rental agreement.

## Applying for a residence card

If you need a residence card, or decide to apply for one, this can be done as soon as you arrive in Spain. Temporary residence cards are issued for stays between three months and one year; people who intend to stay for between one and five years will be issued with a permanent residence card. The process is fairly straightforward, but you cannot expect English or other foreign languages to be spoken by the police and taking along a Spanish-speaking friend or using the services of a *gestor* is a good idea. The application form should be submitted to the local provincial police station (*comisaría de policia*) or foreigners office (*oficina de extranjeros*). You can download an application form from the Interior Ministry website (www.mir.es).

The list of required documents can vary from office to office and from region to region, but some or all of the following documents are often required:

- the completed application form (*solicitud de tarjeta en regimen comunitario*)
- a full, valid passport
- NIE (see page 253)
- proof of employment or other documentation showing how you will support yourself in Spain
- proof of residence such as utility bills and rental contracts
- marriage documents (if applicable)
- three passport-sized photographs
- a standard medical certificate from your doctor
- bank statements showing your regular income
- details of your health insurance (a statement from the insurance company stating that full treatment is covered, or evidence of registration with the Spanish Department of Health/Social Security, the INSS)
- non-EU citizens must also provide proof that they entered Spain on the correct visa

Once you have presented the above documents, the application will be processed and the authorities will contact you when you card is ready. This can happen fairly quickly, or it could take anything up to six months, depending on the region and how busy/efficient the civil servants are. In the meantime you will be issued with a document stating that your application is being processed, which should be sufficient when dealing with official red tape. Upon notification by post, you should return to the police station or *oficina de extranjeros* to collect your card and have your fingerprints taken for police records.

Those who are obliged to apply for a residence card because they are 'inactive', i.e. pensioners and 'persons of independent means' must provide evidence that have sufficient funds to support themselves such as evidence of the pension that they receive from their home country, or an income equal to or above the official minimum wage.

Residence cards must be renewed periodically. Permanent residence cards are automatically renewable after five years. If you move out of Spain or back to your country of origin, your residence card must be handed in to the police station.

More information on all of the above and further advice is available at the Spanish Interior Ministry's website; www.mir.es, or may be obtained by calling the free information number; 900 150000.

**FACT**

- If you move out of Spain or back to your country of origin, your residence card must be handed in to the police station.

# Visas and permits for non-EU citizens

Non-EU or EEA nationals applying to take up residence in Spain have much more red tape to cope with, although the volume and variety of the bureaucracy will vary according to nationality (and if there are reciprocal health and tax agreements for example). All non-EU nationals must apply for a visa through the Spanish consulate in their own country before leaving for Spain. It is wise to apply well in advance.

Non-EU nationals are not meant to go to Spain for the sole purpose of employment without prior permission. Even if the job offer is made while you are in Spain, you need to return home to obtain the residence visa. Without the visa application, it is impossible to apply for a work and residence permit.

Non-EU citizens will require a visa to live in Spain (although not necessarily to visit the country) and both a residence and a work permit if they decide to stay in Spain. Work permits can cost up to €300 and are normally issued for 1–5 years. Details of the different classes of permit are given below.

## Work permits for non-EU applicants

Non-EU citizens are supposed to complete the process of legalising their work and residence status in Spain before starting work in Spain. Note that in recent years the Spanish authorities have tightened up on entry and work regulations for non-EU or European Economic Area citizens, which in practice means that many temporary or short-term workers do not bother to apply, and more and more mainly young people who work in tourism or seasonal jobs and come from outside the EU are being expelled. Illegal residents run the risk of being thrown out of the country straight away and being forbidden to return for three years.

Americans and others from outside the EU will have to know which type of work permit to apply for:

- **Class A**, which covers seasonal or cyclical work
- **Class B**, for 'a given occupation and activity in a given territorial area'
- **Class C**, for those who have already been resident in Spain for some time and covering all categories of employment
- **Class D**, for self-employment in a specific location for up to one year
- **Class E**, for all categories of self-employment.
- **Class F** only concerns you if you do not actually live in Spain but close enough to the Spanish frontier to commute to work in Spain.

For non-EU applicants, the procedures for obtaining a work permit usually take several weeks. Applicants should specify what kind of work permit they are applying for. There are exemptions, for categories of workers from the USA or Canada, and elsewhere for foreign academic staff and media correspondents, for example, or representatives of religious organisations. A full list of these can be obtained from the nearest Spanish embassy or consulate. There are also categories for group work permits, trainees and au pairs.

Applications are not accepted by post in any circumstances, and instead should always be made in person at your local consulate or by a representative who has written consent from the applicant to act on his or her behalf. The following documents are required for each application:

### TIP

It is wise to make sure that all the procedures described in this section are followed, without taking any 'shortcuts' or trying to drift from tourist to resident status.

- a certified copy of the applicant's passport details
- a report on the employer's business and a job profile
- three recent passport-size photos
- a duplicate copy of the applicant's visa application
- any relevant degrees and qualifications held
- evidence (if applicable) that the applicant falls into one of the preferential categories noted above
- evidence that the employer is registered with the Social Security Administration
- the completed application forms
- a medical certificate
- a certificate of your criminal record (if you have one)
- written proof of the offer of employment

If all the documents are in order, a copy of the application form, medical certificate and the photocopies of the passport, certified by the consulate, will be returned to the applicant as proof that he or she has applied for the visa. All three documents must then be sent to the prospective employer in Spain, who in turn should apply immediately for the work permit at the district department of the Ministry of Labour (*Ministerio de Trabajo*) or the relevant department. The granting of the visa is subject to the approval of the work permit by the Spanish authorities and this usually takes between three and six months.

Successful applicants should collect their visas in person as soon as the consulate advises them to do so and must take with them their passports with at least one blank page to affix the visa, the consular fee, and the communication from the consulate stating that the visa is ready for collection. Once in Spain, a work permit can be picked up from the local police station or from the provincial departments of the Ministry of Labour and Bureaux for Foreign Persons; there will be no problem in obtaining this if the residence/work visa is presented.

The type and duration of the work permit will vary according to certain factors, i.e. the type of work undertaken, and the area in which it is done, but in no case will it exceed five years. Work permits will always be issued for the same duration as the residence permit. And their granting and renewal will depend on:

- the level of unemployment in the specific activity for which the permit is applied for; and
- vacancies available in the profession in which the proposed activity is to be carried out.

A Spanish embassy or consulate can advise on the strict rules of taking up employment in Spain, (i.e. foreigners are normally prevented from doing work that could be done by a Spanish person or undercutting wages and conditions that apply locally) and advise on the documents you will need and the forms to be filled in. You may need to present evidence of qualifications or diplomas held; photocopies of your passport and visa application; a certificate relating to your criminal record (if you have one) and a medical certificate. If you can show evidence that your work is needed to 'organise and start up a foreign enterprise moving entirely or partly to Spain', or other documents that might favour your application, so much the better. Excellent detailed information on the legal processes involved can be

### FACT

The granting of the visa is subject to the approval of the work permit by the Spanish authorities and this usually takes between three and six months

seen on the website of *The Broadsheet,* an English-language monthly magazine in Madrid (www.tbs.com.es).

# Residence and retirement

Pensioners from within the EU will now no longer need a residence card (*tarjeta de residencia comunitaria*) if they have retired to Spain, as they are technically classed as 'inactive citizens', and can live in Spain with a valid passport.

Some may find the detailed advice available from the UK Department of Work and Pensions offices helpful; and the Spanish Consulate-General in London can supply a separate leaflet of general information for pensioners who wish to retire in Spain.

 **Department of Work and Pensions:** www.dwp.gov.uk
**Spanish Consulate-General:** www.mae.es/Consulados/Londres/en/home

# Entering to start a business

As explained above, residence permits are no longer necessary for EU citizens who wish to become self-employed or start a business. However, the reality is that you will be spared a lot of bureaucratic hassle if you have one, and it is virtually impossible to get a bank loan without one. EU nationals do not need a work permit to work in Spain.

The situation for non-EU nationals is considerably more complex. They require both a residence visa (*visado de residencia*) and a work permit. There is a special classification of residence visa for those wishing to start a business and non-EU citizens must be able to demonstrate to the consulate in their own country that they have the funds to invest in their Spanish business. Often they must also demonstrate that they will provide work for Spanish nationals. Indeed it is not unusual for the Spanish consulate to insist that the investment is made, the employees are hired and that the business is ready to operate before they will grant the visa. Given the Spanish Ministry of Labour and Social Affairs' concern for job creation, the more Spaniards you intend to employ, the more favourably the visa application will be regarded. The granting of the visa is subject to the approval of the work permit by the Spanish authorities, which usually takes around three months.

Barajas Airport, Madrid

There are 10 different types of work permit for non-EU nationals. Those intending to be self-employed or start a business will need only concern themselves with classes D and E. Initially most people receive a temporary type D permit, which lasts for one year and may limit the holder to a specific activity or geographical area. After the initial year this may be renewed and replaced with a two-year type D permit. Finally, when this permit expires, the self-employed may receive a type E permit, also valid for two years.

## Tax and residency

If you own homes in Spain and in your native country you will be deemed to be resident in the country where your centre of interests lie, i.e. the country where your personal and economic relations are stronger, or in the country where you live most of the time. If you spend more than 183 days in one calendar year in Spain then you automatically become resident for tax purposes in Spain. These days do not have to be consecutive – often temporary absences (for example if you go home to visit friends and family) are ignored for the purposes of the 183-day rule. However, if you genuinely spend less than six months a year in Spain, you will be classed a non-resident but will be required to carry out certain obligations:

- Pay local rates.
- Pay utility bills.
- Pay income tax on any earnings through business activities in Spain.
- Declare all capital assets in Spain and where necessary pay wealth tax on these.
- If you have a car you must pay road tax and have insurance.

Becoming tax resident in Spain is not the same thing as being domiciled in Spain for tax purposes. Your domicile is actually very difficult to change and most people remain UK domiciled regardless of how long they have lived in Spain. To gain Spanish domicile you must prove that you never intend to return to the UK and dispose of most your UK assets.

### Double Tax Treaty between the UK and Spain

Those who have interests in both Spain and the UK may be concerned that they will end up paying taxes to both authorities. To prevent this, the UK/Spain Double Tax Treaty was signed in 1975. Generally this treaty will only need to come into play if you are resident for tax purposes under the rules of both countries. This can sometimes happen during the early stages of your move to Spain due to the fact that the Spanish tax year runs from January to December and the UK tax year runs from April to April, allowing the possibility of overlap. In these circumstances the double taxation treaty will determine the country in which you are deemed to be tax resident, by looking first at your permanent home status, and secondly at your centre of vital interests.

## Residence and citizenship rights

**Residence** in Spain is not the same as **citizenship**. Those who wish to become a citizen of their new host country will need to have lived there for 10 years first. However, Latin Americans, along with citizens of Portugal, Equatorial Guinea, the

**FACT**

■ If you spend more than 183 days in one calendar year in Spain then you automatically become resident for tax purposes in Spain.

Spain retains a mix of stunning traditional and modern architecture

Philippines and Andorra, can apply for Spanish citizenship after only two years of legal residence in Spain.

Residents of Spain with overseas nationality have most of the rights and obligations of a Spanish national in employment, health and other fields; but no right to vote in national elections and no liability to endure military service.

Once resident in Spain, as anywhere in the world, it is also advisable to register with your embassy or consulate: a list of these is provided below. This registration enables the authorities to keep emigrants up to date with any information they need as citizens resident overseas and, in the event of an emergency, helps them to trace individuals. Your embassy or consulate can also help with information regarding your status overseas and advise with any diplomatic or passport problems, and offer help in the case of an emergency, e.g. the death of a relative overseas. However, consulates do not function as a source of general help and advice.

As a rule, British embassies and consulates interpret their role of helping British citizens overseas more strictly than those of many other countries. As many who have needed their help in an emergency have found, diplomats tend to keep within the letter if not the spirit of their duties. Appeals for assistance in matters that fall outside these duties – explained in a leaflet available from embassies/consulates or the Foreign and Commonwealth Office (020 7008 1009; www.fco.gov.uk) – often fall on deaf ears. You will find a list of embassies at the back of this book.

## Useful addresses

**Spanish Education, Labour and Social Affairs Office:** 020 7727 7221; www.sgci.mec.es/uk/. Gives advice on work and social security in Spain, and publishes Regulations for British nationals wishing to work or reside in Spain.
**Employment Service:** Overseas Placing Unit, Rockingham House, 123 West Street, Sheffield S1 4ER; 0114 259 6000; www.jobcentreplus.gov.uk; www.employmentservice.gov.uk. Publishes an information sheet on Working in Spain.

## Becoming a Spanish citizen

EU citizens resident in Spain already have most of the same rights as a Spanish citizen, with the exception of being able to vote in national elections, so there is really little point in applying to become a Spanish citizen. For nationals from countries outside of the EU it may well be worthwhile, as obtaining residence status and having to periodically renew it can be very time-consuming and frustrating.

To apply for Spanish citizenship foreigners must have been resident in Spain for ten years, unless they were born in Spain, have one Spanish parent or grandparent, or have married a Spanish citizen, in which case this period is reduced to just one year. Latin Americans, along with citizens of Portugal, Equatorial Guinea, the Philippines and Andorra, can apply for Spanish citizenship after only two years of legal residence in Spain.

Applications for Spanish citizenship should be made to the local civil registry, who will require numerous documents and a lengthy application process. Most people need to employ a lawyer to handle the paperwork involved. Once the application has been processed, the applicant will be called to interview before a judge, who will decide whether or not to grant citizenship. The applicant needs to demonstrate that they are a good citizen and that they have successfully integrated into Spanish society.

Spanish law does not recognise dual nationality for adults, so in most cases, those who obtain Spanish nationality will have to renounce their previous citizenship. Successful applicants are required to swear loyalty to the Spanish King and obedience to the constitution. For further information on these issues, contact the Servicio de Nacionalidad del Ministerio de Justicia, San Bernardo 45, 28015 Madrid (902 007214; www.mjusticia.es).

### FACT

■ To apply for Spanish citizenship foreigners must have been resident in Spain for 10 years, unless they were born in Spain, have one Spanish parent or grandparent, or have married a Spanish citizen, in which case this period is reduced to just one year.

# ■ THE LANGUAGE

The language that we call Spanish is actually Castilian Spanish, with its roots in the kingdom of Castile, formed in the seventh century. Castile managed to maintain its independence throughout numerous occupations and spread its language through the re-conquest of Muslim Spain. The oldest Castilian texts date from AD 970. The Spanish vocabulary is of Latin origin, but has had heavy Germanic and Arabic influences over time.

These days Spanish is an international language, and is one of the six official languages of the United Nations. After Chinese and English, it is the most prevalent language on earth, spoken by about 400 million people, and as the primary tongue in 21 countries, mainly in Latin America. The 1989 Nobel laureate from Spain, Camilo José Celar, has said:

'We Spanish and Hispano-Americans are the owners and users of one of the four great languages of the future, the others being English, Arabic and Chinese.'

The Latin American variants of Spanish may differ in pronunciation but Castilian Spanish is both widely understood and appreciated there. The difference is not unlike that between British and American English.

Despite the enormous importance of Castilian Spanish worldwide, it is only spoken as a first language by 74% of the country. Three of the autonomous communities – Catalonia, Galicia and the Basque Country – also have their own languages. In the province of Catalonia, the principality of Andorra, parts of the French Pyrenees and the Balearic Islands, Catalan (Catalá), and the various dialects of this language, are widely spoken. The province of Valencia also has its own language, which developed out of Catalan when in the 16th century huge numbers of Catalan-speaking labourers were moved from the north and never returned. Under Franco, Catalá, Galego and Euskera were heavily suppressed – banned from the media, from schools and from all aspects of public life. Franco attempted to eradicate these languages, which he saw as undermining Spain's unity. However, since Franco's death, these languages, which had continued unabated behind closed doors, began to thrive once again in the public domain, in schools, newspapers, and literature and as the language of the autonomous communities' administration.

Spain's warm climate encourages a relaxed pace of life

# Languages in Spain

## Catalan (Catalá)

Catalan dates back to the ninth century and is currently spoken by an estimated eight million people (so is more widely spoken than Danish, Finnish or Norwegian). There is no surer way to offend a Catalonian than to refer to his or her language as a dialect. Although Catalan bears a close resemblance to Provençal, and therefore to French and Spanish, it is as distinct from each of these as, say, Italian, and has as long a history. Schoolchildren in Catalonia are now taught both Castilian and Catalan, and in this region most road signs and documents (as well as tourist office maps) appear in both Catalan and Castilian. The extent to which Catalan is spoken varies depending on where you are. Those living and working in Barcelona are just as likely to hear Castilian as Catalan, but those who find themselves in Catalonia's towns and villages, in Menorca or Mallorca, will need to learn Catalan, which is the language of everyday life. Even in Barcelona, speaking Catalan makes finding work much easier.

## Basque (Euskera)

The Basque provinces also have their own language, known as euskera or euskara, now spoken by around 632,000 people in the País Vasco, Navarra and in the French

Basque region. Although some words have been absorbed from French and Spanish, the basic vocabulary and structure are completely unrelated to any known tongue, so predate the Roman conquest of Spain. Very few English words derive from Basque; one exception is 'bizarre' from the Basque word for beard.

Although a predominantly oral language until the late 19th century, a unified version of the many Basque dialects known as Batua (euskera batua) is now taught in schools. Basque is an incredibly complex language to learn, but those living in the region will find it impossible to integrate fully unless they have some comprehension of the language.

## Galician (Galego)

About four-fifths of the 3,000,000 inhabitants of Spain's northwest province speak Galician (Galego) as at least their second language; it includes elements of both Spanish and Portuguese (with Celtic roots). Again this is a separate language, not just a dialect; within Galicia, three dialects of Galego are spoken. Galicians are less aggressively nationalist than Catalans and Basques, so the language has not been as assertively restored. Of the three, Galego is the most comparable to Castilian, so should be easiest to pick up.

# Learning the language

Knowledge of literary Spanish (Castilian) is much more useful than a knowledge of Catalan, Basque or Galego, since all Spaniards understand Castilian but very few outside their communities can communicate in the regional languages. If you choose to live in the great Catalan city of Barcelona or in rejuvenated Valencia, Castilian Spanish will usually be understood, although at times a certain coolness can be detected towards Castilian speakers. In the more chauvinistic parts of Catalonia and the Basque Country, Castilian is reviled; however, foreigners are forgiven more easily than Spaniards for speaking Castilian. If you have children who are going to go to local schools, be aware that it will be compulsory for them to learn the language of the region, possibly to the exclusion of Castilian.

It is strongly advised that anyone planning to move to Spain try to make some headway learning this useful language before leaving home. Castilian Spanish is one of the easiest languages to learn at a basic level, especially if the student has a prior knowledge of any of the Romance languages (e.g. French, Italian) and some understanding of the basics of phonology. Unlike English, Spanish is a completely phonetic language, and once you have mastered the pronunciation of the individual letters, it is possible to tell simply from the spelling of a word, how it should be pronounced. Beginners will find that tentative attempts are met with a helpful, if sometimes bemused, response once in Spain.

Many types of course are offered by language schools and other organisations, both in the UK and in Spain. Some of the most popular forms of language learning and the organisations that offer these courses or language learning materials are listed below.

## Self-study courses

The advantage of self-study is that it allows students to work and absorb material at their own pace and in their own time.

**BBC:** The BBC produces excellent workbooks and audio cassettes at various levels. You can find out more from BBC Customer Services (0870 2415 490) or via the websites www.bbcshop.com or BBC Education (www.bbc.co.uk/education/languages/spanish). The BBC now offers an online beginners' course called Spanish Steps as well as the self-study course España Viva (among others), an introduction to everyday Spanish based on recordings of what Spaniards actually say.

**Linguaphone:** (0800 136973; www.linguaphone.co.uk) distributes more elaborate (and more expensive) self-study courses in the form of books, cassettes and compact discs, which tend to be geared towards holidaymakers rather than prospective residents. Consequently, the lessons focus on such subjects as sightseeing, how to order meals and drinks, shopping, making reservations and explaining symptoms to a doctor. Linguaphone also now offer Spanish lessons in London and online tutoring.

**Other books with cassettes or CDs:** are Teach Yourself Spanish (Hodder & Stoughton) and Colloquial Spanish (Routledge). These and other book-with-cassette courses are generally priced between £20 and £40 and are available from larger bookshops or in selected libraries.

**Open University (OU):** 0845 300 60 90; www.open.ac.uk (which also runs many courses for expatriates in Spain and around the world) offers courses leading to an undergraduate degree in Spanish. For example, Portales: Beginners' Spanish gives students a solid grounding in the language, runs from November to October and costs £410.

Studying Spanish online has become remarkably popular in recent years and you can find a list of these courses at www.spanishlanguage.co.uk.

You can also find online Catalan courses at http://catalunya-lliure.com/curs/catala.html.

## Language courses in the UK

Evening language classes offered by local authorities and colleges of further education usually follow the academic year and are aimed at hobby learners

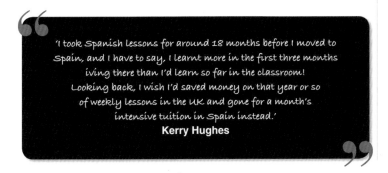

'I took Spanish lessons for around 18 months before I moved to Spain, and I have to say, I learnt more in the first three months iving there than I'd learn so far in the classroom! Looking back, I wish I'd saved money on that year or so of weekly lessons in the UK and gone for a month's intensive tuition in Spain instead.'
**Kerry Hughes**

or those wishing to obtain a GCSE or A-level. Intensive Spanish courses offered privately are much more expensive (expect to pay between £10–£25 depending on the qualifications and experience of the teacher), but have the advantage of being one-to-one. Consider using a self-study programme with books and tapes (which usually cost £25–£35), although dedication is required to make progress. Even if you make slower headway with the course at home than you had hoped, take it with you, since you will have more incentive to learn once you are immersed in the language.

A more enjoyable way of learning a language (and normally a more successful one) is by speaking it with the natives. The cheapest way to do this at home is to link up with a native speaker of Spanish living in your local area, possibly by putting an ad in a local paper or making contact through a local English language school. Remember to check that the tutor can speak enough English to communicate with you in your own language if your grasp of Spanish is patchy.

Total immersion courses in Spanish are offered by international language organisations like Berlitz UK (020 7611 9640; www.berlitz.co.uk) and inlingua (01242 250 493; www.inlingua-cheltenham.co.uk). Both offer crash courses in Spanish which can be started in Britain and completed in Spain on request. The Berlitz School in Madrid is at Gran Via 80/4, while inlingua Madrid is at Calle Arenal 24 (915 413246/7). A useful website for locating Spanish courses in the UK is www.cactuslanguage.com.

There are few opportunities in the UK to learn any of Spain's other languages. However, the University of Birmingham's Department of Hispanic Studies is also a good point of contact for those looking to study Galician or Catalan (Department of Hispanic Studies, University of Birmingham, Edgbaston, Birmingham B15 2TT; 0121 414 6035; www.hispanic.bham.ac.uk).

 For those wishing to learn Basque, a good starting point would be the Basque Association Abroad (The Basque Society, Oxford House, Derbyshire Street, Bethnal Green, London E2 6HD; 020 7739 7339; email basquesociety@btconnect.com).

## Language courses in Spain

Almost all large Spanish towns, language schools and universities offer residential courses for foreigners to learn Spanish. Courses at all levels of ability can last from anything from two weeks to several months and vary in intensiveness. The classes tend to comprise a maximum of 10 pupils and accommodation can be arranged in halls of residence, in local pensions or with Spanish families. You can find such schools can be found by looking in the Yellow Pages (*Páginas Amarillas*) in Spain under *academias de idiomas.*

Details of schools and universities that offer Spanish language courses in Spain are available from the Hispanic and Luso Brazilian Council (see below) and include the current prices and details of the courses, including accommodation if available. Various regional associations of language schools can put you in touch with their member schools, for example the *Associacion de Escuelas de Español para Extranjeros de Andalucía* has links to 16 schools in the main towns of Andalucía such as Cadiz, Cordoba and Granada from its website: www.aeea.es. It also provides language students with online forums in which they can meet and practise their Spanish skills.

Serious language schools on the continent usually offer the possibility of preparing for one of the internationally recognised exams. In Spain the qualification for aspiring language learners is the DELE (*Diploma de Español como Lengua Extranjera*), which is recognised by employers, universities and officialdom. The DELE is split into three levels:

- Certificado Inicial de Español
- Diploma Básico de Español
- Diploma Superior de Español.

Most schools say that even the Basic Diploma requires at least eight or nine months of study in Spain. A prior knowledge of the language, of course, allows the student to enrol at a higher level and attain the award more quickly.

Typically a four-week residential course, including accommodation, will cost between £750 and £1,400 (depending on how intensive the course is and the type of accommodation). Most schools put on a programme of social, cultural and sporting activities to supplement academic study while others offer classes on Hispanic history, culture and art in conjunction with the language course. You may even be tempted by a specialist combination course and in addition to learning Spanish pursue another interest like Flamenco dance or riding, literature or golf.

The cheapest option in the major cities is usually the state-run *Escuela Oficial de Idiomas* (EOI). There is more about the various regional EOIs can be found on the website www.eoidiomas.com. Those wishing to learn Spain's other languages (Catalan, Basque and Galician) are most likely to find a course at one of the EOIs in the region where the particular language is spoken.

Most language schools provide accommodation in the form of home-stays or shared apartments. This can be great for making new friends and socializing; however, those on a tight budget may wish to arrange their own accommodation, as this may work out significantly cheaper for longer courses.

Latin America has in the last few years become another possible destination for those considering Spanish language courses, with lower living costs somewhat offsetting the higher costs of travel to get there; and these courses can be of equal quality. It makes little difference in Spain – if you speak Spanish as a second language – if you have a Latin American accent, although for native speakers there may be some greater problems. In the end, you are learning an international language, rather as those learning English as a second language usually do so to communicate internationally and not just in one country. Most British language agencies have contacts in Latin America as well as Europe.

## UK language travel agents

UK-based language organisations and advisory services that may be of assistance for arranging language courses in Spain.

**Cactus Language:** 0845 130 4775; USA 1 212 404 1846; email via website; www.cactuslanguage.com

**Caledonia Languages Abroad:** 0131 621 7721/2; email courses@caledonia languages.co.uk; www.caledonialanguages.co.uk

**CESA Languages Abroad:** 01209 211800; www.cesalanguages.com

Most language schools provide accommodation in the form of home-stays or shared apartments. This can be great for making new friends and socializing; however, those on a tight budget may wish to arrange their own accommodation, as this may work out significantly cheaper for longer courses.

**Don Quijote:** 020 8786 8081; info@donquijote.co.uk; www.donquijote.co.uk. Intensive (20 lessons a week) and Super Intensive (30 lessons a week) courses for all levels throughout Spain

**EF International Language Schools:** 0207 341 8500; www.efeducation.co.uk

**EuroAcademy Ltd:** 67–71 Lewisham High Street, London SE13 5JX; 020 8297 0505; email studytours@twinuk.com; www.euroacademy.co.uk. Vacation courses and all-year courses for young people and adults in Málaga, Seville, Valencia, etc.

**Eurolingua Institute:** 0161 972 0225; www.eurolingua.com

**Gala Spanish in Spain:** 01252 715319. Information, advisory and placement service for students of any level from age 16 in a number of Spanish and South American cities. Sample prices of family stay with half board would be £700–£920 for 4 weeks

**SIBS Ltd:** 01884 841330; email trish@sibs.co.uk; www.sibs.co.uk

**Spanish Study Holidays Ltd:** 01509 211612; www.spanishstudy.co.uk

# Homestays

Another possibility is to forgo structured lessons and simply live with a family. Several agencies arrange paying guest stays designed for people wishing to learn or improve language skills in the context of family life.

### Homestay agents

These arrange home stays in Spain with or without a language course:

**En Famille Overseas:** 01206 546741; email info@enfamilleoverseas.co.uk; www.enfamilleoverseas.co.uk.

**EIL:** 0800 018 4015; email info@eiluk.org; www.eiluk.org – a non-profit cultural and educational organisation, offers short-term homestay programmes in more than 30 countries.

**Home Language International:** +337 97 707472; email jose@hli.co.uk; www.hli.co.uk.

**International Links:** 01932 229300; email internatlinks@aol.com.

**Relaciones Culturales Internacionales:** 915 417103; email spain@clubrci.es; www.clubrci.es.This youth exchange organisation places native English speakers with families who want to practise their English in exchange for room and board; they also arrange voluntary work for English assistants on summer language/sports camps.

### Language schools in Spain

Out of the thousands of language schools offering Spanish courses for foreigners, a small selection is listed here. If you decide to pursue the language after you are established in Spain, look for relevant adverts in the press, for example in *Lookout* magazine, a useful source of information on living and working in Spain published in Málaga.

**Aula Magna Castellana:** 921 412155; email amagnac@arraki.es; www.transworldeducation.com/ads/aulamagna.htm. Specialised and intensive courses, academic vacation and individual courses in Segovia. From €1,200. Also helps graduates to find paid work or traineeships in local companies.

**CLIC International House:** 954 502131; clic@clic.es; www.clic.es. Recreational Spanish courses in Seville.

**Eat, Sleep and Study Español:** Barcelona; 933 718725. Specialises in one-to-one tuition, living, learning and socialising with the tutor. Full board accommodation and excursions included. Courses from €600.

**ENFOREX Spanish Language School:** Alberto Aguilera 26, 28015 Madrid; 915 943776; email info@enforex.es; www.enforex.es. Courses in 10 locations all year round.

**Estudio Sampere:** 914 314366; www.sampere.es/ One of the most respected Spanish language schools in Spain with branches in Alicante, El Puerto, Madrid and Salamanca (and one in Cuenca, Ecuador).

**Malaca Instituto:** 952 293242; email online@malacainstituto.com; www.malacainstituto.com. Variety of Spanish language and culture courses including practical Spanish for the older student, Spanish and dance lessons (Sevillanas or Salsa), commercial Spanish and intensive or one-to-one tuition.

**Sociedad Hispano Mundial:** Granada; 958 010172; info@shm.edu; www.shm.edu. Spanish language courses, plus Spanish civilisation and Hispanic studies courses.

**Trinity School, Cadiz:** 956 871926; email info@trinitylanguageschool.com; www.trinitylanguageschool.com. Based in a Mediterranean resort favoured by Spanish holidaymakers.

## Spanish societies

It is a good idea to find out if any Anglo-Spanish clubs or societies exist in your area, as these will organise various social events and discussion groups and may help to soften the culture shock when you arrive in Spain. Check with your local further education institute, university, or local library. It is also worth contacting the Hispanic and Luso Brazilian Council (020 7235 2303; email enquiries@canninghouse.com; www.canninghouse.com), a non-profit-making organisation founded to stimulate understanding between Britain, Spain, Portugal and Latin America. They run a number of cultural and educational programmes, including a variety of language courses. They also have a library of 60,000 books, periodicals, videos and DVDs, CD-ROMs and audio CDs/tapes on Spain, Portugal and Latin America, covering geography, history, current affairs, economics, sociology, natural history, literature, art, music and religion.

The Canning House Library is open to the public from 2pm to 6pm Monday to Friday. Borrowing facilities and a postal service are available to members only. The Council can also provide information about Spanish language conversation classes in and around London, including addresses of organisations and private tutors offering day or evening language and conversation classes.

The Instituto Cervantes, the official Spanish Government Cultural Centre, is the largest worldwide Spanish teaching organisation, with headquarters in Madrid (C/ Libreros 23, 28801 Alcalá de Henares, Madrid; 914 367600; www.cervantes.es).

The Cervantes Institute in London, sometimes referred to as the Spanish Institute (102 Eaton Square, London SW1W 9AN; 020 7235 0353; email cenlon@cervantes.es), has an information and audiovisual department to which members have full access. Manchester also has an Instituto Cervantes at 326/330 Deansgate, Campfield Avenue, Arcade, Manchester M3 4FN; 0161 6614200; as does Leeds (169 Woodhouse Lane, Leeds, LS2 3AR; 0113 246 1741). The membership fee includes admission to events on their cultural programme such as flamenco performances, classical guitar concerts and exhibitions of paintings.

**TIP**

■ It is a good idea to find out if any Anglo-Spanish clubs or societies exist in your area, as these will organise various social events and discussion groups and may help to soften the culture shock when you arrive in Spain.

# ■ BANKING

All banking activity in Spain is controlled by the Banco de España, which has branches in all provincial capitals. Banks in Spain are divided into clearing banks and savings banks and there are also a number of foreign banks operating throughout the country.

To open an account in Spain you will be required to present:

- your passport or some other proof of identification
- proof of address
- your NIE tax identification number, see page 56.

It is advisable to open an account in person rather than rely on a *gestor* to do it for you. It is also advisable to open an account with one of the major banks, as they are likely to have far more branches.

The two banking giants in Spain at present are the BSCH (Banco de Santander Central Hispano), which in 2004 negotiated a takeover of Abbey National to create the world's eighth largest bank, and the BBVA (Banco Bilbao Vizcaya Argentaria). Other banks in Spain include the Banco Atlántico, and Banco de Andalucía. Barclays,

Britain's third largest bank, also has a very large presence in Spain, having bought out Banco Zaragozano in 2003.

Most large towns will have at least one branch of these banks and in the cities there will often be several branches, offering all the usual banking facilities, including mortgages and internet and telephone banking facilities, as well as ATM machines and paying-in desks. Standard bank opening times are from 9am–2pm on weekdays and from 9am–1pm on Saturdays, although these may vary from bank to bank.

If you plan to be in Spain for some time, it is best to open a bank account in Spain immediately on arrival – or even before leaving home. This can easily be arranged through the major UK banks – which all have branches in Spain – or through a branch of the larger Spanish banks that have branches in the UK. This will enable you to settle any bills that you may get for any professional advice and for day-to-day costs taken while on, for example, a reconnaissance trip to Spain.

When choosing a bank, it's a good idea to ask friends and acquaintances for recommendations. Banks in resort areas and cities usually have at least one member of staff who speaks English; however, those in rural areas generally don't. Service in small local branches is often more personalised than in larger branches and the staff less harried. However, smaller branches may not offer such a choice of banking services and are less likely to have English-speaking staff.

# Opening a Spanish bank account from the UK

Although some people may be more confident opening an account with a Spanish branch of a UK bank, they will find that the Spanish branches of British banks function in just the same way as the Spanish national banks. HSBC and Barclays Bank are the most widely represented of the British banks in Spain, with branches throughout the country. Those who wish to open an account with one of the branches in Spain should contact their local branch in the UK, which will provide the relevant forms to complete.

The London offices of the largest Spanish banks can also provide the forms necessary to open an account with their Spanish branches. The banks that will provide such a service include Banco De Santander Central Hispano and Banco Bilbao Vizcaya Argentaria.

# Internet banking

Over recent years the use of internet banking in Spain has flourished. Spanish banks offer some of the most sophisticated home banking software in the world. This is largely because Spain was a fairly late developer in this area, so when they finally decided to establish internet banking facilities, they were able to do so with the most up-to-date technology on the market. Almost all banks offer internet banking and once you have set up an account with a username and password, it is possible to carry out most banking transactions online.

There are also a number of internet/telephone-only banks operating in Spain, such as ING Direct (901 020901; www.ingdirect.es); OpenBank (902 365366; www. openbank.es); Uno-e (901 111113; www.uno-e.com).

Internet banks often offer relatively high-interest current accounts and internet banking is very useful for checking on your account and carrying out banking transactions while abroad.

## Cashpoints

There are now cashpoints (*cajero automático*) all over Spain and you can usually even find them in the larger villages. Three automated teller machine (ATM) networks operate in Spain – 4B (the most common), ServiRed and 6000 and you can generally use any ATM to draw money from your account, although there may be a fee charged. As well as cash withdrawals, paying cash into your account and consulting your balance, some ATMs now allow you to carry out other transactions such as renewing your mobile phone card or making theatre reservations. Spanish ATMs offer you a choice of language of instruction.

## Type of bank accounts

Those who are resident in Spain for tax purposes may open the type of current account (*cuenta corriente*) and savings account available to all Spanish citizens. Non-residents may only open the current and savings accounts available to foreigners, which will still allow you to set up direct debits to pay utility bills while you are away from your property and keep a steady amount of money in the country. Note that current accounts pay very little interest on the balance. Sometimes it is as low as 0.1%. It is sensible to keep as little as possible to tide you over in a current account and deposit the rest in a savings account.

The Cajas de Ahorro savings banks are similar to British building societies and American savings and loans organisations. They usually offer a more personalised and friendly service than the clearing banks. They have branches throughout Spain, which, apart from the Catalan La Caixa and Caja Madrid, tend to be regional. Many of the savings banks actually started out as agricultural cooperatives and many still act as charitable institutions – investing part of their profits each year in social and cultural causes. The savings banks all issue a bank card enabling the holder to withdraw money from the cashpoints that they operate.

For a short-term savings account you can open a deposit account (*libreta de horror*), from which withdrawals can be made at any time. Interest will also be added twice yearly to the average credit balance, but this is likely to be negligible unless the account balance is £1,000 or more. For larger amounts of money, long-term savings accounts (*cuentas de plazo*) and investment accounts are also available and will earn more interest, as the money has to be left in the account for an agreed period of time – perhaps six months, perhaps several years. The longer the set period the money remains untouched, the better the interest earned. Interest rates vary and the best rates are obtained from accounts linked to stocks and shares although, of course, there are associated risks of losing some or all of your investment.

Spanish bank charges cover just about every banking transaction imaginable and are notoriously high. Particularly high are charges made for the payment of cheques into your account and for transferring money between accounts and/or banks. Before opening an account, be sure to ask for a breakdown of any charges that may

be made, including annual fees. If you plan to make a lot of transfers between banks and accounts you may be able to negotiate more favourable terms.

# Banking procedures

Bank statements are usually sent out to all customers every month and are available on request at any time. Do not expect to get anything free from the bank. Unlike in the UK, charges are levied on day-to-day banking procedures in Spain, including on all credit card and cheque transactions. Note that cheques are generally not accepted as a form of payment in shops and businesses though credit and debit cards are. Overdrafts and loans are available on request and all the usual services, such as standing orders and direct debit are available from the banks in Spain.

Most Spanish banks will provide cash on presentation of an international credit card (e.g. Visa, American Express). Cardholders are able to withdraw up to their credit limit, which only takes a few minutes, but it is an expensive way of buying euros and it is cheaper, although not as quick, to pay in a sterling cheque to the Spanish bank where commission charges will usually be less. Even if you are moving permanently to Spain, it is a good idea to keep your bank account at home open. This will allow you to transfer money (from a pension, or income accrued from property rentals or business) between accounts if you wish and will be useful when visiting friends and family in 'the old country'.

Overdrafts *(giros en descubierto)* have a peculiar non-legal status in Spain, as officially all debts must be documented so that a bank can take legal action against a customer who defaults on payments. However, overdrafts are readily available and the interest on them is limited to 2.5 times the current bank rate.

If you plan to keep most of your money outside Spain and periodically transfer money from your account back home to your account in Spain, you will need to enquire how long it will take to clear before you can access it and what the bank charges are for this service. Banks tend to take their time transferring money as the longer it swills around in their system the more profit they make. Specialist currency exchange companies can make regular payments for mortgages, salaries and pensions faster and more cheaply than banks.

If you are a resident for tax purposes in Spain, remember that 16% of any interest earned on your account will be retained and paid to the Spanish tax office on your behalf. However, this tax can be deducted from tax payable on the next year's income tax return.

**FACT**

It is illegal to overdraw your Spanish bank account without prior agreement.

| Banking glossary | |
|---|---|
| annual percentage rate (APR) | *tasa porcentual anual* |
| annuity | *anualidad* |
| balance | *saldo* |
| bank account | *cuenta bancaria* |
| bank draft | *letra bancaria* |
| bank statement | *extracto de cuenta* |
| beneficiary | *beneficiario* |

Continued

| | |
|---|---|
| branch | *sucursal* |
| cash | *efectivo* |
| cashpoint or automated teller Machine (ATM) | *cajero automático talonario de cheques* cheque book |
| coins/change | *monedas/suelto* |
| credit | *crédito* |
| counter | *ventanilla* |
| current account | *cuenta corriente* |
| debit | *débito* |
| deposit | *depósito* |
| to deposit money in an account | *ingresar* |
| direct debit | *transferencia* |
| expiry date | *fecha de caducidad* |
| foreign currency | *divisa, moneda extranjera* |
| fees | *comisiones, honorarios* |
| Interest interest rate | *tipo de interés* |
| investment | *inversión* |
| joint account | *cuenta conjunta* |
| mortgage | *hipoteca* |
| overdraft | *giro en descubierto* |
| to be overdrawn | *tener la cuenta en descubierto* |
| savings bank | *caja de ahorros* |
| shares/stocks | *acciones* |
| transfer | *transferencia* |
| valid | *válido* |
| to withdraw money | *retirar/sacar dinero* |

# Offshore banking

Offshore banking is a favourite topic of conversation all over the world among expats looking for high returns on their savings. Offshore banks offer tax-free interest on deposit accounts and investment portfolios through banking centres in tax havens such as Gibraltar, the Cayman Islands, the Isle of Man and the Channel Islands. More and more high street banks and building societies, along with the merchant banks, are setting up offshore banking facilities and the list given below offers only a handful of the most widely known offering such services. Deposit account interest rates work on the basis that the more inaccessible one's money is, the higher the rate of interest paid.

Banks and financial institutions in Spain also offer offshore banking services. In return for a tax-free interest, clients are generally expected to maintain minimum

deposit levels, which can be very high, and restrictive terms and conditions often apply. The minimum deposit required by each bank will vary, the norm being between £1,000 and £5,000. Usually, a minimum of £10,000 is needed for year-long deposit accounts, while the lower end of the minimum deposit range applies to 90-day deposits. Instant access accounts are also available.

For the expat living along the southern coast of Spain, the banks in Gibraltar offer a convenient place to stash cash in a tax-free account. However, you should seek sound financial advice about your financial and tax position before you place your life savings in an offshore account. Buying property through an 'offshore' company is sometimes practised in Spain, although you should be aware that the Spanish Tax Office charges such companies even higher taxes than usual.

It is always best to take advice from financial experts regarding these matters as the divisions between tax avoidance, which is perfectly legal, and tax evasion, which is illegal, can often be quite slim. According to Blevins Franks Financial Management (www.blevinsfranks.com), the Spanish tax authorities are becoming increasingly vigilant with regards to tax evasion, once a national pastime. And the EU's Savings Tax Directive of 2005 means that those who were hoping to avoid tax through offshore banking will now have to choose between being taxed at the point of payment or allowing their bank to notify the relevant authorities of the details of their accounts, including name, account number and payments to the account. The rate of tax deducted at source will rise in 2008 and 2011, making disclosure the more attractive option.

### Useful banking addresses

**Abbey International:** 0845 054 4000; email info@abbeyinternational.com; www.abbeyinternational.com.

**Banco de España:** 913 385000; www.bde.es.

**Banco Santander Central Hispano:** www.santander.com.

**Banco Bilbao Vizcaya Argentaria:** 020 7623 3060; www.bbva.es.

**Bank of Scotland International (Jersey) Ltd:** 01534 825050; www.bankofscotland-international.com.

**Barclays Bank España:** 901 101610; www.barclays.es.

**BDO Stoy Hayward:** 8 Baker Street, London W1U 3LL; 0870 567 5678; email london@bdo.co.uk; www.bdo.co.uk. Fifth biggest accountancy firm in the world, providing tax advice from offices throughout Europe and overseas.

**Bradford and Bingley International Ltd:** 01624 695000; email enquiries@bbi.co.im; www.bbi.co.im.

**Ex-Pat Tax Consultants Ltd:** 0191 230 3141; email les@expattax.co.uk; www.expattax.co.uk.

**Lloyds TSB:** Isle of Man Offshore Centre. 01534 845777; www.lloydstsb-offshore.com. One of their services is the Lloyds Bank Overseas Club.

**Wilfred T Fry Ltd:** 01903 231545; email info@thefrygroup.co.uk; www.thefrygroup.com. A comprehensive tax and compliance service. They may send a copy of their useful free guide *The British Expatriate*

# ◼ THE COST OF LIVING

The cost of living in Spain is generally estimated to be around 20%–30% lower than in England. When talking about Spain's affordability, there is a massive distinction to be made between going to Spain to live on your savings, as a retiree might do, or going there to work and to live on what you earn. The fact is that while Spain is still very cheap by British standards, prices are increasing and wages are not keeping pace, so that many Spaniards are now facing household debt on an unprecedented scale: the average family now owes 120% of their annual disposable income, a figure that is approaching the 160% debt seen in the UK.

**FACT**

◼ While Spain is still very cheap by British standards, prices are increasing and wages are not keeping pace, so that many Spaniards are now facing household debt on an unprecedented scale.

While working in Spain in an average clerical job you are likely to earn between €12,000 and €18,000; in most northern European countries this would be laughable, but in Spain it's enough to live on, and whether you live comfortably or have to pinch pennies depends partly on your location: Madrid and Barcelona have seen some of the biggest increases in the cost of living over the last decade, and it can often feel like a struggle just to scrape by. The coasts are increasingly expensive too, as industries rise to meet the demands, and incomes, of the well-heeled Britons who have retired there. However, those who live in towns or even in the smaller cities will find that it is still relatively easy to live with comfort on a low wage.

One difference between Spain and Britain that makes the cost of living in Spain feel much lower is that in Spain, the little things that make life more pleasurable, such as food and drink, are much cheaper. You can get a glass of wine or a coffee for €1.50 and a decent, no-frills lunch in a restaurant for €10; a bottle of spirits in one of Spain's discount supermarkets can be found for €5. A visit to the cinema will cost around €6 and you can see a live band perform for €3.

Housing, however, is increasingly expensive, and many Spaniards are finding that they spend a large portion of their income on rent or mortgage payments, leaving them with less disposable income than ever before. Property prices have risen by 197% over the past decade, and a house now costs seven times the average person's yearly income. The property boom is now popularly believed to be over, but prices are unlikely to recede to the point where Spain regains its reputation as the place to pick up a prime piece of real estate in the sun for next to nothing, and the repercussions for Spain's economy in terms of personal debt are likely to continue for many years to come.

In terms of foreigners who come to Spain, one factor that also affects the cost of living is your willingness to 'do as the Romans do'. If you want to eat the same foods you are accustomed to eating at home, you will inevitably pay more, as many of them are imported, or are viewed as luxury brands. Even Heinz beans are hard to get hold of and expensive outside the costas. If, on the other hand, you follow the Spanish example of eating small, regular meals featuring plenty of fresh fruit and vegetables and unprocessed, whole foods, you will be able to eat relatively cheaply.

Food bills can also depend heavily on the way in which you choose to shop. Spain, in many ways, is still very much like the UK and America of 30 or 40 years ago, and the most economical way to shop is to visit five or six small specialist shops rather than one large supermarket. Many Spanish people still buy their vegetables from the greengrocer, their meat from the butcher, and so on. It may be more time-consuming to shop this way, but it can result in some real savings, as well as benefits in terms of quality. Fruit from your local outdoor market will be fresh and cheap; fruit from Spanish supermarkets can be very expensive and is often of highly dubious quality. It pays to observe the locals in your area and note where they shop.

Utilities are generally far cheaper in Spain than they are in the UK and, to a lesser extent, the US. You can expect to pay around €30 per month for electricity and €20 for your telephone. Taxes are also relatively low compared with the rest of Europe; for more information, see Taxation, p213.

**TIP**

■ Fruit from your local outdoor market will be fresh and cheap; fruit from Spanish supermarkets can be very expensive and is often of highly dubious quality.

# ■ PETS

## Importing pets into Spain

Spain is very animal-friendly. Many Spaniards keep pets, and dogs are an extremely common sight, even in the big cities where space is at a premium. People are also very tolerant of animals (although their attitudes in everyday life can be somewhat at odds with the way animals are treated in pet markets such as that on Las Ramblas in Barcelona; animal lovers may find these places upsetting).

Before deciding to take your pet to Spain, think carefully about the implications for both yourself and the animal. Local authorities in the regions of Spain have different regulations regarding pets and it is a good idea to check what these are before importing your pet.

In 2000, 'Passports' for pets were introduced. These allow people from the UK to take their animals abroad and to return with them without enduring the compulsory six-month quarantine that was formerly in force. Spain (including the Balearic and Canary Islands, though not the Spanish North African enclaves of Melilla and Ceuta)

is one of the countries that the UK includes in its Pet Travel Scheme. The Pet Travel Scheme (PETS) allows dogs and cats to visit certain countries in mainland Europe and rabies free areas such as Australia and New Zealand provided that they are vaccinated against rabies. Additionally, they are required to have been treated against tapeworm *(echinococcus multilocularis)* – which can pass to humans – and the tick known as *Rhipicephalus sanguineus,* which also carries a disease transferable to humans. Pets must also be microchipped.

The latest details of import conditions for taking your pets to Spain can be obtained by contacting and requesting the contact details of your nearest Animal Health Office. Although the 'Passports' scheme makes travelling with animals more straightforward, getting the necessary documentation can be a lengthy process. At the time of writing, the Department for the Environment, Food and Rural Affairs (DEFRA) – the current name of the old Ministry of Agriculture, Food and Fisheries – was understood to be working to a six-month deadline, so you need to plan ahead.

Some, but not all, ferry companies and airlines will take accompanied pets, though the list of those that do is growing, so check with your carrier. Also, only certain routes are approved for importing pets; these include ferry routes from Calais to Dover, Caen, Cherbourg, Le Havre and St Malo to Portsmouth; by rail, Eurotunnel shuttle services but not Eurostar; by air, certain routes from Europe into London Heathrow. It is wise to check with your airline or tour operator for exact details. Travelling by air from the UK to Spain a pet can travel as excess baggage; however, coming the other way the animal must travel as cargo. Once in the country the animal's documentation will be checked before being taken to the animal aircare centre and then released to the owner. Quarantine is not usually necessary, although regulations may change and you should consult the Spanish consulate in your home country for up-to-date information well before your planned travel date. Note that in some cities in Spain dogs have to be registered and insured and a dog licence required or a tax levied. Information on the registration formalities once in Spain will be found at the local town hall (*ayuntamiento*).

 The Pet Travel Scheme (Department for the Environment, Food and Rural Affairs, Area 201, 1a Page Street, London SW1P 4PQ; 08459 33 55 77; email helpline@defra.gsi.gov.uk; www.defra.gov.uk)

## Importing pets back into the UK

To get your pet back into the UK you will need a PETS certificate to show the transport company when checking in your pet at the point of departure. A PETS certificate is valid six months after the date of the blood test up to the date the animal's booster rabies shot is due (a dog has to be at least three months old before it can be vaccinated). You should obtain the PETS certificate from a government-authorised vet and you can obtain a list of these from DEFRA's website (www.defra. gov.uk/animalh/quarantine/pets/contacts.htm). Immediately (24–48 hours) prior to leaving Spain the animal must be treated against ticks and tapeworm by a vet. This has to be done every time your pet enters the UK. The vet will issue an official certificate bearing the vet's stamp with the microchip number, date and time of treatment, and the product used.

## Pets originating outside UK

If your pet originated from outside UK where different systems for identifying dogs and cats are in force, it will need a microchip insert for entry to the UK. Pets that have had other forms of registration (e.g. an ear tattoo) must be vaccinated; blood-tested and have a microchip insert. To enter the UK the animal must have the PETS certificate showing that the vet has seen the registration document.

### Pet travel insurance

The introduction of the PETS scheme has opened up a niche market in pet travel insurance.

**Pet Plan Ltd:** Computer House, Great West Road, Brentford, Middlesex TW8 9DX; 0845 077 1934; www.petplan.co.uk. Offers cover for pets taking trips abroad. The minimum 30-day cover costs about £22 for dogs and £18 for cats; 60 days' and 90 days' cover is also available.

**Petwise Insurance:** 0800 032 2297; www.petwise-insurance.com.

**Pinnacle Pet Healthcare:** 020 8207 9000; www.pinnacle-pet-health.co.uk.
**MRL Insurance Direct:** 0870 850 0618; www.mrlinsurance.co.uk.

### Pet contacts

**Airpets Oceanic:** 01753 685571; www.airpets.com. Pet exports, pet travel schemes, boarding, air kennels, transport by road/air to and from all UK destinations.

**Independent Pet and Animal Transport Association:** Route 5, Box 747, Highway 2869, 2–364 Winding Trail, Holly Lake Ranch, Big Sandy, Texas 75755 USA; 903 769 2267; email inquiries@ipata.com; www.ipata.com. An International Trade Association of animal handlers, pet moving providers, kennel operators, veterinarians and others who are dedicated to the care and welfare of pets and small animals during transport locally, nationwide and worldwide. Citizens of the USA can contact this address for a list of agents dealing in the transport of pets from the USA to Spain.

**Par Air Services Livestock Ltd:** 01206 330332; email parair@btconnect; www.parair.co.uk. Handles international transportation and quarantine arrangements. Can arrange door-to-door delivery of pets by specially equipped vans.

**Pet Travel Scheme:** Department for the Environment, Food and Rural Affairs, Area 201, 1a Page Street, London SW1P 4PQ; 08459 335577; email helpline@defra.gsi.gov.uk; www.defra.gov.uk.

# ∎ GETTING THERE

## By air

These days, getting out to Spain and back could not be easier. The massive demand for air travel by hundreds of thousands of travellers to Spain each year has created a boom time for airlines offering cheap, no-frills tickets. This stampede of air travellers, lured by the cheap flights, cheap property and guaranteed sun has put an enormous strain on airports and new runways and airports are constantly in progress. Flights to Spain rose by 68% in 2006, to the dismay of environmental campaigners.

Over a third of the millions of international passengers visiting Spain each year travel by air; and many arrive by charter flights. The UK and Spain are the only two countries in the world to record such a high percentage of international charter flights; and the relatively cheap tickets are one reason why many Britons choose to live there. However, the real boom has been seen in bargain-bucket scheduled services to the major cities and to smaller airports as a result of the proliferation of budget airlines that emerged following the deregulation of air travel within the EU.

A huge investment plan for Spanish airports has resulted in many improvements, in particular those at Seville and Barcelona. Madrid's Barajas Airport airport is the centre of domestic traffic (airport information 913 93 60 60) and Barcelona is becoming increasingly important (932 983838). A regular hourly shuttle service – from 7am to 11.50pm in Madrid, from 6.45am in Barcelona – operates between these two cities and transports over two million passengers each year. There are also frequent connections between all the main cities in Spain, including flights between Barcelona, Madrid and the Balearic and Canary Islands, which, after the shuttle service, are the most frequently used.

By using low-cost airlines and booking flights well in advance, the cost of a return flight between Spain and the UK can be much cheaper than a rail ticket between

**TIP**

∎ Scanning the travel pages of newspapers like *The Guardian* and *The Independent* as well as the free London magazine *TNT* is a good way of keeping in touch with the best flight deals, including the many budget airlines offering incredibly cheap flights to Spain.

London and Manchester. Scanning the travel pages of newspapers like *The Guardian* and *The Independent* as well as the free London magazine *TNT* is a good way of keeping in touch with the best flight deals, including the many budget airlines offering incredibly cheap flights to Spain. There are, of course, down sides to the low-cost airlines, such as long check-in times, delays, extortionately priced food and drink on board, inconvenient travel times, airports that are in fact miles away from their declared destination city, tiny airports that you may be forgiven for mistaking as cattle sheds and flights that are not actually as cheap as their advertising suggests (once the incomprehensible taxes and charges have been levied). Also watch out for hidden charges for checking baggage in the hold, or extortionate fines for exceeding weight allowances. This latter charge especially means that using a budget airline when you are moving to Spain and need to transport a lot of possessions is a false economy.

However, for many people, the availability of return flights for as little as £25 more than makes up for the inconveniences mentioned above, and because the tariffs are constantly changing, depending on special offers and when you choose to travel, there is an addictive quality to finding the cheapest possible fares online. Prices will often change daily and it is generally cheaper to fly midweek (and at unsociable hours) than at weekends.

Spain's architectural highlights include Gaudi's unfinished La Sagrada Familia

Depending on when you wish to travel, the no-frills airlines are not always the cheapest, and because they have created such fierce competition in the flight marketplace, some of the mainstream carriers such as BA and Iberia have been forced to reduce their prices drastically on some routes. There are now far more reasonably priced alternatives, so always spend time researching the various possibilities before booking a flight.

 Useful websites that search for the cheapest flights available at any time are www.skyscanner. net and www.airfares.net.

## The airlines

Please note that airline services can and do change, so it is best to check current routes on the internet and to keep an eye on the travel press.

**Aer Lingus:** Flies to Spain from Dublin and Cork. Destinations: Alicante, Barcelona, Bilbao, Gran Canaria, Ibiza, Lanzarote, Madrid, Málaga, Palma Majorca and Tenerife. From the UK and Channel Islands: 0870 876 5000; from Ireland: 0818 365000; www.aerlingus.com.

**BMI Baby:** Flies from Heathrow, Leeds Bradford and East Midlands Airport to Alicante, Barcelona, Madrid, Málaga, Murcia and Palma. 0871 224 0224; www.bmibaby.com

**BMI:** Flies to Spain from Aberdeen, Belfast, Durham Tees Valley, Edinburgh, Glasgow, Leeds Bradford, Heathrow, Manchester. Destinations: Alicante, Madrid, Málaga, Murcia, Palma. 0870 6070 555; www.flybmi.com.

**British Airways:** Flies from various UK airports to Alicante, Almeria, Asturias, Barcelona, Bilbao, Fuerteventura, Granada, Ibiza, Lanzarote, Las Palmas, Gran Canaria, Madrid, Málaga, Menorca, Palma and Tenerife. 0870 850 9850; www.ba.com.

**easyJet:** Flies to Spain from Belfast, Newcastle, Liverpool, East Midlands, Stansted, Luton, Gatwick, Bristol. Destinations: Alicante, Almeria, Asturias, Bilbao, Barcelona, Fuerteventura, Gran Canaria, Lanzarote, Madrid, Murcia, Tenerife, Valencia, Palma, Ibiza, Málaga. www.easyjet.com.

**Excel Airways:** Flies to Spain from Birmingham, Glasgow, Gatwick, Manchester, Newcastle and Stansted. Destinations: Tenerife, Gran Canaria, Fuerteventura, Lanzarote, Alicante, Mahon, Palma, Almeria, Málaga. 0871 911 4220; www.xl.com.

**Flybe.com:** Flies to Spain from Birmingham, Exeter and Southampton. Destinations Málaga, Almeria, Murcia, Alicante and Palma. 0871 700 2000; www.flybe.com.

**FlyGlobespan:** Flies to Spain from Edinburgh and Glasgow. Destinations: Alicante, Barcelona, Gran Canaria, Lanzarote, Málaga, Palma, Tenerife. 08712 710 415; www.flyglobespan.com.

**GB Airways:** (formerly Gibraltar Airways, now owned by BA). Flies to Spain from Heathrow and Gatwick. Destinations: Alicante, Fuerteventura, Gibraltar, Girona, Gran Canaria, Ibiza, Lanzarote, Málaga, Menorca, Palma, Tenerife. 01293 658 004; www.gbairways.com.

**Iberia:** Spain's major international carrier flies to numerous destinations in Spain from Aberdeen, Birmingham, Dublin, Edinburgh, Glasgow, London airports, Manchester and Newcastle. 0870 609 0500; www.iberia.com.

**Jet2:** Flies from Leeds Bradford to Alicante, Almeria, Barcelona, Málaga, Menorca, Valencia and Palma. 0871 226 1737; www.jet2.com.

**Monarch Scheduled:** Flies from Manchester, Luton and Gatwick to Barcelona, Menorca, Palma, Alicante, Lanzarote, Gran Canaria, Tenerife, Gibraltar. 08700 405040; www.flymonarch.com.

**Ryanair:** Flies to Spain from Stansted, Luton, Dublin, East Midlands, Glasgow, Liverpool and Bournemouth. Destinations: Alicante, Madrid, Santander, Santiago de Compostela, Valladolid, Zaragoza, Reus, Girona, Valencia, Murcia, Almeria, Málaga, Jerez, Seville. www.ryanair.com.

**Thomson Fly:** From Aberdeen, Edinburgh, Glasgow, Belfast, Newcastle, Teeside, Leeds Bradford, Manchester, Liverpool, Humberside, East Midlands, Birmingham, Norwich, Luton, Stansted, Gatwick, Cardiff, Bristol, Exeter and Southampton to Palma, Tenerife, Alicante, Ibiza, Málaga, Fuerteventura, Las Palmas, Mahon, Reus, Gran Canaria, Almeria, Costa de la Luz, Lanzarote. 0871 231 4691; www.thomsonfly.com.

## Charter tickets

The immense changes in the European flight industry in recent years have had a knock-on effect on charter flights, which traditionally have been tied in with package holidays. These days there are very few differences between charter and scheduled flights as it is possible to buy flight-only tickets, in many cases all year round. These can be booked direct through companies such as Monarch (www.flymonarch.com) and Excel (www.xl.com), who also offer scheduled flights (see above) or through an agent. The only real difference with flight-only charter tickets

**FACT**

■ These days there are very few differences between charter and scheduled flights as it is possible to buy flight-only tickets, in many cases all year round.

is that they are still usually issued for a fixed period, such as 7 days or 14 days. The largest UK purveyor of flight-only charter tickets is Avro (0871 423 8550; www.avro.co.uk), offering flights from many UK airports to Alicante, Almería, Fuerteventura, Girona, Gibraltar, Gran Canaria, Ibiza, Lanzarote, Málaga, Menorca, Murcia, Palma and Tenerife.

### Websites selling flights

www.airflights.co.uk
www.avro.co.uk
www.cheapflights.com
www.dialaflight.com
www.expedia.co.uk
www.flightcentre.co.uk
www.flightline.co.uk
www.lastminute.com
www.opodo.co.uk
www.statravel.co.uk
www.travelsupermarket.com

# By sea

Depending on your budget of time and money, travelling by sea to Spain is possible, but tickets are not cheap and travel time can be up to 36 hours. P&O runs daily ferries between Portsmouth and Bilbao, which take around 36 hours one way. Contact P&O European Ferries (08716 645 645; www.poferries.com). Ferries operated by Brittany Ferries (08709 076 103; www.brittany-ferries.co.uk) run between Plymouth and Santander twice weekly and take around 18 hours. As a rough price guide, a family can travel at peak rates to Spain and back with a car for around £1,000. However, prices fluctuate dramatically, depending on the time of year.

Ferries also connect Morocco with Algeciras, Almería, Málaga, Tarifa and Gibraltar. A car ferry also serves Tenerife and Gran Canaria, leaving Cádiz once a week. The trip takes around 40 hours.

The Balearic Islands can also be reached by ferry services, operated mainly by Transmediterranea (www.transmediterranea.es) from Barcelona, Valencia, Denia and Vilanova I la Geltru near Sitges.

 **Ferry booking agencies:** www.directferry.com; www.ferrybooker.com; www.onlineferries.co.uk.

# By land

Having your own car while in Spain is very useful and something that many will want to consider. However, those moving to Spain will find that it may be more sensible to buy a Spanish car than register a vehicle brought over from another country (see Daily Life, page 161). Once across the Channel the fast roads in France can get you to the Spanish border in around 20 hours, but realistically you should reckon on two or three days' travel overland to reach southern Spain. Remember that if you stick to the motorways in France and Spain you will have to pay a hefty amount in tolls (the cost of getting from Calais to the Spanish border alone is around £50). It is better to stick to the main trunk roads and take your time, take in the scenery and acclimatise yourself to the life of *mañana* waiting for you. For information about current toll rates, the Spanish motorway system and motoring in Spain, visit the Dirección General de Tráfico website (www.dgt.es).

There are a number of cross-channel ferries to consider as well as the Channel Tunnel, though the time and money saved by taking, say, a ferry from Portsmouth to St. Malo rather than from Dover to Calais is debatable. Getting into a port further south in France will cut out the Paris traffic but you will have to head through the countryside for a time before picking up the main arterial motorways. All ferry services, as well as the Eurotunnel (www.eurotunnel.com), alter their prices depending on the season, the time of travel, the number of passengers, and size of vehicle. Some of the operators offer frequent-user discount schemes and packages aimed specifically at foreign home ownershomeowners. As with the airlines, it is worth shopping around to see what service best suits your particular needs.

*i* Try www.ferrysmart.co.uk and www.eurodrive.co.uk for discounted channel crossings.

With the ease and low cost of flying to Spain from the UK, very few people choose to go all the way by coach or train. However, these options are still available. Eurolines (operated by national express) offers coach services from London Victoria to numerous destinations in Spain (www.nationalexpress.com). Travelling by train is almost always more expensive than flying and takes around 24 hours. The most obvious route is to take the Eurostar from London to Paris Gare du Nord, and then change stations to Paris Austerlitz to get a train to Barcelona or Madrid. Consult www.raileurope.co.uk for further details. Following heavy state investment in the country's infrastructure, Spain's rail network is now very efficient and express high speed Talgo200 services run from Madrid to Málaga, Madrid to Cadiz, Jerez de la Frontera, Huelva and Algeciras, and Valencia. There are high-speed AVE services linking Madrid to Seville via Cordoba. You can find out more from RENFE (902 157507; *www.renfe.es*).

## Spanish Government Tourist Offices

### UK and Ireland

**London:** 22–23 Manchester Square, London W1M 5AP; 020 7486 8077; email londres@tourspain.es; www.tourspain.co.uk.

### Canada

**Toronto:** Bloor Street West, 2 Suite, 3402 Ontario, Toronto M4W 3E2; 416 9613 131/9614 079; email toronto@tourspain.es; www.tourspain.toronto.on.ca.

### United States of America

**Chicago:** North Michigan Avenue 845 (Water Tower 915 E), Chicago IL. 60611; 312 6421 992; email chicago@tourspain.es.

**Los Angeles:** Wilshire Blvd. 3883, Suite 960, Los Angeles, CAL 90211; 213 6587 118/192; email losangelese@tourspain.es; www.okspain.org.

**Miami:** Brickell Avenue 1221, Miami 33131; 305 3581 992; email miami@tourspain.es; www.okspain.org.

**New York:** Fifth Avenue 666, 35th Floor, New York NY10103; 212 2658 822; email nuevayork@tourspain.es; www.okspain.org

**FACT**

■ Following heavy state investment in the country's infrastructure, Spain's rail network is now very efficient and express high speed Talgo200 services run from Madrid to Málaga, Madrid to Cadiz, Jerez de la Frontera, Huelva and Algeciras, and Valencia.

# From the USA and Canada

There are a number of scheduled flights from North America to Madrid and many have connections on to Barcelona. Scheduled carriers from the USA direct to Spain include Air Europa, Air Comet, American Airlines, Continental Airlines, Delta, Iberia and US Airways. Iberia offers the most frequent direct flights out of a range of US cities. Alternatively, you may find better deals flying via other major European cities with the airlines of those countries, for example, Air France via Paris, British Airways via London or Lufthansa via Frankfurt. It may work out cheaper to continue overland from one of these cities, so explore your options.

Those coming from Canada will find that there are no direct scheduled flights, although all major European and North American carriers have connecting flights from Canada to numerous destinations in Spain.

From Madrid or Barcelona you can connect to any major city in Spain. All major European carriers have connecting flights from Europe to numerous destinations in Spain, although fares vary enormously.

### Direct

**Air Europa:** 902 401501; www.aireuropa.com. Daily flights to Madrid from Newark.
**American Airlines:** 1 800 433 7300; www.aa.com. Daily non-stop flights from Miami, Chicago and New York to Madrid.
**Continental Airlines:** 1 800 231 0856; www.continental.com. Daily non-stop flights from Newark and Houston to Madrid.
**Delta:** 1 800 221 1212; www.delta.com. Daily non-stop flights from Newark to Barcelona, from Newark and Atlanta to Madrid.
**US Airways:** 1 800 622 1015; www.usairways.com. Daily non-stop flights to Madrid from Philadelphia.

### Via Europe

**Air France:** 1 800 237 2747; www.airfrance.us/. Fly via Paris to numerous destinations in Spain, from Toronto and Montreal in Canada and many US airports.
**British Airways:** (1 800 AIRWAYS; www.britishairways.com. Flights from Montreal, Toronto and Vancouver in Canada and numerous US airports to Spain via London. Alternatively, once in London, there are a huge number of no-frills, low-cost flights to Spain.
**Lufthansa:** (1 800 399 LUFT; www.lufthansa.com). Connecting flights to Madrid, Bilbao, Barcelona and Málaga via Frankfurt or Munich from many American and Canadian airports.

### Discount travel

**Air Brokers International Inc:** email netsales@airbrokers.com; www.airbrokers.com.
**Airhitch:** email info@airhitch.org; www.airhitch.org. Standby seat brokers. For a non-refundable $29 registration fee, they guarantee to get you a flight as close to your destination as possible. For a flight from the east coast to Europe, costs are currently just $165.
**Airtech:** 212/219 7000; email fly@airtech.com; www.airtech.com. Standby seat brokers.
**STA Travel:** 1 800 781 4040; www.sta-travel.com. Specialists in youth, student and independent travel.

**FACT**

■ Those coming from Canada will find that there are no direct scheduled flights, although all major European and North American carriers have connecting flights from Canada to numerous destinations in Spain.

**Travel Cuts:** 1 888 FLY CUTS; www.travelcuts.com. Canadian company that organises cheap student travel.

**Worldtek Travel:** 111 Water Street, New Haven, CT 06511; 1 800 243 1723; email info@worldtek.com; www.worldtek.com. Discount travel agency.

# ◼ MOVING

## Planning an international move

Many people cite moving house as one of the most stressful times in their life, but for most the move may be just down the road, or to another town; a move does not involve moving to another country with an alien culture! For this reason it is as well to plan your move with as much precision as possible. For citizens of the European Union, there are now very few restrictions on living and working in the EU, and there are no customs duties to pay on personal effects. However, citizens of non-EU member states will need to check with the nearest Spanish embassy or consulate to find out the current regulations relating to their country. With the cheapness and availability of flights between Spain and most other countries in Europe, there is no longer that feeling of great distance between say, Andalucía and Aberdeen that there used to be. These days most of us are used to travelling relatively large distances at least once a year and separation from our family and friends for varying periods of time is a natural part of day-to-day living.

Whether you are moving to your property in Spain for a trial period to see whether you wish (and can afford) to live there full-time, or whether you are moving some of your belongings there to set up a business, it is advisable to make a trip out to your property first, unencumbered with belongings. Check that all services are connected and that all papers and permits are in order. While you are in Spain you could look into the costs involved in hiring removals men or hire cars or a van from the Spanish end. Organise your financial affairs in Spain, set up direct debits to pay the utility companies, and organise the transferral of funds from your bank account at home to your account in Spain. Then go home, let your house, either privately or through a management company, or sell it, and begin your journey into a new life.

## Making the move

When considering what to take with you to Spain and what to leave behind or sell at a car boot sale, start with a list of essential items and then try and cut this down again. Don't be afraid to be brutal! Anything one decides to take must be carefully considered to ensure that it really is practical, and necessary. Electrical items are slightly more expensive in Spain and it may be worth taking yours as long as they are compatible. However, there may be difficulties with electrical repair as some home appliances in Spain are of Spanish design and manufacture, so spare parts for other items can be a problem. Anything of substantial weight will be very expensive to ship abroad, and no matter how carefully you or the removals men wrap an item, breakages occur. A good removals company can avoid or deal with most of the disasters, which can coincide with uprooting yourself, your family and

**TIP**

◼ Citizens of non-EU member states will need to check with the nearest Spanish embassy or consulate to find out the current regulations relating to their country.

all your possessions to a foreign country. The cost of hiring a removals firm to take everything from a home in the UK to a home in Spain will typically cost between £2,500 and £4,000 (€3,200 and €5,500) and take a couple of weeks. Of course, a few brave souls tackle the move themselves, or with help from friends.

For the rest of us, the British Association of Removers (01923 669480; www.bar.co.uk) can provide help and advice about all aspects of planning a move, and can also provide the names and telephone numbers of reputable removals companies throughout the country and overseas that are members of BAR and specialise in overseas operations. The addresses and phone numbers of some of the companies which deal with Spain, whether directly or by sub-contracting to other agencies, are given on page 66.

## Importing goods

Any EU citizen intending to take up permanent residence in Spain may import their household effects and personal possessions free of customs duty. There are now no customs duties to pay on household effects transported from one member country of the EU to another. All reputable international removals firms should be fully aware of the regulations concerning the transport of personal and household items. Anyone thinking of taking their household effects out to Spain in a private truck or van should first consult their nearest Spanish embassy or consulate for the most up-to-date regulations and advice. Much of the paperwork involved in importing goods will have to be in Spanish. The Association of Translation Companies (020 7930 0007; www.atc.org.uk) will be able to put you in touch with translation services specialising in translating documents relating to removals abroad, property purchase, residence, and import/export. Translation service companies are also listed in the Yellow Pages.

You need an application form *(cambio de residencia)* requesting the Head of Customs to allow the goods free entry into Spain (obtainable from the Consulate) as well as an itemised list of the contents in duplicate, written in Spanish, which shows the estimated value in euros. These should accompany the goods or shipment and should have been legalised – stamped – at the Spanish Consulate. If you are sending the goods with a removals company, they will also need a photocopy of your passport, which has been similarly legalised. To import wedding gifts, you will also

**FACT**

■ The cost of hiring a removals firm to take everything from a home in the UK to a home in Spain will typically cost between €2,500 and €4,000 (Ð3,200 and Ð5,500) and take a couple of weeks.

**FACT**

■ If you are moving to Spain permanently you will need to have proof of intended permanent residence in Spain, in the form of a residence permit; if you haven't received this before leaving home the initial visado de residencia will suffice, but a deposit may have to be paid. This deposit exempts the holder from customs duties and will be returned once the permit has been produced.

need a copy of your marriage certificate; and there are similar special requirements for diplomats' removals; gifts by inheritance and, for example, new furniture whose value is greater than €3,000.

Exemption of duties payable on importing effects for non-EU citizens may be possible if the individual has not been resident in Spain during the two years prior to the importation of the goods; if the goods enter Spain within three months of the individual's arrival, that the goods are for personal use, are at least six months old and will not be sold in Spain for at least two years. However, if the individual decides to leave Spain within two years of arrival, he or she will have to export the goods again (a relatively simple process within the EU) or pay duty on them.

Another form of concession on import duties is available for those who wish to import furniture for a second residence or holiday home; this is known as the *vivienda secundaria*. Entitlement to this exemption does not include taking Spanish residency and involves making a deposit (around 50% of the value of the goods), which will be returned on the expiry of a two-year period.

To import a car into Spain, you must provide proof of residence in Spain, prove that the vehicle is taxed and obtain a Spanish driving licence. The relevant forms you will need can be downloaded from www.dgt.es – go to Vehículos.

## The import procedure

This basically consists of compiling a signed inventory, written in Spanish, of all the goods to be transported to Spain. This list should then be presented to the Spanish Consulate with a completed customs clearance form where the inventory will be stamped for a small fee. The removals company should handle a good deal of the paperwork required; however, the basic procedure is outlined below:

- **Inventory:** Make two copies of a complete inventory of all the items to be taken, valuing all of the items at their present value, not cost new, and opting for the low side of the estimate. Even if there are some things you want to take now and others that will not follow for several months, include the latter on the inventory, as once the list is compiled, it cannot be added to later. Remember to include the makes, models and serial numbers of all electrical items on the inventory, plus two copies of a declaration of ownership of the goods in Spanish.

- **Customs clearance form:** *la Dirección General de Aduanas*, must be completed; this will be available from your nearest Spanish consulate.

- *Escritura* **or habitation certificate:** You may also need to present either a copy of the *escritura* to the new Spanish property or, if you have had your own property built, a copy of the habitation certificate from the local authority in Spain that granted the planning permission for building.

- **A full passport:** and photocopies of the pages that have been stamped at the consulate.

Although it is more economical to transport all of your possessions in one go, new Spanish residents are allowed to import all household goods in as many trips as are required. It is worth remembering that it may be difficult to import goods after the expiry of the one-year period; it can take up to a year to obtain a separate import licence and the duty on the import for non-EU citizens can be astronomical. For those who have bought a second home or holiday residence, the procedure for importing personal effects and furnishings is similar to that for

**TIP**

■ It is worth remembering that it may be difficult to import goods after the expiry of the one-year period; it can take up to a year to obtain a separate import licence and the duty on the import for non-EU citizens can be astronomical.

## Checklist for moving house

- Confirm dates with removal company
- Sign and return contract together with payment
- Book insurance at declared value
- Arrange a contact number where you can be reached at all times
- Arrange transport for pets
- Dispose of anything you don't want to take with you
- Start running down freezer contents
- Contact carpet fitters if needed
- Book disconnection of mains services
- Cancel all rental agreements
- Notify dentist, doctor, optician, vet
- Notify bank and savings/share accounts of change of address
- Inform telephone company
- Ask the post office to re-route mail
- Tell TV licence, car registration, passport offices of change of address
- Notify hire purchase and credit firms
- Make local map of new property for friends/removal company
- Clear the loft/basement
- Organise your own transport to new home
- Plan where things will go in new home
- Cancel the milk/newspapers
- Clean out the freezer/fridge
- Find and label keys
- Send address cards to friends and relatives
- Separate trinkets, jewellery and small items
- Sort out linen and clothes
- Put garage/garden tools together
- Take down curtains/blinds
- Collect children's toys
- Put together basic catering for family at new house

long-term and permanent residents, except that the home owner is required to draw up a notarised declaration that he or she will not sell, hire out or otherwise transfer ownership of the property or personal goods within the 12 months following importation.

Finally, it is a commonly held misunderstanding that if you buy an item in Britain (or another EU country), pay VAT (sales tax) and then subsequently export it to another country in the EU such as Spain, there is an entitlement for a refund of the VAT paid on purchase; this is simply not true. The misunderstanding arises from the fact that if you are buying anything to take with you, such as a fridge or stereo, it can be supplied VAT free if the goods are delivered direct to the remover as an export shipment from the dealer.

# Removal companies

The British Association of Removers (BAR) can provide advice on choosing a removal company; and members offer a financial guarantee through BAR if they go out of business. Write to BAR Overseas at the address above.

Although Spanish consulates will supply information concerning the export of household goods and personal effects on receipt of an SAE, you may find that their own information is out of date, as more than in any other European country (with the possible exception of Portugal) Spain constantly amends its regulations regarding the importation of personal and household effects.

**Removal companies can take away much of the hassle of moving if you choose the right one; as one successfully-moved expatriate put it:**

'The secret is to use a really good removal company. Ours was superb and handled everything for us – all the paperwork, form filling, everything we could possibly worry about, was handled by the firm.'

It is particularly important to shop around for a wide variety of quotes as removal companies sometimes subcontract jobs to other companies whose drivers are going to the country in question and charge their client the extra fees picked up along the way. The approximate charge from the UK to Spain is £150 to £170 per cubic metre plus a fixed fee for administration and paperwork. The amount will vary greatly on either side of this estimate however, depending on where in Spain the shipment is going and where it is coming from in the UK. The price per cubic metre should decrease with the volume of goods you are transporting.

It is advisable to take out comprehensive insurance against possible damage to your possessions while in transit. A removals company can advise you about cover and make arrangements on your behalf, and the cost is usually quite modest. Another fact to bear in mind for non-EU citizens is that the customs clearance charges involved in exporting and importing goods can sometimes be more expensive than the shipping charges themselves (also something which a good removal company should advise you of and deal with on your behalf).

Make sure that the removals lorry will be able to reach your Spanish property with ease (check parking restrictions and access). If goods are held up for days at a time at customs in Spain, it may be that another removals firm may be subcontracted to deliver to the Spanish address. Check the contract to see what the clauses (and fees) are regarding such delays.

## Useful addresses – removal companies

**Allied Pickfords:** 0800 289229; enquiries@alliedpickfords.com. A worldwide network with many branches in Britain. In Spain: +34 1 650 4027; www.gb.allied.com.
**Andrich Removals:** 01283 761990; email info@andrichinternationalremovals. co.uk; www.andrichinternationalremovals.com. Associated companies in Spain (Cádiz, and Denia). Regular service to Spain with full and part loads.

**Armishaws Removals and Storage:** 01722 322616; freephone 0800 917 1015; email enquiries@armishaws.com; www.armishaws.com.

**Atlantis Overseas Removals:** 0113 278 9191; email enquiries@atlantisltd. co.uk; www.atlantisltd.co.uk. Depots in Leeds, Birmingham, Fuengirola, Denia and Aguilas.

**Bedwell Removals and Storage:** 01837 83900; freephone 0800 092 1967; email info@bedwellremovals.co.uk; www.bedwellremovals.co.uk. Family-owned business with over 20 years' experience in moving homes to and from Spain.

**Britannia Bradshaw International Ltd:** Manchester; 0161 877 5555; email sales@ bradshawinternational.com; www.bradshawinternational.com.

**Clark and Rose Ltd; Aberdeen:** 01224 782800; www.clarkandrose.co.uk. Also have depots in Stirling and Biggleswade, Bedfordshire.

**Coles Ltd Overseas Movers:** 0800 834446; www.colesremovals.co.uk.

**Cotswold Carriers:** 01608 730500; email bill@cotswold-carriers.com; www. cotswoldcarriers.co.uk. Full or part loads to and from Spain.

**Crown Relocations:** Freephone 0800 393 363, with offices in; Birmingham (0121 380 0910); Bristol (0117 982 1219); Glasgow (01506 468 150); Heathrow (020 8839 8000); Leeds (0113 277 1000); London (020 8591 3388); and Montrose (01674 672 155). Branches in Barcelona and Madrid; www.crownrelo.com.

**David Dale Removals:** 0870 122 1282; www.daviddale.co.uk. Takes part and full loads, has a regular weekly service, and storage available in Spain in Málaga and Alicante.

**Edward Baden:** 01825 768866; freephone 0800 1695309; www.edwardbaden. co.uk. Branches in Croydon, Chelmsford and Biggleswade.

**French Spanish Connexion:** 020 8648 6686; email funnellsremovals@aol.com. Regular removals to and from Spain and throughout the UK; single item to a complete house load.

**Four Winds International Group:** 01494 675588; email info1@ags-demenagement. com; www.agsfourwinds.com.

**Fox International Moving and Storage:** 01633 488100; email international@ fox-moving.com; www.fox-moving.com. Branches at Windsor, Romford, Cardiff, Cwmbran, Stourbridge, Bristol, Preston, Louth, Newtown, Stockton and Edinburgh.

**Greens of East Anglia:** 01449 613053; email overseas@greensremovals.co.uk; www.greensremovals.co.uk. Removals to or from Spain.

**Harrow Green Removals Group:** 020 8522 0101; www.harrowgreen.com. Full removals service, and they can also make arrangements for pets.

**Interpack Worldwide:** 020 8324 2000; www.interpack.co.uk. Services include pet shipping, full/part house contents, motor vehicles, airfreight and storage.

**Matthew James Removals and Storage Ltd:** 0800 040 7907/7908; 952 441556; www.matthewjamesremovals.com. Regular services to and from Spain.

**Movers International (of Preston) Ltd:** 01772 651570; email info@moversint. co.uk; www.moversint.co.uk. Branches in Preston, Málaga and Alicante. A weekly trade service to Spain and Portugal.

**Richman-Ring Ltd:** Eurolink Way, Sittingbourne, Kent ME10 3HH; 01795 427365; email richmanring@dbonner.co.uk; www.richman-ring.com.

**Robinsons International Moving and Storage:** 0800 833638; email via website, www.robinsons-intl.com. Branches in London, Basingstoke, Birmingham, Bristol, Manchester, Southampton, Darlington, and Glasgow.

**Simpsons Removals and Storage:** 0800 515930; email via website; www. simpsons-uk.com. Specialists in removals between Britain and Spain.

**TIP**

■ The most up-to-date information will come from a removal company specialising in exports to the Iberian Peninsula. These can provide quotes, and should also be able to give information on Spanish import procedures on request.

# Setting Up Home

# ■ CHOOSING WHERE TO LIVE

For many years Spain was seen as a property buyer's paradise, especially along the costas, where many Britons have traditionally chosen to move, enticed by the warm weather, long, sandy beaches and laid-back lifestyle. Traditionally cheap property, the availability of timeshares, offshore banking and a welcoming atmosphere for expatriates, all contributed to its attraction for second home buyers and potential residents. Many have bought property in Spain that they would never have been able to afford at home. However, the downside of the Spanish economy consistently outperforming all other large European countries is that house prices have risen over the last decade, increasing by a staggering 18% per annum in 2004.

The result is that some parts of the mass-market costas have effectively priced themselves out of reach of many who would wish to live or retire there. The biggest price increases have occurred in Madrid, where prices have been seen to rise by 30% per year; many Britons, especially those under 30, are drawn to the employment and nightlife opportunities Madrid offers, and for these it is becoming increasingly difficult to find affordable housing. But as the world attempts to adjust to the uncertainties in the financial markets and the prospect of global recession looms, Spain's housing market, along with the country's economy as a whole, is showing signs of at least levelling off, if not slowing down.

Although the costas are becoming less fashionable than they once were and with the bad publicity that mass tourism has attracted, Brits still overwhelmingly opt to buy property along the Costa del Sol and the Costa Blanca because of the ease of access by air, the vast array of available properties, some of the best beaches in Spain and good leisure facilities, particularly for golfers. The Costa Cálida and the Costa del Azahar are less developed, and have traditionally attracted more Spanish buyers than foreigners; however, this is changing as prices on the other costas have risen. Less development means a greater slice of the 'real Spain' as the agents describe it, and a more peaceful way of life.

Another way of avoiding the overly developed areas and finding much cheaper prices is to look inland. The idea of an idyllic rural dwelling in an unspoilt environment, away from the hustle and bustle of modern life, is clearly appealing. Even more appealing are the prices. Property with real character can be bought for prices that have not been seen on the coast for a long time. Many of the major housing developments are now inland, or on sites adjacent to golf clubs or similar facilities to attract the more 'upmarket' purchaser. There are purpose-built complexes for retired people as well, and estate agents have become almost like travel agents, offering everything from inspection visits, car hire, resale and even paying all the bills. Many property developers are now copying the tourist trade and offering an all-inclusive service with the same leisure facilities and amenities that a holidaymaker might expect.

The average price of a second home in Spain is around €246,000, the most sought-after properties being newly built complexes. Prices vary depending on the size of a property and the location. For example, the average cost of a property in Alicante is €250,000, while on the Costa del Sol average properties sell for €270,000. Exchange rate fluctuations in the future and the various effects of your own country adopting the euro (if applicable), is another important factor you should take into consideration before you decide to buy. As this book went to press, the euro was at a record high against the pound, meaning that Britons were paying closer to £1 than 50p for a euro for the first time. Those outside the Eurozone will also have to consider the effect of differential interest rate fluctuations on the amounts they must pay on their mortgages: Spanish interest rates are currently similar to those in the UK.

**Please note:** Those planning to buy property in the Valencian autonomous community should exercise caution due to the complex planning laws still in operation in the region. You can find out more about the controversial Ley Reguladora de la Actividad Urbanistica and its successor, the Ley Urbanistica Valenciana, in the Valencia section on page 128.

# ◼ NEIGHBOURHOOD GUIDE

## Where to live: Madrid

### Lavapiés

After the Jews were expelled from Spain in 1492, Lavapiés, the city's once bustling Jewish quarter, fell on hard times, and was subsequently neglected by city authorities for hundreds of years. In the 1980s and 1990s it became notorious for approaching the condition of a 'vertical slum', with disenfranchised residents living in ugly, unsanitary tower blocks. It was also the centre of the *okupación* (squatting) craze in the 1990s.

But, as prices rose throughout the rest of Madrid, artists, young professionals, students and immigrants began to colonise Lavapiés, and the district has cleaned up its act considerably over the past decade. Although a gritty edge persists, the ruins, which were a tangible illustration of the city's neglect of the area, are a thing of the past, and now the *barrio*'s narrow streets are lined with ethic restaurants, bohemian cafés and dimly lit bars.

Nestling in the south of Madrid, within walking distance of Gran Vía, the Plaza Mayor and the Rastro, Lavapiés' enviable location and the authentic atmosphere of its pedestrianised streets means that prices are rising, although it is still one of the more affordable parts of the city. A word of caution: although the area's reputation is improving, crime is still an issue here, and many young people choose to pay more rent for the peace of mind of living in a more secure area.

Most of the accommodation to be found here is in the form of small apartments or studio flats, and many of the young people who come here choose to share accommodation. An average rent for a studio apartment is currently around €500 per month.

**Best for:** young people
**Less good for:** families with children

TIP

◼ It is essential that you take professional and local advice before you make any financial commitment. This is the first rule of house- or villa-buying in Spain, and you can easily get good advice from property agents in the UK, on-the-spot from solicitors and from others who have already set up home there.

# DISTRICTS**OF**MADRID

1. CENTRO
2. ARGANZUELA
3. RETIRO
4. SALAMANCA
5. CHAMARTÍN
6. TETUÁN
7. CHAMBERÍ
8. FUENCARRAL-EL PARDO
9. MONCLOA-ARAVACA
10. LATINA
11. CARABANCHEL
12. USERA
13. PUENTE DE VALLECAS
14. MORATALAZ
15. CIUDAD LINEAL
16. HORTALEZA
17. VILLAVERDE
18. VILLA DE VALLECAS
19. VICÁLVARO
20. SAN BLAS
21. BARAJAS

SPAIN

MADRID

## Chamartín

Situated in Madrid's northern reaches, Chamartín is a cosy, unobtrusive and perhaps a little uninspiring residential and business district. Rents are on the high side of moderate, but the thirty-something professionals and young families who populate the plush low-rise apartment blocks and stroll down the wide, tree-lined avenues don't seem to mind. There's a significant expat presence here, and the numerous multilingual societies who meet in the area's chi-chi coffee houses and sprawling gardens give the area an international flavour. The local restaurants are renowned for providing good quality, reasonably priced tapas.

Sports facilities are second to none here, and the area boasts an Olympic-size swimming pool. For those who prefer to shop, there's a renowned two-storey market hall where you can buy farm-fresh produce.

Transport connections to the centre of Madrid are particularly impressive, with regular metro services taking you from Chamartín Station to the financial district in under 15 minutes. Expect Operation Chamartín, a big-budget attempt to rejuvenate the north of the city by improving infrastructure, luring in business and creating green space, to push prices up further. Currently you can rent a two-bedroom apartment for €925 per month.

**Good for:** getting out of Madrid
**Less good for:** nightlife

## Moncloa/Argüelles

Located just northwest of Plaza de España and home to the Complutense, Madrid's largest university and one of Spain's most prestigious institutions, Moncloa has everything you could ask for from a student neighbourhood: affordable rents, buzzing nightlife, art-house cinemas showing films in the original language and a friendly, down-to-earth atmosphere. It also has a famous resident – the prime minister of Spain, whose official home is in the Palacio de la Moncloa.

Despite the youthful atmosphere, the chaos and noise of the city centre seems far away here, even though it's just a short bus ride to Madrid's main attractions. There's plenty to do in Moncloa itself, though; Calle Princesa is heaving with intriguing shops selling everything from fresh vegetables to rare 7-inch vinyl, while the Paseo del Pinto Rosales is home to many of Madrid's liveliest summer terraces, where the city's young and young-at-heart drink the night away in the broiling heat, before nursing their hangovers in the laid-back, leafy Parque del Oeste. Just behind this is the somewhat baffling Temple of Debod, a perfectly reconstructed Egyptian temple and potent talking point.

The accommodation here is mostly in the form of large houses broken up into smaller flats or shared between several people, with a room in a shared house currently available for €350 including all bills.

**Good for:** student vibes
**Less good for:** peace and quiet

## Salamanca

A popular choice for those who are wealthy, or elegant, or both, Salamanca is a stone's throw from the fountains and leafy boulevard retreats of Retiro park and

combines a laid-back atmosphere with a chic line-up of art galleries, restaurants, boutiques and cocktail bars. Traditionally, it was the haven of Spain's ultra-conservative upper classes, who lived fairytale lives in its magnificent, multistorey houses, but now you're just as likely to see young families and professionals here, drawn to Salamanca by its cosmopolitan yet local feel, although there are those who find the neighbourhood's studied elegance a little suffocating, and prefer the earthier parts of Madrid.

Nightlife here is refined, but lively – try the internationally renowned El Arbol y *La Tosta,* with its outdoor terrace, smoky, atmospheric basement bar and range of Spanish wines. A studio apartment in Salamanca is likely to set you back around €725 per month.

**Good for:** chic shopping and eating
**Less good for:** youth culture

## La Moraleja

Perhaps best thought of as a Spanish version of Beverley Hills, La Moreleja, on the north-eastern edge of the city, is a moneyed enclave of the rich and famous, including politicians, actors, top businessmen and, until recently, David and Victoria Beckham.

Property prices range from the merely extortionate to the outright laughable here, although it isn't hard to see why: tranquil, green and spacious, La Moraleja has a rarefied air, and seems a world away from the sound and fury of Madrid. Some of the city's best schools, members' clubs and sporting facilities are to be found here, including, for those of a morbid turn of mind, the golf course where Bing Crosby died.

Apartments are available in this area, but the private villa is what La Moraleja does best; expect it to be sprawling, flanked by idyllic gardens, and most likely inhabited by a household name.

Still, it isn't all good, as La Moraleja is distinctly lacking in nightlife, with a dearth of inventive, affordable restaurants and an insipid bar scene. Local shops are also conspicuously absent, as most residents prefer to glide off in their cars to out-of-town malls. However, there is a bus route into Madrid, which delivers you to the city centre in around half an hour.

**Good for:** feeling like a superstar
**Less good for:** your bank balance

## Malasaña

The trendy alternative scene to be found in Malasaña has earnt it comparisons to London's Camden Town or New York's East Village, and, while not being as affordable as it once was, it's still one of the city's most popular residential areas for young people. Located just west of the gay district, Cheuca, and bordering the studenty paradise of Argüelles, Malasaña was the centre of the Movida movement in the 1970s and 1980s, when Madrid's youth emerged from the shadows of Franco's repressive regime to reclaim their national identity and have a lot of fun in the process, and the scent of rebellion still lingers in the streets.

Shops are predominantly small, idiosyncratic and independently owned, and the bar scene is one of the city's finest, including such establishments as Tupperware, Nueva Visión, and La Vía Lactea. The festivities do go on all night here, but those worried about noise and general chaos will be pleased to note that there is also a quieter, more homely feel to Malasaña which emerges in the afternoons and evenings, as locals gather in the cafés or promenade down the *barrio*'s streets.

Malasaña also has a distinct cosmopolitan feel, and is home to some of Madrid's best international restaurants, as well as the city's largest international food market. The most common form of accommodation is in the form of studios and apartments, and these can often be obtained for very reasonable prices.

**Good for:** independent shops and bars
**Less good for:** families

## La Latina

The oldest and without a doubt the most picturesque neighbourhood of Madrid, La Latina is a traditionally working class district which now combines its grittier edge with a new sense of pride. Although not as happening as Malasaña, it has its fair share of bars, cafés and, courtesy of its large immigrant population, affordable international restaurants. However, it's also got a traditionally Spanish feel. The newest wave of immigrants to make their homes here are predominantly from North Africa, India and the Far East, and in recent years artists have moved in too, bringing a new swagger to the area, although the age of the average resident is now higher than in, say, Malasaña.

The area's much-vaunted nightlife includes the tapas bars that cluster around the Metro station and Cava Baja, as well as Las Vistillas, a few blocks of bars and cafés that enjoy stunning views over the sierras. Perhaps most famously, though, La Latina plays host to El Rastro, Madrid's colourful Sunday flea market. If you like weekend lie-ins, La Latina may not be the *barrio* for you – as soon as it gets light, stallholders begin to set out their wares and soon the streets are swarming with people out to buy bargain souvenirs, antiques, leather goods, arts and crafts and knock-off designer sunglasses. After that the shoppers head down to the bars for afternoon drinks that often drag on into evening. Pickpockets also frequent the market.

La Latina is undoubtedly still shabby in places. Many people who are enticed there by its vibrant multiculturalism, affordable rents and picturesque buildings may find that living in one of its ramshackle houses is less romantic when winter has set in. The lack of gas heating and general dinginess becomes more of an issue. Still, for those who want to experience a taste of the real modern Spain on a budget, La Latina is a good bet.

**Good for:** getting a taste of the real Madrid
**Less good for:** mod cons

## Alonso Martínez

To the north of Malasaña lies Alonso Martínez, the playground of young middle-class *Madrileños* with disposable income. It's certainly not as trendy as some of the more central *barrios*, but it's a pleasant place to live, with parks, wide streets and plenty of bars and cafés – try the Cervecería Santa Bárbara to enjoy a cold draught beer in traditional surroundings, accompanied by delicious seafood tapas, or head to Cacao Sampaka, a coffee shop and a chocolate lover's paradise, where you can buy varieties of chocolate from around the world. Rents in this area are a little higher that in the edgier districts closer to the city centre, but it's still relatively affordable, and there are plenty of green spaces and local amenities, making it a popular choice for people with families.

**Good for:** young professionals
**Less good for:** students

## Chueca

With a prime location just off Gran Vía and minutes on foot from most of Madrid's main attractions, Chueca, the city's flamboyant gay district, is loud, proud and welcoming. Most of the city's gay scene is centred here, a large number of gays,

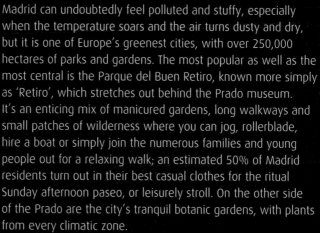

## Green Madrid

Madrid can undoubtedly feel polluted and stuffy, especially when the temperature soars and the air turns dusty and dry, but it is one of Europe's greenest cities, with over 250,000 hectares of parks and gardens. The most popular as well as the most central is the Parque del Buen Retiro, known more simply as 'Retiro', which stretches out behind the Prado museum. It's an enticing mix of manicured gardens, long walkways and small patches of wilderness where you can jog, rollerblade, hire a boat or simply join the numerous families and young people out for a relaxing walk; an estimated 50% of Madrid residents turn out in their best casual clothes for the ritual Sunday afternoon paseo, or leisurely stroll. On the other side of the Prado are the city's tranquil botanic gardens, with plants from every climatic zone.

The city's largest open space is the Casa del Campo, which curves around Madrid's western edge. Those with a head for heights can take a cable car for a spectacular view of the city. The Parque del Oeste, meanwhile, is a favourite for families with children.

Those who are eager to leave the sounds and smells of the city behind for a few hours should make for Faunia, an ecological theme park in the east of Madrid where visitors can interact with the park's 1500 animal residents in natural conditions; see www.faunia.es.

lesbians and bisexuals live in the area, and although it may be a welcome respite for same-sex couples who feel uncomfortable holding hands in the rest of traditionally Catholic Madrid, it doesn't feel at all ghettoised. Everyone can enjoy Chueca's array of local shops, bars, clubs and restaurants, and as well as the gay community, many young professionals choose to live here. Foodies are especially well catered for, and whether it's trendy fusion food or traditional tapas, Chueca is a safe bet. The *barrio* has a cosy, rabbit-warren feel due to the narrow streets and it's easy to get lost here, but it's relatively safe and in recent years investment has been pouring in.

Another point in Chueca's favour is its appealing architecture, which, with its bright facades and intricate wrought-iron balconies, is among the most attractive in the city. Available accommodation here ranges from studio flats to airy, sprawling apartments; renting a one-bedroom flat will cost around €620 per month.

**Good for:** shops and restaurants, the gay scene
**Less good for:** peace and quiet

## Majadahonda

Majadahonda, founded by Segovian shepherds in the 13th century, has historically been a rural town that relied on agriculture and was ravaged by fierce fighting

during the Civil War, but as Madrid has grown over the last few decades some of the city's overspill has migrated here, forcing the town to modernise its infrastructure and move away from its rural roots. It's only 16km from the city, and has become part of the commuter belt, as it's possible to arrive into the city centre in around 40 minutes by the Cercanía network of suburban trains and buses or the Carretera de Coruña motorway; the train journey is particularly picturesque, snaking through the pine trees of the El Pardo national park.

Today, Majadahonda is a well-organised, family-oriented suburb, with plenty of green space and excellent local services such as schools and hospitals, including some good international schools. Much of the town is leaning towards the north American model of big, out-of-town shops and chain eateries rather than the traditional Spanish *barrio* with its local colour; those who are seeking a more 'authentic' Spanish experience may wish to look elsewhere. Although located slightly further out than many residential areas, it is a very popular area and property prices are moderately high as families leave the city behind and head for a quieter life in the suburbs.

**Good for:** creature comforts
**Less good for:** experiencing 'authentic' Spain

## Atocha

While definitely not as buzzing or contemporary in terms of shops and nightlife as some of the city's districts, Atocha, the area surrounding Madrid's main railway station, is a reasonably priced place to live and has everything you could ask for in terms of local amenities. There's easy access to the Retiro park, and the business

district is a few minutes away by bus; the city's main museums are also a short hop away. There are also lots of places to buy food and a good clutch of unshowy local bars, restaurants and cafés serving tapas at reasonable prices. Atocha's accommodation tends to be in the form of studios and apartments in large blocks, and more young people and students than families choose to live here. It is possible to rent a large one-bedroom apartment for around €700 per month.

**Good for:** transport
**Less good for:** atmosphere

## Castellana

Castellana's location puts it right in the thick of Madrid's business world, with the headquarters of numerous banks and international companies a stone's throw away, so Castellana is well suited for those who want to be close to work and don't want the constant noise caused by people drinking, carousing and generally having fun on their doorstep. That's a polite way of saying there isn't a whole lot going on here, although it is secure and there are some upmarket bars and restaurants for those who wish to dip their toes into Madrid's nightlife. However, its central location and its popularity with workers from the city's financial district make Castellana a relatively pricy place to live; expect to pay at least €700 for a studio apartment.

**Good for:** proximity to work
**Less good for:** culture and entertainment

## Las Rozas

Like Majadahonda, Las Rozas is a former hamlet that has been built up into a thriving town in its own right as middle-class families leave behind the hustle and bustle of Madrid for a quieter life in the suburbs; its population doubled between 1991 and 2005, and it currently has one of the highest per capita incomes to be found anywhere in the Madrid municipality. It's served by four railway stations and lies just over half an hour north-west of the city centre by local train. Its residents are attracted not only to its combination of proximity to and distance from Madrid, but also by its excellent schools, hospitals, shopping centres and sporting facilities. As with Majadahonda, this isn't the place for those who want to drink the night away and enjoy the light, colour and hedonism of Madrid, but for those who find the city oppressive it's a good compromise. Rents are high here, and travel costs should also be factored into calculations.

**Good for:** suburban life
**Less good for:** nightlife

## Puerta del Sol

Puerta del Sol, or Sol as it is commonly known, is quite literally the centre of Madrid – the 'km cero' marks the place where all Spain's roads converge, the heart of the capital. Many foreigners are tempted here by the wealth of tourist attractions and for the atmosphere Sol has of being absolutely in the thick of things; however, it's predictably expensive to live here, and residents may be disappointed when they realise that there is actually not a great amount of local infrastructure; Sol caters predominantly to tourists, and not to people who want to buy a pint of milk after eight o'clock in the evening. Still, it's central enough that just about everywhere else is within walking distance, and has a vibrant, if slightly touristy, bar and club scene. You could easily pay €1,000 for a studio apartment here.

**Good for:** tourist attractions
**Less good for:** local amenities

# Where to live: Barcelona

## Ciutat Vella

Centring on La Rambla, the broad boulevard where street performers and market sellers mingle riotously with tourists and locals, the Ciutat Vella, or Old City, is the medieval part of Barcelona: rich in atmosphere, occasionally tacky and overrun by tourists, and ranging between very affordable and extremely expensive. It is divided into three distinct areas, as follows.

## La Ribera

This chic and increasingly trendy district is often referred to as El Born after its main street, the Passeig del Born, which is lined with some of Barcelona's most exclusive shops, restaurants and bars. Historically El Born was the heart of Spain's textile industry, and after a slump during the Franco era the area has recently recovered its crown, with many prominent design houses now based here. The

# DISTRICTS**OF**BARCELONA

1. CIUTAT VELLA
2. EIXAMPLE
3. SANTS–MONTJUÏC
4. LES CORTS
5. SARRIÀ SANT GERVASI
6. GRÀCIA
7. HORTA GUIARDÓ
8. NOU BARRIS
9. SANT ANDREU
10. SANT MARTÍ

SPAIN

BARCELONA

MEDITERRANEAN SEA

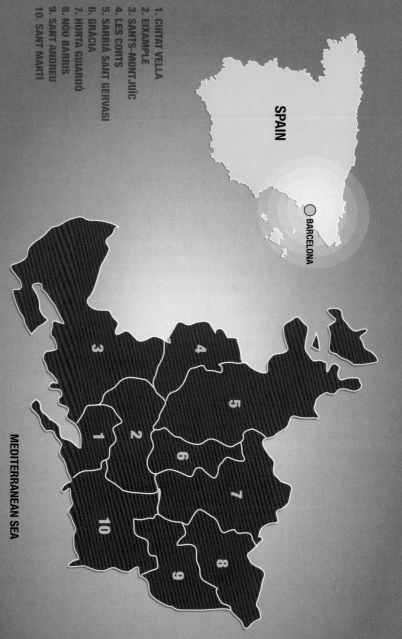

result is a population of moneyed, elegant career men and women who mingle freely with the barrio's long-time residents.

Rents here are relatively high but the location, bordering the sparkling Barceloneta beach complex and sprawling Parc de la Ciutadella, can't be faulted, the area is served by four metro stations, and the stately medieval charm of the architecture is hard to deny. Despite the influx of wealth to the area it still retains a pleasant atmosphere, and feels decidedly local, with a good supply of smaller shops and businesses. A one bedroom apartment averages € 675.

**Good for:** professionals
**Less good for:** those on a budget

## Barri Gótic

For many people, the Barri Gótic represents Barcelona in its most archetypal form: narrow alleyways, broad medieval plazas, wandering musicians and centuries of history seeping out of the cobblestones. As a result, it's a good choice if you want to feel like you're living in a postcard. However, rents are predictably high; in fact, due to the large tourist presence in the area, just about everything is expensive, with some of the city's most extortionate (and not necessarily best) restaurants and bars to be found here, and a distinct lack of useful convenience stores or cheap supermarkets.

However, if you know where to go, the nightlife here can be excellent, and in the past few years the area has become increasingly hip, although not suffocatingly so: the streets behind the tourist-trappy Plaça Reial are home to some great small bars and cafes.

One thing to consider, though, is that the area does tend to attract pickpockets and petty criminals, and after its tourist focussed restaurants and bars have closed for the night Plaça Reial becomes a meeting point for local winos and something of a drug-dealing hotspot. Add to this the stream of revellers moving between the area's bars and venues, and those who like their peace and quiet (and peace of mind) may wish to live elsewhere. A one bedroom apartment averages € 575.

**Good for:** authentic atmosphere
**Less good for:** the quiet life

## El Raval

Traditionally the seedy and somewhat mysterious home of Barcelona's working-class and immigrant populations, as little as ten years ago El Raval was something of a no-go area, renowned for its high crime rate and its problems with drug use and prostitution. However, as rents hurtled up across the city, students, artists, musicians and cultural outsiders of all stripes began to move into the area's spacious lofts and dank basements, and now it's cleaned up its act to become a noisy, vibrant melting pot, combining a strong immigrant flavour (falafel and kebab joints abound) with an arty sensibility which manifests itself through hip restaurants, record shops and trendy boutiques. The colourful facades of the houses here reflect the sense of *joie de vivre* that the barrio undoubtedly exudes, and on summer nights the streets teem with young people moving between bars; the range of venues and galleries mean that residents are never short of things to do.

Although El Raval is a stone's throw away from La Rambla and the heart of tourist Barcelona, it is far from having completely lost its harder edge, and in the knot of alleys away from the barrio's main thoroughfares it's easy to feel far away from the safety of the city's well-lit central squares.

It's possible to find some real bargains in El Raval, although potential residents should note that many of the houses and apartments here are to be found in old buildings, many of which have been poorly maintained and suffer from problems such as damp or lack of amenities.

Noise is another potential issue in this area, as on summer nights the streets team with a rowdy mix of locals, students and savvy tourists making the most of the barrio's nightlife; best to decide in advance whether you prefer edgy ambience to the possibility of a good night's sleep. A one bedroom apartment averages € 500.

**Good for:** nightlife, budget rents
**Less good for:** families

## Gràcia

Although the penniless artists and political non-conformists who traditionally lived in quirky, elegant Gràcia have been somewhat marginalised in recent years by spiralling rents, the *barrio* still represents a relatively affordable way to live within

easy reach of the centre of Barcelona while avoiding the exhausting bustle of the city centre.

A village in its own right until the city swallowed it up around a century ago, Gràcia retains an individualistic, slightly bohemian feel, with narrow streets, picturesque plazas, independent shops and a decidedly local ambience. Amenities are excellent if you don't mind being insular and sticking close to home – you can buy your fruit and veg in the extensive covered market and explore the many cafes and bars after sunset, and Gaudí's sprawling fairytale complex Parc Güell is close by - but those who want to enjoy big city life as well as the local haunts may find the lack of transport into the centre of Barcelona frustrating. For this reason, it may not be the wisest choice for those who will need to do a lot of commuting, as the savings made on rent will be chipped away by the cost of daily metro tickets. However, it's worth remembering that a long commute by Spanish standards looks laughably stress-free to someone accustomed to living in a city such as London or New York, where journeys of up to an hour each way are commonplace.

Those who choose to live here are mostly young professionals or well-to-do creative types, although the area also has a smattering of young families looking to leave behind the heat and dust of Barcelona proper. A one bedroom apartment averages € 750.

**Good for:** young professionals
**Less good for:** city centre life

## Sitges

If city life just isn't your thing but the suburbs look a little too boxy and bland for your taste, join the stream of fancy-free exiles heading for Sitges, a hip, elegant and

pretty beach town just over 35km south of Barcelona and half an hour away by train. Renowned for its riotous carnival and international film festival, the town has a laid-back, anything-goes feel, with its anti-establishment roots stretching back to the Franco era, during which it became the country's countercultural hub. There's a big gay and lesbian community here, and many people come to enjoy the clothing-optional beaches, but the atmosphere never strays over into seediness; Sitges is confident, chic and classy.

The area is also a hotspot for international residents, and approximately 35% of the population hails from France, Britain, the Netherlands and Scandinavia, attracted by the excellent infrastructure and amenities and the several good international schools. Many of them are moneyed families who can enjoy the clean sea air without worrying too much about employment prospects in an area that depends heavily on tourism.

The other downside to Sitges is price: although you may be able to find a cramped apartment on the outskirts of town without having to sell any major organs, the commute to Barcelona will hurt your pocket, and those hoping to rent or buy anything comfortable, let alone luxurious, will be in for a shock: prices are creeping up to the level seen in any major European city. If it's out of your range, console yourself with the thought that

from around March to August, Sitges parties non-stop, and the noise, heat and constant stream of boisterous tourists quickly become exhausting. A one bedroom apartment averages € 850.

**Good for:** sea air, summer celebrations
**Less good for:** life on a budget

## San Cugat

A big favorite with families, San Cugat is very much part of Barcelona's commuter belt. It's close enough to the city to be convenient but boasts a homely atmosphere, picturesque architecture in the form of a Benedictine monastery, and green space in the sort of quantities that city dwellers can only dream of.

Prices are moderate to high here, with both houses and apartments available, but those hoping to find a vibrant cultural scene or hip nightlife here might end up disappointed – the emphasis is very much on peace and quiet and living the suburban good life. Nevertheless, it's a good choice for those with children, and local facilities are excellent, as are transport links both to Barcelona and to the rest of the region. A one bedroom apartment averages €680.

**Good for:** families
**Less good for:** nightlife

## L'Eixample

Dating from 1859 when city planners decided that Barcelona was too cramped and began to mark out new roads, L'Eixample (or 'the extension') is an area of uniformly arranged streets that now covers almost half of the city centre.

Although the area is the centre of Barcelona's commerce, there's a good mix of affordable and more upscale housing, and location is second to none – the heart of Barcelona is within walking distance, and all parts of the city are easily accessible by an excellent network of buses and underground trains. It's home to lots of young professionals, and ideal for those who want to feel like they're really living in the centre of the city – you can barely move without running into some spectacular modernist architecture here, and Gaudi's magnificent Sagrada Familia cathedral, still slowly inching towards completion, looms over the district.

L'Eixample is also home to Barcelona's gay district, with many excellent gay clubs, shops and bars. For families, there is a good range of schools in the area, while the many offices and businesses based here bring job opportunities, and accommodation prices can be surprisingly reasonable bearing in mind the area's enviable location and numerous amenities. However, the area lacks some of the mystery and atmosphere of the old town, and can feel a little uniform at times. A one bedroom apartment averages € 700.

**Good for:** transport and work
**Less good for:** ambience

## Zona Alta

Home to Barcelona's wealthiest inhabitants, Zona Alta is set at a discreet distance from the chaos of the city and is home to some of its most imposing houses and apartments, set on a series of hills at the foot of the imposing Tibidabo mountain. This is a mecca for Barcelona's middle-aged professionals who have made their money in the city's arts or publishing industry, and even though it's resolutely residential, the neighbourhood does have a slight bohemian flavour too.

You're relatively well connected here, with the city centre just a short metro ride away and the Ronda, the city's ring road, giving you access to the suburbs and the countryside beyond, but a car is really necessary to navigate the long leafy boulevards, especially in the dust and heat of the summer. The nightlife here consists mostly of upmarket restaurants and bars that sometimes stray away from elegant and towards snooty, and the prices are another potential downside – the fact that many famous Barcelona residents choose to live in this oasis of urban calm is reflected in the rents, which are the highest in the city. Those who want to feel as if they are in the thick of things or are on a budget may feel happier in some of the city's more central, grittier districts. A one bedroom apartment averages € 950.

# Where to live: Seville

The big decision when moving to the Seville area is whether to live within or outside the city limits. Both have their advantages: Seville's city centre is full of opportunities for nightlife, employment and socialising, but its suburbs are much cheaper, albeit less traditionally 'Spanish' in atmosphere. Seville's transport infrastructure is generally very good, though, and will improve further when the metro opens in 2008 (although its arrival has already been delayed countless times, to the vocal frustration of the city's residents).

## Inside the city

### La Macarena

For those who are planning to live in Seville for more than a few months, and who would like to be central while avoiding the tourist traps of some of the better-known *barrios*, La Macarena is a popular choice. It's 10 minutes from the city's main shopping street, Calle Sierpies, and only 20 minutes from the Cathedral and Giralda, but it feels much further from the picture-postcard image of the city.

Traditionally La Macarena has always been working class, and today it retains its harder edge. Until a decade ago, much of the *barrio* was a virtual no-go area due to high levels of crime and poverty, but the city has since poured money into the area, razing to the ground the slum-like buildings near San Luis and improving the infrastructure; the area will be served by two metro stations when the long-delayed subway system finally opens in 2008.

The area's working-class antecedents have left a legacy of small, unpretentious local shops, cheap and authentically Spanish restaurants – which will pile your plate high for a few euros – and a friendly and local feel. More recently, Seville's alternative community has moved in, and trendy boutiques, alternative record shops and suppliers of goth and hippy clothing have sprung up on Calle Feria and the Alameda de Hercules. The area is also better served by supermarkets than the city's central, tourist-focused districts.

The nightlife in La Macarena is famous, or infamous, depending on whether you're the one out clubbing on a Tuesday night or the one who's trying to get a good night's sleep before work the next day. There is also a heartening supply of small, trendy and very friendly local bars where you can pick up a coffee or a beer for a couple of euros. Another big point in La Macarena's favour are the cheap rents to be found here – it's a popular area with students and there is a ready supply of studio apartments, one bedroom flats and cheap houseshares. Rents are likely to increase over the next few years as the city invests further in the area, but for now it's still very affordable by Seville's standards.

La Macarena isn't as airbrushed as the centre of Seville, and for that reason some people prefer to avoid it in favour of the central *barrios* or the distant suburbs. But for those who want to experience the real Seville without

straying too far from the beauty and history of the city centre, La Macarena is a sound choice. You can find a room in a shared house for as little as €200 here, or a studio apartment for €350.

**Good for:** local atmosphere
**Less good for:** peace and quiet

## El Arenal

Stretching from the Cathedral down to the riverbank, this historic fishing district with its cobbled streets and traditional white buildings is seen by many residents as a pleasant middle ground between the picture-postcard perfection of Seville's central districts and the slightly grittier face presented by areas such as Triana or La Macarena. The area's renowned for its restaurants, and although many are geared towards the tourist trade and are very expensive by Seville's standards, there are some local gems hidden in the narrow side streets if you know where to look; locals will be happy to point you in the right direction.

There's also no shortage of history here, with the magnificent Torre de Oro overlooking the river and the majestic Maestranza bullring perched on the edge of the district. El Arenal is also the cultural centre of the city, and you can find numerous theatres and opera houses here. However, those who are living in the *barrio* long-term might start to tire of the lack of amenities such as large, cheap supermarkets, and may begin to resent the tourists who swarm through the *barrio*'s streets in the summer.

Its centrality and authentic Sevillian atmosphere makes El Arenal a fairly expensive choice, at around €500 per month for a one-bedroom apartment. It's

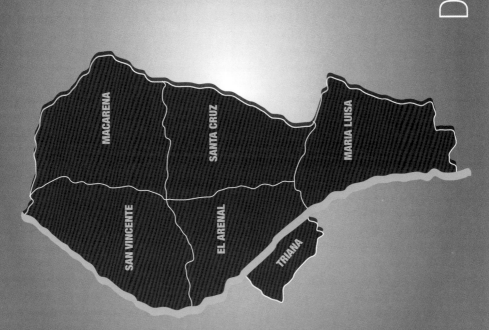

SPAIN

SEVILLE

MACARENA

SANTA CRUZ

MARIA LUISA

SAN VINCENTE

EL ARENAL

TRIANA

popular with older people, families with children and professionals.

> **Good for:** young professionals
> **Less good for:** nightlife

## Santa Cruz

Santa Cruz is the first port of call for anyone who comes to Seville as a tourist. With its whitewashed buildings, narrow, winding streets, ornamental gardens, decorative wrought-iron balconies and spreading palm trees it's a sort of microcosm of the foreigner's dream of authentic Spain, although the area encompasses a strong Moorish influence too, and historically it was the city's Jewish quarter. There are ornate churches, cobbled streets and beautiful blue-and-white Azulejo religious murals.

However, as delightful as Santa Cruz may be to wander through for the weekend, its suitability as a residential area for someone who is planning to live in Seville long-term is a matter of opinion. It undoubtedly is beautiful, but because of this rents are very high here, and residents tend to be wealthy professional families and older people; you can easily pay €800 for an apartment here. There are also a growing number of residents who are investing in property in the *barrio* and then letting it out short-term to tourists, giving the area something of an impermanent feel. The area around Santa Maria de la Blanca is rather bland, a confection of extortionately priced hotels and expensive tourist-focused restaurants serving lacklustre paella.

However, as you move towards Plaza Alfalfa the area picks up considerably, and some of the city's best bars are to be found on Perez Galdos, along with some small and reasonably priced fruit and vegetable shops and two supermarkets. There is also a launderette and a video rental store, and some authentically Spanish (although very pricy) bodegas, where you can pay premium prices to drink a glass of wine, eat some chorizo and be stared at disapprovingly by a sullen waiter.

In the tourist season, though, Santa Cruz can try anyone's patience, as the impossibly narrow streets become packed with slow-moving tourists, the temperatures soar and many locals escape to the coast for their vacation. This is also the time when the pickpockets move in to take advantage of the seasonal trade, and living in the *barrio* can become something of a daily struggle.

> **Good for:** architecture and atmosphere
> **Less good for:** local amenities

## Triana

Although it doesn't boast the same pristine storybook feel of Santa Cruz, Triana has a strong claim to the title of Seville's most atmospheric neighbourhood. It's located just across the bridge from El Arenal, and its most famous street, Calle Betis, the entrance to a former slum and still a sight to behold with its brightly coloured facades, awnings and doorways, stretches along the banks of the Guadalquivir. Traditionally a strongly working-class district, Triana has a distinct hint of mystery about it, and is the closest you can now get to the Seville of the 1930s and 40s, the golden age of flamenco. It has long been the home of the city's gypsy population, and is the birthplace of too many storytellers, flamenco dancers, poets and bullfighters to count. The duende, or mysterious spirit, which flamenco draws on for its emotional power, is strong here, and although parts of the area are distinctly touristy, it's still possible to find dark unlabelled doorways through which the sound of flamenco guitar leaks into the night, and behind them impromptu bars where the drinking and the dancing last all night. Many people choose to live here because, for them, it is the real Seville, more genuine than touristy Santa Cruz and more authentically Spanish than the washed-out commercial and residential districts on the outskirts of the city. Rents are still relatively affordable, and if you move here, your neighbours are likely to be old-timers and families with strong ties to the area rather than hip young professionals.

Its location, a 20-minute walk across the shining Guadalquivir river from the city centre, and its local flavour, make Triana a genuinely pleasurable place to live: there are plenty of shops, many selling clothes and household goods at knockdown prices, and you'll never be short of places to relax with a cool beer or cup of strong coffee. A room in a shared house in Triana is currently available for €300, including some bills.

> **Good for:** flamenco spirit
> **Less good for:** mod cons

## La Cartuja

La Isla Cartuja was the site of Seville's Expo exhibition in 1992, and is now known predominantly for the theme park, which has been built on the foundations of the Spanish pavilion. However, it is a growing residential area, with new apartment blocks springing up, and there is an increasing student presence in the area as new student residences are built around the university campuses that are located here. There's also a pleasant park in the shape of the Olympic Stadium. The Antique discotheque is also a big draw, although nightlife in the area as a whole is somewhat scanty. Apartments in the area are still fairly affordable, and a studio will set you back around €350, something of a bargain if being within easy reach of the city centre is more important to you than a thriving local scene.

> **Good for:** students
> **Less good for:** things to do

## Outside the city

## Bellavista

Seville's southernmost neighbourhood is home to around 20,000 inhabitants, the vast majority of them professionals and young families who commute into the city to work. Local connections are relatively good, with a bus taking you into the city in around 10 minutes. It isn't the most atmospheric place, although the boxy apartment blocks that have been springing up in recent decades are built around a pretty medieval core, and there are plenty of good local amenities. Although geographically very close to the centre of Seville, it's possible to feel very far away from the noise, traffic, nightlife and possibilities for adventure that the big city offers when living here.

> **Good for:** peace and quiet
> **Less good for:** students, young people

## Dos Hermanas

A mid-size town around 15km south of Seville, Dos Hermanas is popular for those who want to live slightly away from the touristy hustle and bustle of Seville and have easier access to the wilds of real Andalucía. It's far cheaper in terms of rent than its better-known neighbour, and has a large number of small, inexpensive restaurants and bars, but this saving will be marginally offset by transport costs for anyone who is planning to commute regularly into the city. There are good shopping facilities,

### The Andalucían accent

Those who have learnt standard Castilian and who then move to Andalucía may be confused by the differences between the local dialect and the language in its textbook form. Confusingly, one of the most difficult-to-grasp features of the Spanish accent, namely the pronunciation of the letters 'c' and 'z' as a 'th' sound, doesn't happen here, where they are both pronounced as 's'. Even more confusing is the Andalucían habit of dropping an 's' when it falls at the end of a word: for example, in Andalucía you will often hear 'Adió' rather than 'Adiós', which can be problematic when trying to distinguish between a singular and plural noun. The thickest Andalucían accents drop the final consonants from many words, and elide the 'd' sound in words such as rosado, resulting in a broad-sounding accent.

Language is a highly political issue in Spain, and Andalucía's government refers to the regional dialect as a 'language' in its own right. Some linguists have lobbied for it to be recognised as a Creole, a mixture between Spanish and the Arabic languages spoken by the Moors. However, throughout the rest of Spain the accent has a mixed reputation, represented both as denoting an authentic Spanishness and also as being the language of the yokel in the country's uncultured backwaters.

Famous Andalucíans often drop their accent in favour of standard Spanish; a notable exception is the actor Antonio Banderas, who speaks in his native accent in interviews as well as in many of his roles.

and an excellent infrastructure, with efficient local schools, hospitals and services. It also has a distinctly provincial feel, populated mostly by families with a fair share of older residents, and younger people may find it slightly suffocating, although anyone in doubt about the town's cultural provenance should remember that it is home to Los del Río, the shiny-shirted duo who perpetrated the international hit single (and accompanying dance routine) 'Macarena'.

When Seville's subway finally opens Dos Hermanas will be connected directly to the city, but until then the numerous train and bus services, taking between 10 and 30 minutes, are perfectly sufficient.

**Good for:** suburban living
**Less good for:** culture and entertainment

## Sevilla Este

As the name suggests, this is a residential and commercial district situated on the eastern side of Seville. It's a relatively new urbanisation, and while it is fairly smart, the area is still somewhat lacking in terms of local amenities; fine if you don't mind travelling into the city when you fancy a night out, but less suitable, perhaps, if you're looking for a vibrant local scene. Transport connections in the area are also not what they could be, although this is expected to improve in the coming years as the area grows in population and popularity.

**Good for:** peace and quiet
**Less good for:** local amenities

## Mairena del Aljarafe

In recent years this southern outpost has become a haven for those hoping to escape the fast pace of life in the big city, and it now boasts around 40,000 inhabitants. The housing is mostly fair quality but unremarkable, with the exception of neighbourhoods such as Simón Verde, which is very upmarket, catering to well-heeled commuters and exiles from the more touristy neighbourhoods of Seville. While it is a good choice for families, young people and students may find the area somewhat lacking in character. But there are plenty of green spaces, schools and local shops in Aljarafe as a whole, and in 2006 the new Metromar mall made the area something of a bargain-hunter's paradise.

However, the area has a problem in infrastructure terms, namely the lack of connections to the city; road networks are very poor, although when the subway opens the town will be linked directly to Seville. Investment in the area is also increasing, and many new buildings are under construction.

**Good for:** facilities
**Less good for:** getting around

## Nervión

Before 1911, Nervión was mostly fields, devoted almost entirely to cotton production. However, as Seville as grown, so has Nervión, and this suburb is now locally known as Seville's 'second centre'. Designed by the renowned Spanish architect Anibal Gonzalez, it's spacious and airy, even if it doesn't quite match the historical centre of the city in terms of atmosphere and authentically Andalucían ambience.

FACT

■ Designed by the renowned Spanish architect Anibal Gonzalez, Nervión is spacious and airy, even if it doesn't quite match the historical centre of the city in terms of atmosphere and authentically Andalucían ambience.

The local amenities can't be faulted; as well as having an enviable supply of food shops and affordable local restaurants, and the Nervión Plaza mall with its cluster of big-name chain stores, Nervión is excellently connected in terms of transport, not only to Seville proper but to the rest of Spain. The largest train station serving the Seville area, Santa Justa station, is to be found here, and you can hop on high-speed trains to Madrid and Barcelona as well as regional services to Granada and Cadiz. There's plenty of green space, notably in the form of El Prado, a series of tranquil gardens.

Nervión also has another claim to fame: it's home to one of Seville's pair of perpetually warring football teams, Sevilla FC, who play in the modern and streamlined Estadio Ramón Sanchez Pizjuan stadium. This, combined with the fact that Seville's business school is close by and students are a common sight in the local bars and cafés, gives Nervión a slightly younger edge. Expect to pay around €500 for an apartment in this area.

**Good for:** shopping and transport
**Less good for:** ambience

## Los Remedios

To the south of Triana lies Los Remedios, a fairly staid residential and business district where many professionals and upper middle-class families choose to live, among them many expats. It's a fairly new area, having sprung up around the Avenida de la Republica Argentina which was built in 1945. There's little of the local colour that is generally associated with sultry Seville, but it's certainly convenient for the city, and will become even more so when the metro opens in 2008: three stations will serve the area. Nightlife is nothing spectacular, and most residents choose to head into the city for a meal or a night out, although it's very well served in terms of supermarkets, chain shops, schools and other local amenities. Its popularity with well-heeled families has pushed up prices in recent years, and when you factor in the cost of regular travel into the city, those on a budget may prefer to look elsewhere.

**Good for:** professionals and families
**Less good for:** students, young people

# ■ RENTING

## Types of properties

Despite the fact that Spain a relatively small rental market, there are thousands of apartments and villas for rent in Spain, available both through commercial agents and through private owners. For those who are planning to live in Spain for anything from a few months to a year or two and who don't want to tackle the bureaucracy involved in buying a house, renting can be a good solution.

Those who are planning to buy in Spain may also choose to rent a property initially, as it represents a less permanent commitment and will allow you time to make up your mind about where you want to live, to see if you like the area, the climate and the amenities and decide what kind of property will suit your needs.

A wide range of properties is available throughout Spain, from bijou studio apartments in the heart of the country's big cities to rural villas and traditional cottages in inland areas. Many people choose to rent a property to spend a winter in Spain, away from the harsh British weather; if you are thinking about renting a holiday villa or apartment, remember that such properties are mainly purpose-built for summer only residence, and that even in the south of Spain winter can still be chilly. Marble floors can be unpleasantly frigid on the feet over the winter months, the walls not particularly thick. Electricity bills can also blow your budget in harsh winters, as some Spanish rental properties rely solely on expensive electric fan heaters.

The disadvantage of Spanish rentals generally is that, price-wise, they can be fairly exorbitant, with prices in sought-after locations such as Mallorca starting at a minimum of €900 per month. Rents in Madrid and San Sebastián are uniformly expensive, and to up to €2000 a month or more for a spacious two or three-bedroom house. Prices in these places are comparable to London but rents in cities such as Valencia and Seville are far more reasonable. Those looking for a room in a shared flat or house in either Madrid or Barcelona should expect to pay €300 or more per month, plus bills. Prices will depend on the size of the property, the time of year, and the location – beach and golf properties command premium rates and as elsewhere the cheapest rents are to be found in the smaller towns and villages inland away from the coasts. Rents on short-term accommodation will be at their highest in July and August (and often over Christmas and Easter), and at their lowest in late autumn and over the winter.

Many apartments for rent in Spain are part of a block of flats or *urbanizaciónes*, which work on the *comunidad de propietarios* (community of owners) principle, similar to the concept of *copropriété* in France. Both concepts involve the sharing of some communal facilities (e.g. swimming pool, car park, garden areas), towards the upkeep of which tenants pay a monthly fee. This fee covers such costs as stair cleaning, rubbish disposal, and garden maintenance, and the level of the fee varies according to the size of the flat: the smarter and larger the flat, the more you pay. This fee can be as high as €230 a month for the more upmarket apartment blocks.

When renting a property within a 'community of owners' as it is known, it is important to get a copy of the deed establishing this communal ownership (called the Deed of Horizontal Division) and to become familiar with the rules of the Community. A meeting of all residents (owners and tenants) of these communal apartment blocks is usually held once or twice a year to plan the following year's budget, elect representatives, and to discuss maintenance, refurbishment and the like. It is your legal duty to attend these meetings, which are a useful way to meet the neighbours, or an interminable waste of time, depending to your point of view.

On leaving a property at the end of a lease the landlord will check the inventory of the contents of the property and has the right to charge the tenant from the deposit for any missing items or breakages. Note, however, that the landlord is obliged to replace and repair items such as water heaters, kitchen appliances and washing machines, at a cost to himself, that have broken through general wear and tear. Additionally, when you leave a rented property the landlord may levy a charge for cleaning.

## Short-term renting

Another option for those who are planning to live in Spain for a short period of time is to take a short let. Short-term lets differ from longer lets in that the rental price will usually include all utilities such as electricity, gas and water. Renting for longer than a month may have reduced weekly rates but you may have to pay utility bills separately.

You will usually be required to sign a contract and pay a deposit to secure a property. Before you hand over any money or sign the contract, check the terms and conditions of the property rental very carefully. The deposit may be refundable either in whole or in part up to one month before your booking. However, if you cancel within a month of your booking, the deposit is rarely returned. Some travel insurance policies may refund your deposit if you have to cancel your accommodation owing to unforeseen circumstances, such as family illness, but others may not. Before you can move into a property you are usually required to pay for the rental accommodation in full, although if your rental is for longer than four weeks you may be able to pay in monthly instalments. Depending on how long you will be staying you may also be required to pay a deposit in case of breakages or damage to the property. If the property needs extra cleaning after you have left, the deposit may be used to pay for this; otherwise, all being well, the deposit will be returned to you after you have moved out of the property. If you are booking a short-term let from outside Spain, check that the company or individual you're planning to book through is reputable before parting with any money or deposits. Be wary of parting with large sums of money to unidentifiable individuals.

## Finding a property

Major tour operators like Thomson (www.thomson.co.uk) and First Choice (www. firstchoice.co.uk) offer many such longer-term stays, and in particular cater for older people. The Spanish Tourist Office (22–23 Manchester Square, London W1U 3PX; 020 7486 8077; www.tourspain.co.uk) can supply on request a list of many companies that offer self-catering holidays in villas, apartments and rural houses. In some resort areas it can be harder to find a long-term rental due in part to the high demand for such properties, but also because property owners prefer the higher returns they can get from short-term holiday lets.

Finding a place to live in the country's capital, Madrid, can be difficult, but one of the contributors to this book, Hal Shaw, recommends a company called Room Madrid (Calle Conde Duque 7, 28015 Madrid; 915 480335), with English-speaking staff, which placed him in an excellent apartment for a reasonable fee.

### Advertisements

You will find advertisements offering property for rent in the property magazines listed in the chapter on Daily Life, in local area newspapers, and even national newspapers and magazines, both in Spain and at home. Some estate agents handle properties for rent as well as for sale and many estate agents now market themselves through the internet . A quick search on Google (www.google.com) will bring up a number of websites offering short- and long-term rents all over Spain. Websites about a specific area or region often have links to sites offering rental accommodation and many owners of property now have their own website to attract customers.

There are many companies offering self-catering holiday lets, though these will invariably work out to be more expensive than renting privately as such companies are looking for a high turnover of clients throughout the high season rather than longer-term tenants. Although these companies may offer out-of-season lets at a

**TIP**

■ Finding a place to live in the country's capital, Madrid, can be difficult, but one of the contributors to this book, Hal Shaw, recommends a company called Room Madrid (Calle Conde Duque 7, 28015 Madrid; 915 480335), with English-speaking staff, which placed him in an excellent apartment for a reasonable fee.

> 'I rented a property for the first six weeks, sight unseen, while I was in England. It was absolutely fine, and by British standards the rent was reasonable, but as soon as I'd got to grips with the country I found a new place, a little further out but much cheaper. I found my apartment in the classifieds section of the city newspaper, but there are also signs in shop windows and taped to lampposts advertising rental apartments; they seem a bit unofficial but I know people who found great places this way. It's definitely worth waiting until you can see a place to make a decision about whether you want to live there long-term.'
>
> **Dan Hancox**

cheaper rate, such lets are often impractical for those seeking to remain in one area for some time as the rental period is only as long as the low (winter) season.

In Spain, dealing with a registered estate agent means dealing with an agency belonging to either the *Agente de Propiedad Inmobiliaria (API) or the Gestor Intermediario de Promociones y Edificaciones* (GIPE). These agencies display their certificate of registration and identification number on the premises and seeing these should give you some confidence in moving forward with that agency. Any API-registered estate agency employs an API accredited lawyer and has paid a bond. Agents who carry the API stamp have received official training from Spain's Ministerio de Fomento. Their fees are regulated, and misconduct by an API agent can result in fines and a revoked licence. A group of long-established property agents based mainly on the Costa del Sol have also formed a group called 'Leading Property Agents of Spain', better known as LPA. All members are professionally qualified. They adhere to a strict code of ethics and are dedicated to giving highly professional and quality service to both buyers and sellers in southern Spain.

When looking for a place to rent, personal recommendation and the 'friend-of-a-friend' approach may be the best way of avoiding unexpected problems, as well as helping you to find the best deal. The locals may well know of someone who has accommodation available for rent. Check the noticeboards of local supermarkets and churches and bars where expats congregate, or try posting your requirements in internet forums on expat websites. Clubhouses on golf courses, shops in marinas and kiosks also often have small noticeboards, which may turn up a suitable property.

One of the best places to look is in the small ad sections of local newspapers (both the Spanish papers and the English-language papers), and free sheets. The classifieds magazine Segundamano (www.segundamano.es) sold in Madrid and central Spain has lists of properties to rent for the entire country.

If you find a property that sounds good, be prepared to act quickly – buy the newspaper in the morning of that day that it is published and make contact with the person who has placed the advertisement immediately to organise a time to view the property. Advertisements in Spanish newspapers for property to let are listed under *alquileres*.

## Useful addresses

**Holiday Rentals Ltd:** 020 8846 3444; www.holiday-rentals.co.uk. Holiday homes booked direct through the owner. Over 45,000 properties worldwide.

**Interhome Ltd:** 383 Richmond Road, Twickenham, Surrey TW1 2EF; 020 8780 6633; email info@interhome.co.uk; www.interhome.co.uk.

**Masia Rentals:** 01439 788899; www.masiarentals.com. Restored Masia guesthouse a few miles inland from Sitges on the Costa Dorada.

**Rent in Spain:** 616 374973/0870 128 9000; www.rent-in-spain.com. Holiday rentals and longer lets across Spain.

**Villas Ferrer:** 965 780263; email info@villasferrer.com; www.villasferrer.com. Winter and spring rentals on the Costa Blanca.

**Villas Spain Rentals:** www.villas-spain-rentals.com

## Rental laws and costs

Spanish renting and letting laws were extensively updated with the enforcement of regulations passed in 1985. These were revised in the Rent Law of January 1995. These regulations have ended some very strict forms of tenant protection, which included what was in effect the tenant's right to an indefinitely extendable rental contract, sometimes at 1964 rates! This situation was regarded as unfair to landlords and made many owners think twice about renting out their property. Rents in some circumstances can now be raised by more than the cost-of-living index. However, there are still some third-generation Spanish families in Madrid paying these low protected rents for centrally located apartments.

The new legislation means that the rights of tenants are very similar to those in Britain, with some additional protection that stops landlords raising the rent unfairly. When a rental contract specifies that the rental period ends, for example, in July, it means just that. All tenants now have the right to renew their tenancy for an initial minimum period of five years and if a tenant fails to vacate the property when the temporary contract expires, the owner does not have the right to evict if a renewal has been sought. So a landlord must offer a tenant a new contract, which can either be temporary or long-term. It used to be that landlords could raise the rent as much as they liked in the process, however, the present situation is that most annual rent rises are in line with inflation and the Consumer Price Index (IPC), which is rarely more than 3% to 4%.

Arrangements are often administered by a rental agency and payments are made to the agency. In Spain as elsewhere all evictions involve the rather time-consuming and costly (for the landlord) process of getting a court order first, but it is the responsibility of a tenant to give one month's clear notice before the end of a contract or he or she may have to pay compensation to the landlord.

There is provision for a tenant to pay a deposit of one month's rent for unfurnished accommodation, or two months for furnished accommodation. This would be lodged with the local autonomous community. Additional guarantees may also be negotiated.

Rental agencies will ask for an extra month's rent in advance, plus a commission for the agency service itself (usually of an additional month's rent). This way of searching for an apartment tends be more expensive, but offers more security and is a way to avoid the interminable search for the 'right' place. Many rentals that are part of an apartment block or *urbanización* work on the *comunidad* principle where communal facilities (and some bills) are shared. Tenants pay a monthly fee for the maintenance of services, so need to be aware of these charges in advance.

**FACT**

■ All tenants now have the right to renew their tenancy for an initial minimum period of five years and if a tenant fails to vacate the property when the temporary contract expires, the owner does not have the right to evict if a renewal has been sought.

# Signing the contract

As is the case in the UK and in many other countries, the rental contract is a foundation of the rent agreement for any kind of property in Spain. While verbal contracts are still valid in Spain, they are not advisable, regardless of the length of the rental. Short-term leases (for a period of six months or less) are known as *por temporada*, while long lets, which generally give tenants more rights than a short-term let, are known as *viviendas*. Longer-term contracts often require tenants living in blocks of flats to pay *comunidad* fees. However, if these charges are not mentioned in the contract, they are wholly the landlord's responsibility and the tenant is under no obligation to pay them or to have them imposed subsequently.

All long-term tenants are legally required to take out house insurance on the property they are renting. The choice of insurance company is entirely his or her own decision and cannot be dictated by the landlord.

Contracts are drawn up through the standard, state-sponsored tenant/landlord agreements which are available from street kiosks and *estanco*s: it is really your responsibility as the tenant to obtain one of these and to make sure the contract type matches the rent you will be paying, as contracts vary. A contract will include personal details of the tenant and the landlord together with information about the property (location, size, and inventory of furnishing and fittings) the terms of the lease and payment and expenses details. It may be advisable to have the contract checked by a solicitor or someone who really knows about rentals before signing. The written contract should clearly state the amount of rent payable and when the tenant should pay it (usually within the first five days of every month). Many rental contracts ask for rent to be paid by direct debit into the landlord's bank account.

When you sign a contract for a long-term let you will usually need to pay between one and three month's rent as a deposit or bond to cover damages to the property. When the contract is terminated, the deposit is returned in full or in part depending on the state of the property. Sometimes the tenant and landlord may agree to use up the deposit in lieu of rent at the end of a lease. You will need to agree on whether the landlord or tenant pays rates, the property tax *Impuesto sobre Bienes Inmuebles* (IBI) and community fees and you will almost certainly have to pay the bills for electricity, water, gas and the telephone. It is advisable to ask to see previous bills for the property to give you an idea of how much you will need to pay each month and also to make sure that all utility charges have been paid up to date.

The landlord's obligations include maintaining the property in good order and offering the services stated in the contract. Anyone who feels that they have a complaint to make regarding their rental contract can – surprisingly – apply to the local tourist office. This is more suitable for those in short lets, while semi-permanent and permanent tenants will do better to enquire at the nearest OMIC (Oficina Municipal de Información al Consumidor, www.omic.bcn.es) – the consumer information office run by the local government or autonomous community. Although the OMIC's function is primarily to deal with consumer problems, they will be able to put you in contact with the most effective place to register a formal rental complaint.

Unlike in the UK, it is fairly uncommon for Spanish landlords to perform formal credit checks on potential tenants. However, if a landlord does wish to perform a credit check and is perturbed by your lack of credit history, you could try pointing

TIP

■ It is advisable to ask to see previous bills for the property to give you an idea of how much you will need to pay each month and also to make sure that all utility charges have been paid up to date.

him to www.insolvency.gov.uk, where it is possible to search by surname for bad debts and past bankruptcies. UK guidelines state that it is reasonable for landlords to charge a small fee for credit checks, but that £80 is the absolute maximum you should ever be charged for such a service; use this figure as an indication of what is reasonable.

## Local taxes

As you do not own rented property, you are not eligible for some of Spain's more significant local taxes. However, you will still have to pay any community charges levied by the apartment block or development in which you live, if applicable. These charges may range from as little as €300 on a flat on a small development where the local authority provides more services, to as much as €3,000 on a large villa on a large development where the development takes responsibility for communal swimming pools and leisure facilities. As a very rough guideline, these charges may range between around 0.5% and 0.75% of the value of your property.

In almost all regions of Spain you will also be liable for Municipal Tax, which is commonly known as basura ('litter') and covers rubbish collection as well as fundamentals such as drain maintenance. The tax is sometimes combined with water consumption; your landlord will be able to tell you if this is the case in your area. It is usually payable in March and generally amounts to between €30 and €90 per year.

The most costly tax a tenant could be liable for is the IBI, which is best thought of as the equivalent of the UK's council tax. It covers local services and administration, and is payable in August or September. In short to medium lets it is customary for the landlord to pay the IBI; however, long-term tenants are often expected to pay it themselves. It is based on the value of the property as stated in the regional records, and is usually between 0.5% and 0.7% of this figure. It is important to note that demands for IBI are sometimes not sent out; the onus is on the liable party to pay the tax, otherwise it becomes a debt on the property.

## ■ SERVICES AND UTILITIES

It is essential to understand that although all public utility services are widely available in Spain, and that the service in question will always be provided in the end, how long it will take to arrive is far less certain. If the property in which you will be living has had electricity, gas and water services fairly recently, a phone call to the relevant companies should see you reconnected fairly quickly; however, if there have been no utilities at the property for some time this may take much longer.

Electricity, telephone and water bills have a payment term of between 15 days and a month, after which a reminder notice will be sent. If payment is still not made, the telephone line, water supply or electricity supply will be cut off and a reconnection fee charged. It is important to give the utility companies notice of a second address if you have one, or set up a standing order from your bank account so that you remain in credit with the utility service companies at all times. It makes sense to set up a standing order to pay this charge, although if you are in the area, paying early and in person can earn you a discount. Make sure that all bills have been paid up to date before you move into a property. If the previous owner has left without paying them then you will be responsible for clearing the debt.

# Electricity

The domestic electricity supply in Spain is mostly 220v or 225v AC, 50Hz and, less commonly in the more remote country areas, 110v or 125v AC. Plugs on electrical appliances in Spain are often two-pin in older properties and three-pin in more modern ones. UK appliances should perform quite adequately, if a little more slowly, using an adaptor while US appliances will need an adaptor plus a 220–110v transformer. Make sure to choose the right socket – flat pins for 220v or 110v. Light bulbs are usually 110v and are of the continental screw-in type. Adaptors can be found in the electrical section of the ubiquitous El Corte Inglés department store for a couple of euros.

Electricity is supplied by the electricity supply company (la compañía de electricidad) that operates in your area through the overhead lines of an extensive grid system linking the hydroelectric and atomic power stations with cities, towns and villages throughout the country. It is essential to organise meter installation or reconnection through your regional branch of the electricity company well in advance, as the waiting lists for both services can be very long. New tenants of a previously occupied property will need to present to the electricity company a Spanish bank account number with which to pay by standing order, and some form of identification document. The compañía de electricidad will come and inspect the electrics on the property and if they need updating you will need to have this done before you can transfer the contract for electricity from the previous owners into your name.

Electricity is priced on the international system of a small standing charge and a further charge per kilowatt-hour consumed, the rate for which diminishes as consumption increases. Bills are issued bimonthly and VAT (IVA) at the standard rate is added.

# Gas

The use of butane gas (butano) is not as common in Spain as in Northern Europe and, except in the larger cities and perhaps on *urbanizaciónes*, there tends to be no piped household supply. However, readily available bottled gas (supplied in cylinders known as bombonas) is still relatively cheap, although it has increased rapidly in price over the last few years (a large 12.5kg cylinder now costs approximately €12) and is commonly used for cooking and heating in most homes. Bombonas can be easily refilled through the butane home delivery service, which operates in most areas. Those in more secluded areas may have to collect their gas supplies from the local depot. As with electricity, if you are in an area where piped gas is provided you will need to sign up with the gas company and arrange to pay the monthly charge and gas bills by standing order. The gas companies are likely to come and inspect your appliances for safety every few years. Gas bills (for piped gas) are rendered bimonthly and VAT (IVA) is added.

Because gas is generally a cheaper form of energy than electricity many properties run as many household appliances as possible on it. There are safety issues when using gas, so check with your landlord that the property has adequate ventilation, that pipes are checked regularly to ensure that they haven't perished and that regulator valves are in good order. Leaked gas sinks and lingers in a room, where a spark or a dropped match will ignite it with disastrous results if there isn't the ventilation to disperse it. Bottled gas has a tendency to run out at the most inopportune times, so it pays to always make sure that you have an adequate supply ready for such eventualities.

# Water

Spanish water is perfectly safe to drink in almost all urban areas as government regulations require public water supplies to be treated with anti-pollutants. For this reason the water can have an unpleasant taste and most expats and visitors to Spain follow the example of the Spanish and drink bottled mineral water instead. This is cheap, of good quality and sold at practically every corner shop in Spain – con gas means carbonated and sin gas non-carbonated.

Although there is surplus rainfall in the north that provides an adequate natural water supply, water shortages can often occur over the summer months along the Mediterranean coast and in the Balearic Islands. The problem mainly arises because the municipalities individually control the supply of water and plans to lay national pipelines are continually frustrated by local political issues. The provision of desalination plants, purification plants and the sinking of wells are common topics of discussion in local politics. The Canary Islands, in particular, have a problem with sourcing enough water for the local populace.

The mains water piped to private premises is metered, with charges calculated either per cubic metre used, or at a flat rate. To have a water meter installed, you will need to apply to the local water company office with your passport, a copy of a previous water bill for the property if you have one, and the number of your bank account. A deposit is payable, and there is a charge made for installing (or repairing) a water meter. Bills are usually issued quarterly. Depending on the hardness of the water it may pay to have filters installed, preferably within the system (as opposed to just on the outlets), to prevent the furring up of pipes and radiators.

# Telephones

Telefónica (www.telefonica.es), Spain's equivalent to BT, was privatised in 1998 and although it has lost its monopoly in Spain, it still retains a powerful hold on the telephone service, with 87% of the market share.

## Installation charges

If you are renting a property, you may be asked to pay a deposit. Charges are currently around €130 for the initial connection fee and approx. €18 + VAT @ 16% per month's landline rental (the standing charge). You can buy or rent a handset. The standing charge will need to be paid bimonthly whether the property is inhabited or not and you should set up a standing order to cover this. If a telephone is disconnected (20 days after the last reminder for payment) there is a fairly hefty reconnection charge but the phone should be reconnected within 48 hours, once the charges have been paid. Connections should not take more than a few days to install, though in more isolated areas it may take longer. Those aged over 65 with a low income are eligible for discounts when using Telefónica services.

## Changing the name on an existing telephone contract

If you are taking over the account of a previous owner, you will need to arrange for the telephone company to close the existing telephone account, and send a final bill to the owners of the property on the day that you take possession of the property (the day you hand over the purchase price to the *notario*). A new account will then be opened in your name from the day you take possession of the property. There is a charge made for this service. It is also important to make sure that there are no arrears to be paid on previous bills sent to the address by the telephone company. If there are, then once you are the registered owner of the property you will be liable to pay them. Note that if you are going to be renting out your property, you should consider how you are going to charge any tenants for the use of the telephone.

## Call charges

Call charges in Spain are no bargain and are higher than those in the UK or USA. Since deregulation in 1998, competing telephone companies have offered alternative services to Telefónica and there is scope for using these other companies' services, especially for long distance and international calls. For a comparison of the rates of the different providers, visit www.teltarifas.com/particulares. The main national providers are BT Ignite (www.bt.es), Jazztel (www.jazztel.com), Tele2 (www.tele2.es) and Orange (www.orange.es). All offer alternative services and tariffs to those of Telefónica (www.telefonica.es). Some providers offer *tarifas planas,* or flat-rate charges. Others offer a discounted indirect phone service, which involves dialling an access code before every call.

Within Spain different tariffs are imposed depending on the time a call is made. Peak rate is from 8am–5pm Monday–Friday and 8am–2pm Saturday; a low rate is in operation from 10pm–8am Monday–Friday and 2pm–8am Saturday as well as all day Sunday and during holidays. Different telephone operators also have different tariffs, which are subject to change due to the competition that exists between the companies. Call charges vary depending on whether you are making a local, provincial or inter-provincial call.

 For a comparison of the rates of the different providers, visit www.teltarifas. com/particulares. The main national providers are BT Ignite (www.bt.es), Jazztel (www.jazztel.com), Tele2 (www.tele2.es) and Orange (www.orange.es).

The various telephone companies operating in Spain all offer various rates for international calls but generally they all offer a cheaper rate between 10pm and 8am Monday–Friday and all day at weekends and on holidays.

## Buy or rent furniture?

Properties are available both furnished and unfurnished in Spain, but, for longer lets especially, unfurnished is more common. However, 'unfurnished' can mean something very different in Spain to what it generally means in the UK, US, Canada and Australia. Whereas you might expect an unfurnished property to lack a bed, a couch, or curtains, many unfurnished properties in Spain are little more than empty shells, lacking carpets, light fittings, a stove, or even the kitchen sink! Check with the landlord in advance. Also, previous tenants may wish to strike a deal with you if they are leaving carpets or fittings: be prepared to negotiate!

Flea markets are a good source of cheap furniture, as is the ubiquitous IKEA, which sells cheap and cheerful furniture through its numerous outlets in Spain; see www.ikea.com.

# Buying a House in Spain

# ■ FINDING PROPERTIES FOR SALE

## Estate agents

Estate agents dealing in properties in Spain and other second-home hotspots such as Portugal, Italy and France are widespread. These agents will be more than willing to offer advice on the costs involved and to help handle the property buying transaction for you.

Discuss your requirements with the estate agent; sound them out about whether what you want is available or whether your ideas are unrealistic. Although the agents will be looking to sell properties already on their books, if they are bona fide they may well tell you honestly that you might do better by going to see their sister company or another estate agency that will be more likely to offer what you want. Giving an agency a clear idea of what you are looking for should save both you and them time and money. You don't want to end up traipsing around being shown totally unsuitable properties. On the other hand, discussing your requirements with an agency will also allow you to find out about possible alternatives. You may think you want a particular kind of property but the agency may come up with other suggestions, or localities that you hadn't considered previously.

Agents can take you to view properties in Spain, but you will need to make sure that you arrange an appointment to view far enough in advance of your trip out there. If you are going to Spain on a househunting trip and will be viewing a number of properties it is a good idea to take a digital camera and a map of the area along with you. Take photographs to help you remember salient points about each property that you view and mark the property on a detailed map of the area so that you can then scout around and get to know whether a particular location is right for you. If an agent is showing you the wrong kind of properties, let them know so that you, and they, can get back on to the right track. If you are on a househunting trip your time will be precious, although in many cases the right property turns up on the last day of such trips ('Well, there is this other property, but we didn't think it would suit you!') necessitating an extension of your trip, or a return to Spain as rapidly as possible.

However, such large companies sometimes deal mainly with large developments (which they may own and manage) in the main resort areas rather than selling more individual properties. If you buy through a Spanish estate agent, it is essential that the company is properly licensed. Their official status will be indicated on their stationery and their licence should be displayed on the premises.

Estate agents' websites and advertisements can give you a rough idea of the types and prices of property dealt with by a certain agent but will often not be bang up-to-date and will only show a small proportion of the properties on the books.

There have been horror stories on TV consumer programmes telling of people who have bought property from 'estate agents' in Spain only to be faced with myriad problems with the property – faulty building work, reneged promises, not being told that a development was planned that would cut off that sea view. These 'estate agents' are not officially registered – British agents do not need to register with the official estate agent body, API, or have achieved any professional qualifications to operate, so it is important to check the credentials of the companies you deal with.

**TIP**

■ The bigger international outfits can lay on every service you can think of once you have invested in one of their properties – from an initial inspection trip to sorting out moving your furnishings to Spain, money matters and residency.

## Getting started

Depending on the timescale you have allowed yourself to find and buy a property in Spain, before dealing with estate agents you should decide first on the area where you want to buy. By all means look in estate agents' shop windows, check out price ranges and property on offer in different parts of the country through property magazines, local English-language newspapers, the internet , and property exhibitions, but don't tie yourself down to one or even several estate agencies before you are sure about where you are hoping to buy.

It will also be far more productive for those looking for an individual property rather than a new build to research properties (and estate agents) on the ground in Spain. Once there, you will be able to get a feel for the reliability and efficiency or otherwise of a particular agent as well as being able to see the most recent properties that have come onto the market.

# UK estate agents

Because estate agents in the UK do not need to be qualified or members of a professional body, anyone can set up and call themselves estate agents. They can work from home, or have an office on a high street. They may market their services through advertisements in the local free press, through English-language newspapers and magazines in Spain, and on the internet . They may act as agents or middlemen for Spanish estate agents who do not have the contacts, the marketing know-how, reach or the fluency in English that a British estate agent has. Because they may well have an office in the UK, contacting such agents is a good starting place for sounding out the prices and property available, above all if they deal with the region/s where you are interested in buying.

Because these agents have experience of dealing with Spanish property law, regulations and red tape they can be very helpful for anyone who is wary of dealing with Spanish estate agents direct. The initial (let's be honest here) suspicion and worry that comes when doing business in a foreign country where you do not know the rules and regulations and way of doing things can be circumvented by dealing with UK-based agents.

Prospective buyers of property should make sure that they are aware of and very clear about everything that is taking place 'on their behalf' during negotiations and to be in control of proceedings. Before entering into a contract through one of these agents, it is wise to find out in advance what charges for services are going to be levied, and to ask for a breakdown of costs and commission. It may work out to be far more expensive going through an agent back home than dealing with a Spanish-based estate agent direct.

## Spanish estate agents – *Inmobiliaria*

In Spain, dealing with a registered estate agent means dealing with an agency belonging to either the *Agente de Propiedad Inmobiliaria* (API) or the *Gestor Intermediario de Promociones y Edificaciones* (GIPE). These agencies display their certificate of registration and identification number on the premises and seeing these should give you some confidence in moving forward with that agency. Any API-registered estate agency employs an API-accredited lawyer and has paid a bond.

A group of long established property agents based mainly on the Costa del Sol have also formed a group called 'Leading Property Agents of Spain', better known as LPA. All members are professionally qualified. They adhere to a strict code of ethics and are dedicated to giving highly professional and quality service to both buyers and sellers in southern Spain.

As in the UK, estate agents in Spain often concentrate on the area around which their office is based. They deal with local properties and have a good knowledge of the possible problems or otherwise associated with planning regulations and utility provision in their locality. Estate agents dealing with properties on the costas are very likely to speak English, and may even be British. *Inmobiliarias* out in the wilds may not be used to dealing with English-speakers, though agents will want to bend over backwards to make a sale. Agencies may be one-office outfits, or part of a large chain, or only deal specifically with the selling of their own developments and properties.

Spanish estate agents in general provide far less detailed descriptions of property than we are used to at home. Photographs of properties and details will be of varying quality, though in general the more expensive the property the better the marketing will be.

Some, but not all, estate agents carry professional indemnity insurance. It is also worth asking whether the estate agent has a bonded client bank account where any monies can be put into until the sale of a property has gone through with the *escritura* signed in front of the notary. This will guard against paying a deposit straight to the vendor who, if the worst-case scenario is evoked, could take the deposit and then sell to another buyer.

The chief role of the *inmobiliarias* is to sell any property that has been placed with them, and they will mostly sell resale properties. Their allegiance is to the vendor from whom they draw their commission, and not to you the buyer. They

### Spanish estate agents

In 2000 a new law was passed in Spain which relaxed the need for Spanish estate agents to be qualified and members of a professional body of estate agents. This has led to an unrestricted market and any potential buyer of property in Spain should be careful with whom they deal. Make sure that all staff, or at least those representatives that you are dealing with, are API members.

may well be able to advise on aspects such as mortgages, residency and the Spanish tax system but such services will come at a cost. Once a deal has gone through, any issues that arise over the property will have nothing to do with the agents. It is therefore imperative to get a lawyer (an independent lawyer, rather than one recommended by the estate agency or the vendor) to check all contracts thoroughly before buying a property.

When dealing with Spanish estate agents, because of the sometimes 'cash in hand' nature of things in Spain, you may be asked to sign a *nota de encargo* before being shown a property or properties. This document protects the agent's interests, and ensures that he will be paid the commission if you go ahead and buy one of the properties on his books. This is because a property may be placed with several agents all of whom are after making their commission from the sale.

## Commission

The commission rate charged by estate agencies can vary from 2% to 10%, with property deposits averaging around 7%. A higher commission is payable on cheap properties than on more expensive ones, and the rate will also vary from region to region, with higher rates being charged in more popular resort areas.

In Spain the commission on a property sale is not always paid by the vendor, so you will need to check whether the purchase price is inclusive of the agent's commission or whether you, as the buyer, have to pay extra to cover the agent's commission. Theoretically, if you are dealing with an agent based in the UK who works as an intermediary for a Spanish estate agent then the commission charged on the sale of a property should be shared between the two of them, rather than you being charged commission twice.

**TIP**

■ If you are sure of the area where you wish to buy, a three- or four-day visit is often adequate, although a longer trip leaves room for the unexpected to turn up.

## Inspection flights

If you know the type of property you want to buy and where you want to buy it, some property firms can arrange inspection flights to Spain. A typical deal involves the estate agency booking the flight to Spain, collecting you from and returning you to the airport and providing free accommodation for the duration of your trip. A consultant will take you round various properties on a one-to-one basis, showing you the area and the facilities on offer. Normally you will only have to pay for your flights (prices will depend on whether you are booked with a budget airline, or a more expensive scheduled flight) and these will be refundable if you eventually decide to buy a property with the agents.

Although there will be no obligation to buy on these inspection trips, expect a certain amount of pressure, and the companies that organise inspection trips advise that they are intended for those seriously wanting to purchase at the time of the inspection.

To begin with you will be shown the various locations that you are interested in and be able to examine the infrastructure, school, medical and leisure facilities on offer. You will get a good idea of the type of properties available in these locations and be shown round a number of them. Towards the end of an inspection trip you will have time to review any properties that you think might be suitable. If you decide to buy a property that you have seen, the agency will be able to introduce you to a local lawyer who will be able to advise on the contracts if you decide to ask them to act on your behalf. Once you are back home the estate agency will continue to liaise between your lawyer, the vendor and yourself.

## When on an arranged inspection trip:

- Don't be rushed around by the agent, but take your time and get a measured response to all properties that you view.
- Try and get some time away from the consultants to go off and explore on your own. Some companies may insist that you spend all your visit under their direction – these are to be avoided as a certain amount of pressure may be brought to bear. You need to be able to hear your own intuitive thoughts about a property and location without the interruptions of a salesman.
- Avoid mass inspections where you are shown a whole load of unsuitable properties. Such an inspection will be a waste of your time and money. Don't waste time looking at properties you have no interest in buying.
- Have a clear notion of what you are looking for in a property in terms of size, location and price, and let the agents know.
- If you decided to buy a property while on an inspection trip it may be difficult to ask to use (or to find) a lawyer other than the one that the agent offers you. You will be under a time limit, and a certain amount of pressure, to close the deal on the property before your return flight leaves.
- Inspection trips take the business relationship between a prospective buyer and an agent into a more complex area. Rather than being able to walk away if you decide that an agent hasn't got what you are looking for, going on an inspection trip means that the agent is investing time and money in you as a client, so you become more important to the agent. They will want a return on their investment.

## Estate agent addresses

**ACD Spanish Properties:** www.acdsp.co.uk. Specialises in freehold property on the Costa Blanca and Costa Calida. Also legal, financial and insurance services.

**Alexander Watson:** 020 8866 0127; email sales@alexanderwatson.co.uk; www.alexanderwatson.co.uk. Specialists in property on the Costa del Sol; also offer mortgage, financial and valuing services.

**Anglo Continental Properties:** 01926 401274; www.anglocontinental.co.uk.

**Atlas International:** email contactus@atlasinternational.com; www.atlasinternational.com. Offices throughout Europe and the US. Specialists in Costa Blanca.

**Bay of Roses:** 972 154359; email info@bayofroses.com; www.bayofroses.com. Properties for sale and to let on the Costa Brava.

**Beaches International:** 01562 885181; email info@beachesint.com; www.beachesint.co.uk. They can send their guidelines to purchasing property in Spain. Costa Blanca and Costa Calida specialists with over 23 years experience.

**Blue Sky Homes Ltd:** 01452 770177; email info@blueskyhomes.co.uk. Costa Blanca specialists.

**Casa Blanca Properties:** 01324 612333; email sales@casablancaproperties.com; www.casablancaproperties.com.

**Casa Del Sol Properties:** 0800 7313893; email emsworth@casadelsol.co.uk; www.casadelsol.co.uk. Properties on the costas, Canary Islands and Balearic Islands.

**David Scott International:** 01279 792162; www.nerjaproperties.co.uk. Specialises in inland and coastal properties around Nerja.

**Diana Morales Properties:** 952 765138; email info@dmproperties.com; www.dmproperties.com.

**Eden Villas:** 0800 7810821; www.edenvillas.co.uk. Properties along the coast from Valencia to Marbella.

**Elite Spanish Properties:** 0800 2941111; email elitesales@espvillas.com; www.espvillas.com. New developments, *urbanizaciónes* and luxury villas on the Costa del Sol, Costa Blanca North, the Balearics and Fuerteventura.

**Escapes 2 Ltd:** 0161 766 218; www.escapes2.com; email propertysales@escapes2.com. Properties on the Mediterranean coastline.

**European Villa Solutions:** 01223 514241; email info@europeanvs.com; www.europeanvs.com. Properties along the Mediterranean coastline and on the Balearics.

**G and R Properties:** 01566 774499; www.chilcott-villas.com. Properties on Costa Blanca North.

**Gran Sol Properties (Europe) Ltd:** 01772 825587; www.gransolproperties.com; Spanish office: 965 835468. Specialise in Costa Blanca North, Madrid and Barcelona.

**Greenbox Properties:** 01670 528258; www.greenbox.co.uk. Residential rural property on the Costa del Sol, Costa Blanca, Costa Calida and Tenerife.

**Horizon Property Group SL:** 922 748313; Birmingham office: 0871 2840035; email info@horizonpropertygroup.com; www.horizonpropertygroup.com. Produces a free property newspaper.

**Iberian International:** 0800 542 4848; email sales@iberianinternational.net; www.iberianinternational.net. Apartments, villas, bungalows, townhouses.

**Images of Andalucía (Spain):** 952 742501; www.imagesofandalucia.com.

**Interealty Canary Islands:** contact via website; www.interealtyes.com.

**IPC Property Consultants:** 0800 1692234; email info@ipcltd.com; www.ipcltd.co.uk. Villas, apartments and townhouses; Costa Blanca and in Tenerife.
**Jaime and Sheldon SL:** 971 696086; email info@mallorcapropertiesonline.com; www.jaimeandsheldon.com. British-owned and run. Specialises in properties on Mallorca.
**John Taylor:** 932 413082; email info@johntaylorspain.coml; www.johntaylorspain.com. Properties in Barcelona and on the Costa Brava
**Kensington Properties International:** 971 713951; www.kensington-properties.com. Top end of the market with villas, mansions and estates.
**Leiner:** 952 667213; email daniela@leiner.net; www.leiner.net.
**Oranges and Lemons:** 962 853112; email info@orangesandlemons.com; www.orangesandlemons.com. Specialise in resale properties in the Oliva/Gandia region.
**Parador Properties Ltd:** 01737 770137. Alicante office: 965 772300; www.paradorproperties.com. Specialise in new and established freehold homes along the entire coastline; full after-sales service includes legal, financial, relocation and completion services.
**Philip Lockwood:** 01562 745082. Philip Lockwood specialise in villa construction and sales of all types of property to the east of Málaga near lake Vinuela.
**Phoenix Overseas Properties Ltd:** 0870 241 4108; email info@phoenix-overseas.com; www.phoenix-overseas.com. Holiday and permanent homes and property for investment on the Costa Blanca, Calida and Almería.
**Pilgrim Homes UK:** 01572 756577; email sales@pilgrimvillas.com; www.pilgrimvillas.com.
**Propertunities:** 01305 757570; email info@propertunities.co.uk; www.propertunities.co.uk. Specialists in villas on the Costa Blanca and Costa Calida.
**Rusticas del Noroeste:** 986 731121; www.rusticas.com.
**Swan International:** 0151 648 3597; email swan@swan.eu.com; www.swanint.co.uk. Property between Marbella and Estepona.
**Tara European Property Consultants:** 928 514094; www.realestatelanzarote.com. Properties in Lanzarote.
**Town and Country South West Ltd:** 01225 755811; www.spanishproperty.uk.com. Specialise in the Costa del Sol, north Costa Blanca and south Costa Blanca.
**Ultra Villas Ltd:** 0845 1305464; www.ultravillas.co.uk; email post@ultravillas.co.uk. Costa Blanca properties.
**Vera Gold:** 08000 711 444; email sales@veragold.com; www.veragold.com. Properties in Almería.
**World Class Homes:** 22 High Street, Wheathampstead, Hertfordshire AL4 8AA; 01582 832001; email info@worldclasshomes.co.uk; www.worldclasshomes.co.uk. Properties throughout Spain including the Costa Brava, Costa Blanca, Costa Orihuela, Costa del Sol, Gibraltar and Ibiza

Names of other agents dealing in Spanish property can be obtained from the National Association of Estate Agents, 01926 496 800; www.naea.co.uk (select the international section). They can send a list (ask for their 'Homelink' department) of members specialising in Spain. Or contact the Royal Institute of Chartered Surveyors, 020 7334 3811; www.rics.org.

The CEI (Confédération Européenne de l'Immobilier: European Confederation of Real Estate Agents) is one of Europe's largest professional organisation of estate agents, now with well over 45,000 members from hundreds of cities in 13 European countries, Austria, France, Germany, Greece, Hungary, Ireland, Italy, the Netherlands, Portugal, Romania, Spain, the United Kingdom and the Slovak Republic, representing a total of over 60,000 operators in real estate. The CEI website (www.webcei.com) has a search facility.

## Adverts

When you begin looking into the possibilities of buying a property in Spain you will very quickly become aware of the vast number of companies out there who are looking to persuade you to do business with them.

The property pages of the weekend national newspapers frequently have articles on buying property abroad and these pieces will include sample prices of properties and details of the companies featured. Note that many property advertisements will include the size of the property (and/or land) in square metres, which allows those interested to compare prices regionally or nationally. Another invaluable resource for both prospective property buyers and service companies is the internet.

## The internet

Although you won't be able (and won't want) to buy properties over the internet, there is a growing number of websites that deal with property, from estate agents' home pages to those of property developers, mortgage lenders, letting agencies,

### Web search tips

Because of the vast amount of information (as well as misinformation) that is posted on the internet , you will need to narrow down any search that you make using a web directory or search engine. Rather than just typing in for example, 'property, Spain' or 'villas for sale, Costa del Sol' name the specific area or town you are looking to buy in.

If you have the name of a property developer or estate agent that you are thinking of doing business with, then use the web as a research tool. Find out as much as you can about their company. You can make initial contact with vendors of property that interests you via email, but be very wary of any company or individual who asks for payment of any kind over the internet .

Although e-commerce has come a long way, smaller operators may not have the latest systems to guarantee the security of transactions. If you decide to continue with negotiations after initial contact over the internet, it is best to set up a face-to- face meeting as soon as possible.

plus websites aimed at the expatriate and the househunter. Estate agents and property developers are increasingly using the internet as a marketing tool, as a relatively cheap way to get their name known internationally. There are now internet portals (websites dedicated to one area of information and/or commerce), which deal exclusively with properties for sale from thousands of leading agents and developers. Using a search engine such as Google or a web directory such as Yahoo will lead you into a selection of websites dealing solely with Spanish property for sale.

The internet can be a great marketing tool – the Hamptons website, for example, has reported getting 120,000 hits (visitors to its website) in one month alone.

## Property websites worth looking at

www.knightfrank.com

www.hamptons.co.uk

www.primelocation.com (which includes property from 250 estate agents)

www.propertyfinder.com (property from 900 agencies)

www.rightmove.co.uk

www.newskys.co.uk

The best of these websites will allow you to search for suitable properties by specifying search criteria such as whether you want a villa with or without a swimming pool, proximity to the beach, hospitals, etc., as well as the desired region in Spain, and of course purchase price. Increasingly, agencies are linking up to property portals. Meanwhile, www.overseaspropertyforum.net allows people to share knowledge and experiences about buying property abroad via online messageboards.

## The press

Daily and weekend newspapers all carry adverts for property abroad – mostly in their property sections, but also sometimes at the back of the travel pages. You may want to take out a subscription to some of the English-language newspapers published in Spain, many of which are regional rather than national in scope. There are also a number of free sheets available from establishments such as bars, estate agents and tourist offices, which carry property advertisements. Another place to look for both property advertisements and articles on living, working and buying property in Spain is in the rising number of glossy magazines published both in the UK and in Spain.

## ■ FINANCE

## Importing currency

You will need to import a large amount of money into Spain to cover the costs involved in buying the property (conveyancing costs, fees and taxes, builders', architects' and surveyors' fees, utility bills and charges, *comunidad de propietarios*, and other fees). When you find a property in Spain to buy, you will of course know the price of the property in euros but until you have bought all of the euros you will need to pay for it you won't know the total costs involved. Depending

on the exchange rate fluctuations between the sterling and the euro during the conveyancing procedures the property could eventually cost you more or less than you had originally thought. Importing money into Spain can take time and there are various ways of transferring funds.

One method of transferring funds is to obtain a banker's draft from your home bank. This is a cheque, guaranteed by the bank, which can be deposited into your bank account in Spain or anywhere in the world. When making the final payment on the purchase of a property at the notary's office it is advisable to hand over a banker's draft made payable to the vendor. Note that a banker's draft works along the lines of a cheque, and once it is paid into an account there will be a short period of waiting before it is cleared and you are able to access the money. You can also transfer money by SWIFT electronic bank transfer. This procedure can take several days and rates of exchange will vary. Unless you are conversant with Spanish banking procedures, transferring money electronically may also lead to red tape problems.

Because of currency fluctuations converting currency from, say, sterling to euros will always be something of a gamble. If the pound falls against the euro you will end up paying far more than you budgeted for on the property. If, as soon as you sign the contract to begin the process of buying, you convert the total cost of the property into euros you may be happy with the conversion rate but you will lose the use of the money while negotiations take place over the settlement of the property.

To avoid this a specialised company such as Currencies Direct (0845 389 3000; www.currenciesdirect.com) can help in a number of ways, by offering better exchange rates than banks, without charging commission, and giving you the possibility of 'forward buying' – agreeing on the rate that you will pay at a fixed date in the future – or with a limit order – waiting until the rate you want is reached.

Payments can be made in one lump sum or on a regular basis. It is usual when building new property to pay in four instalments, so-called 'stage payments'.

If you are having a pension paid into your bank account in Spain make sure that it is transferred into euros before being sent, otherwise you will have to pay commission on the exchange. Specialist currency companies can handle regular

■ For those who prefer to know exactly how much money they have available for their property purchase, forward buying is the best solution, since you no longer have to worry about the movement of the pound against the euro.

payments such as pensions as well as salaries and mortgage payments. Also be aware that money left sitting in a Spanish bank account attracts little interest, so it is advisable to take into Spain only the money that you need and leave the rest offshore or, if you live on or near the Costa del Sol, perhaps open a non-resident account in Gibraltar.

If the vendors of the property are non-resident in Spain, they are likely to want the purchase price paid in the currency of their home country.

## Exchange control

Spain abolished all its laws on exchange control in 1992 and at present there is no limit on the amount of foreign currency or euros that can be brought into Spain, and no limit on the amount of currency and euros which anyone is allowed to take out of the country. However, imports of amounts over €6,000 should be declared to customs within 30 days.

# ◼ MORTGAGES

Although a euro mortgage (*hipoteca*) on a Spanish property provides better security against fluctuations in currency values, fluctuation in interest rates may counteract this advantage. One of the main and uncomfortable aspects of Spanish-based mortgages in the recent past is that interest rates have been maintained at a higher rate than other comparable European countries. Sometimes a fixed UK mortgage will be a better bet, and is usually quite easy to organise. Among those

who can arrange a mortgage are UK banks like the Halifax (www.halifax.co.uk). International and Spanish specialists include Alexander Watson (020 8866 0127; www.alexanderwatson.co.uk) who offer mortgage, financial and valuing services and are also specialists in property on the Costa del Sol; and Philip Lockwood (01562 745082;) who can arrange both euro and sterling mortgages and advise on the benefits and risks of each.

It is easier to borrow money at home and be a cash buyer abroad. If you use your home as equity to fund buying a property in Spain you won't have to deal with overseas lenders and brokers and won't have to worry about the mortgage increasing should the euro appreciate against the pound. If you borrow in euros then when currencies move (which they will do), your asset (the home in Spain) will move in the same direction as the mortgage. It also makes sense to keep your debts in the same currency as your income.

If you are thinking of taking a mortgage with a lender in Spain, remember that there are fewer fixed, capped and discounted schemes operating on the Continent and terms can be more restrictive than those offered in the UK – a high deposit and a maximum repayment term of 20 years is standard. Euro mortgage rates are around 4.6% in Spain, sterling mortgages about 5.75%. You will find that the cheaper interest rates and special deals on offer usually only apply to more high-value properties of between £100,000 and £200,000, and not to the more modest end of the property market.

## UK mortgages

A number of people planning to buy second homes in Spain arrange loans in the UK – taking out a second mortgage on their UK property and then buying with cash in Spain. Alternatively, it is now also possible to approach the banks for a sterling loan secured on the property in Spain. If you are considering borrowing in the UK, then the method of calculating the amount that may be borrowed is worked out at between two and a half, or three and a half, times your primary income plus any

### Your mortgage

Your mortgage will be subject to a valuation on any UK property, and you can expect to borrow, subject to equity, up to a maximum of 80% of the purchase price of the overseas property (compared with the availability of 100% mortgages for UK properties). If you are going to take out a second mortgage with your existing mortgage lender, a second charge will be taken by the mortgage company. Note that some lending institutions charge a higher rate for a loan to cover a second property. You should ensure that if a loan is arranged in the UK then all of the details of this are included in the Spanish property contract deeds (*escritura*).

secondary income you may have, less any capital amount already borrowed on the mortgage. Your credit history will also be checked to assess whether you will be able to manage increased mortgage payments. It is most usual for buyers to pay for their second home with a combination of savings and equity from remortgaging an existing property. Borrowers should bear in mind that many banks are tightening their lending criteria in response to the current unsettled financial climate.

The Norwich and Peterborough Building Society (www.npbs.co.uk) lends a minimum of £40,000 to people wanting to use a sterling-dominated mortgage to buy on the Costa del Sol – along the stretch of land from Gibraltar in the west to Motril in the East. Norwich and Peterborough offers a rate on its Spanish two-year fixed rate mortgage of 6.08, and it also offers a base rate tracker mortgage. They can lend up to 75% for a new property on the stretch of the Costa del Sol mentioned above, but will only lend 65% for an older house in the mountains.

# Spanish mortgages

Many Spanish banks offer euro mortgages both within Spain and through branches in the UK. The conditions relating to Spanish mortgages differ from those in the UK in that a deposit of at least 30% is usually required, with a maximum of 65% of the property value being provided as a loan, unlike the 95% or even 100% available from UK lenders. Those deemed to be non-resident in Spain usually have a lower limit of borrowing of 50% imposed by the lender, and the mortgage repayment period also tends to be shorter – usually about 15–20 years. The buyer must be less than 70 years old by the completion date of the mortgage repayment. Fixed-rate loans usually run for periods of up to 20 years (10–12-year deals are commonplace) and early redemption penalties may apply. These loans also carry introductory commissions of between 1% and 2.5%. Spanish mortgage companies peg their rates to a number of different indexes, offering an index-linked rate plus the company's percentage. You will need to provide the mortgage company with an identification card, a fiscal identification number, evidence of income and details of your financial situation and, if you are married, your spouse's consent may be required. It can take anything from two to six weeks to arrange a Spanish mortgage so four weeks is a good indicator.

Spanish mortgages generally offer fixed or variable interest rate mortgages, mixed interest rate mortgages and fixed repayment instalment mortgages. Interest rates may be lower than at home, but there will be additional costs incurred, related to the registering charge on property in Spain. Acquisition, construction and renovation mortgages are available. Mortgages are on a capital and interest repayment basis, and security will be taken on the property. Most Spanish mortgage lenders work on the basis of repayments being made at a third of the borrower's net income.

Remember that if you take out a Spanish mortgage, you will need to have the currency available in your Spanish bank account to meet the monthly mortgage repayments. There are likely to be tax implications and you will need to ensure that your lawyer explains the legalities in both countries to you. Mortgage lenders deciding how much to advance a potential buyer, both in the UK and in Spain, will not take into consideration any possible income derived from renting out the property. However, it may be possible to offset the cost of the mortgage against the income received from renting out a property and so reducing tax demands. And in effect the rental value on a property should repay the mortgage if problems occur.

Barclays offers euro mortgages through its Spanish subsidiary and other overseas mortgage companies include Banco Banesto; Banco Halifax; Citibank España, Deutsche Bank, Caja Madrid and Banco Atlantico. Spanish banks are not interested whether you have an existing mortgage in the UK.

## Assessing your mortgage

In Spain the method used to assess your mortgage is also a little different from that in the UK. You will have to put all your UK and, if you have any, your Spanish earnings and income forward, and get references from your UK bank. Any other borrowing you have will also be assessed. Although repayment mortgages still predominate, there are endowment and pension-linked options as well. The self-employed must have held such status for a minimum of three years and be able to show fully audited accounts of earnings.

# Offshore mortgages

The principle of offshore companies involves turning a property into a company, the shares of which are held as collateral against a mortgage of up to 75% for a repayment term of up to 20 years by an offshore bank based in a tax haven such as Gibraltar or the Channel Islands. The property owner's name is confidential and the property company is administered on the owner's behalf by the offshore trustees. Previously, the advantage of offshore property purchase was that it reduced tax liability in the country of purchase, as, if and when the property was resold, it merely became a question of transferring the shares confidentially to a new owner, thus avoiding transfer taxes and VAT in the country in question.

However, there are risks. For example, due to legislation passed in 1991, thousands of Britons who bought property in Spain through offshore companies ended up facing potentially huge tax bills in the eventuality of either their selling the property, or of their death. Although, in most cases, offshore property purchase has resulted in the legitimate avoidance of wealth tax, succession duty, transfer tax and capital gains tax, a minority of cases has clearly crossed the fine line between tax avoidance and tax evasion at the cost of the state coffers. You should certainly not try to enter into such an arrangement without the advice of an accountant, solicitor, or other professional adviser.

## Clampdown on tax avoidance

The Spanish government has always been relatively powerless to trace tax evasion carried out in this way, as the confidentiality of the ownership of offshore companies is protected by law. Now, however, even if they are unable to meet this problem directly, the authorities have opted at least to make the avoidance of tax and death duties a costly business for those involved. Offshore companies that own property in Spain are now subject to an annual 3% tax on the property's rateable value (approximately 70% of its market value) unless the owners are prepared to submit the name of the ultimate beneficial owner and proof as to the source of the money used to buy the property. Once this information has been established and the tax levied – or so it is intended – the owners will then not find it so worthwhile to avoid capital gains and inheritance taxes; and the transfer of ownership of property through sale or death will become obvious.

One of the main reasons for Spain clamping down on its own residents is that many have been using money from unpaid taxes to buy property through offshore companies. There is also evidence that offshore companies have been used to launder the proceeds of crime and drugs, and as a convenient way of buying property anonymously. Although the restrictions on offshore companies have seriously inflated some residents' tax bills, tax consultants who advise foreign property owners in Spain have generally welcomed the legislation. They say that it does nothing to alter some of the legitimate advantages of using an offshore company to avoid or reduce some taxes, and is deterring those who wish to operate outside the law.

So, potential property buyers in Spain should be wary of any organisations advertising schemes claiming to be able to circumvent the current legislation or claiming huge tax advantages. In the light of the Spanish authorities' determination to improve tax collection, and considering that all Spanish property is within the territory of the Spanish Tax Authority, which has the right ultimately to seize homes to collect the tax it is owed, it is just as well to take some unbiased professional advice before entering into such an arrangement. In all circumstances, paying for this advice before you make a purchase will almost certainly save you money in the long run; and is the best approach.

All of the above being taken into consideration, offshore property mortgages are now available through many building societies and banks. One such is the Abbey, which has offices in Gibraltar and Jersey (01534 885100). Your local branch of Abbey should be your first port of call. Another building society offering offshore mortgages is the Bank of Scotland International (Isle of Man) Ltd.; 01534 825050; www.bankofscotland-international.com. The Bank of Scotland, like most building societies and banks, has leaflets on offshore mortgages, and other financial matters such as international payments, which will be worth consulting. Lloyds TSB Bank Overseas Club offers a range of services and is based at the Offshore Centre, 08705147789; www.lloydstsb-offshore.com.

Another organisation specialising in Spain is Conti Financial Services (www.mortgagesoverseas.com). Cornish and Co, solicitors, can help you set up an offshore mortgage or overseas trust in Spain; 0870 7871136; www.cornishco.com). In addition Cornish has an office in Spain and associate offices in Gibraltar, Portugal and the USA.

### Useful addresses

**Blevins Franks Financial Management:** 020 7336 1000; email matthew.weston@blevinsfranks.com; www.blevinsfranks.com. Offices throughout the Spanish coastal regions and in the Balearic and Canary Islands. Advise on tax planning, offshore trusts and investments, overseas and UK pensions and mortgages.

**Conti Financial Services:** 01273 772811; email enquiries@mortgagesoverseas.com; www.mortgagesoverseas.com.

**TIP**

■ Potential property buyers in Spain should be wary of any organisations advertising schemes claiming to be able to circumvent the current legislation or claiming huge tax advantages

**Easy2Loan:** 952 827754; email information@easy2loan.com; www.easy2loan.com.

**First Choice Real Estate:** 952 939236.

**John Siddall Financial Services Ltd:** 01329 239111; email enquiries@siddalls.net; www.siddalls.net. Siddalls are independent financial advisers providing expertise across a spectrum of investments, retirement and tax planning for private clients at home and abroad. They have many years experience in assisting British nationals wishing to become resident in Spain with all aspects of their financial planning. Siddalls are part of the IFG Group Plc and authorised and regulated by the Financial Services Authority.

**Mortgages in Spain:** 0800 027 7057; www.mortgages-in-spain.com. Mortgage brokers dealing with Skipton Building Society and Caja Duero – a Spanish mutual savings bank.

**Norwich and Peterborough Spanish Home Loans:** 0845 300 2511; www.npbs.co.uk. Also a branch in Gibraltar; www.npbs-gibraltar.co.uk.

**Solbank:** 902 343888; www.solbank.com. A Spanish bank offering various mortgage and banking services.

**Windram Miller and Co:** 952 820779; email email@windrammiller.com; www.windrammiller.com.

# ◼ PURCHASING AND CONVEYANCING

## Fees

Total inclusive costs (lawyers, land registry, *notario*, taxes, bank charges, associates fees etc.) bring the overall costs of conveyancing to around 10% of the cost price of a resale property in mainland Spain, and between 7–9% on such properties in the Canary Islands. Tax on new property in mainland Spain is 7%, to which must be added 4% additional fees; in the Canary Islands tax on new property is 4%, with another 4% to pay in additional fees. The cheaper the property, the greater the likelihood of that percentage rising due to the minimum charges imposed by lawyers and others involved in the conveyancing.

## Lawyers

It is very important to employ an *abogado* to look after your personal interests. A solicitor should:

- ◼ check that the vendor of the property is the legal (and sole) owner of the property whether there are any outstanding charges or bills on it
- ◼ check that the property has, or is being built with, proper planning permission and has all the necessary licences
- ◼ check that the terms of the contract are fair and reasonable
- ◼ prepare a report of their findings for the potential buyer's information.

Given the go-ahead, the solicitor can then arrange for currency to be transferred to Spain, the title deeds (*escritura*) to be transferred into the buyer's name and registered with the Land Registry and for fees and taxes to be paid.

### Typical costs involved in conveyancing

- **Notary fee:** for preparation of the title deed (usually around €650 for a house costing €200,000).
- **Land registry fee:** dependent on the value of property (around €45~0).
- **plus valía tax:** paid to the municipality on the transfer of property. Depends on the value of the land on which the property sits. The vendor should pay this, but contracts of sale often try to impose the fee on the buyer. It can come to several thousand pounds and is usually around 0.5% on a property that last changed hands ten years previously.
- **VAT/transfer tax/stamp duty:** depends on the value of the property, the type of property and where the property is situated. Usually around 8% of the purchase price on new property.
- Registration with the Spanish Tax Authorities and obtaining a foreigners' identification number (NIE): Your solicitor can do this for a fee.

An independent lawyer should be either a specialist lawyer from home or an English-speaking Spanish *abogado*. Be wary of using the services of a lawyer recommended by the vendor or their estate agent, as their impartiality could theoretically be (though probably isn't) questionable. Also, should you use a Spanish lawyer, even if they speak fluent English, they may be unfamiliar with UK law and the ramifications that buying a property overseas may have on your tax or legal situation back home.

Most *abogado*s are found through recommendation. If your grasp of Spanish is shaky, you should definitely find a lawyer who speaks English.

The lawyer will be able to:

- advise a client whose name should be registered as the owner of a property as ownership will have knock-on effects with regards to taxation
- advise on how to pay for the property – whether through a mortgage, remortgaging, forming a company, cash, etc., and how to minimise costs
- arrange for Power of Attorney should it be necessary
- arrange for the signing of the *escritura* and making purchase payments, and may also be able to organise currency exchange and the transferral of funds from a buyer's home bank account into Spain
- check that there are no cases pending against the property with regards to planning permission not having been obtained when the property was originally built
- draw up the contract for the sale of the property or between a builder, architect and client

## Example of costs on the purchase of a €200,000 property

| | | |
|---|---|---|
| Notary fees | Preparation of *escritura*, registering of ownership, stamp duty | €800 |
| Legal fees | Making searches on registries, preparation of *escritura*, translation of contracts | €2,000 |
| *Plus Valia* | Capital gains tax levied by the Town Hall on increased value of land since last sold | €300 |
| VAT (IVA) 7% | Payable on the declared value of the property | €14,000 |
| Connection charges | Water, electricity, gas, drainage, telephone | €500 |
| | TOTAL | €17,600 |

*Fees exclusive of VAT*

- guide a client through the legal processes involved in buying property in Spain
- look after the conveyancing procedures
- make payments for the conveyancing costs, taxes, etc., on behalf of the buyer
- obtain an NIE number on behalf of the client (this number is needed for the payment of taxes and the purchase of property in Spain)
- recommend local tradesmen, surveyors, agents, mortgage brokers and banks that will suit a client's needs.

In the major Spanish coastal resorts, finding an *abogado* who speaks English will not be a problem. Lawyers in these areas will be used to dealing with foreigners looking to buy property in their locality and may well advertise their services in local free sheets and the English-language press. They will be well aware of potential areas of conflicting interests and will be able to smooth your way to the best of their ability within the confines of Spanish law.

If you are hoping to buy property with land attached in a rural part of Spain, your lawyer will be useful in finding out about the planning restrictions in the area and if there are local bylaws in force with regards to water, grazing or hunting and access rights on the land. You will also want your lawyer to check out where property boundaries end and begin, as these may differ from what has been written in the *escritura*, what the owners of the property believe, and what is registered in the Land Registry. If you are buying into an *urbanización* or an apartment block where you will be part of the *comunidad de propietarios* you will also want the rules and regulations checked by a lawyer.

A traditional hacienda in Andalusia

'We used an abogado for the purchase, but it was still fairly traumatic as he was a city lawyer (there weren't any local gestores who spoke English) and didn't know much about laws affecting property such as ours and what licences we needed. For example we got 'denounced' (the Spanish word is denuncia and refers to being reported to the police by a neighbour for – generally – a minor infraction such as having a dog that barks all night long, or putting up an unsightly satellite dish that 'lowers the tone' of a neighbourhood, etc.) to the river police for having a well dug without their permission.

We'd got four licences (local town hall, local ministry of the environment, mines, water authority) and he didn't know that within half a kilometre of a dried up riverbed we needed another permit too. He got the hunting laws wrong, which led to lots of trouble and he didn't bother to find out about the Andalucían Tourist laws, which affected us greatly, telling us we only had to keep inside the building regulations. For nearly 20 years our business was 'illegal' and I am still unable to develop certain aspects that we had planned for back in 1988 and which he had told us would be "no problem".'

**Lindy Walsh**

You should get your lawyer to check everything that is put on the table by the agents before signing anything. Don't rely on a notary to do the work that a lawyer would normally do. Another good reason for getting a lawyer is that they may well be able to advise you on the most financially beneficial way to deal with the conveyancing process, saving you money by guiding you through the taxation systems of Spain and the UK.

It is a good idea to find a lawyer and get their advice before even starting on the househunt in Spain. They will be able to give you pointers and tell you about the possible pitfalls. They will also be ready to look at contracts before you sign – you may be able to fax them over while you are in Spain and wait for their appraisal before going ahead and signing and committing yourself to something that you may later regret. Remember that you will need to find either a lawyer from home versed in international law and the laws pertaining to Spanish property in particular, or an English-speaking Spanish lawyer versed in the taxation system of your home country. Without this knowledge a lawyer may not be able to organise your affairs to your best advantage.

## Fees

The fees charged by a lawyer for their work on buying a new or resale property are likely to be about 1% of the price of the property, although there may be a minimum charge (perhaps around £1,000). You will need to be aware that apart from the basic fee, should additional negotiations need to be undertaken on your behalf you will be charged. For example there may need to be further clauses added to a contract, or negotiations over the price of a property; if there are irregularities in the *escritura* these will need to be corrected before change of title can take place. There will also be correspondence generated between the solicitors and a mortgage company if you are taking out a mortgage, and all these matters will incur further fees.

For properties that have not yet been built, lawyers will generally charge around 1% of the property value plus an hourly rate on work done on your behalf while the construction continues. Because, as in the way of all things, there can never be a 100% definite completion date, more work may need to be done on your behalf as projects and the legalities involved unfold. The solicitor should give you an estimate of the likely charges to be incurred once s/he has seen the existing paperwork relating to the project.

Consulates and embassies in Spain will hold lists of English-speaking lawyers in your locality. In the UK the Law Society (020 7242 1222; www.lawsociety.org.uk) also holds lists of registered English-speaking lawyers in Spain. The *Consejo General de la Abogacía Española* can be reached on 915 232593; www.cgae.es.

## Useful addresses

### UK-based lawyers dealing with Spanish property

**Baily Gibson Solicitors:** 01494 672661; email Beaconsfield@bailygibson.co.uk; www.bailygibson.co.uk. Susana Diez, head of Spanish Law Dept., is a Spanish lawyer and member of the Bar Association of Bilbao.

**Bennett and Co. Solicitors:** 0870 4286177; email internationallawyers@bennet-and-co.com; www.bennett-and-co.com. Associated offices throughout Spain.

**Cornish and Co:** 0870 7871136; www.cornishco.com. Spanish office: 952 866830; email cornish@mercuryin.es. Gibraltar office: 41800; email cornish@gibnet.gi.

**De Pinna Notaries:** 020 7208 2900; www.depinna.co.uk

**Fernando Scornik Gerstein:** 020 7404 8400; www.scornik-gerstein.com. Also has offices in Madrid, Barcelona, Gran Canaria (2), Lanzarote, and Tenerife.

**Hector Diaz:** 020 7404 9349; email hdiaz@hectordiaz.co.uk. Most of this firm's work is property-related.

**M Florez Valcarcel:** 020 8741 4867

**John Howell and Co:** 020 7061 6700; email info@lawoverseas.com; www.lawoverseas.com. Law firm specialising in foreign property purchasing

**Javier de Juan:** 020 7381 0470; www.spanishlaw.org.uk. Also offices in Alicante and Málaga. All procedures to do with property purchase: conveyancing, wills, mortgages and insurance.

**The International Property Law Centre:** 0870 800 4565; email stefanol@maxgold.com; www.internationalpropertylaw.com. Contact senior partner and solicitor Stefano Lucatello, an expert in the purchase and sale of Spanish, French, Italian, Portuguese, Cyprus, Bulgarian, Turkish, Dubai, Goa and the Cape Verde Islands property and businesses, and the formation of offshore tax vehicles and trusts.

### English-speaking Spanish-based lawyers dealing with Spanish property

**Anderson and Asociados Abogados:** 952 932997; www.anderson *abogados*.com. Specialists in property conveyancing, based on the Costa del Sol.

**Becker-Cid Abogados:** 915 750544. Marbella office: 952 861850.Buño Leon: 965 921853; email mail@cbleon-*abogados*.com; www.cbleon-*abogados*.com/

## Valencian land-grab laws

Those planning on buying property in the Valencian autonomous community should be very careful. Over the last few years an obscure planning law in the region has been hitting the headlines for forcing homeowners to hand over their property to local developers with barely any compensation. As many as 15,000 people who have bought property as holiday or retirement homes in Valencia have had up to 75% of their legally owned land taken from them by developers, and have even been charged up to £100,000 for the privilege. Dubbed the 'Spanish Acquisition' by the newspapers, this phenomenon has been described as one of the biggest illegal land grabs in Europe since the Second World War.

*The Ley Reguladora de la Actividad Urbanistica* (LRAU) was introduced by Valencia's socialist government in 1994 with the aim of making land available for low-cost social housing and t provide space for major public works. Unfortunately the wording of the LRAU was so complex and ambiguous that it was exploited by property developers, who used it as carte blanche for a massive land grab. Any property developer in the area could submit a planning application for a piece of land whether they owned it or not. If no competing plan was submitted, or the town hall did not object or respond within six months, then the developer could proceed with his plan and the owner had to cede part of his land to the town hall, often receiving as little as 10% of the value of the property as compensation.

Worse still, owners could be assessed as liable for a proportion of the cost of the infrastructure of the new development (construction of roads, drains, lighting and other urban development costs). Reports have shown that these ruthless developers were unlikely to build the kind of low-cost houses that the law supposedly required. The idea of LRAU was to provide houses for Spanish people who cannot afford to buy now that northern European property prices have hit the area. In fact, developers were building anything they liked, including expensive luxury housing. As long as the town hall agreed it to be in the public interest, there was little that could be done.

After concerted efforts to challenge the LRAU and a high-profile campaign by an organisation known as *Abusos Urbanísticos No* (www.abusos-no.org), backed by more than 7,000 people (including many Britons), the law was revised in 2006 by the *Ley Urbanistica Valenciana*, making it much more difficult for unscrupulous property developers to claim private land. However, the law still retains some of its headache-inducing complexity, and potential buyers would be well advised to seek trusted legal advice. Only buying land that has been officially designated as 'urban' is another way to safeguard against potential hassles in the future.

ingles. General lawyer based in Alicante. Has a foreigners' real estate transaction department.

**De Cotta McKenna y Santafé Abogados:** 952 931781; email mijasenquiries@decottalaw.net. Offices in Tenerife, Mijas, Neja and Granada. Deals with rural and inland properties, rentals and all conveyancing matters.

## Inspections and surveys

It wouldn't be prudent to buy a property in the UK without having it checked over by a qualified surveyor, so it makes sense to get a property that you are interested in buying in Spain surveyed. That said, the surveying of property before purchasing is not a typical Spanish trait and many buy on sight. However, there are always horror stories of people who have bought a flat that looked 'OK' only to find that during the winter months it became flooded, or the hairline crack that they initially noticed but were told wasn't anything structurally damaging worsened year on year. The old adage, 'when in Rome do as the Romans do...' shouldn't apply when it comes to something as financially risky as buying a house. If you are buying a property on a mortgage, the lenders may well require a survey, even if it is only to provide an appraisal of the purchase price.

When you initially view a property in which you are interested, give it the amateur eye and check for any signs of subsidence, bowing walls, damp patches or strange smells. Check for dry rot (stick a knife into windowsills and other likely areas where damp may have struck), a leaking roof (stains on the ceilings), cracks or fractures in the walls. You will want to make sure that all plumbing, electrics, and water heating systems are in good working order, as well as the drainage and water provision. If there is a well on the land, ask the vendor if it has been tested recently. Be on the look out for any signs of rising damp or signs of condensation/humidity. While viewing a property take your time and get the feel of the place – you will usually be able to tell if there are any glaring structural problems.

**TIP**

■ It wouldn't be prudent to buy a property in the UK without having it checked over by a qualified surveyor, so it makes sense to get a property that you are interested in buying in Spain surveyed.

## Expert opinions

If you need more guidance, you could arrange for a local estate agent (other than the one showing you the property, of course!) to give their opinion of the place and the price asked. Alternatively, a local builder may be able to give their opinion of the structural soundness or otherwise of the property. In any case, if you are looking to buy a derelict property for renovation you will want to get a quote from a few builders as to the likely cost of renovation. A builder will also have local knowledge and be able to comment on the purchase price asked by the vendor. All of these opinions will come at a cost but will be worth it to set your mind at rest.

All the above people will be able to give you their 'expert' opinions on whether your desired property is sound or not, but they are unlikely to be backed up by a professional report. A trained surveyor, on the other hand, will be able to cast a professional eye over the property and give you a full and detailed report on it. Such a survey will cost you perhaps €1,400–€2,200 depending on the surveyor and size of property. Spanish surveyors tend to concentrate on different aspects than their British equivalents, although those who are used to dealing with foreigners are likely to provide you with a report similar to what you would expect to get back home. Be sure to get any report that is presented to you in Spanish translated into English.

Alternatively, you will find British RICS (Royal Institute of Chartered Surveyors)-qualified surveyors such as Andrew Tuckett in Alicante (965 790028; email atuckett@

terra.es) or Gibsons (see below) who have moved to Spain and are able to carry out professional surveys and valuations. These surveyors will often advertise their services in local English-language newspapers and property magazines. Although they will be able to give you a sound structural analysis of the property, unless they have the equivalent Spanish chartered surveying training they will be unable to advise on certain aspects such as building regulations.

Prices, as already stated, are negotiable. Note that most vendors will not sign any contract of sale with a 'subject to survey' clause. They are more likely to demand that you arrange a survey – at your own expense – before they sign anything. If another interested party comes along and signs a contract with the vendor before you have been able to satisfy yourself as to the soundness of the property, you will lose out on the chance to buy.

### Useful addresses – chartered surveyors

**Cluttons Spain:** Marbella; 952 907200; email info@cluttons-spain.com; www.cluttons-spain.com.
**CS Services:** 966 430688; email info@csservicesdenia.com; www.csservicesdenia.co.uk.
**Cushman &Wakefield Healey & Baker:** 917 810010; cushwake.com.

Enjoy the tranquillity of a hillside villa

FPD Savills España SA: 913 101016; savillspain.com.
Gibson's Chartered Surveyors: 952 794628; email info@gibsons-spain.com; www.gibsons-spain.com.
Gleeds Ibérica SA: 951 164909; www.gleeds.es.
Jones Lang Lasalle España SA: 933 185353; email santiago.gutierrez@ eu.joneslanglasalle.com; www.joneslanglasalle.es.
Knight Frank: Madrid; 915 773993; www.knightfrank.com.
Property Works: Mallorca; 971 6333297; email info@propertyworksonline.com; www.propertyworksonline.com.
Survey Spain: Campbell D Ferguson, Chartered Surveyors, Marbella, Costa del Sol; 0870 8003520; email campbell@surveyspain.com; www.surveyspain.com.
Sylvia Kemmeren Sales: 971 891614; www.campion-mallorca.co.uk.
Royal Institute of Chartered Surveyors: 0870 333 1600; email contactrics@rics. org; www.rics.org).

**TIP**

■ Because of the differences in surveying criteria between the UK and Spanish systems you should make sure that you know what should be checked and discuss with the surveyor what aspects you want checked.

# Contracts

Once you have found the right property, you will probably want to act swiftly to ensure that you get it. However, it would be extremely unwise to sign anything without taking independent legal advice. If there is, for some reason, such a pressing time limit that you may lose a property that you are interested in unless you sign **Immediately**, then at least try to fax over a copy of the contract to your legal representatives. Contracts are often short, containing the details of the vendor and purchaser, the purchase price, a legal description of the property, the date set for completion and possession of the property and the type of payment involved in the sale.

## Purchase contracts for resale/new properties

There are three different types of contract that you may be asked to sign at this stage:

**FACT**

■ For new properties, and property that is less than 10 years old the structure will have been guaranteed by the original builders or developers, as all builders must guarantee their work against major structural defects for a decade. However, if you are buying an older resale property, or even a derelict building that you are hoping to renovate, you would be wise to commission a survey.

- **Offer to buy:** A formal offer to buy the property at a fixed price – the contract being valid for a set period of time. If the vendor accepts your offer, then a non-returnable, negotiable, deposit will be payable and the contract will become binding between the two parties.
- **Reservation contract:** An agreement between the potential buyer of a property and the vendor or estate agent. This type of contract dictates that the property is taken off the market for a set period of time. A reservation fee is paid by the potential buyer, which, if a full contract to buy is signed within the set period, will count toward the full price of the property to be paid. If problems concerning the property are unearthed during the reservation period (such as the vendor not being the named owner on the *escritura*) and the potential buyer decides to pull out, the reservation fee will be lost. The clauses in this type of contract, therefore, need to be carefully checked.
- **Private purchase contract:** A full and binding contract to buy. You will pay a negotiable deposit of around 10% of the purchase price, the balance to be paid on the signing of the *escritura*. Before signing such a contract you will want to get your lawyer to check it.

The contract will be prepared by either an estate agent or developer or, if you decide to buy privately from an individual, by the vendor's lawyer. Whichever contract is offered to you, have it presented to you in your mother tongue as well as in Spanish, and make sure that you have your lawyer check it before you sign. There may well be clauses that either you or the vendor will not accept and these will need to be negotiated, as may the purchase price and the amount of deposit payable.

There are strict conditions relating to the repayment of deposits; make sure that you are informed of these by your lawyer. When paying a deposit, ensure that the money is kept by the estate agent or legal representative of the vendor in a bonded account until the sale has gone through. This will guard against a crooked vendor, or estate agent, taking your deposit and then deciding to sell the property to another instead. Although they will be acting illegally, if they do such a thing, getting your money back through the courts may take quite a time and will certainly leave a nasty taste in your mouth – perhaps putting you off ever buying in Spain.

## Purchase contracts for off-plan properties

For properties that are still under construction at the time of purchase, stage payments will be required during the construction period. It may be possible to arrange a payment schedule to suit the purchaser's individual needs, and a typical payment schedule could be as follows:

- On the signing of the contract: a deposit of 20% payable by bankers draft, personal cheque, cash, traveller's cheques or credit card.
- After a set period, or on completion of a certain phase in the building work (e.g. completion of the exterior walls and roof): 25% of the agreed purchase price.
- After a set period, or on completion of another phase in the building work (e.g. completion of interior, fitting of interior furniture and windows and doors): another 25% of the agreed purchase price – the timing of this payment may vary and is generally dependent upon the building project completion date.
- On completion or signing of the *escritura*: outstanding balance payable.

With such contracts it is advisable to negotiate a clause in the contract that allows you to withhold a certain percentage of the cost price – say 10% – for a certain period after you have moved into the property as a guarantee against possible defects. This will ensure that the builders will come back to rectify any problems that crop up, and a good firm should be happy to provide this type of insurance. You may also want to alter the specifications of fixtures and fittings, type and style of tiles, faucets (taps), etc., that have been specified by the builders/developers. If you do alter specifications you will need to make changes to the price structure and also to the completion date. Make sure that:

- the developer is the legal owner of the land.
- the developer has obtained the required building regulations.
- the required payments are held in a bonded account until completion and your taking possession of the property.

## Checks that should be made on a property before completion

### Resale properties

- Are fittings and/or furniture included in the purchase price?
- Are there any planning restrictions pertaining to the property and/or location which will affect your plans should you wish to build on or alter the property?

**TIP**

■ Note that there may be potential tax advantages, as well as other savings, at a later stage by registering the property in the joint names of a wife and husband or partner, or in the name of your child or children, or in the name of the person who will stand to inherit the property, or in the name of a limited company.

- Are there community charges to be paid on the property? Do you understand the statutes of the *comunidad de propietarios*, and are you happy to comply with them?
- Are there restrictions on the uses that can be made of the property?
- Boundaries, access, and public right of way bylaws should be clearly defined and understood.
- Check the *Plan General de Ordenación Urbana* at the town hall to see whether there are going to be future developments (e.g. new lines of communication/ building projects) that may affect the value/view of the property at a later date.
- Check the description of the property in the Land Registry and the Property Registry.
- Check the property is free of any debts or charges; that all utility and community bills, and taxes (including the IBI tax) have been paid up to date. Remember that debts on a property are 'inherited' by the new owner.
- Has there been a completion of a survey to your satisfaction?
- Has there been any alteration done to the property that has not been registered with the authorities?
- How much are the local taxes and charges?
- Is there adequate water, drainage, electricity and telecommunication provision?
- The vendor is the legal registered owner of the property

## Additional checks that should be made on off-plan and new build property

- A full breakdown of the materials, fixtures and fittings used in the building of the property.
- Be clear what you are paying for. What are the finishings? Will the surrounding land be landscaped? What will the property look like (have you seen a show home to gauge this)?
- Make sure that all completion licences (*certificado de fin de obra, licencia de primera ocupación*, and the *boletin de instalación*) have been obtained.
- Make sure that the developers or builders have obtained the necessary planning permissions to build upon the land.
- Make sure that the payment schedule and completion date are clear.
- Make sure the developers or builders are the legal owners of the land they are developing.
- Protect yourself and insure against the possibility of the developer or builders going bankrupt before completing the property.
- Make sure that the property has been registered with the local authorities for real estate taxes.

## Additional checks that should be made on the purchase of plots of land for self-build projects

- Will you be given a permit to build (*permiso de obra*) from the town hall?
- How much will it cost to build on the land, and can you afford the costs? Get sample quotes from architects and builders.

# Registries

The Land Registry (*Catastro*) contains details of the physical and topo graphical details of a property as well as a valuation, while the Property Registry (*Registro de la Propiedad*) only holds the details of ownership and title. These two registries may have differing details of the same property and a potential buyer should check that the description of a property in the contract tallies with that in both the Property and Land Registries. It may take a month or so for the Land Registry to provide a *certificado catastral* outlining the boundaries and measurements of a property, so you should ask for it as soon as you have found the property of your choice.

# The Notary

The Spanish Notary Public – the *notario* – although a lawyer, does not give legal advice to either the vendor or the purchaser of a property. The job of the *notario* is to witness the signing of the title deeds (*escritura*) in his or her office located in the area where the property is being purchased and to deal with other administrative matters. Once the *escritura* has been signed, the purchase price of the property is then handed over to the vendor, or the vendor confirms that payment has already been received. Proof of payment is then noted down in the *escritura*, which is then registered in the local Property Register. Before preparing the *escritura*, a *notario* will ensure that the purchaser has received the property as stated on the contract and that the vendor has received the correct purchase price. The *notario* will also advise on taxes that are due on the property.

Notaries collect their fees from the vendor and the purchaser and these fees are charged in accordance with a sliding scale of charges set by the Spanish government. These will vary depending on the price of a property and the amount of work the *notario* has done on behalf of the two parties in preparing documents. Not all notaries will speak English, so you may need to be accompanied to meetings by a Spanish speaker.

## Power of attorney

The person buying or selling a property does not necessarily have to be present when the title deeds are signed in front of the *notario* and, for a fee, a Power of Attorney can be granted which will allow another person to attend on the vendor's behalf instead. If a Power of Attorney has been arranged outside Spain, it will need to be witnessed and stamped by a *notario* in Spain.

# Signing the *escritura*

The date of the signing of the *escritura* will have been fixed in the contract to buy, though in reality the date may slip a little depending on the status of the checks on the property made by your lawyer. It should normally take place two to three months after signing the contract to buy a resale or new property, but will take longer if you are buying off-plan. If there are problems, such as sorting out ownership of the property or outstanding taxes on the property, this can hold matters up.

When the *notario* has received all the documentation he or she needs to complete the *escritura*, you should receive a draft copy. It is advisable to have this

A quiet mountain village, Mogrovejo in Cantabri

scrutinised by your lawyer to check that all is as should be. Although a notary is a trained lawyer who has taken further exams to qualify for the post of notary, it is not a requirement of the job to do the work of a lawyer. Make a last check on the property to see that everything is in order and that what was agreed as included in the purchase price in the contract of sale remains in or with the property (e.g. fixtures and fittings).

Once everything has been settled, the vendor and the purchaser (or someone acting on their behalf who has been granted Power of Attorney) meet at the *notario*'s office. The notary will read through the *escritura* after which the two parties will sign the document.

For properties that are ready for immediate occupation, full payment is made before signing the *escritura* and taking possession of the property. It may be that the money paid for a property is to be transferred to wherever in the world the vendor wishes to receive it. However, if the purchase price is paid into a Spanish account, the importation of currency will need to be registered with the Spanish authorities and your solicitor should deal with this for you. Many people hand over a banker's draft at this point as it can be witnessed by the *notario* there and then, but other methods of payment are available. At the same time, the notary will collect his fee and inform the purchaser of any taxes payable on the transfer of property. Remember that if the vendor is a non-resident there will be 5% withheld from the purchase price, which will be paid to the Spanish Tax Agency on the vendor's behalf due to capital gains tax liabilities.

After the signing of the *escritura*, the payment of the purchase price and all fees, the notary will pass the purchaser a copy (*copia simple*) of the *escritura* and the keys to the property. The original (*primera copia*) will be sent to the Property Register and the new owner's name registered. It can take several months for the process of registering the change of title deeds as all taxes and fees must be paid before a property can be registered in the new owner's name. Once a certificate has been issued stating that the name of the owner of the property has been registered, the purchaser's lawyer should collect it and forward it on to the new owner.

# ■ LETTING PROPERTY

Letting property is often a good way of accruing income on an investment, or simply helping to repay the monthly mortgage. Buying to let is a boom area at the moment with many people buying properties to rent. When renting out your property it is advisable, as one estate agent has put it, to 'lock away the emotion and look at the maximum return available'. The requirements of the rental and residence markets are very different and it is worth remembering if you intend to buy in the north

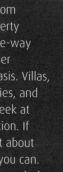

## Rental income

The amount of rental income that can be expected from a property will depend to a large degree on the property concerned. Buying a property in a pleasant, out-of-the-way location will often have an advantage over many other properties for those looking to rent on a long-term basis. Villas, especially those with pools, attract well-heeled families, and can often command rents in excess of €2,000 per week at the height of the summer season depending on location. If you are buying specifically to rent you should find out about neighbouring properties and their letting potential if you can. For holiday rentals, a good position within sight and sound of the sea will also be an advantage. Seafront apartments also generally have easy access to shops and leisure facilities, which is an added attraction for prospective tenants.

If your property is in a major tourist area – the Costa del Sol, the Balearic Islands, Tenerife or the Costa Blanca, then demand is likely to be high. Demand is likely to be much lower for properties in some of the lesser known resorts, or tucked away inland. Grouped houses or apartments in low-rise complexes also tend to do better than individual villas; and there are very high occupancy rates in places like Alicante during the summer where there is a rising demand for long-term leases and quality residences to rent.

of Spain that the holiday rental period really only runs between July and August. Hotter weather in the south means of course that the season can extend into spring and autumn – and even through the winter – so the potential income you may earn from property there is much higher. With future movements in interest rates and house prices highly uncertain, however, buying to rent in Spain is a somewhat riskier prospect than it was even two or three years ago.

The number of property owners looking for short-term tenants, means that there is a lot of competition in the rental market, with hundreds of companies renting out villas and offering a similar service. A good head for business and the right choice of property will be of great importance if you want to make money from your property in Spain. Word-of-mouth may bring some custom (let neighbours, local shop owners and businesses know that you have property to let), as will advertising or asking friendly shop owners to advertise your holiday home in the window of their premises.

Placing an advert in supermarkets, marinas and golf clubs and even in shop windows back home is a cheap or even free form of advertising your property and can often bring in clients. Many properties are now advertised for rent on the internet, and placing

A traditional cottage in rural Spain

ads in local and national newspapers is another option. If you can design your own page, or hire someone to do so, sign up with as many websites as possible, get regional sites to provide internet links to your home page, and register with search engines. Dependent on the budget available, include the location, size and price of the property and talk up the main selling points. Local estate agents may keep properties for rent on their books and it will be a good idea to register with those that do, as well as placing an advert in the local Yellow Pages (*las Páginas Amarillas*). The more time and energy you spend on advertising, the more people will be aware of what you have to offer.

Many golf courses in Spain are surrounded by residential developments, which can provide a healthy return on your investment, although villas or apartments on these are expensive to buy. Golfers flock to Spain to improve their handicap on these courses, especially during the northern European winter. In addition, the golfing fraternity tend to be fairly well off and will pay a good price for the convenience of staying in course-side properties rather than having to travel to a course. For those looking to rent property out as an investment only, and not looking to make use of the property themselves, buying an apartment in one of the larger cities, especially Madrid and Barcelona, though expensive, will guarantee a regular source of tenants.

It is standard practice when letting out any property to charge prospective tenants rent in advance for their stay and to ask for a deposit against possible damage. Telephone and electricity bills can often cause friction between tenant and landlord and it may be as well to remove or lock the phone, or install a payphone while renting out property and to include electricity, water and gas charges – whether this be for two weeks, two months, or longer – in the advance payment to avoid misunderstandings later on. To avoid disputes, it is also a good idea to make a fairly exhaustive inventory of the contents of the property, including a description of their condition. Before you sign a contract, make sure that the details on the inventory correspond exactly with what is in the property at the time. If something is missing, broken or not as stated on the inventory you should agree with the tenant to change the inventory. At the end of the lease, check the inventory and, if items are missing or broken, you have the right to use the deposit (*fianza*) to replace or repair. For short-term rentals the price charged should also include cleaning and linen provision.

A landlord is entitled to evict a tenant for the following reasons:

- failure to pay rent (although courts have a frustrating – for landlords – habit of ruling that the arrears must exceed six months before any action can be taken)
- wilful damage to a property
- the use of a property for immoral purposes
- sub-letting of a property where no such provision has been made in the contract
- for causing a social nuisance to neighbours.

As non-payment of rent can be as much as six months in arrears before a court will rule in the landlord's favour, an efficient approach to managing your property will be your best protection; and the legal approach only a last (and often unsatisfactory) resort.

Apart from advertising for tenants for your property in the local newspapers, it is also worth contacting local letting agencies if they exist, but be sure to check their credentials. Make sure that you are dealing with people who are competent and whom you can trust. All too often you can find that extra fees and charges from the agency begin to mount up, or that maintenance of the property is not attended to properly in your absence. Additionally, some estate agents dealing in Spanish property will arrange lets for Spanish property in the areas in which they specialise (and advertise in expatriate newspapers and elsewhere). Remember that VAT (at 16%) for short-term lets, and income tax, will have to be paid on earnings from rental.

It is a legal requirement for those letting out property on short-term lets to be registered with the tourist authorities. Subject to the property being deemed suitable for letting by the tourist authorities you will be issued with a permit. Although many owners are not registered there are fines imposed for non-registration.

## Short-term rentals (*alquiler de temporada*)

Rental returns on short-term holiday lets are high and this kind of contract is probably the best option for foreign property owners since your property can be available for personal use during the year and it is likely to be less difficult to evict problematic tenants. However, it may also mean that during the low season your property will remain empty and you are receiving no income from it.

Short-term lets require a lot of management time spent on them, as tenants may be coming and going every week or fortnight, especially during the high season. If you are resident in Spain and live near the property then this may not cause much of a problem and the cheapest option will be to manage the property yourself. You will need to be on hand to clean the property before new visitors arrive, welcome the visitors and hand over the keys, troubleshoot and provide information about the area such as where to hire a car, find a bank, the best bars, restaurants, beaches and leisure parks. If you have other work or run other businesses then managing your own rental business on top of this may become onerous.

Bookings for short-term rentals tend to vary according to the season and the highest rates, both for bookings and rents, are during the months of July and August. Some owners often also charge peak rates at Christmas and Easter. If you decide to let your property through a management company, they will be able to tell you what the going rates are. If not, you can always check adverts in the local newspapers or ask other landlords.

Bear in mind that short-term rentals usually mean a lot of wear and tear on fittings and furnishings, and items will have to be replaced on a regular basis. Because short-term tenants are very often on holiday and in a holiday spirit they will probably take less care of the property than a long-term tenant would, so don't furnish your property with anything valuable or irreplaceable. However, this statement may be qualified if you are looking to sumptuous décor to attract very wealthy tenants.

# Long-term rentals (*alquiler de vivienda*)

Tenancies lasting from a couple of months to a year or more will bring in a lower rent than those on a short-term tenancy agreement, but tenants holding them are normally responsible for paying their own utility bills and cleaning costs. Most management companies ask long-term tenants for two months' rent as a returnable deposit plus one month's rent in advance – if you are renting privately you would do well to ask for the same.

Spanish legislation regarding rentals still tends to favour the tenant rather than the landlord and if you need to evict a tenant you are likely to find the process a lengthy one. If a tenant doesn't give the landlord one month's notice before the end of the year, the contract continues. A tenant must inform the landlord in advance, in writing, at least a month before vacating the property.

Recovering a property before the five-year term is up can be problematical. You will need to prove that you own no other properties in the same locality and that you require the property for yourself, for your children or for your work purposes. In practice, it is fairly unusual for a landlord to recover a property from a long-term tenant before the five-year period is up unless, of course, the tenant doesn't pay the rent.

Long-term rentals are really only a good idea if you are not looking to make personal use of your property for several years at least. Think very carefully before going into long-term lets and seek legal advice before committing yourself. Ready-printed rental contracts can be bought from tobacconists (*estancos*). Make sure you understand all the clauses in the rental agreement, have the contract checked by a lawyer, and ensure that you are totally happy with any contract you sign with a tenant. Any contract should state who is responsible for the payment of rates, the property tax (IBI) and community charges (imposed by the *comunidad de*

**FACT**

Long-term rentals, regardless of what the contract may state, are for a minimum period of five years. Even if the contract states that the rental period is for one year, a tenant is well within their rights to renew the tenancy annually for up to five years.

*propietarios*). Usual practice is for the landlord to pay the rates and for the tenant to pay the community charges. Long-term tenants should pay utility bills.

Tenants are expected to pay the rent on time, maintain the property in a good state of repair and may not sublet the property without the permission of the landlord or use the premises for immoral purposes. Failure to fulfil any of these obligations can lead to eviction. As a landlord you will have the right to inspect the property at any time providing you inform the tenant in good time of your proposed visit. Inspect your property every few months to check the general state of repair. The landlord is also obliged to carry out any necessary repair work and general maintenance to the property, and replace any fixtures and fittings that have broken or worn out through general wear and tear. Additional obligations may also be included in the rental contract. Failure to comply with your obligations as a landlord could lead to a tenant demanding compensation.

# Eviction, court orders and the tenant's rights

If a tenant fails to fulfil any of his obligations, the landlord has the right to begin eviction proceedings. In the first instance the tenant should be notified in writing. If this has no effect, the landlord will need to consult a lawyer and start legal proceedings. Note that many courts may rule that arrears in rental payments should be over six months late before action may be taken. A tenant may agree to leave after receiving a letter from the landlord's lawyer, or a tenant will wait until a court order arrives. Once the court has ordered an eviction, the landlord will have to wait for a court official to carry out the eviction. The process of eviction can be very slow and could take several months to reach its inevitable conclusion, so the sooner you start legal action should the worst come to the worst, the sooner the eviction will take place.

It is important to be aware that tenants have a certain amount of rights after signing a rental agreement:

- A tenant has the right to pass on the tenancy to a spouse or child.
- If a landlord puts a property up for sale and does not offer the tenant the opportunity to buy then the tenant has the right to annul the sale of the property.
- If the landlord decides to sell the property, a tenant has the right to buy the property if he or she can match (or improve upon) the offer of another interested party. There will be no obligation to sell to a tenant if they offer a lower bid than another party.

# Taxes

It is perfectly legal for owners of private houses, villas or flats to rent out their property without paying any advance taxes or making any business declarations. However, owners are liable for Spanish income tax if the yearly income from the rent exceeds a certain sum (€5,150), as this is then regarded as taxable income arising in Spain. For more information about this and other tax matters you can contact one of the Spanish consulates or the local tax office (*hacienda*) when in Spain. You can also write to the *Ministerio de Economia y Hacienda* about tax matters (C/ Alcalá 9,

28014 Madrid; 901 335533; www.aeat.es); or from Spain to the *Direccion General de Tributos* (C/ Alcalá 5, 28014 Madrid; 915 221000).

Although the non-taxable limit, or threshold, for earned income is similar to that in Britain, this limit is much less when the income originates from investments or real estate and will depend also on whether you are resident in Spain. Non-residents renting out property are liable for income tax at the rate of 25% from the very first euro of rental income. Even if a tenant pays you rent in a non-euro currency in a bank account outside Spain, this income legally arises in Spain because the property itself is situated there. Although many owners undoubtedly do let their property out on the quiet, taking this risk is really not recommended; and it is advisable to keep records of all income generated through renting.

Anyone intending to make letting property a full-time business, who provides hotel-type services such as bed & breakfast, or deals with a lot of visitors on a short-term basis, is moving away into a whole new area with regards to the tax situation. Such activities will be deemed to be a business, so all income received will need to be declared, with 25% of the rent set aside as a withholding tax paid to the Spanish government and an extra 16% VAT (IVA) added to the rent, which must be paid to the Spanish Finance Ministry. This tax is declared on Form 210, available from *hacienda*s. The positive side of declaring new business status is that maintenance expenses from rental income can be deducted before tax is calculated.

## Services offered by management agencies

- paying all routine bills – electricity, water, community charges, insurance, local rates etc from their own bank account, billing you at the end of each month
- monitoring your local bank account every month and converting your Spanish bank statements to UK-style bank statements, which you will be sent every month.
- looking after the general maintenance of the property, eg routine and emergency, painting, plumbing
- pool cleaning
- gardening – routine or one-off service
- security
- year-round supervision of property
- spring cleaning and laundry service
- providing maid service during holiday-let tenancies
- welcoming holiday-let tenants
- being on hand to offer tenants advice, or in case of emergencies
- finding and vetting tenants for your property.

## Property management companies

Spanish-based rental and property management agencies abound along the Spanish costas and many estate agents will also offer some kind of property management service. Agencies offer a comprehensive range of services – cleaning, maintenance, and payment of utility bills. Management companies may also advertise your property and find and vet tenants for you, but there may be an extra charge for this. Monthly statements are often forwarded on to non-resident owners detailing the income and expenditure pertaining to a property. Rental income may be deposited in the owner's Spanish bank account, sent to owners wherever they may be, or held for collection.

Agents' commission varies but most charge around 15% of the gross rental. Any repairs, cleaning and maintenance costs incurred by the agent will be billed to you and listed on your monthly statement. Management companies are likely to have contacts with the local council, banks and other offices and know about Spanish bureaucracy, which will be to your advantage.

### Useful addresses

**H20 Homes Overseas Countrywide:** 0870 1788066; email info@h20countrywide.com; www.h20countrywide.com.
**Menorca Home Care:** 971 151591; email info@menorcahomecare.com; www.menorcahomecare.com.
**Multi-Property Services:** 0871 7119289; www.multipropertyservices.com.
**Ocean Estates:** Málaga; 952 811750; www.oceanestates.com.

## ■ SELLING PROPERTY

There is a thriving market for resale properties in Spain and the procedure is quite simple. It may be carried out privately or by engaging the services of a registered property agent who deals with all matters including:

■ advertising the property
■ accompanying prospective buyers
■ dealing with the legal technicalities of the sale (including contracts, signing before the notary and paying necessary taxes on the property).

This ensures the smooth progress of the sale and relieves the client of much of the usual worry and concern relating to the sale of a property. As was the case when you bought the property, the vendor (you in this case) does not necessarily need to hire a lawyer, though the purchaser should. Make sure that if you paid the *plus valía* tax on the property when you bought it, the purchaser pays it when you come to sell, otherwise you will pay the tax twice.

You can advertise your property for sale through several estate agencies, and negotiate your own contract with them individually – commission rates charged vary. If you bought the property though local estate agents, it could be useful to ask them to deal with the sale, as they will know the property and you and you will know them.

As always when planning to sell a home, presentation is the key to the process. A lick of paint here and there, the replacement of old or faded interior decorations and fixtures and fittings will create the best impression and move the home faster

## Capital gains tax

Note that capital gains tax is charged on the profit from the sale of property and depending on how long you have owned a property before selling on, this tax could be as high as 35% for non-residents and 18% for residents, though there are exceptions to the rules. It is better to hang on to a property as capital gains tax lessens the longer you own a property, and your property will increase in value the longer you own it. If you can afford to, it is often better to hold on to property and rent it out, rather than go for a quick sale.

than if it is put on the market without being spruced up. Price, of course, is also important, and if you ask for too much, then the property will be difficult to shift. However, if the property is individual enough, or the location spectacular, then it is usually only a matter of waiting for the right customer to come along. Your cast-offs could be another's dream.

# ◼ BUILDING OR RENOVATING

## Self-build

Self-build entails buying a plot of land and then building a house on it yourself. Unfortunately, but perhaps predictably, it isn't as simple as that, and there are a number of bureaucratic hoops to be jumped through to erect that edifice. Potential builders can spend a year or more waiting for the necessary licences to be granted before being given the go-ahead to start building. Finding a site can also be very difficult, and finding land to buy is practically impossible on the Balearic Islands since an embargo on the erection of new property has come into force.

The ratio of build (the size of the house to be built) to plot is determined by local planning authorities, so it makes sense to check this ratio with the authorities before going ahead and buying a plot. At this stage you should run checks on the general status of the land:

◼ Is it on a conservation area where there will be tight regulations on planning permission?

◼ Are there public rights of way over it?

◼ Are there by-laws pertaining to water, hunting, grazing, harvesting rights?

◼ Are there likely to be objections to the building schemes that you may have?

◼ How costly will it be to install services such as sewerage, a telephone, electricity, or a water supply?

◼ Is the ground and resources suitable if you want to put in a swimming pool or tennis court?

Land in Spain is zoned for development. There are green zones and rural areas where development is prohibited. Land on which building is allowed is called *suelo*

## Selling your property on

There are a number of documents that you will need to gather when it comes to selling on your property. These are:

- the *escritura*: You will have received a copy of the title deeds to your property after the original was filed with the *Registro de la Propiedad* (the property registry office) by the notary when you originally bought the property. This details any charges or mortgages listed against the property
- receipt of payment of the *Impuesto sobre Bienes Inmuebles* (IBI): This indicates that the real estate tax has been paid on the property to date and that the property is registered with the local authorities for taxes. The IBI receipt will also show the *valor catastral* – the value of the property as assessed by the local authorities (though this may well be lower than the market rate)
- the *referencia catastral*: This is the file number of the property as kept by the *Catastro* (Land Registry). The *Catastro* has a record of the physical characteristics of the property – boundaries, size of plot, outhouses, pools, etc.
- copies of all utility bills – preferably going back over a period of five months to give the purchaser an idea of what to expect bills-wise
- copies of any community charges imposed by the *comunidad de propietarios* if your property is part of an *urbanización* or apartment block – preferably going back over a period of five months
- copies of the transfer tax, stamp duty and *plus valía* tax that you paid on the property when you originally bought it
- declaration of income tax: Depending on whether you are resident or non-resident in Spain, your tax liabilities through the sale of property will differ. If you are a non-resident the purchaser will retain a 5% tax deposit from the purchase price and pay it on your behalf to the tax authorities. If you are a resident you will want to make sure that your tax status is known by the notary and purchaser.

*urbano,* and it is possible to mortgage this type of land according to the normal terms and conditions. However, if you are buying land where building is not allowed – *suelo rustico* – the maximum mortgage amount is 50% of the value, and the maximum term is 12 years. The best course is to get a lawyer, an architect and a surveyor to check over the plot before you buy, and get price sample ranges for the area in which you are interested. If you are buying the plot through an estate agent then he or she should already know what type and size of property would be allowable.

You will want to consult the town plan (*plan general de ordenación urbana*) at the local town hall. This plan outlines the areas that have already been given over to development where planning permission should be relatively easy and straightforward to obtain. Furthermore, the town plan will tell you at a glance whether the piece of land you are interested in developing has major restrictions imposed on the size or height of proposed building projects. If your grasp of Spanish is not great, take along a lawyer or surveyor who will be able to explain the technical jargon on the plan. Also check the details of the separate plots around the one that you are interested in. Are they set for further development? Find out what types of regulations apply to the surrounding land. These will give you a good idea of what regulations will affect your piece of land. Is the planned view of the sea or spectacular mountain scenery from your planned home liable to being blocked by an *urbanización* planned for completion a few years down the line?

## First steps

Wherever you are proposing to buy land, changes to planning restrictions are often made by local councils in return for a share of a developer's profits, or because of a disagreement between the municipal and regional governments. Once you have checked that planning permission for what you intend building is definitely likely to be forthcoming you can go ahead and buy the plot of land. The vendor must be in possession of an *escritura* or other officially recognised deed of title. It is at this stage that you will need to firm up descriptions of land bordering neighbouring property.

You will also need to get your land surveyed either by an independent surveyor or through the *Catastro* (Land Registry) which holds plans marking boundaries of plots (*parcelas*) of land. When you are happy that all these points have been cleared up to your satisfaction you can sign the *escritura* for the land at the *notario*'s office and hand over the money. Because of their age, some rural properties do not have *escritura*, so buyers need to establish their right to the property through a process known as *expediente de dominio*. This is a complex process involving publication of your claim in the *Boletín Oficial del Estado* (the Official Gazette); a lawyer will be able to advise you how to go about this.

The next step is to apply for a building permit (*permiso de obra*). To obtain this you have to submit the plans for the building to the Town Hall. It is likely to take at least two months for plans of the building project to be ready for submission to the authorities. The permiso de obra may cost you up to 5% of the estimated building costs, so it is worth factoring this in to your budget.

## Building plans

To get a plan for your house you will need to get in touch with a firm of builders or an architect. If you are buying a plot on an *urbanización*, the developers will be able to give you details of local builders, or you can enquire locally. A builder will be able to provide you with details of the type of houses he could build for you and together you can work out any variations you may want, interior designs, etc.

**TIP**

A casually waved arm pointing over towards a row of olive trees and the words 'Your land stops over there' really isn't good enough and is likely to lead to problems in the future. Get boundaries sorted out and marked on the escritura if they aren't already.

Alternatively, you can find an architect and work together to come up with an original design that will answer your needs and pass the building regulations. An architect's fee is typically 6% but may run to as much as 9% of the total cost of the build, which means that they will be in no hurry to design you a cheap house. Architects generally charge 70% of their fees in advance and 30% on completion. Once you and the architect have finalised the plans, building specifications (*memoria*) are prepared. These include such things as the type of materials to be used, the specification of window- and door-frames, guttering and tiles, and are submitted to the Town Hall. Once approved, a building licence will be issued and a fee will be due (around 3–4% of the total cost of the project, depending on the region).

## The Spanish way

In the past it was quite usual for properties to be built or alterations made to existing structures without first obtaining the necessary licences. If the authorities found out about it, then they would impose a fine, but there the matter would end. Today things are tighter and fines are likely to be horrendously large. In the worst-case scenario, and depending on the rules of the local authority, a property could be pulled down if erected without planning permission, as is the case in the UK. It is therefore vital to double-check everything with the town hall as well as with your architect and lawyer.

## Builders

With planning permission granted, you can now look for a builder to take on the contract to build your house. Get several estimates. The builders will look at the plans (*memoria*) and tell you how much they think it'll cost them to complete the job. Estimates will vary both for the time it will take to complete the job and the

**Peter Lytton Cobbold** tried to build a swimming pool in the grounds of his seventeenth century masia (farmhouse) in Catalonia.

We couldn't get permission to build a swimming pool because there was a block on building permissions in our area due to a local urbanización project that is on hold. We went to the ayuntamiento to tell them what we wanted to do and kept going back to try to persuade them. In the end one of the people we saw told us to stop making so much noise, close our gates and get on with it. We did, and once we had finished, we received a letter from the ayuntamiento saying that they had heard that we were building a swimming pool and that we should stop immediately or they would confiscate the building materials. As we had already built it, we went to a local gestor who told us to apply for permission officially and pay the fee for licence application. We did and were refused permission and told that the pool was in a state of illegality. Our gestor said that this was a positive reply because a 'state of illegality' did not mean it was illegal. So we left it, and we have not been forced to fill it in as yet!

price they will ask to do the job. You will need to weigh up the prices as well as the individual builders' reputations.

There are good and bad, reliable and unreliable people all over the world, but if you are trusting someone with a hefty investment of your time and money you need to make sure that your investment is safe in their hands. Be sure to get several quotes on any major job that you need doing. There are many reliable and very professional builders in Spain who will build an individually designed house on your plot of land exactly as you wish, or will sell you a plot of land and build a house chosen from a range of standard designs.

Any builder you employ should be covered by an insurance policy so that if they go bankrupt while in the middle of working on your house you will be able to claim compensation. By law, a builder in Spain must guarantee any work carried out for a period of ten years.

Having decided upon a builder, get your lawyer to look over the contract and make sure that any changes and amendments that arise over the course of the building work (they may be quite a few) are added to the contract and signed by both parties. This will avoid any problems when it comes to the reappraisal of the initial estimate and the final demand for payment. Changes to the initial specifications will also prolong the build time and delay the completion of the work. This will need to be taken into consideration, as the original completion date clause in the contract will have to be changed.

As with all purchases, it is advisable to get a solicitor who speaks fluent English and get all documentation completely translated into English. Don't just settle for a précis or summary of contracts. The process of buying a plot of land will involve obtaining one *escritura*, and the building of a property on that land will necessitate obtaining a second.

**TIP**

If you are trusting someone with a hefty investment of your time and money you need to make sure that your investment is safe in their hands. Be sure to get several quotes on any major job that you need doing

## The building process

Once building starts it is advisable to be on site as often as possible, if possible. If you can't be there to oversee the building process personally, try and find someone who you trust to keep an eye on things, or employ a professional to supervise and troubleshoot. Builders everywhere can occasionally be unreliable, or decide not to turn up for work if something more lucrative can be had that day by doing a spot of building elsewhere. You should also check the plans, make sure that the footings are laid correctly – it would be a great shame if your house ended up facing the wrong way, for example – and check on type and costings of materials. Do you want cheap, chic, expensive, or flash? This is your house that is being built and you will want to be on hand to choose materials and fixtures and fittings. Keep in mind that things rarely go exactly to plan, for instance there may be rock where the footings should go and blasting this out of the way will increase the labour cost, or you may decide that you want changes made to the original designs. It is a good idea to factor in at least 10%–30% on top of the original estimate. Building costs are likely to come in at €1,600 per square metre of build, but remember that land is likely to increase in value before the building work is complete.

Stagger the payment schedule to the builder. For example, make payments on:

- signing of the contract
- completion of the exterior walls and roof
- completion of the interior
- completion of plumbing and installation of electricity and services
- completion of exterior landscaping

Negotiate to hold back a final payment until a certain period has passed once the house has been completed so that if cracks in walls appear, or if there are problems with drainage, plumbing, or electrics, you will have some clout if you need to call the builders back in to repair defects.

Depending on the size and complexity of your design, expect a wait of about a year before being able to gaze upon your dream house. Even after the completion of the house it could take an additional year or two to knock the garden and surrounding land into shape.

## Completion

After the house has been built and the architect has signed the completion of construction certificate (*certificado final de obra*) the final instalment of the architect's fees will need to be paid. You will need to make a declaration of the new building (*declaración de la obra nueva*), which will allow you to add the new building to the original *escritura* relating to the purchase of the land. You will also need to take the *permiso de obra* (building licence), the certificado final de obra (completion of construction certificate) issued by the architect and the *licencia de primera ocupación* (licence of first occupation) to the local town hall. The building must also be registered for real estate taxes.

Because so many foreigners are interested in self-builds, there are currently a lot of clued-up agents and developers buying up plots of land, often with services and *permiso de obra* already obtained, to sell on to clients. Property developers also sell plots on their housing schemes (*parcelas*) for buyers to build their own house on.

A prospective self-builder should look into ways to minimise the amount that will need to be paid in VAT and municipal taxes over the period of the project from its inception to its completion and the registration of the property. There may also be tax-saving ways to finance the building project, whether through funds held in Spain, at home or in an offshore account. Be aware that IVA (Spain's equivalent

**TIP**

- Depending on the size and complexity of your design, expect a wait of about a year before being able to gaze upon your dream house. Even after the completion of the house it could take an additional year or two to knock the garden and surrounding land into shape.

to VAT) will need to be paid on building land at 16% for individuals buying land; companies only have to pay IVA at 7%, so some advisers suggest buying the land as a company if at all possible. IVA at a rate of 7% will be added on to building costs.

## Useful addresses

**Carrington Estates:** 0845 094 1168; www.carrington-estates.com. Self-build specialists with offices in the UK and Spain.
**Househam Henderson Architects:** 01962 835 500, or in Madrid 915 647363; www.hharchitects.co.uk. UK architectural practice with a Spanish office.

# Renovating

If you are looking to renovate rather than build from scratch, then ask yourself whether you have the know-how yourself to renovate a tumbledown property, or the necessary funds to hire builders who do. Depending on the amount of work involved in renovating a property, new build often tends to work out cheaper, by up to a third, than renovation.

When you have found a property that you are interested in, get a survey, or a local builder to come and look at it. Make sure that the external walls at least are sound. Before starting on any major renovation or building work, employ an architect. Shop around and get several quotes as these will vary a lot, and will depend on the size of the property, or the planned building work, and perhaps on how au fait you are with Spain and your ability to negotiate in Spanish. A registered architect, like a builder, must guarantee their plans and the instructions given to the builder for a period of ten years.

An architect's fees will include plans (make sure that you are completely satisfied with them) and the supervision of the project. The fee will also include the copies of the plans necessary for approval by the College of Architects before you can obtain the building permit and should also include the cost of preparing the *memoria*, or building specification. This states such things as the quantity and sizes of tiles, bricks or pipes that are needed for the project, the type of concrete and cement needed, and the rest of the building materials to be used. It is likely that you will want to be involved in deciding on the type of electrical and bathroom fixtures and fittings, the colour and type of the tiles for the kitchen and bathroom. Windows and doors and the kitchen units can all be discussed with the architect or builder while the *memoria* is being compiled.

Once the *memoria* is complete it is then given to the builder/s to get a quote for the cost of the building work involved. This quote will be given after having taken into consideration all the materials listed in the *memoria*, and though it may change a bit as work proceeds, any alterations that you make to it later on will cost you extra – and you will need to amend the contract that you have with your builder accordingly. Quotes that come in will vary and the highest quote will not necessarily guarantee the best results, just as a low quote doesn't necessarily mean that the work or materials will be second-rate. Also be advised that there are plenty of expats living in Spain who are looking for work without having registered with the Spanish tax authorities. If you employ such a person and the authorities find out, both you and your employee may both face heavy fines.

When you sign a contract with the builder, get your lawyer to check it to see whether there are any clauses included that may work to your detriment. The contract should include the *memoria*, the total price for the job with payment schedule and work to be carried out. The cost of the job will need to be negotiated with the builder.

# DIY

### TIP

■ If you are intent on carrying out much of the electrical, plumbing and brickwork on your renovation or building project yourself it is as well to remember that in Spain individual, sheathed cables for Live, Neutral and Earth, run through plastic conduit are used, rather than the standard 'twin and earth' that electricians use in the UK.

For basics such as nuts, bolts, screws, wire and nails, the local *ferretería* (hardware store/ironmonger) is going to be a useful resource, and you will find shops that specialise in electrics and others specialising in plumbing. Additionally, on the outskirts of towns and cities are large industrial estates where you will find workshops and wholesalers who will often be in the building trade. There are also DIY superstores such as Akí and Leroy Merlin, which sell all the kit that you will need to knock up anything from a garden shed to a villa with pool.

For projects that need a professional touch, tradesmen such as plumbers (*fontaneros*), carpenters (*carpinteros*), or bricklayers (*albañiles*) will be listed in the local Yellow Pages (*Páginas Amarillas*) or found through talking to neighbours. As with choosing builders, the best way to find tradesmen is by recommendation. If you live in a rural area there may only be a few specialists around and you might need to tread carefully when choosing the one to carry out work on your property. If you live in a more urban environment, it won't hurt to get several quotes on a job before hiring.

House wiring for sockets is done on radial circuits, not ring circuits as in the UK. And it isn't unheard of for the authorities inspecting property to condemn new wiring installations based upon ring circuits. Remember to fit Spanish two-pin sockets (which will be all you will be able to buy in Spain anyway). Doing otherwise may seem a good idea so that you can run your electrical equipment from the UK, but will be a minus point if and when you decide to sell.

Spanish plumbing uses similar sizes to those in the UK (i.e. 15, 18 and 22 mm) and the water in properties is often heated by an immersion heater, which is invariably unvented and wall mounted, with a two-kilowatt element. Spanish homes also use 'Valiant' style boilers powered by bottled gas; rarely do they have cylinders unless they are headed by solar panels. The heating of houses tends to vary throughout the country but in southern Spain it tends to be electric, as it is rarely needed. New builds in the north of Spain, where it does get chilly in the winter, is often underfloor electric or radiators.

Spanish houses in the south tend not to use much, if any, guttering, basically because it rarely rains. However, when it does rain it pours, so it is a good idea to make sure that you incorporate a roof that has a good size overhang from the walls. This will stop any rain from running down the walls. Any major work carried out on external walls should be done using good quality ceramic blocks. Although these are a lot more expensive than solid concrete blocks, they offer good thermal insulation. Solid concrete blocks let the heat in during summer

and out during the winter. Remember that Spanish houses are built with solid walls, i.e. no cavity to provide the necessary insulation. And if you are redesigning an older property you will want to look into increasing the insulation qualities of the property.

# ▚ INSURANCE

Some questions to ask yourself while looking for an insurance policy on your new property include:

- ▚ Is your villa or flat covered by insurance in the event of your letting the property to someone who accidentally burns the place to the ground/floods the bathroom/steals all the electrical appliances and locks a dog in before vacating the premises?
- ▚ Is the property covered for insurance purposes even if it remains empty for part of the year?
- ▚ Does the insurance policy allow for new-for-old replacements or are there deductions for wear-and-tear?

It is always a good idea to shop around to see what options and premiums are available. Ask neighbours in Spain for recommendations and **always read the small print** on any contract before signing. Do not under-insure property and remember that insurance will also be needed if a property is being built to order by a developer or builder.

It may be better to go with a large insurance company than a small independent company, which may be less amenable when it comes to paying out on a claim. Most companies will demand that any claim must be backed by a police report, which may need to be made within a specific time limit after the accident or burglary. If such an event takes place while the house is empty this may be difficult or even impossible, which is one of the reasons why you should check the small print carefully on all contracts.

In areas where there are earthquakes or heavy flooding or forest fires each year premiums will be much higher than back home, and may not be as comprehensive.

**TIP**

▚ Even though it may seem easier to deal with an architect from home, or someone who's mother tongue is English, a Spanish architect familiar with local building rules and regulations, and the local climate, is likely to be more helpful to you in the long run.

## Insurance                                    *i*

Insuring through a company back home with representatives in Spain will mean that claims will be processed in English rather than Spanish, which can be a great help and will also mean that reading the small print will present no problems. Premiums vary depending on the size, location and age of the property, in addition to factors such as security arrangements, the amount of time it will be occupied over a period of a year, the value of the contents, and the distance from emergency services.

Additionally, buying cover from a Spanish company while in Spain is likely to cost a lot more than taking it from an insurance company back home. Insurance premiums will be cheaper in rural areas than in the larger towns and cities and, wherever your property, you may be required by the company to install certain security arrangements which will need to have been in place should a claim be made.

Insurance premium tax in the UK for instance is about 5% while in Spain it is around 6.5%. Some companies will insure a second home abroad if you are already insured with them.

### UK-based companies insuring second homes abroad

**Norwich Union:** place a premium on the value of a prospective client's main home. www.norwichunion.com.

**Saga:** special premiums for those over 50 (£2 million liability for property, loss of rent provision, full cover of 60 days for untenanted properties, emergency accommodation cover) www.saga.co.uk.

**Schofields:** include public liability of up to £3 million. www.schofields.ltd.uk.

**Towergate Holiday Homes Underwriting Agency Ltd:** 0870 242 2490; www.towergate.co.uk.

**Ketteridge Group Ltd:** 0870 754 2711; www.getawaytravelinsurance.co.uk.

If you are going to let your property to holidaymakers, getting good insurance cover is a necessity that you mustn't overlook and you must inform your insurers that the property will be put to this use, otherwise the policy may be void or an extra premium may be payable. As well as covering the villa or apartment and its contents, you will need to cover your own liability in the event of the unforeseen occurring. It also makes sense to try to find a policy that will cover you for loss of earnings from rentals if your house becomes impossible to rent through problems arising from floods, earthquakes, fires and acts of God. Policies will also need to be updated if your property rises substantially in value. Note that your property will not be covered for theft by a tenant unless you take out a policy that covers larceny. Additionally, the policy will only pay out on theft it there are signs of forced entry. Furthermore, if the property is to be **only** used as a holiday home, where the property will be left empty for months at a time you will need to inform the insurance company to ensure that you are covered throughout the year whether in residence or not. It is also useful to get emergency travel cover so that if there is an emergency concerning your property your travelling costs to Spain will be covered.

With long-term rental agreements either the owner or tenant should always arrange appropriate insurance for a property to cover the cost of rebuilding should it be necessary, contents insurance and third party liability. Apart from being a sensible precaution, third party insurance for property is also a legal requirement. Most insurers prefer a multi-risk policy covering theft, damage by fire, and vandalism. If the insurer has bought into a development, it may well turn out that the building as a whole is already covered. It is advisable to check this before taking out an individual policy. In any event, it is unlikely that the existing cover will include the private property of individual inhabitants.

Anyone who has purchased a resale property may find that the seller's insurance may be carried on by the next owner. However, the new owner will have to check whether the policy is transferable.

**FACT**

■ Note that your property will not be covered for theft by a tenant unless you take out a policy that covers larceny.

## Useful addresses

**Axa Aurora Iberica SA:** 902 404084; email atencion.clientes@www.axa.es; www.axa.es. Mortgages and insurance.

**Direct Seguros:** Ronda de Poniente n°14, 28760, Tres Cantos, Madrid; www.directseguros.es.

**Intasure:** 0845 111 0680; Spanish contact no.s: 900 110680; email enquiries@ intasure.com; www.intasure.com.

**Knight Insurance Centres:** Málaga; 952 660535; email kibsa@knight-insurance.com; www.knightinsurance.com.

**Ocaso SA:** 901 25 65 65; email marketinginfo@ocaso.es; www.ocaso.es. Spanish company specialising in holiday home insurance.

**Right Way Insurance and Finance:** Centro Comercial El Campanario 8b, 29649 Calahonda, Mijas-Costa, Málaga; 952 934963; email info@rightwaysl.com; www.rightwaysl.com.

**Saga:** 020 8282 0330/0800 015 0751; www.saga.co.uk/finance/holidayhome/

**Zurich España:** 902 110330; zurich-seleccion-es@zurich.com; www.zurichspain.com.

#  WILLS

After buying any property in Spain, the purchaser should be sure to draw up a Spanish will with a Spanish lawyer witnessed by a notary. This is essential as under Spanish law if the foreign resident dies intestate (leaving no will) or without having made a Spanish will, the estate may end up being claimed by the Spanish state, as it is a difficult and lengthy process for a British will to be recognised in Spain. When making a Spanish will it is unwise to include any property held outside Spain as this could lead to further complications. In other words, British and Spanish property should be kept entirely separate with two wills being made; one to deal with assets in Spain and another dealing with assets in the UK. To validate a Spanish will you need to obtain a certificate of law (*certificado de ley*) from your consulate which states that the will is being made under the terms of UK national law, which includes a provision for the free disposition of property. Any lawyer will be able to organise this for you.

As a foreign national the Spanish civil code allows you to leave your Spanish assets in accordance with the national law of your country of origin. Once a will has been made you should ask for a copy, known as a *copia simple*, from the *notario* who will keep the original. A further copy will be sent to the Central Wills Registry in Madrid.

> **TIP**
>
> When making a Spanish will it is unwise to include any property held outside Spain as this could lead to further complications.

## Companies working with property and wills in Spain

**Bennett and Co Solicitors:** 144 Knutsford Road, Wilmslow, Cheshire SK9 6JP; 01625 586937; www.bennett-and-co.com

**Cornish and Co:** 020 8477 3300; www.cornishco.com

**Fernando Scornik Gerstein:** 020 7404 8400; www.scornik-gerstein.com

**John Howell and Co:** 020 7420 0400; www.europelaw.com

**Florez Valcarvel:** 020 8741 4867

If you are a part-time resident in Spain, it is a good idea to appoint a fiscal representative who will need to be resident in Spain, and through whom the tax authorities in Spain can deal with your tax liabilities. A fiscal representative can be a lawyer, a bank, accountant or a *gestor*. The organisation *Cuidadanos Europeos* aims to help and advise foreigners living in Spain with regards to financial and other matters. It can be contacted at Apartado 418, 03590 Altea, Alicante, Spain (966 880798; www.c-euro.org).

# ■ THE COST OF RUNNING A PROPERTY

The cost of living in Spain may be as much as 20%–30% less than that in the UK, depending on your lifestyle and where in the country you choose to live. Running a property such as a two-bedroom apartment could cost as little as €850 a year, depending on how much electricity, water or gas is consumed. Electricity is likely to cost between €45–€60 every two months, depending on usage, although harsh winters may bump up your bills as many Spanish properties have poor insulation. Water charges can be as little as €16 for two months. Rates could be as little as €100 a year for a small property, while community charges depend on the size of the property, the number of properties in a *comunidad* and the services provided. These charges could cost around €25 per month in a larger community. In addition, car prices, and car tax and insurance, are lower in Spain than in the UK and petrol at around €1.05 per litre is far cheaper than back home.

# ■ REAL ESTATE TAXES

Buying property is an expensive business. Rather than simply being a deal struck between two individuals, where someone hands over a sum of money to someone

---

## Typical annual running costs of a property in Spain

**Community fees:** Controlled by the committee of owners (*comunidad de propietarios*) and based on a percentage of the cost to maintain the facilities provided, relative to the size of your property. Will vary but usually 0.5%–1% of property value

**Local rates (IBI):** Typically 0.2% of property value but will vary from region to region

**Property tax:** 0.2% of rateable value

**Insurance:** 0.5%–1% of value of property

**Water, electricity, telephone and gas:** standing charge and metering slightly higher than in the UK

**Fiscal representative/ *gestor*:** €170 approx. (dependent on services)

else in return for a flat or a house or a plot of land, there are all sorts of additional payments that have to be made to various individuals and institutions. These payments (taxes, stamp duties, lawyers' fees, notary fees) are likely to add another 10% on to the purchase price of your chosen property. The fees payable on a brand new property in Spain will be slightly (1.5%) higher than those for a resale property. The figures for the individual services involved in buying property in Spain break down as follows:

| | |
|---|---|
| Transfer tax on a resale property: | 6% |
| or IVA (VAT) on a new property: | 7% |
| Stamp duty (if buying a new property): | 0.5% |
| *Plus valía* (local municipal) tax: | 0.5% |
| Legal (lawyers') fees: | 1% |
| Notary fees: | 0.5% |
| Property registry fees: | 0.5% |

In addition there may be extra fees payable for the services of a surveyor, for the connection of utilities (electricity, telephone, water, gas) and for the property agent.

Most of these fees (with the possible exception of the *plus valía* tax) will be paid by the purchaser. Make sure that you are clear on which fees are payable by the buyer and which are payable by the vendor. There is no law in Spain that states one or other of the parties must pay a particular tax or fee; however, most contracts will state that the buyer is liable for *todos los gastos* (all expenses). These fees and taxes are calculated as a percentage of the value of the property as declared in the *escritura*.

## Taxes

Traditionally the price declared in the *escritura* was often much lower than the actual price paid for a property (the difference being discreetly handed over to the vendor in a brown envelope). However, these days, local councils value properties in their area so have accounts of the rateable value (*valor catastral*) of properties.

Under-declaring the price of a property is illegal. Doing so will also mean that if you decide to sell the property at a later date the increase in value of the property will be disproportionately large and you will then have to pay a large capital gains tax bill.

Capital gains tax has recently been reduced from 35% to 18% for non-residents, and is a maximum of 15% for residents. There are also certain exemptions available to the over-65s, who do not have to pay capital gains tax on the sale of a house that they have lived in for three years or more. Most of the fees and taxes (with the exception of the *plus valía* tax) listed above must be paid within 28 days of the signing of the *escritura* at the notary's office. Penalties will be incurred for late payment.

It is quite common for a prospective buyer to deposit 10% of the purchase price declared in the *escritura* with the lawyers dealing with the conveyancing so that they can make the payments on the buyer's behalf. The lawyers must give you the receipts of payment for these costs and should not charge you extra for this service. It may be in your favour to find out how much the total cost involved in the sale is likely to be before handing over a deposit and signing a contract of sale.

## Impuesto Sobre Transmisiones Patrimoniales (ITP)

This is a transfer tax payable on the purchase, from a private owner, of property or land. (If you buy a new property from a developer you will be liable for IVA (VAT) instead – see below). The ITP is usually charged at a rate of between 6% and 7% of the value of a property as declared on the *escritura*.

## Impuesto sobre el Valor Añadido (IVA)

IVA is the equivalent of Value Added Tax (VAT) and is paid instead of ITP (see above) if you buy a new property from a development company rather than a resale property from an individual. IVA on the construction of a building is charged at a rate of 7% of the purchase price. If you buy a house and a plot of land at the same time you will be charged the 7% IVA on both purchases. IVA on building plots, commercial property and on additions to existing buildings (such as the building of a garage or workshop) is currently charged at a rate of 16%.

Note that in the Canary Islands, Ceuta and Melilla there is no IVA. In the Canaries a regional tax (Canarian Indirect General Tax – IGIC) is charged instead at a rate of 5%.

## Impuesto sobre Actos Jurídicos Documentados (AJD)

Stamp duty is paid at a rate of 0.5% of the purchase price of a new property (property bought from a developer). If you are buying a resale property stamp duty is included in the transfer tax (ITP). In some *comunidades autónomas* the rate of stamp duty is 1% of the purchase price.

## Impuesto sobre el Incremento de Valor le los Terrenos de Naturaleza Urbana (plus valía tax).

This is a municipal capital gains tax based on the value of urban land. It is a tax on the increased value of the land since the last sale, and is not a tax on the increase in value of any **buildings** on the land. It is only payable on urban land, not on rural land. The tax is payable on both new and resale property and will vary, depending on how long the property has been in the hands of the vendor, the amount of land being sold and its value as a building plot. Although this tax should, in theory, be paid by the vendor (who has, after all, made the profit) it is more than likely that the purchaser will pay this tax unless a clause is added to the contract of sale and a sum is withheld for the payment of the tax.

If and when you come to sell, you will need to make sure that the purchaser of your property also pays this tax or you will end up paying it twice over. The local municipal tax office will be able to tell you before you sign a contract of sale what the *plus valía* tax will be on the property concerned.

# Other fees and charges

## Legal fees

These will depend on the amount of work carried out by the lawyer (*abogado*) on the buyer's behalf, although there will be a minimum charge imposed. Expect to be billed for about 1% of the purchase price. Each party will pay the fees of the legal representatives acting on their behalf.

## Notary fees

These are dependent on the declared value of the property and the number of pages of the *escritura*, but generally amount to around 0.5% of the value of the property and could be anything between €300 and €700. The fee is calculated using an official sliding scale but there may be further fees applicable depending on the amount of work carried out and the number of documents prepared on your behalf by the notary. Note that if you are buying a plot of land and then having a dwelling constructed on the land you will have to visit the notary (*notario*), and pay his or her fees, twice. The costs of granting the first copy of the *escritura* are payable by the vendor while the costs for the second copy are payable by the buyer.

## Property registry fees

Fees for registering a new property with the Spanish authorities in the Property Register (*Registro de la Propriedad*) vary depending on the size, value and locality of a property. The cost is likely to amount to the same as that payable to the notary (around 0.5% of the purchase price of a property). The initial fee payable is a deposit, and you may get a refund if it is discovered that you have been charged too much.

## Other fees and charges likely to be applicable

- The agent's fee will almost certainly be included in the purchase price and will be between 5% and 10%. If there have been negotiations carried out by an agent's representative back home the fee for this should be included in the agent's fee. Check the contract.
- Surveyors' fees will vary depending on the type of survey carried out (valuation only, or full structural survey).
- Utility fees will need to be paid if a new property is without water, electricity or telephone and gas connections. There may also be charges incurred when changing the names in utility bill contracts from the previous owner's to your own.
- Mortgage and mortgage arrangement costs.
- Insurance – both contents and building insurance will need to be paid for.
- If you have hired a tax consultant, their fees will depend on the complexity of your tax affairs. It is worth finding out the most advantageous way to manage your tax affairs in the matter of buying a property abroad.
- Bank charges relating to the transfer of funds from your bank account at home to your bank account in Spain.
- A 5% tax deposit. If the property is bought from a non-resident then 5% of the declared purchase price is deposited with the Tax Agency as a guarantee against capital gains tax payable on the sale of a property in Spain. In such cases

> **FACT**
>
> Note that if you are buying a plot of land and then having a dwelling constructed on the land you will have to visit the notary (*notario*), and pay his or her fees, twice.

the buyer pays the vendor 95% of the purchase price and the other 5% to the Tax Agency. A notary will need to see proof that the 5% has been received by the tax authorities. This 5% will be included in the purchase price and is not an additional cost – the vendor therefore receives 95% of the agreed purchase price of the property.

## Tasas y Cargas

Some, but not all, municipalities charge a certain amount for services such as rubbish collection and street maintenance. A few also levy a charge for owning a car. Day-to-day running costs of property in Spain will include local council taxes, rates, the annual wealth tax, tax relating to the letting of property, community fees if you are part of a *comunidad de proprietarios*, garden and pool maintenance, fees for a financial consultant or fiscal representative, standing charges for utilities, and caretaker or property management fees.

The average running costs per year for a property amount to around 3–4% of the cost of the property, but will depend on size and opulence. Savings will be made on heating costs of course, but charges for water are higher than in many northern European countries. Expect to pay about €4,000 a year on the upkeep and running costs of a property in Spain.

Spain can offer the opportunity to enjoy the good life

## Local taxes

*The Impuesto sobre Bienes Inmuebles (IBI)* is an annual local property tax calculated on the official rateable value of a property (*valor catastral*). It is payable by both residents and non-residents. The percentage of the property value charged as tax will vary depending on the region/province and takes into consideration such things as the level of local leisure facilities provided, emergency services, population and local services and infrastructure. IBI is raised annually in line with inflation and will be higher in a resort town or city than in a small inland village. Make sure before buying a resale property that all IBI taxes due on the property have been paid to date. Ask to see IBI receipts for the preceding five years if possible. If these charges have not been paid you will inherit any back taxes and penalties liable on the property. If the property that you are buying is new, it is up to you to register it with the town hall. Failure to do so, and late payment, will incur a penalty charge. Payment deadlines of IBI will vary from region to region and from year to year and your fiscal representative should keep you informed of pertinent dates so that you can arrange to pay by standing order.

The IBI receipt will show the *catastral* reference number as well as the *valor catastral* of the property – both of which will be asked for by the notary before a sale of property can go through. The *catastral* reference number refers to details of the property kept at the *Catastro* office.

**FACT**

■ Make sure before buying a resale property that all IBI taxes due on the property have been paid to date. Ask to see IBI receipts for the preceding five years if possible.

# Daily Life

# ■ CULTURE SHOCK

When you go to live in a foreign country, you will immediately find that there is a multitude of daily rituals, previously taken for granted, which now pose a seemingly insurmountable challenge. The intention of this chapter is to provide all of the practical information required to successfully cope with various aspects of Spanish life. The information provided can help you decide if Spain is for you. Note, however, that in most of the aspects covered there are bound to be regional and local variations, so do not take this or any other advice you read or are given necessarily as law. In Spain there are particularly striking differences between town and country which may affect the procedure required in doing even the most mundane things.

One important difference you may immediately notice between Spain and many other European countries such as, for example, Germany or France, is that comparatively few older people speak English. Although English is, of course, spoken almost universally in the expat-heavy coastal areas, in many towns and cities the lack of any English-speaking employees in some shops, restaurants or bars can be bewildering and intimidating, even if you speak passable Spanish.

However, as well as improving your language, it is important to remember that Spanish people are welcoming to foreigners, and are doubly hospitable to those who are willing to make the effort with their language. Spain has integrated a range of immigrant populations over the centuries, and is more than used to newcomers. Asking for English speakers in English will often gather a surly 'no', while asking the same question in Spanish will usually find people much more willing to meet you half way.

Food is also likely to be different from home. Spaniards eat a diet that is rich in fresh produce, legumes and grains, and processed food is, comparatively, far more expensive than it is in Britain. However, if you dislike the new diet, remind yourself that the Mediterranean way of eating – lots of whole foods drizzled in olive oil and washed down with red wine – has been found to be one of the healthiest in the world.

Another difference that might strike Britons and Americans is the fact that drinking heavily is, if not exactly frowned on, not celebrated to the extent that it is in northern Europe and America. Young people in Spain do drink socially, but getting so drunk that your friends have to carry you home is seen as embarrassing, and the foreign students who fall out into the streets as the bars close are the cue for much eye-rolling among Spaniards.

Many people feel disoriented when arriving in a new country; however, for a small minority this confusion develops into full-blown culture shock, and they may begin to isolate themselves from social contact, or become excessively concerned about cleanliness or personal safety. An important way of avoiding this is to avoid projecting your own fears and doubts onto the new culture: just because you are nervous about talking to new people, this doesn't mean that they are hostile

**TIP**

■ The internet is ubiquitous in Spain, so you can always find somewhere to send an email home, and the internet phone provider Skype (www.skype. com) and other similar services are a good option for keeping in close contact with the old country. Skype allows users to make free or very cheap calls to international lines, as well as allowing you to assign a telephone number to your computer that users in a large number of countries around the world can call for a local rate.

or dangerous. Expat groups can be a good way of establishing a social network that will then give you the confidence to explore a broader social life in Spain, although it would be a shame to move abroad only to find you spend all your time with people from your own country.

It's important to remember that although you may feel isolated, in today's global communications climate it is easier to keep in touch with friends and family than ever before.

You may also like to have friends and family to visit, and you will almost certainly find that you have become very popular since you acquired an apartment or villa in Spain! However, although this can be a good way of maintaining your ties to home and tackling homesickness, there are a few things to bear in mind. Firstly, some landlords may be unhappy if they feel that you are entertaining too many visitors, and using their flat or house as the equivalent of a guest house for your friends. As well as this, it's likely that everyone who comes to visit will want you to show them around, and while this can be fun for a while, seeing the local sights for the fifteenth time can get tiresome (as well as expensive). Having too many visitors from overseas can also detract from your incentive to develop a social life within Spain.

*Jamón* is extremely popular in Spain; those who move there will encounter a dizzying array of varieties

So coping with a move to a new country involves striking a careful balance between maintaining links to home and doing your best to fit in with your new environment. The following pages aim to give you some idea what to expect of Spanish daily life and culture, to ease the stress of this transition.

# The Spaniards

It is very difficult to generalise about Spanish people as they embrace at least three different traditions and a range of cultural differences: from the Celtic and Basque peoples of the north to the more typically Mediterranean Spanish of the south. However, it is likely that many of those living and working in Spain will do so on the Mediterranean coast and in the great cities in the southern half of the country.

Traditionally Spaniards have a reputation for self-reliance and self-centredness; for being smouldering and quarrelsome by turns; for being macho, (petulant for women), proud and flamboyant, and on occasions capricious. Having a good time has always been a part of Spanish life. These national traits are still in evidence, but among younger Spaniards especially, an increasing prevalence of a more liberal tolerance of those with differing opinions or a different way of life is noticeable.

Better educated, democratised and with a wider outlook than their forbears, Spaniards can afford to show a certain magnanimity towards the world.

Towards foreigners, Spaniards tend to be open and genuinely helpful. They are as warm and friendly, and show less formality, than the Italians or Portuguese. As in the other Mediterranean countries, even today, it is regarded as an honour to be invited to a Spaniard's home as he or she tends only to ask close friends.

## Spanish manners and customs

The traditional image of Spain is of a country bathed in glorious sunshine and sticky heat, where in the afternoons time slows down as everyone, from young to old, snoozes beneath their hat brims before heading out on the town as the sun sets for a long night of drinking and debauchery.

However, much is changing in Spain, and in these days of air conditioning and global markets, the *siesta* is not as prevalent as it used to be. Many hard-pressed executives, shift workers and busy mothers no longer have time for this once essential afternoon nap.

As in France, it is customary for Spanish families to take a one-month holiday, usually in August, which effectively shuts down the country for that month.

Even the lack of a *siesta* does not seem to affect the Spaniards' passion for nightlife. The climate is one cause of this custom, hence the fact that northerners burn less midnight oil than southerners perhaps. The main reason however is that the Spanish have a lust for life and simply live for every moment. The *mañana* (tomorrow) attitude is often overemphasised in literature such as this, and viewed in a negative light. In fact, it is merely a result of wanting to enjoy the present moment, and put off the tiresome duties to a later date. There is a sense of fatalism to the Spanish zest for enjoyment, a result of so many years of repression. Who knows when the next celebrations will come, so why not enjoy this one to the full?

**FACT**

■ The long, lunchtime siesta break is now being replaced by a shorter, one-hour lunch break in the larger companies and businesses of Spain. However, in line with the shorter lunch hour the working day is finishing earlier; and instead of the traditional 9am–2pm and then 4.30pm–8.30pm day (still maintained, particularly in the summer, by smaller shops) most Spaniards now work what is a comparatively relaxed 9am–6pm or 7pm day with one or two hours for lunch.

Not all Spanish men are as liberated as their womenfolk; men will almost always open doors for women or stand aside to let them past. The Spaniards are also far more tactile than northern Europeans; men embrace their male friends, as well as patting them on the back. Male and female acquaintances kiss each other on the cheek, both cheeks in Madrid and northwards; one cheek in the south.

One aspect of Spanish behaviour that can lead to misunderstanding with the British is the Spanish aversion to queuing. Their style is more of an anarchic mass of humanity of which the queue-jumper is king. In Spain, it is not a question of lining up politely, but of being first.

In Spain there is almost nothing more important than the family and it is not unusual for three, sometimes four, generations to live together. The elderly are revered and cared for in the home and the Spaniards are very indulgent towards their children and like to spend as much time with them as possible. On fiesta nights children accompany their parents to restaurants and bars, and stay up with them until the small hours. Children are not, however, allowed into bullfights.

Young people do not usually leave home until they get married and parents seem quite happy with this arrangement, even though children are not really expected to contribute financially, or even help around the house. Traditionally this period of earning without having to fend for themselves has allowed children to build up enough funds to help buy their first house or start their own business, one of the reasons why bank loans are still much harder to come by in Spain.

However, this situation is gradually changing. Many young people now go away to university, rather than studying at the institution closest to the family home,

> '1 was studying at a language course in Madrid and I went out drinking one night. In class the next morning, my teacher asked us what we had done the night before and when I told him I'd stayed out late clubbing, he said something along the lines of "Yes, you look terrible!" I was taken aback; in Britain there is much more of a culture of politeness and formality, and you go out of your way to avoid making personal comments about people. The flipside is that Spaniards are a lot warmer towards you and a lot readier with compliments, even when you don't know them very well, so I suppose it balances out.'
> **Amishi Patel**

girls now have far more options when they leave school, fewer people are getting married, at least at a young age, and divorce is now a real option. People are also beginning to accept the necessity for residential homes as the aging population increases. It remains to be seen therefore whether the strength of family ties will be able to weather the demands of modern society.

# The role of women

One of the much-needed changes of social attitude to come out of the sexual revolution that has taken place in Spain over the past 30 years has been the steady demise of *machismo*. This often-parodied phenomenon has some deep roots in Spanish society, in a code of honour which, in more northerly countries, died out with the rise of Protestantism (which brought a greater informality in social relations to northern Europe). In the Catholic countries this has lingered on. Honourable behaviour in Britain and America (and our rather outmoded idea of behaving like a 'gentleman') is not quite the same thing as being honourable in Spain, which is a more starkly black-and-white affair.

This peculiar Spanish approach to honour is perhaps best illustrated by the film *Chronicle of a Death Foretold*. The code demands – or demanded – that a man who has been dishonoured by a woman's infidelity or her loss of virginity before marriage, retrieve his honour by challenging his rival. The woman who has prompted this action would subsequently be abandoned. If she were from the aristocratic class she would be hidden away in a nunnery, but if from the poorer classes she would almost certainly end up joining the ranks of the world's oldest profession.

The other iniquitous element of machismo (which is the descendant of this ancient code) is that men were (and often are) respected by their peers for the plurality of their sexual conquests. There are strong overtones of mediaeval Muslim culture in this concept that women can be rated as little more than chattels. Perhaps such attitudes arrived in Spain by way of the Moorish occupation, or perhaps they have more ancient origins. From Spain, machismo spread with the conquistadores to the New World (where it is notable that the Spaniards and Portuguese married the local native Americans to a much greater extent than the British colonists did in North America). Perhaps theirs is a more liberal and 'open' way of looking at things after all...

There is probably less sexism in the workplace in Spain than anywhere else in southern Europe, although it does persist and there are frequent reports about sexual harassment in the press.

Such an about-turn has been effected by a combination of circumstances, including better education and the subsequent emergence of women in the professions (as a rule rather than the exception) as well as the election of women to positions of power in the cabinet, academic institutions and the higher echelons of the police force. The diminishing influence of the Catholic Church and hence an increasingly liberal attitude to issues such as divorce, contraception and abortion have also helped women to gain a more equal footing in Spanish society.

These changes have led to a complete transformation of the family structure and Spain now has one of the lowest birth rates in the world at just 1.16 children per woman. There are far more single-parent families in Spain than ever before, and the single child family is very common. Social legislation is attempting to counter this by offering greater benefits to families with three children or more.

The only negative effect of this liberal evolution of attitudes is that domestic violence in Spain is apparently on the rise. It would seem that behind closed doors women's increasing independence presents a challenge to Spanish men in a society that has traditionally had a strictly determined role for women. However, there are signs that attitudes towards domestic violence are slowly changing, and Prime Minister Zapatero has launched a high-profile campaign to tackle it, including the institution of special women's courts.

**FACT**

■ Fortunately for Spanish women, social progress has wrought encouraging changes in the way society regards them today, in their work and other relations. There are more women than ever before in the workplace, in politics, and in the academic world. Women bullfighters have begun to make an appearance and female troops joined their male counterparts in Iraq in 2003.

Meat plays an important part in Spanish cuisine and you may find cuts you haven't before seen

# ■ SHOPPING

Although the cost of living in Spain a couple of decades ago was one of the foremost reasons why Brits chose to move out there, especially in retirement, this situation has changed. Prices have risen with inflation, while salaries have not risen in tandem, and now in the most expensive areas of the Balearics, e.g. Majorca, the cost of living is even higher than the UK, while on the mainland it is approximately the same. However, markets and small villages still offer bargains; these are the areas the newly arrived resident should also explore to get a flavour of the country, and to live more economically. The Rastro Market in Madrid is particularly recommended; there are similar local markets everywhere and Catalonian textiles are famous around the world. In general all leather goods are of a high quality. Handmade wooden furniture is one of the traditional products of Valencia and fine rugs and carpets can be found in markets and shops in the south.

Shopping hours are gradually changing in Spain and the supermarkets and hypermarkets and other large businesses such as department stores are open between 9am–10am and 8pm–9pm. Throughout most of Spain, however, it is still common for smaller shops to close between 2pm and 5pm for lunch and a *siesta*. New laws on Sunday trading came into force at the end of the nineties and most shops are allowed to open for a certain number of hours, although many shops choose to close on Sundays. Sunday opening is still restricted to protect small businesses, although in the tourist season these rules are relaxed.

# Food shopping

For the less adventurous, Spain's thriving import market means that many of the international brands of canned and frozen foods and drinks are also available in Spain. All large towns have modern, self-service supermarkets which, as well as stocking usual supermarket items, also carry a wide variety of goods as diverse as tableware, clothes, toiletries and hardware. Supermarkets still tend to close for the afternoon *siesta* (from 2pm–5pm) but then re-open from 5pm–8pm every day except Sunday. Those who cannot find their favourite British or American foods (which is fairly unlikely unless you are living in a rural area) have a number of internet options open to them. Websites such as www.expatdirect.co.uk will ship your favourite foods direct to your door, wherever you are in the world, at fairly reasonable prices. Those who simply cannot live without their Heinz baked beans should try www.heinz-direct.co.uk.

However, for those who are determined to integrate more fully into the Spanish way of life, there are the smaller shops which sell food and drink without the extras, and the municipal markets (*ventas*), controlled by the local government, which offer

the best prices and often the highest quality fresh produce. These *ventas* can provide a whole new world of gastronomic discovery. For example, handmade (as oppose to industrially produced) sausages can still be found, offering a staggering variety of names, textures and tastes, ranging from the affordable to the eye-poppingly expensive. The red *chorizo* sausage is the best-known Spanish sausage, consisting of ground pork and fat, paprika or peppers; and pepper, garlic, oregano and nutmeg. *Longaniza* is the long, thin version of the *chorizo*, and the *chorizo de Pamplona* is a smoked variety. These, however, are all merely variations on a theme; the *sobrasada*, *salchichón*, *morcilla* and *butifarra* sausages are still to come.

Indoor or outdoor markets are found in every town and in many of the larger villages, and function as the centre point for the exchange of local news and gossip. They offer a real and rare insight into Spanish, small-town life. A helpful hint is to investigate any nearby countryside, where prices can be lower still than in the markets, which although good value, sometimes raise their prices to suit the look of the foreigner's pockets. Here, the smaller, more parochial shops have managed to retain a genuine local charm, as is shown by the politeness and willingness to help of the various salespeople. Shopping here will bring you more closely into contact with the locals.

Some of the remoter areas of Spain are also served by mobile shops (*ventas ambulantes*). These vans travel around, between them selling most things required by the average household, including really fresh fish and meat. This service, amounting to what is practically a door-to-door supermarket, is especially helpful

### TIP

■ Investigate any nearby countryside, where prices can be lower still than in the markets, which although good value, sometimes raise their prices to suit the look of the foreigner's pockets.

The Spanish often use specialist suppliers for their shopping, such as this butcher

for those of restricted mobility, whether this be due to old age, lack of transport or a young baby to look after.

The tax on alcohol is considerably less in Spain than in the UK and most of the prices in the Spanish shops are lower than the duty-free prices back in Britain.

# Other shopping

Spain, once famous for the quality and low price of its goods, is still known for the quality, but no longer the bargain prices (especially in the larger, tourist areas). The mass-market department stores and boutique-like souvenir shops dominate the larger cities; to find real bargains that combine quality and value for money with authenticity and originality, you will need to travel out to the smaller towns and villages, and into the back streets.

Although there are fewer artisans in Spain today than a few decades ago, the best purchases in Spain are undoubtedly the country's diverse handicrafts. Spain has an ample supply of high quality leather and leather goods, including handbags, jackets, belts and shoes. Leather shoes, produced mainly in Alicante and the Balearic islands, offer very good value. Prices are not as low as they once were so it is best to shop around. Pottery thrives in Andalucía where gaudy, brightly-coloured pots and the regional speciality of *Azulejos* – decorative blue-and-white tiles – are proudly displayed on most balconies. Most forms of ceramics are fairly cheap in Spain and very functional. The Andalucían style has a very attractive Moorish influence, which can be seen most obviously in the intertwining patterns on the region's ubiquitous floor and wall tiles.

Many areas of Spain are renowned for the quality of their intricate lace and linen. Other hand-made products of high quality throughout Spain include embroidery, paintings, porcelain and carved woodwork. Good quality jewellery, cultured pearls, trinkets, ironwork, cutlery and glassware can also be found.

Those looking to buy a high-quality hand-made nylon string guitar will be in their element in Spain. This is the one craft industry that refuses to be beaten into submission by modern factory production techniques. Artisan guitar-makers, known as *luthiers*, exist in their thousands throughout Spain, supplying an enormous domestic demand. Each guitar is lovingly handmade to produce the finest sound, which by far surpasses the sound created on the Far Eastern imports that dominate the classical guitar market in other countries. Handmade Spanish guitars are also much cheaper, with student guitars selling for under €150.

The Spanish fashion industry has come on in leaps and bounds over the last few decades and the Spanish do take pride in their appearance, from the sober elegance of the north to the vibrant colours of the south. National chains offering reasonably priced clothes include Zara (now a massive multinational company), Mango, Pull and Bear, Blanco, Massimo Dutti and Oysho. International chains are also well represented in Spain, for example C&A, Benetton, H&M and Topshop. Buying very cheap clothes is more difficult than in the UK or USA as there are very few bargain, secondhand, or charity shops. However, Spain's numerous markets, complete with fake brands offer a variety of cheap clothes (though the quality varies enormously). At the other end of the scale Madrid, Barcelona, Galicia and Seville have no end of designer boutiques.

Consumer durables, such as refrigerators, washing machines, electronic and electrical equipment and cameras, tend to be as expensive in Spain as in the

**TIP**

■ If you are tempted to indulge in the alcoholic delights of Spain – wines, sherry, brandy, and Spanish champagne – you have only to open your local English-language publication to find a warning: there are long lists of discreet advertisements for Alcoholics Anonymous societies (which are located all along the costas).

Markets are a great place to buy fresh fruit and vegetables

UK, but prices are falling. It is probably advisable to buy electrical appliances (*electrodomésticos*) locally as not only will this save on haulage costs, but the appliances will be compatible with the Spanish power supply, and it will be easier to get local goods serviced or repaired. Furniture (*muebles*) should also be bought locally as there are good quality, hard-wearing products available all over Spain. IKEA has eleven stores in Spain, near to Barcelona, Madrid, Seville, Zaragoza and Bilbao, and there are three more on the islands. Alternatively you could source items online and then ship them directly to Spain. Oka Direct (0870 1606 002; www.okadirect.com) has a large collection of furnishings, china and cutlery, including sofas tables, chairs and beds. John Lewis (08456 049 049; www.johnlewis.com) will also deliver abroad. For all household items, the hypermarkets offer very competitive prices.

FACT

■ The removal of the censorship laws have not changed what can only be described as the apathy of the Spanish towards newspaper reading.

# ■ MEDIA

## Newspapers

Freedom of the press was not established in Spain until 1978, in the aftermath of 30 years of censorship under the Francoist dictatorship. However, the removal of the censorship laws have not changed what can only be described as the apathy of the Spanish towards newspaper reading, at least compared to their more voracious British and American cousins. The circulation of the daily press is far lower than in most other European countries; the only countries in Europe with a lower newspaper readership than Spain are Greece, Portugal and allegedly Albania. The most popular daily newspaper in Spain is *El País* (www.elpais.es), which has a reputation for liberalism and for being supportive of more 'left-wing' causes; it is one of very few Spanish national newspapers to offer any serious political analysis and competent foreign news coverage.

*El País* has an average daily circulation of about 432,000 – which compares not too unfavourably with the most widely read quality newspaper in Britain, *The Daily Telegraph*, which has a daily circulation figure of just under a million. Apathy towards politics is another reason for the ambivalence with which newspapers as a whole are viewed throughout the country. Only eight papers in Spain sell more than 100,000 copies a day. The statistic that only one Spaniard in every ten buys a daily newspaper is also fairly staggering. However, as newspapers in Spain tend to be handed around and read second, third and fourth hand, this statistic is based only on sales figures and is thus not wholly accurate as to readership.

The second biggest selling daily in Spain is *El Mundo* (www.elmundo.es), which has a centrist outlook. *ABC* is the other leading daily newspaper of national circulation; similarly to *El País*; this is published in Madrid with some regional editions in some of the autonomous communities. This, however, is where the similarity ends as *ABC* is aligned very definitely right of centre in its politics as well as in its stringent moral dictums. Other leading national papers include *La Vanguardia Española, El Periódico* (published in Barcelona and read mostly in Catalonia and to a much lesser extent in other parts of Spain) and *AS* and *Marca* – both of which are dedicated to sports coverage. In Spain the newspapers circulated in the week are also published

on Sunday; Sunday sales are generally 50%–100% higher than those for the rest of the week.

Shocking though it may seem to those whose literary staple diet is the *Sun* or the *Daily Mail*, Spain has no real equivalent of our tabloid newspapers. Instead, national curiosity tends to be aroused, not by the latest on the royals, but by current affairs of a rather less frivolous nature, and by sport. The Spanish popular newspapers do cover the lives of the rich and famous, but these articles are left to the back pages rather than taking the role of lead stories as often happens in the UK.

## Magazines

As none of the Spanish newspapers has an equivalent of the social diaries or gossip columns that are found in such abundance in British and American papers, the Spanish magazine market has successfully exploited this gap in the market. There are now countless glossy and profitable women's' magazines devoted to the lives and loves of the famous; a few of the most well-known include, *Hola!* (which spawned Hello! magazine in the UK); *Pronto; Diez Minutos; Lecturas; Semana*; and *Garbo*. These magazines are known as the *Prensa de Corazón* (Press of the Heart) and account for six of the 10 most popular magazines in Spain.

## English language publications

Spain is well served for English-language publications. *Sur in English* is one of the best-known English-language newspapers in the country. It has a large employment section in the classified ads, which is used by many foreign residents in the south of Spain and also a large section of the Spanish population. It is distributed on Fridays through outlets such as supermarkets, bars, travel agencies and banks; 916 221656; www.surinenglish.com. Property is also advertised in *Sur in English*, although this is often aimed at those looking for a holiday home in Spain.

### Other English-language publications in Spain

**Absolute Marbella:** 914 547268; www.absolutemarbella.com. Free monthly magazine featuring news and events on the Costa del Sol.

**Barcelona Metropolitan:** email info@barcelona-metroplitan.com; www.barcelona-metropolitan.com. Guide to Barcelona and Catalonia for English Speaking residents.

**The Broadsheet:** 915 237480; www.tbs.com.es. 'The best of Spain in English', distributed in Madrid, Barcelona and on the costas.

**Costa Blanca News:** www.costablanca-news.com. Weekly paper published on Fridays.

**Costa del Sol News:** www.costadelsolnews.es. Weekly paper published on Fridays.

**Essential Magazine:** www.essentialmagazine.com. Glossy Marbella magazine.

**In Madrid:** www.in-madrid.com. Monthly English-language magazine about what's going on in the Spanish capital.

**Island Connections:** Tenerife; 922 750609; www.ic-web.com.

**Majorca Daily Bulletin:** www.majorcadailybulletin.es.

**The Paper:** Tenerife; 922 736002.

**Tenerife News:** Apartado de Correos 11, Los Realejos, Tenerife; 922 346000; www.tennews.com.

**The Town Crier:** Málaga; www.towncrier.es

The quality of these newspapers and magazines varies enormously, but they are useful for keeping up with expat news and for finding accommodation and jobs.

For those to whom a British newspaper is an indispensable commodity, even when abroad, British newspapers and the *International Herald Tribune* are available in most of the larger Spanish cities. *The Guardian Weekly* subscription rates for Europe are currently €34 from Spain quarterly, with a four-week free trial. See www.guardianweekly.co.uk. *The Weekly Telegraph* is a similar digest of news culled from *The Daily Telegraph*. A year's subscription currently costs £100. *The Telegraph* also has a section of its website devoted entirely to people living abroad: www.telegraph.co.uk/expat (it is also possible to subscribe to *The Weekly Telegraph* here).

Before leaving for Spain there are numerous magazines to whet your appetite. The British property buying boom in Spain and the interest in the country in general has lead to a rise in the number of publications dealing exclusively with life in Spain, aimed at expatriates and those who dream of moving to Spain.

The main magazines listed below all offer a subscription service, so you can continue to receive issues once in Spain:

## Magazines about Spain

**Living Spain:** www.livingspain.co.uk.

**Spain Magazine:** email info@spainmagazine.co.uk; www.spainmagazine.co.uk.

**Spanish Homes Magazine:** www.spanishhomesmagazine.com.

**Spanish Magazine:** 01225 786844.

# Books

Libraries in Spain usually work on a closed-shelf system where readers need to know exactly what they want and then ask for this at the counter. Often, Spanish libraries do not allow readers to take books away, even if they are members of the library. English-language bookshops are scattered along the costas and in the larger cities. Book fairs are often held in town squares. These are good opportunities to buy books on a wide range of subjects and languages at reasonable prices.

The Spanish National Tourist Office in London also publishes an information sheet on Books about Spain including general and regional guides, city guides, books on specialist subjects and the Spanish language. For a list of general reading books about Spain see page 460. Santana books, based in Málaga, publish a wide range of English language books about various aspects of life in Spain. They can be contacted on 952 485838; email sales@santanabooks.com; www.santanabooks.com.

All of the Spain-related English magazines listed above offer reviews of the latest books about Spain and life in Spain and some of them have their own book clubs, from which the latest releases can be ordered overseas. Another good contact is the

Spanish Book Shop, 020 7734 5259; www.thespanishbookshop.co.uk, who have a wide range of books and magazines relating to all things Spanish.

# Television

**FACT**

■ The Spanish are a nation of telly addicts; after the British they watch more television than any other country in Europe.

The Spanish are a nation of telly addicts; after the British they watch more television than any other country in Europe. Nearly every Spanish household contains at least one television set, sometimes where the household lacks several more essential facilities, and approximately 90% of Spaniards over the age of 14 watch television every day. The influence the television has as a media form is intensified by the fact that the Spanish do not read newspapers with the same avidity as the British or Americans.

So far as the history of Spanish TV is concerned, Television Española (TVE), the main Spanish television station, set up as a state monopoly in 1956, was subject to heavy censorship under Franco's regime. This censorship continued well into the 1980s and had the effect of lowering the general quality of the programmes aired. TVE's two channels are called TVE1 and TVE2 and despite being a public service, funded by taxpayers, they still run commercials. The first is directed to a more general public. TVE2 has a flexible programming which lends special attention to sports broadcasts and live broadcasts of important cultural events. Its television coverage and audience have grown considerably, however, TVE1 has the larger audience with more than 20 million viewers (80% of the total).

At the beginning of the 1990s two new national channels started broadcasting, Antena 3 and TeleCinco. There is also a subscription channel, Canal+ (still available as analogue, but the recent merger of Canal+ Digital and Via Digital has led to the new Digital+ service) and various regional television channels also exist in Catalonia, the Basque Country, Galicia, Andalucía, Madrid and Valencia. Added to this, today there are satellite, digital and cable networks, with more than 700 local channels serving the different cities and towns.

Traditionally light entertainment has not enjoyed the same popularity among the Spaniards as it does with most other viewing publics and the audience figures reflected the same interest in current affairs and serious discussion programmes as mentioned earlier.

It is true that Spain's three main broadcasters pump out an average of 13 hours a day of *programas de corazón*: a blend of scurrility, plunging necklines and shouting. However, documentaries are still very popular, as is the current affairs programme *Informe Semanal* on TVE.

Generally the low-budget nature of Spanish terrestrial television leads to some fairly abysmal programming and most expats prefer to watch UK TV. Recently, most British terrestrial television (ie, all BBC and ITV channels) has become free to view in Spain, so there is no need for a Sky service or digital card, although a satellite dish receiving Astra 2 is needed. However, to watch Channel 4 and Channel 5 you will still need to buy a Sky digital receiver; once you have this, it should not be necessary to pay any special subscription charges unless you want to watch pay-per-view channels.

Freeview boxes bought in Britain will not work in Spain; you will need to buy an equivalent Spanish box that has the correct specifications for the broadcasting system. These generally cost around €60.

# Radio

Spanish radio has a reputation for high-quality and entertaining programming and its audience is greater than that in any other European country. The first state network, Radio Nacional de España (RNE), created by Franco in 1937, paralysed the development of the radio as news broadcasts were produced only by this government-controlled station and prohibited on any others. Only groups close to the Franco regime were given licences and in 1960 all radio stations were legally obliged to broadcast simultaneously the news programmes produced by RNE. However, once the censorship laws had been removed, the growth of new networks was so prolific that at one point Spain hosted some 450 radio stations. Currently, however, Spain has a far smaller number nationally, around 15. The largest public network as far as budget, number of stations and personnel are concerned is still RNE, although the audience level is still lower than that of some of the private networks.

The most popular radio networks include SER, which has a number of different stations, broadcasting music, sports and news, both regionally and nationally. COPE (*Cadena de Ondas Populares Españolas*) is the second largest system of private stations and is owned by the Church. Antena 3 is a national network and groups together a number of FM stations, which appeared after the concession of new licences in the 1980s. Most of the stations and networks are now on FM rather than medium wave (Spain has no long-wave stations); and many, like the newspapers and TV channels, also have their own political stance and alignments as well.

Nearly all radio stations can, of course, be listened to over the internet if you have a broadband connection (see page 183.)

**FACT**

■ In recent years, Spanish television has been increasingly dumbed down and the newspaper *El País* recently demanded: 'How much deeper can gossip programmes plunge, with their libel-ridden, rumour-mongering, humiliation and lying?

## Radio Stations *i*

Listening to local radio is a very good way to improve your Spanish, and many of the stations seem to offer continuous discussions and phone-ins. Those who wish to listen to the radio in English will find that in areas where there are large numbers of expats there are a number of English language local stations. Try, for example, Octopus FM (98.3FM), Central FM (98.6FM), Spectrum (105.5FM) and Radio Gibraltar (91.3FM) on the Costa del Sol. It is also possible to get the BBC World Service on short-wave, although the frequency can change. To check the frequency go to www.bbc.co.uk/worldservice/ and click on Radio Schedules and Frequencies.

# ■ COMMUNICATION

## Post

As in the UK, urgent or registered letters and packages must be taken to a post office in Spain. Post is delivered to your door if it weighs less than 500g and by paying a surcharge if the package weighs more than limit. If the excess payment is not made, the package must be picked up from the local post office. For those who have no fixed address the poste restante (*lista de correos*) service is useful; just write the addressee's name, then *lista de correos* and the place name on the envelope; the addressee can then pick up his or her mail from the post office after providing a passport as identification. A PO Box service (*apartado de correos*) also exists whereby, for a fee, correspondence can be picked up directly at the post office most convenient for the addressee.

Airmail letters (*aerogramas*) are available at the post office. Letters may also be sent by registered mail (*carta certificada*); this will guarantee their arrival. It is possible to send money through the post by money order (*giro postal*). Post office business hours are generally from 9am to 2pm, although large cities or towns usually have a main post office with longer opening hours.

Postboxes often have two parts; one marked *ciudad* for local mail and another marked *provincias y extranjero* for the rest of the country and abroad. Stamps are sold at post offices and at tobacconists, easily spotted by the Spanish flag painted outside.

A telegraph service (*servicio telégrafo*) which dispatches telegrams and urgent money orders around the world is also available. A telegram can be sent from the post and telegraph offices, or by telephone for a slightly higher amount. Enquiries should be made at the post office.

## Telephone

Telefónica (www.telefonica.es), Spain's equivalent to BT, was privatised in 1998 and although it has lost its monopoly in Spain, it still retains a powerful hold on the telephone service, with 87% of the market share. In November 2007 it was named the second largest global operator in terms of number of customers. Telefónica also operates the phone booths dotted around the country. These phone booths take coins, credit cards and phone card (*tarjeta teléfonica* (which can be bought from *estancos*, news stands and post offices and come in denominations of €5, €10 and €15). Many of these phone booths have multilingual digital displays and it is possible to use them to make international calls. When calling abroad it makes sense to buy a calling card, which costs €10 but will give you a good five or six hours of talk time. There are also a number of establishments in Spain, especially in the bigger towns and resort areas, which offer low-cost calls, although you should compare prices before using these and shop around.

# Telephone numbers

The full nine-digit number must be used whether calling from within Spain (or even within the same province) or from abroad. Telephone numbers these days are given as three sets of three digits (ie 966 812841), the area code being the first two or three digits of the telephone number. The country code for Spain is 34.

To dial abroad from Spain you will need to dial the internationalprefix (00) followed by the country code (eg. United Kingdom – 44; USA – 1; Australia – 61; New Zealand – 64; Eire – 353; Canada – 15; South Africa – 27) followed by the prefix of the area code minus the initial 0, followed by the number of the subscriber.

Common services telephone numbers are included in the front pages of the telephone directories, which are available by province. There is a charge made for calls to Directory Enquiries. Barcelona, Madrid and some other cities operate an information line, which is often very useful (010).

## Telephone glossary

| | |
|---|---|
| answer machine | contestador automático |
| to cut off | desconectar |
| dialling tone | tono de marcar |
| engaged | ocupada |
| hang up | colgar |
| to leave a message | dejar un mensaje |
| phone bill | factura |
| a phone box | una cabina teléfonica |
| a phone card | una tarjeta teléfonica |
| a phone call | una llamada |
| phone number | numero de teléfono |
| pick up the receiver | descolgar |
| to ring | sonar |
| subscriber | abonada |
| subscription | abono |

## Area telephone codes

| | |
|---|---|
| Aguilas | 968 |
| Albacete | 967 |
| Alcira | 96 |
| Alcoy | 96 |
| Algeciras | 956 |
| Alicante | 96 |
| Almeria | 950 |
| Arrecife | 928 |
| Avila | 920 |
| Aviles | 98 |
| Badajoz | 824, 924 |
| Badalona | 93 |
| Barcelona | 931–938 |
| Benidorm | 96 |
| Bilbao | 94 |
| Burgos | 947 |
| Caceres | 927 |
| Cadiz | 856, 956 |
| Cartagena | 968 |
| Castellon de la Plana | 964 |
| Ceuta | 956 |
| Ciudad Real | 926 |
| Cordoba | 957 |
| Cuenca | 969 |
| Gandia | 96 |
| Gerona | 872, 972 |
| Gijon | 98 |
| Granada | 858, 958 |
| Guadalajara | 949 |
| Huelva | 959 |
| Ibiza | 971 |
| Irun | 943 |
| Jaen | 953 |
| Jerez de la Frontera | 956 |

| | |
|---|---|
| La Coruña | 881, 981 |
| Lanzarote | 928 |
| Las Palmas | 828, 928 |
| Lerida | 873, 973 |
| León | 987 |
| Linares | 953 |
| Logroño | 941 |
| Lorca | 968 |
| Lugo | 982 |
| Madrid | 911, 912, 914, 916–918 |
| Mahon | 971 |
| Marbella | 95 |
| Merida | 924 |
| Málaga | 951, 952 |
| Orense | 988 |
| Palencia | 979 |
| Palma de Mallorca | 971 |
| Pamplona | 948 |
| Pontevedra | 886,986 |
| Reus | 977 |
| Sabadell | 93 |
| Sagunto | 96 |
| Salamanca | 923 |
| San Feliu de Llobregat | 93 |
| San Sebastian | 943 |
| Santa Cruz de Tenerife | 922 |
| Santander | 942 |
| Santiago de Compostela | 981 |
| Segovia | 921 |
| Sevilla | 954, 955 |
| Tarragona | 877, 977 |
| Tarrasa | 93 |
| Tenerife | 822, 922 |
| Teruel | 978 |
| Toledo | 925 |

*(continued)*

| Torremolinos | 95 |
|---|---|
| Tortosa | 977 |
| Valencia | 960–963, 965, 966 |
| Valladolid | 983 |
| Vigo | 986 |
| Vitoria | 945 |
| Zamora | 980 |
| Zaragoza | 876, 976 |

# Mobile phones

If you want to use a mobile phone (*teléfono móvil*) purchased at home during your time in Spain, you will need to check with the service provider what the call rates are when using the phone abroad and whether there is coverage for the service. Spain uses GSM 900/1800 telephones, which are compatible with the rest of Europe, but not with the North American GSM 1900. You may also need to inform your service provider before going abroad to get international access on your handset activated. There may be a charge for this, depending on the phone package that you have. Using your mobile phone while abroad is expensive – you will be charged extra for incoming calls and access to your voicemail may also be restricted.

The mobile phone arm of Telefónica is (www.movistar.com). There are also a number of other operators in Spain including Vodafone (www.vodafone.es) and Orange (www.orange.es).

Mobile phones are very popular in Spain, and phone outlets and agents are not hard to find in the towns and cities. There are two ways of paying for calls: either by setting up an account with a service provider, or by using pre-pay cards bought from supermercados or *estancos*. It will be much cheaper in the long run to buy a mobile

## Useful telephone numbers

| | |
|---|---|
| Alarm call | 096 |
| International directory enquiries | 025 |
| Telefónica fault line | 1002 |
| International operator (Europe/North Africa) | 1008 |
| International operator (Rest of the World) | 1005 |
| National directory enquiries | 1003 |
| *Policía Local* | 092 |
| *Policía Nacional* | 091 |
| Speaking Clock | 093 |
| Weather Report | 365 |

Shopping streets, Figueras

phone from a Spanish operator but whether you want to do this will depend on how long you intend staying in Spain each year. In June 2007 the European Union ruled that the current level of charges for customers who used mobile phones aborad was unacceptable, and these charges are now beginning to decline; however, using a British mobile in Spain is still an expensive option.

You can find more about using mobile phones abroad on www.gsmworld.com and at www.telecomsadvice.org.uk.

# Internet

There are many internet cafés and cybercafés in Spain for you to use if you only plan to spend a few weeks a year in the country, but if you are moving to Spain permanently then you will probably want to get connected to the web. When you install your phone lines, you might want to connect to the internet with the internet service provider (ISP) owned by the telephone company. This usually allows you a free internet connection with calls at local rates. Free connection software is also available from most computer shops, with companies such as Tiscali. The telephone companies also have discount tariffs for heavy internet usage called *tarifa plana*. These charge a flat rate irrespective of usage, that allows you to be connected to the internet either 24 hours a day or only during off-peak times, depending on the deal you choose. It costs around €22 a month for an unlimited connection, but shop around for the best deals. The main providers are www.inicia.com, www.terra.es, www.jazztel.com and www.ya.com.

Broadband is now universal in urban areas and fairly cheap to install (around €100). Often there are offers, which include free installation, so again it is best to shop around. Line rental works out at around €40 per month for 1Mb of bandwidth. The advantage of broadband is that it is considerably faster and allows you to listen to the radio or make phone calls via the internet and allows you to be constantly connected without interfering with your telephone line.

FACT

■ The telephone companies have discount tariffs for heavy internet usage called *tarifa plana*.

## Internet glossary

| | |
|---|---|
| @ (at) | *arroba* |
| to browse/surf the net | *navegar por la red* |
| to cancel | *cancelar* |
| to click | *pulsar* |
| to download | *descargar* |
| to drag | *arrastrar* |
| email | *correo electronico* |
| email account | *cuenta de correo electronico* |
| home page | *la página web inicial* |
| icon | *el ícono* |
| internet | *internet* |
| to install | *instalar* |
| keyword | *la palabra clave* |
| link; to link | *el enlace; enlazar* |
| to log on | *comenzar la sesión* |
| online | *en línea* |
| password | *contraseña* |
| to print | *imprimir* |
| to save | *guardar* |
| search; to search | *la búsqueda; buscar* |
| search engine | *el servidor de búsqueda* |
| spam | *correo basura* |
| toolbar | *barra de herramientas* |
| to uninstall | *desinstalar* |
| web browser | *el navegador Web* |
| web site | *el sitio web* |
| window | *ventana* |

## ■ HEALTH

## INSALUD – the Spanish national health service

The Spanish health service combines both public and private healthcare and everyone who makes social security payments or who receives a state pension, is unemployed, or under the age of 18 is entitled to free medical treatment. The government's public healthcare policy has been oriented towards the universalisation of healthcare, through the recent extension of coverage to a million low-income group residents who have not been protected until recently (98.9% of the population is now covered by the state health system, in contrast to 86% back in the 1980s).

Recent laws have also included illegal immigrants and their dependents in the category of persons given free healthcare. However, free treatment is still only available in certain hospitals, whose waiting lists tend to be long (particularly for those who need hospital treatment for terminal diseases); and coverage for psychiatric illnesses in particular is severely limited. Another difference between Spain and the UK is that much basic non-medical care such as assisted feeding still takes place within the family, with nurses performing a more minor role.

The shortcomings of the system are well exposed by the fact that such preventable diseases as tuberculosus, tetanus and diphtheria are still around in Spain. There are not enough hospitals available (especially in the poorer areas) and the emphasis still lies with curative rather than preventive medicine. The root of the problem lies in the inefficient way in which the social security resources are administered

Traces of Spain's agricultural economy still remain, especially in rural areas

and distributed; it is primarily because of this that various attempts at reform of the system have failed in recent years. Not surprisingly, many Spanish residents, both nationals and expatriates, take out private health insurance, details of which are given on page 188.

Anyone living and working in Spain who is below retirement age must make a monthly contribution to INSALUD, the Spanish national health service. This contribution is included in social security payments (see below), which are deducted from an employee's gross salary by the employer; social security payments account for approximately 5% of a worker's gross income.

The benefits to which anyone subscribing to the Spanish national health service is entitled include free hospital accommodation and medical treatment. As some hospitals (approximately 40%) only treat private patients, it is as well to know which hospitals in your area provide national health treatment. A list of national health centres and hospitals in your area is to be found in the local office of the *Insituto Nacional de la Seguridad Social (INSS) in Spain*, or in the local Yellow Pages (*Páginas Amarillas*) Or write to your Consulate there.

## Using Insalud

It is essential that all UK nationals who are intending to move to Spain – whether to work or retire – register their change of address with the Overseas Branch of the Department of Health before leaving the country. These are the main people to contact. They will then be sent the paperwork to be completed to receive the Spanish national health card from the Spanish social services. If you are working in Spain it is your employer's responsibility to register you for social security and after

> **Martine de Volder** moved to Tenerife 25 years ago to work as a nurse. Previously she worked in Accident & Emergency in a Belgian hospital and believes that Spanish public healthcare compares very favourably with that of other advanced EU countries:
>
> 'The fact that free healthcare is available to all in Spain is a real advantage compared to most EU countries, where the patient always has to pay at least a proportion of the costs of medical attention. In Spain the only thing you have to pay for, unless you are a pensioner, is prescription medicine.
>
> This is not to say that the system is perfect. There are certain disadvantages. For example: long waiting lists; having to go to the doctor at a specific time; having to visit special national health service centres (consulta de seguridad social) which are not necessarily available in smaller towns; the fact that you cannot see a specialist without first visiting your GP. These disadvantages can be major irritations. In my local public doctor's surgery, the doctor is only there from 8am–1pm and after that you have to travel to the next city to find a doctor who is on duty.
>
> Equally the need to make appointments well in advance can be frustrating. For example, if you have 'flu, you may have to wait until the next week before the doctor can see you. It is very important when visiting your doctor to take somebody with you who speaks Spanish. Although you may think that doctors and nurses will be able to speak English, often they don't. Another disadvantage, especially for the elderly and infirm, is that home visits are very rare and only made in exceptional circumstances.
>
> Those who can afford it go private (which is possible whether or not you have private insurance), but private medical care is very expensive and you are generally treated as a client rather than as a patient. Also there is less control over the private sector, nurses are often not as well trained as in the state sector, and those claiming to be specialists often have dubious qualifications.
>
> In general state care is very good, I would say excellent. The system can be a pain and home care is virtually non-existent, but the quality of the doctors, nurses and hospitals is very high.'

a few weeks of working you will automatically receive a social security registration card. Those who are self-employed must register themselves. Once your registration has been processed you will receive the *tarjeta sanitaria*. Whichever of these cards you receive, it must be presented whenever you need medical treatment; and will cover the holder for 100% of medical treatment and 90% of prescription charges.

When you move to Spain it is important to ensure that you and your family are registered at the local health centre. Married couples who are both working will receive a card each, otherwise the non-working partner and any dependents will be covered by one card.

The card will also entitle you to full benefits when on holiday in Britain or in any other EU country. The two systems of national insurance in the UK and social security in Spain are transferable insofar as if you return to Britain at any future time, payments towards one count towards the other; and vice versa. What happens in detail is explained in various leaflets available from the Pensions and Benefits Overseas Directorate in Newcastle (0191 218 7777), or the Euroadviser in your local JobCentre may be able to advise. In Spain, you can find out more about social security can be obtained from the *Instituto Nacional de la Seguridad Social* (INSS); 915 688300; www.seg-social.es.

If you are hospitalised in Spain at any point, then you should be aware that nursing is quite different in Spain. They are available only for their professional medical skills, not for welfare issues such as serving food or dealing with bedpans. While ancillary staff do offer some assistance, this is mainly provided by the patient's family in Spain. The 'two visitors at a time' rule is therefore unheard of in Spain and the entire family often turns up to lend a hand.

# Reciprocal health agreements

## The European Health Insurance Card

Reciprocal medical arrangements that exist between the UK and Spain under EU regulations make it possible to obtain mainly free medical treatment for shorter-term visitors to Spain for no more than three months at one time. This arrangement may well be helpful for those going on a home-searching trip to Spain or those who already have holiday homes there. However, this agreement only covers temporary residence, not the first three months of permanent residence in the new country, and applies only to emergency medical treatment. To qualify for such treatment you need to apply for a European Health Insurance Card (EHIC), which, as the name suggests, is valid across the EU, not just in Spain. Application forms are available online at the Department of Health website: www.dh.gov.uk or from post offices. You will still need to take the downloaded forms to the post office for approval.

Happily, the Spanish authorities have simplified the procedures necessary for foreigners to obtain medical treatment and now you have only to present your EHIC card. It makes sense to make a photocopy of this card, as medical treatment will not be given unless you can prove you are entitled to it. If you do not have an EHIC card, regardless of your status as an EU resident, you will be expected to pay for medical treatment and you will still, anyway, have to pay for non-emergency treatment, e.g. prescribed medicines and dental treatment. Moreover, the EHIC card is not a substitute for travel insurance, which should still be taken out for short trips abroad, as this will provide financial protection against costs that are not regarded as emergencies.

An EHIC card is not valid once you have left the UK permanently or are employed in Spain. Once a residence permit has been applied for (i.e. after three months) you should have made permanent arrangements. Explanatory leaflet SA29 gives details of social security, healthcare and pension rights within the EU and is obtainable from main post offices and also from the Department of Work and Pensions, Overseas Directorate; www.dwp.gov.uk. It may be of use to those intending to move to and work in Spain.

**FACT**

The Spanish authorities have simplified the procedures necessary for foreigners to obtain medical treatment and now you have only to present your EHIC card.

### The E101, E121 and E128

The Inland Revenue, National Insurance Contributions Office, International Services in Newcastle, issues an E101 to UK nationals working in another EU country to exempt them from paying social security contributions in that country because they are still paying them in their home country.

The E128 entitles you to medical treatment in another EU country where you are working, or if you are a student. You have to obtain an E101 before you can obtain an E128. These forms are available from www.hmrc.gov.uk and www.dwp.gov.uk.

The E121 is required by retired people in order for them to receive medical care under the Spanish national health system.

### Sickness and invalidity benefit

Anyone who is moving out to Spain permanently and who claims sickness or invalidity benefit in the UK is entitled to continue claiming this benefit once in Spain. Strictly speaking, to claim either benefit, you must be physically incapable of all work; however, the interpretation of the words 'physically incapable' is frequently stretched just a little beyond literal truth. If the claimant has been paying National Insurance contributions in the UK for two tax years (this may be less depending on his or her level of income) then he or she is eligible to claim sickness benefit. After receiving sickness benefit for 28 weeks, you are entitled to invalidity benefit, which is paid at a higher rate. Although it may seem something of a Catch 22 when you can only claim sickness benefit if you are incapable of working and yet you are only entitled to the benefit through the last two years of National Insurance payments deducted from your income, the benefit is designed to be used by people who have had to stop work due to severe illness.

Anyone currently receiving either form of benefit should inform the Department of Work and Pensions that they are moving to Spain. They will then send your forms to the DWP International Services department (Newcastle upon Tyne, NE98 1YC) who will then make sure that a monthly sterling cheque is sent either to your new address or direct to your bank account. The only conditions involved are that all claimants submit themselves to a medical examination, either in Spain or Britain, on request. You can find out more in the leaflet SA29 'Your Social Security, Insurance, Benefits and Health Care Rights in the European Community and in Norway, Iceland and Liechtenstein', available from www.dwp.gov.uk. Once in Spain, claims for sickness benefits are made through your local INSS office (900 166565; www.seg-social.es/inss).

**FACT**

A growing number of foreign residents in Spain are also opting to remove themselves from the long waiting lists of the Spanish national health service and to take out private health insurance.

# Private health insurance

Although the level of convenience, comfort and attention offered through private insurance schemes is superior to that received by national health patients, the treatment itself will not necessarily be of a higher quality. However, the private sector is constantly growing and around 18% of the Spanish population now have private cover. Many use it as a supplement to the state service rather than a replacement. The private companies have their own hospitals and clinics, although whether these will be better equipped than the state hospitals depends very much on the area. Private prescriptions are not subsidised.

Those who do not work and therefore do not contribute to the Spanish social security system will have no option but to go private, as the state health system is not available to them. It is easy to obtain Spanish health insurance through a UK organisation (see addresses below).

Those who are going to Spain seeking work, or who spend a few weeks or months a year there, will require private medical insurance to cover the balance of the cost not covered by the EHIC card. If you already hold private health insurance, you will find that most companies will switch this for European cover once you are in Spain. With the increase of British and foreign insurance companies offering this kind of cover, it is worth shopping around as cover and costs vary. Those interested can set up the policy from the UK before moving to Spain or on arrival in Spain through a broking agency. One of the advantages of UK health insurance schemes is that their policies cover the claimants for treatment incurred anywhere in Europe, not just in Spain itself.

Spanish insurance policies are widely available and have a distinct advantage over UK ones in that payment for medical treatment is made in the form of vouchers provided by the insurance company rather than having to pay initially and then claim back the treatment cost from the insurance company afterwards. The main private healthcare companies in Spain are Adeslas (www.adeslas.es), Asisa (www.asisa.es) and Sanitas (owned by BUPA – see below). Prices for private coverage depend on a number of factors such as your age, sex and state of health, but more importantly the company you use and the degree of cover you require.

Although the premiums on Spanish insurance policies may appear much cheaper and more attractive than those offered by the British companies you may well find that the policy is limited to specific local hospitals – not very helpful if you are in urgent need of treatment and are driven to a hospital not on their list and refused treatment. Additionally, the small print needs to be read very carefully; perhaps treatment is only refunded if surgery is performed, or outpatient treatment is not included in the policy (i.e. visits to the local GP and the dentist). Other policies may offer limited cover on surgery, medicines and accommodation.

## Useful health addresses

**AXA PPP Healthcare:** 0870 6080850; www.axappphealthcare.co.uk.

**British United Provident Association (BUPA):** 0800 600500; www.bupa.co.uk. BUPA International offers a range of worldwide schemes for individuals and companies of three or more employees based outside the UK for six or more months.

**Community Insurance Agency Inc:** IL 60062, USA; 1800 3449540; email info@visitorsinsurance.com; www.visitorsinsurance.com. International health coverage agency.

**Exeter Friendly Society:** 01392 353535; 08080 556575; email sales@exeterfriendly.co.uk; www.exeterfriendly.co.uk.

**Expacare:** 01344 381650; email: info@expacare.com or visit www.expacare.com. Specialists in expatriate healthcare offering high quality health insurance cover for individuals and their families, including group cover for five or more employees. Cover is available for expatriates of all nationalities worldwide.

**Goodhealth:** 0870 4427376; email enquiries@goodhealth.co.uk; www.goodhealthworldwide.com. Offers private healthcare plans to expatriates worldwide.

**Healthcare International:** 84 Brook Street, London W1K 5EH; 020 7590 8800; email enquiries@healthcareinternational.com; www.healthcareinternational.com. Global medical insurance for expats and travellers.

**Sanitas:** 902 102400; www.sanitas.es.

**FACT**

■ Although the premiums on Spanish insurance policies may appear much cheaper and more attractive than those offered by the British companies you may well find that the policy is limited to specific local hospitals

# ■ CHILDREN AND THE EDUCATION SYSTEM

Deciding how and where to educate your children poses a quandary for parents, wherever or however they live. Moving abroad with young children is, in some ways, easier than moving with teenagers, as younger children are remarkably adept at picking up languages and fitting into new situations. As their education has not yet begun in earnest, the problem of juggling two curricula does not exist. Although the Spanish education system is perfectly adequate, it will not follow the same syllabus as the UK or American one; this will create difficulties if a child in the middle of a GCSE course is suddenly uprooted to Spain and expected to do well in Spanish examinations. For this reason, many parents choose to send their children to international schools while abroad (see below), while families who can afford it sometimes choose to keep their children at UK boarding schools so as not to disrupt their education. However, the opportunity to mix with Spanish children and to attend a Spanish school is both rare and exciting, and one well worth considering.

The Spanish education system has undergone a radical transformation in recent years. Previously élitist and badly organised, the system is now built on a structure which has opened up education to all classes, and to people of all abilities. Responsibility for education in Spain is shared between the state and the 17 autonomous communities or regions. Some of these autonomous regions have

**TIP**

■ The opportunity to mix with Spanish children and to attend a Spanish school is both rare and exciting, and one well worth considering.

assumed full control over education, and it is likely that decentralisation will go further in future.

It is ironic that a country that for so many years has fallen behind its European neighbours in education should at the same time possess a deep and inherent respect for study and education not found in many other countries, including the UK. The structure of the Spanish education system is still based primarily on Article 27 of the 1978 Constitution, which recognised education as a fundamental right to be upheld by public powers and distributed educational powers between the State administration and the autonomous communities. Subsequently there have been numerous additions and modifications to the laws relating to education, including most recently the *Ley Organica de ordinación General del Sistema Educativo* (1991), otherwise known as the LOGSE, and in 2002 the *Ley Orgánica de Calidad de Educación* (OCE). In general terms, the Spanish education system has moved away from a centralised and highly traditional system to a decentralised and more modern one. The central tenet of the system is that a high quality, free education should be readily available for children up to the age of 16. This includes vocational training.

School attendance in Spain is compulsory by law between the ages of six and 16 (and it is no longer possible, as it was, to opt out of education at 14). Both state and private education exist; families in state education are expected to pay only for school books (which are only free in special cases), school supplies, a certain proportion of transportation services and for some voluntary extracurricular activities. The academic year usually runs from September to June, with vacations at Christmas and Easter; religious instruction is voluntary.

The spectacular growth of the Spanish educational system over the past few years has resulted in many changes; but there are still four basic levels of education in Spain: pre-school, primary, secondary, and university level.

In contrast to the present non-élitist structure of education, what pre-school education existed in the 1970s was very limited and secondary education, beginning at the age of 10, was mostly restricted to private sectors. As well as this, failure rates in schools were very high, with over three-fifths of students failing to attain a qualification; this was attributed to poor teacher training and low levels of pay in the teaching profession.

It was true at that time that a significant number of Spaniards were illiterate. But the new system has brought levels of illiteracy more into line with other European countries. Nowadays, university is no longer seen as nothing more than a place of study for the privileged minority, and both of these routes – the vocational and academic – allow the student to apply for the university of their choice, dependant of course on their results, and their passing the entrance exam.

The reformation and improvement of the system when Spain became a democracy has resulted in nearly all children from four to five years old attending pre-school education; compulsory education up to 16 years of age is universal; and more than 72% of young people stay on until the age of 18 while 40% receive professional training. University has become a form of education which anyone may enter, with a student body of over one million people. Interestingly, this growth is principally a result of the number of female students at university, who exceed the number of males in secondary education and in the first years of university.

**FACT**

■ University has become a form of education which anyone may enter, with a student body of over one million people.

# State and private education

Both state and private education are available in Spain, although the former accounts for by far the larger percentage of students. However, the fees charged by the private schools are usually not monstrously large, although international schools do tend to be more expensive than private schools in the UK. There is also the option of *concertados*, private schools that receive state subsidies. State education is free and is available by law to all children resident in Spain. More details of the Spanish education system (state and private) can be obtained from the Spanish Embassy Education Office in London (020 7727 2462; email conseduca.lon@dial.pipex.com) or the *Ministerio de Educación* in Madrid (www.mec.es). At present, a large minority of all non-university education is private and Catholic education represents approximately 20% of the whole educational system, but is more widely prevalent in school than university education.

# The structure of the education system

## Pre-school

*Educación Preescolar* is for children up to 3 years of age and *Educación Infantil* is for children aged 3–6 years. Both groups are voluntary and free in public centres. Private schools charge a fee, which tends to be most expensive in the unsubsidised international schools. Despite the rapid growth in recent years in the number of state pre-school facilities, anyone considering this form of education for their children will have to research the area of Spain in question to find out what facilities are available as these tend to vary greatly from region to region. Although it is not always the case, children who have been to pre-school classes do tend to be at an advantage over those who have not, once they enter primary school.

The objective of pre-school education is to develop basic personal aptitudes and cooperative social attitudes through games and other non-didactic methods; instruction in reading and writing tends to be left to the primary schools.

**FACT**

■ Although it is not always the case, children who have been to pre-school classes do tend to be at an advantage over those who have not, once they enter primary school.

## Primary

Primary education (*Educación primaria*) is both compulsory and free in Spain in the state sector, catering for children from the age of six to the age of 12. Children are taught a range of subjects including art and music, mathematics, physical education and 'the natural, social and cultural environment'. From age eight, children are also taught a foreign language, which is usually English, or the co-official language in those areas. Classes usually have a maximum of 25 pupils. There is a constant process of evaluation and those classed as under-achievers will be forced to repeat a year. School ends at 2pm, although most children take part in activities such as music or sport in the afternoons.

## Secondary

From the age of 12 to 16, the curriculum is known as ESO (*Educación Secundaria Obligatoria*) or compulsory secondary education. This stage of education prepares children for either the baccalaureate (*Bachillerato*) (see below) or for vocational training (see below). There are a number of compulsory subjects at this stage, such as the humanities, sciences and the arts, but there are also several optional subjects. Again, there is a constant process of evaluation and at the end of the course students who pass receive the *Graduado en Educación Secundaria* certificate, which allows them to go on to either vocational training or the baccalaureate.

## 16–18 years

The *Bachillerato Unificado Polivalente* (BUP) is a two-year course covering four areas of study: arts; natural and health sciences; humanities and social sciences; and technology. This course prepares students for university entrance exams. The *Título de Bachiller* is awarded at the end of the course if no more than two subjects have been failed in the final examinations. Some students go on to technical training centres rather than entering university.

An alternative route is to leave school and go in for the *Profesional de Primero y Segundo Grado*, the two levels of vocational training, with Intermediate and Higher Grades each comprising two years of study. Those leaving school without qualifications would have to go in for an initial year of training called the Social Guarantee Programme (*Garantia Social*), which would act as a foundation course for the Intermediate Grade Training Cycles (*Ciclos formativos – Grado Medio*) and subsequently the Higher Grade Training Cycles (*Ciclos Formativos – Grado Superior*).

## Technical training

The Formación Profesional comprises two levels, known simply as FP1 and FP2, and is free for most students, whether they attend a public centre or a private institution financed by the state. The technical training courses have a strong practical emphasis and take students from the age of 14. FP1 consists of a two-year course and is compulsory for those who fail to gain the Título de Graduado Escolar. The course provides a general introduction to a specific vocation such as clerical work, or electronics. FP2 is the second level or cycle of technical training and offers specialised vocational training. In the past about twice as many children chose to take BUP over the FP course, but as vocational training becomes more and more precious the balance is changing and the ratio is now closer to three to two.

The high percentage of failures and dropouts combined with the reluctant acceptance of the certificate in the job market and the class consciousness in the make-up of the student body have also made FP1 the most problematic and criticised area in the Spanish education system. However, those who continue to FP2 and successfully complete the course receive the further Técnico Especialista certificate and this enjoys a much better reputation in the job market. Usually, students on this course have divided their time between school studies and working in some kind of business concern.

## Study and exchange

The ASSE programme gives school students in Britain the opportunity to spend a year in Spain (and other countries), living with a local family and attending school there. This is for sixth-form students aged between 16 and 18. They can provide details of possible placements and have representatives on the ground to assist students once they are there. Contact: ASSE UK, 01952 460733; email maureen@ asseuk.freeserve.co.uk.

Teachers interested in exchange programmes should contact Teacher Exchange Europe, The British Council, 020 7389 4447; email teacher.programmes@britishcouncil.

org; www.britishcouncil.org. Those eligible for the programme are teachers of modern languages with a minimum of two years experience working at secondary school level. An exchange can last for six weeks, one term, or a full academic year. To take part in the exchange, teachers must find an exchange partner in Spain. The British Council can provide advice and guidance as to how to do this.

## Enrolment in a Spanish state school

Most schools have a certain number of places available each year and allocation is usually on a first-come, first served basis. Schools often begin admissions from January to April, but this varies so it is best to contact the schools in the area. As in Britain, schools have catchment areas from which they enrol pupils. You need to be registered on the *padrón* for your area to enrol your child in a local school; your *ayuntamiento* can help you to do this. Generally to enrol your children you will require:

■ copies of the child's birth certificate or passport

■ copies of the parents' passports

■ proof of residence

■ the child's immunisation records

■ two passport-sized photos.

Children entering the Spanish state school system at an older age may also need exam certificates, or at least a record of their academic achievements. You can find out more in Spain from the Ministerio de Educación y Ciencia and in the UK from the Spanish Embassy Education Office in London. The bureaucracy involved in enrolling your child in school can be tiresome. The Department of Education can take between three and six months to process the paperwork and theoretically the child will not be admitted until all of the red tape has been completed. Those moving to Spain with children should therefore begin the process well in advance.

# University

The Spanish university system, like many of its European counterparts, dates back to the Middle Ages. The oldest Spanish university is Salamanca, founded in 1218. In the last 20 years, the university system has experienced its greatest growth in history while at the same time advancing towards a self-governing and decentralised system. There are presently 73 universities in Spain, 23 of which are private. Seven of these belong to the Catholic Church, and one in particular, the Opus Dei University in Navarre, carries far more influence than its size would warrant, most of its intake comprising the sons and daughters of the powerful, wealthy and aristocratic.

The Complutense in Madrid and the Central in Barcelona are by far the largest Spanish universities; the former comprising nearly 100,000 undergraduates while the latter has a total intake of nearly 80,000. Despite their size, these two universities are generally regarded as being the best in Spain. In 2006, Barcelona's university was ranked as one of the *Times Higher Education Supplement* THES-QS World University Ranking's top 200 universities in the world.

To enter a Spanish university, a student must have passed either the educational or vocational levels of secondary education (see above); a university entrance exam (*selectividad*) must also be taken (this is held in the university itself). The subject of study is determined by academic criteria and depends on the average grades received and on the grade received in the university entrance exam; this combined grade is known as the *nota de corte*.

There is a clear division between academic and practical courses; some universities (*facultades and colegios*) offer five- or six-year academic courses leading to a licenciatura (equivalent to a bachelor degree) while the *Escuelas Universitarias* provide shorter, three-year, vocational courses, leading to a diplomatura, for teachers, nurses, etc. Historically many more students undertake purely academic courses than those who enter for vocational ones, and those who have high enough academic grades usually chose to enter the former, although this is now changing, and shorter courses such as Business Studies are very popular. A high percentage (80%) of all Spanish students who complete secondary education go on to university.

Within the EU, theoretically the educational institutions are open to all and an EU national may enrol in a Spanish university in exactly the same way as a Spaniard might. Fluency in Spanish will of course be an additional requirement. Foreigners who choose to work within the courses offered by the Spanish education system at university level must sit the *selectividad* examination either at the university where they wish to study or, if they live abroad, at the Spanish Embassy in that country. Before taking this entrance exam, foreign students must have their qualifications (GCSEs, A levels, etc.) officially validated through the Ministerio de Educación y Ciencia in Spain (C/ Alcalá 36, 28014 Madrid; 902 218500; www.mec.es) or through the Spanish Embassy in the applicant's native country. A-levels are recognised by most universities as sufficient qualifications to enter university. However, Americans should be aware that high school diplomas are often not accepted.

Almost all Spanish universities offer special courses for foreign students. It is not necessary to validate foreign qualifications for these courses but the certificates gained through following this type of course are not recognised within the state education system. Courses take place both during summer vacations and throughout the year and universities may be able to offer accommodation in student halls of residence or at least provide some assistance in this respect. Information on both standard Spanish courses and those specially designed for foreigners, and details of how to apply for them, may be obtained directly from the universities in question. Note that a prior knowledge of Spanish will be required by most universities.

## Study and exchange schemes

There are a number of such schemes for those already studying or intending to study at a British university and wishing to spend up to a year at college in Spain as well. The British Council in London should be contacted (see address above) or your UK university. The Erasmus scheme is part of the EU's Socrates programme, intended to encourage cooperation between universities as well as student exchanges. Students and UK institutions should contact the UK Erasmus Students Grants Council, (02920 397405; email via the website; www.erasmus.ac.uk). In Spain contact the *Agencia Nacional Sócrates* (Ministerio de Educación, Cultura y Deporte, Subdirección General de Programas Europeos, 915 065685; email a.socrates@educ.mec.es; www.mec.es/sgpe/socrates).

# International schools

International schools were once regarded as the best alternative by expatriates considering the long-term education of their children. However, times are changing,

**FACT**

■ Historically many more students undertake purely academic courses than those who enter for vocational ones, and those who have high enough academic grades usually chose to enter the former, although this is now changing, and shorter courses such as Business Studies are very popular.

**TIP**

■ Information on both standard Spanish courses and those specially designed for foreigners, and details of how to apply for them, may be obtained directly from the universities in question.

and an estimated 80% of expat children now attend Spanish schools, as international confidence in the Spanish education system increases. However, it is worth bearing in mind that international schools offer the qualifications better known to selection bodies for UK or American universities. Spanish law requires all foreign schools to be supported by their embassies. For this purpose, The National Association of British Schools in Spain, (www.nabss.org), works with the British Council to arrange that all of its member schools are visited regularly by British inspectors who then report to the Spanish Ministry of Education. On receipt of a satisfactory report, the school is authorised to continue as a foreign centre of education.

Below you will find a list of international schools in Spain which either teach the UK or American curriculum or a combination of the Spanish and international systems; the age range of the pupils is also listed. The list is updated constantly at the website of the European Council of Schools (ECIS), 01730 268244 or 263131; email ecis@ecis.org; www.ecis.org.

Parents should expect to pay fees of around €3,250–€4,500 per child for primary schools and €6,000–€7,000 for secondary schools.

International schools also teach French and German curricula; ECIS also lists such schools. There are around 10 American schools in Spain, which are a possible choice for all expatriates. However, the multitude of British schools in Spain, along with what is the overall high quality of education that they offer, will probably make this unnecessary for British citizens, as it easier to switch back into the British education system from a UK, rather than a US, school abroad. Other schools offer a dual system of Spanish and English language teaching and curricula which provide the opportunity for children to be equally well qualified to live and work in Spain or in the UK in future life; these schools are required to allocate at least 20% of the total number of places available to Spanish students. Different again are those schools that teach the UK curriculum but also include some Spanish studies, taught in English in the same curriculum.

In the list below, the address and phone number are generally followed by the age range of the pupils. If the school offers teaching in both Spanish and English, and the curriculum offered covers both UK and Spanish subjects, then this is indicated by the words, 'mixed curriculum' at the end of the entry. Most of the American schools are also included. Most schools are day schools only, but the few that do take boarders have been marked as doing so.

### International schools – addresses

**The Academy International School:** Mallorca; 971 605008; email acad@ocea.es; www.theacademyschool.com; ages 2–14.

**Aloha College:** Málaga; contact via the website; www.aloha-college.com; ages 3–18+.

**Baleares International School:** Mallorca; 971 403061; email office@bis-int.org; www.balearesint.net; ages $3^1/_2$–18. US and UK curriculum.

**Bellver International College:** Mallorca; 971 401679; email bellver@bellver. baleares.net; www.bellvercollege.com; ages 3–18.

**British Council School of Madrid:** 913 337612; www.britishcouncil.es; ages 3–18.

**The British Kindergarten:** Madrid; 916 370127; 915 617213.

**The British School of Barcelona:** 936 651584; email info@britishschoolbarcelona. com; www.britishschoolbarcelona.com.

**British School of Gran Canaria:** 928 351167; email hardes@bs-gc.net; www.bs-gc.net; ages 4–18.

**Caxton College:** Valencia; 961 424500; email caxton@caxtoncollege.com; www.caxtoncollege.com; ages 3–14.

**Col-legi Europa International School:** San Cugat del Valles; 935 898420; email europa@intercom.es.

**The English Educational Centre:** Tenerife; 922 738638; email englished centre@arraki.es; www.englishedcentre.com.

**Hastings School:** Madrid; 913 590621; www.hastingsschool.com; ages 3–18.

**International British Yeoward School of Tenerife:** Parque Taoro, Puerto de la Cruz 38400 Tenerife; 922 384685; email office.secondary@yeowardschool.org; www.yeowardschool.org; ages 3–18.

**International College Spain:** Madrid; 916 502398/99; email admissions@ icsmadrid.org; www.icsmadrid.org; ages 3–18.

**International School of Madrid:** 913 592121; email ismspain@teleline.es; ages 3–14. Mixed curriculum.

**King's College Madrid:** 918 034800; email info@kingscollege.es; www.kingscollege.es; ages 2–19. Takes boarders.

**King Richard III College:** Mallorca; 971 675850; email office@kingrichardcollege. com; www.kingrichardcollege.com.

**Newton College:** Alicante; 966 610238; email info@newtoncollege.es; www.newtoncollege.org/ingles.

**Numont School:** Madrid; 913 002431; email numont@telefonica.net; www.telefonica.net/web/numontschool.

**Oakley College:** Las Palmas de Gran Canaria; 928 354247; email oakley@ teleline.es; www.oakleycollege.com; ages 2–11.

**El Plantio International School of Valencia:** 961 321410; email plantiointer national@retemail.es; www.plantiointernational.com; ages 3–16.

**Queen's College, The English School:** Mallorca; 971 401011; email info@ qcmallorca.com; ages 3–18.

**Runnymede College:** Madrid; 916 508302; email office@runnymede-college.com; www.runnymede-college.com; ages 2–18.

**Sierra Bernia School:** Alicante; 966 875149; email duncan@ctv.es

**Sotogrande International School:** Cadiz; 956 795902; email info@sis.ac; www.sis.ac; ages 3–18. Takes boarders.

**Sunland International School:** Málaga; 952 424253; head@sunland-int.com; www.sunland-int.com.

**Sunny View School:** Torremolinos; 952 383164; www.sunnyviewschool.com; ages 4–18.

**Xabia International College:** Javea, Alicante; 966 471785; email info@xabia internationalcollege.com; www.xabiainternationalcollege.com; ages 2–18+. UK-based curriculum.

## American schools

**American School of Barcelona:** 933 714016; email info@a-s-b.com; www.a-s-b.com; 3–18.

**American School of Bilbao:** Bizkaia; 946 680860/1; email asb@asb.sarenet.es; www.sarenet.es/asb; ages 3–16.

**American School of Madrid:** 917 401900; email asmcc@asmadrid.org; www.asmadrid.org; ages 3–18.
**American School of Valencia (Colegio Hispano NorteAmericano):** 961 405412; email therdon@asvalencia.org; www.asvalencia.org
**Benjamin Franklin International School:** Barcelona; 934 342380; email bfranklin@bfis.org; www.bfis.org; ages 3–19.
**Evangelical Christian Academy:** Madrid; 918 865003; ecaspain@telefonica.es; www.ecaspain.com; ages 5–18.

# ■ SOCIAL SECURITY AND JOBSEEKER'S ALLOWANCE

## Social security

The Spanish system of social security (*Seguridad Social*), which was set up in 1966, is not the only welfare system in Spain, but it is the largest. There are separate social security systems for members of the civil service and the armed forces and a variety of other bodies like the *Fondo Nacional de Asistencia Social* (FONAS), which provides old age pensions for those who do not qualify under any of the other schemes. The national social security system covers over 90% of the population and offers a complete range of welfare provision. Cash benefits (for unemployment,

| Group | Professional category | Minimum base | Maximum base |
|---|---|---|---|
| 1 | Engineers and graduates | €799.80/month | €2,731.50/month |
| 2 | Technical engineers and assistants | €663.60/month | €2731.50/month |
| 3 | Clerical and workshop supervisors | €576.90/month | €2731.50/month |
| 4 | Unqualified assistants | €537.30/month | €2731.50/month |
| 5 | Clerical officers | €537.30/month | €2731.50/month |
| 6 | Messengers | €537.30/month | €2731.59/month |
| 7 | Clerical assistants | €537.30/month | €2731.59/month |
| 8 | Foremen classes 1 and 2 | €17.91/day | €91.05/day |
| 9 | Foremen class 3 and craftsmen | €17.91/day | €91.05/day |
| 10 | Labourers | €17.91/day | €91.05/day |
| 11 | Workers under 18 years of age | €17.91/day | €91.05/day |

**Social security bases for general contingencies 2004**

sickness, housing, etc.) are distributed through the *Instituto Nacional de Seguridad Social* (INSS); medical care is administered through the *Instituto Nacional de Salud* (INSALUD) and the *Insituto Nacional de Servicios Sociales* (INSERSO) is responsible for social services. The benefits are among the highest in the EU, but unfortunately, so are the contributions.

Salaried workers have most of their contributions paid for by the employer and the rest comes out of their salary. Unless one of the special programmes applies, employees are subject to the general social security programme. Under this programme, personnel are classified under a number of professional categories to determine their social security contribution. The contribution is based on the *nómina*, which is the official salary for a particular type of work. Each category has a minimum and a maximum contribution base, which is generally reviewed each year.

## Autonomous workers

The self-employed and business owners are required by law to pay into the Spanish social security system under the *autónomo* scheme. In 2004, the minimum contribution base for *trabajadores autónomos* was €755.40 per month and the maximum, €2731.50. In 2004, social security contributions for the self-employed were set at 29.8% of the contribution base, although it is less if you choose not to have cover for short-term incapacity benefit. Self-employed workers under 50 years of age are free to set their own contribution base anywhere between the minimum and the maximum, depending on the level of pension they wish to receive upon retirement. Autonomous workers aged 50 or over cannot pay contributions on more than €1,416 per month.

All self-employed people, even those who work part-time, must contribute to social security. If no work is done for any period longer than a calendar month, then it is not necessary to pay social security contributions for that time. For example, many small businesses close for a summer break during August.

Not only are social security contributions under this scheme higher than for salaried employees, there are also fewer benefits. For example, should the business fail, then the company directors, under the *autónomo* scheme, are not eligible for unemployment benefit. One way around this is for the company to give you a fixed contract. However, this should be discussed with a qualified accountant, as it is only possible in certain circumstances such as when a director owns less than 24% of the company.

It is possible to keep up national insurance contributions (the equivalent of Spanish social security) in the UK on a voluntary basis on moving to Spain. This can be quite a canny move for anyone who isn't working but who hasn't yet reached retirement age. If you do keep your payments up then you will be eligible to claim a UK pension from the age of 65 (for men and women) throughout your time in Spain. However, this will be unnecessary for those who intend to work in Spain. EU regulations ensure that social security contributions made in one member state are counted as a contribution period to the contributor's own country's social security system for the purpose of determining their future benefits from that system. The two systems are now supposed to be more or less interchangeable.

You can find out more about social security from the *Instituto Nacional de la Seguridad Social* (INSS), 915 6888300; www.seg-social.es.

**FACT**

■ EU regulations ensure that social security contributions made in one member state are counted as a contribution period to the contributor's own country's social security system for the purpose of determining their future benefits from that system.

# Benefits

## Health benefits

Social security payments entitle you to medical benefits through the Spanish national health scheme, the *Instituto Nacional de Salud* (INSALUD). Once registered as a member of INSALUD, you will receive an electronic social security card, a list of local medical practitioners and hospitals and general information regarding the services and charges. Registered members are entitled to general and specialist medical care, hospitalisation, laboratory services, discounted drugs and medicines, basic dental care, maternity care, appliances and transportation. While you may have to pay a percentage of the cost of things like drugs and medicines, most of this care is totally free.

## Sickness and maternity benefits

A worker may receive sickness pay, which is a percentage of his or her salary, depending on various factors. If you are self-employed, you may also receive sickness pay when ill at the rate of 60% of base payments for the first 20 days and then 75% thereafter, as long as you can present a doctor's certificate testifying that you are unable to carry out your profession.

Maternity and paternity benefits are also available for workers. Mothers can receive 100% of their benefit base for 16 weeks, of which six weeks must be taken immediately after the birth. Paternity leave can also be taken for six weeks after the birth at full salary.

## Pensions

Salaried workers and the self-employed are entitled to Spanish state pensions, which are the highest in Europe after Sweden. In 2007 the minimum pension at age 65 was around €600 per month for a single person. Remember that just as workers receive 14 pay packets a year, pensioners also receive 14 payments including the two extra payments in July and December.

To qualify for a full pension as a self-employed worker (*trabajador autónomo*), you must have worked for 35 years. The minimum period you must work to qualify for any sort of pension is 15 years, for which you would receive half the full pension. Foreigners who contribute to social security for less than 15 years receive no pension at all. However, if you move to Spain after working in another EU country, these state contributions can be transferred. Each country pays the percentage of the pension for which it is liable. UK citizens should obtain certificate E301 which shows the amount of social security contributions they have made. This can be obtained from the Department of Social Security Overseas Branch (Newcastle upon Tyne, NE98 1YX; 0191 2253963).

Should he or she so choose, the self-employed worker can set their salary base as high as €2700 a month and pay more into the system each month, to qualify for the maximum pension after 35 years. The pension is calculated mainly on the last 15 years of working life and especially on the last two.

Pensions are also set aside for those with permanent disabilities caused by work injury or an occupational disease, for widows and widowers and for orphans.

## Unemployment benefit

Almost all categories of employees are covered by unemployment insurance. The self-employed on the other hand, are not, unless they are medically incapacitated for work. Entitlement to unemployment benefit is based on having twelve months of contributions during the last six years and unemployment not being due to the refusal of a suitable job offer or training. Social security payments made in another EU country are taken into consideration.

The duration of the benefit varies with the amount of contributions. Regardless of previous earnings, the amount paid out to the unemployed currently stands at 75% of the minimum wage. These benefits cease after one or two years, except in the case of families, who receive a reduced amount for two more years.

Currently, Spain has a relatively high unemployment rate by European standards although nowhere near as high as it was in the 1970s and 1980s. Nearly half of the total number of unemployed are young people who have never had a job and who, because of this, do not qualify for benefit. The thinking behind this is that young people can remain with and be supported by their family until they do find a job. Many choose to go abroad, where prospects may be brighter.

As Spain is a full member of the EU, it is possible, however, for someone claiming unemployment benefit in the UK to transfer this claim to Spain. As discussed earlier, sickness and invalidity benefit as well as child benefit can be maintained and transferred to Spain at the present time.

# Claiming UK Jobseeker's Allowance in Spain

One of the advantages of labour mobility within the EU is that it is possible for those who are currently unemployed and claiming benefit, or eligible to claim it, to have it paid in another EU country if planning to go there to look for work. Those who have been claiming UK unemployment benefit for at least four weeks before departure are entitled to receive Jobseeker's Allowance (JSA) for up to three months, paid at the UK rate, while looking for work in Spain. To do this, you should inform the UK office through which you are claiming benefit, of your intention to seek work elsewhere in the EU. You will need to do this at least six weeks in advance of your departure. It is helpful if you have a precise date of departure and definite destination, preferably with an address. Note that if you go on holiday to Spain and decide to stay on to work, the benefit cannot be transferred.

Your local job centre should have a leaflet (ref. JSAL 22) for people going abroad or coming from abroad, plus an application form for transferring benefit. When you have told your local job centre your plans, they will supply a letter in English and Spanish explaining you are eligible to claim benefit. This letter is called a DLJA 402/403. Within seven days of arriving in Spain you must register with the Instituto Nacional de Empleo (INEM).

Your local job centre will inform the Department of Work and Pensions in Newcastle, who will then decide if you are eligible for an E303 which authorises INEM to pay JSA for up to three months. The E303 is sent directly by the DWP to Spain. Further details can be obtained from the Department of Work and Pensions, Jobseekers and Benefit Enhancement, Overseas Benefit Directorate, Tyneview Road,

Benton, Newcastle-upon-Tyne NE98 1BA; 0191 218 7147 and they can send you a fact sheet if your local job centre has not supplied you with one.

Anyone tempted to chuck in their present job to go on the dole for the requisite number of weeks before departing for Spain will be disappointed: by making themselves voluntarily unemployed they render themselves ineligible for Unemployment Benefit for six months.

# ■ CRIME AND THE POLICE

Sadly, democracy in Spain has appeared to come hand-in-hand with a crime rate that has been rising steadily over the last 30 years. However, the Spanish figures for car crime and burglary are still significantly lower than Europe's most crime-ridden country in this respect: Britain. These are lower than in much of the rest of Europe as well. The use of firearms in street crime is still practically unheard of, and rape and sexual assaults are still very rare. The only real concern for most people living in Spain is petty crime: pickpocketing, muggings, scams and other forms of robbery.

One factor that has contributed to the increase of crime in Spain is the growing drug problem. Drugs are relatively easy to come by and cannabis (known as *chocolate*) is widely used among the young, and largely tolerated by the Spanish police. This problem was born in the transition to democracy, and the relaxation of social *mores* that followed. It was the Socialists who, in 1983, effectively decriminalised the use of cannabis for a time; a measure which was largely responsible for the

'easy-going' attitude taken towards the use of soft drugs in the 1980s. This law was then revoked; and now all non-prescribed drug use is illegal; but the effect has been irreversibly stamped on drug-users and police alike. The core of the drugs epidemic, however, lies in the spread of hard drugs such as cocaine and heroin. Madrid's Barajas airport is a particularly popular entrance point for drugs from Latin America destined for the whole of Europe. Other soft drugs tend to be smuggled in from Morocco.

One focus for crime is, unsurprisingly, tourism, with much petty theft located along the costas and directed at the thousands of tourists who visit them each year. The varieties of crime indulged in range from purse snatching and car break-ins to theft of property left on the beach to armed burglary. A classic form of robbery in Spain is bag-snatching carried out by the passenger of a moving motorbike, or even from a car; so be aware of carrying bags over your shoulder when walking along the road. Pickpockets are at their most comfortable in a crowd, so be careful in places like the metro.

There is little you can do after the event; and it is best to prevent such unhoped-for traumas by taking sensible precautions. The British Foreign Office recommends that travellers keep their passport, credit cards, travel documents and money separately. And you should ensure that you have a good insurance policy. It is better to 'travel light', preferably without a large, inviting-looking bag. However, in pleasant contrast to this rather bleak picture, those who choose to live away from the popular and tourist-saturated coastal areas will most probably enjoy a blissfully crime-free existence.

# Police

While Spain may no longer be as crime-free as it was 30 years ago, the Spanish police have improved markedly. Spain has three different types of police. The *Policía Municipal* (the approximate equivalent of Britain's local police forces – with a gun) is the least intimidating and most sympathetic force, and can be found in every small town. These are definitely the people to approach in cases of minor disaster; if you are hopelessly lost; or need to ask the time. They can be recognised by their dark blue uniforms with either white or light blue shirts.

The *Guardia Civil*, a 60,000 man force which patrols the rural areas of Spain – who also act as customs officers and frontier guards – are less approachable and many people advise that you avoid them unless you have had a road accident, in which case you must report this to them and just grin and bear it. Established in 1844 to combat banditry in the countryside, the Guardia Civil is a predominantly military force that has failed to lose its reputation as a reactionary and somewhat hostile militia, called out to combat riots or strikes as well as more peaceful demonstrations. However, in recent years they have been partially demilitarised and their reputation is slowly improving. These are the most readily identifiable police force, wearing a green military-style uniform.

The third police force, the *Policía Nacional*, was much hated for the violence and repression for which it was responsible in the Franco years. However, in what was a largely successful effort to clean up their image, the government renamed and redressed the *Policía Nacional* in 1978 (they were previously known as the *Policía Armada*). The *Policía Nacional*, and their machine guns, can be found mounting

zealous vigil over embassies, stations, post offices and barracks in most cities. Serious crime, such as theft, rape or mugging should be reported to the nearest *Policía Nacional* station. The *Policía Nacional* also devotes resources and manpower to the *policía de proximidad*, who are old-fashioned beat police.

Lastly, the Basques and Catalans both have their own police forces, a hangover from the Spanish flirtation with devolution in which both these communities were granted home rule.

Spanish police are permitted to hold anyone suspected of a serious crime for up to 10 days before charging or releasing them; and they have 72 hours before they are required to bring the suspect before a court. In practice, however, three days can easily become three weeks, months or even years in some, more notorious cases.

Although everyone is entitled to some legal advice in prison, whether it is provided privately or by the state, those who cannot afford their own solicitor often forgo even the smallest hope of gaining legal representation. What may seem the chaotic nature of the Spanish prison system is largely due to overcrowding; this is being tackled by the present government. It is not a very good idea to run the risks involved in drug smuggling or of committing any other dire crime and ending up in a dilapidated Spanish prison awaiting trial for an indefinite number of years. The British Embassy is notoriously unsympathetic towards those who have committed a crime and are hoping to get help or advice. Lorry drivers returning from Morocco should pay particular attention to what they are carrying; and you should not carry bags for others at airports.

# ■ CARS AND MOTORING

## Roads

The Spanish road system is radial, stretching out in all directions from the centre point, Madrid. The country's system of motorways presently has several branches, stretching out along the Mediterranean coast and up to Barcelona in the east, to the west of Madrid as far as the Portuguese frontier, and linking up with the Basque country, Valladolid and Burgos in the north. Some statistics illustrate the extensive road revision, stimulated by the need to transport cash crops quickly, and spurred on by Spain's rapid modernisation: in 1984, the country had only 1,800km of motorways; by the end of the twentieth century it had 11,000km. The road revision programme also includes widening roads, to introduce special lanes for heavy traffic, improving traffic signs and road markings, and to build town bypasses around the most built-up areas.

Tolls are required on all motorways except urban ones; a useful map of all the Spanish toll points is available, free of charge, from ASETA, www.aseta.es, or may be supplied by local tourist offices. Current Spanish toll rates can be obtained from www.dgt.es.

The essential driving signs to recognise to avoid chaos and potential disaster on the Spanish roads include: *Peligro* (danger) and *Cuidado Estacionamiento Prohibido* (no parking). Car parks are indicated by the letter P in towns. In blue zones the maximum waiting period is one and a half hours; parking permits for 30, 60 or

Traffic congestion is a problem in bigger cities

90 minutes are available from tobacconists. A more arcane regulation concerns parking in one-way streets. On dates that are an odd number, you should park on the side of the road with odd house numbers; on even-number dates you should park on the opposite side of the street where the even-number houses are, leaving it an open question where you should park if you are staying more than a day.

# Driving regulations

The minimum driving age in Spain is 18. Drivers and front-seat passengers are required by law to wear seat belts in built-up areas (the fine for not doing so is currently €90) and children under 12 are not permitted to travel in the front seat of the car. Three-point turns and reversing into side streets are forbidden in towns; and at night sidelights alone must be used in built-up areas (unlike in the rest of Europe where dipped headlights are required). In daylight dipped headlights must be used on motorways and on fast dual carriageways. A spare set of headlight bulbs must also be carried. One tip is always to carry enough cash with you to pay on-the-spot fines. For speeding, these amount to €6 for each kilometre above the speed limit. Lorry drivers in front of you will indicate right when it is safe for you to pass. If they then switch the indicator off or are indicating left – but heading straight on – this means there is oncoming traffic.

Speed limits are 50kph in towns; 90kph out of town; and 120kph on dual carriageways. In Spain, the alcohol limit for drivers is 50mg per 100ml of blood. The Guardia Civil, or Civil Guard, has set up a roadside rescue service, which operates on major roads throughout the country. The roadside SOS telephones are connected to the nearest police station which sends out a breakdown van with first aid equipment. The van driver can also radio for an ambulance if needed. There is a small charge for labour and any spare parts required. Alternatively, in cases of accident, contact the nearest Guardia Civil station.

## New traffic laws

A recent sharp rise in accident figures has led to some fairly draconian new fines for offending motorists. New penalties now in force include a €1,053 fine and a suspension of the driver's licence for up to a year for using a mobile phone while

### Documents to carry in the car

Anyone driving in Spain should carry the following documents, just in case they are stopped by the traffic police:
- driving licence
- spanish vehicle tax (paid annually at the *ayuntamiento*)
- *permiso de circulación* – car registration document
- *ITV* certificate; the Spanish equivalent of the MOT, which proves that your car is roadworthy
- insurance documents proving that your insurance is paid and up-to-date

driving, driving without a proper licence or driving an unregistered vehicle. Fines from €302 to €602 and suspension of licence for up to three months may be enforced for driving under the influence of alcohol or drugs, refusing to take the breathalyser test, exceeding the speed limit by 50%, reckless driving, racing or carrying 50% more passengers than there are seats. There are also a number of less serious violations which incur fines from €92 to €301 (including parking the vehicle in a dangerous position) and minor violations which incur fines up to €91.

Non-residents should be aware that the Spanish police are legally allowed to demand on-the-spot payment of fines for any traffic violations and the police can impound your car if you are unable to pay.

## Driving licences

Non-UK and non-EU nationals may drive with their own driving licence for up to six months in Spain. If you intend to live permanently in Spain, you can extend this period by applying for an international driving permit or an official translation of your original licence, both of which are valid in Spain for one year. An official translation of your licence can be obtained from the Spanish Consulate in your home country. However, after one year you will need a Spanish driver's licence.

Unsurprisingly, a mountain of paperwork is involved (as for those seeking work there from outside the EU). Just for starters, Americans and others from outside the EU will need to present a medical certificate, a letter specifying which kind of

In many Spanish cities bikes are available for hire

licence they are applying for, the residence permit, current driving licence, and the inevitable three or four passport-sized photos. During the few months it takes for the new licence to be processed you will be given an official receipt for your old one and a photocopy of it.

For Britons and EU citizens the procedure is much easier. All licences issued in the EU are now valid in any other EU country. This means if you got your licence in France, Britain or Ireland you no longer have to exchange if for a Spanish one if you decide to take up residence in Spain. Official regulations governing motoring matters are available at the local traffic department in Spain, the *Jefatura Provincial de Tráfico*. However, if you are in Spain for a long time it does make sense to get a Spanish licence, available from the *Jefatura de Tráfico* of your province. You will need your present licence and a copy, your residence card and one photograph. This exchange procedure, known as *canje*, only takes a few hours and costs around €22.

Note that licences in Spain are not sacrosanct until the driver reaches the age of 70 as in Britain. Instead they have to be renewed according to your age and the type of licence held. A car licence is usually granted for 10 years if the driver is under 45, and for five years if he or she is between 45 and 70. Drivers over 70 years old must renew their licence each year.

## Importing a car

Anyone thinking of importing a foreign-registered car into Spain should first of all consider carefully the drawbacks: the inconvenience of having a right-hand drive car in a country where people drive on the right, and the inevitable tortuous red tape that complicates the import procedure.

A UK or Irish citizen who feels that they cannot possibly part with their UK car and decides to import this permanently into Spain does not need to apply for authorisation to use the vehicle for a period of up to six months.

If you decide to import your car officially, it will have to be re-registered as a Spanish vehicle. Britons should surrender their registration document to the DVLA and in return obtain a Certificate of Permanent Export (V561). You will also require a roadworthiness certificate, known as the ITV in Spain (*Inspección Técnica de Vehiculos*). The procedures are fairly complex, but you can get advice and information from RACE (Real Automobile Club de España, Calle Jose Abascal 10, 28003 Madrid; 914 473200). The process of importing a car usually takes between three and six months.

One big advantage of bringing your own car from any EU or non-EU country is that the car can be imported duty free, providing that the vehicle has been used and registered in your name for at least six months prior to moving. Added to exemption from import duties is the exemption from VAT (16%) and from Spain's own vehicle registration tax (12%). Note that the exemptions are given on condition that the vehicle will not be sold or transferred within a period of one year after the registration date in Spain.

## Buying a car

As importing your car into Spain brings with it a number of problems, many people choose to simply buy a new car once in Spain. Brand new cars are far cheaper in Spain than in the UK. However, second-hand cars can often be quite expensive, although Spain's good weather does mean that cars tend to last for longer. Many of the used cars available along the costas are ex-hire cars, which are generally sold on by the hire-car companies after two years. It is therefore possible to find some real bargains.

As in the UK, it is possible to buy cars on an instalment plan, although dealers may be less likely to offer credit to those who have recently arrived in Spain and do not yet own property or have a full-time work contract.

When buying a second-hand car, remember that you need to transfer the car's ownership. Many dealers will do this for you for a small fee, but if you buy privately then it may be necessary to employ the services of a *gestor*.

Many new residents manage to avoid paying the hefty VAT charged on cars bought in Spain by buying a car in Spain with tourist plates; this is quite legal as anyone who moves to Spain is classified as a tourist for the first six months of residence anyway. Many residents manage to renew the tourist registration plates for more than four years, even though they have now become fully-fledged Spanish residents. The disadvantages of this are that although a greater VAT cost is avoided, the buyer must pay for the total cost of the car in foreign currency and immediately; the car cannot be bought through a hire purchase agreement.

In many ways, selling a UK car and simply buying another one in Spain, with Spanish registration plates, saves a lot of paperwork and bother. Until recently anyone buying a car, be it new or second-hand, was required to have a residence permit. Although the rules have changed, many dealers are still not aware of this.

A comprehensive road network supplements Spain's efficient public transport system

# Insurance

As many vehicles have historically been driven uninsured in Spain, the authorities now come down hard on anyone who does not have insurance, levying fines of up to €3,000. The basic legal requirement for Spanish car insurance is third party only (*terceros*); thus drivers are insured for claims made against them, but not for any accident which may befall driver or car. This type of insurance can cost as little as €400 a year and covers third party claims for bodily harm and collateral damage. If you feel that you don't have enough security with only third party insurance, you can take out more comprehensive insurance which either raises the limit on the amount the insurance company will pay out on third party insurance, or insures the car owner, his or her family and the car. You can also buy cover for fire, theft and damage.

Fully comprehensive car insurance, known as *todo riesgo* policy will cost more (€1,200–€2,000 per year). If the policyholder agrees to pay an excess (i.e. they are liable for the first hundred euros or so) of the costs in any accident not only will they receive substantial protection in return but the protection will cost less than it would without this agreement. As in other countries, policyholders are entitled to a no-claims bonus – a discount on their insurance premiums if there have been no claims against the policy.

In the case of an accident, either party must bring any charge against the other within two months. This simply involves going to the local police station, making a statement (you must know at least the registration number of the other car involved) and then letting the insurance companies on either side battle it out. However, if it comes to a court case then you may have to wait, literally, for years, as the Spanish judicial system heaves its way towards justice.

For those on a temporary visit to Spain, the country's membership of the EU has made the international insurance certificate (green card) no longer necessary. However, you may find that your individual policy gives only minimum coverage without it, so check to be sure. Green cards are available on request from all insurance companies.

## Breakdown insurance

If you are simply visiting Spain on a regular basis, your own breakdown assistance company will provide foreign cover for a premium. Most offer 24-hour multilingual assistance, and there are annual policies available for those who travel frequently abroad. Those living in Spain permanently should consider taking out a Spanish breakdown insurance policy *(seguro de asistencia en carretera)*. Policies are provided by Spanish car insurance companies and Spanish motoring organisations such as RACE (Real Automobile Club de España, Calle Jose Abascal 10, 28003 Madrid; 902 404545; www.race.es). Membership of RACE is round €32 (registration fee), plus an annual fee of around €118. Their services are very similar to those of the AA or RAC in the UK.

# ■ OTHER TRANSPORT

## Train

The Spanish national rail network, RENFE (*Red Nacional de los Ferrocarriles Españoles*) has a length of around 13,000km; it stretches out from the centre point of Madrid where its three principal lines begin, two of which extend to the French frontier crossing the Basque country and Catalonia and the third to Andalucía and Levante. The junctions within the rest of the network are Medina del Campe Venta de Baños and Zaragoza in the northern half and Alcázar de San Juan in the South.

All train fares and times can be viewed on the website www.renfe.es, which has a booking service in English, or telephone 902 240202 (domestic) or 934 243402 (international) for information and reservations.

There are three types of train:

■ local trains, *cercanías*

■ regional trains, *regionales*

■ long-distance trains, *grandes lineas*.

Long-distance trains are graded and priced according to their speed. Talgo 200, TER, AVE, InterCity, Trenhotel and Estrella require the largest supplements. Cercanías run very frequently and cover the surrounding towns and villages. It is possible to buy a season ticket for these trains, which is also valid on the city buses and metro.

An ongoing project (which began with the 1992 Seville EXPO 92 exhibition) is the *Alta Velocidad Española* (AVE) which is the Spanish equivalent of the TGV in

France. It is a high-speed train linking initially Madrid and Seville (in just 2 hours 30 minutes) but destined to cover most of the intercity routes in Spain. An AVE route is currently in the final stages of construction from Madrid to Barcelona, and it is already possible to get as far as Lleida from the capital.

The Talgo 200 is also a fairly new innovation and although not as quick as the AVE, operates a service between Málaga and Madrid that takes just over four hours, three times daily. In the north-east of Spain, the Euromed is also fairly rapid, connecting Barcelona, Valencia and Alicante on a line that runs parallel to the coast.

RENFE also has a service known as the Trenhotel: trains which run overnight for greater distances and offer very compact rooms with bunk beds crammed into them. This is a useful service for those who wish to cut down on hotel and transport costs by combining them, and it is very pleasant to be able to fall asleep in the cultural capital of Madrid and wake up the next day in the party capital of Barcelona. These trains are also run on a number of direct international routes including: Madrid–Paris, Madrid–Lisbon, Barcelona–Paris, Barcelona–Zurich and Barcelona–Milan.

Almost all trains have first- and second-class compartments: first class costing approximately 30% more than second. Supplements can almost double this. Then there are a wide range of saver tickets, including young saver, child saver, large family and family pass tickets. In addition, there are many more local and long-distance tourist train routes that will be of interest to enthusiasts, like the Al Andalus Express and, in the north, El Transcantabrico. A list of all these RENFE services, and how to make reservations for them, is available from the Spanish Tourist Office in London (www.tourspain.co.uk/)

Trains are clean, comfortable and generally reliable. Booking in advance is best. If you board a train without a ticket you may be able to pay the conductor on the train itself, but you are liable to be charged double for this. It is always advisable to reserve your seats as ticket offices have erratic opening hours. Go to the RENFE office in town or to any travel agent. You can also book online very easily at www.renfe.es. Another useful reference site is www.spanish-rail.co.uk.

**FACT**

■ Single track lines (Ferrocarriles Españoles de Vía Estrecha, FEVE) still crisscross much of the north and east, picturesque for tourists but for the locals more often frustrating as they are highly susceptible to delays.

# Air

There is a comprehensive range of internal flights available between the various Spanish airports run by the major Spanish carrier Iberia (www.iberia.com; 902 400500) as well as by the smaller independent companies: Spanair (www.spanair.com; 807 001700) and Air Europa (www.air-europa.com; 902 401501). Internal air travel in Spain is still quite expensive and as yet Spain does not have a 'no-frills' alternative. Flights are therefore only really for those who need to save time: the flight between Madrid and Barcelona takes just over an hour, whereas the train takes seven hours. Those travelling between Spain and the Balearic Islands, however, will find that air travel is only marginally more expensive than the ferries, although it is usually necessary to reserve these flights a long time in advance.

## Metro

Barcelona, Bilbao, Madrid and Valencia each have their own underground railway network, known as the metro, and a metro system is currently being completed in Seville. These are open from around 6am until midnight or 1am the following day. There is a 'carnet' ticket you can buy which is valid for 10 trips. Most metro stations have ticket-vending machines but you can also buy tickets at the counter.

Generally, the metro is safe and well lit, with security guards patrolling the stations.

## Coach and bus

Spain has a very comprehensive bus and coach service and many of the smaller villages are accessible only by bus if you are reliant on public transport. Prices are very reasonable, and although the quality of the services varies, buses are usually fairly reliable and comfortable. Local journey times are often faster than trains, depending on the route, and at around €5 per 100km, they are certainly cheaper.

The only real drawback with coaches is that there are a variety of different companies operating different routes and finding comprehensive travel information can be difficult. Although the local bus station provides timetables and sells tickets for all of the coach companies, many towns still have no main bus station, or they have several, and buses can leave from a variety of places. As in many European countries, bus stations and the areas around them can have a slightly unsavoury atmosphere, and are not relaxing places to spend time after dark.

If you rely on public transport, bear in mind that buses offer a drastically reduced service on Sundays and holidays.

Generally, bus and coach tickets within Spain cannot be booked outside Spain, and seat reservations for the long-distance routes can be made only a day or two in advance from the bus/coach station or departure point. The relevant local tourist office can supply details of bus services in the area.

Within large towns and cities there is generally a very good public bus service, offering clean, safe transport at a very reasonable price. There is usually a flat-rate fare for all journeys within the central zone. It is also possible to buy either a monthly ticket, or a 10-journey ticket. In the cities that operate an underground metro (Madrid, Barcelona, Bilbao and Valencia) these tickets cover use of both buses and the metro. Buses usually run until 11.00pm or 11.30pm.

## Taxis

Taxis are cheap, reliable and – most importantly – metered. Prices can vary from area to area, though, and drivers should have an approved list of charges for intercity or airport journeys. There is usually a surcharge for luggage, and for travelling at night, weekends, and during public holidays. There are also supplements for being picked up at an airport or station. All taxis are licensed by the local government.

## Useful websites

The web is awash with information about the various aspects of daily life in Spain for tourists and expatriates, although not all of it is correct, well researched or up-to-date. The following is a list of the more helpful and informative sites relating to Spain, to help you sort the wheat from the chaff. In addition to the regional sites each local tourist authority has its own website, all of which are listed in the Regional Guides (page 426)

### Tourist and expat sites about Spain

www.spainexpat.com
www.idealspain.com
www.tourspain.co.uk
www.tuspain.com
www.travelinginspain.com
www.aboutspain.net
www.spainforvisitors.com
www.typicallyspanish.com

### Regional sites

www.andalucia.com
www.xbarcelona.com
www.webmalaga.com
www.granadainfo.com
www.ibiza-spotlight.com
www.madridman.com

### General expat sites

www.escapeartist.com
www.expatnetwork.com
www.britishexpat.com
www.expatexchange.com
www.expatexpert.com
www.livingabroad.com
www.expatworld.net

# ◤ TAXATION

Spain is no longer a tax haven for those with a lot of money and few nationalistic or altruistic tendencies. Over recent years the Spanish taxation authorities have tightened up on foreigners coming to Spain to dodge income tax in their own country by not declaring certain assets and income. Currently, foreigners resident in Spain will find that they pay approximately the same amount of tax as they would have done in the UK; and more at the top rate of tax. There is no special tax relief for foreigners residing in Spain; capital gains and disposable assets are included as part of income and are taxed accordingly; and residents are liable for Spanish tax on their worldwide income. This means that all income is taxable, whether it be a pension, private investments, dividends, or interest.

Any person who spends more than 183 days a year in Spain is considered a resident and will be liable to pay Spanish tax. Contrary to popular belief this unpleasant reality holds true whether or not you have a formal residence permit; faking tourist status will not, therefore, exclude unwilling contributors from paying their share of taxes. Another refinement of the 183-day rule is that anyone who is not resident in Spain, i.e. who spends fewer than 183 days in the country each year, is still liable for Spanish tax on income arising in Spain, e.g. from renting out property. In this case, the recipient of the income will be taxed in Spain and will have to apply for relief when they pay income tax in their own country.

Although Spain's taxes (especially indirect taxes) have been steadily increasing over recent decades, overall taxation remains reasonably low and still below the EU average.

Spanish taxation is very complex; until recently it was compulsory in law for Spanish citizens to have a professional representative to handle their taxes, and even now many Spaniards choose to have a lawyer or *gestor* perform this role for them. What follows is intended as a guide and certainly not as a substitute for professional advice, especially as Spanish tax rules have a nasty habit of changing from year to year.

## Accountants and professional advice

Sorting out one's accountancy affairs can be a complicated matter in your native language, let alone in Spanish, and with the added confusion of an ever-changing tax regime. Those with interests in two countries, or who move permanently from one country to another, will need to consider the tax systems in both countries and the best ways to minimise their tax obligations in both. International advisers are able to offer advice on how to enjoy the tax advantages in both countries without incurring any serious drawbacks.

Each individual will have a different set of priorities, depending on the extent of their assets and taxable income in Spain. Certainly those who are self-employed, or who have established a business presence in Spain, would be well advised to consult an accountant (*contable* or *asesor fiscal*). Many self-employed people simply hand everything over to their accountant and trust them with the day-to-day running of their accounts. Those with small-scale business concerns or few assets will find that a *gestor* will very provide reasonably priced tax advice and look after your books.

An ordinary accountant is called a *contable* in Spain and the *asesor fiscal* (literally a fiscal advisor) is the equivalent of a chartered accountant. A good accountant will save you money and make sure that you are kept up to date with changes in taxation law. Accountants can be found in the Spanish Yellow Pages (*Páginas Amarillas*), and the embassies and consulates have lists of English-speaking accountants in your area. It is a good idea to take advice from local businessmen as to the most reliable consultants in the area. A list of financial services firms with English-speaking staff is also provided below.

The main accountancy body in Spain is the *Instituto de Auditores-Censores Jurados de Cuentas de España*, which is responsible for drafting accounting and auditing standards throughout the country. There is an office in every autonomous community and the contact details of your local department can be found online at www. www.icjce.es.

Free tax advice is available from the information section (*servicio de información*) at your local tax office in Spain. Offices located in resort areas usually have English-speaking staff. The tax office also provides a telephone information service open 9am–7pm, Monday to Friday (901 335533).

## Useful addresses

**Instituto de Contabilidad y Auditoria de Cuentas:** 913 895600; www.icac.mineco.es

**Adesso Res Asesores:** Marbella; 952 782625; email adesso@terra.es.

**Asesoría Económica:** Marbella; 902 995993; email info@asec.es; www.asec.es.

**BDO Fidecs Insurance Management Ltd:** Gibraltar; 00350 42686; www.bdo.gi.

**Blevins Franks Financial Management:** 020 7336 1000; www.blevinsfranks.com.

**Bravo Asesoría:** Avenida Condes de San Isidro 23/1º, Fuengirola, Málaga; 952 473062; email francisco@*gestoria*bravo.es; www.*gestoria*bravo.es.

**Conti Financial Services:** 0800 970 0985; email enquiries@contifinancial.com; www.overseasandukfinance.com.

**Delgado Y Canudas Associats:** Barcelona; 934 261550; email gcanudas@retemail.es.

**Gestoría Ripolles:** Sevilla; 954 577558; ripolles@gestures.net; www.ripollesgaliano.com.

**John Siddall Financial Services Ltd:** 01329 288641; email: enquiries@siddalls.net; www.siddalls.net. Siddalls are independent financial advisers providing expertise across a spectrum of investments, retirement and tax planning for private clients at home and abroad. Siddalls have many years experience in assisting British nationals wishing to become resident in Spain with all aspects of their financial planning. Siddalls are part of the IFG Group Plc and authorised and regulated by the Financial Services Authority.

**Spain Accountants:** Estepona; 952 791113; email info@spainaccountants.com; www.spainaccountants.com.

# Moving to Spain

## Procedure for UK residents

If you are moving abroad permanently, the situation is reasonably straightforward. You should inform the UK Inspector of Taxes at the office you usually deal with of your departure and they will send you a P85 form to complete. The UK tax office will usually require certain proof that you are leaving the UK and hence their jurisdiction, for good. Evidence of having sold a house in the UK and having rented or bought one in Spain is usually sufficient. You can continue to own property in the UK without being considered resident, but you will have to pay UK taxes on any income from the property. You should also go to your bank and fill in a 'not ordinarily resident' declaration so you will not be taxed on your savings.

If you are leaving a UK company to take up employment with a Spanish one, the P45 form given by your UK employer and evidence of employment in Spain should be sufficient. You may be eligible for a tax refund in respect of the period up to your departure, in which case it will be necessary to complete an income tax return for income and gains from the previous 5 April to your departure date. It may be advisable to seek professional advice when completing the P85; this form is used to

## Spanish tax residence

In Spain the issue of whether you are considered resident for tax purposes determines the way you are treated by the tax authorities and the types of tax you will have to pay. Tax residence in Spain is known as *domicilio fiscal* and is determined by a number of rules. You will become resident for tax purposes in Spain if:

- You spend more than 183 days in Spain during one calendar year, whether or not you have taken out a formal residence permit; or
- You arrive in Spain with an intention to reside there permanently, you will then be tax-resident from the day after you arrive; or
- If your 'centre of vital interests' is Spain, although this rule is hardly ever applied; or
- If your spouse lives in Spain and you are not legally separated, even if you spend fewer than 183 days in Spain.

determine your residence status and hence your UK tax liability. You should not fill it in if you are only going abroad for a short period of time. Once the Inland Revenue are satisfied that you are no longer resident or domiciled in the UK, they will close your file and not expect any more UK income tax to be paid.

Spain has a double taxation agreement with the UK, which makes it possible to offset tax paid in one country against tax paid in another (see below). Find out more in the Inland Revenue publications IR20 Residents and non-residents. Liability to tax in the United Kingdom which you can download from www.hmrc.gov.uk. Booklets IR138, IR139 and IR140 are also worth reading; you can get these from your local tax office or from: Centre for Non-Residents (CNR): tel 0845 070 0040; *www.hmrc.gov.uk/cnr*.

## Double taxation agreements

Fortunately Britain has a reciprocal agreement with Spain, which avoids double taxation and thus the possibility of someone being taxed twice, once by the Spanish and once by the British tax authorities on their income or pension. The exception to this is during the initial period of Spanish residency when, as the UK and Spanish tax years run from April to April and from January to January respectively, UK nationals in Spain may be taxed by both the Spanish and UK authorities in the overlapping months of their first year in the new country. In this case, you are able to claim a refund of UK tax by applying to the Inland Revenue through your local tax office. They will supply you with the elusively-titled SPA/Individual form, which offers relief at source for tax refunds concerning interest, royalties and pensions, or with the yet more obscurely-titled SPA/Individual/Credit form which provides repayment on dividend income for anyone who has suffered double taxation on moving to Spain.

When you have filled in the form, take it to the local *hacienda* (tax office); they will stamp it and then you can return it to the British tax authorities as proof that you have paid Spanish tax and are therefore no longer liable for British tax. You should do this while you are in Spain and not after your return to the UK; and it is important to keep good records of your income, etc., while in Spain, to meet any problems should these arise.

The main point is to keep these records of salary and other income; and there are specialist accountants who can advise you on your tax situation in Spain, mainly for those starting or running a business (see the chapter on this for some useful addresses).

For more information on the Spanish tax system, contact the Spanish Embassy or Consulate, or the *Agencia Estatal de Administración Tributaria* (901 335533; www. aeat.es).

# Income tax (IRPF)

Income tax is known in Spain as IRPF (*Impuesto Sobre la Renta de las Personas Físicas*) and only applies to residents. Non-residents are taxed under a separate scheme. Those running a business and the self-employed will certainly need to file a return for income tax, no matter what their actual income is. Rates of income tax have been going down in Spain in the last decade and in the last four years, IRPF cuts have led to a 25% reduction in the tax burden.

Residents are taxable on all sources of worldwide income, both earned and unearned, at a rate that varies between 15% and 45%. The total taxable income is composed of income from various sources, which include:

■ Trading income from professional or business activities.

■ Income and other benefits derived from a contract of employment.

■ Investment income from property.

■ Investment income other than from property.

■ Capital gains and losses.

■ Deemed income from real property holdings for own use.

■ Income imputed from companies operating under the fiscal transparency regime.

The system has been reorganised and a vital minimum introduced (*mínimo vital*). Before you become liable for income tax you deduct the minimum from your gross income and also deduct various other allowances, depending on your circumstances. You can get up-to-date information about the minimum earnings before tax is liable from the Spanish Tax Office website (www.aeat.es).

Income tax is generally assessed on the household but there are no longer different tax rates for couples who choose to be taxed individually or jointly. IRPF rates for individuals start at 15% on income up to €4,000 and rise to 45% on income above €45,000. This tax is divided between central government (85%) and the autonomous regions (15%). However, some regions offer deductions from tax due.

### The tax system

The Spanish system of personal taxation is based on three kinds of levies:
- *impuestos* (true taxes)
- *tasas* (dues and fees)
- *contribuciones especiales* (special levies).

The last two are much lower; and residents will mainly be concerned with the *impuestos*.

There are around 15 separate taxes for which that Spanish residents are liable: the most significant are:
- income tax (*Impuesto sobre la Renta de las Personas Físicas* (IRPF) or simply *'la renta'*
- wealth tax (*impuesto sobre el patrimonio*)
- capital gains tax.

There are three levels of taxation in Spain:
- central government taxation
- autonomous community taxation
- local taxation.

*The Agencia Estatal de Administración Tributaria* (901 335533; www.aeat.es), is based in Madrid and collects government taxes via centres in provincial capital towns.

The Spanish tax year follows the calendar year and therefore runs from 1 January to 31 December.

## Allowances and deductions

Various deductions are available from income totals. For example, all social security payments are tax deductible and there is a personal minimum allowance (the amount considered necessary for you and your dependants to live on). In 2007, this figure was €3,400 per individual, or €6,800 a couple. Further allowances and deductions include:
- professional and trade union fees
- legal expenses up to €300
- a percentage of an annuity (life or fixed period) depending on your age
- child support payments made as a result of a court decision
- 60% of any dividends
- deductions for dependents (e.g. €800 for someone aged 65–75 living with you; €1000 for someone aged over 75 living with you; €1,400 for a first child; €1200 for each child aged under three)
- disability deductions – €2,000 if the disability is between 33% and 65% and €5,000 if the disability is above 65%

| Income tax rates 2007 | | | | |
|---|---|---|---|---|
| From (€) | To (€) | General rate (%) | Autonomous Community rate (%) | Total applicable tax rate (%) |
| 0 | 17,707 | 15.66 | 8.34 | 24 |
| 17,707 | 33,007 | 18.27 | 9.73 | 28 |
| 33,007 | 53,407 | 24 | 5 | 37 |
| 53,407 | and above | 31 | 6 | 43 |

- 75% of any *plus valía* tax paid as a result of a property sale
- 15% of the cost of purchase or renovation of your principal residence up to €9,015
- deductions for mortgage payments up to €9,015
- foreign tax deduction – if you have already paid income tax abroad you can also deduct that from your Spanish tax bill
- properties let to young people between 18 and 35 are now exempt from taxation.

## Tax returns

Those whose financial situation is relatively uncomplicated can draw up their own tax return – you can get advice on how to do this from your local *hacienda*. You can purchase tax return forms from the tobacconists (*estanco*) for around €0.30 or from your local *Agencia Tributaria* office. There are three kinds of tax return form. Form 103 is the abbreviated declaration, form 101 is the simple declaration and form 100 is the ordinary declaration. Business and professional activities must be recorded on the last, the *declaración ordinaria,* which is the longest and most complex of the three and will usually require the help of an accountant to complete. The fees charged by an accountant to file a tax return can vary, but you should expect to pay around €40 for a simple return and around €70 for a more complex return.

Many taxpayers or their advisers now complete income tax returns electronically using a programme that runs on Microsoft Windows. The Spanish tax authorities sell this quite cheaply and it has a number of advantages, such as the fact that certain allowances are inserted automatically.

Returns should be made between 1 May and 20 June. The self-employed pay their income tax quarterly (*pago fraccionado*). If you employ any staff, it is also your responsibility to deduct your employees' income tax at source. Late filing of a tax return leads to a surcharge on the tax due. It is possible, however, to request payment deferral.

Returns should be submitted to the district tax office where you are resident for tax purposes. Or you can file the return and pay at designated banks in the area, which allows you to transfer the cash to the tax authorities straight from your account.

## Wealth tax

Unlike in France, where wealth tax is something that affects only the lucky (or unlucky) few, the Spanish wealth or 'net worth' tax (*impuesto sobre el patrimonio*) is a small tax levied on every individual's assets and property. For a rural home it could be as little as €80, rising to around €1500 for a large villa. The tax was originally introduced as a means to force many Spanish citizens to declare previously hidden assets, especially property; anyone who does not declare all his or her assets is subject to fines. It is also a way of stamping out tax evasion on other levies such as income tax, capital gains tax, and inheritance tax. By gathering regular information on all of your assets, it is possible for the Spanish tax authorities to check that the figures add up when it comes to paying other taxes. For example, as a result of your wealth tax payments, when it comes to your heirs paying inheritance tax on your assets, the Spanish authorities should already know what is due.

**FACT**

■ By gathering regular information on all of your assets, it is possible for the Spanish tax authorities to check that the figures add up when it comes to paying other taxes.

Wealth tax is calculated on the value of an individual's assets in Spain on 31 December every year and is imposed on residents and non-residents alike. Residents are taxed on all of their worldwide assets, whereas non-residents pay wealth tax on all of their assets in Spain. The amount payable runs on a sliding scale from 0.2% for assets valued at €167,129, to the top bracket of 2.5% on assets worth over €10,695,996.

Liability to wealth tax is calculated by totalling the value of all of your assets including business ownership, property, vehicles, cash, life insurance, jewellery and financial investments. An end-of-year bank statement will therefore be required showing any interest and an average balance. If you do not declare your total assets, you may face a fine.

Residents will be pleased to know that they will pay nothing on the first €108,182.18, with an additional €150,253 for a principal residence. Those with a principal residence in Spain therefore have a wealth tax allowance of €258,435.18. Very few assets are exempt from this tax, although if you have bought property with a loan or mortgage, there are deductions from your wealth tax liability. There is no allowance for non-residents.

## VAT

VAT, known confusingly as IVA (*Impuesto sobre el Valor Añadido*) was introduced in 1986, as a prerequisite to Spain joining the then EC. Transactions subject to VAT are sales and importation of merchandise and services rendered; exports are exempt from the tax. There are currently three rates of IVA, ranging from a super-reduced rate of 4% for basic foodstuffs, to a reduced rate of 7% for a number of goods such as water, fuel, or medicines; through to a standard rate of 16% for most goods and services. Health, education, insurance and financial services are all exempt from VAT, as is the transfer of any business providing the buyer continues the existing business concern, rental of private property, etc. It is worth mentioning that VAT is not levied in the Canary Islands, Ceuta and Melilla. The Canary Islands have an equivalent Canary Islands Indirect General Tax (IGIC). The standard IGIC rate is 5%.

# Capital gains tax

Every time property, business, or stocks and shares change hands in Spain, capital gains tax is incurred. Capital gains tax is calculated on the net gain in the declared purchase price when bought, and the price that it fetches when it is subsequently sold. There are certain allowances available on this tax, but those resident for tax purposes in Spain will need to include the capital gains in the income tax return of the year in which the gain occurred (subject to a maximum of 15%). Capital gains tax on the sale of a property for non-residents was reduced for non-residents in 2007 from 35% to 18%.

When buying a property, it is always best to declare in the *escritura* the full purchase price when you buy, so that you do not have to pay a high capital gains tax when you sell. If you own a property through a company and the property has not risen in value when you come to sell, it is possible to change the ownership structure without incurring a large capital gains tax bill.

Capital gains is generally paid via the buyer of the property, who retains 5% of the agreed purchase price and pays this to the Tax Agency on account of the vendor's capital gains tax liability. The purchaser therefore only pays 95% of the purchase price to the vendor. Depending on the amount of tax due, the vendor may request a tax refund from the Tax Agency once the sale has gone through. There are several circumstances where the vendor of a property in Spain is exempt from paying capital gains tax and is not subject to the 5% tax deposit:

**TIP**

■ When buying a property, it is always best to declare in the *escritura* the full purchase price when you buy, so that you do not have to pay a high capital gains tax when you sell.

- Those 65 years of age or over, who are resident in Spain and whose property has been the principal residence of the individual for at least three years, pay no capital gains tax on the sale of the property.
- If a resident of Spain sells his or her principal residence in Spain of at least three years and reinvests all of the proceeds of the sale into another property that will become his or her principal residence, s/he is exempt from paying capital gains tax.
- Residents and non-residents who bought the property they are selling before 31 December 1986 will not have to pay capital gains tax.
- If a resident is 65 years old or over and sells his or her principal residence to a company in exchange for the right to reside in the property till death and makes a monthly payment, there will be no capital gains tax to pay.

There are several circumstances where the vendor of a property in Spain has partial exemption from paying capital gains tax:

- If a resident of Spain sells his or her principal residence in Spain of at least three years, and reinvests part of the proceeds of the sale into another property that will become his or her principal residence s/he will be entitled to tax relief on a proportion of the proceeds.
- Anyone who bought a property in Spain between 1987 and 1994 has the right to a reduction of 11.11% per year, beginning from two years after the purchase up until 1996.
- Those who bought property after 1996 can apply an inflation correction factor that saves them a certain amount of money on capital gains tax liabilities.

# Wills and taxation

It is very important that anyone who buys property in Spain should make a Spanish will to avoid the time-consuming and expensive legal problems that will other otherwise result from Spanish inheritance laws and taxes. Having a Spanish will for Spanish assets also avoids the hassle of waiting for the granting of probate from your country of origin, and allows the will to be dealt with immediately under local laws, thereby speeding up the will's execution. It is therefore advisable to make two wills, one which disposes of Spanish assets and another which deals with any UK assets, rather than trying to combine the two. However, it is vital that these two wills do not contradict one another.

Problems arise when people die intestate, i.e. without a will. Usually Spanish law will be applied to the Spanish assets of the deceased, although this could give rise to legal wrangling as there may be a case for applying the rules of the home country to the estate. The cost of these arguments between lawyers and tax officials will be borne by your heirs, so it is always best to make a will. If a person dies intestate then the Spanish law of succession determines who shall inherit. According to the law of 'compulsory heirs' (*herederos forzosos*) in Spain, two-thirds of the deceased's estate must be left to his or her children. Spanish inheritance rules are far more restrictive than those that apply under British law. Only one-third of the estate can be disposed of freely.

However, if a foreigner makes a will in Spain, then they are not subject to these restrictions and may dispose of their assets as they please. The only consideration to bear in mind however is that non-relatives may be liable for larger amounts of inheritance tax. A Spanish will does not exempt the inheritors from Spanish inheritance tax (see below), although this will only affect those who have inherited a sum that exceeds the current non-taxable tax threshold; even then, inheritance tax rates are only really very high in the case of property being left to non-relatives. The closer the relationship between the deceased and the heir, the lower the rate of inheritance tax. Unmarried couples are treated as complete strangers in the eyes of the Spanish legal system! It is for this reason that executors and trustees are unusual in Spain.

It is always advisable to use a Spanish lawyer to draft your will and to advise as to its contents. The cost of drafting a simple will is around €150, plus the cost of the notary. All Spanish wills can be made out in two columns, one in Spanish and one in English, as long as this is approved by an official translator.

The most common form of will in Spain is the **open will** (*testamento abierto*). This type of will is made before a notary, who keeps the original document in their files. The notary will also send a notification of the will to the Central Registry of Spanish Wills (*Registro Central de Última Voluntad*). The notary may require the presence of two witnesses, who must also sign the will. Once the will is drawn up, you will be presented with a copy (*copia autorizada*). It is also possible to draw up a closed will (*testamento cerrado*), the contents of which will remain secret until your death. Unlike an open will, this **must** be drawn up by a Spanish lawyer. This will is presented before the notary in an envelope. You must then declare before the notary that the provisions are contained within the envelope, whereupon the notary will seal the envelope in the presence of witnesses. The notary then files the will and sends a notification of it to the Central Registry in Madrid.

**TIP**

■ It is always advisable to use a Spanish lawyer to draft your will and to advise as to its contents. The cost of drafting a simple will is around €150, plus the cost of the notary.

There is a third type of will in Spain, although this is not recommended as the processes for its execution are more complicated. The holographic will (*testamento ológrafo*) is written entirely in the handwriting of the testator, who must also sign and date it. No witnesses or other formalities are required, although it is sensible to voluntarily register the will in Madrid. Upon the death of the testator the will must be verified as genuine before a judge, who will require the closest relatives of the deceased to authenticate the handwriting.

Having made the will, you should ideally keep it in a safe place along with bank accounts and insurance policies. Another copy should be held by the executor of your estate, or by your lawyer. However, it is fairly uncommon to appoint an executor in Spain. If at any point you decide to change your will then it is possible to revoke provisions made in a will, even if you had previously declared your intention not to revoke them.

# Succession tax

Gifts on the death of an individual can still bring high rates of taxation in Spain – sometimes at a rate as high as 82% on inherited wealth. The Spanish inheritance tax (*Impuesto Sobre Sucesiones Y Donaciones*) is paid by the persons inheriting, and not on the value of the estate of the deceased. If the deceased was resident in Spain for tax purposes, all his or her assets worldwide will be subject to Spanish inheritance tax; if the deceased was a non-tax resident then only the property in Spain will be subject to tax – the rest of the assets being subject to the tax in the country of residence. If the beneficiary is a resident of a country that has a double taxation agreement with Spain, he or she will not be taxed twice.

Property is valued by the Tax Agency at the market rate, or the *valor catastral*, depending on which is the higher. Furnishings are usually valued at 3% of the value of the property. Outstanding debts are deducted from the value of the assets, and stocks and shares and bank balances are valued at the date of death.

The Spanish tax authorities impose penalties if matters are not cleared up quickly. For example, there is a window of six months in which to pay taxes on the Spanish estate after death. If taxes are not paid within this time limit a surcharge of 20% will be applied, and further, additional interest on the original demand will be charged.

If a joint owner of a property in Spain dies, there is no automatic inheritance by the other owners of the property. Even if the property is left to a beneficiary in the owner's will, there will be a tax payable. Because the tax is based on the size of the gift, the more you inherit the more you will be taxed. However, the nearer the relative is to the deceased, the less tax payable on inherited gifts. Near relatives are also entitled to receive a proportion tax-free. One way of making sure that a beneficiary of a will is not liable for crippling taxes is to register a newly purchased property in the name of the person/s who will eventually inherit. Because the property will stay in the name of the original named owner on the death of the buyer of the property, the taxes and fees usually incurred on transference of title deeds will be minimal.

The tax payment is calculated on the degree of kinship between the deceased and the person inheriting. Allowances (at differing rates) are given to direct descendants less than 21 years of age, direct descendants (spouse, parents, children, siblings) over 21 years of age and other relatives (uncles/aunts, cousins, nieces/nephews).

The rate of tax payable after the allowances on kinship is then multiplied by a rate ranging from 1–1.4% dependent on the existing wealth in Spain of the person inheriting. However, if the recipient is not resident in Spain, they will pay no added tax if they have no wealth in Spain. There is also tax relief available on family homes and businesses and 95% of the net value of such properties if the recipients are either the children or spouse of the deceased. However, the property will need to remain in the hands of such recipients for 10 years – and continue to be used as a family home or business – if inheritance tax is to be avoided.

Please note that the inheritance tax rules can differ wildly between the different autonomous communities. For example, the tax authorities in the community of Valencia have recently unveiled plans to abolish all inheritance tax for spouses and children and it is always best to take expert legal and financial advice on your own particular circumstances.

# Bereavement

In the unfortunate event that a relative, partner or close friend should die while in Spain there are a few essential formalities that you will have to deal with. If the person dies in hospital, the hospital authorities will take care of the administrative details. However, if the person dies at home, the first step is to inform the municipal police (*Policía Municipal*) who in turn will advise the forensic judge (*juez forense*) who will have to come to the home to authorise the removal of the body. If the deceased has been receiving medical care, you should also contact his or her doctor. As in the UK, an autopsy is not necessary unless the forensic judge or the doctor is in any doubt as to the cause of death.

You will need to contact a funeral director (*pompas fúnebres*) who will often deal with a lot of the paperwork on your behalf. For example, it is quite common for a funeral director to obtain the consulate death certificate on behalf of the deceased's relatives. He or she will frequently also ensure that the necessary official certificates are delivered to the family and contact a British pastor to perform the burial service.

Funerals in Spain are usually held within 24 hours of death, but they can be delayed to allow for friends and family to arrive. In these circumstances the body will be kept in a morgue at additional cost. It is possible to have the body repatriated for cremation in the country of origin, but such procedures are expensive as the body must be embalmed and transported in a lead-lined coffin.

**FACT**

■ British and international cemeteries have the familiar subterranean burial plots to which we are accustomed, while Spanish cemeteries consist of raised graves with the bodies placed in niches.

A foreigner can be buried in most Spanish cemeteries, whether or not he or she was a Catholic. However, other options include a British cemetery in Málaga, an international one in Benalmadena and crematoriums in Madrid, Seville and Málaga. You will find that the British and international cemeteries have the familiar subterranean burial plots to which we are accustomed, while Spanish cemeteries consist of raised graves with the bodies placed in niches. A funeral service will cost a basic rate of around €1,000 although this can rise quickly with transport costs and other fees. Most Spanish cemeteries rent out burial plots for varying time periods and, while you will find that municipal cemetery rates are quite inexpensive, purchasing a plot can be very pricey; so it's worth enquiring at the town hall for price details.

The death certificate is issued by the Civil Registry (*Registro Civil*) or at the offices of the local justice of the peace (*juzgado de paz*) depending on the locality. The certificate is usually available for collection within 2–3 days. It is a good idea to get a number of original copies of the death certificate as many authorities may require a copy. These may include, for British citizens: the British consular office in your location, Department of Work and Pensions in Newcastle, Paymaster General, Inland Revenue, probate office, banks, and insurance companies. It is also a good idea to keep a copy for your own records.

# Executing the will

To start the procedures involved in the execution of a Spanish will, it is first necessary to apply to the *Registro Central* in Madrid for the *Certificado de Ultimas Voluntades*. Most people use a *gestor* for this process, who will send an original copy of the death certificate with full details of the deceased. However, those with sufficient Spanish can find the official form that needs to be completed in any *estanco* (tobacconists). The death certificate will be returned, along with the appropriate certificate, within 2–3 weeks. If you do not know whether the deceased had made a will, the *Registro Central de Última Voluntad* will be able to tell you as every will is kept on file here. If the will exists, the registry will be able to supply you with the document's certificate number and the name of the notary who authorised it. If there is more than one will, only the last one made is legally valid.

Once received, the certificate must be taken to a notary who will prepare the inheritance deed (*Escritura de Aceptación de Herencia*). This deed must be signed simultaneously by all heirs, or a representative who has been issued power of attorney. The notary will require full details of all assets plus a number of other documents such as deeds, receipts for property tax, details of bank accounts, shares, etc. Once the *escritura* has been signed a copy must be taken to the tax office to pay the death duties. This should be done within six months of the death, otherwise surcharges will be applied. If the assets include property, then the inheritance deed must also be presented at the Property Registry (*Registro de Propiedad*) so that the names of the new owners of the property may be registered. Another copy of the deed should then be presented at the local town hall and the plus valía tax paid (this must also be done within six months of the death). Inheritance tax must be paid before the assets in Spain can be released. You may need to take out a loan to pay the taxes and ensure the release of the assets.

**FACT**

■ Inheritance tax must be paid before the assets in Spain can be released.

# Working in Spain

# ■ FINDING A JOB

## A guide to the market

For most foreigners the most trying aspect of moving to Spain is finding a new job. Jobhunting and interviews can be difficult enough in your own language, let alone in a second language. The good news for EU citizens is that they enjoy exactly the same rights as Spaniards and cannot be discriminated against during the application procedure (this is not the case for a non-EU citizen, whose employers must prove that there is no suitable Spanish or EU worker for the job). The bad news is, of course, that those who are not fluent in the language are at a distinct disadvantage when going up against those who are (i.e. the Spanish). Also, foreigners may not be directly discriminated against, but simply by not knowing the right people, or having the right contacts, they may find that they are marginalised. A great deal of recruitment in Spain still relies on personal relationships and informal networks.

Equally disconcerting for the potential employee is the relatively high level of unemployment in Spain. In terms of regional variation, Navarra, the Balearic Islands, Aragon, Rioja and Catalonia have the lowest unemployment rates at around 6.5%, whereas Andalucía and Extremadura present the highest unemployment rates, sometimes reaching 20%. The details of the employment scene in each autonomous community are discussed on page 279.

However, nationally the unemployment rate is gradually falling and currently rests at around 8.3% (a marked improvement on the 15.5% level just a decade ago, and a world away from the 30% unemployment seen in the 1980s). You need to bear in mind that this figure is only the official one and does not take into account the black economy – at least 20% of all work in Spain escapes the notice of the taxman and the social security office, according to a recent study by the Institute of Tax Studies, and some commentators suggest that the real unemployment rate is at least 5% lower than the official figures suggest.

Areas highly regarded by employers are the master of business administration (MBA), marketing, and human resource management. Overall there seem to be good opportunities in the Spanish market, especially for graduates. Sales and marketing positions are still at the forefront of the international job market, largely based in Madrid and Barcelona.

Spain needs workers from abroad in the next 10 years to maintain its expanding economy; however, the current uncertainties in the global financial markets and the spectre of recession in Europe were casting a pall on the country's outlook as we went to press. But opportunities do exist, whether you intend to work in Spain as an employee, employer or entrepreneur, and overall, the time is ripe for foreigners, especially those who are qualified, innovative and tenacious, to make the most of this favourable moment in Spain's economic development.

**FACT**

■ The time is ripe for foreigners, especially those who are qualified, innovative and tenacious, to make the most of this favourable moment in Spain's economic development.

## Job search resources

Looking for work in Spain is not an easy task, especially if you do not yet have sufficient Spanish skills to trawl through the local newspapers and the Spanish employment agencies' websites. Being fluent in the language is undoubtedly a huge

## The black economy

The *economia sumergida* is a salient feature of the Spanish labour market. Recent estimates suggest that there are around 800,000 illegal workers in Spain, positioning Spain's black economy as one of the largest in the developed world. The rising number of immigrants, who now account for at least 6% of the population, have added to this problem. Many are willing to accept low cash payments for unskilled work, often working long hours in unpleasant conditions, and unscrupulous employers have exploited this situation to the extent that the black economy accounts for around 20%–25% of the official GDP.

With one in three people in Spain expected to have come from another country by 2015, this trend is set to continue. So acute is the problem that the Spanish authorities recently offered an amnesty to illegal immigrants to keep track of foreigners and increase tax revenue. This resulted in an estimated 800,000 illegal immigrants registering as official Spanish taxpayers.

However, it is not just the illegal immigrants who are working illegally – many EU and particularly British residents of Spain are thought to dodge the taxman. Most of these are self-employed and simply do not declare their earnings. Be warned: in recent years there has been a severe clamp down on illegal labour, and inspectors are now making regular checks. Also, if you do not receive an official paycheck and are not registered as paying tax on your earnings you will not be eligible for healthcare, pensions and other social security benefits. The Spanish economy has generally been expanding over the past decade, increasing in 2004 by a healthy 2.9%; however, there are now signs of slowdown, with repossessions and unemployment rising. Salaries have fallen behind rising living costs in unskilled areas, but have risen with demand in areas of skills shortage, as in the flexible labour markets of Britain or the United States. When considered against the political background of years of dictatorship and relative economic and industrial isolation, Spain has already achieved a massive step forward in attaining its current, stable form of democracy and low inflation.

*continued*

## The black economy *(Cont'd)*

Although pockets of relative poverty still exist, and despite the commonly held image of a rural and backward country – which still holds true in some more remote areas – wealth is gradually spreading; poverty nowadays is as much urban as rural; whole new industries have sprung up, in information technology for instance. Others (like the telephone company Telefónica and the public utilities) are being or have been privatised. All of this is subject to the vagaries of politics, and economic progress throughout the rest of Europe, but already Spain boasts the position of fifth largest industrial power in Europe.

The service sector employs the greatest number of workers in Spain, although it has a high level of seasonality due to the tourism and catering sectors. Construction also continues to register an increase in employment after a few years of strong expansion and a period of stability.

The downside of Spain's economy being based more and more on tourism and services is that there is a growing trend for heavy industry to leave Spain in favour of emerging markets such as India, China and Eastern Europe. This trend is likely to increase as a result of the expansion of the EU and Spain's increasingly expensive workforce.

The jobs that are heavily oversubscribed are the low-skilled positions. High immigration in recent years has intensified competition for casual employment. Spanish businesses struggle to find staff to fill vacancies requiring specific training or experience. Those with qualifications, experience, language abilities and a good range of computing skills should have little difficulty in obtaining a job, especially if they are willing to demonstrate flexibility and adaptability. The reason for this is that the Spanish economy has grown so rapidly over the past 20 years that there is a shortage of skills in many white-collar functions.

advantage. There may be some multinational companies who offer jobs without a prerequisite of fluency, but improving your language skills will give you a far wider window of opportunity.

The foreigner also suffers an added disadvantage in Spain in that recruitment is often conducted through informal networks such as family and friendship ties, and word of mouth. As a result many of the best jobs never even reach the job pages. However, it is obligatory for all companies to register **any** vacancies, whether skilled or unskilled, permanent or short-term, full-time or part-time with the INEM (www.inem.es), the National Institute of Employment, or *Instituto Nacional de Empleo* (see below). Once you have been in Spain for some time and have made some contacts, the Spanish system of networking (known as *enchufe*) may well work to your advantage. It is always a good idea to get some business cards made up and distribute them liberally.

One of the easiest ways to do this is to visit your local jobcentre office and investigate any openings listed with EURES (the European Job Mobility Portal – see below), which posts job vacancies all over Europe. Alternatively jobs in advance can be found at any of the websites listed below. Some of these allow you to post your own CV online for potential employers to view.

Many foreigners are not so well prepared and make the move to Spain first, then take their chances in the job market. This is only advisable if you have deep enough pockets to fund several months of potentially fruitless job hunting. However, once in Spain there are far more jobseeking resources available to you.

### Useful websites

Increasingly the trend for jobhunters is to use the internet. Indeed, according to www.jobtoasterspain.com, 124,000 people look for work in Spain via the internet every month. A wealth of online databases and resources exists, but as is often the case with the internet , some resources are very useful, whereas others are out-of-date or poorly maintained. Some of the best websites are listed below, but it is a necessary evil to trawl the net for new and specialised sites that may be of greater use to your specific circumstances.

www.inem.es: The website of Spain's National Employment Institute (Instituto Nacional de Empleo).

www.monster.es: Spanish section of Monster.com with jobs all over Spain.

www.anyworkanywhere.com: Mostly jobs with tour operators in Spain.

www.jobtoasterspain.com: Site catering specifically for expats. Most jobs are on the Costa del Sol.

www.eurojobs.com: Pan-European job-search facility.

www.infojobs.net: Spanish language site with a range of jobs.

www.trabajo.org: Spanish language site with a range of jobs.

www.laboris.net: Spanish language site with a range of jobs.

www.tecnoempleo.com: Spanish language site specializing in IT and telecommunications jobs.

www.excoge.com: Launched by the national Spanish newspaper El País, helpful guide for career development.

www.oficinaempleo.com: Spanish language site with a range of jobs.

www.exposurejobs.com: Specialists in searching, selecting and recruiting key business personnel for jobs in Spain and Gibraltar.

www.recruitspain.com: Recruitment consultancy on the Costa del Sol for English-speaking candidates.

www.wemploy.com: Recruitment specialists on the Costa del Sol for English-speaking candidates.

www.balearic-jobs.com: Vacancies for English speaking seasonal workers in the Balearic Islands.

www.britishchamberspain.com: Website of the British Chamber of Commerce in Spain. British companies in Spain often register jobs here and for €25 it is possible to register as a potential candidate.

## UK newspapers and directories

Although some jobs for Spanish-speakers are advertised in the UK press, these tend in the main to be UK-based (with perhaps some potential for relocation to Spain in future). Occasionally jobs in Spain will appear in the major British daily newspapers, although these are more likely to be very senior positions. It is quite reasonable, though, to consider working for an international company with Spanish connections. Use your own contacts, or see the list at the end of this chapter. An exception to this general rule is teaching English abroad, which will certainly mean that you are based in the country. You can find vacancies for English language teachers in the Times Educational Supplement, published every Friday, and the Education pages of The Guardian on Tuesdays.

A wide range of casual jobs, including hotel work, campsite leaders and nannies and au pairs are advertised in the annual directory Summer Jobs Abroad published by Crimson Publishing. Teaching English Abroad lists schools worldwide that employ English-language teachers each year. These books are available in most bookshops or contact Crimson Publishing, 020 8334 1660; www.crimsonpublishing.co.uk.

## International newspapers

International newspapers circulate editions across several national boundaries and usually carry a modest amount of job advertising. Again, the amount of ads carried and the number of these publications is likely to increase. The newspapers to consult include *The Wall Street Journal*, *Financial Times* and *International Herald Tribune*. The major US newspapers carrying international recruitment advertising are *Chicago Tribune*, *Los Angeles Times* and *The New York Times* (see below). As well as employers advertising in these papers, individuals can place their own adverts for

**TIP**

■ A wide range of casual jobs, including hotel work, campsite leaders and nannies and au pairs are advertised in the annual directory Summer Jobs Abroad published by Crimson Publishing.

any kind of job, although bilingual secretaries and assistants, marketing managers and other professionally qualified people looking to relocate abroad are in the greatest demand. With the current vogue for privatisation and restructuring in the Spanish economy, UK management consultants are presently much in demand, as are more traditional areas of expertise like engineering and information technology, or tourism.

Advertising rates vary, but are usually around £10 a line for a week's coverage. This kind of advertising can become expensive, though, so readers should go through the more conventional channels first, of replying to situations vacant ads; then trying more 'creative' approaches, which include contacting individuals and companies direct, before investing heavily in situations wanted ads. Anyone interested in doing so should contact the advertising department at the addresses listed below.

### Useful addresses

Chicago Tribune: www.chicagotribune.com.
International Herald Tribune: www.iht.com.
Financial Times: 1 Southwark Bridge, London SE1 9HL; 0800 028 1407; www.ft.com.
Los Angeles Times: www.latimes.com.
The New York Times: www.nytimes.com.
The Wall Street Journal: www.wsj.com.

## Spanish newspapers

There are more than a hundred newspapers published both locally and nationally in Spain and most of these carry job advertisements. The most important newspapers, which have distribution throughout Spain and overseas are *El País* (www.elpais.es) and ABC (www.abc.es), *El Mundo* (www.elmundo.es) in Madrid, and *El Periodico* (www.elperiodico.es) and *La Vanguardia* (www.lavanguardia.es) in Barcelona. All of these newspapers are distributed throughout Spain and may be found in the larger cities and in public libraries in the UK. Job advertisements are usually published in the Sunday supplements, although these papers have a daily section dedicated to positions vacant.

A number of specialist jobseekers' publications are also distributed nationally in Spain. These include *El Mercado de Trabajo* (www.mercadodetrabajo.com), which offers over 1,000 temporary and permanent jobs per week, plus information on job fairs and training opportunities. It also offers an extensive demandas de trabajo or situations wanted column covering everything from lawyers to translators. Another weekly tabloid including many job advertisements is *Laboris* (www.laboris.net). Finally, the *Exchange and Mart*-style publication *Segundamano* also offers a wide variety of jobs and has the added advantage of being published three times a week.

Those with limited Spanish skills will probably not be able to find anything of use in the Spanish-language publications, although advertisements for very senior positions will occasionally appear in English. This usually occurs when the company is looking for very specific skills and does not wish to limit itself to the Spanish labour market. For most, however, the most likely source of jobs will be the local expat publications. Unfortunately, hard copies of these publications can be difficult to get hold of within the UK, even at places like the Spanish Embassy and Hispanic and Luso Brazilian Council library. It will be best to write directly to the publishers to obtain copies, or search the internet for online versions.

## Advertising in newspapers

Job offers resulting from advertisements placed in either the Spanish press of English-language newspapers published in Spain are not very common. A job wanted ad can be placed in many Spanish newspapers through the London-based publishers representative, Powers Turner Group (020 7592 8315; www.publicitas.com/uk) who deal with many Spanish newspapers ranging from the nationally-read *El País* and *La Vanguardia* published in Barcelona to more obscure regional publications.

But they do not deal with any English-language newspapers in Spain, so these will have to be purchased while on a reconnaissance trip or directly from the publishers (or again you can request an inspection copy).

# Professional and trade resources

## Professional journals and magazines

If you are a member of a professional or trade body, or even if you are not, but one exists, then there may well be a professional journal or magazine that carries advertisements for jobs in Spain. Examples include *Architects' Journal* and *The Bookseller*.

Many professional journals and magazines circulate free of charge and are not tied to any specific professional body. Some such magazines may carry suitable advertisements, for example, those in the air transport industry should consult *Flight International*, while those in the catering trade could try *Caterer and Hotelkeeper*; and anyone working in agriculture, *Farmers Weekly*. Some of these magazines, although they are published in the UK, are considered world authorities in their field, and they are widely available in public libraries and newsagents.

An exhaustive list of trade magazines can be found in media directories, for example, *Benn's Media Directory Europe* volume, which is available from major UK reference libraries. To track down all UK-based professional and trade publications *British Rates and Data* (known as 'BRAD') will be your source; and the European Media Directory also covers Spain, with entries for journals and periodicals arranged by country and subject category.

## Professional associations

Many professional associations do not provide any official information on working overseas as such. However, many of them will have had contact with their counterpart associations in other EU countries, often during negotiations involving the mutual recognition of qualifications mentioned above, and should be able to provide names and addresses for their opposite numbers in Spain, or even some individual help. Trade unions are also generally members of international bodies and have useful contacts overseas. You may consider joining one, if you are not already a member and already in employment. Many have sections for unemployed and freelance workers as well. Their publications and vacancy lists sometimes include jobs abroad as well as in the UK.

Details of all professional associations are to be found in the directory, *Trade Associations and Professional Bodies of the UK* (Gale, 2004), available at most reference libraries. In more specialist libraries the *European Directory of Trade and Business Associations* may also be consulted, and as mentioned above, it is also worth trying to contact the Spanish equivalent of UK professional associations: the UK body may be able to provide a contact. Alternatively, consult the Spanish Yellow Pages (*Páginas Amarillas*) at major UK reference libraries or online, or approach your trade union for information about its counterpart organisation in Spain.

## Specialist publications

A few specialist publications in both the UK and Spain contain job vacancies. In the UK, *Nexus Expatriate Magazine* handles many foreign vacancies; and provides other valuable information for expatriates. This publication is available from Expat Network Limited (020 8256 0311; www.expatnetwork.com; email nexus@expatnetwork. com). Membership of the Expat Network costs £66 a year in the UK, £72 in Europe, and also includes an online jobs newsletter.

Your local Jobcentre should not be overlooked. It will have access to useful resources such as the Eurofacts and Globalfacts series of International Careers Information, and Exodus, the Careers Europe database of international careers information produced by Careers Europe (01274 829600; www.careerseurope. co.uk). Another source of information on European programmes is Eurodesk, which has an online database (www.eurodesk. org.uk).

## Chambers of commerce

The Spanish Chamber of Commerce (020 7009 9070; www.spanishchamber.co.uk) publishes a list of addresses of its member companies, many of whom recruit in Spain. Information is provided free of charge to members; and charged to the general public to cover administration, printing and postage costs. The Chamber may send you its Trade Directory, Directory of Chambers of Commerce in Spain and can be helpful in providing other useful information.

Chambers of commerce exist to serve the interests of businesses trading in both Spain and the UK and most should provide a lot of potentially invaluable information about their member companies for those enmeshed in the jobhunting process. Your local UK Chamber may also have Spanish contacts. In Spain, local and regional branches can be found throughout the country, in virtually every city and town. Many of these provide enthusiastic support for local industries and companies and, on request, will provide details of these and a list of government incentives for new industry. The central Chamber of Commerce in Spain is known as the *Consejo Superior de Cámaras de Comercio, Industria y Navegación de España* (902 100096; email via website; www.camaras.org).

It is even possible that the local chamber of commerce might know which companies currently have vacancies in that area, although in the process they will no doubt rightly inform any hopeful jobseeker that they don't function as an employment agency. For those interested in doing business in Spain, too, these will be invaluable contacts. The addresses for the main chambers of commerce (*Cámara oficial de comercio e industria*) are listed in the Regional Employment Guide, page 279.

## Employment agencies

### Eures

A Europe-wide employment service called EURES – European Employment Service (http://ec.europa.eu/eures) operates as a network of more than 500 euro-advisers who can access a database of jobs within Europe. These vacancies are usually for six months or longer, and for skilled, semiskilled and (increasingly) managerial jobs. Language skills are almost always a requirement. On average, 500 new posts are registered with EURES each month, although if you have a specific destination in mind, they are unlikely to be able to offer much choice of vacancy. However, at the time of writing there were 522 registered vacancies in all fields throughout Spain. These can be accessed through the EURES website given above.

**FACT**

■ Chambers of commerce exist to serve the interests of businesses trading in both Spain and the UK and most should provide a lot of potentially invaluable information about their member companies for those enmeshed in the jobhunting process. Your local UK Chamber may also have Spanish contacts.

Rather than settle for consulting a EURES adviser at home, you might get a more complete picture by telephoning the EURES office in your destination. Again the EURES website (http://europa.eu.int/jobs/eures) provides contact details for all EURES Advisers including the 41 in Spain, indicating which ones speak English. Otherwise ask at your local Jobcentre how to contact a EURES Adviser either at home or abroad. In the UK most of the expertise is based in the headquarters of the national employment service. The Overseas Placing Unit (0114 259 6051/fax 0114 259 6040) coordinates all dealings with overseas/EU vacancies.

## INEM

The state-run *Instituto Nacional de Empleo* (INEM) is the Spanish equivalent of the UK Jobcentre and it used to be the only employment and recruitment agency that was allowed to operate officially in Spain. Branch offices are pretty evenly distributed throughout Spain and can be found online at www.inem.es or in the telephone directory. The INEM advertises mostly local positions but there are often a few national posts displayed. The offices generally have a good resource library and it is possible to obtain advice on jobhunting from a work counsellor.

In addition to operating a job placement service they give assistance to budding entrepreneurs. Although primarily a service for Spanish nationals, the job centres have an obligation, imposed by EU regulations, to be of assistance to nationals of other EU countries. It is worth seeking out the more important centres with a EURES adviser on staff. However, once again, they are unlikely to help anyone who is unable to communicate in Spanish. As elsewhere in Europe, government employment offices can be unhelpful to foreigners; so don't expect them to bend over backwards to help, even if you do speak the language well.

Any newly arrived EU citizen has the right to sign on as a jobseeker (*demandante de empleo*) with the INEM. It is no longer necessary to produce a residence card to sign on, just a passport.

**FACT**

■ Although primarily a service for Spanish nationals, the job centres have an obligation, imposed by EU regulations, to be of assistance to nationals of other EU countries.

## Private placement agencies

An *agencia privada de colocación* is a non-profit making organisation and may only charge fees relating to expenses arising from the services provided. These agencies act as an intermediary in the job market. These have increased in number over the past few years. The INEM keeps a record of all authorised work placement agencies. Most them are based in Madrid and – for English speakers – in Málaga, and are listed in the Spanish Yellow Pages (*Páginas Amarillas*). Bear in mind, however, that there is little point in applying for most jobs unless you are bilingual or have specialist skills needed for the job.

## Temporary employment agencies

Short-term work is available in Spain from numerous *empresas de trabajo temporal*, or ETTs. These are private companies that facilitate temporary employment by contracting workers themselves and then transferring or lending their services to other companies. ETTs often specialise in certain areas such as the hospitality and construction industries. Usually workers are only hired out during periods of great demand, so this kind of work is far from stable. ETTs can be found in the Spanish Yellow Pages (*Páginas Aurarillas*). The Manpower temporary employment agency (www.manpower.com) has 20 or so branch offices in Spain but specifies the following conditions to potential applicants:

- Their Spanish offices deal only in temporary work.
- They will accept enquiries from within Spain only.
- All applicants must have references with them.
- All applicants must be able to speak fluent Spanish as their service largely provides office, catering and industrial jobs where communication skills are essential.

Other major ETTs in Spain are Adecco (www.adecco.es) and Randstad (www.randstad.es).

## The application procedure

Speculative letters of application to Spanish companies can be written, using as a source the Directory of Employers list which follows. The *Directory of Jobs and Careers Abroad* (Crimson Publishing) also has a useful list of British companies with Spanish connections and subsidiaries. Another useful source of British companies operating in Spain is the British Chamber of Commerce in Spain (933 173220; email britchamber@britchamber.com; www.britishchamberspain.com). Speculative letters to larger companies may seem like a long shot, but many companies prefer to recruit this way. A CV that arrives on its own, rather than among an enormous bundle of replies to an advertised post, will certainly attract more attention.

If you feel that the letter should be sent in Spanish, perhaps a Spanish-speaking friend can help. Alternatively the Institute of Translation and Interpreting (01908 325250; email info@iti.org.uk; www.iti.org.uk) can put people in touch with freelance translators who will provide a fluent translation, for a fee.

Letters of application will be expected, as in the UK, to be formal, clear and polite with little creative or personal content. The letter, whether speculative or direct, should always be sent with a CV. It is common to open a covering letter with formal expressions such as *'Muy Señor Mío'* or *'Estimado/a Sr/Sra'*. The main text of the letter should explain why you are applying for the job and highlight the most relevant aspects of your CV. When signing off it is usual to use formal expressions such as *'En Espera de sus noticias, le saluda atentamente'*.

The style of CV should not be much different from the kind found in Britain or in a US resumé. The CV should be structured, clear and concise (no more than two sides of A4). Spanish employers will not usually be interested in information about hobbies and interests. Generally the emphasis is on qualifications. It is fairly common practice in Spain to attach a recent photograph with your CV. You can find services which assist in the preparation and presentation of CVs under the heading CV or Secretarial Services in your local Yellow Pages or in employment and expatriate publications like *Nexus Expatriate* magazine. After the CV has been compiled (and usually translated), look at any abbreviations or terms that may confuse a foreign reader; there should be a clear presentation of your qualifications and what these actually mean. Model CVs and advice on how to write your CV are available on most public employment websites in Spain.

Generally it is better to provide a CV that is too short rather than too long! This might prompt further enquiries from an interested employer. Don't send any original certificates or documents with an enquiry or application, of course, as these stand little chance of being returned.

**TIP**

■ Companies will usually want to know how good your Spanish is. There is no point in claiming fluency if this is not the case, as the truth will be discovered at interview.

Another word of warning: Spanish companies are notoriously bad at answering letters or faxes and copious amounts of persistence and patience will have to accompany each speculative application. A follow-up call is always a good idea. See the chapter The Creative Job Search in the *Directory of Jobs and Careers Abroad*, published by Crimson Publishing, for more about this aspect of your jobseeking.

If you are offered an interview, remember that first impressions and appearances count. Whatever the number of interviewers, the meeting is still likely to be a formal one in Spain; you will find that a casual approach to interviews is an Americanism that has yet to find a vogue with most Spanish employers. An interview in Spain can also be a test of language ability as much as job ability. This applies in the case of more basic jobs, as well as to more high-flying executive positions, and will sometimes be the major challenge. Remember that handshaking is popular in Spain and that it is polite to shake hands both on arrival and departure. Always use the more formal *usted* form during interviews (see Language, page 38).

As with any job in any country, it is important to find out as much background information as possible about the company and the position for which you have applied, in advance of the interview. An interest in the company and its activities (based on knowledge and hard facts) is more likely to impress your potential employer than your general enthusiasm. It wouldn't hurt to give a good shot at your best Hispanophile impression either. It is advisable not to mention anything to do with salary until you are asked, which is usually during the final stages of the interview procedure. For more senior positions it is not unusual, as in the UK, for the interview procedure to involve psychological and psychometric testing as well as several interviews before a panel.

During the Franco era English was not commonly taught as a foreign language and a general estimate is that even today 70% of Spanish business people don't speak English; this figure is much higher throughout the general population. Adverts

**TIP**

■ Remember that handshaking is popular in Spain and that it is polite to shake hands both on arrival and departure. Always use the more formal *usted* form during interviews

Traditional ways of life can still be observed in rural areas

for English language courses abound in Spanish newspapers, as older people try to catch up. The amount of English spoken, however, will vary enormously depending on your location. For instance, virtually no English is spoken (even in the world of business) in the Bilbao region, only some in Madrid, substantially more in Barcelona, and an awful lot in tourist-saturated Málaga or the islands. The level of English ability will also vary with the different professions: for example, much more English is spoken as the norm in chemical and engineering or computer industries, where it is part of the job, and a lot of the textbooks and information required are only available in English. This 'globalisation' of the language is a worldwide trend.

Young people generally are more proficient than their parents, as in many other countries. These demographic and professional variations are something that the less linguistically talented jobseeker may do well to consider when considering what job they are most suited to in Spain.

The *Directory of Jobs and Careers Abroad*, available from good general bookshops, is an invaluable source for anyone who feels that they need a hands-on guide on how to research the job market, or what career direction to take, with advice on CVs and the best ways to go about your job search, with sections on Specific Careers and Worldwide Employment, and including a chapter on Spain.

# ■ JOB IDEAS

## Teaching English

The late 20th century was a period of unprecedented economic growth in Spain as business and industry forged ahead, prodding Spanish schools and companies into a frenzy of English language learning. Even now major companies in every sector from transport to fashion employ English teachers to improve their staff's English skills. As a result more and more academies and agencies are springing up to serve the language needs of company clients with such familiar names as Lloyd's Bank, Universal Studios, L'Oreal and IBM.

There is also a national push to introduce English early; it is compulsory in state schools from the age of eight, and the Spanish Ministry of Education in conjunction with the British Council has been recruiting experienced EFL teachers to work in primary schools. This trend has filtered through to private language providers, some of whom organise summer language camps for children and teenagers. Many children are enrolled in private English lessons to improve their chances of passing school exams.

There are thousands of foreigners teaching English in language institutes from the Basque north (where there is a surprisingly strong concentration) to the Balearic and Canary Islands. The entries for language schools occupy about 18 pages of the Madrid Yellow Pages and 585 listings in the online Yellow Pages. Almost every back street in every Spanish town has an *Academia de Ingles*. Technically *academias* are privately run and largely unregulated and *institutos* teach children aged 16 to 18.

All schools prefer their teachers to have European Union nationality (and most will not consider applicants without it) and to have a university degree, Cambridge Certificate (or equivalent) and knowledge of Spanish. Although some may be prepared to consider less, especially from candidates with some business experience or experience teaching children, the ever-increasing number of qualified applicants means that the occasions when schools need to do so are diminishing. The days are gone when any native speaker of English without a TEFL background could reasonably expect to be hired by a language academy. Many schools in the major cities echo the discouraging comments made by the director of a well-established school in Barcelona who said that he has found that there is a large supply of well-qualified native English speakers on hand so his school cannot possibly reply to all the CVs from abroad that they receive as well.

Other schools report that the number of applications from candidates with a TEFL Certificate has soared simply because so many more centres in the UK and worldwide are offering the training courses. Opportunities for untrained graduates have all but disappeared in what can loosely be described as 'respectable' schools, although there are still plenty of more opportunistic language academy directors who might be prepared to hire someone without qualifications, particularly part-time. A great many schools fall into this category. To take a random example, the expatriate director of a well-established school in Alicante estimated that of the 20 or so schools in town, only four operate within the law (i.e. keep their books in order, and pay social security contributions for their staff).

Many Britons and Irish people with or without TEFL qualifications set off for Spain to look for work on spec, preferably in early September. A high percentage of schools, especially those that have been termed 'storefront' schools, depend on word-of-mouth and local walk-ins for their staff requirements. Anyone with some experience and/or a qualification should find it easy to land a job this way. With a knowledge of Spanish, you can usually fill one of the many vacancies for teachers of children (with whom the total immersion method is not always suitable). Some of the big chains (see Useful Addresses below) are a good bet for the novice teacher on account of the stability of hours they can offer. The usual process is to put together a timetable from various sources and be reconciled to the fact that some or all of your employers in your first year will exploit you to some degree. Those who stay on for a second or further years can become more choosy.

The English language training (ELT) business is constantly evolving in Spain. One important development in recent years has been the failures of two of the major chains, Opening Schools and Wall Street Institutes. These chains revolutionised the market with multimedia teaching that relegated the language teacher to a back seat in the learning process, and at one point seemed to threaten the very existence of traditional language schools, until students eventually figured out that they weren't learning all that much, and these centres started closing down. Most of these chains have either closed their doors altogether or are in the process of doing so.

In some places, the ELT business has become cut-throat with academy owners doing their best to squeeze out every last euro of profit, which can lead to poor working conditions.

Candidates who know that they want to teach in Spain should consider doing their TEFL training with an organisation with strong Spanish links. Better still, do a TEFL training course in Spain. There are many training centres in Spain who can offer positions after the course has finished to their better students, take for example the Advanced Institute (address below), which has centres in Madrid and Barcelona.

For a listing of English language schools in Spain, a good place to start is the Education Department of the Spanish Embassy (020 7235 5555). As well as sending

FACT

■ A high percentage of schools, especially those that have been termed 'storefront' schools, depend on word-of-mouth and local walk-ins for their staff requirements. Anyone with some experience and/or a qualification should find it fairly easy to land a job this way.

an outline of Spanish immigration regulations and a one-page handout Teaching English as a Foreign Language, it can send a list of the 350 members of FECEI, the national federation of English language schools (*Federación Española de Centros de Enseñanza de Idiomas*), although they may not always have the most up-to-date list available. FECEI is concerned with maintaining high standards, so its members are committed to providing a high quality of teaching and fair working conditions for teachers. To become a member, a school has to undergo a thorough inspection. Therefore FECEI schools represent the élite end of the market and are normally looking for well qualified teachers. FECEI comprises 16 regional associations integrated in ACADE (*Asociación de Centros Autónomos de Enseñanza Privada*, 902 104080; www.acade.es).

Check the TEFL advertisements in the Education section of *The Guardian* every Tuesday, especially in the spring and early summer. Also try *The Independent* on Thursdays and *The Times Educational Supplement* on Fridays, but don't expect more than a sprinkling of international job ads. The monthly *EL Gazette* is also a good source of news and developments in the ELT industry, although it is pitched at the professional end of the market. An employment section, *EL Prospects*, comes free with the gazette, although there are far fewer advertisements than there used to be. An annual subscription costs £32 in the UK and £44 worldwide. Contact *El Gazette* (020 7481 6700; editorial@elgazette.com; www.elgazette.com).

Searching for *escuela de idiomas* on www.paginasamarillas.es (Spanish Yellow Pages) will produce lists of schools in the places you search, some with email and website addresses. Most of the regional British Council offices in Spain maintain lists of language schools in their region apart from Madrid, does not keep a register

The popularity of Spanish beaches has lead to continued strong growth in the tourism sector

of schools. The offices in Valencia, Bilbao, Barcelona and Palma de Mallorca also produce useful lists.

British or Irish nationals with a TEFL qualification or postgraduate certificate of education (PGCE) might want to make use of a recruitment agency, whether a general one or one which specialises in Spain such as English Educational Services (see address below). The owner recommends that candidates with just a degree and Certificate of English Language Teaching to Adults (CELTA) come to Spain in early September and contact his agency on arrival. He works in conjunction with schools all over Spain.

Most teaching jobs in Spain are found on the spot. With increasing competition from candidates with the Cambridge or Trinity Certificate (now considered by many language school owners a minimum requirement), it is more and more difficult for the underqualified to succeed. The best time to look is between the end of the summer holidays and the start of term, normally 1 October. November is also promising, since that is when teachers hand in their notice for a Christmas departure. Since a considerable number of teachers do not return to their jobs after the Christmas break and schools are often left in the lurch, early January is also possible.

The beginning of summer is the worst time to travel out to Spain to look for work since schools will be closed and their owners unobtainable. There are some language teaching jobs in the summer at residential English camps for children and teenagers, but these are usually more for young people looking for a working holiday as camp monitors than for EFL teachers.

Although most jobseekers head for Madrid or Barcelona, other towns may answer your requirements better. Language academies can be found all along the north coast and a door-to-door job hunt in September might pay off. This is the time when tourists are departing, so accommodation may be available at a reasonable rent on a nine-month lease.

Private tutoring pays better than contract teaching because there is no middleman. But it is difficult to get started without a network of contacts and a good knowledge of the language and when you do get started it is difficult to earn a stable income due to the frequency with which pupils cancel. The problem is particularly acute in May when school pupils concentrate on preparing for exams and other activities fall by the wayside. Finding private pupils is a marketing exercise and you will have to explore all the avenues that seem appropriate to your circumstances. You can advertise on noticeboards at universities, public libraries, corner shops and wherever you think there is a market. A neat notice in Spanish along the lines of '*Profesora Nativa de clases particulares a domicilió*' might elicit a favourable response. Compile a list of addresses of professionals (e.g. lawyers, architects, air traffic controllers) as they may need English for their work and have the wherewithal to pay for it.

Salaries are not high in Spain and have not increased significantly over the past decade. A further problem for teachers in Madrid and Barcelona is that there is not much difference between salaries in the big cities where the cost of living has escalated enormously and salaries in the small towns. The minimum net salary is about €900 per month, although most schools offer €850–€1000 after deductions for 25 hours of teaching a week. A standard hourly wage would be €10–€12. The very best paid hourly wages, say €20, are paid by centres specialising in sending teachers out to firms or those teaching short courses which are funded by the European Union.

**TIP**

■ The best time to look is between the end of the summer holidays and the start of term, normally 1 October. November is also promising, since that is when teachers hand in their notice for a Christmas departure.

> **Joanna Mudie** was a private language teacher in the Midlands before trying the same thing in Spain. She found her first job in Spain through the British press, and then subsequent jobs simply by phoning or visiting schools listed in the yellow pages. We asked her how working as a teacher in Spain compared to the same job in Britain:
>
> *'In one word, good; but there's much more uncertainty and insecurity about all aspects of work: hours, days, rates of pay, insurance, contracts (invariably, if you're lucky enough to get one, a load of rubbish because employers put down less hours on paper to avoid paying so much insurance, and also to protect themselves if business dwindles and they can't offer you much work). All of this is compensated for by mostly pleasant students interested in learning, small groups, and the pleasure of working in an attractive foreign country.'*

## Useful addresses

### TEFL recruitment organisations and major schools in Spain

**Advanced Institute:** Fernandez de Los Rios 75, 28015 Madrid; 915 448800; email tefljobs@terra.es.

**British Council:** 913 373500; email madrid@britishcouncil.es; www.britishcouncil.es

**EF Education:** 900 102209; www.ef.com.es.

**Escuelas de Idiomas Berlitz de España:** 915 425466; email via website; www.berlitz.es.

**English Educational Services:** 915 329734; email movingparts@wanadoo.es.

**Inlingua:** 914 451984; email madrid@inlingua.es; www.inlingua.es.

**Linguarama Iberica:** 915 550485; email madrid@linguarama.com; www.linguarama.com.

### Training centres

**Advanced Institute Teacher Training Centres:** 605 133378; email trainingspain@terra.es; www.targetedgrad.com/advanced. Intensive TEFL courses.

**British Language Centre:** 917 330739; email ted@british-blc.com; www.british-blc.com. CELTA centre.

**Campbell College:** 963 524217; email infor@campbellcollege.com; www.campbellcollege.com. CELTA centre.

**CLIC International House Seville:** 954 500316; email training@clic.es; www.clic.es. CELTA courses year round.

**International House Barcelona:** 932 684511; email training@bcn.ihes.com; www.ihes.com/bcn. Regularly offers CELTA courses.

**International House Madrid:** 913 101314; email training@ihmadrid.com; www.ihmadrid.es. Full-time and part-time CELTA courses.

**Chester School of English:** 914 025879; email cert.tesol@chester.es; www.chester.es/tesol. TESOL centre.

**Windsor TEFL:** 01753 858995; email info@windsorschools.co.uk; www.windsorschools.co.uk. TESOL courses offered in Barcelona and Madrid.

TEFL International: Seville; email info@teflintl.com; http://teflinternational.com. 130 hour+ certificate course.

### TEFL recruitment organisations in the UK

Berlitz (UK) Ltd: 020 7611 9640; www.berlitz.co.uk.

International House: 020 7518 6970; worldrecruit@ihworld.co.uk; www.ihworld.com/recruitment.

Linguarama: 01420 80899; 01420 83243; email personnel@linguarama.com; www.linguarama.com.

Saxoncourt: 020 7491 1911l email recruit@saxoncourt.com; www.saxoncourt.com.

For many more addresses of recruitment organisations, training centres and individual language institutes in Spain, consult the most recent edition of *Teaching English Abroad* by Susan Griffith (Crimson Publishing, 2008).

## Au pair work

Spain's demand for au pairs and mothers' helps is booming. The number of agencies inside Spain and of UK and European agencies that have added Spain to their list of destination countries has increased significantly over the past few years. Many Spanish families want more than an au pair; they want a young English speaker to interact with their children on a daily basis. The emphasis on conversational English means that some families are happy to consider young men for live-in positions.

Au pairs are usually expected to work for a minimum of six months, although many families will require an au pair for the entire school year. Summer au pair programmes are also on offer, lasting from two to three months. The best time to apply for a position as an au pair is around September when the school year begins. Those applying for summer positions should do so in March.

Hours tend to be on average longer than in other countries. Officially working hours are limited to 30 per week, although some au pairs report that they have ended up working the same hours as a mother's help but for au pair pocket money (which is normally paid on a monthly basis in Spain). The minimum pay at present is €56 per week, although agencies urge families who live in suburbs some distance from the city centre to pay €60. No perks are built into the arrangement, so au pairs can't count on getting any paid holidays, subsidised fares or a contribution towards their tuition fees except at the discretion of their employers. However, au pairs do receive free food and board with the family. Au pairs should have a basic knowledge of Spanish and are required by law to attend Spanish language classes during their stay in Spain.

Au pair positions can be arranged with an agency either in Spain or the UK. It is generally a good idea to use an agency, as the better ones provide useful services such as vetting the family, helping you to overcome any problems you might encounter, organising cultural activities and making regular checks on your welfare. One of the biggest au pair and student exchange agencies with partner agencies around the world is *Club de Relaciones Culturales Internacionales*, a member of the International Au Pair Association (www.iapa.org).

Some au pair agencies are listed below, but many more are listed in *The Au Pair and Nanny's Guide to Working Abroad* by Susan Griffith (Crimson Publishing). It is always advisable to contact a number of agencies to compare registration fees and pocket money.

**FACT**

Many Spanish families want more than an au pair; they want a young English speaker to interact with their children on a daily basis.

## Useful addresses

### Au pair agencies in Spain

Au Pair Service: 933 219512; email info@aupair-barcelona.com; www.aupair-barcelona.com.

Au Pairz.com: email contact@aupairz.com; www.aupairz.com.

CEAE: 972 221693; email ceae@grn.es; www.idiomesestranger.com

Club de Relaciones Culturales Internacionales (RCI): 915 417103; email spain@clubrci.es; www.clubrci.es.

Eurolingua Consulting: 902 636903; email info@eurolingua-spain.com; www.eurolingua-spain.com.

Europair Agency: 020 8421 2100; email info@europair.net; www.euro-pair.co.uk.

Globus Idiomas, Formacion y Ocio: 968 295661; email globus@ono.com; www.globusidiomas.com.

Infort Instituto para la Formacion: 915 624346; email idiomas@infort.org; www.infort.org.

Interclass: 934 142921; email info@interclass.es; www.interclass.es.

International Au-Pair and Language Abroad Group: 952 901576; email ia.la@spanishlanguagec.com; www.languageabroad.info.

Juventude y Cultura: 915 312886; info@juvycult.es; www.juvycult.es.

Kingsbrook SL: 932 093763; info@kingsbrookbcn.com; www.kingsbrookbcn.com.

### Au pair agencies in the UK

Angels International Au Pair Agency: 01202 313653; email earnot@btinternet.com; www.aupair1.com. Member of the Spanish-based International Organisation for Quality in Au Pair Services (IOQAPS).

Childcare International Ltd: 0800 6520020; email office@childint.co.uk; www.childint.co.uk.

Jolaine Au Pair and Domestic Agency: 020 8449 1334; email aupair@jolaine.prestel.co.uk.

## Secretarial work

Opportunities are both widely available and lucrative for bilingual secretaries in Spain. According to the personal assistant (PA) and secretarial recruitment specialists the Angela Mortimer Agency (www.angelamortimer.com) in a recent article in *The Times*, it is now far more common for both PAs and secretaries to move to jobs all over Europe. They estimate that around 12% of their clients move regularly from country to country, sampling different lifestyles in exchange for their office skills. In Spain the most popular destinations for this type of work are Barcelona and Madrid. While the salaries may not quite live up to those encountered in the UK (the average PA earning £20,000 in the UK, can expect to earn about £16,500 in Madrid), most agree that the lifestyle more than makes up for it. However, the agency also points out that the market has become far more competitive, with 38% of their clients being fluent in a second language, compared with 5%–10% ten years ago. Many speak three or even four languages, although fluent English and Spanish will be sufficient for most jobs in Spain.

For anyone thinking of doing this kind of work it is often worth trying the Spanish Tourist Authority (www.spain.info), which employs a multitude of linguistically-able secretaries. A few London agencies place bilingual secretaries abroad such as Merrow Language Recruitment (0845 226 4748; email recruit@merrow.co.uk; www.merrow.co.uk) and Appointments BiLanguage (020 7836 7878; email info@ appointmentsbilanguage.co.uk; www.appointmentsbilanguage.co.uk).

# Tourism

Tourism is undoubtedly one of Spain's largest industries, employing around 11% of the Spanish workforce, over 1.5 million people. Large British tour operators like Thomson and First Choice employ hundreds of representatives to work abroad as managers, sports instructors, chefs, bar and chamber staff each summer. First-time reps working for major tour operators, whether British, German or Scandinavian, have a 60% chance of being sent to a Spanish resort. Although it is sometimes easier to arrange a job with an organisation if you have a proven commitment to a career in tourism, this is not essential. Although you won't make a fortune (and will have to work hard), and although you may see decidedly little of real Spanish culture and life while working very long hours, these kinds of openings provide some potential for getting a job later on in tourism or related areas; and, if for nothing else, then for a long, hot and enjoyable Spanish summer. The Spanish infrastructure is generally well organised which makes your work much easier.

Most of the British camping tour companies such as Canvas Holidays, Club Cantabrica, Keycamp Holidays and Eurocamp have sites in Spain. Siblu (formerly Haven Europe) needs Spanish-speaking couriers and children's staff to work at mobile home and tent parks from early May to the end of September. There are also a number of smaller family businesses who employ in Spain such as Harry Shaw City Cruiser Holidays, Solaire Holidays and Bolero International Holidays. My Travel run self-catering holidays on Spain's foremost holiday islands and provide an extensive children's programme, employing nannies and animators. In some cases, a knowledge of German can be more useful than Spanish as many holiday villages cater primarily for the 13.5 million Germans who visit Spain annually.

In addition to the cheap packages, a vast array of special interest tours and upmarket villa holidays is available in Spain.

### Holiday operators

Companies like these sometimes look for staff who speak good Spanish and know the country:

Headwater: 01606 720033; email info@headwater.com; www.headwater.com. Activity holidays.

Individual Travellers (Spain and Portugal): 08701 921322; www.individualtravellers.com

Mundi Color: 020 7828 6021; www.mundicolor.co.uk

Other companies operate upmarket walking tours, wine appreciation tours or trips for pilgrims to Compostella in Galicia. The agency Select Spain in Reading has links to many interesting operators running cycling, hiking, yacht charter or other specialist tours (www.selectspain.com).

English-speaking guides for horseback expeditions in Spain may be needed by Inntravel Riding Holidays (01653 617949; www.inntravel.co.uk), which takes riding tours into the Sierra de Guarda and Andalucía. Try also In the Saddle (01299 272997; www.inthesaddle.com).

**TIP**

■ Ideally, you should arrange to visit the resorts you are considering, in advance of the tourist season, which usually begins about Easter, and ask at all hotels, restaurants and tourist shops.

It is always worth checking the English-language press. Ideally, you should arrange to visit the resorts you are considering, in advance of the tourist season, which usually begins about Easter, and ask at all hotels, restaurants and tourist shops.

A major employer near to Barcelona is the Universal Studios theme park, Port Aventura. This enormous theme park employs around 3,000 people annually and is certainly worth contacting for seasonal work (Universal Studios, Port Aventura, Dpto RR.HH, Avda Alcalde Pere Molas,km. 2, 43480 Vila-Seca, Tarragona (Ap 90), email recursos.humanos@portaventura.es; www.portaventura.es).

Those with relevant sports instruction qualifications may find work with one of the many companies offering activity holidays in Spain. For example Acorn Adventure (address below) needs seasonal staff for its two water sports and multi-activity centres on the Costa Brava. Royal Yachting Association (RYA) qualified windsurfing and sailing instructors, British Canoe Union (BCU) qualified kayak instructors and SPSA qualified climbing instructors are especially in demand for the season April/May to September. PGL also needs staff for Spanish holiday centres and TJM Travel hires qualified instructors and ancillary staff for hotels and activity centres in Spain.

Sailors from around the world congregate in the hundreds of marinas along the Spanish coast and create some opportunities for employment on yachts. Minorca Sailing Holidays (www.minorcasailing.co.uk) hires nannies and other staff for its sailing centre in the Bay of Fornells, Menorca.

There are also opportunities for ski instructors in the winter season, especially at resorts such as Cerler, La Molina or El Formigal in the Pyrenees. The ski industry is flourishing in Spain and a few British tour operators such as Thomson and First Choice require qualified instructors, as does the UK company Ski Miquel (01457 821200; www.miquelhols.co.uk) which has ski chalets in the Spanish resort of Baqueira.

## Useful addresses

There are more contact addresses in the book, *Working in Tourism, the UK, Europe and Beyond* by Verité Reily Collins (Vacation Work Publications, 2004).

Acorn Adventure: www.acorn-jobs.co.uk. Management and support staff needed to work at camps, mainly on the costas.

ATG-Oxford: 01865 315678; www.atg-oxford.co.uk/working.php. Walking and cycling tours. Seasonal workers required from March to August.

Canvas Holidays: 01383 629012; www.canvasholidays.co.uk. Season lasts from March to October. Recruitment takes place from October to March.

Cosmos Coach Tours: 020 8695 4724; www.cosmos.co.uk/about/careers.

Club Cantabrica Holidays Ltd: 01717 866177; www.cantabrica.co.uk. Couriers and resort managers required from May to October.

Eurocamp: Overseas Recruitment Department, 01606 787522; www.holidaybreakjobs. com. Part of the Holidaybreak Group which includes Keycamp Holidays. Recruit up to 1,500 seasonal staff; www.holidaybreakjobs.com.

MyTravel UK: 0870 241 2642; www.mytravelcareers.co.uk. Giant UK tour operator. Brands include Airtours Holidays, Direct Holidays, Panorama and Manos Holidays. Require huge numbers of staff from April to October; www.thomascookvacancies. co.uk.

Much of Spain's produce is locally grown

**Siblu (formerly Haven Europe):** 01442 239231; www.siblu.com. Seasonal staff required March to September.
**Solaire Holidays:** 0121 778 5061; email jobs@solaire.co.uk; www.solaire.co.uk. Require site couriers from April to October.
**Tall Stories:** 020 8939 8739;13; email info@tallstories.co.uk; www.tallstories.co.uk/jobs.shtm. Adventure sports holiday operators in Spain and Mallorca.
**Thomson:** See www.thomson.co.uk/jobs/travel-jobs.html to search for opportunities and apply online.

## Casual work

Tourism in Spain is such a vast industry that simply by turning up to the right place at the right time it is usually possible to find casual positions made available by the influx of 50 million or more visitors per year. The types of positions where there are always openings during the tourist season include hotel and restaurant work, couriers and representatives, bar, club and disco work, public relations, work in holiday camps, and shop assistants. Fluent English is an advantage for such jobs and explains why foreigners are often able to find work in areas of high Spanish unemployment.

If you can arrange to visit the Spanish coast in March before most of the budget travellers arrive, you should have a good chance of fixing up a job for the season. The resorts then go dead until late May when the season gets properly underway and there may be jobs available.

TIP

■ If you can arrange to visit the Spanish coast in March before most of the budget travellers arrive, you should have a good chance of fixing up a job for the season.

> **Louis Henderson and Nancy Ryan** spent a summer working in Barcelona. Both were able to secure positions fairly quickly; Louis worked in an art gallery catering mainly to tourists, and Nancy found work in an Irish bar:
>
> 'Finding work was fairly easy. We both wrote CVs in Spanish, with photos attached (as is increasingly the custom in Spain), and handed them out to as many places as we felt was appropriate. I found it a lot easier than I thought it would be to find work. I was worried because I knew very little Spanish before moving to Spain and I thought the language barrier would be a problem, but it wasn't at all.
>
> I worked in an Irish bar, which had a very mixed range of customers. There were obviously lots of tourists visiting the bar looking for English speaking places to relax, but there were also lots of Spanish customers and I found the language pretty easy to pick up. When I applied for the job, I had to explain to them that I knew little Spanish and they were fine with that as long as I was keen to learn, which I was.
>
> The work was very similar to any bar work in England, except that because of Spain's licensing laws I ended up working until very late, but this wasn't really a problem as I was able to sleep late and take plenty of siestas!'

The hotel and restaurant trade employs most casual workers. Kitchen hands, chefs, hotel managers, waiters, maids, receptionists and cleaners are required and although experience, qualifications and language skills are required for the better-paid positions, there are numerous positions open to the inexperienced. Unfortunately, with this kind of work, long hours and low pay are fairly standard. Many casual workers are employed illegally, so have no job protection and very few rights.

In the Canary Islands the season runs from November to March and Lanzarote and Tenerife offer the best chances for employment. Along the beachfront at Puerto del Carmen in Lanzarote and Playa de las Americas in Tenerife, almost every building is a bar, pizzeria, or hamburgeria. Just walk along the front until you come to a place whose client language you speak and go in and ask. There are ample opportunities in the year-round resorts of the Canary Islands for bar staff, DJs, beach party ticket sellers and timeshare salesmen. Many young people make ends meet by working as a 'PR' or 'prop', i.e. someone who stands outside trying to entice customers to come in.

A good starting point for finding out about seasonal job vacancies in Ibiza is the website of the Queen Victoria Pub in Santa Eulalia (www.ibizaqueenvic.com) which posts jobs and accommodation both on its site and on the pub notice board which anyone can drop by and consult. The Queen Vic itself-employs a large number of European fun seekers. Two other websites worth checking are www.balearic-jobs.com and www.gapwork.com.

Seasonal and casual work in Spain can also be found in the Crimson Publishing books: *Summer Jobs Abroad* (David Woodworth and Victoria Pybus) and *Work Your Way Around the World* (Susan Griffith).

## Agriculture

Reports of people finding harvesting work in Spain are very uncommon, mainly because of the huge pool of immigrant labour from North Africa and of landless Spanish workers. Occasional opportunities do present themselves on organic farms especially those owned by back-to-the-land expats looking for congenial company as well as hard workers. These arrangements are normally taken on a work-for-keep basis.

The most likely way to find agricultural work is by visiting farmers and landowners and offering your services. The work can be backbreaking and you should expect to earn no more than €20–€70 per day. Bear in mind that there are many immigrants to Spain who are willing to do this sort of work for next to nothing, so you are not in a strong negotiating position. Tomatoes and many other crops are grown on Tenerife. The Canaries are normally valued by working travellers only for their potential in the tourist industry, but there is a thriving agricultural life outside the resorts. Just a bus ride away from Los Cristianos, the farms around Granadilla, Buzanada, San Isidro and San Lorenzo may take on extra help between September and June. Most harvest workers camp and work on three-month contracts.

Wine is an important export for Spain

The organic farming movement (*Coordinadora d'Agricultura Ecològica*) in Spain no longer helps prospective volunteers. You can get a list of farms that accept people to work in exchange for board and lodging from AEAM (Amics de l'Escola Agrària de Manresa; 938 749060; www.agrariamanresa.org). They stress that member farmers want to hear only from people whose main interest is organic farming, not learning Spanish.

## Voluntary work

Working as a volunteer in Spain is a good way to get to know the country and learn the language, while contributing to Spanish society. Although unpaid, most volunteers receive meals and accommodation in exchange for their skills. There is great demand for volunteers in Spain in a variety of projects ranging from rural regeneration to archaeological and conservation projects. Finding volunteer work is far easier than finding paid work, and usually does not have the same level of language requirement. Non-EU citizens will also find that they are not required to obtain a work permit for voluntary work.

International work camp organisations recruit for environmental and other projects in Spain for programmes as various as carrying out an archaeological dig of a Roman settlement in Tarragona to traditional stone quarrying in Menorca. The co-ordinating work camp organisation in Spain is the *Instituto de la Juventud's Servicio*

**TIP**

■ The Sunseed Trust, an arid land recovery trust, has a remote research centre in southeast Spain where new ways are explored of reclaiming deserts. The centre is run by both full-time volunteers (minimum five weeks) and working visitors (minimum one week) who spend half the day working. See Voluntary Work, below.

*Voluntario Internacional* (913 637700), which oversees 150 camps every year. You can approach them independently as well as through a partner organisation in your own country (see below). International work camps usually operate from April to October and offer voluntary placements for two to three weeks.

Those looking for work in the Madrid region should contact the *Dirección General de Cooperación al Desarollo y Voluntariado* run by Madrid's regional government (900 444555; email dgvoluntariado@madrid.org; www.madrid.org/voluntarios). This organisation co-ordinates voluntary projects in the area involving working with the disabled, the elderly, and working in conservation projects. They may also be able to help you to find projects in other parts of the country and have a useful online directory of non-governmental organisations (NGOs)

There are many NGOs in Spain, known as ONGs (*organizaciones no gubernamentales*) and these usually offer voluntary work, which can sometimes lead on to paid positions. Search the online directory mentioned above or contact the *Coordinadora de ONG para el Desarollo España*, (CONGDE) (902 454600; www.congde.org) to find an organisation that may suit your interests.

An interesting opportunity for young volunteers with an interest in languages is the relatively new Englishtown project (913 913400; email anglos@puebloingles.com; www.vaughanvillage.com). Englishtown is a group of venues, among them an abandoned Spanish village, that have been transformed into villages 'stocked' with native English-speaking volunteers who live together with an equal number of Spanish people for an intensive week of activities, sports, games and group dynamics. The English native volunteers exchange conversation for room and board.

Two very different projects of particular interest to those concerned with sustainable environments are Sunseed Desert Technology and Ecoforest Education for Sustainability. Ecoforest (Málaga; 669 227447; email ef@ecoforest.org; www.ecoforest.org) is a charitable organisation set up to provide education about living and working in simple, natural and sustainable ways. The community of voluntary residents aims to demonstrate ecologically sound and self-reliant methods of food production. The Sunseed Desert Technology project (Almería; 950 525770; www.sunseed.org.uk) is located in the tiny village of Los Molinos in Southern Spain and aims to develop low-tech methods of sustainable agriculture in a semi-arid environment. Both projects rely heavily on volunteers.

You can find many more voluntary organisations and opportunities for volunteer work in Spain in a number of books all published or distributed by Crimson Publishing (www.crimsonpublishing.co.uk): The International Directory of Voluntary Work; World Volunteers; Green Volunteers; Archeo-Volunteers.

## Useful addresses

**International Voluntary Service:** (IVS Field Office) 0113 2469900; email youthwork@ivs-gb.org.uk; www.ivs-gb.org.uk

**Concordia Youth Service Volunteers Ltd:** 01273 422218; 01273 421182; email info@concordia-iye.org.uk; www.concordia-iye.org.uk

**UNA Exchange:** 029 2022 3088; email info@unaexchange.org; www.unaexchange.org

**Youth Action for Peace/YAP:** www.yapinc.org

# ■ EMPLOYMENT REGULATIONS
## Work regulations

Full details of visa requirements are given on page 30. EU nationals are at liberty to enter Spain to look for and take up work without requiring a work permit or residence visa. However, people without a European passport will find it extremely difficult to find an employer willing to tackle the immigration bureaucracy with no guarantee of success. Note, however, that au pairs, academics employed by Spanish universities and teachers employed at American or international schools are all in categories where work visas may be more easily granted.

Remember that whether or not you are an EU citizen, to work in Spain, the first thing you must do is apply for the NIE (*Numero de Identificación de Extranjeros*). This is a tax identification number and allows you to undertake any form of work or business activity, file tax returns, vote in local elections, or open a bank account. The NIE is obtainable from the *oficina de extranjeros* or police station. An application form can also be downloaded from www.mir.es. The filled out form and a passport are usually sufficient to obtain the NIE, which will be sent to you by post as soon as it has been processed. The application process is the same for both EU and non-EU citizens, although non-EU citizens must have entered the country with the correct visa.

If your NIE takes some time to come through and you wish to start looking for work, then possible employers will usually be satisfied as long as you can prove that you have applied for one.

## Professional mobility

If you want to work for yourself in Spain, as, for example, a doctor, surveyor, lawyer, plumber, carpenter, journalist, or language teacher, or if you run a business in your own name as a sole trader (*empresario individual*) you will come under the category of *cuenta propia* or 'working on your own account'. This is also known as *autonomo* for the purposes of the Spanish social security system. EU nationals and permanent residents with a residencia can be self-employed in a profession or trade in Spain, although they must meet the legal requirements and register with the appropriate organisation. For example, professionals must register with their professional *colegio* (see below).

> 'To get an NIE all we had to do was obtain proof of identity and of a permanent address, some passport photos, etc. and hand them in at the police station along with some forms. We were told that our NIEs would arrive within a month, but they never turned up. This didn't matter too much because the police gave us a form that said that we had applied for one. This was vital when looking for work as every prospective employer asked for proof of the NIE application.
> **Nancy Ryan**

### Professional bodies in Spain

Architects: *Consejo Superior de los Colegios de Arquitectos de España*, 914 352200; email info@cscae.com; www.cscae.com

Commercial agents: *Consejo General de Colegios de Agentes Comerciales de España*, 902 366956; email via website; www.cgac.es

Doctors and Dentists: *Consejo General de Colegios Oficiales de Médicos*, 914 317780; email webmaster@cgcom.es; www.cgcom.org

Estate agents: *Consejo General de los Colegios Oficiales de Agentes de la Propiedad Inmobiliaria de España*, 915 470741; email cgcoapi@consejocoapis.org; www.consejocoapis.org

Lawyers: *Consejo General de la Abogacía Española,* 915 232593; www.cgae.es.

Nurses and midwives: *Consejo General de Colegios Oficiales de Enfermería de España*, 913 345520; www.ocenf.org

Pharmacists: *Consejo General de Colegios Oficiales de Farmacéuticos*, 914 312560; email buzon@redfarma.org; www.portalfarma.com

Veterinary surgeons: *Consejo General de Colegios Veterinarios de España*, 914 353535; email via website; www.colvet.es

## Mutual recognition of qualifications

In recent years, the recognition of foreign qualifications for EU citizens has been rationalised. The General System for Mutual Recognition of Professional Qualifications was introduced to enable fully qualified professionals from one EU country to join the equivalent profession in Spain without having to re-qualify. If you hold a qualification entitling you to practise a regulated profession in your Member State of origin, this is sufficient to establish that you are eligible for consideration under the general system.

A comparison between foreign qualifications and those recognised in Spain can be obtained from any Spanish employment office (INEM) where there is a representative of NARIC, the National Academic Recognition Information Centre, *NARIC España*, 915 065593; email nieves.trelles@educ.mec.es. It is better to contact your UK or Spanish employment agency rather than contact NARIC directly as you should not be charged for the service. You can find out more, in English, at the NARIC website, www.naric.org.uk. You should not contact NARIC in the UK if you are going to work in Spain.

You can find a great deal of information on professional bodies and EC directives on the EU website http://ec.europa.eu/citizensrights.

Foreigners who wish to become self-employed will go through exactly the same procedure as a Spaniard. All self-employed people must register for income tax, social security and VAT. To register at the local Tax Office as self-employed, you will usually need a copy of your NIE and passport and completed forms 037 (tax registration) and 845 (business tax – IAE – registration).

Self-employed workers are required by law to pay into the Spanish social security system under the *autónomo* scheme and as a result they are entitled to medical benefits through the Spanish national health scheme. They may also receive sickness pay when ill, at the rate of 75% of the minimum wage, on receipt of a doctor's certificate testifying that they are unable to carry out their profession. Self-employed workers also qualify for a pension but they cannot qualify for unemployment benefit.

> 'There is a big problem with registration out here. It took me 12 months and a good deal of expense, what with the cost of the verification certificate, the cost of the solicitor, the postage and the telephone calls. It really was a nightmare. I followed the guidelines given by the Spanish government to the UK Nursing and Midwifery Council. I had all of my qualifications translated, filled in the forms, paid the money and sent it all off to Madrid. I then took everything to the Ministry of Sport, Education and Culture in Málaga who stamped it and sent it back to Madrid. It took seven months before I got any response and when I did, I took everything to the nursing council here, who told me my documents were out of date! So I had to spend even more money on getting another certificate, having it translated and stamped. It was then sent to England to be verified and then to the Foreign Office, just to make sure it was official. Finally it all came back to me, I took it to the nursing council and I think they agreed just because they felt sorry for me. I was then able to start practising. I am now a member of the College of Midwives here, the Colegio de Enfermería.'
>
> **Liz Arthur, Registered Midwife, Costa del Sol**

To register as self-employed with the Social Security Office, you will need the original and copies of your NIE and passport, a copy of Tax Office form 845 and the completed form TA.0521.

# ■ ASPECTS OF EMPLOYMENT

Employment in Spain is subject to many regulations and what follows is merely a general overview. Any specific queries relating to the obligations of the employer and the rights of the employee should be directed to the Spanish Ministry of Labour and Social Affairs at one of the addresses listed below. The *Ministerio de Trabajo y Asuntos Sociales* also produces an annual *'Guide to Labour and Social Affairs'*, the latest version of which is available online (in Spanish) at www.mtas.es/Guia/es/entrada.htm; the 2006 version is available in English at www.mtas.es/Guiaingles2006/texto/index.htm.

## Useful employment addresses

Spain: *Ministerio de Trabajo y Asuntos Sociales* 913 630000; email ministro@mtas.es; www.mtas.es.

UK and Republic of Ireland: *Work and Social Affairs Department*, 20 Peel Street, London W8 7PD; 020 7221 0098; email constrab.londres@mtas.es.

United States: *Labour and Social Affairs Advice Bureau*, 2375 Pennsylvania Avenue, NW Washington D.C. 20037; 452 01 00; email embespus@mail.mae.es.

Canada: *Labour Section*, 74 Stanley Avenue, Ottawa ON K1M1P4; 613 742 7077/8257; email laboral@docuweb.ca.

## Types of contract

In Spain, a contract may be made verbally or in writing, although in certain cases such as part-time, temporary and training contracts lasting more than four weeks, the contract should be in writing. Spanish labour law will usually regard the relationship between employer and employee as legally binding whether or not there is a written contract, and the worker is protected from dismissal even if a business is heading towards bankruptcy. It is vitally important that both parties understand the contract. Generally, the employment contract will include:

- details of the employer and the employee
- the length of time that the contract is valid for
- type of contract
- professional category
- description of work conditions, the work centre, working hours, work schedule
- duration of holidays
- level of compensation for dismissal.

Employment contracts in Spain can be made either for an indefinite term or for a specific duration. This has not always been the case but anger among Spanish businessmen at the government's rigid protection of the worker's right to job security led to a series of measures in 1994 and 1997 designed to create a more flexible labour market. The difficulty and expense of dismissing workers was creating real problems for seasonal businesses such as hotels, and was actually making bosses reluctant to take on extra employees for fear of being stuck with them through difficult periods. An indirect contract provides for 45 days of redundancy pay for each year worked. The government therefore made provisions for hiring workers on short-term contracts as well as the standard indefinite contracts.

Under a short-term contract the employer is liable only for a small redundancy payment when dismissing a worker. In general, contracts are made for an indefinite term and there must be specific circumstances to justify temporary hiring.

Unless a temporary contract takes one of the legal forms shown below, it will be deemed to be permanent.

### Short-term contracts

Contract for a specific project or service: The time period for this type of contract is uncertain and depends on the length of the project or service. This type of contract should clearly set out what work needs to be done. Its termination entitles the employee to receive an indemnification of eight days of salary per year worked.

Casual contract due to production overload or backlog: This type of contract may only last for a maximum period of six months, or 12 months if extended. Again the project should be set out clearly

Moncloa, Madrid

in the contract and its termination entitles the employee to eight days of salary per year worked.

Contract to substitute employees entitled to return to their job: This type of contract must name the employee being temporarily replaced and the cause of his or her substitution, and may only last until the return of the replaced worker.

Two further short-term contracts exist for training purposes:

Work experience contract: This type of contract may last for a minimum period of six months and a maximum period of two years and is only open to recent graduates. The salary for such a contract must be between 60% and 75% of the salary of a worker holding an equivalent post. Once the term of the contract has expired, the same person may not be hired again under the same type of contract in any company.

Trainee contract: This contract allows young people to acquire the theoretical and practical training necessary for a certain work post. It is specifically for workers aged between 16 and 21 who do not have the qualifications necessary for a work experience contract and may last between six months and two years. The employer must ensure that a trainee spends a minimum of 15% of his or her working hours undertaking theoretical training. Again, an individual may only work this type of contract once.

## Incentives for indefinite contracts

While businesses have been happy to take full advantage of short-term contracts, the trade unions are less enthusiastic about what they refer to as *basura* or 'rubbish' contracts offering the worker little security. Gaining *fijo* status has become increasingly difficult as employers are well aware how expensive it can be to fire a *fijo* worker. In many professions, one year short-term contracts have become the norm. These are renewed annually, but may not be renewed for more than three years, after which period the employer is legally obliged to either terminate the employment or grant a *fijo* contract. Unfortunately many employers simply choose to let the employee go after the third contract has expired.

In an attempt to counter trade union criticism and to reduce unemployment, the Spanish government offers incentives to encourage long-term employment contracts. These incentives are available to the employer if an already existing temporary contract is transformed into a permanent contract or if the permanent employee is from any of the following disadvantaged groups:

- young people aged 16 to 30
- workers aged between 30 and 45 who have been unemployed for at least six months
- unemployed women
- women in sectors where they have traditionally been under-represented
- the unemployed aged over 45
- unemployed workers who have been registered as jobseekers at the National Employment Institute (INEM) for at least six months
- workers with disabilities.

The use of such contracts entitles the employer to tax benefits and subsidies of up to 75% on the employer's social security contribution. It also reduces the amount of severance pay for improper dismissal to 33 days' salary for each year worked, rather than 45.

**FACT**

In an attempt to counter trade union criticism and to reduce unemployment, the Spanish government offers incentives to encourage long-term employment contracts.

## Part-time contracts

Employment contracts may be made full-time or part time. The part-time contract is defined as a contract in which the number of hours of work has been agreed with the worker per week, month or year and is less than that of a full time worker in the same work place, performing similar work. Part-time workers have the same rights as full-time workers.

## Trial periods

Spanish employment law also allows for trial periods, which are becoming increasingly common practice. At any point during this trial period, the length of which should be specified in the contract, the worker may be dismissed without notice. For graduates and qualified workers this trial period may last for no longer than six months, for all other workers it may last for no longer than two months.

# Employee representation

Out of a total population of just over 40 million people, there are approximately 15 million registered workers in Spain, of whom only two million belong to trade unions (*sindicatos*). The two major unions are the Socialist Union, the UGT (*Unión General de Trabajadores*) and the communist-leaning CCOO (*Comisiones Obreros*). Of less importance are the USO (*Unión Sindical Obrera*) and other markedly nationalist unions such as the Basque nationalist union, ELASTV.

Unlike some European workers' councils, the local union is not considered a joint management–employee structure, and neither unions nor employees as a rule have a direct voice in management decisions. The idea of co-determination, which is found in Germany, does not really exist in Spain. Instead, unions are concerned with negotiations for base salary and standard salary rates (the latter is invariably higher than the state legal minimum salary) and for salary payments (most agreements require 14 monthly payments but some can demand up to 16 payments during the year, with the base salary split accordingly). Unions also deal with social aspects of work, technical training and fringe and retirement benefits. Despite the low overall union membership in Spain, the two main trades union confederations play a key role in these industrial negotiations. Generally, industrial relations are relatively stable with few unauthorised strikes.

Agreements made with unions are legally binding as the minimum working conditions for the organisation in question. No employee is obliged to join a union, but all business entities with 50 or more employees are required to have some kind of workforce representation.

At company level, employees are represented by company committees or by employee delegates depending on whether the number of employees exceeds 50. These representatives have a right to information on the employer's financial situation and to copies of the business's annual report.

## Workers' delegates

Workplaces with more than 10 employees but fewer than 50 require workers' delegates. Between one and three delegates are elected from within the workforce by a majority vote of the entire workforce. Delegates have a number of powers and responsibilities, including:

**FACT**

■ No employee is obliged to join a union, but all business entities with 50 or more employees are required to have some kind of workforce representation.

- the right to negotiate company or workplace agreements
- the right to information or consultation on financial, commercial and labour matters
- responsibility for supervising and monitoring compliance with regulations on labour matters, social security, employment and health and safety
- the right to take administrative and legal action.

## The workers' committee

This is an organ of representation in enterprises or workplaces with 50 or more employees and its purpose is to defend and promote employees' interests at work. The committee has between five and 75 representatives, depending on the size of the enterprise or workplace, who are elected by the employees and hold their mandate for four years. In contrast to the situation in many other countries, the committee's role is largely one of opposition, rather than of involvement in joint management. While not union-based, the committees have been influenced and sometimes dominated in the past by trade unions.

## Wages and holidays

In unfortunate contrast with the escalating cost of living, wages have tended to remain static over the last few years. However, it is fair to say that although Spain does not presently offer instant riches, it does have one of the most rapidly developing economies in Europe and as the struggle to keep inflation down and to develop Spanish industry progresses, opportunities for industrial growth and financial success will be even greater.

Spain has a statutory inter-industry minimum wage, which is established every year by the government. In 2007 it amounted to €666 per month or €9324 per year for persons over 18 years of age, including 12 monthly and two extra payroll payments. However, this is fairly low and most employees are paid more; in 2007, less than 1% of the population earned the minimum wage.

Your employer will pay you at a time established within the contract and supply you with a *nómina*, or wage slip. Earnings must not be paid at an interval of more than a month and any late wages are subject to 10% interest. Your employer will deduct tax and social security contributions from your wages.

Workers are entitled to one month's vacation, as well as 14 paid public holidays. The worker must disclose holiday dates at least two months in advance, though it is very common for staff to take their annual holiday in August. As a result many local amenities, especially in the larger cities, close for all or part of August, of particular note when dealing with bureaucracy. Public holidays differ from year to year and from region to region, but generally an autonomous community will designate 12 national holidays and two local ones, such as an individual town's fiesta. During public holidays very few businesses, other than bars and hotels will be open.

Should your employer go bankrupt, then your wage is be guaranteed by an independent body known as the *Fondo de Garantía Salarial*, or the Wage Guarantee Fund. All employers are obliged to contribute 0.4% of wages to this fund, to ensure that wages and compensation are paid out to employees in the case of a company going into liquidation.

## Working conditions

Spanish labour legislation is codified in the *Estatuto de los Trabajadores* (Workers' Statute), which has been in force since 1980. This covers most basic aspects of conditions of work, employee representation in companies, strikes, etc. Pay and conditions of work are normally governed by collective agreements, negotiated either nationally or regionally in each sector.

The standard working week in Spain is 40 hours. Overtime cannot be forced and cannot exceed 80 hours per year. There is an official 40% pay increase for overtime, with double time for Sundays and national holidays. According to Spanish law, workers are not entitled to paid holiday until they have been working for 12 months (hence the popularity in some lines of work, such as English teaching, of nine-month contracts). An annual paid holiday of 30 calendar days is then obligatory; this does not include the 14 national public holidays that are celebrated each year, and one or two regional holidays as well.

The traditional long lunchtime *siesta* break is now being replaced by a shorter, one-hour lunch break in the larger companies and businesses of Spain. However, in line with the shorter lunch hour the working day is finishing earlier and instead of the traditional 9am–2pm and then 4.30pm–8.30pm day (still maintained, particularly in the summer, by smaller businesses) most Spaniards now work what is a comparatively relaxed 9am-6pm day with one hour for lunch.

## Health issues

It is generally accepted by Spanish employers that you may call in sick for up to three days. However, from the fourth day, most employers will require a note from your doctor. Those who are absent from work for between four and 20 days are entitled to 60% of their salary. Once you reach the 21st day, this increases to 75%. However, if your illness is work-related then you are entitled to 75% of your salary from the first day. The self-employed must be able to show that their ailment prevents them from working and are entitled to 75% of the minimum legal salary.

The Spanish social security system is dealt with on page 198. It is worth reiterating that nearly all workers are covered for healthcare, workplace accidents, sick leave and invalidity. Free healthcare is, therefore, provided by INSALUD doctors and hospitals and most prescribed medication is free. It is not common for companies to provide private health insurance for their employees, but some of the larger companies may have an agreement with one of the health insurance companies, offering discounted insurance to employees.

## Leave of absence

Leave of absence is granted to employees for a number of reasons, mostly personal. These include getting married, moving house, serious illness, union duties, unavoidable public and personal duties, and death or hospitalisation of relatives.

Around half of Spanish women under 40 work. This phenomenon has been developing over recent years and is partly a result of the increasingly high percentage of female university graduates. Female lawyers and doctors are particularly in evidence and many women now occupy middle and senior management positions. Despite the traditional image of the macho and chauvinistic Spanish male, there generally tends to be less sexism in the professions there than in other Latin countries. Having said this, the great majority of Spanish working women still occupy the less senior and less powerful levels of their professions (unless they are the daughter of the founder).

A kind of self-deprecatory attitude is still in evidence in day-to-day office life as female professionals often introduce themselves in a business context by their first names, while Spanish businessmen would never dream of encouraging the same kind of liberty. However, businesswomen do expect the same level of professionalism that would be extended to a man.

Women are protected from discrimination by the Workers' Statute of 1980, which prohibits discrimination on the grounds of sex, marital status, age, race, social status, religious belief, political opinion or trade union membership. Discrimination in the case of physical or mental disability is also illegal, so long as the work being performed will not be negatively affected by the disability. Legislation has also been introduced that further protects pregnant women's rights at work.

Maternity leave is fairly generous in Spain. Women are entitled to 16 weeks of leave and until the child is nine months old, the mother is entitled to an hour a day 'feeding time'. Fathers do not receive such generous treatment, being entitled to only two days of paternity leave. However, the mother can transfer two of her weeks to her husband.

# ◼ WORKING CULTURE AND ETIQUETTE

When it comes to Spanish working practices, it really is best to throw all of your Anglicised preconceptions out of the window. Spain has a distinct working culture, which at times barely resembles its British or American counterpart and may leave the unsuspecting foreign businessman utterly bewildered. While you may find Spanish customs time-consuming and frustrating, the alternative is to carry on exactly as you would in your home country, and almost certainly fail.

## Business hours

These will vary from business to business and from location to location, but there are some points worth noting about Spanish working habits. The normal business hours are 8am–1pm and 4pm–6pm, Monday to Friday. Offices generally open slightly later than in the UK, but will often remain working until 8pm with a long lunch break between 2pm and 4pm. Business discussions may even spill over into a nearby bar. From mid-June to mid-September, many offices adopt 'summer hours', especially in the hottest areas of the country, where offices are open from 8:30am to 3pm.

Lunch in Spain is by far the most important meal of the day and traditionally families would get together for a long break between 1 pm and 3 or 4pm. Although this practice is dying out in the larger cities due to greater commuting distances and traffic congestion, it still persists in small towns and rural areas. If returning home for lunch is impractical, Spaniards will still take a long lunch break, often visiting a restaurant or café. They would never consider eating at their desk. Even drinking coffee at one's desk is considered to be unsophisticated and unsociable. Instead it is perfectly acceptable to leave the office and go to a café with a colleague. However, it would be unusual to go out for coffee or lunch with someone of a different rank. Many working environments now have lunchrooms for all the staff. Again, Spanish colleagues tend to mix with people at the same level, even if they are on the same team.

The Spanish are famed for keeping very late hours, with young *Madrileños* often not going out in the evening until 11pm or later. Similarly, if you are being entertained by a business associate, don't expect dinner to start before 9pm or to finish before midnight.

## Punctuality

It is true that procrastination and delay are an endemic part of Spanish business life. However, it would be wrong to view this in a negative light, it is nothing to do with indolence or apathy, but is usually because the Spanish try to cram too many things into too short a space of time. While the clichéd *mañana* attitude may still be found in the state sector, with its impenetrable web of bureaucracy, it is less obvious these days in modern, private firms. In fact the Spanish work incredibly hard, especially within middle management. Always try to be on time to appointments and business meetings, but do not be too surprised if you are made to wait.

## Formality

Some aspects of the Spanish working world are still fairly formal. In a business environment particularly, formal dress is required and the Spanish will be quite taken aback by someone who turns up to a meeting or appointment in casual dress. Most Spanish businessmen wear conservatively coloured suits with shirts and ties. Suit jackets are very rarely removed, even during a business lunch. Style is considered fairly important and quality and taste in personal possessions (clothes, jewellery etc.) are a symbol of success in the eyes of a Spaniard. For women suits, trouser suits or business dresses are considered appropriate, although this is relaxed to a certain extent during the extremely hot summer months. Any business introduction demands a formal handshake, rather than a pat on the back or kiss on the cheek, although these may come later with the progression of a business relationship.

## Working relationships

Whereas the British tend to follow that old maxim of not mixing business with pleasure, the Spanish, in contrast, like to build up a relationship with their colleagues and business partners. Good relations between colleagues are maintained by regular chats, and anyone who spends too much time at their desk is regarded with suspicion.

Spanish businessmen much prefer to work with people they know, like, and therefore trust, so that any working cooperation is a mere formalisation of an ongoing relationship. It really is worth making the effort to develop business relationships.

Entertaining and eating out are important aspects of Spanish business life and they are used to establish personal relationships. Usually on a first business meeting everything except business is discussed until coffee is served, when the host will move onto the real reason for the invitation. Until that moment it is best not to appear too formal. Spanish protocol dictates that whoever has extended the invitation foots the bill for the meal. If you have been invited out for a meal, it is always a good idea to return the gesture at some point.

> 'Be open and honest and don't try to be greedy. People would prefer to hold onto their money or have less, than deal with someone who they did not like or who they felt was getting too good a deal out of them.'
> **Peter Cobbold**

## Negotiations

Business meetings in Spain are not informal. On the contrary, professional attire is expected and a handshake is customary upon initiating and closing a meeting.

You will have to learn to approach your business negotiations in a much more relaxed manner, because things may well take considerably longer. The Spanish are often inefficient because there is no structure to their meetings. Foreign businessmen and women often find that whereas in their own country they could conduct three or four important meetings in a day, in Spain one meeting may last the entire day and still prove fruitless. It is vital to go into a meeting with Spanish businesspeople with an agenda of points that you wish to discuss or you may waste a lot of time.

On the other hand, the actual decision-making process in Spain is often very speedy.

Another potential frustration is that the Spanish are often unwilling to commit anything to paper, preferring face-to-face discussions or conversations over the phone.

It is therefore good practice to follow up a letter with a telephone call to ensure a response, but there is really no substitute for a personal meeting.

## Working values

In most Spanish companies, loyalty and friendships outweigh intelligence; character and amiability are rated higher than business acumen; and modesty is valued over assertiveness. The four words used most frequently in connection with comments on individual colleagues or clients are:

> ❝
> Where the Spanish get very frustrated with foreign businessmen and vice versa during meetings comes down to the percentage of spontaneity allowed in a negotiation. Generally what happens in the UK and the USA is that decisions are not made in a single meeting. The information is taken away, evaluated and then a counter proposal is presented at a further meeting. This can take a lot of time, but generally when a decision has been made, it does go ahead.
>
> In Spain, the reverse is true. Spontaneity is highly valued. The ability to make a decision at a meeting, a snap judgement with no counter proposal, is highly valued. This galls the British especially, because we are not used to having that kind of decision-making freedom. The downside however, is that just as decisions can be made quickly, they can also be unmade at the very last minute.
>
> **Richard Spellman, Ambient Media and Communications SL, Madrid**
> ❞

- *Valiente* – The quality most admired in business is courageous decision making. Sharing decision making is often interpreted as weakness.
- *Bueno* – This is the best compliment; if you are referred to as *un tipo bueno* you are considered clever, honourable and *valiente*.
- *Inteligente* – That the Spanish put little stock in intelligence as a business trait is shown by the fact that this is used to imply solid and boring.
- *Listo* – Sharp but perhaps not altogether trustworthy.

## Language

It is important to remember that less than 30% of local managers are fluent in English. While English is recognised as the international business language in Spain, on a smaller, more local scale you will have to brush up on your Spanish or even the local language. Only 74% of the Spanish population speak Castilian Spanish as a first language, and you may need to learn Catalan, Galician or Basque. Conducting negotiations in a second language can cause embarrassing and even expensive misunderstandings. Even if your Spanish is fluent, there will always be cultural references and contexts that may pass you by, so be sure not to make any assumptions.

Note however that in the south of Spain, manners are slightly more formal than in the north and it may take slightly longer to get on to *tu* terms. One point worth remembering if you are employing Spanish staff is that to refer to subordinates as *usted* would be considered very insulting, putting them around the same level as the domestic staff.

## Communication

Within Spanish companies it is not considered necessary to communicate to colleagues or subordinates anything other than what is strictly necessary for the job in hand. Correspondence, staff noticeboards and memos are conspicuously absent from all but the largest of companies.

Similarly there is not really a culture of meetings in Spain – when they do exist, their function is primarily to communicate instructions. The business environment is therefore lacking in team spirit, as the Spanish like to be independent and make decisions on their own.

There is a lingering fear of sharing information and people tend not to hand over knowledge to a younger apprentice, out of fear for their own job. Companies have very flat hierarchies of only two or three tiers and in the upper echelons people are often so intent on keeping their position that they will not delegate. For the outsider doing business with a company, this can be useful as it is fairly easy to identify the right person to talk to, and they will usually give you an interview. On the other hand, they usually have an enormous pile of work to get through. For those hoping to 'climb the ladder' in a particular company, it can be very frustrating.

Construction work continues as many of Spain's cities modernise

## Forms of address

The Spanish system of having two surnames is not as baffling as it first appears. Children receive both the first surname of their father and the first surname of their mother. Women do not change their names when they get married. For example, the son of Sr José Lopez Garcia and Sra Maria Pizarro Vega could be called Juan-Pablo Lopez Pizarro. While it certainly won't cause any offence if you get this wrong it may cause some embarrassment, but in every day business correspondence there is no need to use both surnames. Official paperwork, however, will require the full Spanish name.

To be addressed as Don or Doña is considered a mark of respect. Academics, lawyers and other professional people will be referred to as Don. This term is used before the Christian name, for example Don Eduardo or Doña Almudena.

## Correspondence

For your working correspondence to appear more 'Spanish', and to avoid any misunderstandings, it is a good idea to become familiar with the conventions of Spanish business letters:

### The envelope

When addressing the envelope, the correct way is to begin with the name of the company. This is followed by Atn (like the English Attn, for the attention of) and then the name of the person. The job title follows and then the address. Note that in Spanish, unlike in English, the postcode always comes before the town.

If you wish to include your return address on the envelope, it should be written on the back, following the word *Remite*.

**TIP**

■ One constant source of confusion is the use of *tu* and *usted* in work situations, especially as 'usted' said in a sarcastic tone can be very insulting. Generally usage is based on familiarity, and most Spaniards will drop the use of the formal usted after an initial meeting.

## Beginning the letter

The letter should be laid out similarly to an English letter. Your own address and name, without title, should be at the top on either the left or right hand side. The addressee's name and address should be inserted on the left-hand side of the paper, above the opening greeting. The date should follow this address, and in a formal letter should be written out in full, e.g. *12 de enero de 2008*.

It is customary to begin a letter with *Estimado/a*, followed by *Señor*, *Señora*, *Señorita*, followed by the surname of the person, followed by a colon. For example, *Estimado Señor Juarez*: If you do not know the person you are writing to, it is sufficient just to write *Estimado/a Señor/a* or if you would like to write the equivalent of Dear Sirs, the plural form is *Estimados Señores*. However, if you are writing to someone in Cataluña, the phrase *Estimado* is usually replaced with *Apreciado/a*. Once you have built up a good relationship with the addressee, it is perfectly acceptable to use a first name, e.g. *Estimado José*. The phrase *Querido/a*, which translates as Dear, is only used when you know the addressee well.

## Signing off

There are a number of potential letter endings for formal correspondence, however modern business Spanish is much less flowery than it used to be and usually sticks to the following endings:

- Formal – Yours faithfully/sincerely = *Atentamente or Le saluda atentamente.*
- Less formal – Kind regards = *Cordialmente or Un cordial saludo.*
- More personal – Best wishes = *Un abrazo* or even *Un fuerte abrazo.*The ending, *Un abrazo*, which translates as 'an embrace', is often used in business correspondence where a friendly relationship exists between the parties.

## Emails

Spanish business emails do not generally differ too much from business letters. However, they are quite often less formal and may begin with *Estimado/a Amigo/a* (dear friend) or even *Hola* (Hi). In the UK and the USA much of the formality is removed from emails and people get straight to the point, as if they were speaking. In Spain, this is also largely true, but the Spanish do also expect a working email to be slightly more long-winded and friendly.

# ■ DOING BUSINESS IN SPAIN

Many foreigners who move out to Spain choose to start up their own business, but for those who already have business interests in the UK or America, and wish to extend them to Spain there are a number of opportunities available. For example, a foreign businessman might form an association with other entrepreneurs already established in Spain, known as a joint venture, or a foreign parent company might choose to set up a branch of the company in Spain. Indeed, an investor wishing to operate or distribute goods in Spain need not even physically establish a centre of operations in Spain. There are various alternatives including signing a distribution agreement, operating through an agent and operating as a franchisor. Each of these forms of doing business in Spain offers distinct advantages and problems from both a legal and fiscal perspective.

For British investors, the best way to gather information on such enterprises is by contacting UK Trade and Investment, either at the British Embassy in Madrid (917 008200; email commerce@ukinspain.com; www.ukinspain.com), or before you leave, in London (020 7215 8000; www.uktradeinvest.gov.uk). They have staff working throughout Spain whose aim is to help British exporters of goods or services win business in the Spanish market. They will be able to advise you on appropriate strategies to enter the market and put you in touch with key contacts in Spain such as local representatives, agents and distributors. They can also advise you on setting up a branch in Spain.

# Branch offices

As well as the numerous forms of business enterprise created under Spanish law, foreign investors may operate in Spain through a branch (*sucursal*). Unlike a company, this organisation is not a legal entity of its own, but depends on a head office. It is therefore subject to the legislation of its country of origin. The branch must have a legal representative, empowered to administer the affairs of the branch.

Generally speaking, the requirements, procedural formalities, accounting and initial costs for a branch are very similar to those for a corporation, and a branch operates much like a corporation in its dealings with third parties.

The choice between forming a branch or a legal entity in Spain may be affected by commercial reasons. For example, some may see a company as providing a more solid presence than a branch. The main legal differences between a branch and a separate company are set out below:

- Legal status: a branch is not a legal entity and has the same legal identity as its parent company.
- Minimum capital: whereas an SA (*Sociedad Anónima*) requires a minimum capital of €60,101 and a Sociedad de Responsabilidad Limitada (SL) requires €3,005, a branch does not require any minimum assigned capital.
- Tax: both a branch and a company are generally taxed under Spanish corporate income tax at 35% on their net income. However, there are some other aspects of taxation which require special mention. If the parent company is non-EU-resident, it is possible that remittance of branch profits may be taxed at 15%, although many non-EU countries have tax treaties with Spain, in which case remittance is not taxable in Spain. Also, in general it is easier for the parent company's overheads to qualify as deductible in the case of a branch.

## Registration of a branch office

The requirements for the constitution of a branch office are the same as for setting up any other business in Spain. As with a new Spanish company, a branch must be set up through a public deed, executed before a public notary and registered at the Companies' Registry. As well as the documents required at the incorporation of a new company (i.e. evidence of the identity of the person appearing before the notary, their power of attorney, the method of contribution), the following documents will also be required for the registration of a branch:

- a copy of the deed of incorporation and articles of association of the foreign partner
- a copy of the minutes of the foreign company's Board of Directors' meeting establishing the decision to open a branch in Spain, including the capital assigned to it, the name of the general manager and his powers
- a certificate from a Spanish bank showing that the transfer of capital assigned to the branch has been deposited in a bank account.

The incorporation deed and the foreign company's bylaws must be translated into Spanish. As with the formation of a new company, the following procedures must be followed before beginning operations:

- The branch must be assigned with a tax identification number.
- Transfer tax must be paid.
- The branch must be registered at the Companies' Registry.
- The branch must be registered for the tax on economic activities (IAE).
- The branch must be registered for VAT purposes.
- Payment of opening licence tax.
- Registration for social security purposes.
- Compliance with labour formalities.

## Joint venture

Foreign investors often find that a joint venture with a Spanish company allows the parties to share risks and combine resources and expertise. Many choose to use a Spanish corporation or limited liability company as the vehicle for joint ventures. However, there are a number of different options available according to Spanish legislation when it comes to cooperation between companies.

### Temporary business associations (UTEs)

Such projects are very common for engineering and construction projects, although they can be used in other sectors as well. UTEs are defined under Spanish law as temporary business cooperation vehicles set up for a specified or unspecified period of time to carry out a specific project or service. They allow several companies to work together in one common project, although each company will keep its legal status. They are not corporations and they have no legal personality, but they are formed by deed in the presence of a notary public and are registered in a special UTE register held by the Spanish Ministry of Finance. They may also be registered at the Companies' Registry.

UTEs must comply with all the accounting and bookkeeping requirements with which a company usually complies.

### Economic Interest Groupings (EIGs)

These differ from UTEs because they are separate legal entities. However, they are not-for-profit companies and may only be created to help the members achieve their objectives. The EIG is most commonly used to provide a centralised service within the context of a wider group of companies, for example centralised purchasing, sales, information management or administrative services. Like a UTE, they must be formed by a deed of incorporation witnessed by the notary and entered in the Companies' Registry. The members of an EIG are personally and severally liable for the entity's debts.

There is also a European EIG (EEIG), with its own legal personality, which was established in the European Commission as a means of encouraging cross-border cooperation between businesses in different parts of the EU. It differs from the EIG because it is governed by EU regulations rather than Spanish company law. The EEIG is totally free to move around the EU member states.

## Silent partnership (participation account agreement)

Many foreign entrepreneurs choose this route, which involves providing monetary or 'in kind' contributions to another entrepreneur to share an interest in the activities carried out. This interest may be either positive or negative, depending on whether there is a profit or loss on the business activity. These contributions are not the same as capital contributions – investing as a silent partner does not, therefore, make you a shareholder. This type of agreement does not require any legal formality such as incorporation or registration. However, in practice, it is fairly common for both parties to reflect the agreement in a public deed.

# Other methods of investing in Spain

## Distribution agreements

Under a distribution agreement a company operating in Spain will undertake to achieve wide distribution of a product or service belonging to the foreign investor. This method offers foreign investors an attractive means of entering into commercial cooperation with previously existing entrepreneurs for carrying out their operations in Spain, as the initial investment required is very low. There are several broad categories of distribution agreements:

- Exclusive distribution agreements: The supplier provides his product to only one distributor within a specified territory.
- Sole distribution agreements: As above, but the supplier reserves the right to supply the products himself to the specified territory.
- Selective distribution: This applies only to certain products that require special handling and distributors are carefully selected to preserve an image or brand name.

Generally, distribution agreements are fairly unregulated and allow the parties discretion to decide on the contents of the contract. However, the provisions that may be included in a distribution agreement are as follows:

- details of supplier and distributor
- payment terms in an agreed currency
- a minimum volume of sales
- supplier's liability for defective products
- duration of the agreement
- law and jurisdiction applicable in the case of a dispute
- the geographical area covered by the agreement.

Note that it is important to protect your intellectual property when signing a Spanish distribution contract, as your home country protection may not be valid. Local legal assistance on this issue is essential.

The income for the non-resident supplier of goods is usually not taxable in Spain.

## Agency agreements

These are agreements where an agent negotiates commercial operations on behalf of another, without assuming the risk of those operations. This is another useful method of expanding your business operation into Spain without the complications of establishing a legal entity there. An agent is duty bound to safeguard the interest of your company and not act for companies offering similar goods or services without agreement. They can be paid a fixed sum, a commission or a combination of the two.

Agency contracts can be indefinite or they can last for a specified period of time. Indefinite contracts may be terminated at any time by either party, as long as there is prior written notice. Under some circumstances it is possible for the agency agreement to include a non-competition provision to restrict the professional activities of the agent for up to two years after a contract has ended.

Generally a non-resident of Spain using a Spanish agent will record business income in Spain on the sale of goods and this tax income will usually not be taxable in Spain. The law and jurisdiction applicable in the case of a dispute is usually that of the company's home country, rather than Spain.

## Franchising

Another possible way of marketing goods and services in Spain is to franchise. As a franchisor, it is possible to sell the concept of your business to those wishing to set up in Spain. The Spanish business will be legally and financially independent from you, but there will be close cooperation between the two enterprises. Franchisees pay to use your brand name or trademark and business procedures in return for ongoing provision of commercial and technical assistance. The individual franchisees are obliged to do business under your rules and guidelines.

The 1998 Royal Decree on franchises in Spain set out the following stipulations:

- that the franchisee has access to a common business name or sign and standardised presentation of the premises or transport.
- that the franchisor transfer his or her business know-how.
- that the franchisor gives continued provision of commercial or technical assistance during the term of the agreement.

The franchisor must have written information which franchisees are sent before deciding whether or not to sign a contract. As a franchisor you will receive:

- the initial registration fee, a one-off payment for joining the franchise network
- royalty fees which continue as long as the franchise lasts and which may range from four to 20 per cent of the revenue
- advertising fees are often paid annually to the franchisor. These rarely exceed three per cent of gross sales.

Anybody operating a franchise in Spain must be registered with the Franchisor's Register run by the Directorate-General of Internal Trade of the Ministry of the

Economy, who will issue you with a certificate and supply public information to the Autonomous Communities and to interested parties. This must take place a maximum of 20 days before the signing of the franchise contract, otherwise the franchisor is liable for serious fines for non-registration.

The tax status for the franchiser, however, is fairly complex and should be analysed by an accountant, as the amount paid by the franchisee could be considered royalties rather than business income and therefore taxed in Spain at 25% or the reduced tax treaty rate.

# ■ BUSINESS AND INDUSTRY REPORT

Spain is an extremely dynamic country and has traditionally achieved very high economic growth rates over the past decade, over and above the average for other industrialised countries. In 2006 Spain's Gross Domestic Product (GDP) increased by 3.9%, making it the seventh highest in the Organization for Economic Cooperation and Development (OECD). According to the International Monetary fund (IMF) the Spanish economy weathered the difficulties created by the recent world economic slowdown remarkably well, proving resilient and rich in job creation. The services and industry sectors are the main contributors to Spain's GDP, accounting for 85%. Agriculture accounts for 3% of GDP, a figure that is expected to decline over the next few years. Spain's entry into the European Union forced the country to open its economy and expose its companies to foreign competition. As a result, Spanish companies went through a period of restructuring and have increased their level of competitiveness and technological innovation.

According to the Spanish Office for Economic and Commercial Affairs Spanish industry at present reflects three main tendencies: integration into the euro zone, globalisation and the liberalisation of its markets.

What follows is an analysis of some of the main sectors of business and industry in Spain. You can find out more about individual sectors from the Office for Economic and Commercial Affairs at the Spanish Embassy in London (020 7467 2330; email buzon.oficial@londres.ofcomes.mcx.es; www.comercio.es). Many addresses and phone numbers for the main companies operating in Spain are listed in the Directory of Major Employers at the end of this chapter.

## Agriculture

Despite the massive shift to urban areas that has taken place over the last 40 years, agriculture is still present in the Spanish economy and employs around seven per cent of the labour force. Spanish final agricultural production amounts to about 12% of all EU member state production.

The image of farming in Spain is quite different from the UK or USA. The countryside and farms are still a fundamental aspect of the Spanish identity, with 27% of the population living in rural areas. There is a sense of great pride that Spain is still, for example, the world's largest producer of olive oil (45% of all olive trees grown in the EU are in Spain), and that Spain's vineyards are the largest in the world (60% larger than France's). The leading agricultural products, after grapes and olives, include a huge variety of fruits as well as cereals, vegetables and root crops.

## Spain's top 10 companies:

1. **Grupo Telefónica.** Spain's biggest employer, with more than 95,000 people on the payroll, and one of the largest telecommunications compainues in the world. Telefónica was privatised in 1997 but, despite losing its monopoly over telecommunications in Spain, still holds the lion's share of the market and has expanded geographically and diversified into other media, making it the company with the largest net profit in Spain.

2. **Grupo Santander.** This banking giant has an enormous presence in Spain, Portugal and Latin America. Companies include Santander Central Hispano Bank, Banesto, the Bank of Venezuela, and Río de Plata Bank. In 2004, Santander also took over Abbey, the British building society. Grupo Santander is the largest banking group in the Euro zone, employing 126,000 people, 68% of whom work outside Spain.

3. **Repsol YPF.** Spain's largest producer of oil and gas, with an international presence in 29 countries; it employs over 30,000 people worldwide.

4. **Iberdrola.** Leading private electric utilities provider, with over nine million customers in Spain. In 2006, the merger between Iberdrola and Scottish Power created the world's third largest energy company.

5. **BBVA.** Global financial group with 35 million customers in 40 countries worldwide. Employs around 91,000 people.

6. **Endesa.** Spain's largest electricity company with a presence in Spain, Portugal, Italy and Latin America.

7. **El Corte Inglés.** Spain's biggest chain of department stores and hypermarkets. The company also offers financial services, insurance, online shopping, retail consulting and telecommunications services. Also expanding into Portugal, France and Italy.

8. **SEAT.** Spain's first big car manufacturer, founded in 1950, now owned by Volkswagen. The company produces 460,000 cars per year and is a major employer. The Seat Ibiza is the best-selling car in Spain, and the company plans to enter the US market in 2008.

9. **FASA Renault.** Spanish branch of Renault.

10. **Opel.** Spain's third largest car manufacturer (known as Vauxhall in the UK).

Find out more about growing olives from the Olive Oil Agency (*Agencia para el Aceite de Oliva*), website: http://aao.mapa.es. There are also opportunities in forestry, with help available for the reforestation of formerly productive agricultural land.

Organic production has been so successful in Spain because the natural conditions of the land allow for a higher diversity of production, there is a favourable climate for early cultivation, numerous ecosystems and a relatively moderate use of agro-chemicals in most parts of the country. Currently 666,000 hectares of Spanish land are farmed organically, generating produce worth €173.9 million. Andalucía is the area most dedicated to organic farming with 225,600 hectares under organic cultivation, followed by Extremadura, Valencia, Navarra, Murcia, Catalonia, Aragon and the Canary Islands. Each of the autonomous communities has a regulatory body for organic crop production (*Consejo Regulador de la Agricultura Ecológica*). Find the address of your local organisation on www.vidasana.org/autoridades.html.

## Biotechnology

The Spanish biotechnology sector has an annual turnover of €1.6 billion and employs over 12,000 people. The industry has been experiencing rapid growth over the last few years and there are currently over 120 companies in Spain dedicated to biotechnology, with 49% working in the health sector, 27% in food and the remaining 14% in environmental or bioprocessing sectors. Staff in this sector are highly qualified, with 80% being graduates and 20% dedicated purely to research and development.

This industry is based mainly in Madrid, Catalonia and Valencia. Significant companies in this sector include Natraceutical and Puleva Biotech (food), Abengoa, Amgen SA, Genentech, Sero and Glaxo SmithKline.

You can find out more from: www.csic.es (Spanish Higher Centre of Scientific Research); www.cnb.csic.es (National Biotechnology Centre); and www.asebio.com (Spanish Association of Biotechnology Enterprises).

## Chemicals and petrochemicals

The value of Spanish chemical production is around €32 billion per year, around 10% of the Spanish GDP. Chemicals are Spain's second biggest export after cars, and this sector generates 500,000 indirect or direct jobs.

The chemicals sector is highly globalised. About half of the business is in the hands of the multinationals including Michelin, Pirelli, ICI, Unilever and Shell; while the smaller firms face an uncertain future or have merged with larger ones. However, the Spanish company Repsol YPF produces around 50% of the total national output of ethylene, propylene, butane and benzene.

Spain is a country naturally blessed with the raw materials for these industries, with an abundance of pyrites, sodium and potassium salts, although its coal deposits are generally low quality and almost all oil has to be imported. The principal production areas are the Basque country, Catalonia and the Madrid region, as well as Huelva, Cartagena and Puertollano.

There is more about this industry on www.feique.org (Federation of the Spanish Chemical Industry).

## Construction

Construction makes up round 9% of Spain's economic activity and over the past decade the sector has expanded rapidly. Nearly two million people are employed in Spain's construction industry, which amounts to nearly 12% of the working population, and this figure is growing year on year. Spain's motorways have more than tripled in length since 1982 and high-speed trains have become a priority. The boom in the construction industry has also been fuelled by the enormous demand for tourist-related buildings and second homes.

However, fears are beginning to grow of a slowdown in the housing market, which will have a knock-on effect on construction. Diana Choyleva, an analyst from Lombard Street research, says in a BBC interview that there is currently a surplus of 800,000 houses in Spain, describing the country as 'over-housed and over-indebted'. Those seeking to enter this sector should be aware of its somewhat less-than-rosy prospects as much of Europe threatens to slide into recession.

The construction industry in Spain can be divided into the following sub-sectors: residential construction, which makes up 31% of the total activity, non-residential construction (18%), civil engineering (26%), and renewal and maintenance (25%). All of these sub-sectors have excellent growth forecasts for the coming years.

Find out more about this industry from: www.cnc.es (National Construction Federation); www.mfom.es (Ministry of Infrastructures); www.seopan.es (National Building Companies Association); www.apce.es (Association of Spanish Property Developers); www.ancisa.com (National Independent Builders Association).

## Electronics and IT

The electronics industry in Spain can be subdivided into four groups: consumer electronics, electronic components, professional electronics, and telecommunications and computer equipment. The industry employs around 80,000 people and is still largely located around Barcelona and Madrid.

The electronics sector in Spain is dominated by foreign firms which are managed locally in wholly or partly owned subsidiaries. Telecommunications accounts for 19% of the sector. World leading companies such as Alcatel, Ericsson, General Electric, Lucent Technologies, Manufacturers Services Limited, Pioneer, Philips, Siemens, Sony and Samsung all have a presence in Spain.

The total market for Information Technology (including hardware, software, services, supplies) was estimated at around €11 billion in 2003, representing 5% of the entire European market. Most market leaders in Spain are US firms such as HP, Dell and IBM, but the number of IT firms owned by Spanish capital represents 30% of the market, mainly concentrated in small and medium-sized companies. The best prospects for growth in this industry are to be found in servers and portable equipment for smaller companies, new requirements for e-commerce, software for business integration and consulting and implementation services. So far, the sector has remained fairly robust in the face of slumps across much of the economy.

The home sector has also experienced growth in the last few years, thanks largely to the impressive development of internet access in Spain and the market for CD-ROM readers for private use and multimedia PCs. This has created opportunities in related sectors such as laser printers, laptops and palm PCs.

**FACT**

■ Most market leaders in Spain are US firms such as HP, Dell and IBM, but the number of IT firms owned by Spanish capital represents 30% of the market, mainly concentrated in small and medium-sized companies.

# Food and beverages

The Spanish food and drink industry's gross production is around €58.6 billion per annum, making Spain the fifth largest EU producer, and production is currently growing by around 4.1% per year. The main sub-sectors are the meat industries (which make up 21.18% of sales value), dairy products (10.53%), animal food (9.51%), wine (7.76%), fats and oils (7.42%), bread, cakes and biscuits (7.21%) and processed fruits and vegetables (6.95%). The other 29% is made up of processed fish, the milling industry, sugar, chocolates and others.

The industry is made up of around 36,000 companies that between them employ half a million people. However, most of these companies are small concerns, with only around 6,000 of them employing more than 10 people. The last 20 years have seen many smaller companies disappear as Spain's full accession to the EU liberated fruit, vegetables and cereals from all restrictions (previously they were subject to import licences from the other European countries). This made it far easier for the foreign market to fulfil the considerable potential for importing selected UK and US-brand foods to Spain, especially cereal products and confectionery.

Although major multinationals such as Nestlé, Coca-Cola, Heineken and Unilever play a substantial role in the Spanish food and drink industry, there are several very large companies with Spanish capital. These include Ebro-Pulva, Campofrío and SOS Cuétara.

Spanish vineyards are the most extensive in the world, although the yield per hectare is comparatively low. Wine represents, on average, 5% of the value of total agricultural production, as compared to 10% in both France and Italy. The main wine-producing regions are la Mancha, Castille, Extremadura and Andalucía, although probably better known to the British palate are the wine and sherry-producing areas of Rioja, Jumilla, Jerez and Málaga.

Beer is becoming more popular, with a negative impact on the wine market. Heineken and United Breweries have brought a much-needed injection of capital to Spanish breweries as well as much new technology and marketing techniques. However, breweries elsewhere in the EU still tend to be more competitive and to produce better beverages more cheaply, which means exports are small. Until recently, transport costs and Spanish tariff barriers had succeeded in alienating the foreign beverage market from Spain but now all the famous international brands are represented, with many being produced under licence in Spain.

Find out more about the food and drink industry from the website of the Spanish Food and Drink Industry Federation – FIAB (www.fiab.es), where it is possible to download a report giving a detailed statistics about the industry's composition and performance; and the Ministry of Agriculture, Fisheries and Food website (www.mapya.es).

**FACT**

■ Heineken and United Breweries have brought a much-needed injection of capital to Spanish breweries as well as much new technology and marketing techniques.

# Mining

The main mining areas of Spain are the north (Asturias) for hard coal and anthracite; and Catalonia, Aragon and Andalucía for lignite. The quality of Spanish coal is poor (low in calorific value) and production costs are relatively high so better quality coal is imported from Poland, Australia and the USA. However, Spain is expanding its home mining industry as the demand for coal has risen and research and exploration operations have discovered new coal sources in Arenas de Rey, Padul, Mallorca and

León. The industry is planning to improve the quality of its coal with new coal-fired power stations and to encourage greater coal consumption by internal transport (Spain has a relatively low proportion of electrified railways). Nuclear energy (and oil imported from Algeria) also makes its contribution to Spain's energy sector. Despite the expansion of home production in coal, Spain will continue to import high quality coal and also to provide a good, ongoing market for advanced mining machinery and equipment imported from abroad.

## Motor vehicles and components

Spain has emerged as a leading country in the automotive industry. It is the world's sixth largest car manufacturer and the EU's third, behind Germany and France. Annual national output amounts to around 2.86 million motor vehicles. The industry is therefore a major sector of the Spanish economy with a 5.7% sector share of the GDP, and employs 11% of the total labour force.

Ever since the 1970s the Spanish motor industry has been almost entirely controlled by multinational companies and production in Spain is carried out by well-known groups such as Renault, Ford, Opel, Mercedes Benz, Peugeot-Citroën, Volkswagen and Nissan. SEAT, owned by Volkswagen, has production plants in Barcelona, Ford has a base in Valencia, Renault are based in Seulte and Citroëns are manufactured in Orense and Vigo. Nissan has plants in Avila, Barcelona and Madrid, and General Motors has a plant in Zaragoza.

This solid manufacturing industry is in close connection with a spare parts and components industry made up of over 900 companies, employing 250,000 workers.

Find out more about this industry from the website of the Spanish Association of Car and Truck Manufacturers – ANFAC (www.anfac.es); and the website of the Spanish Association of Manufacturers of Equipments and Parts for the Automobile Industry (www.sernauto.es).

## Pharmaceuticals

As many as 375 firms (262 of which have manufacturing facilities), employing around 39,000 people, make up the Spanish pharmaceuticals industry. This sector, which makes up 26.4% of the chemical industry in Spain, is made up of fairly small concerns, with only 2% of companies employing more than 1,000 people.

While this industry is not what it once was, it is currently experiencing sustained growth and ranks fifth in Europe. This sector has the advantage of being one of the most innovative in Spain, with enormous expenditure and job creation in research and development. The jobs available in this industry largely require a high degree of professional training.

Foreign investors have a significant presence in Spain, including multinational companies such as Novartis, Pfizer, Lilly, Merck, Bristol-Myers Squibb, Roche, Abbott, Johnson & Johnson and Bayer. Recently Genentech, the leading American biotechnology corporation has set up in Pontevedra and specialises in the production of monoclonal antibodies and cellular structures. Also the British company Glaxo SmithKline, one of the biggest pharmaceutical companies in the world, is in the process of setting up a new pioneering research and development centre in Madrid.

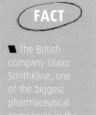

**FACT**

■ The British company Glaxo SmithKline, one of the biggest pharmaceutical companies in the world, is in the process of setting up a new pioneering research and development centre in Madrid.

Find out more about this industry from: www.farmaindustria.es (National Association of the Spanish Pharmaceutical Industry, which publishes an annual report on the industry, plus a series of statistics); www.msc.es (Directorate General for Pharmaceuticals); and www.agemed.es (*Ministerio de Sanidad y Consumo*).

## Retail

Small, family-run shops still dominate the retail arena in most areas of Spain. However, these small privately run family businesses are coming up against increased competition from hyper- and supermarkets, especially since the major changes to the retail laws at the end of the nineties. The Spanish government has played an active role in liberalising Spanish retail and bringing it into line with European standards and legislation. It has adopted measures to increase competition, open up trading hours, control prices and improve consumer rights. Many of the changes are driven by socio-demographic and lifestyle factors, including the development of an out-of-hours culture, growth in the number of working women and falling household sizes. The increasing number of working women has resulted in more family members making purchasing decisions. Fathers, sons and daughters are less likely to opt for the social option of the local shops, but for the convenience of the supermarkets.

The food retailing sector in Spain is now dominated by leading international players such as Carrefour, Lidl, Aldi and Alhold and Tengelmann. Other major chains include Mercadona, Eroski, Auchan and El Corte Inglés.

International companies have also been successful in the restaurant trade. Despite Spain's seemingly impenetrable culture of local, family-run restaurants, the fast-food industry is making steady progress in Spain especially among young people. Leading operators such as McDonalds, Burger King and Pans and Co. have developed strong expansion strategies, covering not only the main cities and tourist areas, but the whole of Spain. Fast food restaurants, especially those who manage to combine both quick service and Spanish culinary culture, are becoming

New industries such as wind farms are offering new investment opporitunties in Spain

a convenient daily solution for the increasing number of Spaniards who dine out of home frequently. Twenty-three per cent of Spaniards eat out regularly and this figure is on the increase. Work is the main reason for eating in restaurants, a trend which has significantly increased due to changing working hours. As more businesses bring their hours of trading in line with much of Europe, the traditional long meal at home with the family is disappearing and workers are opting for the convenience of eating establishments near their place of work. Another factor is the continued strength of the tourism sector, with seasonal visitors demanding a variety of eating establishments during their stay.

Clothing retail is also undergoing a process of change, which has been particularly driven by the increase in disposable income for women. Womenswear outlets have been very dynamic over recent years, as can be seen by the massive international success of the Zara chain. Women with disposable income also tend to buy for their husbands and children, creating a boost to male fashion stores. New boutiques catering for a more affluent, younger clientele and specialising in designer and brand-name merchandise have sprung up around the major department stores and are increasingly appearing in expensive, prime high street locations, which has increased consumer interest.

In general terms, steady growth within the Spanish economy, together with an increase in consumer confidence and personal income, as well as the decline in the unemployment rate, have impacted positively on all areas of retail, providing a promising source of employment for appropriately qualified professionals.

**FACT**

■ New boutiques catering for a more affluent, younger clientele and specialising in designer and brand-name merchandise have sprung up around the major department stores and are increasingly appearing in expensive, prime high street locations, which has increased consumer interest.

## Telecommunications

The liberalisation of Spanish telecommunications in 1997 generated strong investments in the infrastructures and services of telecommunications, and created a remarkable increase in the number of operators, higher speed communications, and a significant diminution of prices. This has been an area of enormous growth over the last few years, increasing by around 13% per annum. The telecommunications industry now employs over 46,000 people in Spain.

The major player in this industry is Grupo Telefónica, the second biggest telecom company in the world, which owns the companies Telefónica de España, Telefónica Móviles, Telefónica Sistemas, Telefónica Data, Movistar and Telefónica Cable. Other companies include Grupo Retevisión, Vodafone, Grupo Sogecable, Cable and Wireless and Jazz Telecom. Competition within the industry is supervised by the Telecommunications Market Commission (www.cmt.es), which produces an annual report (in English) on the industry as a whole.

## Tourism

One of the Spanish economy's most dramatic success stories is the tourist trade. In 2007 Spain played host to 60 million visitors, an enormous amount considering that the indigenous population of Spain is only around 40 million. The annual revenue that tourism brings into Spain is around €46 billion and the tourist trade employs 1.5 million workers, contributing over 12% to the country's gross national product. The industry currently shows no signs of slowing down and in 2002, Spain overtook France for the first time as the most popular holiday destination for UK residents.

Spanish tourism today is a solid, well founded sector which has learnt to grow, consolidate and undertake large investments to improve quality.

Spanish tourism has evolved to meet the demands of 21st century travellers. Although the sun, sea and sand package holidays to Spain are still important, many independent travellers are bagging cheap flights on the no-frills airlines and rather than spending a fortnight on the beach they are taking city breaks, spa breaks and walking holidays; they are visiting vineyards and art galleries and staying in working farms and converted monasteries. This change is partly due to the effects of the low-cost flight revolution. In 2003, Ryanair flew to Spain for the first time. In 2005 it flew five and a half million people to a range of new destinations, and it currently flies to 15 destinations.

However, the changes are also the result of a huge amount of government investment. *The Plan Integral de Calidad del Turismo Español* 2000–2006, or the Spanish tourism integral quality plan, was established by the *Ministerio de Economía* to address the challenges facing Spanish tourism. It was co-ordinated by both the private sector and the public administration and was heavily supported by EU funds. The aim of the plan has been to promote business opportunities in the tourism sector in two ways: firstly by investing in the recovery and regeneration of an already mature Spanish tourism, i.e. the traditional sun, sea and sand holidays based largely around the costas; and secondly by promoting alternative kinds of tourism in new destinations. These include:

- **Sports tourism**, consisting of new golfing, adventure, sailing and skiing ventures
- **City and cultural tourism**, focusing on language courses, museums, gastronomy, heritage sites and festivals
- **Rural and active tourism**, focusing on guest houses in rural areas and the national parks and biosphere reserves
- **Business tourism**, focusing on business meetings, conferences and conventions held in Spain
- **Health tourism**, focusing on beauty treatment and relaxation
- **Residential tourism.** There are already three million second homes in Spain, as well as a million European, non-Spanish residents. It is hoped that the large number of European citizens buying property in Spain will lower the seasonality of the industry.

Find out more about the Spanish tourist industry from: Tourspain (www.spain. info); *Instituto para la Calidad Turística Española* (www.calidadturistica.es).

# REGIONAL EMPLOYMENT GUIDE

The number and type of jobs available will vary from region to region. For example, the communities of Madrid, Catalonia, Valencia, Andalucía, País Vasco and Galicia are usually the areas of strongest growth in employment, and especially graduate employment.

The information provided here gives some idea of the dominant industries and the types of jobs that are most readily available in each area. In each case, several sources of further information on the region in question are given. The press listing is for the regional newspaper in that area which may also be a source of jobs and information. The Chamber of Commerce may be able to provide information and the listing usually gives the details of the largest branch in that region – there will be others in adjacent towns.

## Andalucía

**Provinces:** Almeria, Cádiz, Córdoba, Granada, Huelva, Jaén, Málaga, Sevilla.
**Main city:** Sevilla.
**Regional newspapers:** *El Faro Informacion, Europa Sur* (Algeciras); *Ideal, La Voz* (Almeria); *Andujar Informacion; Antequera Informacion; Arcos Infomacion; Entertainer* (Benalmadena); *Informacion, Diario* (Cadiz); *Chiclana Informacion; Cordoba, El Dia de Cordoba; Estepona Informacion; Ideal* (Granada); *Guadix Informacion; Huelva Informacion; Ideal, Diario* (Jaen); *Diario; Informacion* (Jerez); *Diario, La Opinion, Sur, Sur in English* (Málaga); *El Faro, Ideal* (Motril); *Puerto Real Informacion; Ronda Semanal Informacion; San Roque Informacion; Sanlucar Informacion; Diario, El Correo; Triano Los Remedios; Torremolinos Informacion; Villamartin Informacion.* . A very useful website is http://classified.andalucia.com.
**Chamber of Commerce:** Camara de Comercio Málaga; C/ Cortina del Muelle 23, 29015 Málaga; 952 211673; email info@camaramalaga.com; www.camaramalaga.com.
**Major companies:** Delphi Automotive System España (automotive), Carbonell (food industry), Cruzcampo Grup (food industry), Abengoa Grup (construction), Siderúrgica Sevillana, Alcatel Citesa (telecommunications), Siemens Matsushita Components (electronics), Tioxide Europe (chemicals and pharmaceuticals), Fujitsu (electronics/computers), Visteon (automotive).
**Employment prospects:** The vast region of Andalucía is currently in a phase of expansion. Andalucía is traditionally an agricultural region and the industrial sector is less developed than in other regions. However, in recent years it has been the services sector that has predominated in Andalucía (accounting for around 65% of the workforce), especially with regard to tourism, commerce and transport. The construction sector is very dynamic and continues to grow, giving rise to an unmet labour demand for bricklayers and stonemasons, floor layers and tile setters, heavy truck and lorry drivers, and machine-tool operators.

Although Andalucía is the region with one of the highest unemployment rates in Spain, this is largely due to a lack of a skills and qualifications among the local population. The greatest lack of professional qualifications is to be found in sheet metal and electrical mechanical work, and in tourism and hotels.

Other professions in demand in the region include veterinarians, lawyers, translators and interpreters, sales and marketing department managers, domestic helpers and cleaners, agricultural mechanics and fitters, accounting and bookkeeping clerks and electrical engineering technicians.

**FACT**

■ The construction sector is very dynamic and continues to grow, giving rise to an unmet labour demand for bricklayers and stonemasons, floor layers and tile setters, heavy truck and lorry drivers, and machine-tool operators.

## Aragón

**Provinces:** Huesca, Teruel, Zaragoza.
**Main city:** Zaragoza.
**Regional newspapers:** *El Heraldo de Aragon; El Periodico de Aragon.*

Chamber of Commerce: *Cámara Oficial de Comercio e Industria de Zaragoza*, Pº Isabel la Católica 2, 50071 Zaragoza; 976 306161; email cci@camarazaragoza.com; www.camarazaragoza.com.

Major companies: General Motors (automotive), Adidas España (textiles and footwear), Schindler (mechanical industry), Saica (paper and press), Valeo Térmico (automotive), Lecitriler (automotive), Siemens Elasa (electronics).

Employment prospects: Zaragoza is an important economic centre in Spain, being central to the automotive, mining and machinery industries. Most current industrial job offers concern activities relating to metal work and the manufacturing of capital equipment, such as machinery, cars and products connected with the peripheral car industry such as electronic components, leather, and plastics. While unemployment levels in Aragón as a whole are among the lowest in the country, the evolution in employment has been a little stagnant in recent years. In general there is a dearth of skilled workers, technicians, managers and senior staff to fill the vacancies in industry in the region.

Recent public investment in infrastructure in Aragón has created a positive outlook for employment in this sector as well as in related sectors such as transport, where there are a number of job offers for lorry drivers of all kinds and in logistics and storage.

The job vacancies that have been difficult to fill in recent years due to a lack of applicants include: mechanical engineers, masons, plumbers, public works machinery operators, heavy industry welders, industrial sheet metal workers, lorry drivers, industrial pipe fitters and waiters.

## Asturias

Main city: Gijón.

Regional Newspapers: *El Comercio* (Gijon); *La Voz de Asturias* (Lugones); *La Nueva España* (Oviedo).

Chamber of Commerce: *Cámara de Comercio Oviedo*, Quintana 32, 33009 Oviedo, Asturias; 985 207575; www.camara-ovi.es.

Major companies: Alsa (transportation), Suzuki (motorcycles), Naval Gijón (naval construction), Thyssen Industrie (metallic and mineral products), Hunosa (coal mines), Du Pont (chemical), Fluor Daniel (engineering), Celulosas de Asturias (paper and press), Danone (food), Saint Gobain (glass industry), Limpac Plastics (plastics and rubbers), Tenneco (automotive).

Employment prospects: The two main motors of the regional economy in Asturias are the services sector and the construction sector. Industry is also important in the region, but has witnessed a decline in recent years due to the diminished importance of the region's energy production. However, the outlook is positive for the Asturian labour market. The pace of job creation has speeded up over the last year and unemployment rates have fallen.

FACT

■ The two main motors of the regional economy in Asturias are the services sector and the construction sector.

In the construction sector, there are a dearth of skilled applicants for certain positions such as bricklayers, shutterers, plumbers and pipe fitters and carpenters. This is especially true in Avilés, Grado, Tineo, Infiesto and Lugones. In the western part of Asturias there is a severe lack of forestry workers and loggers. Avilés particularly suffers from a lack of architects and printing workers. In Siero and Lugones there is a demand for drivers of heavy trucks and lorries. The lack of a pharmacological university faculty in the region also means that there is a demand for qualified pharmacists.

## Cantabria

Main city: Santander.

Regional newspaper: *El Diario Montanes.*

Chamber of Commerce: *Cámara de Comercio Cantabria*, Plaza Velarde, 5. 39001 Santander (Cantabria). 942 318000; www.camaracantabria.com.

Major companies: Eléctrica de Viesgo (electricity, water, gas), Teka Industrial (metalliC/ mineral products), Alcatel Cable Ibérica (electronics), Plásticos Españoles (plastics and rubber), Transportes Gerposa (transportation), Edcha España (automotive), Derivados del Fluor (chemicals and pharmaceuticals), Solvay (chemicals and pharmaceuticals).

Employment prospects: The services sector heavily predominates in Cantabria, providing work for around 71% of the region's total employees. This trend is most pronounced in the region's capital, Santander, and in hotels in the coastal towns. Jobs for which vacancies are not filled are mainly cooks, and on a seasonal basis, waiters and head waiters. The catering industry in the region requires responsible professionals who can demonstrate considerable experience in supplies, nutrition and dietetics, international cuisine and the use of new cooking technologies. There is also a professed need for waiters and waitresses with some knowledge of languages, especially English.

There is also a demand for IT professionals in Santander and its hinterland. Most in demand are those with knowledge or experience of new programming languages, databases, local networks and maintenance, as well as programming of applications geared to multimedia.

Other professions in demand in the region include technical and commercial sales representatives, metal workers and operators, welders (especially in the Torrelavega and Camargo district) and drivers and mobile plant operators. The region has a glut of the following trades and professions, making it hard to find difficult: education professionals, administration professionals, healthcare professionals, assembly and manufacturing labourers.

## Castilla-la Mancha

Provinces: Albacete, Ciudad Real, Cuenca, Guadalajara, Toledo.

Main city: Albacete.

Regional newspapers: *La Cerca, La Tribuna, La Verdad* (Albacete); *Lanza* (Ciudad Real); La *Cronica de Guadalajara.*

Chamber of Commerce: *Cámara Oficial de Comercio e Industria de Ciudad Real*, C/ Lanza, 2, Ciudad Real 13004; 926 274444; email info@camaracr.org; www.camaracr.org.

Major companies: Basf Coating (chemicals and pharmaceuticals), Magneti Marelli Ibérica (automotive), Liebherr Ibérica (mechanical industry), Thomson TV España (electronics), Schmalbach Lubeca Pet Cont. Ibérica (chemicals and pharmaceuticals).

Employment prospects: Castilla-la Mancha is an enormous region encompassing a diverse range of industries. Generally speaking, services absorb over two-thirds of the largest enterprises in the region but it is in Cuenca that the greatest concentration of workers is employed within the service industry (69%). In Toledo, the percentage of workers employed in industry (31%) is above the provincial level.

The main industries in the region are foodstuffs, clothes manufacturing, timber, and the production of metal and non-metal mineral products.

Employment opportunities in the region are also diverse. There is a surplus of applicants for jobs requiring low qualifications such as shop assistants, clerks, cleaners and textile workers; but skilled workers have a far greater chance of finding work. In particular demand are specialists in the construction industry, machinery drivers and operators, sheet metal and painting specialists, security guards.

Hotels also occupy a prime position in this region, and this is a sector that continues to grow. There is, therefore, a constant demand for cooks, waiters and waitresses and bartenders. However, such work tends to be fairly seasonal.

## Castilla y León

**Provinces:** Avila, Burgos, León, Palencia, Salamanca, Segovia, Soria, Valladolid, Zamora

**Main city:** Valladolid.

**Regional newspapers:** *Diario de Burgos; Diario de León; El Adelanto, La Gaceta Regional, Tribuna* (Salamanca); *El Norte de Castilla* (Valladolid); *La Opinion de Zamora.*

**Chamber of Commerce:** *Camara de Comercio Valladolid*, Avda Ramón Pradera, s/n, 47009 Valladolid; 983 370400; www.camaravalladolid.com.

**Major companies:** Nissan Vehículos Industriales (automotive), Antolín Irausa Grup (automotive), Siro (food), Rhone Poulenc Animal Nutrition España (chemicals and pharmaceuticals), Fasa Renault Grup (automotive), Michelin (plastics and rubbers).

**Employment prospects:** The vast region of Castilla y León offers a wide range of jobs, the main centres of employment being Salamanca, Zamora, Valladolid, Burgos, León and Soria. The greatest concentration of employment is Valladolid, where 24% of the total workers are employed. However, unemployment is highest in Salamanca and Valladolid. In the region as a whole, the service sector predominates, employing around 60% of workers, whereas industry and construction are less important. Agriculture still plays an important part in the regional economy employing around 9% of the region's workers.

The region as a whole is in need of the following categories of workers: chemists, manufacturing labourers, freight handlers, domestic helpers and cleaners, cooks, waiters, bartenders, bricklayers and postal workers.

## Cataluña

**Provinces:** Barcelona, Gerona, Lérida, Tarragona.

**Main city:** Barcelona.

**Regional newspapers:** *El Periódico de Catalunya, La Vanguardia, Avui* (Barcelona); *Diari de Girona, El Punt* (Girona); *Segre* (Lleida); *Diari de Tarragona; L'Ebre* (Tortosa).

**Chamber of Commerce:** *Cambra de Comerç de Barcelona*, Avda Diagonal, 452. 08006 Barcelona; 902 448448; www.cambrabcn.es.

**Major companies:** Seat (automotive), FCC (construction), Gas Natural (electricity, water, gas), Nissan Motor Ibérica (automotive), Bayer Hispania (chemicals and pharmaceuticals), Basf Grup (chemicals and pharmaceuticals), Nestlé (food), Sony (electonics), Henkel Ibérica (chemicals and pharmaceuticals).

FACT

■ The catering industry in the region requires responsible professionals who can demonstrate considerable experience in supplies, nutrition and dietetics, international cuisine and the use of new cooking technologies.

Employment prospects: Barcelona is a huge industrial centre and port, and the opportunities for work in the city are endless. Over recent years Barcelona has continued to generate employment and has expanded rapidly over the past few years. This has largely been due to a forward-looking local government keen to promote an 'economy based on knowledge and specialisation in the sectors of the future', largely concentrating on information and communication technologies. The services sector clearly predominates in Barcelona, accounting for almost 80% of jobs in the city. Unemployment levels for both the city and Catalonia as a whole are well below the average for Spain. However, Barcelona is a magnet for young people seeking work in the service industries, so those planning to seek work there may find themselves up against a fair amount of competition.

In Catalonia as a whole, analysis of unfilled vacancies from recent years shows that the following jobs are in greatest demand in the area: social workers and assistants, administrative workers, proofreaders and clerks, cashiers and ticket clerks, telephone switchboard operators, waiters, waitresses, bartenders, auxiliary nursing staff, security guards, bricklayers, helpers and cleaners for offices and hotels, freight handlers.

## Extremadura

Provinces: Badajoz, Cáceres.

Main city: Badajoz.

Regional newspapers: *Hoy* (Badajoz); *El Periodico Extremadura* (Caceres).

Chamber of Commerce: *Cámara Oficial de Comercio e Industria de Badajoz*, Avda de Europa 4, 06004 Badajoz, Extremadura; 924 234600; email camarabadajoz@camaras.org; www.camarabadajoz.com.

Major companies: Acorex (agriculture and livestock), AG Siderúrgica Balboa (iron and steel), Alfonso Gallardo (metallic and mineral products), Deutz Diter (automotive), Christian Lay (Trade), Mercoguadiana (agriculture and livestock), Industrias y Promociones Alimenticias (food).

Employment prospects: The labour market in Extremadura lacks specialists in almost every sector, and the only surplus of applications is found in areas not requiring specialisation such as agricultural labourers, factory workers, construction labourers, cleaners, shop assistants. Operations in Extremadura are finding it difficult to find skilled staff in the construction sector, where there is a distinct lack of floor tilers, plasterers, stonemasons, painters, plumbers and electricians among others. There is also a demand for graduates in sectors such as new technologies (for example, technicians, programmers and designers), hotels and tourism (cooks and guides), and, due to new legal requirements, graduates in occupational risk prevention. There is also a demand for doctors, social workers and home-based personal care workers in the region.

## Islas Baleares

Main city: Palma de Mallorca.

Regional newspapers: *Diario, Ultima Hora* (Ibiza); *Es Diari, Ultima Hora Menorca* (Mahon); *Diari de Balears, Diario de Mallorca, El Mundo, Majorca Daily Bulletin, Ultima Hora* (Palma de Mallorca).

Chamber of Commerce: *Cámara de Comercio de Mallorca, Ibiza y Formentera*; 971 710188; email ccinmallorca@camaras.org; www.cambresbalears.com.

FACT

■ Operations in Extremadura are finding it difficult to find skilled staff in the construction sector, where there is a distinct lack of floor tilers, plasterers, stonemasons, painters, plumbers and electricians among others.

Ibernostar Grup (hotels and tourism), Sol Meliá (hotels and tourism), Barceló Grup (hotels and tourism), Riu Hotels Grup (hotels and tourism), Air Europa (air transportation), Gesa Grup (electricity, water, gas) Coflusa (textiles/footwear), Casa Buades (iron and steel).

**Employment prospects:** The Balearic Islands rely heavily on tourism, and in particular German tourism, so the regional economy is vulnerable to changing trends in travel. However, the islands' economy is currently fairly sound, having one of the lowest rates of unemployment in Spain and better employment prospects than the EU as a whole. Low-skilled vacancies are easily filled and the job market for hotel, shop and cleaning staff is fairly saturated. However, skilled workers should find the job market in the Balearics to be fairly prosperous. Those with experience and/or qualifications and those with languages will find that there are numerous vacancies for the following posts: technicians (electricians, plumbers, mechanics, etc.), lifeguards, leisure activity monitors and sport monitors with diplomas, skilled construction workers, skilled hotel workers with languages.

## Islas Canarias

**Main city:** Las Palmas de Gran Canaria.

**Regional newspapers:** *La Voz* (Arrecife); Canaria 7, Island Sun, La Provincia (Las Palmas); El Dia, Fortnightly Tenerife News, La Opinion (Santa Cruz de Tenerife).

**Chamber of Commerce:** *Cámara de Comercio de Las Palmas*; C/ León y Castillo 24, 35003 Las Palmas de Gran Canaria; 928 391045; email informacion@camaralp.es; www.camaralaspalmas.com.

**Major companies:** Unelco (electricity, water, gas), Freiremar (seafood), Binter Canarias (air transportation), Flick Canarias (automotive), Disa Red de Servicios Petrolíferos (petrochemical).

**Employment prospects:** The economy in the Canary Islands is almost exclusively reliant upon tourism. Industry has scarcely any impact in terms of job creation, largely due to the distance from the mainland and the lack of raw materials on the islands. Agriculture is also in decline and is largely dependent on banana production. However, positions for agricultural labourers on the islands often remain unfilled. Despite tourism being of vital importance, the sector is largely saturated and the vacancies that do exist are seasonal. However, jobseekers with specific skills and qualifications in tourism or languages are in demand.

Although the Canary Islands have traditionally been a safe bet for those seeking employment in the construction sector, the recent falls in property prices on the islands and the stagnation of the market across Spain in general have resulted in many new developments being shelved or abandoned, and analysts predict significant construction layoffs in the near future; Spain already has a surplus of almost a million houses, and as Europe's economic future begins to look uncertain, companies are unwilling to invest in new builds.

## Galicia

**Provinces:** Corunna, Lugo, Orense, Pontevedra.

**Main city:** Vigo.

**Regional newspapers:** *Diario de Ferrol; La Opinion A Coruña, La Voz de Galicia, El Progreso* (La Coruña); *Diario de Ponteverda; El Correo* (Santiago de Compostela); *A Nosa Terra, Faro de Vigo* (Vigo).

Chamber of Commerce: *Cámara de Comercio de Vigo*, República Argentina 18a, 36201 Vigo; 986 432533; email camaravigo@camaravigo.com; www.camaravigo. com.

Major companies: Inditex Group (textiles/footwear), Financiera maderera (wood/ furniture), Calvo Group (fish canning), La Lactaria Española (milk), Astilleros y Talleres de Noroeste (naval construction), Coren Group (food), Adolfo Domínguez (textiles/ footwear), Citroen Hispania (automotive), Pescanova Group (food).

Employment prospects: The labour market for Galicia is relatively stable, with moderate but constant growth figures for the economically active population. Most jobs are to be found in Vigo. Citroën's car production plant is based in Vigo and is the largest of its type in Spain. Fishing is also very important to the city's economy. However, most workers in Vigo are employed in the service sector.

According to figures supplied by employment offices in Galicia, the jobs in which there are most vacancies in the region as a whole are bricklayers and construction labourers, waiters, waitresses and bar staff, carpenters, manufacturing labourers, typists and shop assistants.

## Comunidad De Madrid

Regional newspapers: *ABC, Cinco Dias, El Mundo, El País, El Telegrafo, Expansion, La Gaceta de los Negocios, La Razon.*

Chamber of Commerce: *Cámara Oficial de Comercio e Industrua de Madrid*, C/ Ribera del Loira, 56–58, 28042 Madrid; 915 383500; www.camaramadrid.es.

Major companies: Repsol Group (petrochemical), Telefónica Group (telecommuni-cations), El Corte Inglés (department store), Endesa Group (electricity, water, gas), Cepsa (petrochemical), Aceralia Group (iron and steel), IBM España (computers), Saint Gobain (glass).

Employment prospects: Employment prospects for foreigners are fairly high in Madrid, not least because many UK and American companies operate within the city. Madrid has seen a rapid rise in unemployment levels, which jumped by 15% in 2006, although this is due in the most part to an increase in the number of workers coming to the city. According to 2006 figures from the European Commission, the service and construction sectors are the most oversubscribed, and unemployed foreigners make up 13% of Madrid's total unemployed population.

The services sector is far and away the most important in the country's capital, employing around 75.9% of workers, followed by industry (13.8%) and construction (12%). The biggest industries in Madrid are publishing and graphic arts, manufacturing of metal products, furniture making, textiles and clothing.

Recently the greatest demand for employees was in the following sectors: agriculture, architecture and related services, hotels and restaurants, social services, the furniture trade, financial brokerage. There is also a significant need for administrative, managerial and service staff with technical skills, and especially for bilingual business people.

## Murcia

Main city: Murcia.
Regional newspaper: *La Verdad.*

FACT

■ The biggest industries in Madrid are publishing and graphic arts, manufacturing of metal products, furniture making, textiles and clothing.

*Cámara Oficial de Comercio*, Industria y Navegación de Murcia, Plaza San Bartolomé 3, 30004 Murcia, 967 229400; email camara@cocin-murcia.es; www.cocin-murcia.es.

El Pozo (food), Hero España (food), Misiva anvases (bottles, cans), Garcia Carrión (food), GE Plastics de España (plastic/rubber).

Unemployment in Murcia is one of the lowest in Spain, at around 6%. Most jobs in Murcia are to be found within the construction and agriculture sectors, with organic food a rapidly growing offshoot of traditional farming in the area. Murcia is fast becoming a popular destination both for tourists and second-home buyers. This trend has been aided by improved roads and the development of San Javier airport from an ex-military airport with one flight a week to an international airport delivering 1.5 million visitors a year to the region. This demand is set to continue when the new regional airport, close to Corvera, opens in 2009. In terms of construction these developments have led to a shortfall of plasterers, plumbers, electricians, carpenters, concrete placers and finishers, and bricklayers. Increased tourism to the area has also created an unmet labour demand in the services sector. Hotels have problems finding waiters and experienced chefs in the main cities and in the coastal towns. In the retail sector, there is also a demand for shop assistants.

Traditionally agriculture has been of great importance to the regional economy in Murcia and workers are needed in every category, especially around Cartagena, Mar Menor and the Alto and Bajo Guadalentin districts. These mainly seasonal vacancies are often filled by immigrants.

# Navarra

Pamplona.

*Diario de Navarra, Diario de Noticias*.

*Cámara Oficial del Comercio e Industria de Navarra*, C/ General Chinchila 4, Navarra. 948 077070; email marketing@camaranavarra.com; www.camaranavarra.com.

Volkswagen Navarra (automotive), BSH Electrodom España (electronics), Aceralia Transformados (iron and steel), Viscofan (plastic/rubber), Delphi Unicables (automotive), Cementos Portland (cement factory), SKF Española (automotive), Nissan Forklift España (electronics), Sanyo España (electronics).

The regional economy in the *Comunidad Foral de Navarra* has enjoyed sustained growth and consolidation over recent years, leading to an unemployment rate as low as 5.7% (less than the national average). In 2007, unemployment fell again, although job creation is slowing as the construction industry battens down the hatches. Prospects for employment in the region are relatively good. The importance of industry in Navarra cannot be underestimated. It absorbs 28.3% of the total number of employees. The presence of Volkswagen's large factory near Pamplona is of particular importance, employing around 5,000 workers, and promoting related industries in the area. The industrial sector of this region has a high demand for experienced welders and steelworkers, and skilled automation and machine tool workers for both production and maintenance.

In the construction sector, there are vacancies for skilled jobs such as stonemasons, plasterers, plumbers, gas installers, electricians and earthmoving plant operators.

In the agricultural sector workers are required for seasonal work during harvesting of horticultural products and fruit in the La Ribera del Ebro area. Workers are also needed for the agri-foodstuffs industry during the harvesting season.

## La Rioja

Main city: Logroño.

Regional newspaper: *La Rioja*.

Chamber of Commerce: *Cámara de Comercio de Rioja*, C/ Portales 12, 26001 Logroño, La Rioja; 941 248500; email camararioja@camararioja.com; www.camararioja.com.

Major companies: Delphi Componentes (automotive), BTR Sealing Systems Ibérica (plastics/rubber), Bodegas Dinastia Vivanco (wine), Tobepal (paper and press), Barpimo (chemicals and pharmaceuticals), Ramodín (metallic and mineral products).

Employment prospects: The level of unemployment in Rioja is, at around 6.9, almost two percentage points below the national rate, so prospects for jobhunters are good. The best prospects for employment are in the following sectors: construction, foodstuffs and beverages industry, manufacturing of metal products, machinery and equipment, hotels, retail trade, real estate, health and veterinary care, social services.

Generally speaking, the common denominator in all sectors is that there is a possibility of employment for those workers with qualifications as technicians or advanced technicians and who are familiar with the profession in question. Vacancies that have been recently advertised in employment offices and have proved difficult to fill include technical and commercial sales representatives, stonemasons and related construction workers, beauticians and related workers, plumbers, welders, and pipefitters.

## Comunidad Valenciana

Provinces: Alicante, Castellón, Valencia.

Main city: Valencia.

Regional newspapers: *Alacant Express, Informacion, La Verdad, Weekly Post* (Alicante); *Costa Blanca News* (Benidorm); *Mediterraneo* (Castelllon); *El Temps, Las Provincias, Levante* (Valencia).

Chamber of Commerce: *Cámara Oficial de Comercio, Industria y Navegación de Valencia*, Poeta Querol 15, 46002 Valencia; 963 103900; email info@camaravalencia.com; www.camaravalencia.com.

Major companies: Famosa (toys), Reebok Leisure (textiles/footwear), Francisco Ros Casares Group (iron and steel), MB España (toys), Porcelanosa Group (construction), Johnson Controls España Group (automotive), Plastic Omnium (plastic/rubber), Ford (automotive), Ube Industries (chemicals and pharmaceuticals).

Employment prospects: Commercially speaking, Valencia is the most important city on the Spanish Mediterranean coast. Recent years have seen a huge amount of investment and modern development and, as Spain's third largest city, it has a thriving business district and over 40 international trade fairs are staged in the city every year. In the region as a whole, industry is quite diversified, with the following products being predominant: furniture, transport equipment, textiles, metal products.

**FACT**

■ Commercially speaking, Valencia is the most important city on the Spanish Mediterranean coast.

In Castellón the manufacturing of ceramics and chemicals associated with ceramics is prevalent. In Alicante, the most dynamic sectors are textiles, shoes, paper, rubber and plastics, foodstuffs and construction materials.

Of course the services sector is of enormous importance in this region, with tourism especially creating huge numbers of (mainly seasonal) jobs along the Costa Blanca and the Costa del Azahar. Commerce, transport and communications are also important service industries in the region. In agriculture seasonal jobs are still being offered during harvest time, relating to the picking of citrus fruits, fruit and vegetables.

In recent years, there has been a shortage of labour supply in the Community of Valencia in the following areas: construction (stonemasons, electricians, plumbers, painters), industry (welders, lathe operators, mechanics and fitters, carpenters, car mechanics, electronic technicians), services (lorry drivers, hairdressers, waiters, qualified cooks, administrative clerks with languages).

## País Vasco

**Provinces:** Alava, Gipuzcoa, Vizcaya.
**Main city:** Bilbao.
**Regional newspapers:** *Berria* (Andoain); *Deia, El Boletin de Bolsa Economia y Finanzas, El Correo, Gara* (Bilbao); *El Diario Vasco* (San Sebastian).
**Chamber of Commerce:** *Cámara de Comercio de Bilbao*, Gran Via 13, 48001 Bilbao; 944 706500; email atencionalcliente@camarabilbao.com; www.camarabilbao.com.
**Major companies:** Gamesa (aeronautics), Tubos Reunidos (iron and steel), Sidenor (iron and steel), Petróleos del Norte (petrochemicals), Bridgestone Firestone Hispania (plastic/rubber), GKN Transmisiones España (automotive), Pepsi Cola España (food).
**Employment prospects:** Although the region has been through an economic slump in recent years, there is still a labour demand in certain areas. Industry has traditionally been the sector that has experienced problems filling all the jobs it needs. For example the region has a strong demand for welders, steelworkers, sheet metal painters, electronic technicians, and mechanics and fitters. There is also a shortfall of crafts workers within the construction industry, including stonecutters, marble cutters and in quarries. These positions are being filled by the numerous foreign workers seeking work in the sector, and by self-employed workers from other Spanish provinces.

Agriculture still plays an important part in the region's economy and specialised workers such as tractor drivers, machinery operators, cattle workers and, in the coastal regions, fishermen, are in demand. In terms of short-term work, the two harvests in Álava (potato-picking and grape-picking) requires a large work force for a short period of time.

Much of the foreign labour in the region is absorbed by the services sector, mainly in jobs in hotels and domestic service. For example, there are regularly jobs available for cooks and kitchen helpers, waiters, carers for the elderly and childcare workers. However, the Basque country has historically been the first region in Spain to succumb to recession and the slowest to recover, and has always struggled with unemployment.

# ■ DIRECTORY OF MAJOR EMPLOYERS AND FIRMS WITH UK OFFICES

## Accountancy

Aced Asesores SL: Barcelona; 934 877142.
Argent International Asset Management SL: Huelva; 959 322125;
www.argentinternational.com.
Asesoria Economica SC: Málaga; 902 995993; email info@asec.es; www.asec.es.
BDO Audiberia: Madrid; 914 364190; email bdo@bdo.es; www.bdo.es.
Bove Montero y Asociados: Barcelona; 932 180708; www.bovemontero.com.
Cook-David: Barcelona; 678 702369; www.spainaccounting.com.
Deloitte: Madrid; 915 145000; www.deloitte.es.
Ernst & Young: Madrid; 915 727200; www.eyi.com.
Eurocontrol Asesores Contables y Tributarios SL: Las Rozas; 916 406138;
email andrew_hall@infonegocio.com.
Grant Thornton España SA: Madrid; 915 763999; www.audihispana.com.
KPMG: Madrid; 914 563400; www.kpmg.es.
Martin Howard Associates: Barcelona; 932 022534; www.mhasoc.com.
PriceWaterhouseCoopers: Madrid; 915 684400; www.pwc.es.

## Agriculture and food processing

Agricola Mar Menor SL: Murcia; 968 574025.
Agricola San Blas de Ribaforada SC: Navarra; 948 864086.
Bodegas Age SA: La Rioja; 941 293500.
Bodegas Viveda SA: Ciudad Real; 926 322351.
Bodegas Pirineos: Barbastro (Huesca); 974 311289; email info@bodegapirineos.
com; www.bodegapirineos.com.
Coca Cola España: Madrid; 913 481700; www.conocecocacola.com.
Codorniu SA: Barcelona; 935 051551; www.codorniu.com.
Compañia de Bebidas Pepsico S.A: Madrid; 913 829300; www.pepsi.es.
Conservas Napal SA: Navarra; 948 867060; email comercial@conservasnapal.com;
www.conservasnapal.com.
Cooperativa Agircola Virgen del Rocio: Cádiz; 956 387242; www.vrocio.com.
Fortuna Frutos Ltd: Kent, UK; 01892 837587; www.fortuna-frutos.com.
Freixenet SA: Joan Sala 2, 08770 Sant Sadurni D'Anoia; 938 917000;
email freixenet@freixenet.com; www.freixenet.com. Cava producers.
Heineken España SA: Sevilla; 917 149200; www.heineken.es.
Heinz Iberica SA: Madrid; 913 692207; www.heinzweb.com.
Juan Castillo Ltd: Herbery Lodge, Blackminster Business Park, Evesham,
Worcestershire, WR11 7RE; 01386 833091.
Kellogg España SA: Madrid; 913 768030.
Kraft Foods España SA: Madrid; 913 254750; www.kraft.es.
Lola España Ltd: Manchester, UK; 0161 873 8001; www.lolaespana.com.
Mahou Fabricas de Cerveza y Malta San Miguel Group: Madrid; 915 269100.
Moreno SA: Cordoba; 957 767605; email Moreno@morenosa.com;
www.morenosa.com.

Pescanova Alimentación SA: Pontevedra; 902 999333; www.pescanova.es.
Primaflor SA: Kent, UK; 01622 695314; www.primaflor.com.
Ruinart España SL: Madrid; 917 818957; www.ruinart.com.
Snack Ventures SA: Barcelona; 934 840500; www.fritolay.com.
Sucesores de Arturo Carbonell SL: Murcia; 968 643745;
email jesus@suc-carbonell.com; http://suc-carbonell.com.
Unilever Foods España SA: Leioa; 944 818600; www.unilever.es.
Wrigley España SA: Gran Canaria; 928 202740.

## Architecture and interior design

Broadway Malyan España, Designers y Arquitectos SL: Madrid; 913 750049;
www.broadwaymalyan.com.
FM Arquitectos: Madrid; 915 770664; www.fmarquitectos.com.
Pilgrem I Blasco Arquitectes Associats SL: Barcelona; 933 181371;
email rosebud@coac.es.

## Banking

ABN Amro Bank, NV Sucursal en España: Madrid; 914 236900;
www.abnamro.com.
Banco Bilbao Vizcaya (BBA): Bilbao; 915 375312; www.bbva.es.
Banco de Finanzas e Inversiones, SA: Madrid; 902 152595;
www.fibancmediolanum.es.
Banco Finantia Sofinloc SA: Avda Menéndez Pelayo 67, 28009 Madrid;
902 575057; www.bfs.es.
Banco Inversis Net SA: Madrid; 914 001400; www.inversis.com.
Banco Santander Central Hispano: Madrid; 915 581111;
www.gruposantander.es.
Banco Urquijo SA: Madrid; 914 366900.
Bancoval SA: Madrid; 913 609900.
Bank of Scotland: Madrid; 917 454150; www.bankofscotland.com.
Barclays Bank: Madrid; 901 100055; www.barclays.es.
Caixa de Galicia: A Coruña; 981 187000; 981 188179; email info@caixagalicia.es;
www.caixagalicia.es.
Ibercaja CAMP de Zaragoza, Aragón y Rioja: Zaragoza; 976 767595.
JP Morgan Bank SA: Madrid; 915 161200; www.jpmorgan.com.
Lloyds TSB Bank: Madrid; 902 024365; www.lloydstsb.es.
HSBC: Madrid; 914 566100; www.hsbc.es.
Royal Bank of Scotland: Madrid; 917 015110; www.rbs.co.uk.
SG Hambros Bank and Trust (Gibraltar) Ltd: London, UK; 020 75973000;
www.sghambros.com.
Unicaja: Málaga; 952 138494; www.unicaja.es.
Banco de Sabadell SA: Barcelona; 902 323777; www.sabadellatlantico.com.

## Business consultancy firms:

Advance Communication SL: Barcelona; 932 387140;
www.advancecommunication.biz.

Essor Professional Development Group: Barcelona; 933 179551; www.essorpdg.com.
English Business Unit SA: Barcelona; 935 088783; www.ebuspain.com.
Iberian Management Consultants: Madrid; 915 326639.
International Intergest S.R.L: Barcelona; 934 674910; www.intergest.es.
Isidro López Molina: Barcelona; 933 220443.
IVC SA: Barcelona; 934 817200; www.ivc.es.
Schubert Consulting SL: Barcelona; 936 756260; www.schubertconsulting.com.

## Chartered surveyors

Costa Blanca Surveyors: Alicante; 966 460063; email nmrobinson@ terra.es.
Cushman & Wakefield Healey & Baker: Barcelona; 932 724495.
FPD Savills España SA: Madrid; 913 101016; www.savillspain.com.
Gibson's Chartered Surveyors: Gibraltar; 952 794628; email info@gibsons-spain.com; www.gibsons-spain.com.
Gleeds Ibérica SA: Madrid; 914 356949; www.gleeds.com.
Hamptons International: Marbella; 952 933825; email info@hamptonsfielding.com; www.hamptons-international.com.
Jones Lang Lasalle España SA: Barcelona; 933 185353; email santiago.gutierrez@eu.joneslanglasalle.com; www.joneslanglasalle.es.
Knight Frank: Madrid; 915 773993.
Property Works: Mallorca; 971 6333297; email info@propertyworksonline.com; www.propertyworksonline.com.
Survey Spain: Campbell D Ferguson, Chartered Surveyors, Marbella, Costa del Sol; 650 599701; email campbell@surveyspain.com; www.surveyspain.com.
Sylvia Kemmeren Sales: Mallorca; 971 891614; email sks@campion-mallorca.co.uk; www.campion-mallorca.co.uk.
Contact the Royal Institute of Chartered Surveyors (0870 333 1600; email contactrics@rics.org; www.rics.org) for further information.

## Construction and property services

Bellwater SL: Madrid; 914 261915.
Contratas y Obras Empresa Constructora SA: Barcelona; 934 142814; www.contratasyobras.com.
F. Gutierrez Bustinduy: Pontevedra; 86 223661; www.geocities.com/fgbustinduy. Slate exporters.
FPD Savills España SA: Barcelona; 932 724100; www.savills.com.
Gleeds Iberica SA: Madrid; 914 356949; www.gleeds.com.
Grupo Proalpe SL: Murcia; 968 181587; www.grupoproalpe.com. Construction company.
Grupo Infinorsa: Madrid; 914 264200; email infinorsa@infinorsa.com; www.infinorsa.com.
Industrias Roko SA: 981 631159; www.rokagar.com.
Jones Lang Lasalle España SA: Madrid; 917 891100; www.joneslang lasalle.es.
Juan Porsellanes SA: Enfield, Middlesex EN1 2PE; 020 8367 0050; email info@montepego.co.uk; www.montepego.co.uk.

CB Richard Ellis SA: Madrid; 915 981900; www.cbre.com.
Riel Chyc SL: Alicante; 902 411111; www.rielchyc.com.
Watts and Partners Consultores SL: Madrid; 914 355459;
www.wattsandpartners.com.

# Estate agents

Aguirre Newman Barcelona SA: Barcelona; 934 395454;
www.aguirrenewman.es.
Cushman & Wakefield Healey & Baker: 917 810010; Madrid;
www.cushmanwakefield.com.
Estudio Perez Galdos, SL: Valencia; 963 0853006; www.espegal.net.
Gesinar: Madrid; 914 549700; www.gesinar.es.
Gran Sol Properties Europe Ltd: Lancashire; 01772 825587;
email info@gransolproperties.com. Spanish office: Alicante; 965 835468;
email gspspain@terra.es. www.gransolproperties.com.
Images of Andalucía (Sierra Doña Ana Real SL): Málaga; 655 910194;
www.imagesofandalucia.com.
Imisa SA: 932 160501/972 652528; www.grupoimisa.com.
Inmobiliaria ABC International: Alicante; 966 691778;
www.abc-*inmobiliaria*.com.
Inturdor SA: 971 167088; www.inturotel.com.
Macdonald GMDC: Málaga; 952 863819.
Procosona SL: 950 431680; www.procosona.com.
Promociones Begosal SL: Alicante; 966 726181; www.fidalsa.com.
Torremas Internacional SL: Alicante; 966 761086.
United European SL: Canary Islands; 922 753406/7; www.ueproperties.com.
Names of other agents dealing in Spanish property can be obtained from the
National Association of Estate Agents, Arbon House, 21 Jury Street, Warwick
CV34 4EH; 01926 496800; email info@naea.co.uk; www.naea.co.uk (select the
international section).

# Insurance

Axa Aurora Iberica SA: Málaga; 956 630261.
Brumwell–Bevan: Barcelona; 932 384499; www.brumwell.com.
Direct Seguros: Madrid; 902 400800; www.directseguros.es.
Intasure: Croydon; 0845 1111 0670; Spanish contact nos 900 110670;
email enquiries@intasure.com; www.intasure.com.
Knight Insurance Centres: Málaga; 952 660535; email kibsa@knight-insurance.
com; www.knightinsurance.com.
London General Insurance Co Ltd Sucursal en España: Barcelona; 932 419830;
932 009724.
Ocaso SA: London; 020 7377 6465; www.ocaso.es.
Prosperity Standard Life SA: Barcelona; 932 928181; www. prosperity.es.
Right Way Insurance and Finance: Málaga; 952 934963; email info@rightwaysl.
com; www.rightwaysl.com.
Zurich España: Barcelona; 933 067300; www.zurichspain.com.

## Law firms

Ashurst Morris Crisp: Madrid; 917 456819; www.ashursts.com.
Christopher Lee: Barcelona; 934 150677; www.domenechmascaro.com.
Clifford Chance SC: Barcelona; 932 442200; www.cliffordchance.com.
De Cotta McKenna y Santafé Abogados: Málaga; 952 527014.
Dechamps Abogados: Málaga; 952 903270; www.dechamps*abogado*s.com.
DLA Piper Rudnick Gray Cary Spain SL: Madrid; 913 191212.
Ecija y Asociados Abogados SL: Madrid; 917 816160; www.ecija.com.
Eshkeri and Grau SCP: Tarragona; 977 249960; www.solicitorsinspain.com.
Fernando Scornik Gerstein: London; 020 7404 8400; email cedilla@fscornik.
co.uk; www.scornik-gerstein.com. Offices in Madrid, Barcelona, Gran Canaria (2),
Lanzarote, and Tenerife.
Gomez-Acebo y Pombo Abogados: Madrid; 915 829100;
www.gomezacebo-pombo.com.
Graham Consitt: Alicante; 965 791158.
Iura Despacho Jurídico SL: Málaga; 952 477108; 952 477116; www.iura.es/.
Jausás: Barcelona; 934 150088; email law@jnv.com; www.jnv.com.
KPMG Recursos, SA: Barcelona; 932 532900; www.kpmg.es.
Linklaters SL: Alicante; 965 980080.
Lovells: Alicante; 965 144105.
Marti y Associats: Barcelona; 932 016266; www.martilawyers.com.
Michael Soul y Asociados Abogados: Málaga; 952 900323; email mjs@
spanishlawyers.eu.com; www.spanishlawyers.co.uk.
Monero, Meyer and Marinel-lo Abogados SL: Barcelona; 934 875894;
www.mmmm.es.
Mullerat: Avda Barcelona; 934 059300; www.mullerat.com.
Simmons and Simmons: Madrid; 914 262640.
Thomas Cooper and Stibbard: Madrid; 917 816670.
Wilton and Partners SL: Barcelona; 934 150957; www.wilton-es.com.
A list of English-speaking lawyers may be provided by the Law Society (113
Chancery Lane, London WC2A 1PL; 020 7242 1222; www.lawsociety.org.uk).

## Manufacturing and marketing

Almirall Prodesfarma SA: Barcelona; 932 913091; www.almirallprodesfarma.es.
Amifarma SA: Barcelona; 932 172425. Chemical products.
Antonio Pernas SA: La Coruña; 981 641082.
BASF Española SA: Barcelona; 934 964000.
Biocosmetics SL: Madrid; 913 071554.
CadburySchweppes España SA: Zaragoza; 976 332262;
www.cadburyschweppes.com.
Confecciones Carmen Melero SL: Pontevedra; 986 292949.
Construcciones y Auxiliar de Ferrocarril: Madrid; 915 756403; www. caf.es.
Central FM English Radio: Málaga; 952 566256; www.centralfm.com.
Ezpeleta SA: Pontevedra; 986 293922; www.ezpeleta.com.
Fansa SA: La Rioja; 941 440000.
Formica Española SA: Madrid; 916 839900.
Gorina SA: Sabadell; 937 450720; www.gorina.es.

ICI España SA: Fogars de la Selva; 937 669800; www.ici.com.
Industrias Gabar SL: Valencia; 962 257035; www.gabar.es.
Industrias Roko SA: La Coruña; 981 631163.
KLK Electro Materiales SA: Asturias; 985 321850; www.klk.es.
Loramendi SA: Alava; 945 242462; www.loramendi.com.
Malta SA: Vizcaya; 946 250050.
Manufacturas Tompla SA: Madrid; 918 872200.
MG Rover España SA: Madrid; 916 789000; www.mg-rover.es.
Michelin España Portugal SA: Valladolid; www.michelin.es.
Nestlé España SA: Barcelona; 934 805100; www.nestle.es.
Productos Dolomiticos de Málaga, SA: Málaga; 952 450450;
www.prodomasa.com. Chemical products.
Proyectos Limited: Barcelona; 678 050479; www.proyectos.co.uk.
Repsol YPF SA (UK): 24 Grosvenor Gardens, London SW1W 0DH; 020 7730 2044;
www.repsolypf.com. Petrol and gas.
Rolls-Royce International Ltd: Madrid; 917 356736; www.rollsroyce.com.
Sammic SA: Guipuzcoa; 943 157236; www.sammic.com.
Sanyo España SA: Barcelona; 937 182000; www.sanyo.es.
Shell Española SA: Madrid; 915 370100; www.shell.com.
Sur in English Newspaper: Málaga; 952 649741; in the UK: S.S.M. Global Media,
First Floor, Premier House, 1 Cobden Court, Wimpole Close, Bromley, Kent BR2 9JF;
020 8464 5577; www.surinenglish.com.
Telemark-Spain SL: Leon; 902 360737/0800 8353 6275;
www.telemark-spain.com.
TI Group Automotive Systems SA: Barcelona; 932 419696;
www.tiautomotive.com.
Tubos Reunidos SA: Alava; 945 897100; www.tubosreunidos.com.
Unilever España SA: Madrid; 913 983000.
Union Quimico Farmaceutica SA: Barcelona; 934 879477; www.uquifa.com.
United Biscuits Iberia SL: 935 719100.
Waymouth-Peter Michael: Girona; 972 835111.

## Shipping, transport and freight

Christian Salvesen Gerposa SA: Cantabria; 942 352352; www.salvesen.com.
Crown Relocations SL: Madrid; 914 850600; www.crownrelo.com.
Fleetway Ltd T/A Mudanzas España: London; 020 8767 2050;
www.mudanzaespana.com.
Framptons Iberica SL: Parets del Valles; 935 731337.
Hijo de Alfredo Rodriguez Ltda: Puerto de Almeria; 950 243044.
Papi Transitos SL: Alicante; 965 206233; www.papitransitos.com.
Transcotex SL: Barcelona; 932 964408; www.transcotex.es.

## Travel and tourism

British Airways SA: Madrid; 913 769625; www.britishairways.es.
Iberia Airlines: London; 020 8222 8900; www.iberia.com.
Jet2: Barcelona; 932 265157; www.jet2.com. Low cost airline.
Lifestyle Barcelona SL: Barcelona; 932 702048; www.lifestylebarcelona.com.

Paradores de España (Keytel Int.): London; 020 7402 8182; www.keytel.co.uk.
Sol Melia Hotels: London; 020 7391 3000; www.solmelia.com.

## Other

Aceites Borges Pont SA: Lérida; 973 501212; www.borges.es. Olive oil exporters.
AIS Diseño SL: Barcelona; 932 151568; www.ais-bcn.com. Design consultancy.
Burberry Spain Retail SL: Barcelona; 932 158104; www.burberry.com. Fashion retailing.
Currencies Direct: London; 020 7813 0332; www.currenciesdirect.com. Currencies exchange house.
Expo Global: Almería; 950 851141;6; www.saloninmobilario.biz. Events organiser.
Fragil SA: Barcelona; 933 893451. Decoration and design.
Iberpress España: Madrid; www.johnsons-spain.com. Import/export of newspapers and magazines.
Ketchem/SEIS: Madrid; 917 883200; www.ketchum.com/spain. Public relations.
Masters-Robert: Barcelona; 934 284357; www.bobmastersphotography.com. Photography for advertising, design, corporate, multimedia and web.
Marcus Evans España Ltd: Barcelona; 933 934600; www.marcusevans.com.
SCR Relaciones Publicas SA: Barcelona; 934 342920; www.scr-rrpp.com.
Source 23 Internet Design and Consultancy SL: Barcelona; 932 155392; www.source23.com.

# Starting a Business

# ■ INTRODUCTION

Recent estimates suggest that around half of British people who move to Spain choose to set up their own businesses or work as self-employed craftsmen or professionals.

There are a number of reasons why this new generation of young entrepreneurs has grown up alongside the more traditional expatriate community, but perhaps the most important of these is the sense of freedom associated with making the move to Spain, of breaking free of the shackles of a nine-to-five working day and becoming your own boss; of working less but enjoying a culturally richer lifestyle. Those who make the move will be in good company. There is a deep-seated entrepreneurial spirit in Spain. A recent survey on Spanish work habits shows that over 60% of Spaniards would prefer to be their own boss than to be a salaried employee. The reality of the situation in Spain reflects this attitude, as 94% of all businesses in Spain are *micro-empresas* with fewer than 10 salaried workers and 52% of businesses have no salaried workers at all. Spain is traditionally a country of small companies, sole traders and family-run businesses.

The fact that there is already an enormous community of foreigners is also a tremendous advantage. You only have to glance at the classifieds of an English-language newspaper such as *Sur* or the *Costa Blanca News* to see the plethora of English-speaking plumbers, electricians, translators, hairdressers, satellite television engineers, dog groomers and every other imaginable service. The number of foreigners emigrating to Spain shows no signs of diminishing so, for the foreseeable future, there will always be a demand for those offering, in English, the kinds of services to be found at home.

Many foreigners choose to tread the well-worn and perilous path of opening a bar, restaurant or café in an attempt to turn Spain's seemingly constant festivities into a way of life. It should be noted, however, that some find that being on the other side of the bar does not quite meet their expectations, and given the level of competition, many struggle to make a living. The most successful businesses run by foreign entrepreneurs in Spain are those that fill a necessary gap in the market and cater to both the expatriate market and the Spanish market. The key to success in Spain is creativity and an original approach, coupled of course with an enormous amount of preparation.

Spain has modernised incredibly quickly over the last few decades, graduating from the rural backwater of Western Europe to the world's ninth largest industrial power. Spain's economic achievements of recent years are remarkable and although the economic outlook is uncertain across Europe as a whole, Spain shows signs of being prepared to weather the coming storms. This is encouraging for potential investors who choose to operate in Spain.

Although Spain once presented a maze of complex procedures and formalities to those wishing to start their own business, this situation has improved immeasurably. A persistent rationalisation of Spanish bureaucracy is taking place, and a wide range of information and advice is available to foreign businessmen to help them succeed. Whether your aim is to provide a business service for expatriates or to find a more general niche in an economy that is still developing and diversifying, as long as you have a creative approach and a little business acumen, your prospects of establishing a successful business in Spain have never been better.

**TIP**

■ The most successful businesses run by foreign entrepreneurs in Spain are those that fill a necessary gap in the market and cater to both the expatriate market and the Spanish market. The key to success in Spain is creativity and an original approach, coupled of course with an enormous amount of preparation.

## Why start a business in Spain?

**The economy.** The Spanish economy has grown consistently over the past decade, with 2006 marking its 13th consecutive year of growth, and prospects for the future are solid. Spain has the eighth largest economy in the OECD with a modern network of transport and telecommunications, a highly qualified local labour force and growth above the EU average. It is also the second most important tourist destination in the world, and the most visited country by Britons. It is second only to the US in terms of income generated by tourism.

**Success of small businesses.** The number of new business startups is currently increasing by around 3.8% each year, whereas the number of businesses going into administration has reduced by around 10% in recent years. The large expat population means a wealth of opportunities for business and self-employment.

**Low fixed costs.** Spain is a fairly cheap country in which to do business. Almost all of your fixed business costs will be lower than in the UK, including the cost of renting/buying premises, utilities, and staff wages. However, the initial costs involved in setting up a business are much higher than in the UK.

**Encouragement for businesses.** Last year 123,484 new businesses were established. This is, at least in part, due to the important efforts of the Spanish government to promote small and medium-sized businesses and procure the most favourable business environment for their success. The procedures for incorporating a company have also been dramatically simplified.

# Residence regulations for entrepreneurs

Residence permits are no longer issued to EU citizens who wish to become self-employed or start a business. Neither do EU nationals need a work permit to work in Spain.

The situation for non-EU nationals is considerably more complex. They require both a residence visa (*visado de residencia*) and a work permit. There is a special classification of residence visa for those wishing to start a business and non-EU citizens must be able to demonstrate to the consulate in their own country that they have the funds to invest in their Spanish business. Often they must also demonstrate that they will provide work for Spanish nationals. Indeed it is not unusual for the Spanish consulate to insist that the investment is made, the employees are hired and that the business is ready to operate before they will grant the visa. Given the

Reliable trades people are in demand across Spain, although construction has slowed in 2008

Spanish Ministry of Labour and Social Affairs' concern for job creation, the more Spaniards you intend to employ, the more favourably the visa application will be regarded. The granting of the visa is subject to the approval of the work permit by the Spanish authorities, which usually takes several weeks.

There are 10 different types of work permit for non-EU nationals. Those intending to be self-employed or start a business need only concern themselves with classes D and E. Initially most people receive a temporary type D permit, which lasts for one year and may limit the holder to a specific activity or geographical area. After the initial year, this may be renewed and replaced with a two-year type D permit. Finally, when this permit expires, the self-employed may receive a type E permit, also valid for two years.

# ■ SOURCES OF INFORMATION

## Government sources of information

The bureaucracy associated with starting a business in Spain can be both onerous and tedious. With a complex array of documents and procedures, and a dreary wait of around four months, it is no surprise that in previous years only 10%–15% of those who started the procedure managed to successfully incorporate their company. However, the difficulties involved in establishing a business presence in Spain can be minimised simply by taking professional advice and talking to the right people.

The Spanish government actively encourages investment. There are several good governmental sources of information available to the potential entrepreneur, and they will be happy to deal with initial enquiries and provide general orientation:

## Government information sources

**General Directorate for Trade and Investment** at the Spanish Ministry of Economy, Madrid; 913 493983; email buzon.official@sgiex.dgcominver.sscc.mcx.es.

**Commercial Office of the Spanish Embassy, Invest in Spain:** Office for Economic and Commercial Affairs, Spanish Embassy, 66 Chiltern Street, London, W1U 4LS; 020 7467 2387; email buzon.official@londres.ofcomes.mcx.es. Good source of advice and information for those in the UK.

**Spanish Institute for Foreign Trade:** ICEX, Madrid; 913 496100; email icex@icex.es. Publish the official 'Guide to Business in Spain', available online at www.investinspain.org.

**UK Trade and Investment:** British Embassy, C/ Fernando el Santo 16, 28010 Madrid; 917 008200/913 190200; www.uktradeinvest.gov.uk.

Although their main remit is to help British companies who are looking to trade with Spain, or to set up a branch in Spain, they will be happy to help individual businessmen, providing information and contacts and generally directing people towards relevant associations, trade fairs and publications.

On a more local level, there are numerous organisations offering advice on business creation and setting up in a self-employed capacity, including employment services, autonomous community authorities and even your local *ayuntamiento* (town hall).

It is also advisable to contact the local Chamber of Commerce (details in the Regional Employment Guide on page 279) to benefit from their expertise on the economic conditions of the local area.

If you are thinking of buying an already established business then you will have far less red tape to deal with, but you are running a completely different set of risks and will benefit enormously from professional advice, especially considering the pitfalls of Spanish leasehold law and the rate at which businesses change hands on the costas.

**TIP**

However, it is always a good idea to take legal advice specific to your business idea either from a gestor or a lawyer.

## Useful official websites

**www.ceoe.es:** Spanish Confederation of Entrepreneurial Organisations.

**www.cepyme.es:** Spanish Confederation of Small and Medium-Sized Enterprises.

**www.ipyme.org:** General Directorate of Policy for Small and Medium-Sized Enterprises.

**www.camaras.org/publicado:** High Council of the Spanish Chambers of Commerce, Industry and Shipping.

**www.camaramadrid.es:** Chamber of Commerce, Madrid.

**www.investinspain.org:** General Directorate for Trade and Investment at the Ministry of the Economy.

**www.spainbusiness.com:** Spanish Embassy Office for Economic and Commercial Affairs in the USA.

**www.imade.es:** Madrid Development Institute.

**www.icex.es:** Spanish Institute of External Trade.

**www.vue.es:** *Ventanilla Unica Empresarial* (one-stop shop for business).

www.mir.es: Ministry of the Interior.
www.mcx.es: Trade and Tourism Secretary of State.
www.map.es: Ministry of the Public Administrations.
www.mineco.es: Ministry of the Economy.
www.europa.eu: European Union.

# Professional assistance

*Gestores* are particularly useful for negotiating the procedures relating to starting and registering a business. If you go to them with any questions about permits, licences, or insurance, for example, they will explain the correct procedures to follow and often suggest shortcuts that you may not otherwise have found. With a signed letter of authorisation, the *gestor* will also act in your name to carry out tortuous procedures such as presenting necessary papers at relevant departments.

Similarly a *gestor* is very useful when buying a business as they can pass a qualified eye over the contract and also investigate whether the business has all of the necessary licences and whether there are any outstanding debts in the name of the business that would be transferred to the new owner.

A good *gestor* can be a valuable asset. It is very worthwhile to establish an ongoing relationship with them so that you have a useful contact whenever a problem arises. *Gestores* can also offer a range of other useful services such as accounting, assistance with completing tax returns and bookkeeping. Some even act as small business advisors.

The fees of a *gestor* are generally reasonable, especially considering the amount of confusion they will save you. However, as the quality of the service that they provide can vary considerably and they do not always do a professional job, it is worth asking around for personal recommendations.

## Lawyers

Inevitably the prospective businessman will at some point during the setting up, buying, or running of the enterprise, need specialist legal advice from a qualified, English-speaking lawyer. This applies no matter how large or small the business is.

> 'The earlier you seek professional legal advice regarding your business venture, the better. If you don't, the consequences can be terrible. A client of ours came to us with what he thought was a small legal problem. He had been on holiday to the Canary Islands many times and noticed that there were no ice cream vans there. Spotting a potential money-spinner he bought a fleet of vans and a warehouse to store the ice creams and then entered into supply contracts with Italian and Spanish ice cream distributors. When he came to us, he was having problems obtaining the licence. We did some investigation and found that the reason that he couldn't get a licence was that it is in fact illegal to sell ice cream from vans in the Canaries! As a result he lost a lot of money.'
> **John Howell and Co. solicitors and international lawyers**

Do not confuse the lawyer (*abogado*) with the notary public (*notario*). The *notario* is a public official in charge of officially registering certain events such as property purchases and the incorporation of a company. The notary's fees are fixed by law.

If you are willing to spend the money, it is possible to give a lawyer power of attorney to deal with all the necessary procedures involved in establishing a business presence. It is well worth investing the money in seeking professional advice, because the authorities are becoming increasingly vigilant and will not hesitate to close down or heavily fine a business that does not have the correct papers to trade.

Lawyers' fees can vary enormously in Spain, depending on the amount of work involved. It is best to ask in advance and try to agree on a fee or a percentage before choosing a lawyer.

There are a number of UK law practices with knowledge of Spanish company law and some international law firms with offices in Spain. However many small businesses will be best served by a local Spanish practice and although these are numerous, English-speaking lawyers are still fairly rare. What follows is a selection of UK lawyers and English-speaking lawyers in Spain who deal with commercial law. A full list for your local area can be obtained from the British Consulate.

## UK legal practices

**Baker and Mckenzie:** 020 7919 1000; www.bakernet.com; Spain office: Paseo de la Catellana 33, Edificio Fenix Planta 6, 28046 Madrid; 912 304500.

**Bennett and Co. Solicitors:** Cheshire SK9 6JP; 0870 428 6177; www.bennett-and-co.com; Associated offices throughout Spain.

**Fernando Scornik Gerstein:** Holborn Hall 193–197, High Holborn, London WC1V 7BD; 020 7404 8400; email cedilla@fscornik.co.uk; www.scornik-gerstein.com. Also has offices in Madrid, Barcelona, Gran Canaria (two), Lanzarote, and Tenerife.

**Florez Valcarcel, Lawyer and Notario:** 130 King Street, London W6 0QU; 020 8741 4867. Notary public and licentiate with over 35 years' experience in Spanish law.

**John Howell and Co Solicitors and International Lawyers:** Holborn Hall 193–197, High Holborn, London WC1V 7BD; 020 7061 6700; email info@lawoverseas.com; www.lawoverseas.com. Team of English and European lawyers specialising purely in overseas work.

**The International Property Law Centre:** Suffolk House, 21 Silver Street, Hull; 0870 800 4565; email stefanol@maxgold.com; www.internationalpropertylaw. com. Contact senior partner and solicitor Stefano Lucatello, an expert in the purchase and sale of Spanish, French, Italian, Portuguese, Cyprus, Bulgarian, Turkish, Dubai, Goa and the Cape Verde Islands property and businesses, and the formation of offshore tax vehicles and trusts.

## Spanish legal practices

**Adarve Corporacion Juridica:** C/ Presidente Alvear 5, 1°, Las Palmas de Gran Canaria; 928 361072; email info@adarve.com; www.adarve.com.

**Becker-Cid Abogados:** Chantal Becker-Cid, Madrid office: C/ Ayala, 4–3° izda., 28001 Madrid; 915 750544; Marbella office: Travesía Carlos Mackintosh s/n, Edif. Puerta del Mar, Portal A 7°4, 29600 Marbella; 952 861850; email chantal@becker.jazztel.es.

**Consult Card Law Office:** C/ del Capitan 12, 29640 Fuengirola, Málaga; 952 463081.

**Delgado Canovas, Juan Bautista:** Alameda de Cervantes 1, 30800 Lorca, Murcia; 968 467996.

**Gabernet and Blanco Abogados:** Benalmádena-Costa; 952 446456;
email gabernetblanco@teleline.es.
**Gomez, Acebo y Pombo, Ignacio Alamar:** G.V. Germanias 49, 46005 Valencia;
963 513835; www.gomezacebo-pombo.com.
**Martin Bruckhaus:** C/ Castanos 22, 5B, 03001 Alicante; 965 161606;
email abogados@abogados.de.

# ■ IDEAS FOR NEW BUSINESSES

The type of business that you choose will depend on a range of factors, such as whether you decide to buy an existing business or start a new one from scratch, whether you decide to cater for the tourist market, the expatriate market, or the local market, and your own personal skills and interests. Starting a business in Spain requires a good deal of determination and initiative and making a go of it will entail thorough preparation and planning, hard work and a healthy dose of luck.

Many people feel more comfortable setting up a service for other foreigners, but you cannot afford to ignore the local market completely. There is a risk that you simply will not have enough customers during the low tourist season, and even in high season any serious downturn in the tourist market could leave you struggling. Blending in with the Spanish and catering for their tastes will invariably be a more enriching experience, but it depends heavily on where you choose to establish your business. If, for example, you choose a town like Javea where around two-thirds of the population are British, then you may well wish to capitalise on your 'foreignness'. Ultimately, though, your business will succeed or fail on the basis of what you are rather than your nationality.

The procedures involved in opening a particular type of business in Andalucía may differ enormously to opening the same business in Madrid. The Ventanilla Unica Empresarial (one-stop shop for business) website has a useful search engine for each region and each type of business. To access this go to www.vue.es and click on Biblioteca de Trámites (procedures library). Here you can enter your region followed by the type of business you wish to start and view the most recent regulations.

Each type of business has its own specific set of regulations and procedures for starting up. Unfortunately Spain's overly bureaucratic regime delegates overall responsibility for these procedures to the autonomous communities.

## Be creative

In some lines of business and in some areas of Spain, the competition for trade is so great and the number of customers so greatly reduced out of season that businesses close within months of opening up; bar and restaurant owners can work horrendously long hours just to scrape a living and do not have the time to enjoy the sunshine just outside their front door; and some businesses are simply killing themselves off by undercutting to the point of making a loss, just to entice customers away from the competition.

The expatriate community, especially along the costas, will furnish you with any number of horror stories about unsuspecting foreigners who came to start a business in Spain with the sun in their eyes and lost everything. There are also a small but significant number of financial advisors, particularly along the costas, who are willing to capitalise on foreigners' lack of knowledge of Spanish business and tax procedures, so it is important to be certain that you can trust the people who you do business with.

To avoid these potential pitfalls, you need to be a little bit creative in your choice of business. The tourism and service sectors are the obvious business choice for most people who want to live the holiday lifestyle by the beach; there is no need to learn Spanish because your customers will speak English; and you will able to benefit financially from the fact that tourism is still booming in Spain, even as many other industries are slowing down. All of these things may well be true, but the saturation of trades and services in resort areas is very common, and often the only people who are making money are the estate agents buying and selling businesses and the landlords taking a cut every time the leasehold on their property changes hands. There are simply too many bars, restaurants, and shops catering to the tourist market in the resort areas, and not

enough customers to go around, particularly in the winter months. This is not to say that such a business is not viable, but simply that a new business will need to have a unique selling point to distinguish it from the competition, and that potential entrepreneurs should always do some comprehensive market research before rushing into anything.

It is important that entrepreneurs think carefully about their motives for starting a particular type of business.

It is important to maintain a reasonable balance between 'living the dream' and good business sense. Many people make the mistake of going into a business of which they have very little experience, a notion which they probably would not even contemplate in their home country.

The most important consideration when deciding on the type of business you will open is whether or not it is viable. Is there is a market for your product or service and will you be able to compete against similar products or services in the area? An innovative business, or a business catering to a previously untapped market in Spain, will always prove to be more lucrative in the long run.

# Tourism

Tourism is booming in Spain. In recent years, Spain has overtaken France to become the most popular holiday destination for UK residents and around 60 million tourists visit every year, providing the Spanish economy with an annual revenue of €46 billion. It is the second most visited country worldwide, and the tourist industry shows no signs of flagging. Not only has the government (supported by EU funds) invested in regenerating its already mature tourism sector (sun, sea and sand) but

You should never open a rural bed and breakfast because you would like to be a guest at one, nor should you open a bar because you enjoy drinking (a shocking number of foreign-owned bars close because the landlord has been drinking the profits). If you do, the reality of the hard work involved in either venture will be a horrible blow.

it is also promoting alternative forms of tourism in new destinations, for example, rural, sports, business, health and cultural tourism. There are plenty of new business opportunities springing up.

Rural tourism is an area that has particularly blossomed in recent years. The traditional beach holiday will always be popular with tourists but for some, the crowded resorts, the heavy traffic of the coastal roads and the late-night noise of youthful revellers have lost their appeal. Radically improved transport systems in the interior of the country have allowed the backwaters of Spain to enter the limelight and demand for hotels and other services in areas of natural beauty and tranquillity is increasing.

## Camping and caravanning

There are around 740 *campings* or *campamentos turisticos* in Spain, which receive around six million guests per year, and the number of guests choosing to stay at campsites has been on the rise over recent years (especially as many local authorities have now prohibited 'wild' camping). One thing to consider is that this is a highly seasonal business, with most sites closing for the winter months.

The best place to start if you are planning to set up a campsite is the Spanish Federation of Campsites (*Federación Española de Empresarios de Camping y Centros de Vacaciones* – FEEC, www.fedcamping.com). In Spain campsites are highly regulated and each region has its own specific rules. You can find full contact details for the FEEC office in your region on www.fedcamping.com.

## Hotels and guesthouses

A fair number of hotels and guesthouses in Spain are run by foreigners. As with a bar or a shop, a hotel business can be bought and sold separately from the building, which is then rented. Those who buy a property and decide to turn it into a hotel or guesthouse will have to obtain an *autorización de centros hoteleros* from their *ayuntamiento*, who will inspect the property to ensure that it is suitable for guests.

A useful source of advice for the hostelry industry is the *Federación Española de Hostelería* (913 529156; www.fehr.es).

## Rural bed and breakfasts

More and more property owners are setting up rural accommodation facilities (*alojamiento rural*) as the backwaters of Spain begin to enter the limelight. Rural properties can be very cheap, and with a bit of work can be converted into B&Bs and

> 'It was an advantage taking over an existing business because I already had customers who had been coming for years and years. That gives you a head start, but after that it's your responsibility to keep the clients. If they all run away, then you know that you are doing something wrong!'
> **Rita Hillen runs a small hotel in Torremolinos**

guesthouses, and grants are often available for building work on rural properties. This is a highly seasonal business and not likely to generate a massive income, but there are opportunities to supplement your income by setting up as a mountain biking, hiking, fishing, or horseriding centre.

Rural accommodation is highly regulated in Spain and each region has its own legislation. For regularly updated information from all of the regions, visit www.toprural.com/propietario/legislacion.cfm.

## Sports and adventure tourism

The Spanish government is keen to promote alternative types of tourism, and sports tourism is specifically listed as being ripe for investment. Spain's climate, its mountainous topography and 5,000km of coastline make it the ideal location for sporting holidays. On the coasts sailing, fishing, diving and windsurfing are becoming increasingly popular, and in rural areas trekking, rock climbing, descending rivers and air sports are all taking off. For those with the enthusiasm for sports and a little entrepreneurial spirit, there are plenty of opportunities to be found.

## Tourist attractions

There will always be a market for keeping the growing number of visitors to Spain entertained. Tourist attractions of any kind usually require a huge amount of investment, although you may find the municipal authorities to be encouraging towards new enterprises that help to bring visitors to the area.

# Eating and drinking

An enormous percentage of foreigners moving to Spain choose to make their living running a bar, restaurant, café or nightclub for tourists and expats. In the resort areas of the Costa Blanca and the Costa del Sol, it is hardly possible to take a step without encountering a British bar with Tetley's on tap or a café selling a full English breakfast. In such areas the market is completely saturated, and buying a business could be the fastest possible route to bankruptcy.

Despite all of this, there are many success stories, and the right amount of planning, preparation and research can lead to a prosperous and happy lifestyle in the hospitality industry. With so many bars, cafés and restaurants in Spain, it is unlikely that you will have to start a business from scratch, a visit to any of the

**Philippe Guémene** is a Frenchman who runs the Crocodile Park on the Costa del Sol

'The local council were keen on the idea because it encourages tourism. The land here is municipal, so they gave us the lease for 50 years. In return they take a percentage of the entrance fee rather than a fixed rent. A tourist attraction is quite a seasonal business. This is something that you have to take into account. So we are quite lucky that our rent is a percentage of our takings as it means that we pay the council less when trade is slow,'

> **Jos Arensen,** a business consultant on the Costa del Sol, estimates that in certain areas 90% of new bar and restaurant businesses fail within months of setting up. If you want to make a go of it, research the area and the competition very, very carefully before buying, and try to find a way of distinguishing your business from the competition. The reality of running a bar in the sunshine often involves working incredibly long hours and struggling to make a profit.

commercial estate agents will yield a wide selection of businesses for sale. For further advice and orientation, contact the Spanish Federation of Hostelry (Madrid; 913 529156; email fehr@fehr.es; www.fehr.es).

# Information technology and e-commerce

The lure of living in Spain is even greater for those who have the luxury of being able to operate their business from anywhere in the world, and some surveys suggest that as many as 30% of the British working in Spain are involved in IT. Spain has rapidly caught up with the European market leaders in terms of technological developments, billions have been invested in communications and Spain is now a sophisticated, well equipped and modern country. Broadband access is now fairly cheap and is widely available in urban areas. Recent laws in Spain have established certain legal regulations regarding information services and electronic business, dealing with issues such as copyright, the protection of personal

data, business registration and tax. You can find these in English on the website of the Spanish Economic and Commercial Affairs Office in the United States (www. spainbusiness.com).

# Agriculture

Despite the massive shift to urban areas that has taken place over the last 40 years, agriculture is still a mainstay of the Spanish economy and employs around seven per cent of the labour force. Spain is the world's largest producer of olive oil and Spain's vineyards are the largest in the world (60% larger than even France's). The Spanish government is keen to diversify agricultural production and over recent years Spain has become one of Europe's largest organic food producers, generating produce worth €173.9 million per year. The number of organic farms rose by 10% between 2001 and 2006. Increasing numbers of foreigners are taking advantage of Spain's reputation for high quality wines and setting up their own vineyards. Running a commercially viable vineyard requires an enormous amount of investment of both time and money and it can take several years to start making a profit.

Farming in Spain will probably not reap vast financial rewards. Farmers have been particularly badly hit in recent years by falling prices and drought. There is particular concern about the future impact on agriculture of new EU resolutions on water use. However, land is very cheap by British standards, and can start from as little as €2,000 per hectare. Farming also creates opportunities for sidelines such as plant nurseries, and landscape gardening. Cortijos and Fincas (farmhouses) in attractive rural areas are also in great demand as B&Bs. The Spanish authorities welcome those with agricultural skills, a sense of entrepreneurial spirit and a commitment to live in and contribute to rural communities. There is a range of grants and incentives available to farmers. For further details contact the Ministry for Agriculture, Fisheries and Food (Servicio de Información Administrativa, Ministerio de Agricultura, Pesca y Alimentación; 913 475368; www.mapa.es).

Read more about the trials and tribulations of a foreigner running a farm in Spain, Michael Harvey's story on page 13.

# English teaching and translation

Teaching English is a well-trodden path for newcomers to Spain. Most EFL teachers come to Spain primarily to travel and experience the culture for a few years, but for those who decide to make a career of it, opportunities abound to start up your own school, or to work as a freelancer (*autónomo*). Despite the glut of English language centres in Spain, the Spanish interest in and need for English continues unabated, and the industry is adapting to the changing requirements of the market. Language schools continue to attend to the massive demand from students and young adults just out of university keen to improve their CVs, but more and more academies and agencies are springing up to serve the language needs of company clients.

English schools are comparatively easy to set up as the only bureaucracy you need concern yourself with is the opening licence. Language schools also have the advantage of having low overheads (all you really need are premises, teachers, books and stationery).

The translation market place is very competitive, and unless you are completely bilingual, it is not worth kidding yourself that you can make a living. Those setting

**FACT**

■ Despite the glut of English language centres in Spain, the Spanish interest in and need for English continues unabated, and the industry is adapting to the changing requirements of the market.

themselves up as translation freelancers usually have qualifications in an area of specialisation such as law, finance, engineering or medicine, as well as fluent Spanish.

## Property-related businesses

There are three million second homes in Spain and of these 1.2 million belong to foreigners. Since 1997, property prices in Spain have risen by 170%. This booming market has created a vast number of business opportunities. These include setting up as an estate agent, property management companies (who manage the properties of absentee landlords), gardening and maintenance services, and of course private rentals. However, it is now becoming clear that the astronomical price rises seen in Spain are unsustainable; in 2007, many areas saw property prices stagnate, and some regions even saw the first price drops for over a decade. The fear is that investors will begin to offload their properties, adding to the glut of empty homes already on the market and putting further pressure on the industry. Those who would like to work in the property market in Spain would be wise to keep themselves informed as to the outlook for the industry.

Renting out property is one of the more obvious ways for second-homeowners to exploit their recurring visits to Spain. Terms and conditions of rent agreements and the tax implications of renting out second homes are discussed in full on page 119.

**TIP**

■ Property in the north will only be viable as a holiday home through July and August; June can actually be quite cold in this part of the country. In contrast, however, the holiday season in the south extends from spring through to the end of autumn, by virtue of the weather, which consequently involves higher property prices.

## Shops and services

Spain's growing economy is in part fuelled by a continued increase in household consumption, helped by low interest rates, a steady decrease in unemployment and rising wages. The retail sector is a particularly buoyant part of the Spanish economy and offers a wealth of business opportunities. Despite the influx of chains and supermarkets, Spain still has one of the highest percentages of independent retailers in Europe, especially when it comes to food.

Many entrepreneurs have chosen the route of setting up shops to sell goods imported from the UK to homesick Britons who miss their Marmite and digestive biscuits. There is also a market among the local population for everyday British items that appear quite exotic to the Spanish.

The vast number of British expats in Spain has created a market for every imaginable service in English, including builders, carpenters, electricians, plumbers, piano tuning, removals, TV installation, signwriters, insurance, central heating specialists, car sales and mechanics, kennels and catteries, hairdressers, and lawyers, to name but a few. If you have experience providing a service elsewhere, there is no reason why it should not translate to the expatriate market in Spain, many of whom are uneasy about employing the services of the Spanish due to the language barrier. Once you have established a reputation and begun to grapple with the language, you should also be able to offer such services to the local population.

## ■ START OR BUY A BUSINESS?

One decision that you will have to make before deciding on the type of business that you want to establish is whether to start up from scratch or to buy an existing

> 'Existing businesses come with too much baggage, such as differing management styles, décor, staff policies and a possibly undesirable customer base. People find that it takes them a lot of hard work, changing things around, before they get it right. Starting a business from scratch allows you to establish the business exactly as you want it, from the outset'.
>
> **International legal expert John Howell**

business. There are pros and cons to both options, see table below. The reality is that it is quicker and easier to buy an existing business but this has to be balanced against the fact that when buying you are limited to the businesses that are on

## Starting *v.* buying

| Advantages of buying an existing business | Advantages of starting a new business |
|---|---|
| Most businesses fail within the first two years of operation. Existing businesses have already gone through this difficult period and hopefully established a good reputation, recognised products, loyal clientele, proven management techniques, a place in the market and a clear and visible profit margin. | The business will be entirely your own project – you are free to open exactly the business that you want to open, where you want to open it and you are free to run it exactly as you wish. It will not have any of the baggage that goes with buying an existing business. |
| Existing businesses involve less paperwork. Having bought the business you simply need to transfer the licence to your name. Legal fees are much lower and you should be up and running in a matter of weeks. | All of your options are still open. There are a number of legal entities available, which allow you to minimise your personal liability. |
| **Disadvantages of buying an existing business** | **Disadvantages of starting a new business** |
| It is very difficult to value an existing business. How do you know how much the 'intangible assets' such as client base and reputation are really worth? Many people fail to keep proper tax records and their official accounts may bear little resemblance to the reality. | Start-ups can fail due to a host of reasons that could not possibly have been foreseen and most new businesses take around a year or even more to show a profit. During the initial period, all your time energy and funds must be invested into the business. You may need to cover the business's expenses without taking a salary for yourself. |
| Your choice of business is limited to those on the market. Quite often, especially in the coastal resorts, these businesses are for sale because they are struggling to survive in a saturated market. | Starting a new business involves a lot of bureaucracy, paperwork and hence legal fees. Even if you decide not to incorporate a company, you could find yourself waiting six months or so for the town council to approve an opening licence. |

sale, you have a greater chance of being targeted by conmen and you may buy a business that has very little chance of success because the account books you saw were pure fiction.

Of course, balanced against this is the fact that the legal fees relating to starting from scratch are much higher, and it can take much longer.

Ultimately, it will come down to a purely personal decision based on the type of business that you wish to establish. If the business you hope to start is fairly original and there is nothing like it on the market, then you will have no choice but to start from scratch.

# ■ HOW TO START A NEW BUSINESS

## Advice and assistance

### Chambers of commerce

The network of chambers of commerce in Spain offers a variety of information-based services to the potential entrepreneur. However, bear in mind that these can vary in terms of the services offered, the quality of those services and the ability to speak English not only between autonomous communities but also between individual chambers.

All of the chambers of commerce offer an information service (*servicio de creación de empresas*) for those who are thinking of starting a business. They will be able to advise you on all aspects of business creation, from the types of legal entity that can be formed to the different incentives available locally for business creation. The chambers will also be able to help you to research the market before you make your business plan. Usually these services are completely free, although occasionally you may be charged a small administration cost.

While all chambers of commerce will be able to offer advice and orientation to potential entrepreneurs, those chambers that include a *Ventanilla Unica Empresarial* (VUE, one-stop shop for business) will also guide them through the processes involved in incorporating and registering a business. Further information on the network of VUEs is provided below.

Chambers of commerce offer another service for the creation and development of business in the area, known as the *Instituto Cameral de Creación y Desarollo de la Empresa* (INCYDE). The INCYDE foundation is financed by the European Social Fund and offers free advice and personalised assistance to people wanting to set up a company and also to those who wish to set up as self-employed. Included in this service is support with complex procedures such as making a business plan. The foundation also offers special programmes for certain groups including women, the long-term unemployed and the disabled.

The INCYDE provides ongoing support for entrepreneurs once they have established their business enterprise. There are around a hundred consultants attached to the foundation who travel around the country visiting businesses and offering free advice regarding their development and consolidation.

General advice about the network of chambers and the services that they offer can be obtained from the High Council of the chambers of commerce (*Consejo Superior de Cámaras de Comercio*, Madrid; 915 906900/906974; email info@

cscamaras.es). To locate your nearest Chamber of Commerce visit the website www.camaras.org, click on *buscador de cámaras* and select your region.

## Ventanillas unicas empresariales

(One-stop shops for businesses). For years the process of establishing a business presence in Spain for both Spaniards and foreigners alike was characterised by the need to invest a great deal of time and patience into visiting a vast array of different offices, all with inexplicable opening hours and lingering queues. The rationalisation of this process, has been aided greatly by the development of the network of *Ventanillas Unicas Empresariales*; an integrated system providing future entrepreneurs with information and advice. What makes this service so innovative is that all the facilities for setting up a business are provided in a single location, precluding the need to travel great distances and produce an inordinate number of duplicated documents. It should also reduce set-up costs as the service is government-sponsored and therefore free.

The VUE can help with the following procedures:

- *Obtaining municipal licences:* Opening licence, licence for minor work on the premises, licences for tables, chairs and umbrellas for bars and restaurants, etc.
- *Fiscal obligations:* Obtaining the CIF (company tax identification number), registering for IAE (tax on business activities), registration at the *Agencia Tributaria* for tax purposes etc.
- *Labour and social security obligations:* Registration of workers for social security, making sure that you are covered under the prevention of occupational risks regulations.

Row of lettuces

> 'The VUE is the product of a great deal of collaboration, combining representatives from the Chamber of Commerce, the Treasury and the Ministry of Labour and Social Affairs. We can provide, in one physical space, co-ordinated advice relating to starting any kind of business and most of the necessary administrative procedures to create a small to medium-sized business. All the customer has to do is change seats!'
> **Pilar Solana Elorza, – coordinator of the VUE in Madrid**

There are now 26 such offices in Spain, and between them they have facilitated the creation of more than 9,300 businesses and have dealt with over 44,000 enquiries. There is also a virtual online VUE, which provides detailed information and help for those wishing to set up a business, and a 'virtual adviser'. However, the site is only available in Spanish (www.ventanillaempresarial.org).

The system is not yet perfect, as the offices are targeted at helping only those businesses that fall within the local area. So far only twelve of the 17 autonomous communities are included in the scheme, leaving important areas such as Catalonia and Galicia without a similar service. The network of VUEs also appears not to have grown since 2005. Furthermore, the service makes no language concessions to foreign entrepreneurs and if your language skills are not up to it, you will have no

### Ventanilla Unica Empresarial

Visitors to a *Ventanilla Unica* go through three separate phases:

- **Information and guidance.** This area acts as a 'first filter'. Entrepreneurs are pointed in the right direction, based on their requirements and provided with basic information on starting businesses.
- **Advice.** A personal adviser then studies the business plan and following a personal interview, gives an assessment of the project and a range of alternatives. Advisors provide entrepreneurs with information about the suitable legal form for their business, labour obligations, private financing and government aid and subsidies.
- **Formalities.** Suitable projects are then forwarded to the procedure management centre, where the officer-in-charge, in close cooperation with representatives of the tax and social security authorities and the regional and local authorities, will co-ordinate all of the procedures needed to set up the business.

choice but to employ the services of a translator. Contact details for the 26 current offices are on www.ventanillaempresarial.org, click on oficinas. The website also says which areas and organisations are covered by the scheme. There is a central number you can call for general advice: 902 100096.

# Researching the market

Whatever the size of a business, making a comprehensive study of the proposed market is the best way to avoid failure and disappointment. Good market research is necessary for the entrepreneur to ascertain who are the potential consumers for his product or service, both their quantity and their qualities. This will include information on the target population's location, needs and tastes, buying power, age and sex. This information is also very useful when deciding how to target your marketing strategy.

However, clients and consumers only make up around half of the market research. It is also necessary to make a thorough study of the competition. The type of questions that need answering include:

- Who are the market leaders and what are the reasons for their success?
- Which businesses in the sector are having difficulties and what are the causes?
- How can we offer our products in a form that is perceived as more attractive than the competition?
- Which products perform similar functions to ours or satisfy the same need?
- Which businesses offer products or services that are complementary to ours and is collaboration possible?

Finally, a good study of the market should include information on possible suppliers of materials or stock for your business. Often suppliers can be an important source of information regarding the characteristics of the market.

If there is a deficient market, then it really is necessary to abandon the project before you've even started, or at least modify it dramatically. It is sensible to put as much time and effort as possible into identifying your potential customers, suppliers and competition.

There are a number of specialised market research companies who will do the work for you, but they are expensive and, for a smaller business, usually unnecessary, given the amount of information that is publicly available and on the internet. The type of research that you do and the questions that you ask will vary enormously depending on the business. If, for example, you are starting a country hotel, you need to consider the variables affecting the number of visitors you are likely to have such as the traffic throughput, the weather conditions, and local attractions. If your business is fairly small-scale, all this information will be available simply by asking local businessmen and observing trade in the area.

If your business is on a larger scale, you may need to do some more in depth investigation. A good place to start for general information is the local Chamber of Commerce (see above). Some of the better equipped chambers, such as those in Madrid and Zaragoza, will be able to carry out a full study of the geographical area and the level of competition within it, although they may well charge you for a full market study (*estudio de mercado*). Smaller chambers may only be able to give you a general guide and offer advice on further sources of information.

> 'It is far better to spend time seeing what you are going to do before rushing into setting up a company. Otherwise, you could get caught up in all the bureaucracy before you fully understand the market. You have to remember that it is a different country and that you are an immigrant. It takes time to do even the basic things and you cannot use previous experience at home as a basis for what you think other people will spend their money on in a completely different market.'
>
> 'Spain has some of the best business schools in the world, so there is no shortage of skilled young entrepreneurs. Don't see it as a market ripe for the taking. Live here for a while and try to understand the way the markets work before starting a business.'
>
> **Peter Lytton Cobbold, Masia Rentals near Barcelona**

Consumer associations, trade publications and trade fairs and exhibitions are all good ways of investigating the market, and your local Chamber of Commerce or the British Embassy in Spain will supply details of these. If you are setting up in Spain as a professional, then the professional college (*colegio*) which you join will be able to tell you exactly what other similar businesses are operating and where.

## Making a business plan

**FACT**

■ Spain's decentralised system of government means that some of the legal steps will vary between the autonomous communities, so it is vital that you seek advice that is specific to your particular area. The procedures may also differ depending on the type of legal entity that you choose to form although there are few differences in the legal steps for incorporating an A or an SL.

Producing a business plan is not obligatory for new businesses as it is in France, nor will it guarantee your business success. However, what it will do is to force you to examine the viability of the business proposal in a realistic way. According to John Howell and Co solicitors and international lawyers, one of the main reasons for people going bust is that they do not have a realistic business plan. It will also provide you with a useful document to present to third parties when for example asking for the opinion of a business advisor, looking for private investment or applying for public subsidies, and also when looking for collaborators for the business. Even if you are planning to take over a business that is already up and running, the business plan will help you to consider the logical and viable steps for development in the future.

It will involve a great deal of work, speaking to potential clients, gathering information about the competition, making a projection of all the possible costs that the business will have to confront, and of the capital needed to start up. Maximising the depth of your investigation should mean minimising the risks involved later on.

A mistake people often make, even if subconsciously, is that they fool themselves. They are very optimistic about their income and tend to minimise their projected outgoings. Even if you are realistic about everyday outgoings, you should also leave yourself a buffer zone to cope with any unexpected expenditure. It may well be worth seeking the help of a qualified accountant (*contable* or *asesor fiscal*) or even a *gestor* to help you to avoid these pitfalls and to make sure that your plan follows an accepted format and is realistic. In the UK, solicitors John Howell and Co. (020 7420 0400; www.lawoverseas.com) have a lot of experience drawing up business plans in Spanish and in the format expected by Spanish banks and other institutions.

# Necessary steps to establish and incorporate a new company

To create a new business entity from scratch, perhaps the most important prerequisite is an enormous amount of time and patience. It is often necessary to visit a vast range of offices and officials, such as the lawyer, the national tax agency or *hacienda*, and the social security office. David Searl, author and broadcaster on Spanish law, suggests that the procedures associated with starting a business may

| Costs involved in setting up an ordinary SL or SA | |
|---|---|
| **Stamp duty** | **1% of capital contributions** |
| Share capital (minimum) | €3003 (SL) / 25% of €60,101 (SA) |
| Certificate of company name | €12 |
| Company registration | Approx. €150 – fees are assessed on the capital investment and may not exceed €2,181. |
| Legal fees | Min. €1000 |
| Opening licence | Price depends on a number of factors, such as the location and size of the business premises. |

include as many as 57 different steps. For this reason, he estimates that around 40% of businesses remain unlicensed.

However, the whole frustrating process will be far more palatable if you make use of an experienced professional. There are a great number of qualified and English-speaking lawyers and *gestores* who will guide you through the apparently impenetrable web of bureaucracy.

## Step 1 – Pre-registration of the company name

The first step on the path to obtaining the deed of incorporation is to register the name of the company at the commercial register (*Registro Mercantil Centro*). Having decided on a name, you need to ensure that no other company has the same, or a similar name and to obtain a certificate documenting this (*Certificacion Negativa del Nombre*; CNN). The cost of this certificate currently stands at around €12. This process may seem fairly minor, and indeed should only take about forty-eight hours, due to a new simplified procedure. However, without the certificate it is impossible to proceed.

The *Registro Mercantil Central* can also be checked online and in English on www.rmc.es/default_ing.htm. The site allows you to consult existing names and submit new ones. It is also possible to find your nearest office.

## Step 2 – Application for the taxpayer's ID number (NIF)

Before you can open a bank account in the company's name, you need to register with the central tax agency, known as the *Hacienda*, or more correctly as the Agencia *Tributaria*. Here you will receive the *Numero de Identificación Fiscal*, which identifies the new company for tax purposes. It is possible to apply for the NIF online at www.aeat.es. Otherwise, the owners of the company or their legal representatives should contact the Tax Authorities' Office corresponding to the address where the company intends to be incorporated. You can find full contact details for your local *Hacienda* at www.aeat.es/agencia/direC/ .

You will be provided at this time with a provisional tax number. Once the company has been fully registered in the Mercantile Registry, it must obtain the definitive NIF within a maximum period of six months from the issuance of the provisional number.

## Step 3 – Deposit

To incorporate a company you need to decide on the amount of capital with which the company will be formed. There are established minimum capital amounts depending on the type of legal entity chosen (see *Which business structure?* page 324). For an SL all of the minimum capital of around €3003 must be paid in, and for an SA 25% of the €60,000 minimum must be paid in. This capital must be deposited in a bank account made out in the name of the company, and for this you will receive a certificate – the *Certificado del Desembolso Efectuado*. It is mandatory to obtain this certificate before a company can be incorporated.

## Step 4 – Execution of the public deed of incorporation

The deed of incorporation must be signed before a Notary Public. The following fundamental documents must be submitted to establish the company, within the eyes of Spanish law:

**FACT**

■ There are established minimum capital amounts depending on the type of legal entity chosen

- a certificate registering the name of your company
- a certificate from the bank showing that the necessary share capital has been deposited in an account in the name of the company
- the company statutes containing all of the agreements reached by the shareholders.

The Notary Public will also require the persons who appear before him to demonstrate evidence of their identity and, where applicable, power of attorney to represent a third party. It is also necessary to provide the notary with the bylaws of the company.

The deed of constitution will present the following crucial points:

- **Name, nationality and residence** of all shareholders.
- **Company name:** This should also indicate the legal form of the business, such as SL or SA.
- **Company aim:** Setting out all of the proposed activities of the new business.
- **Start of business activity:** Indicating the official date that the business will start to operate.
- **Duration of the company:** An estimate of the period of time that you intend to operate.
- **Company headquarters:** Detailing the address of where most business activities will occur and a point of contact for the shareholders.
- **Share capital:** You must indicate the exact amount of capital invested at the moment of incorporation.
- **Board of directors:** Indicating the person or persons who will be responsible for the administration of the business.

If the company is being incorporated as an SL, it will need to present additional information such as:

- the capital contribution of each shareholder as well as the nominal value attributed to it
- method of establishing and summoning the general meeting of shareholders and the form which the decision making process will take.

If the company is being incorporated as an SA, the deed of incorporation should also clarify elements such as:

- personal details of all shareholders and a declaration of their desire to form an SA
- the contribution of money, assets or rights of each shareholder
- the cost of incorporation.

## Step 5 – Payment of the transfer tax

This duty must be paid within 30 business days of the execution of the public deed of incorporation. A special form must be filled in and presented along with a copy of the deed of incorporation at the tax office corresponding to the company's address for tax purposes (www.aeat.es). The tax is levied at 1% of the current value of the capital contributions made.

## Step 6 – Registration at the Companies' Registry

Once the above steps have been completed, and within 30 days of the execution of the deed, the new company must be formally registered with the *Registro Mercantil*

*Central* (www.rmc.es). The following documents must be presented to register the company:

- the public deed of incorporation
- the *Certificacion Negativa del Nombre* obtained from the companies' registry.
- evidence of having paid the stamp duty.

Registration fees are assessed on a sliding scale of officially approved charges according to the amount of capital contributed (the larger the capital, the lower the rate). The total amount of the fee may not exceed €2,181.

### Step 7 – Obtaining the permanent tax identity number

One final trip to the tax office is required before the company is considered to be a fully incorporated legal entity. For the purposes of exchanging the temporary CIF for a permanent one, the tax office will need to see:

- the certificate of the temporary CIF number
- a copy of the deed of incorporation
- a photocopy of the registration entry in the companies register.

# Necessary formalities before beginning operations

Having followed the above steps, the business is now fully incorporated and registered. However, before the company can start operating there are a number of legal and fiscal obligations that must be fulfilled. Again these obligations can vary depending on the type of business and where it is based. There are also a number of specially regulated activities that may require additional administrative authorisation such as restaurants, travel agencies, security, or toxic substances storage. However, a good *gestor* or lawyer will advise you as to the specific details of such operations.

## Municipal licences

### Opening licence

To obtain the licence, the first step is to approach the *ayuntamiento* (town hall) with your proposition to see whether in theory they would approve such a change. It is then necessary to employ an architect, who would approach the High Council of Colleges of Architects (*Consejo Superior de los Colegios de arquitectos de España*; www.cscae.com) or the local *colegio* to ascertain the current planning regulations for such a business. The architect would then submit a project, and the suggested work, such as installing the correct amount of toilets and following fire regulations, would have to be carried out to the letter. Only then could you apply to the local council for the licence allowing you to operate the business from those premises.

Usually the council will visit the business premises and make sure that they fulfil all legal and sanitary conditions. The *ayuntamiento* will not even consider granting the licence before the necessary work has been done. The cost of the opening licence depends on the location of the premises and its size in square metres, but it can be as little as €100 for a small shop, or €200 for a bar or restaurant.

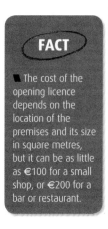

**FACT**

The cost of the opening licence depends on the location of the premises and its size in square metres, but it can be as little as €100 for a small shop, or €200 for a bar or restaurant.

### ■ Works licence

Any construction work that needs to be done on the premises requires the appropriate works licence obtained from the local council office. The granting of this licence implies that the local council accepts that the planned works are in accordance with the existing town planning regulations.

## Fiscal obligations

### ■ Registration of the company for the purposes of business activities tax

The *Impuesto sobre Actividades Económicas* (IAE) is levied annually on any business activity conducted within the territory of the municipality. It is likely that the company, if it is a fairly small enterprise, will not have to pay any IAE contributions as, in a move to stimulate small business, the government has abolished this tax for anyone with a turnover of less than €1 million per year. However, it is still necessary to register as you must have a tax category assigned for your business. A special form must be filed at least ten days before the company starts its business. If payable, the tax is levied at the moment of inception and annually thereafter.

### ■ Registration of the company at the census of taxpayers

The company must be registered or listed for control of its subsequent tax obligations at the *Agencia Tributaria*. A special form must be filled in at the tax office documenting various data on the company's future activities.

### ■ Legalisation of official books

Every company must keep a number of tax and accounting 'books' such as the Journal (*Libro Diario*) and the Inventories and Annual Accounts Book (*Libro de Inventarios y Cuentas Anuales*). These must be physically taken to the nearest Companies' Registry for stamping, before business activities commence. As well as the accounts journals, companies should have a Minutes Book (*Libro de Actas*) recording all of the agreements taken at general meetings. SLs also need a *Libro de Registros de Socios* recording the quantity of participation units held by each company owner. A *Libro de Matricula* logs personnel registration as well as the visits that the labour inspectors (*Inspección de Trabajo*) pay to the work centre. These books and any others which your accountant or *gestor* advises to be necessary must be presented at the Companies' Registry.

**FACT**

■ Every company must keep a number of tax and accounting 'books' such as the Journal (*Libro Diario*) and the Inventories and Annual Accounts Book (*Libro de Inventarios y Cuentas Anuales*).

## Labour obligations

### ■ Registration of the company for social security purposes

It is obligatory for all businesses to register with the Social Security Treasury prior to starting their activities so that the company will later be able to employ workers. You will need:

■ the original and copies of the business owner's NIE and passport
■ a copy of the insurance policy for accident and health cover (paid for out of social security contributions)
■ a copy of the deed of incorporation (*escritura*)
■ a copy of the form from the tax office (845) showing that you have registered for business tax
■ the completed form TA6.

The company will be issued with a social security identification number and advised as to their social security obligations. If you already have a labour supply, then you must file first-time registration of the workers who do not have a social security number (*afiliación*), or a renewal of those who are already registered (alta). For each new employee, you must supply the Social Security office with the original and copies of the employee's NIE and passport and a completed form (TA2/S).

### ■ Registration at the provincial office of the Ministry of Labour and Social Affairs

The labour authorities must be made aware of the start of operations in a work place within 30 days. The relevant form must be completed and delivered to the above office (*Ministerio de Trabajo y Asuntos Sociales*). You can find the address of your nearest provincial office on www.mtas.es/infgral/provin/espana.htm.

# ■ WHICH BUSINESS STRUCTURE?

## Choosing the correct legal entity for your business

One of the first decisions that the entrepreneur should make, having analysed the viability of his or her business, is which form of business enterprise to adopt. There are a number of legal entities that a Spanish business may assume and choosing the right structure for your business should be the subject of extensive study. Taking legal advice on this subject is a must.

One of the main considerations is finding a good balance between keeping the administration simple and protecting your personal assets. It is impossible to establish general criteria to determine the legal form that your business should take, as each particular project will have its own characteristics and requirements. The decision you make will determine aspects such as the individual liability of the shareholders, the form of taxation payable and the amount of capital invested.

Many small businessmen operate as sole traders or *empresarios individuales*. This format accounts for around 68% of the new businesses that are created each year. The main disadvantage of operating as a sole trader is that the owner of the business is personally liable for any debts the business may accrue. To limit personal liability it is necessary to operate as a corporate entity. The most significant forms of larger business enterprise are:

■ Corporation (*Sociedad Anónima* or SA)

■ Limited liability company (*Sociedad de Responsabilidad Limitada* or SL)

■ General partnership (*Sociedad Colectiva* or SC)

■ Limited partnership (*Sociedad Comanditaria*).

Traditionally the SA was by far the most commonly used form. However, in recent years the SL has gained popularity as a result of its lower minimum capital requirement and it is certainly the most convenient legal form for a small or medium-sized business. The most commonly used entities are discussed below.

## Different types of Spanish company

| Entity | Type | Number of partners | Working capital | Liability | Taxation |
|---|---|---|---|---|---|
| individual | *Empresario Individual* (sole trader) | 1 | no legal minimum | unlimited | individual income tax |
| individual | *Comunidad de Bienes* (group of owners) | min. 2 | no legal minimum | unlimited | individual income tax |
| corporate | *Sociedad Colectiva* (co-partnership) | min. 2 | no legal minimum | unlimited | corporate taxation |
| corporate | *Sociedad de Responsibilidad Limitada SL* (limited-liability) | min. 1 | min. €3,005 | limited to the capital contributed | corporate taxation |
| corporate | *Sociedad Anónima SA* (Corporation) | min. 1 | min. €60,101 | limited to the capital contributed | corporate taxation |
| corporate | *Sociedad Comanditaria por Acciones* (limited partnership) | min. 2 | min. €60,101 | unlimited for some partners, limited for others | corporate taxation |
| corporate | *Sociedad Comanditaria Simple* (limited partnership) | min. 2 | no legal minimum | unlimited for some partners limited for others | corporate taxation |

# Individual forms of enterprise

## Empresario individual (sole trader)

The *empresario individual* is a sole trader, offering goods or services without being bound by any labour contracts or to any other business and assuming both the risks and the profits of his or her labour. Most very small business concerns will be better with sole trader status as it is the most efficient form for them, and can be more economical. It is also the form with the fewest bureaucratic procedures involved in setting up, given that no legal entity must be established that is distinct from the entrepreneur himself. Despite the name, a sole trader does not have to operate on his or her own; it is possible to take on employees.

The main advantages of this type of operation are as follows:

- Sole traders make their own business decisions and do not have to answer to anybody else.
- The fiscal obligations are much simpler. The taxes you have to pay are reduced only to the individual income tax, known as IRPF and VAT, known in Spain as IVA.
- There is no minimum amount of working capital required and no initial registration tax.
- There is much less red tape involved in setting up the business. You merely need to register for social security under the *autónomo* scheme and register for the IAE (tax on business activities). It is likely that you will not need to pay the IAE, which was abolished for smaller businesses in 2003, but it is still necessary to register. In certain cases, the sole trader may also have to obtain

municipal licences, for example if you operate out of business premises you will need a licencia de apertura, an opening licence which certifies that the business premises are suitable for your business activity. *Empresarios individuales* are not obliged to register at the *Registro Mercantil* as other businesses are, but your lawyer may advise you that it is opportune to register anyway.

The major disadvantages of working as a self-employed person or a sole trader are as follows:

- You do not have the protection of a limited company if your business fails. You are personally responsible for any business transactions, which in effect means that your personal income from whatever source, your house, your car and even your estate after your death can be used to pay off the debts of the business.

- You are also not entitled to unemployment benefit should the business fail, so it is important to consider worst case scenarios and seek professional advice before deciding on sole trader status over limited company status.

# Limited liability companies

## Sociedad Anónima (SA)

The equivalent of a British public limited company (plc) or an American corporation (Inc.). This is a widely used form of business entity in Spain and is used for investments in major projects. This option is only really advisable for experienced businessmen making a large investment. The minimum amount of share capital required is €60,101, as opposed to the €3003 needed to establish an SL The capital must be fully subscribed and at least 25% of it must be paid in at the time of incorporation.

Participation is represented by shares that qualify as negotiable securities. Furthermore, shares of an SA may be quoted on the stock exchange (*Bolsas de Valores*). Shareholders can be individuals or companies of any nationality and residence. There is no minimum number of shareholders required by Spanish law, although sole shareholder companies are subject to a special system. Contributions may be made in the form of money, goods or intellectual property, which can be valued.

Shareholders are not personally liable for the company's debts other than to the extent of their capital contribution.

The shareholders or their representatives are obliged to appear before a notary public to execute the public deed of incorporation. This deed is subsequently registered in the Mercantile Register giving the company legal status and capacity.

The disadvantage of the SA is that the business is held accountable to its shareholders. The shareholders have some basic rights, which must be observed under Spanish corporation law. These include the right to a share in corporate earnings and also in the assets in the event of liquidation, as well as preferential rights to subscribe new shares. However, they also have the right to obtain information about the company's affairs and to attend and vote at shareholders' meetings, held every year, and to challenge corporate resolutions.

## Sociedad de Responsabilidad Limitada (SL)

A far simpler form of incorporation with a reduced capital and often a reduced number of shareholders. As a result, it is the ideal way to enter the entrepreneurial

## Sole shareholder companies

Both SAs and SLs may be set up as, or can consequently become, a company having a sole shareholder or a sole participation unit holder. However, it is important to get specific legal advice. Unless you follow the correct procedures, the company may lose its limited liability status and you may find yourself personally liable for the company's debts. It must be written into the company's articles that the business is unipersonal to give some defence against creditors.

Sole shareholder companies are subject to a specific regime involving special reporting requirements and registration requirements. These include the obligation to acknowledge single owner status on all company correspondence and commercial documents.

world without running huge risks and this is the form that most smaller and medium sized companies in Spain will assume. It is also worthwhile noting that an SL can always be upgraded to an SA after a few years, if the business is very successful. Around 80% of newly incorporated companies are SLs.

Technically, the capital of an SA is divided into shares whereas the capital of an SL is divided into participation units. These units may not be represented by means of certificates, nor considered securities. The participation units need not all be equal and consequently they carry different voting weight. The liability of the shareholders is limited to the individual portion of capital invested. Whereas shares in an SA are usually freely transferable, this is not the case with the participation units of an SL, which may only be transferred to other unit holders. Only shares of an SA can be listed on a stock exchange. Participation units of an SL cannot.

The minimum capital required for incorporation of an SL is €3003. There is no maximum capital and some larger companies choose this business structure as a result. Again, the share capital must be fully subscribed but in contrast to the SA the capital must be fully paid up at the moment of incorporation. Only one shareholder is required but there is no limit on the number of shareholders.

Shareholders have the right to participate in company decisions and the right to be elected as company administrators. They also have the right to company information at regular intervals, which are established in the deeds of incorporation.

A further advantage is that the SL is subject to fewer reporting and auditing requirements than the SA. SLs are incorporated in much the same way as an SA.

# Partnerships

Setting up a partnership allows two or more people to set up in business together sharing profits, management burdens and risks. The partnership must be based on ties of personal trust between the associates and for this reason it is the ideal legal entity for a family business, or a business run by friends with high aspirations but little capital. A partnership should not be undertaken lightly. Partners need to have complete confidence in one another, as partners remain liable for all the debts of the business, not just for the half or third relating to their partnership share. Spain has two main types of partnership.

## Sociedad Colectiva (general partnership)

The simplest of the commercial entities. It is essentially an independent legal entity owned by two or more general partners, all assuming unlimited responsibility for the company. All partners are duty bound to participate in the management of the company, contribute that which was agreed at the moment of formation, refrain from competing against the partnership and accept joint liability for the company's debts. In return, partners take a share of the profits.

The partnership must be formalised by public deed and registered in the Companies' Registry. The steps necessary to form a partnership are almost identical to those for forming a company. The name of a partnership is made up of all of the names of all the partners or some of them with the expression 'y compañia' added. The names of non-partners may not be included.

## Sociedad Comanditaria (limited partnership)

Very similar to the general partnership described above, in that it is an independent legal entity owned by more than one partner. However, in this case, ownership is divided between one or more general partners who assume unlimited responsibility and one or more limited partners whose liability is limited to the amount of capital contributed but who play no part in managing the company.

There are two types of limited partnership. The first is called a *Sociedad Comanditaria Simple*, and the second a *Sociedad Comanditaria por Acciones*. In the latter, the contribution of the silent partners is divided into public shares. The minimum capital necessary to form this kind of partnership is €60,101, which must be fully subscribed and at least 25% of it paid in at the time of incorporation (as with an SA).

In a *Sociedad Comanditaria*, the general partners are subject to exactly the same rights and obligations as partners in a *Sociedad Colectiva*. Again the name of the partnership is made up of the names of the general partners. The names of the silent partners cannot feature.

# ■ BUYING, LEASING OR RENTING AN EXISTING BUSINESS

The number and variety of existing businesses for sale in Spain is quite staggering. While the majority are undoubtedly bars, cafés and restaurants, even the most cursory of glances in the window of a commercial estate agency will expose the enormous diversity of businesses available to foreign buyers. For lease there are fully stocked supermarkets at around €50,000 and bars with licences for around €110,000. For sale, there are charter boats for €200,000 and car parks for nearly

€6m. Almost every imaginable business comes up for sale at some point if you know where to look.

Buying an established business can be less risky and much easier than setting up a new one. The obvious advantage is that you are buying a business that is already producing an immediate cash flow and has an established customer base. The risk is also reduced because studying the accounts of a business will allow you to analyse the past performance of a business before buying.

As well as reduced risk, an immediate cash flow and an established clientele, there are numerous other advantages. These include an established location, existing licences and permits, existing suppliers and equipment and sometimes even trained employees.

In spite of all of these apparent advantages, buying a business that is a going concern is not by any means easy and the need for comprehensive research cannot be overemphasised. Thriving Spanish businesses are not usually sold without a very good reason. It is imperative that the buyer finds out what this is before signing anything. More often than not the reason will be that the business is failing, or there may be a hidden motive such as imminent construction works, which would adversely affect the performance of the business. You should always check local planning permissions for roads, housing developments, rival businesses, factories and anything else that may affect your business.

Anyone planning to buy a business should certainly obtain an independent valuation. Never take actual or projected turnover or profit figures at face value, especially if they are provided by either the current owner or the estate agent. Theoretically the company's books will show the past performance of a business before you buy it. Unfortunately this benefit is almost entirely negated by the fact that in certain businesses, very few people keep accurate tax records. The declared turnover for tax purposes is often lower than the actual turnover. According to John Howell and Co, solicitors and international lawyers, the tendency to under-declare income to pay less tax is so rife that it is very difficult to

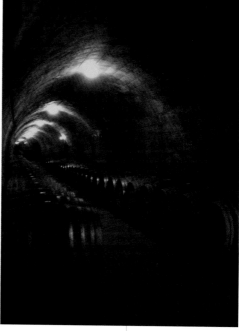

Sherry barrels. Vineyards are often family-owned enterprises

obtain an accurate idea of the value of the business. The business owner will usually tell you what they consider to be the actual turnover, but whether they are telling the truth is an entirely different matter.

Many factors affect the value of a business. It is fairly easy, for example, to put a value on the tangible assets such as equipment, fixtures, and inventory. However, intangible assets such as the reputation of the business, its customer base and its strength in its own competitive market, are the most valuable. It is these assets which will produce your cashflow and are the best indicator as to whether the business will sink or swim. Other factors, which a buyer should take into consideration, include location, lease terms or possible ownership of premises, competition, reputation, years in business, the industry's outlook for the future, special permits and terms of sale.

To ensure that you are paying the correct price for a business, it is better to take professional advice about the viability of a business from an accountant, *gestor* or lawyer.

## Finding a business

There are a huge number of specialist business agencies throughout Spain, and many real estate agents also sell businesses. The best place to start looking is the publication *Dalton's Weekly*, sold in newsagents, which comes out every Thursday and costs £1 (www.daltons.co.uk). The 'Business Abroad' section is made up mostly of companies and individuals selling businesses in Spain and its islands. Other UK national publications also list a few businesses for sale, such as *Exchange and Mart* (www.exchangeandmart.co.uk) and *The Daily Telegraph* (www.telegraph.co.uk).

The English-language press in Spain is a useful source of classified advertisements offering leasehold and sometimes freehold businesses. If you are researching from outside Spain, some of the newspapers' websites include classified advertisements. For example, it is possible to access the business opportunities advertised in both the *Costa Blanca News* and the *Costa del Sol News* at www.costablanca-news.com/classified. More specifically aimed at the Costa del Sol, *Sur in English* is Málaga's daily English language newspaper and its website, www.surinenglish.com, has a classifieds section including businesses for sale. For the Canary Islands, try *Island Connections* (www.newscanarias.net).

Major Spanish newspapers such as *El País* (www.elpais.es) and *ABC* (www.abc.es) also include some advertisements for businesses for sale.

Although some preliminary research and investigation can be done from outside Spain, it is essential to visit the country on at least one inspection trip before making a shortlist.

## Commercial estate agents

It may seem very tempting to buy privately, especially with so many businesses on the market, but unless you speak the language very well and have a great deal of experience in business, it is advisable to use an agent. A reputable agent will ensure that your business has all the relevant paperwork and will make you less vulnerable to some of the con merchants that operate, especially on the costas where businesses change hands very rapidly.

**TIP**

■ For those considering the purchase of any business connected with tourism or leisure, as many expatriate businesses tend to be, it is particularly important to see how the business varies seasonally. Remember that you will still have to pay the rent, rates and salaries for any employees even in periods when there are far fewer customers.

Agents take a commission from the vendor rather than the potential buyer, so you should not hand over any money to them. Potential buyers should thoroughly check the credentials of the estate agent that they intend to use before employing them. Some agents will sell businesses that they are fully aware are not viable, safe in the knowledge that the buyer has little or no protection against things going wrong. There are even a large number of illegal agents. For example, around 44% of the commercial estate agents selling businesses to foreigners in Mallorca operate illegally out of small apartments, so be sure to check them out carefully.

Many agents, however, do offer a full pre- and after-sales service, and some even offer domestic support packages, helping you with non-business related matters such as finding somewhere to live, healthcare and schooling.

If you do decide to buy a business without the help of an agent, then it is essential that you employ a *gestor* to help you establish that the business is free of debts and holds the appropriate licences, which can be simply transferred. One of the most common errors that people make when buying a business without using an agent, is that they hand over the 10% deposit to the vendor, thereby running the risk of losing that money if the vendor decides to sell to someone else. Most agents will ensure, and you can personally ensure, that the deposit is lodged at the *gestoría* until the day of completion, when the money is transferred to the vendor.

There are hundreds of specialist business agencies selling businesses of all kinds and also empty *locales* (premises). What follows is merely a selection.

## Specialist business agencies

**A2Z Properties:** Alicante; 965 733492; email a2zproperties@wanadoo.es; www.a2zpropertiesspain.com.

**Bizbalears:** 0871 222 3626; email office@bizbalears.com; www.bizbalears.com. Business sales and support in Mallorca, Menorca and Ibiza.

**Business Finder Mallorca:** 971 234543; freephone from UK 0870 0444445; email info@businessfindermallorca.com; www.businessfindermallorca.com.

**Costa Blanca Business Consultants:** 966 812190; www.costablanca business consultants.com. One of Spain's foremost commercial property brokers, dealing with the sale, lease and rental of bars, cafés, restaurants, hotels and all other types of business.

**Diamond Commercial Specialists SL:** 951 900354; email info@diamond commercials.com; www.diamondcommercials.com.

**Global Property Services SL:** 01362 687910; email info@globalproperty services. co.uk; www.globalpropertyservices.co.uk. Costa del Sol and inland.

**Jaime and Sheldon SL:** 971 696086; email info@jaimeandsheldon.com; www.jaimeandsheldon.com. Professional, ethical and friendly, British owned and run legally registered Spanish company.

**Lanzarote Bar and Restaurant Agency:** 928 827291; email info@lanzabar-agency.com.

**Medbars:** 952 593510; email info@mpsproperties.com; www.medbars.com.

**Portico Properties SL:** 0871 717 4224; www.porticoproperties.com.

**Property Network Spain SL:** 952 447722; email benalmadena@property networkspain.com; www.propertynetworkspain.com. The website links over 75 agents across Spain and the Balearic Islands selling both businesses and commercial and residential property.

**Salvador Perez Gestion Inmobiliaria:** 966 4211656; email sperez@salvadorperez. com; www.salvadorperez.com.

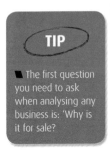

# Choosing a business

The first question you need to ask when analysing any business is: 'Why is it for sale?' Around 40% of new businesses fail so it is not unlikely that the answer will be that the business is losing money, whether or not that is what the accounts show. There are many other reasons why a business could be on the market, but it is in your interests to ask searching questions of the owners. Clearly you do not want to find yourself lumbered with a poorly located business that has changed hands several times in a short space of time.

Because of the intangible nature of the 'goodwill' involved in a business transfer and the unreliability of Spanish accounts, it is not an easy task to assess an existing business.

In most cases the vendor of a business will dictate the price based not on the intrinsic value of the business's tangible and intangible assets but based on recovering what he paid for it with a little extra to cover the transfer fee to the freeholder and the agent's fee. This leads to the fairly ludicrous situation where the price of businesses snowballs by 5% or so each time it changes hands, whether or not the business has been successful.

Many entrepreneurs will sell a business on at the same price, or even higher even if the business has been failing. Unfortunately the demand for businesses is so great that they can usually get away with this. It is essential that the potential buyer has his wits about him as paying more than a business is worth is one of the principal reasons for businesses failing at an early stage. Most of the businesses sold to foreigners are bars and restaurants in the resort areas and these are notorious for changing hands every six months or so. Agents have very little influence over the price of a business but the good ones will inform you if a business has been on the market for a long time, or if they consider it to be overpriced.

The 'goodwill' includes the customer base and the reputation of a business, but there are other intangible assets included in a business transfer such as the name of the business, the location, and the right to continue a lease. The contract should state exactly what these intangible assets are. Even something as simple as a promise from the existing owner that he will not set up a similar business around the corner has value and should be negotiated into a contract. There are numerous horror stories of former leaseholders taking all of their clients with them and decimating the clientele of the new business. The equipment needed to run the business and the stock are tangible assets and are simpler to value.

## Location

The most important of the intangible assets is almost certainly location. A greengrocer's has little future if it is next door to a supermarket, and bars and cafés rely on passing trade. Admittedly, businesses that have built up a reputation rely more and more on people seeking them out, so location is not so important. In the early years of a business, though, location can make the difference between success and failure and potential entrepreneurs should research the area and its potential, both during and outside the tourist season. If not, you could end up losing everything.

## Turnover

The Spanish often do not keep accurate records of the business turnover. Many businesses will not even allow you to see the books and even if they do there is no guarantee as to their accuracy. According to Jerry Whitehouse of Jaime and Sheldon, commercial estate agents, there are ways around this.

Ask also to look at purchase invoices, see how much stock the business regularly needs to buy and the value of the assets the business has invested in. Another handy tip is to look at the takings on any games machines or jukeboxes in a bar or restaurant. Although you cannot investigate this personally, your agent can contact the companies that distribute and manage these machines and such information will give a rough approximation of the business's client base.

Because of the intangible nature of the 'goodwill' involved in a business transfer and the unreliability of Spanish accounts, it is not an easy task to assess an existing business.

> 'When you are buying a new business you have to put the location first. This is difficult because you are new to the country and you don't know the nuances of different areas. You have to wait. You have to stick around. You cannot buy a business within three weeks or a month. You have to look, talk to people, do some investigation for yourself. People come here in a great rush – they want to start making money straight away. No. It's better to take a couple of months to take in the different areas and the amount of trade for a particular business. People come and look at bars in the summer when the sun is shining and the sky is blue. You have to wait until it's raining to get a true picture.'
> **Rita Hillen, Hostal Los Geranios, Torremolinos**

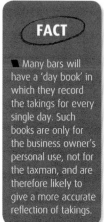

# Which type of contract?

The Spanish make a strict distinction between the business and the premises. Those who buy existing businesses tend to pay a lump sum for the 'goodwill' or reputation and customer base of the business and then rent the building that houses it (leasehold). It is also possible to buy the business and its premises (freehold). Rental businesses also occasionally appear on the market. By far the most common situation is the leasehold, largely because it is considerably cheaper and is easy both to buy and to sell on later if required. Even if it is within your budget to consider buying a freehold, it might be worthwhile to opt first for a lease and then trade up later, especially if this is your first Spanish venture. Some contracts offer a leasehold with a view to purchase, which allows the buyer to agree a price with the vendor at the start of, for example, a five year lease. When the lease expires the buyer can then trade up at the original agreed freehold price.

Unless you are buying a freehold, you will not need to employ the services of a Notary Public because the contract you sign will be a 'private contract'. However, it is advisable to employ the services of a solicitor or *gestor* to check the contents of the contract and ensure that the business is free from debt.

## Leasehold

The Spanish lease is known to most as a *traspaso* (transfer), although it is now officially called a *cesión* (cession). If you buy a *cesión*, the landlord still owns the shell of the building, for which you will pay him a monthly rent but you own everything else. The lease can be anything from 5–25 years and sometimes it is for an indefinite period. However, 5 or 10 years is the normal lease period and leases can usually be renewed for another term without payment of a further premium. Note that the operator of the business who sells you the leasehold in many cases is not the actual owner of the premises. If you lease directly from the owner, then you usually have the automatic right to renewal when the term is up.

When taking on a lease it is a good idea to negotiate as long a contract as possible. Although the landlord will usually renew the lease for another term, often the contract says that this is only *con mutuo acuerdo* – by mutual agreement – so the landlord can refuse to renew the lease if he is not happy. Also, when a lease does run out, the landlord can raise the rent considerably, whereas during the term of a lease he can only raise it with inflation.

## Costs of the lease

A 10% deposit will be required to secure the purchase of the lease and the balance is usually payable in 30–60 days. If you change your mind once the deposit has been paid, then you will lose that money, although if you do not complete because there is a problem with the contract, then you should not lose your deposit. Upon completion, the landlord must be paid a security deposit of two month's rent and your rent will be paid monthly in advance.

For a normal business transfer you should allow approximately €1,220–€1,400 (£750–£850) for legal fees, which will include the preparation of the new lease contract on the premises, licence transfers, *residencias* and NIE, social security and census registrations, plus any other necessary documents.

## Terms of the lease

The term *traspaso* sometimes causes confusion to foreign entrepreneurs and Spaniards alike. Many seem unaware that the law has changed and that the word *traspaso* itself no longer has any legal significance. All lease agreements are called *cesións* and have no set formula. The exact terms of the lease must therefore be specified to the letter in the contract.

There are still *traspaso* contracts around which people may try to sell you, but unless the contract specifies the exact terms of the lease, it is worthless.

During the agreed period of your lease, the rent can only increase by the annual 'cost of living index' as published by the Spanish government, currently around 2–3%. During your term as the leaseholder, you will be responsible for the service charges of the business but the landlord will usually be responsible for real estate taxes, but study the contracts to make sure of this.

One important difference between the *traspaso* and a UK lease is your position if the lease is broken. In the UK you can be held responsible for the full term, whatever happens, but in Spain you normally need only give two months' notice and you are then able to pass the property back to the landlord. As the leaseholder, it is possible to sell the lease to someone else as long as it is written into the original contract. However you must first offer it to the landlord at the same price as your prospective purchaser has offered. The landlord always has first refusal. If you do sell the lease, you normally have to pay a commission to the landlord of between five and 20 per cent of the sale value. The landlord will normally agree a new lease term to the buyer as per your original contract, for example ten years, rather than the balance of the years remaining.

As the leaseholder you must abide by certain laws. You are responsible for the licensing of the business; you cannot structurally alter the building without the owner's permission; nor can you sublet the business. The landlord cannot terminate the lease for any reason other than non-payment of the rent. If you miss three payments, the freeholder is entitled to take you to court and have you removed from the premises.

For many businesses such as bars and restaurants, sufficient working stock is normally included in the sale price. If not, you will have to calculate the initial price of stock.

On the agreed date, the outgoing tenant will sign a release document relinquishing the rights of the lease and the purchaser will sign a new lease agreement with the landlord. Payment in full should be made at this stage and the lease, business and fixtures pass to the new owner.

## Freeholds

Freeholds are far more difficult to obtain as quite often the Spanish consider rental income from leasing a business as their pension or inheritance for their children.

The freehold is more expensive than a lease but has the obvious advantage that there is no monthly rent to pay. Another benefit is that the freeholder always has the option of selling the leasehold of his business, for which he will receive a one-off payment for the lease and a monthly rental income. Freeholders also often write a sell-on fee into the contract, so that they profit every time the business lease changes hands. The value of this fee varies, but it can be as high as 20%.

A further advantage of owning a property is that while the real estate boom continues, even if the business is not a success, you are likely to make money on the property, which may be rising in value by as much as 10% each year. Those who lease a business also have the disadvantage that they may not get back any money that they spend on improving the premises. With a freehold this is not the case.

Estate agents tend to advise that if you have the money and you are sure about the property, then take the freehold when it is offered. Freeholds are so rare that many businesses still find themselves leasing after 20 years or so.

## Costs of the freehold

You should allow an extra 8%–10% of the purchase price for transfer taxes, legal and notary fees. The purchase of a business is almost identical to that of buying property. The only real difference is that when purchasing an existing business the cost will be much higher than if you were simply buying a property because you are paying for tangible assets such as existing licences and also the intangible assets such as the reputation and existing client base of the business.

On the agreed completion date both parties will attend the office of the notary public to sign the *escritura de compraventa* (the title deed). Note that the notary public will not check the details of the purchase but will confirm that both parties have agreed to them. Payment is made in full at this stage, usually via a bankers draft or guaranteed bank cheque and possession passes immediately to the purchaser.

## Rental businesses

These occasionally appear on the market and the contracts are usually renewable on an annual basis. Some contracts have a 'try before you buy' option to purchase the freehold, built into them. Often landlords will ask for a year's rent in advance and the deposits required are often substantial, although refundable upon return of the business to the owner. This is because with a *traspaso*, you have effectively bought all of the fixtures and fittings within the building. With a rental, however,

the landlord needs some guarantee against any potential damage done to the premises, fixtures and fittings. A fair amount of initial capital is therefore required to rent a business.

# ■ BUYING A FRANCHISE

Anyone who is tempted by the idea of running their own business, but who is deterred by the high failure rate, may consider taking on a franchise. 'Business format franchising' is the granting of a licence by the franchisor to the franchisee allowing

## Under-declaration of taxes – a word of warning

Any potential buyer of either a commercial property or a going concern should be aware of the heavy cash culture that exists in Spain. The reality is that often, Spanish accountants do not see their job as to present accurate accounts for their clients, but to minimise their clients' tax obligations. As a result, when buying you may well be advised to only declare around 70% of the price, so that the vendor receives a reduced capital gains tax and *plus valía* bill and you, the buyer, pays less VAT at 7%. Buyers of a leasehold may even find that they are advised by the vendor, the agent or their accountant to pay the entire amount in cash and avoid paying tax altogether.

The short-term advantages of this method are clear, but the procedure is highly inadvisable. Apart from being illegal, you are also running the risk of shooting yourself in the foot later on when you come to sell. Capital gains tax is calculated by subtracting the purchase price from the sale price. If you have under-declared at purchase then clearly you will have to pay capital gains on a far higher amount.

## Advantages and disadvantages of becoming a franchisee

| Advantages | Disadvantages |
|---|---|
| One of the simplest ways of running your own business if you have limited knowledge of the business world. Good franchisors will offer comprehensive training programmes. | Although it is your own business, you will be constrained by the franchisor's system. |
| You can talk to existing franchisees before you buy and investigate the pros and cons of a particular chain. | Your business is part of a chain and the image and reputation of that chain as a whole is in somebody else's hands. |
| The business already has a proven position in the market and a recognisable brand, making it easier to obtain start up capital and premises. | The franchisor has access to your figures and may run regular security and quality checks. |
| There is less risk because your business will benefit from the brand name and you will be following a path that has proved to be successful in the past. | You must commit to a certain number of years on the franchise contract. If you decide to quit, to re-sell or lease the franchise, you will be subject to any penalties agreed in the contract. |
| You will benefit from the financial backing of a large organisation. Small businesses cannot usually afford to buy in bulk or spend large amounts on research and development or marketing. | You must pay a franchise fee to join the network and then continue paying royalties throughout the contract period. |
| You will receive ongoing technical support. | You may be required to make publicity contributions. |

them to trade under a specific trademark or trade name. This licence usually includes an entire package comprising all the necessary elements to establish a previously untrained person in the business and to run it for a predetermined period. Each business outlet is owned and operated by the franchisee but the franchisor retains control over the way in which the products and services are marketed and sold. The franchise is one of the most rapidly growing business concepts in Spain.

## Franchise costs

To help analyse the viability of your franchise agreement, the likely franchise costs are set out below:

- **Canón de Entrada.** The franchise fee is paid at the outset is usually between €4,000 and €65,000, depending on the company. Some of the smaller Spanish franchises will not charge a franchise fee and will simply skim off royalties.
- **Royalty de Explotación.** Franchisors' ongoing management service fees. Most franchises charge a monthly percentage of the turnover, which is usually around 5% (although it can be as much as 10%), although some franchises take a fixed monthly charge.
- **Royalty de Publicidad.** A charge for marketing costs, on a local, regional or even national scale. Larger franchises will charge from 0.5% to around 5% of turnover. Others make a fixed, annual publicity charge.

- **Inversion Inicial.** All franchises require a minimum amount of investment capital to help get the business started. This is not a payment, but your money which you are investing into your business, although how you spend it is generally dictated. The initial investment will vary depending on the size and reputation of the franchisor. Some demand an investment of as little as €25,000 and others could require as much as €500,000.

These are just the costs of the franchise. Remember that you may have to pay more money in legal fees if you decide to run the business as a legal entity rather than run it on your own. Also remember that the business premises will be a huge expense. Although the franchisor gives guidelines as to the minimum size of the premises (*local*) and the characteristics of its location (*ubicación*) and may help you to find the most appropriate local, ultimately the premises are your responsibility.

Having found a suitable franchise agreement, it is always a good idea to have it checked over by a specialist lawyer.

### Useful addresses
**The British Franchise Association:** 01865 379982; www.thebfa.org. Useful for general advice on franchises.
**European Franchise Association:** +32 2523 9707; email eff-franchise@euronet. be. Promotes franchising in Europe exchanges information between the European national federations and associations.
**Spanish Franchise Association (AEF):** 963 861123; email aef@feriavalencia.com; www.franquiciadores.com. Lists all of the franchise chains currently operating in Spain, complete with company information, details of the franchise terms and requirements for the business premises.
**Tormo and Asociados, Consultores en Franquicia:** 913 834140; email mjimenez@ tormo-asociados.es; www.tormo-asociados.es. Specialist franchise consultants in Spain.

# ■ FINANCING YOUR BUSINESS

Most people starting new enterprises sell up at home and put everything into their new lives abroad. There are, however, a number of other ways to finance your new venture that may allow you a greater comfort zone.

While loans, mortgages and incentives are all available, no matter what the EU regulations say, as a foreigner any prospective financiers will regard you with much greater suspicion. Even the Spanish rely predominantly on personal and family financing. It is therefore advisable that you take local advice on your business finance options and use a *gestor* or accountant to guide you through the procedures.

## Official business incentives, grants and subsidies

The decentralised nature of Spain's government creates a tangled web of grants offered by the European Union, the federal government, the autonomous regions and even municipal regions. Add to these a confusing array of region-specific subsidies, industry-specific grants, employment and training subsidies and tax credits, and it all appears just a little too mind-boggling to cope with.

The good news is that in theory there is plenty of aid available for new initiatives and there are a number of sources of advice and information to turn to. In practice however, actually obtaining the money seems to be far more difficult and even when a grant has been promised, it may be withdrawn at the last minute. Often, receipt of the subsidy is dependent on work having already started, or the money having already been paid. If you manage to get the grant, it may well arrive up to two years after the investment has been made. It is advisable not to factor official subsidies and grants into your plans when studying the viability of a business. The project should always be viable without the grant or subsidy and if one arrives it should be treated as a bonus.

# How to find official grants and subsidies

A good source of free information on official funding for businesses is your local chamber of commerce office, or the *Ventanilla Unica Empresarial* (VUE) part of the chamber of commerce in certain locations in Spain. These will be able to guide you through the types of funding available to your specific business and they will be happy to help, although they will not necessarily be able to do so in English. To find your nearest chamber of commerce, visit the website www.camaras.org and click on *Buscador de Cámaras*.

For information on regional grants and incentives, your first port of call should be the nearest local investment promotion agency. These are listed below.

To search for European Union grants and incentives visit the website of the *Dirección General de Política de la PYME* (www.ipyme.org) and click on '*Inform. Europea*'. This allows you to search for European aid programmes relevant to your business. Alternatively visit the European Union online (www.europa.eu), select 'enterprise' and then 'grants and loans'.

# Incentives aimed specifically at small and medium-sized enterprises (PYMEs)

In recent years there has been a distinct increase in the interest shown both by the Spanish government and the autonomous community governments in promoting and developing *Pequeña y Mediana Empresas* (PYMEs). A plan for 'the consolidation and competitiveness of the small and medium-sized enterprise' was launched for the years 2000–2006 and promotes the granting of certain incentives and aid schemes designed especially for the PYME. Small businesses may be the direct beneficiaries of funds for projects relating to innovation in business techniques.

2008 sees the launch of the Spanish government's Corporate Promotion Plan, aimed at incentivising small and medium-sized enterprises. The scheme has been allocated €7,275m to help get small businesses off the ground, and has cut interest rates on start-up loans.

A further aid instrument for PYMEs sponsored by the public sector is the 'Linea PYME', allowing preferential access to official credit. PYMEs can finance up to 70% of their net investment projects with money borrowed from the Official Credit Institute (ICO, 915 921600; www.ico.es). In 2007, the ICO provided financing for 136,000 projects to the tune of a total of €8,770m. The rates of interest were 0.4% for businesses with between one and nine workers and 0.5% for businesses

with between 10 and 250 workers, to be paid back in a period of three, five or seven years.

The European Commission also runs programmes to help finance small and medium-sized enterprises; one such scheme is run by the European Investment Bank (EIB). The EIB grants loans to intermediary banks, which in turn provide funding for small-scale business initiatives. Specifically in Spain these loans are routed through the ICO (see above), BSCH and BBVA (Spain's two largest banks) and Banco Popular. There are many types of loans and credits with varying maturities, amounts and interest rates, but generally they will cover up to 50% of the overall investment costs. Amounts awarded range from €20,000 to €12.5 million and must be repaid over a period of between four and 20 years. These loans are free of fees and other charges, except for minor administrative expenses.

Grants dealing specifically with the creation of small businesses (PYMEs) are co-ordinated by the *Dirección General de Política de la PYME* (915 450937; *www. ipyme.org).#*

# State incentives

There are a number of industry-specific incentives granted by the central government, but most of these are aimed at much larger businesses and industry, and cover sectors such as energy, mining, research and development, the audiovisual industry and tourism. However, smaller businesses may be able to take advantage of a number of incentives, including:

- **employment** incentives aimed at the promotion of stable hiring of workers
- **initiatives to promote activities of rural interest**, granted by the Ministry of Agriculture, Fisheries and Food (www.mapa.es)

■ **regional incentives** (three-quarters of Spain lags far behind Catalonia and Madrid in terms of economic development).

There are a number of websites, available only in Spanish, that will help you to locate state grants and subsidies and allow you to tailor the search to a particular business or area. These include the virtual *Ventanilla Unica Empresarial* site (www. ventanillaempresarial.es, click on ayudas y subvenciones).

State business creation grants are administrated by ENISA, Empresa Nacional de Innovación SA (915 708200; email enisa@enisa.es; www.enisa.es).

# Autonomous community and local initiatives

The Spanish autonomous community governments provide similar incentives on a much smaller scale for investments made in their region. These are usually granted on an annual basis. Each community has very distinct incentives, and information on these can be obtained from local chambers of commerce and the above local investment promotion agencies. Job creation is almost always a vital prerequisite for such benefits. The main types of incentive are non-refundable subsidies, special loan and credit terms and conditions, technical counselling and training courses and tax incentives.

## Local employment initiatives

There are numerous projects sponsored by autonomous communities and municipal governments aimed at generating economic activity and new jobs in local areas. Applications for these incentives must be filed with the National Employment Institute (www.inem.es), who select eligible projects. These projects must provide for the incorporation of a new company, for the hiring of new workers, for the production of products or services which either relate to emerging economic activities, or which cover unsatisfied needs of the area in the case of traditional activities.

If the INEM agrees that a project meets all of these requirements, it is possible to receive reduced interest rates on loans granted to the company relating to its incorporation, a subsidy for the support of management activities, subsidies for the hiring of highly-qualified technical experts and a one-time subsidy for each indefinite term employment contract amounting to €4,808 for each worker hired on a full-time basis. There is also a similar subsidy available for firms that hire workers with disabilities.

### Useful addresses – local investment promotion agencies

**Andalucía:** *Instituto de Fomento de Andalucía (IFA):* C/ Torneo 26, 41002 Sevilla; 955 030700; www.ifa.es.

**Aragón:** *Instituto Aragonés de Fomento (IAF):* C/ Teniente Coronel Valenzuela 9, 50004 Zaragoza; 976 70 21 01; www.iaf.es.

**Asturias:** *Instituto de Desarrollo Económico del Principado de Asturias (IDEPA):* Parque Tecnológico de Asturias, 33420 Llanera (Asturias); 985 980020; www.ifrasturias.com.

**Balearic Islands:** *Oficina de Promoción Industrial:* C/ Reina Constanza s/n, 07006 Palma de Mallorca; 971 176507; www.idi.es.

**Basque Country:** *Sociedad para la Promoción y Reconversión Industrial SA (SPRI):* C/ Gran Vía 35-3°, 48009 Bilbao; 944 037000; www.spri.es.

**Canary Islands:** *Sociedad Canaria de Fomento Económico, SA (SOFESA):* Consejería de Economía, *Hacienda* y Comercio, C/ Nicolás Estévanez nº 30-2°, 35008 Las Palmas de Gran Canaria; 928 307456; www.invertirencanarias.com.
**ZEC Tenerife:** Avenida José Antonio, 3-5°, Edificio Mapfre, 38003 – Santa Cruz de Tenerife; 922 298010; www.zec.org.
**Cantabria:** *Sociedad para el Desarrollo Regional de Cantabria, SA (SODERCAN):* C/ Eduardo Benot 5-1°-C, 39003 Santander; 942 312100;/273240; www.sodercan.com.
**Castilla La Mancha:** *DG Promoción y Desarrollo Empresarial:* Avda Río Estenilla s/n, 45071 Toledo; 925 269800; www.jccm.es.
**Castilla- León:** *Consejería de Industria, Agencia de Desarrollo Económico (ADE):* C/ Duque de la Victoria 16-2°, 47001 Valladolid; 983 361233; www.jcyl.es/ade.
**Cataluña:** *Centro de Innovación y Desarrollo Empresarial (CIDEM):* C/ Provenza 339-5°, 08037 Barcelona; 934 767284; www.cidem.com.
**Consorcio de Promoción Comercial de Cataluña (COPCA):** Paseo de Gracia 94, 08008 Barcelona; 934 849627; email info@copca.com; www.copca.com/infoexport.
**Extremadura:** *Sociedad de Fomento Industrial (SOFIEX);* Avda José Fernández López nº 4, 06800 Mérida (Badajoz); 924 319159; www.sofiex.es.
**Galicia:** *Instituto Gallego de Promoción Económica (IGAPE):* Complejo Administrativo San Lázaro s/n; 15703 Santiago de Compostela (La Coruña); 981 541180; email dg@igape.es; www.igape.es.
**La Rioja:** *Consejería de Hacienda y Promoción Económica, Agencia de Desarrollo Económico de la Rioja:* C/ Muro de la Mata 13-14, 26001 Logroño; 941 291500; email ader@ader.es; www.ader.es.
**Madrid:** *Instituto Madrileño de Desarrollo Económico (IMADE):* José Abascal 57-2°, 28003 Madrid; 913 997400; www.investinmadrid.com.
**Murcia:** *Instituto de Fomento de la Región de Murcia;* Avda de la Fama 3, 30003 Murcia; 968 362207; www.murcia-inversiones.com.
**Navarra:** *Sociedad de Desarrollo de Navarra (SODENA):* Avda Carlos III 36, 1° Dcha, 31003 Pamplona; 948 421942; www.sodena.com.
**Valencia:** *Instituto Valenciano de Exportación (IVEX):* Plaza América 2, 7°, 46004 Valencia; 961 971500; www.ivex.es.

# Bank loans

Despite the fact that Spanish banking has come on in leaps and bounds in the last two decades, it is still very difficult for a foreigner to get a bank loan (*préstamo*) for a business start-up. The banks are very wary of anyone who has no credit history with them and often they will only offer loans against some kind of personal guarantee such as a house or some other asset (see below).

This is not to say that it is impossible to get a loan, however, and those who are able to demonstrate some business ability, who have a well thought-out business idea and a cash flow forecast do stand a chance of obtaining a loan. Theoretically, both residents and non-residents should be eligible for loans in any EU country, in any currency. However, this will usually be no more than the amount the business itself injects in cash. Such a loan would normally need to be repaid over a period of between five and seven years.

The chances of obtaining a loan are far higher at one of the savings banks (*cajas de ahorro*). It is worth doing a little research before approaching the bank,

**FACT**

■ Despite the fact that Spanish banking has come on in leaps and bounds in the last two decades, it is still very difficult for a foreigner to get a bank loan (*préstamo*) for a business start-up.

as you will definitely need a well-constructed business plan and it would be useful to detail exactly how you intend to pay the money back. Some banks may be more favourable to certain businesses than others, so ask around.

Interest rates on loans vary depending on the bank, the amount and the period of the loan. The cost of a loan is calculated using the *tasa annual equivalente* (TAE), which must be quoted by law. This figure is the actual rate of interest, which includes all charges and varies according to the frequency of payments. The commission a bank can charge when a client pays off a loan prior to the due date is limited.

## Secured loans

While Spanish banks are often unwilling to offer loans for new business ventures, and banks in general are treading more carefully where lending is concerned, you will find them to be far more amenable if you have something to offer them as security against the loan. This could be a mortgage against the freehold of the business premises you are buying. If you have equity, such as a Spanish property, you may be eligible for a secured loan. These are usually at a lower rate of interest than an ordinary bank loan. However, it is important to remember that if you use a personal asset as security for the loan, then whether or not a limited liability company has been formed, you are personally liable for the repayments on that loan. This is a risk that many sole traders and directors of small companies take but it is a move which should be considered carefully as staking everything on the success of a new venture can be disastrous. It is often safer, if you have formed a limited company, to borrow money against the company's assets such as the business premises.

Unfortunately, while fixed residential mortgages are fairly easy to obtain in the UK, many of the UK lenders specialising in mortgages in Spain will not deal with mortgages on commercial properties, due to the fact that the risks involved are much higher and that they require a record of income for the last three years. Even if you intend to buy a hotel or B&B, the official line from Halifax International is that if the property is used to generate any income at all, it will not qualify for a

> '*For me, the main advantage to working in Spain is that my fixed costs are very low. There is no way that I could work in the centre of London, in a suite of offices for the same price as I do here in Madrid. Away from the capital prices are even lower!*
> *It is a general rule of business here in Spain that you never re-dimension yourself more than you need to. Spain, although it is a growing economy, is still quite volatile and it is very difficult to make sales projections, so keep your fixed costs low. There is no compunction here about operating out of small premises, even an apartment, and you don't need pot plants and girls in mini-skirts to make the business work. Start small, sign short-term rental contracts (you can always renew them) and build up slowly.*'
> **Richard Spellman, Ambient Media and Communications SL, Madrid**

mortgage. As yet there are no companies aimed specifically at providing business finance specifically for the expatriate market. You may be lucky and find a local lender who will finance your business premises, but most people find that they have to take a Spanish mortgage, take a loan secured against personal property in Spain, or remortgage their first home to invest in the business in Spain. Specialists in business finance such as ASC Partnership PLC (020 7616 6628; www.asc.co.uk) will be able to help you to raise finance on any commercial assets that can be used to fund a business venture in Spain.

Commercial mortgages from a bank or lender in Spain are available, especially if you go to one of the larger banks such as BBVA, Banco Santander or Barclays España. If you are forming a Spanish branch of a foreign company then, according to Barclays España, the procedure will be much simpler and you are likely to get a better rate, based on the accounts and guarantee of the parent company.

For example, a high deposit and a maximum repayment term of 20 years is standard. You will also find that cheaper interest rates and special deals on offer usually only apply to more high-value commercial properties.

Many Spanish banks will offer mortgages on commercial property. However, the conditions relating to Spanish mortgages are often quite different to those in the UK. For example, a deposit of at least 30% is usually required with a maximum of 70% of the property value being provided as a loan (in the UK as well as in the US it is common for lenders to agree to 95% or even 100%).

**TIP**

■ If you are thinking of taking a mortgage with a lender in Spain, remember that there are fewer fixed, capped and discounted schemes operating on the Continent and terms can be more restrictive than those offered in the UK.

# ■ BUSINESS PREMISES

Business premises, known as *locales*, can be found in the local press and in most estate agents in Spain (although some deal solely in residential properties). There is a list of commercial estate agents on page 113 but in any given town, there are always plenty of agents offering empty locales to rent or buy.

A major disadvantage of starting a new business from scratch is the paperwork involved in obtaining the opening licence for your premises. The *Licencia Municipal de Apertura* or opening licence certifies that the planned facilities and the business activity are in accordance with the applicable municipal regulations. It must be obtained from the municipal or district council (*ayuntamiento*) where the offices are to be located.

Unfortunately, when applying for an opening licence, you are completely at the mercy of your *ayuntamiento*. It is not unusual for a town council to take six months or more examining the project before issuing a licence. Additionally, there is no guarantee that they will approve the project, even if all of the refurbishment has already been done.

However, if you are taking over existing business premises, there is a possibility that the licence can simply be transferred, as the licence is for the premises rather than the business itself. This is not possible if the two business activities are very different, but there is usually a standard licence for any kind of office.

Finally, because obtaining an opening licence relies on the local council, who are often fairly lax in making inspections and granting licences, many people operate merely on the basis of a stamped application for a *licencia de apertura*. If you take this route you should be aware that it is not altogether legal, but is often tolerated by the authorities.

# Buying business premises

For new companies, it is far more common to rent business premises than to buy due to the initial expense. However, this decision depends very much on the type of business that you intend to run and in the current economic climate, buying any property can be a good investment. Buying commercial property follows identical regulations and procedures to buying residential property. Spanish law stipulates that if any income is derived from receiving customers at the premises, then it is a commercial property and this will be stated on the deeds. For example, businesses with accommodation such as a hotel or a shop with a flat above are classed as commercial properties.

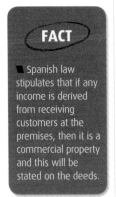

**FACT**

■ Spanish law stipulates that if any income is derived from receiving customers at the premises, then it is a commercial property and this will be stated on the deeds.

# Renting business premises

When buying an existing business, leasehold contracts are very common and rentals are very rare. The reverse is true with premises for a new business. One bad practice that still exists in Spain is that estate agents and individuals will occasionally try to sell you a lease for empty business premises and offices. In most cases if you buy a lease for an empty local all you are purchasing is the rental contract. The lease is often worthless, so if you do pay an initial lump sum for the premises, make sure that the contract specifies exactly what you are paying for.

## Cost

The cost of renting office space, retail outlets and other commercial premises in Spain compares very favourably with other European countries. Clearly the cost of renting premises in the centre of Madrid is far higher than it would be in a small town, but even in the capital, rent is far lower than many other European capitals and has been coming down over recent years due to new commercial developments.

In 2007, office space in Madrid cost around €529 per square metre, per annum. This compares very favourably with €2,009 in London's West End and €1,012 in Paris. The cost of a high street retail outlet was also far cheaper, standing at around one third of the cost of Paris and one quarter of the cost of London.

## The rental contract

Renting business premises is very similar to renting a residential property. The main difference is that there is no such thing as short-term and long-term lets when it comes to commercial premises. All contracts are for a fixed term, which is agreed between the two parties. A further difference is the VAT situation. Spanish VAT (IVA) is not applicable to a domestic property, but it is applicable to commercial property. The law states that 1% of VAT must be paid to the landlord as part of the rent and the remaining 15% must be paid quarterly to the VAT office. The VAT returns of the landlord and tenant are then compared to make sure that they correspond. This method was established to try and prevent landlords avoiding VAT by claiming that the premises were unoccupied.

The legal provisions on renting and letting business premises in Spain are contained in the Law of Urban Lettings (*Ley de Arrendamientos*) of 1994, which applies to all rental contracts made after 1 January, 1995. A lawyer should always be consulted before any contracts are signed. The landlord and tenant may make oral agreements about both parties' rights and obligations but it is always advisable to state the rental conditions in a written contract, drawn up by a lawyer or *gestor*.

## Working from home

Recent estimates suggest that as many as 60% of new businesses operate out of their own homes. Unlike France, where there are strict regulations about operating a business out of residential premises, in Spain it is perfectly acceptable to register a business at your own residence or at rented accommodation as long as the landlord agrees to it. Many landlords would object to a point-of-sale business in a residential property due to the wear and tear caused by people tramping through the building. Offices, however (*oficinas y despachos*), are usually perfectly acceptable and do not require an opening licence (*licencia de apertura*) from the town hall.

Company directors have the right to work from home under the same conditions as self-employed people. The company must have a registered headquarters, but there are no restrictions as to where this is. Unless there is a clause in your lease preventing you from doing so, then you can continue to work from home indefinitely and have your company registered at your home address.

From the point of view of taxation, the law allows you to deduct a proportion of your joint home and business expenses from your taxable profits. You will need to declare the percentage of space that is taken up by business activities in your home and that percentage of the rent is then deductible. The same is true with utility bills: you can deduct a percentage of the total from your taxable income; your accountant will be able to advise you as to how much you can get away with.

Your principal residence is protected against creditors in the event of bankruptcy as long as it has not been purchased in the company's name.

Operating a point-of-sale business from your home (a business which receives customers or has regular deliveries) is quite a different matter and requires permission from the local council. For example, if you chose to operate a small shop or restaurant out of part of the building, then it would be considered a change of use and you would have to apply for a *licencia de apertura* (see above).

# Running a Business in Spain

# ■ ACCOUNTANTS AND BOOKKEEPING

One piece of advice that entrepreneurs who have made the move to Spain always give is to get a good accountant (*contable* or *asesor fiscal*). Most foreign businesspeople simply hand everything over to their accountant and let them get on with the job of dealing with income tax returns and so on. If your business is fairly small-scale, you may find that a good *gestor* will be sufficient to look after your books and draft tax returns. However, larger scale businesses should employ a tax consultant as well to make sure they are fully informed. Look for accountants in the Spanish Yellow Pages, *Páginas Amarillas*.

Spanish law requires that all business enterprises in Spain keep orderly accounts that are appropriate to their activity. Your accountant will be able to advise you as to your particular business needs. It is mandatory for all enterprises to keep inventories and a financial statements book and companies with shareholders must keep a minutes book recording any resolutions adopted at shareholders' meetings. Any accounting books required must be taken to the Companies' Registry where the business is registered in order for them to be stamped and legalised.

Corporations, limited partnerships and limited liability companies must also have share or participation unit registers, which may be computerised.

**FACT**

■ It is mandatory for all enterprises to keep inventories and a financial statements book and companies with shareholders must keep a minutes book recording any resolutions adopted at shareholders' meetings.

| Business glossary | |
|---|---|
| accountant | *contable* |
| audit | *auditoria* |
| bad debts | *deudas incobrables* |
| bookkeeper | *tenedor de libros* |
| branch | *sucursal* |
| business | *negocio, empresa* |
| business expenses | *gastos del negocio* |
| capital assets | *bienes de capital* |
| cash flow | *flujo de fondos* |
| chamber of commerce | *cámara de comercio* |
| demand for payment | *requirimiento de pago* |
| deposit | *fianza* |
| deed (as in a deed of incorporation) | *escritura* |
| fiscal advisor | *asesor fiscal* |
| full-time employee | *empleado de tiempo completo* |
| gross profit | *utilidad bruta* |
| income | *ingreso* |
| invoice | *factura* |

| | |
|---|---|
| loan | *préstamo* |
| local council/town hall | *ayuntamiento* |
| location | *ubicación* |
| market research | *estudio de mercado* |
| monthly payments | *pagos mensuales* |
| municipal business tax *(IAE)* | *Impuesto sobre Actividades Económicas* |
| notary | *notario* |
| net profit | *utilidad neta* |
| opening licence | *licencia de apertura* |
| part-time employee | *empleado a jornada parcial* |
| payroll | *nómina* |
| premises | *local(es)* |
| salary | *sueldo* |
| self-employed person | *trabajador autónomo* |
| self-employment | *cuenta propia* |
| sole trader | *empresario individual* |
| Spanish Tax Office | *Agencia Tibutaria* |
| stamp duty | *Impuesto de Actos Jurídicos Documentados* |
| stocks/shares | *acciones* |

## Payment terms

Payment terms in Spain are notoriously bad. An EU law passed in 2000 states that unless the parties agree otherwise, interest becomes automatically payable 30 days after the receipt of the invoice. In Spain however, many companies ignore this, so small businesses need to have deep cash reserves. Indeed, throughout Europe, one in every four businesses that fail does so because of late payments. One way to relieve the cashflow pressure is to have a *linea de descuenta* with your bank with which you can receive an advance on letters of credit and invoices for a small charge.

# ◼ BUSINESS TAXATION

There are three levels of taxation in Spain: central government taxation, autonomous community taxation and local taxation. The *Agencia Estatal de Administración Tributaria* (901 335533; www.aeat.es), or *Hacienda* as it is popularly known, is based in Madrid and collects government taxes via its centres in provincial capital towns.

A five-year statute of limitations exists on the collection of back taxes, so if no action has been taken during this period to collect unpaid tax, it cannot be collected. The tax year in Spain is the same as the calendar year: from 1 January to 31 December.

■ One problem
that you may have
when paying taxes is
Spain's cash culture.
The country has a
terrible problem with
black money, to the
extent that even
accountants may
advise you to make
some deals in cash.

One problem that you may have when paying taxes is Spain's cash culture. The country has a terrible problem with black money, to the extent that even accountants may advise you to make some deals in cash. Fiddling the books is fairly standard practice. While it is illegal, those who take the moral option may find that their business cannot compete with other businesses that are only declaring a percentage of their income for tax purposes. Take recommendations from a good accountant and listen to his advice. Free tax advice is available from the information section (*servicio de información*) at your local tax office in Spain. Those offices located in resort areas usually have English-speaking staff. The tax office also provides a telephone information service open 9am–7pm, Monday to Friday (901 335533).

## Corporation tax (IS)

Corporate taxation, or *Impuesto sobre Sociedades* (IS) only applies to companies, not sole traders or the self-employed (unless they have formed a company), that are resident in Spain. A company is deemed to be resident in Spain for tax purposes if it was incorporated under Spanish law, or its registered office is located in Spain, or its effective management headquarters are in Spain. Taxation of non-resident entities is regulated separately under the Non-residents' Income Tax Law.

Resident companies are taxed on their worldwide income both earned and unearned, including all the profits from business activities, income from investments not relating to the regular business purpose and income derived from asset transfers. Spain's current standard corporate income tax rate is 30%, although there is a reduced rate of 25% for small and medium-sized companies with a turnover less than €120,202.

The accounting year runs from 1 January to 31 December and tax is payable within 25 days of the AGM, which must be held within six months of the end of the company's accounting year.

### Provisions

Under Spanish tax law, provisions are established for certain, but unrealised, losses, or to cover future expenses. These provisions are deductible, provided that they are properly recorded in the accounts and comply with tax legislation. These deductible provisions include: provisions against the value of portfolios of investment, against bad and doubtful debts, for various legal obligations and duties, for costs

> " Payment terms in Spain really are terrible. There's no payment at 15 days. Thirty days really means 45 or 60; 60 days is really 75–90; and 90 days can mean anything up to six months. Although that is ostensibly illegal, in practice the people who abuse these terms the most are the largest companies and government agencies who will pay at anything up to a year. It's shocking. You need very deep pockets and a tidy cash flow in Spain if you want to work for the big boys.
> **Richard Spellman, Ambient Media and Communications SL, Madrid** "

incurred due to inspection and repairs under warranties and for costs relating to the return of goods.

## Capital gains reinvestment

It is possible to defer paying tax on the sale of tangible and intangible fixed assets and investments, as long as they have been owned for at least a year and amount to at least five per cent of the company capital and that the profit is reinvested within the permitted period. This profit will not be taxed in the period of sale, or for the following three years. However, it must be paid within 10 years following the year of disposal of the asset.

## Tax incentives for PYMEs

Spain's standard corporation tax rate is 30%. However, small and medium-sized companies receive a reduction, and pay only 25% for the first €120,202 of taxable income and thereafter 30%. To qualify for this reduction and the following incentives, the company must have net sales (*cifra de negocio neta*) in the immediately preceding tax period, or in the case of newly incorporated companies – in the current tax period, of less than three million euros. There are a range of other tax incentives for PYMEs, which include: accelerated depreciation of their tangible fixed assets, accelerated depreciation of new fixed assets, a 10% tax credit for investments and expenses in internet, information technology and communications, and a 10% tax credit for environment-related investments. Consult your tax adviser for further details of these incentives.

Other deductions applying to all companies in Spain, small and large, include those for scientific research, development and technological innovation, export

There are usually incentives for the first three years of a small business, allowing you to reinvest any profit rather than pay corporation tax on it. This is a very good idea, allowing you to build up the company's net worth in the early years.

> 'Here is a practical example of what you can do to help ease the burden of corporation tax on a new company. As the director of a company, it may be a good idea not to take a salary for the first months, to keep the company's finances looking healthier. As you get to the year end you can then employ yourself as a freelancer for December only and invoice the company for that amount. If that money stayed in the company, you would be paying corporation tax on it, but as it goes into your private income, you will be paying a much lower rate of personal income tax. This is a fairly simple tip, but one which I only learnt from bitter experience.'
>
> **Richard Spellman, Ambient Media and communications SL, Madrid**

activities, investments in items of cultural interest, investments in assets used for the protection of the environment, costs of professional training and creation of employment for disabled persons.

The exact terms of tax incentives change from year to year and your accountant will be able to advise you on the current deductions.

## Income tax

Those running a business should be aware that their personal income from professional or business activities must be declared for IRPF purposes. Many small businesses that have not formed an incorporated entity find that they are obliged to start off paying their taxes using the *modulo* system. Under this system, the tax agency decides what your business income (taxed as a part of your personal income tax) should be and you are charged tax on this amount each quarter. Only the tax agency could explain the complex analysis that allows them to come up with this figure, but in the case of a bar or restaurant, for example, it would take into account the number of tables, waiters, your location, and so on.

It is still necessary to file an ordinary tax return at the end of the fiscal year stating actual income and any business deductions. The tax agency will then return any money owing (it is usually the case that they overestimate rather than underestimate). There are not many advantages to this system, although you do not have to present detailed quarterly statements, which is helpful for small operations dealing in thousands of small transactions. After a year of this system, it is possible to change to the direct estimation system (*estimación directa*) requiring complete quarterly bookkeeping.

Those whose financial situation is relatively uncomplicated can draw up their own tax return and advice on how to do this is available from the local *hacienda*.

There are three kinds of tax return form. Form 103 is the abbreviated declaration, form 101 is the simple declaration and form 100 is the ordinary declaration. Business and professional activities must be recorded on the last, the *declaracion ordinaria*, which is the longest and most complex of the three and will usually require the help of an accountant to complete. The fees charged by an accountant to file a tax return can vary, but you should expect to pay around €40 for a simple return and around €75 for a more complex return.

Returns should be made between 1 May and 20 June. The self-employed pay their income tax quarterly (*pago fraccionado*). If you employ any staff, it is also your responsibility to deduct your employees' income tax at source. Late filing of a tax return leads to a surcharge on the tax due (see Penalties and Infringements below). It is possible, however, to request payment deferral.

In response to widespread grumbling about the complexity of tax returns, the Spanish authorities have introduced an automated computer programme, known as PADRE, which calculates your tax for you. It isn't being generally distributed yet but your local tax office will have a copy and will be more than happy to let you use it. An advantage of doing this is that, to promote the programme, those who use it will get any refunds due to them before those who have filed using the paper method.

Returns should be submitted to the district tax office where you are resident for tax purposes. Alternatively you can file the return and pay at designated banks in the area, which allows you to transfer the cash to the tax authorities straight from your account.

## VAT

Businesses have a number of obligations with regard to IVA. They must:

- have applied to the tax authorities for a tax identification number
- issue and deliver invoices and keep copies
- keep accounts and records of IVA transactions
- file quarterly or monthly returns.

Unlike in the UK, all businesses must register for IVA, regardless of turnover. Businesses with a turnover of less than €3 million must file a quarterly return and pay tax due within 20 days of the end of the quarter. If your annual turnover is more than this you should file an IVA return monthly.

Health, education, insurance and financial services are exempt from IVA, as is the transfer of any business, providing the buyer continues the existing business concern, and rental of private property. Exports are also exempt from IVA.

## Business tax (IAE)

The *Impuesto sobre Actividades Económicas* (IAE) is levied annually on any business activity conducted within the territory of the municipality. This tax takes into account neither the regularity of operations nor the existence of a profit. It is calculated taking into account several factors, including the type of activity, the number of employees and the status of the activity.

The good news is that in 2003, in a move to stimulate small business, the government abolished this tax for anyone with a turnover of less than €1 million per year. It is likely, however, that the IAE will be replaced in the future with an alternative, to compensate local councils for a vast loss of revenue. The administration of this tax has also been removed from the municipalities and returned to the central Tax Agency, so you need to apply to register at the *Hacienda* office.

## Infringements and penalties

As recently as 20 years ago, tax evasion was rife in Spain. These days, however, it is far more difficult to avoid paying taxes and there are severe penalties for infringements.

Current legislation establishes significant requirements for furnishing information to the tax authorities and there are heavy fines for non-compliance.

A delay in the payment of tax debts leads to an additional surcharge. If payment is made within three months, the surcharge is five per cent, 10% within six months, 15% within twelve months and 20% plus late payment interest after twelve months.

Failure to pay taxes to the authorities can be penalised with fines ranging from 50% to 150% of the unpaid amount. Non-monetary penalties may be applied on top of a fine and these include forfeiting the right to tax relief, to receive state subsidies and to conclude contracts with the state or other public agencies for a period of up to five years. Directors of legal entities are jointly and severally liable for fines.

If there is a fraudulent tax non-payment of more than €90,151.82, or if a state subsidy of more than €60,101.21 is fraudulently obtained, then a tax offence has been committed. Tax offences are punishable by fines of up to six times the amount defrauded and imprisonment for between one and four years. For companies, this tax offence is deemed to have been committed by the director's or the company's legal representative.

Copies of your tax returns should be kept for at least five years, which is the maximum period that returns are liable for audit by the tax authorities.

Despite the fact that you probably will not have to pay the IAE, you still need to register as you must have a tax category assigned for your business or profession.

## ◼ SOCIAL SECURITY

The self-employed and business owners are required by law to pay into the Spanish social security system under the *autónomo* scheme. In 2007, the average contribution for a sole trader was €235 per month and the maximum, €2731.50.

Social security contributions for the self-employed are set at 29.8% of the contribution base, although it is less if you choose not to have cover for short-term incapacity benefit. Self-employed workers under 50 years of age are free to set their own contribution base anywhere between the minimum and the maximum. Autonomous workers aged 50 or over cannot pay contributions on more than €1,416 per month.

All self-employed people, even those who work part-time, must contribute to social security. If no work is done for any period longer than a calendar month, then it is not necessary to pay social security contributions for that time. For example, many small businesses close for a summer break during August.

Not only are social security contributions under this scheme higher than for salaried employees, there are also fewer benefits. For example, if the business fails, then the company directors, under the *autónomo* scheme, are not eligible for unemployment benefit. One way around this is for the company to give you a fixed contract. However, this should be discussed with a qualified accountant, as it is only possible in certain circumstances such as when a director owns less than 24% of the company.

There are various levels of social security payable, depending on the amount of pension you wish to receive on retirement, but most people choose the minimum. Your social security office will supply you with a book of payment slips and payments can be made directly by your bank. It is important to note that if you have two unconnected jobs you must pay social security twice. Social security benefits are not taxed (with the exception of sickness benefits).

You can find out more about social security from the *Instituto Nacional de la Seguridad Socia* l (INSS), 900 166565; www.seg-social.es.

# Registration

All companies must be registered in the Social Security Treasury office corresponding to the business address or head office before any work commences. You will need:

- the original and copies of the business owner's NIE and passport
- a copy of the insurance policy for accident and health cover (paid for out of social security contributions)
- a copy of the deed of incorporation
- a copy of the form from the tax office showing that you have registered for business tax.

The company will be issued with a social security identification number and advised as to their social security obligations.

All employees must also be registered for social security purposes. The company director or business owner is responsible for carrying out this requirement. This involves presenting the appropriate social security office with an application form and a photocopy of the national identity card, if the worker is Spanish, or the NIE if the worker is foreign. Registration must take place before an employee starts work, although it cannot be done more than 60 days before.

You must also register yourself under the special *autónomo* scheme within 30 days of starting work. Registration should take place at the social security office corresponding to the area where the work will be done.

**FACT**

■ It is important to note that if you have two unconnected jobs you must pay social security twice. Social security benefits are not taxed (with the exception of sickness benefits).

# ■ INSURING YOUR BUSINESS

There are hundreds of insurance companies and brokers (corredor de seguros) including those who specialise in business insurance or in certain fields of business and those who cater mainly for the expatriate market, whatever their insurance needs. Take care when choosing an insurance company. It can be difficult to obtain impartial advice from insurance brokers as they often work on a commission for selling a particular policy. Also, a number of insurance companies have gone bankrupt in recent years, and insurance fraud does occasionally occur. It is a good idea to take recommendations and to shop around. Making a few telephone calls could save you quite a lot of money.

The type of insurance policy you require will be very specific to your own business requirements. The main insurance considerations are the building, its contents, public liability, employer's liability, goods in transit, loss of earnings due to an incident leading to a claim, and professional negligence. The main insurance companies offer general multi-risk policies, which are fairly flexible and can be adapted to your individual needs. They may also offer special policies for certain lines of work. For example Axa Seguros (see below) has special policies for a number of businesses, including hotels and hostels, wine producers, mechanics and agriculture.

One difference between Spain and other countries is that professionals such as doctors, surveyors and accountants, usually arrange insurance through their own *colegio*, the body which regulates their profession. Insuring professionals is a slightly more complex matter as the policy must include clauses regarding professional negligence.

**FACT**

■ The main insurance considerations are the building, its contents, public liability, employer's liability, goods in transit, loss of earnings due to an incident leading to a claim, and professional negligence.

## Insurance contracts

These usually last for a year. The cost varies considerably depending on the level of cover required and factors such as the location of the premises. However, a figure of about €250 per year is a rough average for small businesses.

It is fairly common for insurance policies in Spain to be automatically extended for a further year if they are not cancelled two or three months before the expiry date. Make sure that you are aware of the amount of notice required for cancellation or you could be stuck with an unnecessary expense. There are certain conditions where a policy can be cancelled before the period of cover has expired, such as a change in the terms of the contract, or an increase in the premium. All cancellations should be made in writing and by registered post.

## Making a claim

The insurance company should usually be informed within two to five days of an incident, depending on the terms of the contract. In the case of criminal damage to the business or theft, then you need to inform the local police and obtain a police report (*denuncia*) as evidence for the claim. The incident should be reported to the insurance company within 24 hours in such cases and they will usually send someone out to assess the extent of the damage.

# Complaints

Complaints about your insurance policy should be directed firstly to the company itself, and the larger companies will have a complaints department (*defensores del asegurado*). However, if the company does not rectify your complaint, you should contact the Dirección General de Seguros y Fondos de Pensiones, the body charged with regulating Spanish insurance companies and foreign companies with a registered office in Spain (Servicio de Reclamaciones, Dirección General de Seguros y Fondos de Pensiones, 913 397000; www.dgsfp.mineco.es).

## Companies offering Insurance for businesses

**Axa Seguros y Reaseguros:** email atencion.clientes@axa.es; www.axa-seguros.es.
**Caser Seguros:** 902 454595; email comunicacion@caser.es; www.caser.es.
**Direct Seguros:** 902 404025; email operaciones@directseguros.es; www.directseguros.es.
**La Estrella Seguros:** 902 333433; www.laestrella.es.
**Knight Insurance:** 952 660535; www.knight-insurance.com. Specialists in insurance for expatriates.
**Seguros El Corte Ingles:** 901 122122; www.elcorteingles.es/seguroseci.

#  EMPLOYING STAFF

## Recruitment

Although recruitment in Spain is still largely conducted through informal networks with many key posts never reaching the job pages, it is obligatory for companies to register any vacancies, whether skilled or unskilled, permanent or short-term, full-time or part-time with the INEM, the National Institute of Employment (*Instituto Nacional de Empleo*). The INEM is a useful free source of information regarding the labour market and will advise businesses on the correct recruitment procedures to follow, including regulations for drawing up contracts.

 To find your local employment office, visit the INEM website (www.inem.es) and click on Direcciones y Teléfonos.

The employer must indicate the following to the local employment office: what the work entails, type of contract, and the place, date and procedure of the selection process.

Having consulted its database, the employment office will send the employer a shortlist of suitable candidates for interview. Sometimes the employment office will carry out a series of tests on candidates to gauge their professional ability. All services provided to the employer by the INEM are free.

Other than the INEM, there are a number of other recruitment options open to the small business owner.

■ **Private placement agencies** are non-profit-making organisations who may only charge fees relating to expenses arising from the services provided. The INEM keeps a record of all of the authorised work placement agencies.

■ **Temporary employment agencies** (ETT) are private companies that facilitate temporary employment by contracting workers themselves and then transferring or lending their services to other companies. You can find their names and addresses in the Yellow Pages under 'Temporary Employment Agencies'.

If you are looking to fill a very specific position then it may be useful to use the services of a human resources consultant. They offer a highly specialised service, recruiting professionals for permanent vacancies. These consultants can be found via the chambers of commerce, town halls, telephone directories or contact the HR managers association, *Asociación Española de Dirección de Personal* (AEDIPE), 914 200612; www.aedipe.es.

Finally, the media can be a useful recruitment tool. There are more than a hundred newspapers published in Spain, and many have a daily section dedicated to job offers.

## Social security

One of the most crippling costs of employing staff is the payment of their Spanish social security contributions. While these contributions are split between employer and employee, it is the boss who pays the greater share.

All new employees must be registered immediately with the social security authorities. It is illegal to hire workers without having registered them for social security. It is also necessary to register their employment contract with the Spanish Institute of Employment (INEM) within the next ten days.

**FACT**

■ Employment contracts in Spain can be made either for an indefinite term (*temporal*) or for a specific duration (*fijo*).

Special social security programmes exist for agricultural workers, seamen, self-employed workers, civil servants and military personnel, coal miners and students. For everybody else there is a general social security programme. Under this programme, personnel are classified under a number of professional categories to determine their social security contribution. The contribution is based on the *nómina*, which is the official salary for a particular type of work. Each category has a minimum and a maximum contribution base, which is generally reviewed each year. The minimum contribution base, in practice, means that if you are paying an employee the absolute minimum wage of you will still have to pay contributions based on the minimum base of around €665.70.

Contributions are set for general contingencies in 2007 at 29.8%. An employee's contributions are in the region of 4.7 % and the employer's contributions are much higher at around 23.6%. However, the calculations are complex, with each of the percentages varying dependent on salary changes. As an employer, you must pay the contributions for each employee and you must also deduct the 4.7% contribution from their salary. This will be recorded by the Social Security General Treasury.

## Types of contract

Spanish labour law will usually regard the relationship between employer and employee as legally binding, whether or not there is a written contract, and the worker is protected from dismissal even if your business is heading towards bankruptcy. It is vital that both parties understand the contract.

Employment contracts in Spain can be made either for an indefinite term (*temporal*) or for a specific duration (*fijo*). This has not always been the case but anger among Spanish businessmen at the government's rigid protection of the worker's right to job security, led to a series of measures in 1994 and 1997 designed to create a more flexible labour market. The difficulty and expense of dismissing workers was creating real problems for seasonal businesses such as hotels, and was actually making bosses reluctant to take on extra employees for fear of being stuck with them through difficult periods. The government therefore made provisions for hiring workers on short-term contracts as well as the standard indefinite contracts.

Under a short-term contract, the employer is liable only for a small redundancy payment when dismissing a worker. In general, contracts are made for an indefinite term and there must be specific circumstances to justify temporary hiring. The types of short-term contract that may be employed are:

- contract for a specific project or service
- casual contract due to production overload or backlog
- contract to substitute employees entitled to return to their job
- work experience contract for recent graduates
- trainee contract for unqualified workers aged 16–21.

While businesses have been happy to take full advantage of such short-term contracts, the trade unions are less enthusiastic about what they refer to as *basura* or 'rubbish' contracts offering the worker little security. In an attempt to counter trade union criticism and to reduce unemployment, the Spanish government offers incentives to encourage long-term employment contracts. These incentives are available to the employer if an already existing temporary contract is transformed into a permanent contract or if the permanent employee is from a number of disadvantaged groups, including young people, women, those over 45, long-term unemployed, or people with disabilities.

The use of such contracts entitles the employer to tax benefits and subsidies of up to 75% on the employer's social security contribution. It also reduces the amount of severance pay for improper dismissal to 33 days' salary for each year worked, rather than 45.

**FACT**

- In an attempt to counter trade union criticism and to reduce unemployment, the Spanish government offers incentives to encourage long-term employment contracts.

## Dismissals and labour disputes

One of the most troublesome and expensive aspects of employing staff in the past has been firing them. Traditionally it was almost impossible to dismiss a worker for any reason other than gross incompetence without facing a large redundancy sum and possible legal action. Although the situation is gradually changing, the costs of redundancy and the fines for unfair dismissal in Spain are still among the highest in Europe.

An employment contract may be terminated for certain reasons which usually do not give rise to a dispute such as mutual agreement, death, retirement, or a contract ending. However, Spanish law also regulates three principal grounds for dismissal of an employee:

- **Collective payoff.** This category allows employers to dismiss a group of workers through a specific administrative procedure. The entire payroll can be dismissed under this category if the business ceases entirely. The employer pays 20 days of salary per year worked, up to a maximum of 12 months' salary.
- **Objective causes.** An employer may dismiss a worker for a number of objective reasons such as the known ineptitude of the worker, intermittent absences from work or a need to cancel posts due to economic, technical, organisation

or production reasons. The employer should serve at least 30 days of advance notice in writing, or at least pay the salary of the notice period. The employer pays 20 days of salary per year worked, up to a maximum of twelve months salary. The worker may appeal against this decision.

- **Disciplinary action.** If there is a serious and wilful breach of the contract by the employee, the employer may fire a worker without compensation. Such breaches of contract include repeated and unjustified absenteeism, insubordination, physical or verbal abuse, and habitual drug or alcohol abuse. The employee must be given written notice of dismissal, stating the causes and effective date of dismissal. Again, the worker may appeal this decision.

Any dispute over a labour issue should be taken to the Labour Courts, the *Magistratura de Trabajo*, who will sit in judgement, although a conciliation hearing must first be held between the worker and the employer to attempt to reach an agreement. The Labour Courts will classify a dismissal as fair, unfair or null.

If the Labour Courts rule that a dismissal is unfair then the employer must either reinstate the worker or pay an indemnification of 45 days of salary for every year worked, up to a maximum of 42 months of salary.

The labour courts will pronounce a dismissal null for a number of reasons, including failure to comply with the formalities for objective dismissals. In such cases the worker must be immediately reinstated and paid any due salaries.

## Prevention of occupational hazards

The general framework for health and safety at work was established in 1995 and regulates the obligations or duties of employers and employees in relation to risk prevention. Increasingly stringent regulations on the prevention of occupational risks are being implemented in Spain.

Employers of any kind are responsible for the health and safety of their employees. From the outset of business activities, employers are obliged to remedy situations of risk and plan preventive action. This includes the obligation to perform risk assessments, adopt measures in emergency cases, provide protective equipment and to ensure the health of the employees.

In companies with more than 50 employees, a health and safety committee must be established and consulted regularly on procedures. However, in smaller companies it is necessary only to have a 'prevention service', for which the employer should nominate one or more workers. In companies with fewer than six workers, this role can be assumed directly by the employer. Safety representatives should monitor the compliance with regulations on the prevention of occupational hazards and be consulted on any employer decisions regarding such matters.

Failure to comply with these obligations may give rise to substantial fines by the Ministry of Labour and Social Affairs.

**FACT**

Employers of any kind are responsible for the health and safety of their employees. From the outset of business activities, employers are obliged to remedy situations of risk and plan preventive action.

## ■ MARKETING

Whatever the size and nature of your business, the level of competition in Spain is such that good marketing is a must. The most suitable method of promoting your business depends very much on the goods or services that you offer and your target audience.

# Directories

Ensuring that the business is included in the appropriate directories is a good place to start. The Spanish version of the Yellow Pages is published in each province and provides details of local businesses (*Páginas Amarillas*; 902 202202; www.paginasamarillas.es). Euro Pages (900 131131; www.europages.es) is a useful tool for businesses with a more international perspective, with details on some 150,000 suppliers. On the Costa del Sol and in Gibraltar, businesses should register with the English Speakers' Telephone Directory (956 776958).

# Business cards and leaflets

It is always useful to have some printed material to hand out to potential clients or to distribute as leaflets, posters or flyers. Digital printing in Spain is very cheap and simple leaflets or business cards can be designed on any home computer and then taken to the local copyshop for mass production. Once printed, leaflets and flyers need to be distributed, and many tourism-related businesses employ reps either to hand them out in the streets or stock hotel lobbies and tourist information centres. An alternative to private reps is to employ the services of a company representing a number of businesses. Companies such as Promarketing SL (952 383140; info@promarketing.es; www.promarketing.es) on the Costa del Sol, ensure a regular supply of promotional material in all areas with a glut of tourists.

# Newspapers and magazines

Another useful avenue for marketing is the local and national media. The pages of the English language press in Spain are filled with every imaginable expatriate service in English. The costs of advertising depend on factors such as circulation and the size and type of the advertisement. As an example, the *Costa Blanca News*, which is read weekly by around 100,000 residents and tourists, currently charges from €4 per line for small ads to €380 for a quarter page display, to €1,600 for a full page.

# Radio

Radio advertising is also an effective marketing medium. Unfortunately the quality of advertising on local expatriate radio is still fairly amateur. As an example, Octopus FM on the Costa del Sol (952 667742; info@octopusfm.com; www.octopusfm.com) offers five daily plays of a 30 second advertisement for around €500 per month (less in winter).

# Direct marketing

Those looking to target their marketing at a specific group should contact either their local chamber of commerce or the Association of Direct and Interactive Marketing Agencies (*Asociación de Agencias de marketing Directo e Interactivo*, 932 402720; email info@agemdi.org; www.agemdi.org), both of whom can help provide sector guides and databases. Selective advertising improves marketing efficiency, and allows you to be very precise in your material.

## Mailshots

Mailshots, usually comprising a brochure and letter of introduction, remain a popular method of publicising businesses in Spain, although they traditionally have a very low response rate. However, if sent to specifically targeted groups and addressed to the correct person, the response rate should be higher. The Spanish tend to simply bin anything not addressed to a specific person. It is always a good idea to follow up a targeted mailshot with a phone call. The Spanish far prefer to do business over the phone than to commit anything to paper.

## Personal contact

Trade fairs are held regularly in Spain and are the only occasion when people from the same sector get together. At an early stage, taking a stand is unnecessary. Simply take a stack of business cards and speak to as many people as possible. You can find out about forthcoming fairs in trade magazines and periodicals, or search for trade fairs on the website: www.spainbusiness.com.

## Internet marketing

Lower call charges and cheaper computers have created an enormous increase in internet usage throughout Spain. Over 60% of small and medium-sized businesses have some sort of Internet presence, either in the form of advertisements or their own website. Internet presence is of particular importance for businesses related to the tourism trade, as there is a growing rend for tourists to plan their holidays online. Tourism websites receive thousands of visitors every day and many of these offer business directories for all manner of services. Some will offer to list your business for free, while other sell advertising space.

For most businesses today, having a website is fundamental. Small Spanish holiday let businesses receive around two thirds of their bookings online.

Unlike print media, radio or television, a website acts as a permanent and highly accessible, worldwide showcase for your business, and after the initial set-up costs, monthly maintenance charges are marginal.

The most important consideration for any website is accessibility. If the site does not appear near to the top of the major search engine, then people simply will not find it. A good web designer will register your site with the major search engines and construct the site in such a way that it will achieve as high a position as possible; this is known as SEO, or search engine optimisation, and is achieved by including in your text the sort of words or phrases that internet users are likely to search the web for. Websites should also be attractive, but not too flashy.

> 'The internet is the most important marketing tool that we have. More than 50% of our customers have seen our website, so we spend around €100 a month on updating the site. I would be happy to pay double that because it brings in so much business.'
> **Peter Deth, Happy Divers; Club, Marbella**

Research shows that if a site takes longer than eight seconds to download then people will look elsewhere.

Website set-up costs vary enormously, but Mike Stickland of Stickland Web Studio (+44 01424 775021; email mike@sticklandweb.co.uk; www.sticklandweb.co.uk) suggests spending around £500–£600. Once a website is running, the hosting costs can be as little as £8 per month, although maintenance costs will depend on how often the site needs to be updated.

### English-speaking website designers in Spain

Pro Digital Media Internet Design Agency: 952 885985; email sitelink@website-designers-spain.20m.com; website-designers-spain.20m.com.

Peppercorn Ltd: 01234 834746; email diseno@peppercorn.co.uk; www.peppercorn.co.uk.

Mas Adelante: 647 533833; email info@masadelante.com; www.masadelante.com.

Venga Venga Worldwide Web Weavers: www.vengavenga.com.

#  SELLING ON

There is a thriving market for resale businesses in Spain and if you have made a success of your business and your efforts have crystallised into a valuable asset, then it may be time to sell on. Entrepreneurs choose to sell a business for many reasons, including wishing to invest the capital into a new project. Whatever your reason, the procedures involved in selling are fairly simple and you should be able to demand a reasonable price for your business.

The costs involved in selling a business are minimal but will include:

■ capital gains tax

■ fees to professional advisors (lawyers and accountants)

■ business agent's fee

■ any liabilities not being assumed by the buyer.

## Preparing the business for sale

Any business needs to allow itself some time for preparation before selling. Issues such as setting the right price for a business, getting the accounts in order and ensuring that the business looks as attractive as possible will take a good deal of forethought and hard work. It will save you time and money if you get these things right at the outset.

Business records can be an effective tool for luring potential buyers. It can take time to prepare the books in such a way as to show maximum profitability, and ideally you should start preparations a year or more in advance. The most recent financial year's results are critical when a buyer is evaluating a business. Most small businesses operate in such a way as to minimise tax liability, for example receiving tax credits by reinvesting any profit immediately. Unfortunately accounting practices that minimise tax liability can also minimise the apparent value of the business. As a result, there is often a conflict between running a company the way an owner wants to and making the company attractive to potential buyers. Consultation with an accountant or *asesor fiscal* will help you to reflect optimum performance. Financial records should be compiled neatly and clearly for ease of viewing.

Good financial statements do not eliminate the need for making the company aesthetically pleasing. The premises should always be clean, the inventory current and the equipment in good working order. Presentation plays a crucial role when selling a business, so a lick of paint here and there, the replacement of old and faded decorations, fixtures and fittings are all important.

Certain labour law provisions are particularly relevant when selling an ongoing business in Spain. When a business is transferred, the employees are also transferred and the new employer takes on all of the former employer's labour and social security rights and obligations, including pension commitments. The employees must be informed in advance of the proposed date of transfer, reasons for the transfer, the legal, economic and social consequences of the transfer for the employees and any measures that are envisaged for the employees. There is also an obligation to arrange for a period of consultations with elected employee representatives if new labour measures are adopted. It is important to keep your employees on side as the loss of any key employee could be crucial to the success of the new owner and hence the deal.

## Pricing the company

Determining the value of a business is a process fraught with potential differences of opinion and difficulties. Unlike in other countries, there is no set format for pricing your business. The Spanish use a very informal system of evaluating a business based on the price of similar businesses in the area. For those entrepreneurs reselling a lease they have bought previously, the trend is to charge the same amount as they paid for the business, plus perhaps a little more if they have invested a lot of money or been successful in building up a regular clientele. This should be demonstrable in the business accounts. If you wish to get back the amount that you originally invested, remember to include the agent's fee (usually between 5% and 10%) and the landlord's transfer fee (written into the contract, usually between 5% and 20%) in the price. You will of course be liable for capital gains tax on the difference between the purchase and sale value.

Those who are selling on a business which they have built up from scratch themselves will have greater difficulties in assessing the value of their business and it may well be worth employing the services of an accountant or asking the agent to evaluate the business. Starting with an assessment of the value of other similar businesses, you should then factor into the calculations a number of other variables including:

- recent profit history
- general condition of the company (e.g. the facilities, and the accuracy of books and records)
- market demand for the particular type of business (including an evaluation of the competition)
- economic conditions of the area
- the intangible assets of the business such as client base, location, reputation, years in business, and licences
- future profit and expansion potential.

A further consideration when pricing the business is the amount of cash that you will personally require for the next stage of your life. Many business sellers want enough cash to repay all their personal debts, such as their mortgage, personal loans, and credit card debts. Additionally, they may be looking to invest the profits from the sale into a further business venture. Whatever your personal needs, be sure to estimate the amount that you need from the sale before fixing a price.

## Selling the business

The Spanish make a clear distinction between the business premises and the business itself, no matter how apparently intertwined they may appear, for example, in the case of a hotel. If you are selling a business with freehold premises, then you must treat the two aspects separately. The sale of the property will be dealt with in the deeds executed by a public notary. The sale of the – often intangible – business assets is a private agreement between vendor and purchaser.

You may sell privately but most people employ the services of a registered agent, who will deal with all matters including advertising the property and accompanying prospective buyers. Agents will also deal with the legal technicalities of the sale such as contracts, signing before the notary (for a freehold), and paying necessary taxes on the property. Using an agent ensures the smooth progress of the sale and relieves the client of much of the usual worry and concern relating to the sale.

It is possible to advertise the business for sale through several estate agencies and only pay commission to the one that makes the sale.

Commission rates vary between the various agencies, so it pays to shop around. As a rough guideline, expect to pay around 5%–10% of the sale price to the agency. The more valuable your business, the lower the rate of commission. The commission is usually accounted for in the asking price so although it appears that the vendor pays the agent's commission, in fact it is the purchaser who bears the actual cost. If you bought the property through local estate agents, it could be useful to ask them to deal with the vending process, as they will know the business and the property.

Although the purchaser of a business should always seek legal representation, it is not always necessary for the vendor, but it may be advisable, especially if you are selling a business you have built up from scratch and wish to add any special clauses. For example, some vendors may wish to include a clause protecting their rights to open up another similar business and their rights to take clients with them. Unless the buyer specifically demands clauses regarding these issues in the contract, however, your rights will not be affected. Even if such practices are specifically prohibited in the sale contract, the Spanish often get around the problem by obtaining a business licence in someone else's name!

When it comes to striking a deal with a prospective buyer, they will usually put down a 10% deposit with an arrangement to pay the balance within an agreed time period. If the buyer pulls out at the last minute

or does not complete payment, he or she will lose their deposit. However, if the vendor pulls out of the agreement having accepted a deposit, it is usual for the vendor to have to pay twice the amount of the deposit back to the prospective purchaser.

| **Explanation of Spanish business terms** | |
|---|---|
| Certificado del . Desembolso Efectuado | Certificate stating that the minimum capital necessary to incorporate a company has been deposited into a bank account in the company name |
| Certificacion Negativa del | Certificate documenting that no other |
| Nombre | company holds your company name |
| Cesión | Transfer of a lease – includes the goodwill, fixtures and fittings of a business (known colloquially as a *traspaso*) |
| Código de Identificación Fiscal (CIF) | Company tax identification number required by all incorporated companies |
| Comunidad de Bienes | A business that is not an independent legal entity and belongs to two or more proprietors who assume unlimited responsibility |
| Dirección General de la Politica de la PYME | Organisation dealing with the promotion of small and medium-sized businesses in Spain. |
| Empresario individual | Sole trader |
| Impuesto sobre Actividades Económicas (IAE) | Municipal tax on business activities. |
| Impuesto sobre Sociedades (IS) | Corporation tax paid by companies |
| Instituto Camaral de Creacion y | Found in certain chambers of commerce, |
| Desarollo de la Empresa (INCYDE) | INCYDE offers free advice and personalised assistance to people wanting to set up a company. |
| Instituto de Crédito Oficial (ICO) | Official credit institute |
| Instituto Español de Comercio Exterior (ICEX) | Spanish Institute of Foreign Trade |
| Libro de reclamación | Complaints book. Many regional authorities insist that small businesses that deal with the public have a complaints book and a notice proclaiming that it is there |
| Licencia de Apertura | Opening licence |

| | |
|---|---|
| *Linea de descuenta* | Bank facility allowing the businessman to obtain an advance on any money owed, similar to factoring. |
| *Memoria de actividades* | Activity report. A written explanation of the business activity you intend to carry out |
| *Micro empresas* | Businesses with fewer than 10 salaried employees |
| *Módulo* | A tax system designed for small businesses. The tax agency decides what your business income should be and you are charged tax on this amount each quarter |
| *Pagas Extraordinarias* | Extra payments of a month's wage in the summer and at Christmas. |
| *Pagarés* | A special type of cheque that can be postdated |
| *Punto de Asesoriamiento e Inicio de Tramitacion* | New automated technology (not yet widely available) that helps entrepreneurs to set up an SLNE quickly and easily |
| *Pequeña y Mediana Empresas (PYMEs)* | Small and medium-sized businesses |
| *Registro Mercantil Centro* | Companies'/mercantile registry where all companies must be registered before they can begin trading |
| *Sociedad Anónima (SA)* | The equivalent of a British public limited company (plc) or an American corporation (Inc.). This is the most widely used form of business entity in Spain and is used for major investments |
| *Sociedad Colectiva (SC)* | General partnership. The simplest of the commercial entities. Essentially an independent legal entity owned by 2 or more general partners, all assuming unlimited responsibility for the company |
| *Sociedad Comanditaria* | Similar to the general partnership but ownsership is divided between one or more general partners who assume unlimited responsibility and one or more limited partners whose liability is limited to the amount of capital contributed but who play no part in the managing of the company |
| *Sociedad de Resonsibilidad Limitada (SL)* | The most common form of business entity for smaller enterprises |
| *Sociedad Limitada Nueva Empresa (SLN.E.)* | A specialised version of the SL designed to be set up quickly and at a lower cost |
| *Unipersonal* | A limited company formed with only one owner/shareholder |

Continued

| | |
|---|---|
| *Ventanilla Unica Empresarial (VUE)* | 'One-stop shop for business' – combines all of the necessary departments of the chamber of commerce in one location to facilitate simpler business creation |
| *Zona Especial Canaria (ZEC)* | The Canary Islands Special Zone – a low tax regime created with the objective of promoting the economic and social development of the islands |

## Resources guides to business in Spain

A Guide to Business in Spain: (ICEX, 2006) This useful guide is available to view online at www.investinspain.org. A very useful source of information, but aimed primarily at large business and industry.

Cómo Crear una Empresa: (Boletín Oficial del Estado, 2002) €3. Part of the 'Conoce tus derechos' (know your rights) set of booklets issued by the Official State Bulletin. Fairly simple but in depth look at the options and solutions available to entrepreneurs.

Crea tu Propia Empresa: *Estrategias para su Puesta en Marcha y Supervivencia* (McGraw-Hill; 2003); €17. A Spanish-language guide for first-time entrepreneurs, dealing with the key aspects of business and the processes involved in business start-ups. Very good section on business financing.

Doing Business with Spain: (Kogan Page, 2001); £40. Aims to help international companies take advantage of the Spanish market. Needs updating.

Guide to Labour and Social Affairs: (Ministry of Labour and Social Affairs; 2004); €14. A list of all the employment and social security regulations. Published in English and available from Labour and Social Affairs Advice Bureau, 20 Peel Street, London W8 7PD; 020 7221 0098; email spanlabo@globalnet.co.uk.

Starting a Business in Spain: (Vacation Work, 2004); £12.95. By the author of this book, a complete guide to the practicalities and legalities of starting a business that covers all the possibilities in greater detail than is possible in this chapter. Available from www.crimsonpublishing.co.uk.

Tu Propia Empresa: Un Reto Personal. Manual Util para Emprendedores (ESIC Editorial, 2003) €16. Very good, Spanish-language, general analysis of the processes involved in starting a new company in Spain.

## Legal and accounting guides to Spain

The Blevins Franks Guide to Living in Spain: (Blevins Franks, 2003) £6.99. Useful financial guide to Spain by international financial advisers, Blevins Franks.

You and the Law in Spain: (Santana Books, 2003) £19.95. Fourteenth edition of the very helpful and readable guide to Spanish law for foreigners.

# Retiring
# in Spain

# ■ RETIRING ABROAD

Retiring abroad has such an allure that one in five of us will take this route by 2020, according to research by the Centre of Future Studies. There are, at present, more retired foreigners than retired local people along the Spanish coasts, and a staggering 75% of all expatriates in Spain are said to be of retirement age. These statistics certainly guarantee no lack of companionship for the older expatriate and the majority live comfortably, feeling that they have greatly improved their quality of life in their twilight years. A recent survey of retired British residents living in purpose-built estates in areas such as Torremolinos, Mijas and Fuengirola found most to be 'happy with their move' and even 'pleasantly surprised'. Retirees to Spain often become more 'robust, independent and sociable' than their counterparts in Britain. In many ways the Costa del Sol has become Europe's equivalent of America's retirement sunbelt for those from Britain and other European countries who prefer a life in the sun.

However, anyone considering such a move should thoroughly investigate the main issues involved. There has recently been a plethora of TV programmes describing the dire straits in which many British expats find themselves after a few years of what was to be their ideal retirement in Spain. The difficulties of coping on a fixed income with spiralling inflation and an often dismal absence of welfare and aftercare services for the elderly can, in the worst cases, combine to make life in Spain more like a fight for survival. Financial hardship can be even worse when you are away from home. Emotionally, loneliness and isolation can often set in, especially when one partner outlives the other, leaving the survivor alienated and often without enough funds to return to family and friends in the UK.

However, many retired migrants refute the reports of loneliness, poverty and ill health as exaggerations of the sensationalist press and are quick to point out that they are enjoying a far more positive experience of ageing than they would have had in their home country. There is a strong feeling among the communities of retired Brits that older people in Spain are an accepted part of mainstream society and not marginalised as they are in the UK. There is certainly a perception that the elderly are more respected, and hence looked after by the family, rather than being shipped off to an old people's home (of which there are few).

The ability to be active is certainly one aspect that older residents cite as having improved their lives tremendously. Mobility is eased by the warmth of the climate and there are numerous leisure activities and social clubs that people can become involved in. Rather than being stuck at home all day waiting for visitors, older people

> **Naomi Greatbanks**, who spent many years selling property to retired couples in Spain, explains that although there is no doubt that moving to Spain and living in its wonderful climate is therapeutic for many, living costs and inflation have succeeded in bringing both hardship and regrets into the lives of many retired couples.

tend to become a part of a community in which they feel valued, with many taking on important roles in social clubs.

There is no need for a retirement in Spain to be anything but a happy experience if all the necessary and sensible precautions are taken before departure and sufficient homework is done about where, when and how you intend to live once in Spain. Some of the benefits of retiring to Spain include a quality of life which is quieter and often higher than that offered in the UK; property costs are often lower than the equivalent UK prices; and while the climate is generally more temperate, the attraction of a new culture and way of life may act as a great incentive to Brits who are tired of the endless rain, traffic and distinctly uncontinental ambience which often seem to be a part of British life.

## The decision to leave

First and foremost, anyone considering retiring to Spain must be able to afford the move financially. Although in general your living expenses will be lower in Spain, it is vital to calculate what your retirement income will be, allowing for exchange rate fluctuations and inflation. This involves requesting a State Pension Forecast (see below) if you are not already receiving your pension, finding out which other benefits you may continue to claim once in Spain and seeking independent tax advice regarding your investments.

Older people should also consider health issues before deciding to move to Spain. The Spanish are classed as one of the world's healthiest peoples, with male average life expectancy at around 76 and female at around 81. Dietary factors in Spain lead to a far lower number of cases of heart disease, as does the relaxed way of life and reduced stress levels. Those who are healthy and active on arrival in Spain can therefore hope to remain so for longer. Even those who arrive in Spain with minor health issues often find the climate and way of life beneficial.

Certainly those living in the south of Spain will find that there is a much lower incidence of the colds and flu that affect UK residents during the cold damp winters.

However, while the Spanish climate and lifestyle may well be beneficial to your general health, and the public health system first-class, it is important to consider the future, and what will happen if you become seriously ill or no longer able to care for yourself. The Spanish have great reverence for the elderly and as a result older people are almost always cared for by their families.

FACT

■ The ability to be mobile, to take leisurely walks in the fresh air and warm sunshine also has obvious health benefits and statistics do show that older people stay healthy for longer in Spain's stress-free climate.

> **Karen O'Reilly** in her sociological study, The British on the Costa del Sol (Routledge, 2000) sees an enormous contrast between the elderly in Britain, who may sit in a chair all day, staring at the grey skies, without the motivation to go out for walks, play bowls, swim, or simply chat with friends in a nearby café or bar:
>
> 'It often struck me how different the elderly migrants in Spain looked compared with elderly people in Britain. They wore bright colours, suntans, shorts and T-shirts, lots of jewellery, and smiles. They looked fit and healthy...the migrants were aware of a feeling of freedom from restriction on dress and behaviour. I overheard Joan, a full resident in her fifties, tell her new migrant friend, "You can wear what you like, no-one takes any notice really. I couldn't dress like this back home, not at my age!"

**FACT**

■ The family unit is much tighter in Spain than we are used to in the UK or USA so traditionally there has not been the need for networks of nursing homes and personal homecare services.

While social and economic developments in Spain are forcing this situation to gradually change, the infrastructure is still insufficient in all but the most heavily expat-concentrated areas. This is an important issue, especially as the UK government is considering ways of enforcing the rule that people who have lived abroad for more than six months are no longer immediately eligible for free NHS care upon returning to the UK.

You will also need to possess copious amounts of energy and enthusiasm to deal with the move practically and emotionally. Problems often arise when children and grandchildren are left behind. Women often feel this wrench much more than men and for some the homesickness can have a very negative effect on the new life in Spain. For this reason and because many decisions to move abroad are based on a love of the country discovered through past holidays, it is quite a good idea to consider a long stay of, say, six months which includes the winter period, in the area in which you are interested before moving permanently.

Many retired people have a lifestyle that takes them to Spain during the winter months (when holidays and longer stays are cheap) returning to Britain only for the more pleasant spring and summer. Alternatively, if you have sufficient funds, you

> According to Cyril Holbrook, in his book Retiring to Spain (Age Concern, 2004), the climate has a markedly beneficial effect on many who suffer from arthritic or rheumatic ailments, and many people find relief from the aches in their joints within a few weeks.
>
> 'It has been known for crutches and even wheelchairs to be left behind in bars or restaurants after a hearty night out, the refreshed foreigners obviously forgetting that they needed such assistance on the way there.'

## Age Concern España factsheets

**ACE offers the following fact sheets, available free of charge if you send a large SAE:**

- Tele-alarm
- Breast cancer screening
- Help with incontinence
- Palma de Mallorca European Social Services
- Mallorca Social Services
- Menorca Social Services
- Ibiza Social Services
- What to do in case of death
- Personal check sheet
- Precautions against falls
- UK habitual residence test
- Keeping well and keeping warm
- Social Security Offices in Palma de Mallorca
- Hospital visiting service
- British War Disability Pension
- Benefits from UK charities
- Healthcare in the Community
- Cataracts and eye surgery
- Clinics and hospitals in the Balearics
- Spanish Telefónica answerphone service
- Healthcare for cats and dogs
- Glaucoma
- Diabetic retinopathy in the home
- Retiring to Spain
- Lanzarote SocialServices Centres
- Hospitals in Lanzarote

Further details of their main activities are on the website: www.acespana.org. Listed below are the contact details of the main branches in Spain:

*Federación Age Concern España:* 971 231520; email federation@ageconcern-espana.org.

*Age Concern Costa Blanca Sur:* 965 710506.

Age Concern Estepona y Manilva: Málaga; 952 897251.

*Age Concern Ibiza y Formentera:* 971 303106; email acibiza@ageconcern-espana.org.

*Age Concern Lanzarote:* Apartado 287, 35571 Macher, Lanzarote.

*Age Concern Mallorca:* 971 777179; email acmallorca@ageconcern-espana.org

*Age Concern Menorca:* 971 377023.

could buy a second home in Spain and then sell your UK residence and move abroad permanently after a trial period of staying there. Both of these suggestions should be considered, as many parts of Spain that are bustling and cheerful in the summer are correspondingly deserted and desolate in the winter.

## Residence requirements

Despite the changes to residence regulations in 2003, pensioners from within the EU are still required to obtain a residence card (*tarjeta de residencia communtaria*) if they have retired to Spain. However, those who have paid into the Spanish social security system and receive their pension from the Spanish government no longer need a residence card and can live in Spain with a valid passport. Nevertheless, the British Embassy in Spain advises that all residents obtain a residence card even if it is not obligatory for them, as it simplifies many of the administration procedures for new residents. Also, a residence card is required to be able to use the Spanish public health system.

Full details of all residence and entry requirements for Spain are on page 30, Residence and Entry Regulations. However, pensioners should be aware that when applying for their residence card they will need to supply the nearest *oficina de extranjeros* with proof of their pension as well as the usual required documents. One way of proving that you are in receipt of a UK state pension is to arrange for it to be paid into your Spanish bank account, and then display a stamped letter from the bank as proof.

Some may find the detailed advice available from the UK Department of Work and Pensions offices helpful, and the Spanish Consulate-General in London can supply a separate leaflet of general information for pensioners who wish to retire in Spain.

## Age Concern España

A useful source of guidance and information for older people living in Spain or thinking of moving to Spain is the charity Age Concern España. ACE was established in 1994 to promote the well-being of older English-speaking people living in Spain, and has been growing ever since. The charity is run by English-speaking volunteers and provides a number of services including information, assistance to people who find themselves in difficult circumstances, often due to bereavement or poverty, a home visiting service and equipment loan.

**FACT**

■ There are numerous groups around the country that offer expats a chance to learn new things and meet new people.

# ■ HOBBIES AND INTERESTS

## Pensioners' clubs

You will find a pensioners' club (*hogar de pensionistas*) conveniently and centrally located in most Spanish towns and villages. Each club has its own bar, television and newspaper facilities, while some are so well organised as to arrange for a local doctor to call on the club, for the convenience of its members. While membership is primarily Spanish, the warmth with which expatriates are received within these clubs is a testament to Spanish hospitality. Anyone over 65 is eligible to join and apart from the obvious social possibilities, drinks are usually subsidised and offered at prices slightly lower than those found in most other bars or cafés.

# English-speaking organisations

There will be many English-speaking community organisations, wherever you are, centred around cultural organisations, newcomers clubs, theatre groups, churches and places of worship. There are so many local clubs that the best way to find out the most information is via the local English-language press. For example, the *Costa Blanca News* lists hundreds of English-speaking social clubs each week. Most clubs organise any number of activities for their members, such as bridge and chess evenings, outings, dances and social events. Social clubs are a very good way of meeting people and of gleaning information and advice.

Membership fees vary enormously from around €10 to up to €100 per year, depending on their facilities (some social clubs offer a clubhouse, library, bar, or restaurant). As an example of the number and variety of social clubs available to expatriates, a recent listing for the Costa del Sol included, among others, dancing clubs, theatre groups, spiritual awareness societies, an oompah band, a breakfast business club, craft classes, a Chelsea supporters' club, a digital camera club, gardening clubs, a glass painting club, writers' groups, slimming clubs, a computer club, a Morris dancing club, over-50s singles clubs, a number of sports clubs including sailing, walking, bowls, running, cycling, table tennis, tai chi, archery, cricket, darts, golf, diving and watersports. On top of this many of the social organisations that function in the UK exist in Spain, such as Lions clubs, Rotary International, the Royal British Legion, and the Royal Naval Association. Whatever you want to become involved in, the network of expatriates in Spain can help you.

# University of the Third Age

Those who crave intellectual stimulation during their retirement will be interested to know that there are numerous groups around the country that offer expats a chance to learn new things and meet new people. One of the most important of these groups is the University of the Third Age (U3A), an educational and social association that began in France in the 1970s. There are now around 1,773 U3As in 39 countries, offering educational courses very cheaply for pensioners and others. Courses range from languages to genealogy, creative writing and history, and also serve as a good opportunity to meet new people. There are currently three branches of U3A operating in Spain – on the Costa Brava (www.u3acostabrava.org); and on the Costa del Sol (www.u3acostadelsol.org).

# Sport

As far as sporting activities go, these are many and varied. Golf enthusiasts in particular need look no further: in southern Spain the climate lends itself ideally to the sport, and you will find that virtually all of the popular resort and retirement areas have golf courses within easy reach, as do many of the new housing complexes, although the membership fees are becoming more and more pricey. You will find a list of golf clubs in the local Yellow Pages (*Páginas Amarillas*) and the national or local tourist offices can provide information about courses.

Beach life in Spain offers yet more opportunities for the sporty; and swimming, sailing and fishing are all easily available along the coasts. Tennis is very popular; and hard courts, both public and private, can be easily found in most areas.

So a retirement in Spain can be as sociable and gregarious as the person considering it. The life around the pubs and bars offers another way to meet people and form a circle of friends and acquaintances. Then there is travel. Being based in Spain offers a good opportunity to explore this vast and scenically diverse country. Camping and caravanning facilities are generally good and most public transport and other leisure facilities offer generous discounts for senior citizens. For those who drive, it is relatively easy to get to Portugal, Andorra and France. Morocco is a short boat ride away. Pensioners can receive concessionary cards from their local rail and bus stations upon proof of age and residence.

### International places of worship

British Embassy Church of St. George: C/ Nuñez de Balboa 43, 28001 Madrid; 915 765109; email stgeorgemadrid@telefonica.net.

Community Church of Madrid: C/ Viña 3, 28014 Madrid; 655 031857.

Immanuel Baptist Church: C/ Hernandez de Tejada 4, 28027 Madrid; 914 074347; email info@ibcmadrid.com; www.ibcmadrid.com.

Mountainview International Church: C/ Playa de Sangenjo 26, 28230 (Las Rozas), Madrid; 916 305137; email info@mountainview-church.com; www.mountainview-church.com.

Our Lady of Mercy Catholic Church: C/ Drácena 23, 28016 Madrid; 913 503449; email ourladyofmercy@terra.es; www.ourladyofmercy.info/.

Synagogue: C/ Balmés 3, 28010 Madrid; 915 913131; email info@ comjudiamadrid.org.

## ■ CHOOSING AND BUYING A HOME FOR RETIREMENT

The main point to make about buying a retirement property in Spain is to choose something that is both within your reach financially and which, unlike a holiday home, is suitable for year-round living. You will also need to take into consideration the running and upkeep costs of the property in question. Buying an apartment within a block of flats which works on the *comunidad* principle, for instance, can help ease some of the budgeting costs involved in house maintenance. Proximity to facilities is also an important consideration for anyone reliant on public transport. The availability of buses, and general accessibility – even if you yourself own a car – should be part of your decision to buy or not to buy. Once you have decided on your new home you will need to follow all the procedures for property purchase which are explained in full on page 123.

## Where to buy

Both the British Consulate and Age Concern España advise people to look ahead when considering where to buy their retirement home. Although none of us likes to think about the possibility of ill health in our later years, these facts have to be faced, and while it may be ideal to live in a beautiful but remote spot in your 50s, in your 60s the long trek to the nearest health centre may become a real burden. Also bear in mind that if you need home help in later life, then only municipalities with a population greater than 20,000 have a legal obligation to provide home help for the elderly and infirm, although many smaller towns and villages do so anyway.

Proximity to amenities and the best services, particularly English-speaking services, will probably also mean living in one of Spain's many pockets of foreign residents. The best known of these are the Costa del Sol, the Costa Blanca (especially around Benidorm) and the Balearic and Canary Islands. While many will relish the thought of living within a community of expatriates, being able to buy Marmite and decent tea, many others find this an unbearable thought and will be intending to get away from other foreigners to live among a real Spanish community. This is a very personal decision, but a possible compromise is to live in one of the more cosmopolitan cities such as Madrid, Barcelona, Seville or Valencia, all of which have English-speaking amenities and are large enough to either avoid the expatriate population or become a part of it.

## Retirement villages

The over-55 age group make up over 50% of the total number of foreign owners of property in Spain. However, this fact, so far, is not reflected in the number of retirement homes being built in the country (see below). This gap in the market has led some developers to build top-end retirement developments and sheltered housing with 24-hour medical facilities on site, particularly along the Costa del Sol around Marbella and along the Costa Blanca. These properties have much the same features as similar outfits back home – swimming pools, restaurants,

Retiring in Spain can improve your quality of life

medical block, shopping centre, gym – and as with *urbanizaciónes* there are additional service charges payable (around €30–€80 per month) on top of the purchase price of the flat. The difference is that there is 24-hour security and medical care on site, as well as home cleaning services, room-service food, and a laundry and grocery service.

Most these residential developments have all of the luxuries expected from an *urbanización*, but being age-specific they have the added advantage that residents will be surrounded by people with similar interests. Many of these developments organise cultural and sporting activities for their residents including arts and crafts, music, languages, computer courses, bridge, chess, and walking.

Depending on what you are looking for – whether you are happy to live out your last years away from your family back home – nursing costs in Spain are likely to be lower and residential nursing homes far more appealing than those in, for instance, the UK. If you are only a temporary resident in Spain, you may even be able to generate some income by renting out a sheltered property to senior citizens back home in need of a bit of sun.

One such residential resort home, with 24-hour medical service, being advertised at the time of going to press was Sol Andalusí (Málaga; 952 963096; email info@ solandalusi.com; www.solandalusi.com). Another is Sanyres (www.sanyres.es), part of the Prasa Property Group (Córdoba; 957 475676; www.grupoprasa.es), with 10 residential developments already open in the provinces of Córdoba, Madrid, La Coruña, La Rioja, Málaga, Alicante, and Léon, and 15 more centres planned by 2009 all over Spain.

# ◼ PENSIONS

## Receiving Spanish or UK state pensions

Although there is no set retirement age in Spain, workers may retire and become eligible for a state pension when they reach the age of 60 for women, and 65 for men. Spanish pensions are among the highest in Europe. The minimum pension at age 65 is around €400 per month for a single person, and the maximum is over €2,000. Another bonus is that just as workers receive 14 pay packets per year, pensioners also receive 14 payments including the two *pagas extraordinarias* usually paid in December and in the summer.

Anyone who moves to Spain before reaching retirement age should continue to pay National Insurance contributions in the UK to qualify for a British state pension once they do reach 65. Failure to do so may result in not being eligible for a UK pension on reaching retirement age, depending on the number of years' contributions made. This is a thorny issue and it is best to seek advice from the Inland

Revenue National Insurance Contributions Office (Benton Park View, Newcastle upon Tyne NE98 1ZZ).

To receive a Spanish state pension, you must have worked and paid social security contributions in Spain for a minimum of 15 years. However, contributions made previously in another EU country are transferable to Spain and count towards your entitlement. Even a few years working in Spain can produce a worthwhile pension. The qualifying period for a full pension in Spain is 45 years (in the UK it is 44 years). Any pension will therefore be paid as a proportion of that total.

Usually each country will pay the percentage of the pension for which it is liable. For example, if one-third of the social security contributions you have made were in the form of UK national insurance contributions, then the UK would pay one-third of the total state pension it has worked out you could get. The other two-thirds, presumably made in Spain, would come from the Spanish government. The pension is calculated mainly on the last 15 years of working life and especially the last two. UK citizens should obtain certificate E301, which shows the amount of social security contributions they have made. This can be obtained from the Department of Social Security Overseas Branch (Newcastle upon Tyne NE98 1YX; 0191 2253963).

The self-employed in Spain, who pay their social security contributions under a different scheme, as a *trabajador autónomo* are able to set their contributions at a higher level to receive a greater state pension upon retirement. For example, a salary base as high as €2,700 per month may be chosen, thereby making contributions pertaining to that base and receiving the maximum pension upon retirement. However, most people still choose the minimum level of payment.

Those planning to start receiving their UK state pension in Spain should request a Retirement Pension Forecast, which will tell you the amount of state pension you have already earned and the amount you can expect to receive at state pension age. This will help you to plan exactly how far your pension will go in Spain. To receive a forecast, obtain form BR19 from your local social security office or contact the Retirement Pension Forecasting and Advice Unit (DWP, Newcastle upon Tyne, NE98 1BA; 0191 218 7585). If you are already in Spain, contact the Inland Revenue and ask for form CA3638.

Before moving to Spain, contact the Pensions and Overseas Benefits Directorate of the Department of Work and Pensions in Newcastle upon Tyne, NE98 1YX; 0191 218 7147 to obtain a couple of forms which must be completed to arrange the transfer of your UK pension to either an address in Spain or a bank account in either the UK or Spain.

The DWP Overseas Benefits Directorate office in Newcastle also publishes Leaflet SA29 (available if you send an SAE), which provides details on EU pension and social security legislation. You can download the leaflet from www.dwp.gov.uk/international/sa29/index.asp. Further help and advice is available from the International Pension Service (0191 218 7777).

You can be paid a UK state pension in Spain and will receive exactly the same amount

**FACT**

■ Note that pensions are not frozen at the level they reached on arrival in Spain; instead the pension will rise in accordance with any increases which take effect in the UK.

as you would have done in Spain. This pension can be paid directly into your UK bank account or into your account in Spain. Alternatively you can choose to receive payment by payable orders sent by post. Payment is made every one (only in the UK), four or 13 weeks in arrears. Non-EU citizens are also able to receive a pension from abroad in Spain.

UK company pensions are paid as per the rules of the individual company. They may say that your company pension may only be paid into a UK account, in which case it will be necessary to set up a standing order from your UK account to your Spanish account.

It is important to examine your payment options when receiving a pension from abroad as the bank abroad may charge for making the transfer, and your bank in Spain may also apply a commission. It pays to shop around. Those living on the Costa del Sol often use the banks in Gibraltar to avoid the charges that Spanish banks make on sterling payments. It may also be more sensible to have the money transferred in quarterly instalments rather than monthly, as the charge is often less. Alternatively a currency dealer, such as Currencies Direct (020 7813 0332; www.currenciesdirect.com) will allow you to make an annual arrangement that fixes the exchange rate for a year, insuring you against currency fluctuations.

## Exportable UK benefits

On top of your UK pension, once you have received Spanish residence, you are still entitled to some UK benefits such as any Bereavement Allowance (payable for up to one year), and Widowed Parent's Allowance.

You can find out more in two leaflets; Going Abroad and Social Security Benefits (GL29), available from your local social security office, and the DWP's leaflet SA 29, mentioned above. A useful source of advice and information on any of the above issues is the International Pension Centre (0191 218 7777; www.dwp.gov.uk).

## Private pensions

Spain's ageing population means that a growing number of retirees are being supported by fewer and fewer workers. The future of the state pension is therefore in jeopardy, especially as they remain comparatively generous and more people receive income from the state than from the private sector. It is estimated that by 2015 there will be over 7.5 million pensioners in Spain and the state pension fund, which has verged on bankruptcy before, may run into problems. The Spanish government is trying to encourage people to pay into private pension funds to supplement their social security benefits.

Given that you must contribute to Spanish social security for 15 years before becoming entitled to a Spanish private state pension, it may be a good idea to sign up to a private pension scheme. The Spanish banks and some private companies offer a range of pension funds. It is also possible to continue contributing to a personal pension plan abroad and many of the European private pension companies

**FACT**

■ There are a number of benefits that you can no longer receive once living abroad. These include Disability Living Allowance, Income Support, Pension Credit, Attendance Allowance, and Carer's Allowance. Some pensioners find their income substantially reduced when they move to Spain.

have offices in Spain. Spanish taxpayers may normally deduct pension contributions up to a maximum annual limit of €9,015 from their taxable income.

Spanish pensions usually require a small minimum monthly payment, sometimes as low as €30. Lump sum contributions can be made whenever you like, although they must usually be more than around €600. Pensions should be index-linked so that they keep pace with inflation. Index-linked policies ensure that capital is tax-free after contributions have been made for 15 years, but there is an increasing scale of tax penalties for early surrender. Some of the main Spanish pension providers are listed below.

Some of the larger companies in Spain have set up supplementary pension schemes for their employees. These *planes de pensiones* are set up voluntarily and are deemed by Spanish law to be of a private nature. They may be set up and administered by corporations, companies, enterprises, associations, trade unions and many other bodies. Although there is no compulsory retirement age in Spain, some company pension schemes are designed to induce employees to retire at a certain age, usually between 60 and 65.

### Private pension plan providers

Axa Seguros y Reaseguros: www.axa-seguros.es.
Caser Segruos: 902 222747; email comunicacion@caser.es; www.caser.es.
Direct Seguros: 902 404025; email operaciones@directseguros.es; www.directseguros.es.
La Estrella Seguros: 902 333433; www.laestrella.es.
Seguros El Corte Ingles: Madrid; 901 122122; http://seguroeseci.elcorteingles.es.
Winterthur: 902 303012; email winterthur@winterthur.es; www.winterthur.es.

### Useful addresses

John Siddall Financial Services Ltd: 01329 288641; email: spain@johnsiddalls.co.uk; www.siddalls.net. Siddalls are independent financial advisers providing expertise across a spectrum of investments, retirement and tax planning for private clients at home and abroad. Siddalls have many years experience in assisting British nationals wishing to become resident in Spain with all aspects of their financial planning. Siddalls are part of the IFG Group Plc and authorised and regulated by the Financial Services Authority.

# ■ FINANCE

Anyone considering retiring to Spain should take specialist financial advice about their own situation. Most people in a position to retire overseas have an amount of capital to invest, or will have once they sell their UK home; and it is essential to take good advice on how and where this may best be done. Those who intend to maintain connections with both the UK and Spain will need advice on how their taxation affairs can be sorted out to their own advantage. Usually, there is no reason why you should not continue with bank accounts or investments already established in the UK, and in most cases interest will be paid on deposits paid without deduction of tax where you are non-resident. A good source of information and advice on all financial and tax matters is *the Blevins Franks Guide to Living in Spain* by Bill Blevins and David Franks, available from www.blevinsfranks.com.

One of the major issues regarding your investments is currency fluctuations. If you have investments that are sterling-based or dollar-based, then as you will be spending euros from now on, the value of your investments may go up and down with the exchange rate. Of course, the value of your investments will not crystallise until such a time as you sell them. However, any revenue generated from these investments will fluctuate in value. It is best to consider offshore options for your investments, or to think about obtaining investments that pay out in euros. For all of these considerations, you will need a tax adviser who has expertise in both your home country and Spain.

## Taxation

Taxation is inextricably linked with investment considerations. Reasonably impartial advice can be obtained from the UK Inland Revenue (the Spanish equivalent tends to be less helpful), which has no wish to tax people on income to which they are clearly not entitled. Those in need of taxation advice should contact the Inland Revenue Office with which they last dealt.

Because the UK tax year runs from April to April and the Spanish one from January to December there are certain advantages and disadvantages, from a tax point of view, in choosing a particular removal date. Whereas employees are not usually able to indulge in such freedom of choice, the retired person should consider this seriously.

UK pensions paid to British expatriates are subject to Spanish tax, unless the pensioner is exempted by a double tax agreement, or he or she is a former public service employee who worked abroad (in which case the pension is taxable in the UK, although sometimes not liable to any tax at all). The double taxation agreement only relates to pensions in Spain if you are resident there. Whether your pension is liable for UK income tax or Spanish tax, it may be better in either case to elect to take a tax-free lump sum pension option, thereby reducing the level of pension liable to tax.

## Offshore banking

From a retired person's point of view, if he or she has a sum of money they wish to invest or put into a long-term deposit account (for a minimum of 90 days) it is well worth looking at the tax-saving options like ISAs (Individual Savings Accounts) that banks and building societies all offer in Britain in addition to the offshore account. Banks, building societies and merchant banks all offer accounts through offshore banking centres in tax havens such as Gibraltar and the Channel Islands. The basic difference from an onshore account is that these investments pay income gross of tax, which of course is ultimately taxable, but they do offer legal ways of paying less tax.

These ways of paying less tax are mainly through roll-up funds, an investment vehicle in which you buy shares; and offshore life insurance, which practitioners like to stress is really an integral part of Britain's tax planning industry. For how much and when to sell you certainly need the advice of a financial planning expert, or a company to administer the fund for you. You can also defer paying tax to a time of your own choosing, perhaps when you anticipate you will need the money or when you enter a lower tax bracket income-wise. Offshore life insurance policies offer similar tax savings.

Most of the banks and building societies offer useful explanatory leaflets.

## Offshore trusts

One important tool for the investor moving to Spain is offshore trusts. Shares, bonds, funds and bank deposits can all become free from Spanish income tax, wealth tax, inheritance tax and capital gains tax, simply by putting them into trust. Trusts, although complicated, are possibly the most effective tool for individuals wishing to minimise their tax liability. Put simply, setting up a trust involves giving assets to 'trustees' – usually a trust company located in a low tax regime. The way in which trustees manage your assets will be stipulated when the trust is set up. Some people hand all control over their assets to the trustees and others prefer to play more of an integral role in the management of their assets.

#  HEALTHCARE

It is generally agreed that the Spanish system of public healthcare, available free to all pensioners with a residence card, is very efficient and the quality of care of an extremely high standard. Many British expats living in Spain claim that the system is more advanced than the NHS in the UK, and that waiting lists for operations are far shorter. This is a fairly subjective viewpoint, but it seems fair to say that medical facilities in Spain are excellent. Many doctors and nurses speak English and most hospitals and clinics in the main tourist areas provide interpreters.

However, it is vital that those with any health issues look into the level of care available to them before moving to Spain. The availability of certain services does vary from locality to locality and if facilities are not available to meet your specific needs, you may have to travel to another area for treatment. Those who fear a shortfall in public healthcare, could consider taking out private insurance. There is more about Spanish medical care on page 184.

A list of English-speaking doctors will be available from the local British Consulate: this will, however, often involve using private facilities. You may choose your own general practitioner, provided that the GP's number of patients does not exceed the limits established in that particular area. Pensioners in Spain are entitled both to free medical care and free prescription medicine. However, Spanish social security does not cover dental treatment, dentures or spectacles.

Remember to take copies of your medical records with you to present to your new doctor. It is also a good idea to find out the generic name for any prescribed medication that you are taking, as this can vary from country to country.

When in hospital in Spain, it is the job of nurses to provide medical attention only, and not to deal with welfare issues, which are usually provided by the patients' family. Age Concern España provides a hospital visiting service for those who require it.

## The E121 and E106

The first step for retired UK citizens, before moving to Spain, is to obtain the form E121 from the Pension Service (0191 218 7777; email tvp-ipc-customercare@thepensionservice.gsi.gov.uk). This form gives access to the Spanish health system for British state retirement pensioners, their spouses and dependent children, and for anyone receiving the UK incapacity Benefit. Without it, you will be charged for

> **Judy Arnold-Boakes** of Age Concern España
> in a recent article in The Observer:
> 'In some areas the authorities don't pick up the bill when a person runs out of money and in some areas they do. Some areas provide the full range of social services help. Others don't. And what is the policy today may not be the policy in 15 years'.

treatment. Your form must be registered at the local social security office (*Instituto Nacional de Seguridad Social*), for which you will need your residence permit. If you are submitting the E121 for registration before the application for residencia has been approved, you should submit a copy of the residencia application form.

Many retired British people simply rely on their EHIC card for healthcare. However, this card is really intended only for emergencies. Until recently the authorities did not really bother to control this, and the EHIC card was sufficient (many hospitals barely bothered to look at it). These days the rules are far more likely to be enforced, and patients may well be asked for flight tickets as proof of when they arrived in Spain. It is therefore far more sensible to obtain and register the E121.

Those who move to Spain before UK state retirement age are able to obtain temporary cover for healthcare for up to two and a half years by filling in form E106. This form is also available from the Department of Work and Pensions, or the Inland Revenue.

## Care in the home and residential care

As mentioned earlier, Spain has a long tradition of looking after its old people in the family home. This has presented a major problem for many retired expatriates who have reached the stage where they can no longer care for themselves. In most areas of Spain the infrastructure for caring for the elderly is simply not yet in place. It is only in the last few years that any long-term care homes have sprung up in any number, many of them to cater solely for Britons and Germans. With the infrastructure for caring for the elderly and infirm in its infancy, this can become a major issue for retirees a little further down the line, when struck by illness, or the death of a partner. The provision of social care can vary enormously from one local authority to another.

British consular officials recommend that people should make provisions long in advance for the point when they will no longer be able to look after themselves.

As Martine mentions, homecare is available from social services. Indeed, it is a legal requirement that town councils (in communities with a population of more than 20,000) provide home help for those who are unfit to look after themselves properly. The council sends a carer (often unqualified) to provide assistance with, for example, cooking, cleaning and shopping. However these carers can often only come in for 15 minutes a day, with no services provided in the evenings, at weekends, or during public holidays, which may be insufficient. These services can vary dramatically in quality from one area to another, so when planning for the future it is important to consider what is available in the area you have chosen.

> 'The influx of retirees to Spain has created quite a problem. I have seen too many people in a terrible state because they could not afford proper nursing. If the elderly are healthy then there is no problem, but issues arise when one or both partners need some help. Many people are forced to return to their country of origin to receive full-time care. There are very few public nursing homes and even the private homes have enormous waiting lists. Homecare can be provided by social services in the town where you live, but this is a minimal service.
> Further problems arise when people are living illegally in Spain. Many are forced to pay for people who are not professionals to visit them in their own homes, as they are not eligible for support from social services. Often these people have no training and are simply earning extra money by offering caring services. This is potentially disastrous as the patients may be very vulnerable.'
> **Martine de Volder, nurse in Tenerife**

To qualify for this kind of assistance, the expatriate must have a residence card, and also be registered at the local town hall.

Those concerned for their own vulnerability may like to consider the Red Cross Tele-Alarm system, which is operated in several areas of Spain. This allows the elderly to be in contact with someone who can help them 24 hours a day. Subscribers wear a button, either on a pendant or wrist band, which if pressed sends a signal down the telephone line to the control centre, who will be able to see the person's details immediately and ask them the nature of the problem or, if the person is unable to speak, contact the emergency services. Subscribers to this potentially lifesaving facility pay a one-off installation charge and monthly rental and service charge. Further details can be obtained from Age Concern España.

Also of interest to the increasingly immobile is the growing availability of the types of mobility aids we are used to in the UK, such as stair and bath lifts, mobility scooters, and wheelchairs. These are becoming much easier to locate in Spain, especially in areas with a high concentration of expatriates. Prices tend to be much lower than in the UK. One company with a number of shops in Spain is Mobility Abroad (01375 377246; lo-call 0845 644 2892; email enquiries@mobilityabroad. com; www.mobilityabroad.com).

Residential and nursing homes are available, but as yet there is a vastly insufficient number of them in Spain. As a result there are large waiting lists for most of these places. If you do manage to get a place in a home, many people report that the facilities lag way behind UK standards. Another problem is that very few local councils provide homes and most are private. Subsidies are not usually available, so it means bearing the entire cost yourself, which can be very expensive. According to Age Concern España, monthly costs for 24-hour care in a home are likely to be between €2,000 and €2,800 per month, and most residents will have to pay this themselves. An alternative is to live in a retirement village (see above), which allows pensioners to own their own apartments, but within a luxury development including 24-hour medical care and various services.

# Time Off

# ◼ TIME OFF

Despite the tens of millions of foreign tourists visiting Spanish resorts each year making Spain one of the most popular tourist destinations in the world, surprisingly few of these visitors have ever explored beyond the confines of the most 'touristy' areas. However, if you live in Spain, opportunites to explore the country, and to get to grips with its culture, traditions, customs and manners – and to have a lot of fun in the process – are limitless.

One way to discover Spain is by consciously making an effort to travel even a little way from the coast or the big cities, where social distractions are geared to international tastes as much as local demands. The radically improved road network has succeeded in making the interior accessible to everyone; and as the costas experience a slight decline in popularity, so the National Tourist Office in Spain is successfully promoting a rather different image of the country and its many unspoilt and undiscovered regions inland, as a destination for cultural and special interest holidays, as well as a summer vacation by the beach.

Anyone thinking of living and working in Spain certainly needs to experience some of the real Spanish flavour, which is among the liveliest and most colourful in Europe. If you are now living on the coast, you can plan excursions inland; getting away from it all will now, for many, mean getting away from all those tourists! And the Spanish Tourist Office *Turespaña* can provide some helpful leaflets (www.tourspain.es). To travel successfully, it is also helpful to have a knowledge of Castilian (or perhaps one of Spain's other languages, see page 39. The Spanish Languages). To understand the Spanish character and attitudes, a knowledge of the history, ancient as well as recent, is also a must. Spain has changed so rapidly in the last 20 odd years that it is hard even for the Spanish themselves to come to terms with all these changes and the liberties they now possess after decades of repression.

This is so among older people at any rate. The greatest changes have been in the lifestyle of the young. The 'economic miracle' of Spain has been achieved in part through these changes in society, and to some degree of dislocation as well, in particular the movement of inhabitants from one region to another to fulfil the labour demands of the big cities. Spain, like Britain, is now mainly an industrial country (with an agricultural sector in decline). This has left vast tracts of countryside virtually abandoned; and the customs and traditions pertaining to them may soon require scholarly research to preserve their memory, as Spaniards become increasingly homogeneous and separated from their roots. However, there is still a pastoral nostalgia in Spain, even among younger people, for the *pueblo*, or home village.

Meanwhile there are still plenty of traditional customs to be found in the villages and smaller towns, where the social life often revolves around cafés and bars, and also outdoor *fiestas*, in which the whole community takes part. In the bars and clubs of the big cities, life is more like that to be found in any city, anywhere in the world. One difference is that nightlife begins late (perhaps because of the daytime heat), and goes on into the early hours.

The two main categories of foreign resident in Spain are the retired expatriate who may or may not run a small business, and the person who goes there to take up employment, temporary or long term. The expatriate community for either has its own social network. For those who arrive without any contacts there are ways of forming them: through the local English churches and through activity clubs (e.g. bridge, golf and painting) and pubs and bars in the area. The newspapers and magazines that serve the English-speaking community in Spain (see Newspapers, page 172) provide an invaluable source of information, listing various social activities and events taking place in the area.

# ■ PUBLIC HOLIDAYS AND *FIESTAS*

Celebration is second nature in Spain. There are literally hundreds of *fiestas* and holidays with ancestral rites that have been preserved for centuries to maintain regional identities. If there's one thing the Spanish are good at, it is celebrating, and they do it as enthusiastically and vibrantly as possible. Indeed, the number of *fiestas* throughout Spain is growing year on year as local people set about energetically recovering customs and ceremonies that had been long forgotten.

**FACT**

■ Most towns in Spain have their own festival, usually linked to the patron saint.

Most of these celebrations have a religious origin, others are based on historical events, and other *fiestas* have origins that have been lost in the mists of time, but in almost all cases the most important aspect is the coming together of the community and having a party.

Some of the *fiestas* are simply days off, but others are week-long carousing sessions, where all work stops and the people take to the streets. Some of these have become famous worldwide, such as San Fermínes (Pamplona's bull-running festival), or the ferias of Seville.

The total number of legal national holidays per year, including the many regional ones, is 14. In addition, the various regions and localities have their own festivals and carnivals which may not officially be public holidays but when most facilities will be closed. The national holidays are shown below. If a holiday falls on a Tuesday or Thursday, most people take an extra day's holiday on the Monday or Friday to give them a long weekend (known as *puente* – bridge).

## Christmas (*Navidad* ) and New Year (*Año Nuevo*)

Christmas in Spain is a magical affair and far less commercial than in the UK or America. The lights, decorations and glut of sumptuous Christmas supplies in the shops do not really appear until around 8 December, the Feast of the Immaculate Conception (*inmaculada*), which marks the beginning of religious Christmas celebrations. There are some notable celebrations in the build up to Christmas, for example *Inmaculada* in Seville and Hogueras in Granada (a celebration which takes place on the winter solstice and involves people throughout the city leaping through bonfires to protect themselves from illness).

However, the main celebrations begin on Christmas Eve, known as *nochebuena*. This is the most important family gathering of the year and families sit down to a long evening meal, typically of shellfish starters, followed by roast lamb, and rounded off with *turrón* for desert (a nougat made of toasted sweet almonds). Many people then attend midnight mass (*la misa del gallo*). Throughout Spain there are various traditional processions, nativities and celebrations on *nochebuena*. One particularly appealing tradition, *caga tió*, takes place in towns in Catalonia, where

## Public holidays

| | |
|---|---|
| 1 January | New Year's Day |
| 6 January | Epiphany |
| March/April | Good Friday |
| 1 May | Labour Day |
| 15 August | Assumption |
| 12 October | National Day |
| 1 November | All Saints' Day |
| 6 December | Constitution Day |
| 8 December | Conception |
| 25 December | Christmas Day |

a tree trunk stuffed with sweets and presents is installed and then attacked by children with sticks, eager to extract the goodies.

Christmas Day is not a day of great celebration in Spain, more one of relaxation and a long family lunch. In more traditional households there are no presents until 6 January, the day when the three wise men arrive (riding horses and camels in spectacular parades throughout most towns) and then at night come in through the windows of households sharing out presents. However, most children have now heard of Santa Claus and so receive at least some of their presents on Christmas Day.

The day of *Santos Innocentes* (holy fools) takes place on 28 December and is the equivalent of April Fools' day in the UK. People throughout Spain play tricks on one another and the national media often include a number of bogus stories. *Noche Vieja* (New Year's Eve) is a huge celebration all over the country.

## *Carnaval*

*Carnaval* takes place across Spain in various guises, although the biggest celebrations take place in Cádiz, Santa Cruz de Tenerife and Barcelona. The celebrations have their roots in a period of overindulgence, debauchery, madness and general subversion of the established order, before the fasting and sobriety demanded by Lent. It was partly for this reason, and partly because masked participants could not be recognised during times of insurgency, that Franco banned *Carnaval* and it is only since 1975 that the festivities have returned.

The only real common denominator of *Carnaval* throughout Spain is the huge array of food consumed (especially meat – of which traditionally they will soon be deprived). Other than this the processions and rituals vary enormously, heavily influenced by local customs. The most lavish carnival is held in Santa Cruz de Tenerife, which includes colourful fancy dress and a flamboyant procession,

**FACT**

■ At the stroke of midnight it is customary to eat 12 grapes, one on each stroke of the clock, to bring good luck for the New Year. These should be washed down with cava. Most people stay at home until after midnight and then the young hit the street parties and clubs until the early hours.

which could easily be mistaken for carnival in Rio. In Cádiz *Carnaval* managed to avoid being banned throughout history and its festivities bear a strong resemblance to the carnival in Venice, with whom the city had strong trade links in the 16<sup>th</sup> century. Particularly spectacular are the float parade, fancy dress, jokes and choruses.

# Easter

During *Semana Santa* (Holy Week), the week leading up to Easter, there are thousands of processions covering the length and breadth of the country. Carefully constructed decorations and elaborate costumes are fundamental to these processions, which wind through town streets complete with enormous images representing the last days of Christ. In some regions of Spain these processions are fairly sombre affairs and even include acts of penitence and self-abasement. In Andalucía, however, and particularly in Seville, which is renowned for the mystery and solemnity of its Holy Week celebrations, the emphasis is far more on the splendour of the costumes and floats. The different stages of the events leading to the crucifixion are also represented in 'passion plays' that take place throughout Spain, especially in Catalonia.

On Easter Sunday in Castilla-La Mancha, Castilla-León, País Vasco and Andalucía, straw effigies of Judas are burnt, often filled with rockets and explosives, creating a spectacular effect at the moment of truth. On Easter Sunday, Monday and Tuesday outdoor festivals take place throughout Spain.

# San Juan

On 23 June, Midsummer's Eve, the feast of Saint John takes place in towns across Spain. Again the festivities vary from place to place, but the most common aspect to these festivities is that bonfires are lit and often jumped over for luck. In San Pedro Manrique (Soria), men walk over the burning embers barefoot, often carrying people on their backs, apparently without harming themselves at all. Often the streets are decorated with branches and leaves, especially above the balconies of young girls in love who are serenaded by their suitors.

# Corpus Christi

This feast day, celebrated throughout Spain, observes the Real Presence in the Eucharist. The form these celebrations takes varies from town to town, but generally there is a procession in which the main feature is the Host, often housed in magnificent pieces of silverwork. The ceremonies usually involve flowers, and in Córdoba, the private patios filled with flowers become an enormous attraction. In Catalonia, Galicia and the Canary Islands it is not unusual for flower carpets to cover the route of the Host.

## Los Moros y Cristianos

Across 150 towns in Spain and throughout the year, mock battles between the Moors and the Christians take place to commemorate the battle for each particular town between these two sides. In some regions the festivities are more like choreographed dances than fighting and make quite a spectacle. These rituals are most common in Alicante, where they become increasingly lively.

## Local festivals

There are so many local fairs and festivals in Spain that it would be impossible to cover them all here, but the best-known certainly deserve a mention. The most famous, if only for the reports of deaths and injuries every year, is certainly **San Fermín** in Pamplona. Locals, overenthusiastic tourists and the clinically insane run with the bulls through 825 metres of Pamplona's streets to the Bull Ring and attempt to get away with as few injuries as possible. The bull run takes place every morning from 7–14 July and has become the focus of the festival, although there are also fireworks and festivities which continue well into the night for the entire week.

Another fiesta that has received international infamy is **La Tomatina** in Bunyol, essentially an enormous tomato fight between the townsfolk. There are numerous urban legends as to how this bizarre ritual started, but it is commonly held that the festival dates back to 1945 when a carnival of *Gigantes y Cabezudos* (giants and bigheads – traditional characters in Spanish festivals since medieval times) turned into an enormous brawl, as fate should have it, very close to the tomato vendor. The riot was broken up by the police, but the following year, on exactly the same day, the same thing happened. Despite being officially banned by the police at this time, the tomato fight has continued unabated every year since.

One of Spain's most colourful and vibrant festivals takes place in Valencia every year in the week around St Joseph's Day, 19 March. **Las Fallas de San José** consists of a week of endless processions, bullfights, fireworks displays and most importantly fire. Each *barrio* (neighbourhood) of Valencia produces its own giant papier-mâché representation of popular satirical figures (*las fallas*), which they have worked on all year. The judges choose a winner and all of the others are ceremoniously burnt at the finale of the festival, the **nit de foc.** At midnight the entire city is ablaze with enormous fires in every street, the sky lights up with fireworks and the smell of gunpowder is everywhere. The people of Valencia then dance and drink in the streets until the early hours.

Spain's biggest annual party however, takes place in Seville two weeks after Semana Santa, (also an excuse for carousing and frivolity in Seville). **La Feria de Seville** is an extraordinary spectacle of flamenco dancing, horseback parades and

The festival of San Fermín in Pamplona, better known as running with the bulls, attracts the brave and foolhardy

bullfights. Although the **feria** began as a market fair, a means of exchange between the local towns in the Middle Ages, it has blossomed into an extravaganza that lasts all day and all night for a week. During this time the *Real de la Feria* on the far bank of the river fills with rows of *casetas*, tents that bulge with singing and dancing, and the sounds of Sevillanas spill out into the night. Most of the women wear traditional costume, which consists of brightly coloured gypsy dresses. Many of the *casetas* are booked by private groups and associations but there are a number of public tents set up by the town council. During the day the fair moves to the streets of Seville where music plays on every corner and bars serve food and drink in the streets.

# ■ ESTABLISHING A SOCIAL LIFE

Although moving to a new country is undoubtedly difficult, and establishing a social life will take time and effort, newcomers to Spain should not be deterred from exploring the country, its customs, manners and traditions, by their lack of a readymade social network. Spain is a genuinely welcoming country, and although the groups of laughing Spanish men and women who stroll down the *Avenidas* arm in arm may seem forbidding and cliquey to the new arrival, strangers, foreigners included, are accepted with warmth into the social circles of most Spaniards.

Integration is made easier by the fact that Spain devotes a lot of energy to leisure, and opportunities to enjoy yourself, to learn new skills, to drink the night away, or to meet new people on the sports field are never far away. If you choose to work in Spain, it will soon become clear how important socialising and leisure time is: long, lazy lunches with your new co-workers will soon cement new friendships, and to many Spanish people, being personable and cheerful is an important a factor as any in being successful at work.

However, if you are not planning to work, or if you would simply like the security of having a group of English speakers to socialise with, you may wish to contact your local expat group. These organisations are very common in Spain, particularly on the costas, but also in the major cities and increasingly in the towns and rural areas too. Below are the contact details of some of the main expat clubs and societies in Spain; however, there are so many of these that the best way to find out the most information is via the local English-language press. Most clubs organise any number of activities for their members, such as evenings, outings, dances, and social events. Many clubs provide information packs for newcomers. Membership fees vary enormously from around €10 to up to €100 per year, depending on their facilities (some social clubs offer a clubhouse, library, bar, or restaurant) .

Booksellers on the Paseo del Prado, Madrid

## Useful addresses – social clubs

**American Women's Club Madrid:** Plaza de la Republica del Ecuador 6, 28106 Madrid; 914 571108; email awcmadrid@awcmadrid.e.telefonica.net.

**American Women's Club Seville:** Monthly luncheons and ladies' nights out; Contact via website, www.awcseville.org.

**The American Society of Barcelona:** Barcelona; 696 751645; email amersoc@amersoc.com.

**Association of Foreign Property Owners:** Annual membership €10; 965 830106; http://afpo.org/.

**Barcelona Women's Network:** Volunteer organisation helping women to adjust to life in Barcelona. Annual membership €55. www.bcnwomensnetwork.com.

**British Hispanic Cultural Foundation:** Cultural and social events. 913 456344.

**British Ladies Association:** Monthly meetings and social activities.918 034713.

**British Society of Catalunya:** Providing channels of information among the British community. 972 770517; www.bsce.freeservers.com.

**Cambridge Club:** Ex-university members, social activities. 914 316497.

**The Good Companions Club:** Fuengirola-based social, cultural and travel charity; 952 471562.

**The English Speaking Club of Málaga:** Provides social evenings and Spanish/English conversation groups. 952 222144.

**International Newcomers Club:** Provides information about community activities and services. email info@incmadrid.com; www.incmadrid.com.

**Madrid Players:** English-speaking amateur theatre group; 913 262439.

**Madrid Toastmasters Club:** (other branches all over Spain); 615 888634; www.toastmastersmadrid.com.

**X-Barcelona Club:** free monthly meetings for expatriates. Further info at www.xbarcelona.com.

# ■ SPORT AND FITNESS

Soccer rates highest on the list of spectator sports for Spaniards. The major teams, Real Madrid and FC Barcelona have large and fanatical followings and foreigners may join the crowds without worries for their safety. Even the British expatriate community in Spain is represented by its own football club, FC Britanico, not yet known in international competition, but which has participated in one of the Madrid amateur leagues for many years.

The Spanish are also keen participants and observers of basketball, tennis, golf and a number of other sports. Peculiar to Spain is the popular pastime *balonmano*, which is very similar to football but involves throwing the ball rather than kicking it. Cycling is very popular, especially in the north and Spain's topography means that mountain bikers can find plenty of rugged terrain to enjoy. September sees the

**FACT**

■ Peculiar to Spain is the popular pastime *balonmano*, which is very similar to football but involves throwing the ball rather than kicking it.

annual Tour of Spain Cycle Race, *La Vuelta*. This is the third biggest race of its kind in the world (after the Tour de France and the Giro d'Italia). Formula One has also gained in popularity in recent years and each year in May the Spanish Formula One Grand Prix is held at Montmeló near Barcelona. The success of Spanish tennis players such as Rafael Nadal, Alex Corretja and Arantxa Sanchez-Vicario have made the sport very popular in Spain. You can find out more about playing tennis in Spain on www.playtennisspain.com.

Sports facilities in Spain are excellent around the main tourist areas, where communal swimming pools and tennis courts are nearly always attached to apartment blocks. Wherever there are large concentrations of Brits and other expatriates, there are numerous rugby, football, cricket and even lawn bowls clubs. Golf clubs abound, especially on the Costa del Sol. However, as in France, golf is somewhat exclusive if the fees are anything to go by. Many British aficionados prefer to take golfing trips to neighbouring Portugal, which is cheaper. You can find out more about playing golf in Spain on www.golfspain.com.

At weekends the street are crammed with shoppers

Outdoor sports in Spain are plentiful, largely due to the country's climate and wealth of natural wonders. Hiking, trekking, rock climbing, hunting and fishing are all readily available, as are more adventurous sports such as hang gliding and bungee jumping. Spain's miles of coastline also make water sports very accessible and surfers, sailors, windsurfers, waterskiers and scuba divers will all find plenty to keep them busy. Windsurfers should visit the website www.windsurfspain.com for information.

Spain also has several skiing resorts in the Pyrenees: Cerler, La Molina, Formigal and Panticosa. Perhaps the best-known resort is Sol y Nieve (Sun and Snow) in the Sierra Nevada, a mere 30km/19 miles from Granada. The mountains are also popular with walkers in summer. Detailed maps and guides to these areas can be obtained from the Spanish Mountain Federation (*Federación Española de Montañismo*) or the Spanish Tourist Office.

Some of the main national sporting federations are listed below, but for general information about sporting activities in Spain contact The Spanish Sports Council: Consejo Superior de Deportes: (915 896700; www.csd.mec.es).

## National sports federations
**Athletics:** Real Federación Española de Atletismo, 915 482423; www.rfea.es.
**Basketball:** Federación Española de Baloncesto, 913 832050; www.feb.es.
**Cycling:** Real Federación Española de Ciclismo, 915 400941; www.rfec.com.
**Fishing:** Federación Española de Pesca, 915 328352; www.fepyc.es.
**Golf:** Real Federación Española de Golf, 915 552682; www.golfspainfederacion.com.
**Riding:** Real Federación de Hípica Española, 914 364200; www.rfhe.com.
**Rugby:** Federación Española de Rugby, www.ferugby.com.

> 'Spaniards are noisy and friendly, even in Madrid where city life makes anyone a little more arrogant and impatient. I have found the Spaniards hospitable and open to contact although perhaps a little insular – is this any surprise when they have a climate which ranges from that of Ireland in the North, through Alp-like ski country, to flat endless plains and mile upon mile of beaches? The Spanish quite simply do not have to go abroad to get away from it all, so many don't. Although it is possible to live and work in Spain without ever understanding a word of Spanish this tends to encourage an arrogance towards the Spanish and their culture, which will only serve to alienate you. British 'colonies' are to be found all over Spain, but by joining one of these groups you will not learn very much about the language or the country.
>
> The Spanish take their social life seriously, have beautiful manners, want to have a good time and take their time in doing so. In terms of nightlife, there is no reason to miss anything that you enjoyed in London and of course you can go on doing whatever it is much later into the night here! Alcohol remains very cheap for the huge quantities that are poured into your glass.
>
> The best piece of advice I can give is to come to Spain with an open mind.'
>
> **Peter Siderman,** an economic researcher, moved out to Madrid when he was offered a job researching European Latin-American relations for a small, private research institute

**Sailing:** Real Federación de Vela, 915 195008; www.rfev.es.
**Tennis:** Real Federación Española de Tenis, 932 005355; www.rfet.es.
**Water-Skiing:** Federación Española de Esquí Naútico, 934 520895; www.feen.es.
**Winter Sports:** Real Federación Española de Deportes de Invierno, 913 769930; www.rfedi.es.

# ■ ENTERTAINMENT AND CULTURE

## Bullfights

By far the most notorious Spanish entertainment is highly ritualised bull killing. Regarded as a disgusting spectacle of cruelty by many foreigners, its popularity shows no sign of abating among Spaniards themselves, who continue to flock to the *corridas* (bullrings). However, it seems as though the official tide may have begun to turn against this national institution, with the state broadcaster TVE stating in 2007 that it no longer thought it appropriate to show live bullfights in the afternoon (the time at which children arrive home from school). A bullfight is also an indispensable part of many village *fiestas*, when main squares become improvised

Barcelona Olympic Stadium

*corridas*. At the other end of the spectrum from the village fights are the main *corridas* of Seville and Madrid where the stars of the art (it is not really considered a sport in Spain), the matadors, are treated and paid like opera stars and have enormous followings. Bullfighting season runs from April to October, and fans of what Hemingway called 'Death in the Afternoon' are treated to six deaths (usually of bulls) per fight, dispatched by three matadors with assistance from picadors and apprentice bullfighters. Spectators should try to get a seat on the shady side of the ring in the *tendidos* (shaded stands) as, if the blood and evident suffering doesn't bring on faintness, heatstroke will.

## Flamenco

Perhaps Spain's best-known music and dance is flamenco, which originated in Andalucía. This flamboyant dance, with its accompanying guitar music and songs, is performed in theatres and night clubs, especially in the tourist resorts. It can be seen also at *fiesta* time being performed spontaneously in the streets. The best flamenco can still be found in Andalucía, where the general public are so passionate about the art that they demand only the best, but flamenco can be found all over Spain. The best place to see flamenco is in a *tablao* – a flamenco club.

The *gitanos* (gypsies) are the acknowledged founders and aficionados of flamenco, an art

that arrived in Spain in the 15th century evolving from many sources. The first flamenco schools were established in Cadiz, Jerez de la Frontera and Seville in the late 18th century and Flamenco has gained in popularity ever since, experiencing a 'golden age' from 1869–1910, a renaissance in the 1950s and a period of enormous innovation in the 1980s and 1990s.

## Cinema

Before José Luis Garcí won an Oscar for *Volver a Empezar* in 1983, the reputation of the Spanish cinema had rested on the undisputed and surreal mastery of Luis Buñuel. Recent Spanish 'classics' enjoyed by an international audience include the anarchic, urbane comedies of Pedro Almodóvar (*Women on the Verge of a Nervous Breakdown, Tie me up, Tie me down, All About My Mother, Bad Education* and most recently *Volver*) and the *Carmen* of Carlos Saura. Sexuality and repression are themes of modern Spanish cinema, as they are in many ways the themes of Spanish life. With the breakthrough of Spanish film to an international audience has come the worldwide acclaim of Spanish actors such as Antonio Banderas and Penelope Cruz, both of whom worked in Almodóvar's films.

Only about 25% of films shown in Spanish cinemas are home-grown. The rest are usually dubbed into Spanish, which can be a problem for foreigners with a minimal grasp of the language. Going to see real Spanish films can be one way of improving this, though. Watching how a language is spoken and how its sounds are made can be as instructive as listening to it; even if you do not always understand all the dialogue! Foreign films shown in the original version are indicated, as in France, with the letters 'vo' (*versión original*). The best place to see Spanish films and absorb Spanish culture at the same time is in the local plaza during the summer months, when many small towns have a *cine de verano* (summer cinema) festival.

**FACT**

■ There is a lot of folklore and mythology surrounding flamenco and its irrepressible spirit known as duende. Those interested in trying to understand the spirit of flamenco from an outsider's point of view, should read Jason Webster's incredibly personal and passionate quest: Duende: A Journey in Search of Flamenco (Black Swan, 2004).

# Art

Spain is universally recognised as having produced some of the world's greatest and most startlingly original painters, including Velásquez, El Greco, Murillo, Ribera, Picasso, Dali and Miró. One of the most famous art museums in the world is the Prado in Madrid, which houses works by all the great Spanish artists and Flemish and Italian masters. Near the Prado is the Reina Sofía National Museum, which was opened in 1986, basically as a museum of contemporary art. In Barcelona there is the excellent Picasso Museum and the Museum of Catalonian Art. In recent years modern art has become something of a passion with the Spanish and the annual Contemporary Art Fair (ARCO) in Madrid arouses huge national interest.

# Music

Spain's best-known piece of classical music is probably the hauntingly beautiful, *Concierto de Aranjuez para guitarra y orquesta*, by Joaquín Rodrigo (usually known as Rodrigo's Guitar Concerto), which even reached the British Top 20. This remarkable composer outlived his two great friends, the composer Manuel de Falla and Spain's most famous classical guitarist, Andrés Segovia.

At present Spain has almost completed a massive construction programme for musical auditoria, which has meant more halls for symphony and chamber orchestras around the country. For opera fans there are regular seasons in Madrid at the Gran Teatro de Liceo; also in Barcelona, Oviedo, Bilbao and other cities. Opera is very popular in Spain and the internationally famous Spanish tenors, José Carreras and Plácido Domingo are revered nationwide. A national operatic tradition is the *Zarzuela*, a form of comic opera (similar to Gilbert & Sullivan), which can be seen in the Teatro de Zarzuela in Madrid.

Spain's popular music scene is growing, although as yet few of the bands and solo artists adored by the Spanish youth have crossed over into the English-

Bull fighting in southern Spain

Barcelona is home to some of Spain's best museums and galleries

speaking world (with the exception of Enrique Iglesias). This is not to say that it's not worth listening to, and Spain has produced numerous bands who deserve greater international recognition. On the pure pop scene, Alejandro Sanz and Monica Naranjo are both very popular for their passionate voices and striking compositions and Jarabe de Palo's now classic album La Flaca was groundbreaking at the time. The music scene in Barcelona is going through an exciting period of innovation and offers the best clubs, record labels and music magazines, much to the chagrin of *Madrileños*. Barcelona is also considered to be at the forefront of electronic music and hip-hop, both of which are showcased in the annual Sonar festival. The indie music scene is also thriving, inspired by bands such as Los Planetas from Granada.

Whether or not you are enthralled by Spanish music, international pop music is extraordinarily popular and over the last 15 years Spain has added itself with alacrity to the European summer festival scene. Barcelona offers Sonar every March, attracting more than 50,000 festival-goers to concerts spread around the city, Madrid offers Festimad, a more rock-based festival, but the jewel in the crown is the *Festival Internacional de Benicassím*, known to its fans as FIB. Over the last 10 years, this cross-genre, cross-cultural festival held in a beach resort near Valencia has exploded to become, to those in the know, one of the best festivals in Europe, attracting some of the biggest names from all over the world. The festival is a welcome relief from the oversized and overly commercial summer festivals that Britain offers these days, and attracts a small crowd (around 40,000 in 2007) of music lovers, happy to spend their days lazing on the beach and their nights dancing until dawn. The festival also offers a free beach party on the final night, headlined in 2007 by The Arctic Monkeys.

## Theatre

The most important theatres in Madrid are the Teatro de Zarzuela, the Teatro Español, the Centro Dramático Nacional, the Teatro María Guerrero, the Centro de Nuevas Tendencias Escénicas and the Compañia Nacional de Teatro Clásico. Unfortunately much will be incomprehensible to foreigners, unless they are already familiar with the works being performed. However, English translations of the works of Frederico Garcia Lorca, Spain's famous pre-civil war playwright and poet, and Lope de Vega, 16th century playwright, are available.

Chueca is madrid's gay district, and is also known for its shops and restaurants

In areas where there are expatriate communities, English and American plays are regularly performed by amateur theatre groups. Details of forthcoming productions in English may be found in the English-language publications.

# Nightlife

Spanish nightlife is legendary. Anyone who has passed an evening with young *Madrileños* will have really come to appreciate exactly what a late night is. Most of Spain's bars do not close until the last people leave at two or three in the morning; luckily, this is just when the clubs start to get going at the weekends and many of these do not close until at least five or six in the morning. In Madrid, still Spain's most vibrant and exciting city when it comes to nightlife, many people then go on for *churros* (like long thin doughnuts) dipped in hot chocolate, but the hardcore few go on to the early morning clubs that open at around this time and play chilled tunes until well after the sun has come up. Despite the apparent hedonism of Spain's nightlife, what makes it so refreshing is that whereas in the UK all-nighters are usually fuelled by excessive alcohol and drug binges, in Spain they are often (although not always) fuelled by pure verve and enthusiasm. Spain's nightlife is a pure and unadulterated expression of the post-Franco era of freedom and liberalism for the Spanish youth, (a notion supported by the recent opening of Europe's first nudist disco night in the Spanish town of Corneall!)

"

'The nightlife in Spain is totally out of control! It's a blast! In Madrid there is something going on seven days a week. Furthermore, the Spaniards know how to have a good time and embrace those who enjoy their country. It helps tremendously to branch out beyond the areas where foreigners hang out and to meet some locals who can show you the fun places to go and introduce you to their friends.

It takes a bit of time to learn how to pace oneself when enjoying the nightlife in Spain. Whereas American nightlife tends to end at around 1–3am, in Spain it goes on until 5–8am. Needless to say, when I first arrived in Spain I was quickly burning though my money and energy. After about six weeks, I started to calm down a bit and adjust to a more leisurely way of life. I believe it's pretty common for people to go a bit wild when they first arrive in Spain because the scene and the festive atmosphere lure you in.'

**Hal Shaw,** 25, from South Carolina, spent his time in Madrid burning the candle at both ends, working hard and playing hard, and sampled most of the delights of the capital's riotous ambiente nocturno:

"

# ◼ MARRIAGE

Spanish law recognises both civil and religious marriages, and people under 18 are not allowed to marry. To get married in Spain, you will need:

- your passport
- original birth certificate
- application to marry form
- proof that the two parties are single. A form can be obtained from the civil registry of your home country
- if previously married, the original final divorce decree or death certificate
- certificate of residence: If you are non-resident, you may sign an affidavit before your consular officer
- certificate of Consular Inscription: Can be obtained from your embassy or consulate.

A baptismal certificate is also needed when arranging Catholic marriages. The required documents must be presented to the priest performing the ceremony. All documents that are not written in Spanish may need to be officially translated and authenticated. Approval for a marriage licence may take up to eight weeks.

In 2005, Spain also passed a controversial new law permitting marriage between same-sex couples; the administrative procedures are the same as those described above.

# About Spain

# ■ HISTORY

The key to Spain's recent political development lies in its rich and varied history. For those who are interested, *A History of Spain* (Palgrave Macmillan, 2003) by Simon Barton outlines the main events from early times to the modern day. If you are going abroad, some research into the history and culture is invaluable. We recommend a trip to your local bookshop or library or a call to the Spanish Tourist Office brochure line – 0891 669920 – for some excellent brochures on your chosen destination or region and its history.

Important events that have shaped Spain's past (and present) include the fascist dictatorship of General Franco; the country's imperial expansion during the 16th and 17th centuries; and the earlier domination by Islamic invaders for over 599 years from AD 718, which left behind a unique legacy unique of Moslem art and architecture in such cities as Granada, Córdoba and Seville and which has influenced musical traditions, and Spanish literature.

It took the Christians 36 years to complete a military reconquest of Spain in the 13th century (although the Arabs retained their final stronghold of Granada until the 15th century); there was a period of colonial expansion and the colonising of vast territories in Latin America and Asia; more recently, a bitterly fought Civil War and the right-wing military dictatorship of General Franco have coloured the Spanish experience in the 20th century. Franco's death in 1975 ended a period of stagnation and oppression, although for some Franco embodied a 'restored' (as they saw it in the 1930s) and united Spain. Arguably, the scars of fascism have not yet fully healed in Spain, and many Spanish people are still unwilling to talk about the horrors and hardships of Franco's regime.

However, over the last 30 years Spain has emerged from dictatorship and international isolation, built a successful economy and established an effective democracy. Few countries could claim to have achieved so much, on so many fronts, in such a short space of time.

## The development of the modern Spanish economy

**FACT**

■ Spain remained neutral in World War II and even provided active aid to the Axis Powers in return for their support for Franco's dictatorship. As a result, Spain did not receive post-war aid from the Marshall Plan as the main protagonists did, and was penalised by a UN economic blockade that lasted until 1950.

Spain was exhausted by the Civil War of 1936–1939 – an internal military rebellion against the elected government, which turned into an international affair. The war was brutal and by the time the army finally seized power, half a million lives had been lost. Among those casualties was the economy, which was left in a state more ruinous than that of Spain's neighbours in the aftermath of World War II six years later.

Spain remained neutral in World War II and even provided active aid to the Axis Powers in return for their support for Franco's dictatorship. As a result, Spain did not receive post-war aid from the Marshall Plan as the main protagonists did, and was penalised by a UN economic blockade that lasted until 1950. The extreme hardships of the post-war years came to be known as *los años de hambre* (the years of hunger), when cats and dogs disappeared from the streets and it was said that only handouts from Perón's Argentina kept the country from total starvation.

Economic isolation and disastrous mismanagement had a devastating effect on living standards throughout the fifties and it was not until the later stages of

Roman ruins, Extremadura

Franco's dictatorship that there were some signs of economic progress. The period from 1961 to 1973, known as *los años de desarollo* (the years of development) saw the economy grow annually at a rate of 7%, second only to that of Japan. International companies such as Chrysler, John Deere and Ciba-Geigy set up operations in Spain and tourism became a huge earner for the country as the coasts were opened up for international visitors and high-rise apartments sprung up in places such as Benidorm and Torremolinos. The onset of mass tourism inevitably led to an expatriate property-buying boom, which began in the 1960s and continues to this day.

During this period, an estimated 1,700,000 Spaniards left their homes to work abroad and their earnings, sent back to swell their bank accounts at home, contributed to their country's economic expansion. At the same time, there was a mass rural exodus to the cities by craftsmen and artisans as the disparity in living standards between rural and urban areas became more apparent. The resulting depopulation of the countryside and especially the *meseta* (central Spain) caused an extreme imbalance in Spain, between the wealth and high population of the cities and the desolation and poverty of the countryside.

Franco's death in 1975 led to a period of rapid liberalisation of the economy. By this time, five of the 19 provinces (Madrid, Barcelona, Valencia, Biscay and Oviedo) were producing nearly half of the country's industrial output, concentrating the wealth of the country in the North and East. Today that position is very similar, except that Navarre (in the North) has taken over from Oviedo as a centre of industrial development.

In the last three decades Spain has undergone an enormous transformation from a backward, rural country with an agriculturally based economy, to a nation with a diversified economy made up of strong retail, property, industrial and tourism sectors. As recently as 1964, the United Nations classed Spain as a developing nation, yet today Spain takes its modernity for granted.

Recent economic developments such as the joining of the European Monetary Union in 1998, followed by the adoption of the Euro in 2002, have placed Spain in a position of strength in the world markets. The ongoing programme of privatisation has brought a new wave of workers skilled in areas like finance, consultancy, electronics, information technology and industrial design which have little to do with the service sector and tourism. The accession of countries such as Poland, Bulgaria and Lithuania to the EU and the extension of the Schengen zone has also been instrumental in bringing cheaper labour to Spain.

## The current economic situation

**FACT**

■ According to a recent study by the accountancy firm PriceWaterhouse-Coopers, Spain is Europe's fastest growing economy and consistently beats its European counterparts in terms of economic performance.

Spaniards today are about 75% richer than they were 30 years ago, and have seen their economy grow faster than the European average for nearly ten years.

By late 2006 the GDP growth had accelerated to 3.3%, whereas in much of Europe growth has stagnated. The Spanish economy is now the eighth largest in the world.

Spain's buoyant economic growth has been fuelled in recent years by successful supply-side reforms, the growing purchasing power of consumers, service improvements, .an influx of cheaper immigrant labour and the quick pace of innovation. One of the most significant changes over the last 30 years or so has been the growth of the services sector at the expense of more traditional sectors such as agriculture and fishing. The services sector now accounts for more than 65% of the GDP. Clearly the most dramatic success story in the services sector has been tourism. Today Spain plays host to a staggering 60 million visitors per year and this shows no signs of slowing down, despite the decrease in popularity of traditional package holidays. Also of enormous importance to this sector are banking, retail and telecommunications.

Industry contributes just over 21% to the Spanish GDP. The most important manufactured goods are textiles, metals, chemicals, machine tools and shipbuilding. One area in which Spain's relative youth in terms of economic development is obvious is in the attitude of big business. Spanish business is fairly timid and deferential towards government. Only the clothing company Zara, the hotel chain NH Hoteles and the stainless steel manufacturer Acerinox have really made an impact outside the Spanish-speaking world. Spain has very few big international companies. On the other hand, many British and American companies have large operations in Spain and there is a British and American presence across a wide range of industries and business activities.

Construction makes up round 9% of Spain's economic activity, but after a decade of expansion, this industry looks set to stagnate and possibly even go into recession. However, as well as unbridled property building, an extensive renewal of Spain's infrastructure has taken place over the last decade. Spain's motorways have more than tripled in length since 1982 and high-speed trains have become a priority. The boom in the construction industry has also been fuelled by the enormous demand for tourist related buildings and second homes.

Unemployment remains at one of the highest levels in the EU, but it has reduced dramatically over the last decade and particularly in the last three years, currently standing at 8.3%, less than two per cent higher than the European average of 6.9%. In the last five years, half of the new jobs in Europe have been created in Spain.

Overall, Spain's economic achievements of recent years are remarkable and the current situation reflects solid and sustained growth, which shows no signs of diminishing. However, the end of 2007 saw inflation reaching an all-time high in Spain as consumer confidence plummeted; like many world economies, Spain's faces an uncertain future as the global financial markets attempt to weather the credit storm.

# ■ GEOGRAPHY

## Mainland and offshore Spain

Spain occupies 85% or 194,885 sq miles/504,750 sq km of the great landmass that forms the south-western extremity of Europe, the Iberian Peninsula. Including the Balearic and Canary Islands, Spain is the third largest European nation (after Ukraine

### Regional divisions and main towns

The 19 autonomous regions of Spain and their provinces are:
**Andalucía** (Andalusia) – Almería, Cádiz, Córdoba, Granada, Huelva, Jaén, Málaga And Sevilla (Seville)
**Aragón** – Huesca, Zaragoza (Saragossa), Teruel
**Asturias** – Oviedo
**Cantabria** – Santander
**Castilla la Mancha** – Albacete, Cuenca, Ciudad Real, Guadalajara, Toledo
**Castilla y Léon** – Avila, Burgos, León, Palencia, Salamanca, Segovia, Soria, Valladolid, Zamora
**Cataluña** (Catalonia) – Barcelona, Girona, Lléida (Lerida), Tarragona
**Ceuta**
*Comunidad* **de Madrid** – Madrid
**Extremadura** – Badajoz, Cáceres
**Galicia** – A Coruña, Lugo, Orense, Pontevedra
**Islas Baleares** (Balearic Islands) – Palma
**Islas Canarias** (Canary Islands) – Las Palmas De Gran Canaria, Santa Cruz De Tenerife
**La Rioja** – Logroño
**Melilla**
**Murcia** – Murcia
**Navarra** (Navarre) – Pamplona
**País Vasco** (Basque Country) – Bilbao, Donostiasan Sebastian, Vizcayagasteiz
**Valencia** – Alicante, Castellon, Valencia

and France) and, perhaps more surprisingly, is second only to Switzerland in its average altitude. The Pyrenees form a natural barrier between Spain and France to the north-east while to the west lies Portugal. To the north is the Bay of Biscay, and the north-western province of Galicia has an Atlantic coast. In the south and east is the Mediterranean; a mere 10 miles/16km separates it from Africa (and its two tiny enclaves of Melilla and Ceuta) across the Straight of Gibraltar. The Balearics, which comprise the four islands of Mallorca, Ibiza, Menorca and Formentera, lie off Spain's north-eastern coast and occupy 1,936 sq miles/5014 sqkm. The Canaries, about seven of which are inhabited, are situated about 60 miles/97km off the coast of Africa and occupy 2,808 sq miles/7273 sqkm. Here, the population is Spanish, and a variety of climates and landscapes in each island, as well as long sandy beaches, have made islands like Tenerife and Gran Canaria familiar to tourists from all over Europe.

## Population

While the populations of several EU countries, notably Italy, France and Germany have been falling, by contrast the population of Spain has been increasing despite the fact that the Spanish birthrate has fallen dramatically. From being a nation synonymous with big families and despite the Catholic Church's hostility to contraception, Spain has seen its birthrate fall to just 1.37 children per woman of childbearing age (compared with 1.84 in the UK). This is perhaps because Spanish women work longer hours, face mounting childcare costs and delay having children until their 30s. However, Spain continues to have one of the fastest rates of population growth in Europe.

Two factors help to explain this apparent contradiction. The first is life expectancy, which is very high in Spain. In 2007, figures from the National Statistics Institute showed that the average overall life expectancy in Spain has reached 80 for the first time, with women living an average of six years longer than men. A recent report by the pharmaceutical company Pfizer suggested that Spain's excellent healthcare system, and a diet with lots of olive oil and red wine were together responsible for the longevity of its people.

The second factor is high immigration and the numbers of children born to immigrants in Spain. For Spain such high immigration is a new experience, driven both by globalisation and Spain's internal demand for cheap labour. By 2007 there were over 3.6 million foreigners in Spain, mainly coming from Latin American countries (38.6%), especially the Andean countries; Africa (19.6%); and the EU (22%).

The current population is around 40.4 million. However there is a wide disparity in the population density region by region: the Basque country and Madrid province together comprise only 3.02% of the total surface area but house around 16% of the population. However if you put together the provinces of Extremadura, Castilla la Mancha, Castilla-León, Aragon and Navarre which, together, represent over half the surface area of Spain, their total populations would still not exceed the combined population of the Basque Country and Madrid. This population imbalance and the wide variations in prosperity between regions are the result of decades of internal and external migrations, the former from the rural to the industrialised areas, where the cities continue to expand their populations at the expense of the countryside. The largest conurbations are Madrid (3.2 million people), Barcelona (1.6 million), Valencia (796,000) and Seville (704,000).

**FACT**

■ A recent report by the pharmaceutical company Pfizer suggested that Spain's excellent healthcare system, and a diet with lots of olive oil and red wine were together responsible for the longevity of its people.

Bajamar beach, Tenerife

## Climatic zones

Spain is a country of climatic extremes. However hackneyed the phrase, there is no other way to describe a country where in the north-west (Galicia) the climate is as wet and the landscape as correspondingly verdant as parts of Wales (though the mountains are higher); while in the south much of the province of Almería is so arid that westerns have been filmed there. The nearly subtropical climate of Almería means it can be a pleasant holiday destination even in December. Another sunny area not yet spoiled by tourism is the Costa de la Luz (Coast of Light), which runs from Huelva near the Portuguese border in the south to Cape Trafalgar overlooking the Straight of Gibraltar. The town of Seville in Andalucía has the highest temperatures in Spain reaching 94°F/34°C between July and September, when the sun beats down ceaselessly from dawn to dusk. By contrast, in the north of Spain, Santander in Cantabria has a climate and temperatures similar to Britain. The vast area of central Spain is known as the *meseta* (tableland), and though not a precise geographical area it embraces the Castilles (La Mancha and León) and Extremadura as well as the edges of Navarre and Aragon. Here the inhabitants are baked by the sun in summer and endure freezing temperatures in winter. The capital, Madrid, which is in the centre of Spain, also has the lowest winter temperatures and expatriates there may not be prepared for the colder conditions.

Along the Mediterranean coast there are rarely such extremes of climate as in the *meseta*; but the costas in the north and east may be subject to the cold winds that bring the snow to the Pyrenees and the *meseta* in winter. It is said that the mountainous ranges of the hinterland protect the costas in some measure from extremes of climate and funnel warm air to the costas through the summer.

The offshore provinces of Spain, the Balearics and the Canaries, have their own weather patterns. The Balearics usually have warm comfortable summers, tempestuous autumns and chilly winters, while the Canaries, situated off the coast of Africa, are nearer to the equator than the Bahamas; and their winter climate is correspondingly warm and welcoming to visitors in search of winter sun. In spite of the relatively long flying time from the UK of five hours, the popularity of the

Canaries as a destination and a place to live or retire is growing, mainly the islands of Gran Canaria. Lanzarote and Tenerife.

| Average maximum temperatures | | | | |
|---|---|---|---|---|
| Area | Jan | Apr | Aug | Nov |
| Cadiz | 15°C | 21°C | 30°C | 20°C |
| Málaga | 17°C | 21°C | 30°C | 20°C |
| Sevilla | 15°C | 23°C | 36°C | 20°C |
| Murcia | 12°C | 19°C | 29°C | 20°C |
| Alicante | 16°C | 22°C | 32°C | 21°C |
| Valencia | 15°C | 20°C | 29°C | 19°C |
| Barcelona | 13°C | 18°C | 28°C | 16°C |
| Santander | 12°C | 15°C | 22°C | 15°C |
| Pontevendra | 14°C | 18°C | 26°C | 16°C |
| Madrid | 9°C | 18°C | 30°C | 13°C |
| Mallorca | 14°C | 19°C | 29°C | 18°C |
| Gran Canaria | 21°C | 23°C | 31°C | 24°C |

# ■ POLITICS

## Political parties

Historically, Spanish politics has a Byzantine complexity. The main elements of the fascist regime headed by Franco in the 1930s included his own Falange (fascist) party, the church and the monarchists, who were fused into an unusual coalition. The many political parties which comprised these groups were known collectively as the *Falange Española Tradicionalista y de las Juntas de Ofensiva Nacional-Sindicalista*, mercifully shortened to *FET de las JONS* but also known as the *Movimiento Nacional*.

The Falange progressively became the most dominant element and the coalition itself was the only legal political entity under the dictatorship. Illegal opposition parties without political power could only seek influence through street demonstrations, which were invariably suppressed by the police. Barely a year after Franco's death, political parties were legalised; the Socialists in February 1977 and the Communists in April. Along with these reforms came legalisation of trade unions and the right to strike. The Movimiento was abolished and the new constitution was drawn up in 1978 through all-party consultation.

While all this was going on the new political parties were organising themselves for the forthcoming election which was won by Suárez and his coalition the UCD (*Unión de Centro Democrática*) which could be described as comprising the vestiges of Francoism with elements of liberalism. In the election of 1982, the UCD not only lost but did so spectacularly, its 168 deputies and 119 senators being reduced to 13 and four respectively. The ascendant party was the PSOE (*Partido Socialista Obrero Español*) led by Felipe González, giving the socialists an overall majority in parliament for the first time. The PSOE has its origins in the Spanish Socialist Workers' Party which was started in 1879, and it is the oldest political party in Spain. It enjoyed a rebirth in the twilight years of the dictatorship and held the balance of power from 1982 to 1996. After eight years out of office, the PSOE returned to power in April 2004 under Jose Luis Rodriguez Zapatero's premiership and celebrated a victory in the March 2008 General Election.

The current opposition party is the centre-right PP (Partido Popular), the ruling party from 1996–2004. The PP has roots in the Francoist Alianza Popular, although during the 1990s it moved to a more centre-right position. The current PP leader is Mariano Rajoy, an experienced and well-regarded politician.

# Government

Throughout his dictatorship, Franco held the disparate elements of Spanish politics together in a coalition and enforced rigidly centralised government. Franco himself was also a monarchist, and having made himself head of state with the power to appoint his successor, he began to groom Prince Juan Carlos to take over the reins of power. In spite of these efforts it remained a generally held belief that the young Juan Carlos was not up to much and that the political future of Spain was uncertain. During the last months of the dictatorship it became obvious that all the distinct peoples of Spain, some with their own language and culture like the Basques, Catalans and Galicians (who had experienced a measure of autonomy under the Republic) were working themselves up to bid for their old autonomy back; no doubt some of this activity resulted from the fear that the kind of monarchy envisaged by Franco was not likely to be any more liberal than his dictatorship.

Even regions that had formerly not been overly concerned with self-rule jumped on the bandwagon, and the prospect of a loose federation of states (derived in part from the pattern of the old mediaeval kingdoms) caused a mounting *fiebre autonómican* (autonomy fever) throughout Spain.

After Franco's death in 1974, King Juan Carlos transferred power to a democratically elected parliament and Spain has ended up as what can best be described as a federal-monarchy, which the Spaniards call an *estado de las autonomías*. Their king pays taxes in keeping with his constitutional role and has powers strictly limited to the promulgation of laws and decrees, the calling of elections and referenda, and the appointment of prime ministers and ministers. However, it is said that he wields considerable personal influence on politics; and he is Commander-in-Chief of the armed forces.

In 1978 the Spanish constitution was drawn up, largely at the behest of Juan Carlos. The most important task of the constitution was to make possible the devolution of power to the regions, which were (and still are) entitled to have their own governments, parliaments, regional assemblies and supreme legal authorities. This radical transition to a democratic and devolved system of government was carried out to form the 17 autonomous communities of Spain, each with their own flag, capital city and president.

However, these procedures for devolution have been carried out more slowly in some regions than others. Spain is really a mosaic of parliaments and regional identities. The Spanish film-maker Victor Erice used Frankenstein's monster as a

FACT

■ Spain is really a mosaic of parliaments and regional identities. The Spanish film-maker Victor Erice used Frankenstein's monster as a metaphor for Spanish nationhood in his 1973 masterpiece The Spirit of the Beehive; regions here are often distinct from one another in language, culture, terrain, climate and lifestyle.

metaphor for Spanish nationhood in his 1973 masterpiece The Spirit of the Beehive; regions here are often distinct from one another in language, culture, terrain, climate and lifestyle. Catalonia, the Basque Country, Galicia and Andalucía were the first of the regions to become autonomous communities. Nowadays there are still variations in the level of independence among the regions. The central parliament, or Cortes, retains overall control of such matters as foreign policy and defence, although it is true to say that in Spain local politics normally arouse more interest than national ones.

The first Prime Minister of Spain, Carlos Arias Navarro, a political appointee chosen by Franco, lasted barely six months in office and was replaced by Adolfo Suárez, chosen by King Juan Carlos as the best person for the job of transforming Spain from a dictatorship to a democracy. Suárez was responsible for political reforms including the creation of a two-tier parliament, the Cortes, comprising a lower house, the Congress, and an upper house, the Senate. Meanwhile a plethora of political parties were formed to contest the forthcoming election in 1979. Suárez resigned shortly after the elections for a variety of reasons arising mainly from the government's proposed liberalisation of various laws. He was honoured with a dukedom by Juan Carlos in recognition of his achievement in setting up the new democracy.

Between the dissolution of the Suárez government and the creation of the next, reactionary elements of the army, alarmed by what they saw as political turmoil and the end of Spanish unity, launched a theatrical attempt at a coup when Antonio Tejero Molina, a lieutenant-colonel in the Civil Guard, marched into the lower house of Parliament at the head of his men brandishing a pistol and proceeded to hold the entire Congress hostage for 24 hours.

The situation was saved by King Juan Carlos, who still commanded the loyalty of monarchists. He announced that the attempted coup did not have his backing; and this probably tipped the balance against Tejero, who was isolated from more senior officers who had orchestrated the coup attempt and he was sufficiently demoralised to surrender, without bloodshed, to the police.

A long period of rule by the 'moderate' socialist party the PSOE (Partido Socialista Obrero Espanōl) followed and its leader Felipe González, originally a lawyer from Seville, presided over the renewal of the Spanish economy and society and a process of privatisation and economic reform which was only partially completed. It brought riches to some but at a cost of high unemployment and discontent among those who wished to see more power at the centre, and among some other nationalists in Catalonia and the Basque Country who are still seeking full independence. The González government was responsible for taking Spain into the EU and also into NATO. However, there was widespread corruption as well as other scandals that are often associated with a long period in office, culminating with the election in 1996 of a government led by the Popular Party (Partido Popular) of José María Aznar.

The PP's eight years in power should not be discredited entirely by the party's apparently shameful behaviour of 11–14 March 2004 (see below). Aznar was able to turn the PP, which had been suspected by many as being Francoist in its sympathies, into a respectable centre-right organization. He also presided over eight years of economic growth (at an impressive average of 3.2% per year), sound management of the public purse (no budget deficits like those of France, Germany and Italy), fairly low inflation and a cut in the unemployment rate from 22% to 11%. During the first term, Aznar successfully continued the devolution of power to the autonomous communities. However, it was in the second term that the PP began to provoke fierce criticism and lose some of its support. This was perhaps largely due to the fact that Aznar became increasingly inflexible in his approach and his arrogance needlessly antagonised numerous groups who might have worked with him. His belligerent and aggressive stance is perhaps most clearly demonstrated in the decision to oppose, with Poland, any change to the majority-voting provision of the EU's Nice treaty, which gave Spain and Poland nearly the same number of votes as Britain, France, Germany and Italy. The refusal to compromise led to a deadlock over the proposed EU constitution, which was consequently in limbo when the 10 new states joined the EU in May 2004.

Two events of 2002 had also eroded confidence in the government. The first was the misjudgements over proposed changes to the right to unemployment benefit, which meant that people would risk losing their benefits if they were not prepared to accept jobs as far as an hour and a half's journey from their homes. These proposals led to a general strike in June and the government, while denying that the strike had had any effect, was forced to redraft many of their proposals. The second issue was the government's failure to react effectively to the Prestige oil tanker disaster, which polluted a long stretch of the Atlantic Coast. Aznar's arrogance even shone through in more trivial actions. For example, the electorate was intensely annoyed by the holding of a flamboyant wedding for his daughter in the Escorial monastery, which is traditionally where Spain's monarchs are buried.

The political opportunism of the PP became increasingly obvious in its second term. During its first term, the government had been dependent on regional parties in government such as the Catalan nationalist party, Convergence in Union (CiU). It was this dependence that many suggest drove the continued devolution of power to the regions. However, with the absolute majority achieved in the 2000 general election, Aznar turned on the nationalists. He increasingly treated all Basque nationalists with equal disdain whether pro- or anti-violence, and from 2001 even refused to talk to the non-violent Basque premier Juan José Ibarretxe. The nationalist demands of the CiU were also ignored in the second term, as Aznar increasingly appeared to view all nationalist demands as equally contemptible.

The issue that most alienated the electorate, however, was the decision to support the invasion of Iraq. Although Spain's involvement was minimal, the very gesture of sending Spanish troops to Iraq provoked outrage. In poll after poll, 90% of Spaniards opposed the war and Spain's part in it. Had the prime minister been more willing to explain his reasons for his steadfast support of Bush and Blair, then the electorate may have been placated. However, Aznar refused to make his case before parliament and only grudgingly allowed a secret parliamentary vote. It was only eight months after the war in Iraq had begun that Aznar addressed parliament regarding Spain's involvement.

By early 2004, the polls suggested that despite many of the contentious issues described above, most Spaniards would vote the PP in for a third term, under Aznar's chosen successor Mariano Rajoy. However, the events of March 2004 were to change all of that.

## The Madrid bombings and the 2004 elections

March 2004 proved to be one of the most dramatic months of recent Spanish history, sending Spain spiralling into a period of transition and uncertainty. In the early hours of 11 March, a dozen bombs exploded on four Madrid commuter trains, killing 191 people and injuring 1,430. The events of the next few days were to prove the undoing of Prime Minister Aznar and the *Partido Popular*, as he attempted to contain and even turn to his political advantage an overwhelming feeling of horror and outrage surging through the country. Around 11 million Spaniards (over a quarter of the population) took to the streets in throngs to take part in dignified demonstrations and express their disgust with the perpetrators of terror and their sympathy for the victims. Aznar's attempted manipulation of this enormous outburst of public feeling in the period between the bombings of 11 March and the elections on 14 March so infuriated a large group of Spaniards that they voted Socialist in disgust, changing the course of Spanish history in one fell swoop.

The PP were all but guaranteed to win the election before the bombings. Despite the loss of popularity during Aznar's second term, the PP had held up well in the 2003 local and regional elections. Zapatero's socialists, on the other hand, having spent eight years in the political wilderness, were far from prepared to take up office, and their election manifesto was mainly the bluster of opposition, promising a host of reforms that no prudent finance minister would want to pay for. Nobody could have foreseen such an enormous turnaround of public opinion.

One of Aznar's main achievements was his hard line against the Basque terrorist group ETA (*Euskadi Ta Askatasuna*), the Separatist organisation responsible for many terrorist attacks in Spain since its formation in 1959 (for further information on Basque separatism and ETA, see the *País Vasco* section of the regional guide on page 445). The organisation was, according to the government, 'on the ropes'. Its political wing, Batasuna, had been outlawed, and the PP had shown very low tolerance to the organisation, making around 200 arrests in 2003 alone. Had ETA been responsible for these latest attacks, this surely would have provided Aznar with a popular mandate to continue his zero-tolerance policies, and create a wave of support for a government that had proved so unwilling to endure nationalist terrorism. These thoughts were probably in Aznar's mind when he chose to promote indiscriminately the theory that ETA were behind the blasts and suppress any evidence suggesting that Al-Qaeda was responsible. The PP embarked on a policy of 'superspin': the media were contacted and assured of ETA's guilt, the Foreign Minister, Ana Palacio, requested a specific condemnation of ETA in a UN resolution of sympathy, and sent telegrams to all Spanish ambassadors asking them to give the impression that the attacks were the work of ETA; the state television station inexplicably replaced its scheduled programming with a documentary detailing the evils of ETA.

Despite all of this spin, the official story did not quite fit. Firstly, as the PP themselves had pointed out, ETA had been beaten back in recent years, and it was highly unlikely that they could have mustered the funds, manpower and explosives for such an ambitious attack. Equally curious was the lack of telephone warning before the explosions, and the failure to claim responsibility afterwards, both standard ETA tactics. ETA vigorously denied that they were involved and even repudiated the attacks.

When the news was revealed, despite government attempts to suppress it, that those connected with the bombings had been arrested and that they had suspected Al-Qaeda links, there were enormous demonstrations outside the PP headquarters in Madrid. People felt that they had been betrayed by a government acting purely in its own interests. Turnout at the elections was huge and the PP were defeated by Zapatero's *Partido Socialista Obrero Español* (PSOE).

## The current government and the future

Jose Luis Rodriguez Zapatero has been Spain's Prime Minister since April 2004, and has a very different style to his predecessor, preferring consensus to confrontation. However, his first act as Prime Minister, pulling Spain's 1,300 troops out of Iraq, was certainly controversial. Many expected him to renege on this election commitment in the light of the terrorist atrocities, or at least postpone it. In fact, Zapatero acted far quicker than anyone had expected, abandoning his initial condition that the withdrawal would only happen if the UN had not taken control of Iraq by 30 June. Despite being accused of cowardice by Donald Rumsfeld, and despite international concern that the withdrawal would be perceived as a victory for terrorism, Zapatero stuck rigidly to the very clear desires of the great majority of Spanish people. The Socialists had been promising to bring the troops home for over a year, and the cries of 'don't fail us' from the post-election crowds were certainly a deciding factor.

However, his actions cannot simply be seen as electoral opportunism (attempting to seal his bond with the two million or so people who had voted for the first time in the March elections). It had become clear to Zapatero not only that there was no prospect of a UN handover, but also that Spanish troops were not taking part in stabilisation and reconstruction, as set out by the original mandate, but were required for 'an offensive strategy' in Najaf.

Zapatero's critics suggested that the events of 11 March have thrust him into a position for which his lack of government experience and relative youth make him unworthy. However, the PSOE government has pursued an agenda of social reform and has made numerous notable changes to Spanish law, including the legalisation of same-sex marriage; the granting of adoption rights for gay and lesbian couples; and the creation of the Spanish Courts for Violence against Women to tackle the domestic violence that has been a problem in Spain for many years. He has also pursued classically Socialist policies such as increasing funding for state welfare and raising the minimum wage.

Zapatero has always seen himself as negotiator, and had previously spoken out against his predecessor's staunch policy of refusing to engage in dialogue with groups such as ETA. However, his premiership has seen his resolve tested after ETA broke its official ceasefire in December 2006 by planting a car bomb in Madrid's Barajas airport. Even though Zapatero immediately broke off all dialogue with the group, angry demonstrations followed across the country as people expressed their discontent with a government which they felt had allowed ETA to regroup and had granted it too many concessions in the months leading up to the bombing.

Zapatero has also courted controversy abroad, most notably with his immigration amnesty, which has allowed an estimated 800,000 illegal immigrants to register as official Spanish taxpayers. Some commentators saw this as a refreshingly clearheaded way to deal with the problem of worker exploitation in Spain's shadow economy. However, other European countries, most prominently Italy and France, have complained that what they see as Spain's lackadaisical attitude towards immigration is undermining their own attempts to control their borders, as once immigrants are registered in Spain they are free to travel throughout the EU. Zapatero has also failed to make any sort of significant dent in the huge numbers of immigrants, mostly of north African origin, who arrive on the shores of the Canary Islands in rickety makeshift boats in search of a better life in Europe. During the immigration amnesty the numbers of new arrivals skyrocketed, with over 2,200 people arriving in boats from Senegal over a single weekend in September 2006.

Immigration is still a burning political issue in Spain. Spaniards are generally welcoming towards foreigners, but the country has transformed in little more than ten years from a largely homogeneous nation into a multicultural one, and the infrastructure is struggling to cope. Relatively high unemployment means that the job prospects in Spain are not as good as many new arrivals anticipated. However, it is not just the infrastructure that cannot cope, the Spanish people have no experience of mass immigration, and the issue has divided them. Among older people there is a definite hangover from the Franco era. Much of Franco's rhetoric demonised foreigners and glorified the quintessence of Spanish-ness and this has left a lasting legacy. Far-right groups have been active in displaying their rejection of the newcomers through racist slogans and violent crimes against immigrants. Spanish motor racing fans shocked the sport with racist chants against the UK's Lewis Hamilton in February 2008, and racist incidents at football matches still occur with worrying frequency.

However, this was by no means the first such public display of racism of recent years. In February 2000, in El Ejido near Almería, where Moroccan immigrants were working as fruit pickers in dreadful conditions for around €3

an hour, some of the worst race riots in Spain's history broke out. These were
precipitated when a mentally ill Moroccan killed a local woman, and in response
local gangs went on an indiscriminate 'Moor-bashing' spree. Racial attacks are
certainly on the increase in Spain, and the strain has only intensified after the Madrid
train bombings by Islamic extremists. There are also claims that the police and
judiciary are biased against minorities, especially following a case in Huelva in late
2004, in which three men were absolved of killing an elderly Moroccan at a bus
station. At the same time, however, the great majority of the population rejects
such viewpoints and many see the immigrants as enriching the country's cultural
diversity. Spain remains a country of contradictions.

Zapatero surprised many by rising admirably to the challenge of leading Spain
through a time of social and economic transition, instituting numerous social reforms
and pursuing broadly redistributive policies; however, at the time of going to press,
Europe is watching with bated breath as Spain prepares to hold its general election.
It will be the first EU nation to do so since the credit squeeze hit the financial markets
in the summer of 2007, and as the campaign swings into action Madrid is humming
with of rumours of spiraling house repossessions and impending recession. After
falling steadily for years, the unemployment rate jumped suddenly at the end of
2007 as retail sales declined and real estate and construction firms laid off workers,
and private sector economists have slashed their growth forecasts for the country.
Whether the Socialists can make good on their reported 6% poll lead and win
another term in office remains to be seen.

# Local government

'Autonomy' is a difficult word in a political context. The heady, near neurotic drive
for local home rule that gripped Spain as the years of Franco's repressive dictatorship
drew to a close was to cause years of political controversy, unrest and negotiation.
The result of these troubled years (which climaxed in the failed military coup of

1981, the military's response to the seemingly all-embracing move to a federal Spain) was the carving up of the country into 17 autonomous communities. The devolution of power to the regions was the outstanding innovation of the 1978 Constitution although this was not effectively achieved until 1983.

The Basques and Catalans were the first to achieve autonomy; they were both given control of education in their area and won the right to plan their own economies and set up their own police forces. A difference between the two is that in the Basque country the regional government collects taxes and hands them over to the central government, retaining what it needs for its own purposes; whereas in the Catalan provinces, as in the rest of the country, the central government collects the money and then gives the regional government its share.

In the lead up to the March 2004 election, the debate over the autonomous communities heated up considerably and certainly had an effect on voting patterns in the Basque region and Catalonia. Many of the regions now feel that the statutes drawn up in the early 1980s are out of date and need to be re-examined. In Catalonia and the Basque region particularly, there are strong calls for further autonomy and Juan José Ibarretxe, president of the Basque government, intends to hold a referendum on the creation of an independent Basque state, only loosely linked to Spain.

Zapatero's government is far more reliant on the nationalist groups for his parliamentary majority than Aznar was in his second term, and he has taken a more amenable stance towards such groups, for example allowing Catalonia to vote on partial devolution. However, he has come under fire for what many Spaniards see as his pandering to Basque separatists; there are still a great many Spanish people who believe that the autonomies already have more than enough power, and resent Zapatero's willingness to negotiate with groups such as ETA.

Although all of Spain is now divided into autonomous communities, and each of these enjoys a varying degree of autonomy, the concept of self-rule has come to have very little direct effect on the man in the street. Locals and expatriates often find that power is really devolved further in Spain, down to the city administration; and to get things done will find a visit to the *ayuntamiento* (town hall) more useful. This functions as part of the regional administration; and will answer queries on local taxes, and dispense advice on both central and federal government matters. In terms of daily life, many Spaniards will admit to having a stronger allegiance to their region that to the concept of Spain as a whole.

# ■ RELIGION

The Catholic Church in Spain has a long and rich, if sometimes intolerant history, which reaches far back to the Church's spearheading of the Counter Reformation. The years of the Inquisition resulted in the virtual elimination for a time of Protestantism in Spain (and forced Jews and Muslims to convert). The right to worship freely and of freedom of conscience was not granted to other religious denominations until as recently as 1978; and even then the centuries of power and influence which the Catholic Church had enjoyed through its close association with the state (particularly in the early Franco years) persisted, meaning that by this time there were few strongholds of any other religious denomination left.

The lay religious order, Opus Dei, was primarily responsible for the influence over the secular authorities which some would say the Catholic Church still wields in the 21st century. Founded in 1928 by José María Escrivá Balaguer, this semi-secret organisation succeeded in infiltrating Spanish society at many professional levels, in schools, government and business, and became tremendously powerful in the 1960s. A tax scandal exposed in 1969 by a government official succeeded in reducing but not extinguishing the rather sinister power of this group. One of their greatest strongholds is in the education sector, and their universities and colleges provide an initiatory education for the sons and daughters of the many aristocratic and influential Opus Dei members.

However, Catholicism in Spain has been forced to adapt to a modern secular society since the 1978 constitution, and changes in

A Catholic mass

Spanish society such as legal divorce, contraception and abortion have forced the church to rethink its approach. Spanish society has become markedly more liberal in the last few decades, a change that has been most visibly demonstrated to an international audience by the success of Pedro Almodóvar's films dealing with issues such as relaxed sexual morality, drugs, prostitution, homosexuality and transsexuals. Under Aznar and the PP, there was an attempt to restore some of the church's influence on public life, especially in education, where religious instruction was controversially restored to the state curriculum. However, Zapatero's government has done its best to mitigate the church's clout, and Spanish bishops have blasted the Prime Minister for his liberal policies on issues such as divorce, abortion, same-sex marriage and religious education in schools.

Unsurprisingly, newly fledged Spanish residents will find themselves immersed in Roman Catholicism in almost every town in the country. Notices of services are posted not only outside the churches, but at strategic viewing points throughout the town to attract as many churchgoers as possible. There are many festivals and holy days which are popular with visitors and locals, as in Seville. The effect of Catholicism in Spain is not only to be felt in the church (with the number of churchgoers now in sharp decline: only 18% go to church every Sunday); its culture and values are an integral part of many social attitudes within the country. Even those Spaniards who claim agnosticism have the Catholic culture as part of their heritage.

Christianity in Spain is all but synonymous with Catholicism. There are a mere 350,000 Protestants in the country, while 94% of the population is Catholic. However, there are resident Anglican clergy in a number of tourist and retirement areas and many Anglican services take place throughout Spain, which are attended by expatriates and visitors. These are usually listed in the local paper. Such services often take place in buildings borrowed from other denominations or in schools or church halls, even in hotels. There are also synagogues, temples and mosques in the main towns and cities.

## ◼ REGIONAL GUIDE

Historically, Spain has been assembled from a number of states or kingdoms, making it a mixture of peoples and cultures more complex than many of its near neighbours. Apart from Spanish (Castilian), there are at least three other distinct languages spoken by the so-called 'historical nationalities': the Basques, Gallegos and Catalans. The regions described below represent the current political set-up of Spain; many of them are based on the old kingdoms, like Asturias, which was founded in the 10th century. Although most of those living and working there are likely to find themselves in the better-known areas, there are vast areas of Spain like Extremadura which seem practically deserted. *Spain Off the Beaten Track* by Barbara Mandell and Roger Penn (Moorland Publishing) is an excellent guide to some of these more out-of-the-way destinations.

Spain's provinces are grouped into 17 autonomous communities, plus the two semi-autonomous enclaves located just across the water in North Africa, Ceuta and Melilla. Officially they are all *comunidades*, but for historical reasons Navarra is a *Comunidad Foral*, Murcia is a *Región* and Asturias is a *Principado*.

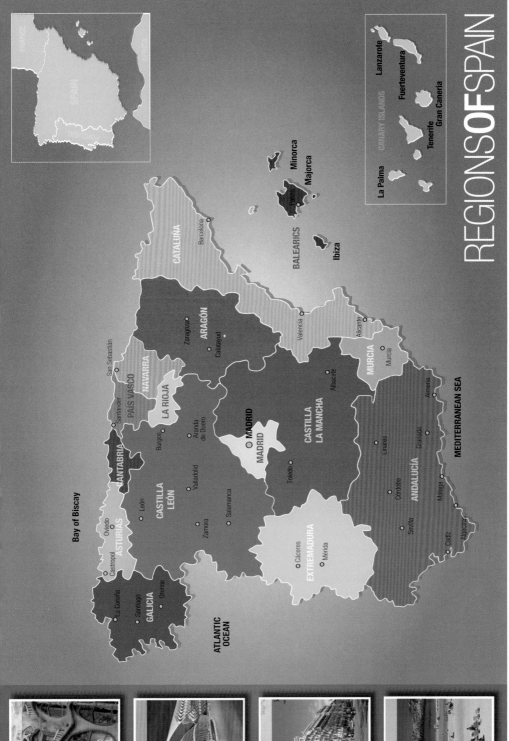

# REGIONS**OF**SPAIN

FRANCE
SPAIN
PORTUGAL

CANARY ISLANDS

Lanzarote
Fuerteventura
Gran Canaria
Tenerife
La Palma

Bay of Biscay

ATLANTIC OCEAN

GALICIA
- La Coruña
- Santiago
- Orense

ASTURIAS
- Castropol
- Oviedo

CANTABRIA
- Santander

PAÍS VASCO
- San Sebastián

NAVARRA

LA RIOJA

CASTILLA LEÓN
- León
- Zamora
- Valladolid
- Salamanca
- Burgos
- Aranda de Duero

ARAGÓN
- Zaragoza
- Calatayud

CATALUÑA
- Barcelona

BALEARICS
- Minorca
- Majorca
- Palma
- Ibiza

MADRID
- MADRID

EXTREMADURA
- Cáceres
- Mérida

CASTILLA LA MANCHA
- Toledo
- Albacete

VALENCIA
- Valencia
- Alicante

MURCIA
- Murcia

ANDALUCÍA
- Linares
- Córdoba
- Sevilla
- Cádiz
- Algeciras
- Málaga
- Granada
- Almería

MEDITERRANEAN SEA

Barcelona, Cataluña

Sevilla, Andalucía

Valencia, Cataluña

Cantabria

The constitution created in 1978 provided for a large amount of devolved power for the original 17 regions (Ceuta and Melilla gained limited autonomous status in 1994). However, this system has never become totally stable, as there is no uniformity to the powers that a region can have. Some of the larger regions act almost like separate countries, operating their own police forces and controlling the education and health systems. Others, however, operate far more like the local governments that the British are used to. Basque politicians have recently been calling for a renegotiation of their autonomy, and in June 2006 Catalonia voted in favour of greater autonomy and more devolved control over its legislative and judicial system.

The autonomous regions are further divided into *provincias* and then into smaller *municipios*. The municipalities are governed by a system of elected town councils with mayors, from the *ayuntamiento* (town hall). Even in quite small villages these institutions wield a surprising amount of power and are responsible for all aspects of daily life within the community. EU citizens that have registered for the electoral roll at the *ayuntamiento* are entitled to vote in municipal elections.

Unlike France, where the distribution of foreigners living and working is more widespread, in Spain the expatriates are concentrated on the Mediterranean costas, and to a lesser extent on the Balearics and Canaries, often living in all-foreign purpose built complexes (*urbanizaciónes*). The exception would be those teaching

Medieval buildings, Extremadura

regional guide aims to introduce the different areas of Spain mentioning their salient points, general characteristics and advantages and disadvantages to be taken into consideration when choosing an area to live, work and or retire to.

There is information on the industries and employment potential in each region on page 279.

# Information facilities

A good starting point is the Spanish National Tourist Office (SNTO) in your own country, or visit the website www.spain.info/ (in English) for a supply of national maps, railway guides and brochures for all the main Spanish towns and regions. In Spain itself, you will find an SNTO in every larger town and from these you can get specific local guidebooks and information on hotels, car hire, and the principal sights. In addition, there are the tourist information bureaux (*Turismo*), which are run by the municipality. Generally speaking, the tourist offices and bureaux do not carry information for places outside their region. *The Mapa de Comunicaciones España* which can be supplied by the SNTO lists each of the local tourist information offices, with information on customs posts, driving and speed limits, motorway assistance, railway information telephone numbers, and the *paradores*, which are the government-run hotels luxury hotels in castles and other buildings of historic importance.

The central reservation number for Spanish paradores is 915 166666; email reservas@parador.es; www.parador.es. In Britain, Keytel International, 020 7616 0300; info@keytel.co.uk; www.keytel.co.uk, will send you a booking form and general information including insurance and car hire details, and a Directory of Paradors in Spain. To arrange accommodation in advance try Sun Hotels, admin@sunhotels.net; www. sunhotels.net, is a hotel consolidator offering reasonable rates on accommodation throughout the country, including Madrid, Andalucía, Santander, Santiago and Toledo, and others. Flights, car hire and tailor-made itineraries can also be arranged.

# ▣ THE MEDITERRANEAN REGIONS
## ANDALUCÍA (ANDALUSIA)

**Provinces:** Almería, Cádiz, Córdoba, Granada, Huelva, Jaén, Málaga and Sevilla (Seville).
**Main city:** Sevilla.
**Airports:** Almeria, Córdoba, Gibraltar, Granada, Jerez de la Frontera, Málaga, Sevilla.
**Regional tourist office website:** www.andalucia.org.

Andalucía is the second largest autonomous region of Spain covering 17% of Spain's total area. It is the most populated region with around seven million inhabitants, all enjoying 300 days of sunshine per year. Andalucía takes its name from al Andaluz, which was the stronghold of Muslim Arabs and Berbers who crossed from North Africa in the eighth century, virtually took over the Iberian Peninsula in less than four years, and were finally driven from their last stronghold in Granada by the Christians in the mid-15th century. The region's Moorish past can be seen in the great monuments that survive from the period, such as the Mezquita in Córdoba and the Alhambra palace in Granada, regarded as one of the world's greatest buildings.

By contrast with its rich past, Andalucía today can be said to embrace extremes of poverty and wealth. The Costa del Sol is one of the most popular tourist destinations on earth and areas such as Marbella have long been the playground of the rich and famous. However, unemployment here is at one of the highest rates in Europe (around 14%, although this is a vast improvement on the 34% unemployment rate seen in the 1980s) and peasants are forced to eke out an existence on smallholdings and through seasonal work.

Those who choose to live in Andalucía, away from the enclaves of expats, may find it hard to blend in and adapt to the many customs and traditions of local life.

Some of Spain's largest mountain ranges are located in Andalucía. The Sierra Nevada and the Sierra Morena dominate the Moorish town of Granada. There are ski resorts in both ranges. The province of Jaén behind Granada is famed for its olive growing, while Almería is partly desert. There is a small collection of foreign-owned villas in and around the hill town of Mojácar near Almeria: most are inhabited during the mild winter months as summers tend to be too hot and dry.

Foreigners who relocate to Andalucía tend to gravitate to one of the region's four costas: the Costa de la Luz, the Costa del Sol, the Costa Tropical and the Costa de Almería. These areas are discussed below:

### The Costa de la Luz

The 'Coast of Light' is gaining popularity among property buyers and those seeking to relocate permanently, largely because property prices are still somewhat lower than on the neighbouring Costa del Sol. The region offers traditional whitewashed villages and fine golden beaches which are more spread out than on the Costa del Sol, and often backed by sand dunes and pine trees. One real advantage of this area is that it has not as yet seen the high-rise hotel development of other areas, and inland there are still plenty of cheap properties for renovation. Some of the most popular destinations, certainly for those looking to buy property are the villages of Conil de la Frontera, Chiclana de la Frontera, Sanlúcar de Barrameda and Arcos de la Frontera.

Ski town, Sierra Nevada

## The Costa del Sol

The Costa del Sol is by far the most populous part of Andalucía, accounting for 76% of the region's total inhabitants, and is one of the fastest growing areas of population in Europe. UK residents account for 220,000 of the permanent population here and more than 60% of British people looking to relocate to Spain choose to join them.

Most of the development so far has taken place around and to the west of Málaga, where there is perpendicular concrete virtually all the way to Marbella, amidst which may be found the infamous resorts of Torremolinos and Fuengirola. At the most westerly point of this costa lies Gibraltar, still British and a banking and money moving centre. Many British expats are choosing to live in the vicinity of this British enclave, and new luxury housing developments have sprung up in the area, notably at Sotogrande and La Duquesa.

East of Málaga development has been a little less rampant, although concrete does proliferate, especially around the resort of Nerja. Property prices here are generally cheaper.

Property prices hit their peak here in 2003 and have begun to level out since then, although some areas are still seeing increases of 10% each year, and for many the area has become prohibitively expensive. Some are choosing to move to this same area, but a little inland, to some of the white-walled unspoilt villages around Antequera.

The advantage of the Costa del Sol for anyone thinking of living and working in Spain is that there is a ready market for anything from bookshops to barbers – it's just a question of finding a suitable gap in the market. There are over 10,000 registered foreign businesses on this coast alone.

## The Costa Tropical

The 60km of coastline running from just east of Nerja to Adra was, until a few years ago, lumped together with the Costa del Sol, but it has now been re-branded in an attempt to highlight the region's distinct character. This coastline takes its name from the sub-tropical climate, which allows the cultivation of exotic fruits and crops such as avocadoes, mangoes and bananas.

While there are similarities with the Costa del Sol, Tropical has managed to avoid mass tourism and some of the uglier high-rises. The warm micro-climate found here is created by the shelter of the Lujar and Chaparral mountains and the Sierra Nevada behind, helping to trap the warm winds drifting across from North Africa. As a result the coast is filled with dense orchards, which are guarded by Moorish watchtowers and fortresses nestling on the cliffs.

The coast is a mere 45 minutes from Granada and it takes just over an hour to get to the Sierra Nevada, leading to the fairly bizarre situation between October and April when you can, if so inclined, ski in the morning and sunbathe in the afternoon.

From Salobreña to Motril the coastline remains entirely undeveloped, although work is underway to extend Motril's golf course, which is expected to be completed in late 2008.

Fifty kilometres inland from this coast lies the Alpujarras region, a beautiful and unspoilt area of mountain villages and deep valleys tucked away in the foothills of the Sierra Nevada, where whitewashed houses built haphazardly on top of one another tumble down steep slopes, strewn with geraniums, carnations and wild roses. The area is a real draw for foreigners, many of whom are inspired by Chris Stewart's best seller, *Driving Over Lemons*. Foreigners living here describe the area as a microcosm of traditional Spanish life.

Those looking to work on the Costa Tropical are most likely to find opportunities in Castell de Ferro, the area's centre for trade and commerce. There are new-build apartments around the town, with views of the sea and mountains for around €250,000.

## The Costa de Almería

Although parts of Almería are arid and desert-like, this is the cheapest area of Andalucía to buy a coastal property, up to 40% cheaper than the better developed costas, and the estate agents are claiming there is great investment potential here, with annual growth as high as 25% in recent years. Almería missed out on the seventies boom and as a result the region is not yet spoilt or overcrowded, although some new high-rise developments are now underway. It offers some very pleasant beaches and the most sunshine hours of any part of Spain. Many foreigners have

| Some Andalucían specialities | |
|---|---|
| *alfajores* | nut and honey dessert |
| *habas con jamón* | fava beans with ham |
| *heuvos a la flamenca* | baked eggs with sausages and vegetables |
| *menudo* | chick-pea and vegetable stew |
| *pestiños* | fried pastries with honey |
| *polvorones* | sugar biscuits |
| *rabo de toro* | oxtail soup |
| *riñones al Jerez* | kidneys in sherry sauce |
| *tocino de cielo* | caramel flan |

chosen to settle in coastal resorts such as Roquetas del Mar, Mojácar and San Juan de los Terreros. However, those looking for work are most likely to find success in Almería itself, which is a fairly unattractive industrial city which was given an investment boost through its hosting of the Mediterranean Games in 2005.

# Murcia

**Main city:** Murcia.
**Airports:** San Javier Airport (47km from Murcia). Work is currently under way on a new regional airport near to Corvera, which is due to open in 2009.
**Regional tourist office website:** www.murciaturistica.es.

Murcia, the driest part of Spain, is quite a contrast to Valencia, its neighbour to the north, which is one of the most fertile. It is still a very agricultural region, with crops as diverse as tomatoes, citrus fruits and cotton grown here. Many of the previously desert-like areas have been irrigated and covered with plastic tunnels, much as in Almería. Murcia consists of a single province of that name; and neither historically nor currently does it have as strong a regional identity as its Valencian neighbour. In the 13th century the area was a part of the united territory ruled over by the dynasties of Castille and Aragón. The Aragonese kingdom at that time also encompassed Catalonia.

It was the historical linkage of Catalonia and Murcia that led many inhabitants of the region to pour into Catalonia after the Civil War, to search for jobs. It was at this time, too, that Murcians seem to have acquired an unfortunate and unmerited reputation for being uncouth and violent which has become part of national lore, to the extent that to many Spaniards 'Murcian' is a term of abuse. The main port in Murcia is Cartegena, named after the Carthaginians who founded it. Cartagena is a large naval base whose nightlife is described by one guidebook as 'lively, if somewhat dangerous'.

The region has a lot to offer. For nature lovers there is the stunning Sierra Espuña National Park and the Sierra de Carrascoy mountain range. For beach-lovers, the Costa Cálida, which runs from Aguilas to La Manga, boasts white sandy beaches and crystal clear water, deserted coves and a yearly average temperature of 18°C. For those interested in sport, the region offers excellent facilities. At the upmarket La Manga Club there are international golf courses and tennis centres and the Mar Menor, Europe's largest saltwater lagoon offers sailing, windsurfing, diving and jetskiing. Inland the landscape is dominated by vineyards, rivers, mountains and apricot trees. The city of Murcia is the commercial centre of the region and as such offers the most career opportunities. Very few tourists visit the city and as a result it has a peaceful, unspoilt air and a traditional slow pace of life. The city is renowned for its Baroque cathedral, museums and beautiful 19th century architecture.

The Costa Cálida is currently being billed as an up-and-coming area. The Spanish themselves have been buying holiday homes here for generations, so pie and chips and all-night karaoke are blissfully absent from the region, but foreigners are beginning to catch up. Growth in the region is currently the highest in the country, and Murcia is currently the fastest-growing area in Spain for new *urbanizaciónes*, custom-built villa communities, mainly for the expat market. New marinas, golf courses and hotel developments are all in the process of being built, but it is hoped that the developers here will have learned from the 'too much too soon' construction of some of the other costas and will manage to retain some of the coast's present charm.

**FACT**

■ Growth in the region is currently the highest in the country, and Murcia is currently the fastest-growing area in Spain for new *urbanizaciónes*, custom-built villa communities, mainly for the expat market.

### The Mar Menor

To the north of the Costa Cálida, La Manga ('the sleeve') sits on a narrow strip of land that stretches 22km out into the Mediterranean sea creating the largest saltwater lagoon in Europe – El Mar Menor. With a maximum depth of only eight metres, the water in the Mar Menor remains at a constant 18°C and is calm all year round making it ideal for children.

One of the more bewildering sights to be found on the shores of the Mar Menor is that of people wallowing in the mud. The climactic conditions of the area have created deposits of mud and clay in certain areas and these muddy deposits are said to have healing properties, curing everything from arthritis and rheumatism to skin complaints.

These warm waters have been recognised as having health benefits ever since the time of the Romans who built a number of baths in the area, but until recently the sea's healing properties were considered nothing more than local legend. However, in 1995 Murcia University made a study of the sediment and found it to contain unusually high levels of chlorine and sulphate as well as calcium, magnesium and potassium. The presence of so many minerals in the mud provide scientific evidence for long-established local beliefs.

The best place to experience the Mar Menor mud therapy is at the thermal baths in Los Alcazares.

In the past, development in the Costa Cálida was restricted by poor infrastructure. However, improved roads and the evolution of San Javier from an ex-military airport with one flight per week, to an international airport delivering 1,995,000 visitors a year to the region have improved accessibility. As a result house prices here are on the up, and demand is set to continue, especially when the new custom-built international airport opens at Corvera in 2009, with the capacity for 22 planes per hour.

## Valencia

**Provinces:** Alicante, Castellón and Valencia.
**Main city:** Valencia.
**Airports:** Alicante, Valencia, New Castellón de la Plana.
**Regional tourist office website:** www.comunitat-valenciana.com.

The País Valenciano has strong historical associations with the Catalonian/Aragonese partnership which conquered it in the twelfth century; it shares a linguistic heritage with Catalonia, and Valencian is commonly accepted to be a dialect of Catalan, although this assertion belies the strong political links that Valencians feel they have to what they see as their distinct native tongue.

Valencia itself is Spain's third largest city and is a truly exciting and vibrant place, accurately labelled by many as the 'City of Contrasts'. Founded by Roman legionaries in 138 BC, Valencia has a traditional atmosphere with an impressive array of architecture going back to the Middle Ages. However, in recent years there has been a huge amount of investment and development in the city. The brand new City of Arts and Sciences has been praised for having brought ultra-modern urbanism right into the heart of its traditional town.

Valencia may not have the same diversity and vitality as Madrid and Barcelona, but it is a city that thrives on festivities, colour and noise. The city's emblem is a bat, and its residents are joyously nocturnal; some of the best nightlife in mainland Spain, if not in the country as a whole, is here and the *Las Fallas* festival, which takes place in March, is one of the most important festivities in Spain. During the week of *Las Fallas de San Jose*, there are endless processions, bullfights and firework displays, terminating in the *Nit de Foc* when the entire city lights up with bonfires in every street, burning enormous caricatures of popular satirical figures.

Those relocating to Spain for professional reasons will discover that Valencia is one of the most important cities on the Spanish Mediterranean coast. It has a thriving business district and over forty international trade fairs are staged in the city every year, offering professionals from a variety of economic sectors the ideal platform for launching and distributing their products. The city is pushing hard to meet the demands of the 21st century and the use of English is higher in Valencia than in many other Spanish cities.

Valencia has enjoyed such a remarkable regeneration in recent years that it is now being hailed as the next big thing; some commentators are even calling it the new Barcelona, and no-one can be immune to the sense of optimism and self-confidence that now pervades the region. Valencians are enthusiastically buying up run-down properties and transforming them into elegant residences, and the America's Cup in 2007 spawned an overhaul of the shabby seafront and the opening of a sparkling new cubist marina, a stunning confection of steel, glass and light named the Port America's Cup.

## The Costa Blanca

British visitors will be most familiar with the province of Alicante, which, after Andalucía, is the home of the largest number of British residents in Spain. The beaches and resorts of the Costa Blanca, Denia, Javea, Calpe, Altea, Benidorm and Villajoyosa, to name but a few, are incredibly popular with both tourists and property buyers alike. Access to the Costa Blanca is easy from Alicante airport.

The 'White Coast' gets its name from Greek traders who founded *Akra Leuka*, or the blank foothill, there around 2,500 years ago, but it was only really in the 1960s when the picturesque village of Benidorm began attracting package tourists that the area started to take shape as the holiday haven it has become today. The Costa Blanca may have been overdeveloped in places, but this does not detract from its natural beauty and serenity. Indeed, the World Health Organization cites this stretch of coastline as one of the healthiest places on earth due to its climate, recreational facilities and relaxed way of life. Environmental issues are now at the forefront of local politics in the region and as a result further development has been restricted in many areas and construction companies are being forced to show a commitment to a sustainable environment.

The main city on the Costa Blanca is Alicante. While tourism has replaced port activity as the main source of revenue in the region, Alicante still has a bustling and vibrant harbour. The city has benefited from continuing investment, creating high quality residential and business developments. There are plans for further redevelopment of the area, including a high-speed train line from Valencia, which is currently under construction and an expansion of green areas in the city.

There is a quite large north/south divide on the Costa Blanca. Property prices are far cheaper in the south and, as a rule, the north attracts a more refined crowd searching for a villa with private swimming pool, whereas in the south property buyers are usually young families or couples looking for an apartment. On the Costa Blanca as a whole, property prices are currently increasing by an average of 17% per annum, so it is still a good place to invest.

## The Costa del Azahar

The other coastline in this region, in the provinces of Valencia and Castellón, is the Costa del Azahar (the Orange Blossom Coast), so called because it is lined with magnificent orange plantations amidst lush green vegetation. The strong smell of pines drifting down from the mountains mixed with the intoxicating smells of orange trees in blossom and the almond groves really brings this 112km stretch of coastline to life. Dotted along the shoreline are small summer resorts, perhaps the best known of which is the ancient fortified town of Peñiscola. The coast here boasts miles of sandy beaches and very calm waters, particularly safe for bathing and for practising all kinds of water sports.

Properties along this less-known coastline are bought mainly by Spaniards, but appeal to foreigners as prices remain reasonably low and access is relatively quick and direct from Valencia airport. The new airport at Castellón de la Plana is has made the area far more accessible to foreign home buyers, and new developments are springing up as a result. For example a huge theme park, Mundo Ilusion is currently being built near to Torreblanca and aims to cater for 2 to 3 million visitors annually.

## Islas Baleares (Balearic Islands)

**Main cities:** Palma (Mallorca), Mahon (Minorca), Ibiza Town, Sant Francesc Xavier (Formentera).
**Airports:** Palma, Mahon, Ibiza Town.
**Regional tourist office website:** www.visitbalears.com.

The Balearic Islands (Las Islas Baleares) off the Valencian and Catalonian coast, have been associated with Spain since the Romans incorporated them into their province of Hispania, which comprised the whole Iberian Peninsula. Together, the four main islands, Mallorca, Menorca, Ibiza and Formentera comprise less than 1% of the area of Spain with a total population of around 870,000.

The biggest island is Mallorca, which attracts an estimated 15 million tourists a year and also has around 15,000 British residents and workers. Fortunately, the tourist development is concentrated in small areas of the coast, notably around Palma and in the northeast around Pollensa. The other islands are mainly summer resorts and extremely quiet (and sometimes chilly) out of season. The liveliest and most upmarket is certainly Ibiza (main town Eivissa), which gained its reputation for tolerance towards foreign visitors in the 1960s when it was popular with hippies; several rock stars also bought properties there. More recently, aficionados of house music and dance culture have made it a popular destination among the young, although those who pioneered the scene in the 1990s now bemoan its impersonality and commercialism. Menorca is more sedate and family-oriented; and the smallest island, Formentera, is also the quietest and the least developed.

Because of government restrictions on development and limited land availability, prices on the islands are higher than on the mainland and it is difficult to find a well located property for less than €150,000. The islands are the number one choice for buyers looking for luxurious properties, glamorous surroundings and the best weather. Homes on the islands are coveted by the rich and famous and Formula 1's Schumacher brothers are among the many owners of multi-million pound villas.

Access to the Balearic Islands from the UK is easy as there are numerous charter flights all year round. There are ferry connections to Ibiza from Denia and Barcelona and from Valencia to Ibiza and Palma. It is also possible to reach Mahon in Menorca by ferry from Barcelona.

## Mallorca

This island has become an extremely desirable place to live, attracting the likes of Michael Douglas, Claudia Schiffer and Richard Branson, and literary pilgrims still come here to see the former house and the burial place of the English writer Robert Graves. The unfair myth that the island offers little more than high-rise hotels and cheap package holidays is simply not true. Admittedly there are certain areas of the island that were ravaged by developers in the 1960s and 1970s, but

Preparations for a procession during Semona Santa (Holy week)

these are more or less confined to a handful of large resorts. Most of the island retains its staggeringly diverse natural beauty, with the striking cove beaches of the northwest coast, the rugged peaks of the Serra de Tramuntana, and an array of charming old towns. The island's capital, Palma, has also been much maligned. Those who visit are often surprised to find a lively, vibrant city steeped in history and culture.

The largest number of foreign homebuyers on the island has always been the Germans, followed by the Scandinavians and Dutch. However, the slump in the German economy has led to many Germans selling up and it is the British who are snapping up these resale properties. The southwest corner of Mallorca has proved the most popular for property buyers, largely because it offers better weather, a popular coastline and exclusive residential areas. The inland villages are also popular due to the lower prices and the lack of tourist activity.

## Menorca

Menorca is the Balearics' second largest island. Unlike parts of Mallorca, it has remained largely untouched by tourism. It has also avoided the 24-hour club culture that plagues Ibiza. Menorca's charms lie in its relaxed atmosphere, picturesque towns, stunning scenery and deserted beaches with crystal clear waters. There are more than a hundred idyllic beaches on Menorca and although the government here has been trying to improve access to the more remote ones, there are still a handful of beaches that can only be reached by foot.

The entire island was designated a biosphere reserve in 1993, and it is largely a rural green paradise, filled with ancient relics and monuments. Romans, Arabs, Catalans, British and French rulers have all at some point made their mark on Menorca.

Around 70%–75% of property buyers in Menorca are British. According to estate agents on the island, their market has changed entirely over recent years. Whereas previously most people were looking for a holiday home, these days people are seeing the long-term advantages of living on the island and are looking to either retire there or split their time equally between a home in Menorca and a home elsewhere. Expatriates cite such aspects of island life as the minimal crime index, peace and quiet and the friendly familiarity of the locals as the main reasons for choosing Menorca as the location for their second home or full-time residence.

## Ibiza

Ibiza offers something to please everyone, from the culture, fashion and superb cuisine in Ibiza town and the stunning coves and beaches on Ibiza's coastline to the wild 24-hour clubbing in San Antonio and hippy chic in Santa Eulalia. Those worried about Ibiza's culture of excess will find that the clubbers and revellers are concentrated in Ibiza Town, San Antonio and Santa Eulalia. Away from the resort areas is a stunningly beautiful island with dense pine forests, towering cliffs and some of the best beaches in the Balearics. The over-development that plagued Mallorca in the 1960s is far less visible in Ibiza and most of the island has an unspoilt rural air. Ibiza also offers a climate of almost perpetual sunshine.

Property on Ibiza is very expensive. The restrictions on development in the Balearics have caused prices in Ibiza to soar even more than on the other islands.

**FACT**

■ There are more than a hundred idyllic beaches on Menorca and although the government here has been trying to improve access to the more remote ones, there are still a handful of beaches that can only be reached by foot.

# Formentera

The tiny island of Formentera is the smallest of the inhabited Balearics. It can only be reached by ferry from Ibiza Town, although there is a regular service every two hours. The island is only 35 square miles and is home to only 5,300 people, but for those really looking to get away from it all, Formentera feels like a new world waiting to be discovered. The island is yet to be spoiled by tourism development and there are only a handful of hotels and hostels, all of which close for the winter. The beaches are long, sandy and flanked by palms and pines, and they are never overcrowded.

Property on Formentera is not easy to come by, but those who are willing to persevere will find that there are a few small apartment developments and some villas and converted farmhouses.

| Some specialities of the Balearic Islands | |
| --- | --- |
| *arroz brut* | rice, pork and vegetable casserole |
| *butifarrón* | cured sausage with pine nuts and herbs |
| *caldereta de langosta* | lobster stew |
| *escaldums* | chicken and meatball stew |
| *frit* | sauté of liver, peppers and potatoes |
| *greixonera* | bread pudding |
| *queso de Mahón* | semi-soft cow milk cheese |
| *sobrasada* | soft seasoned sausage |
| *sopas Mallorquinas* | thick vegetable soup |
| *tumbet* | sautéed potatoes, peppers, eggplant and zucchini |

Other Balearic specialities include fluffy pastries known as ensaimadas; the islands also gave the world mayonnaise (*salsa Mayonesa*).

# Catalunya (Catalonia)

**Provinces:** Barcelona, Girona, Lléida (Lerida), Tarragona.
**Main city:** Barcelona.
**Airports:** Barcelona, Girona, Reus.
**Regional tourist office website:** www.catalunyaturismo.com.

Catalonia, whose first ruler was the hirsutely-named Guifré el Pelós (Wilfred the Hairy), is one of the regions of Spain which has its own distinct historical – and some would say national – identity, with its own culture and language, Catalan. Although covering less than 7% of the total area of Spain, Catalonia is home to over seven million inhabitants, 61% of whom live in Barcelona province. This has long been one of the most exciting and cosmopolitan parts of Spain, and Barcelona itself is a hotbed of politics, fashion, commerce and culture.

In the 12th century, Catalonia was an autonomous part of the kingdom of Aragón, an alliance that enhanced its political influence, and brought far ranging cultural influences to Aragón from Provence and Roussillon by way of Catalonia. The Catalan language is closely related to the Langue d'Oc, still spoken in some parts of

Boats in Port Vell, Barcelona

southern France, which once formed part of a single kingdom with Catalonia. There is even a Catalan-speaking outpost in Sardinia: in the Middle Ages Catalonia was one of the Mediterranean powers.

The decline of Catalonian wealth and power in the 14th century weakened Aragón to the extent that Castile became the dominant regional power. For the next five centuries the Catalonians attempted to consolidate their autonomy in an on-and-off fashion as successive Spanish dynasties tried to stake a claim to it. Towards the end of the 19th century, the broad based nationalist movement of Catalanism began to gather momentum and attracted the attention of Madrid which offered a limited autonomy to the region, which was subsequently repressed by the dictator Primo de Rivera. Any further thoughts of autonomy were interrupted by the Civil War during which Barcelona became the final refuge of republicanism and anarchism, and held out against Franco's armies until the bitter end in 1939.

Franco's retribution against the Catalan language and culture took the form of book-burning and the changing of street and place names. However, in the decades following the end of the Civil War, Catalan nationalism mellowed, and Catalanism became characterised by bravura rather than violence and extremism. Perhaps one of the reasons for this change is that, throughout the 20th century, many migrant workers from poorer parts of Spain settled in Catalonia, attracted by the industry and wealth of the area. The result is that about half of the population are descended from immigrants, which has led to a bilingualism not unlike that of Wales, with Spanish universally spoken but Catalan favoured in schools and universities. This immigration also contributed to the dilution of some of the stronger nationalist feelings in the region.

The town of Tarragona is a large industrial port with chemical and oil refineries and can be divided into two parts: an old walled city and an ugly modern one. Historically, Tarragona has had trading links across the Mediterranean. The Romans built a splendid city here, and many fine examples of their architecture remain in the old part of the town and its environs, notably the forum, Scipio's Tower (Torre de Scipio) and a triumphal arch (Arco de Bara).

Barcelona (the province) includes part of the Pyrenees. It is also home to one of the national symbols of Catalonia, the monastery of Montserrat built around the legend of the Black Virgin, an icon reputedly hidden on the site by St Peter and rediscovered in the ninth century amidst the sort of miraculous happenings usually associated with such shrines. During the Franco era the monastery clandestinely published the Montserrat Bible in Catalan and became a centre of nationalist gatherings. It can be visited by bus or train from Barcelona.

Barcelona city, much to the chagrin of the capital Madrid, is held by many to be the most lively and interesting city not only Spain but also in Europe. It is a huge industrial centre and port (population three million), and the spiritual home of individuals of such startling originality as the architect Gaudí and Pablo Picasso. And it is also the most liberated (or decadent, depending on your viewpoint) city in Spain. The notorious red light district, the *barrio* chino, is now used as the term for similar districts elsewhere in the country. Students, young people and hedonists of all ages flock here, and the sheer energy and sophistication of the place are a great attraction. Barcelona is also close enough to the Costa Brava, where many foreign residents are based, to make it a regular port of call for those who want a change of pace.

Work on the famous Gaudí cathedral, La Sagrada Familia, started in 1882 and was left uncompleted after the architect was killed by a tram in 1926. Work has continued, controversially, and the cathedral is likely to be finished within the next 20 years or so. For years it remained open to the skies – although work proceeds apace – and many Barcelonans would have preferred to see it left that way as a monument to its creator. The facilities left behind by the Olympic Games in 1992 are another attraction. Another is the Picasso Museum on the Carrer de Montcada.

Barcelona airport, Prat, is 14km from the city centre; and there are ferries from Barcelona to the Balearics. The airports of Girona and Reus are further away, but the low cost fares available to these airports may make the extra journey worthwhile.

Of interest to jobseekers are the many English language schools in Barcelona – as in many other Spanish cities – and the recent growth of high-technology industries to match those across the Mediterranean in southern France, where the region also has many commercial as well as historical links (see page 240 for details of English language teaching in Spain). However, the number of English teachers looking for jobs in Barcelona heavily outweighs the number of positions available. Catalonia is a fairly rich area and opportunities for foreigners to find work are distributed widely through the region's small but prosperous towns.

A religious procession during holy week

The growth in the property market in Barcelona has leveled off slightly over the past few years, and prices are now rising steadily by around 8.3% per annum. In the city centre it is very rare to find anything other than apartments. For those looking to buy townhouses and villas, these are mainly located in the north (Pedralbes, Tres Torres and Sarria) and west (Les Corts) of the city.

The northern costas, the Costa Brava and the Costa Dorada were the first to be invaded in the 1950s by tourism and property development. There is a large Spanish presence among the property owners in this region, so it has remained fairly culturally intact, unlike the Costa del Sol.

## The Costa Brava

For many the Costa Brava ('the rugged coast') is the only place in which they would consider buying property. The beauty of this coastline, with its cliffs and coves led to the beginnings of mass tourism in Spain, which in turn has led to the over-development of the area. Between Blanes and Sant Faliu de Guixols some of the worst aspects of mass tourism can be seen, but the further north toward the French border you travel, the less sprawling the development. In this area lie the small and unspoilt resorts of Calelle de Palafrugel, Figueres and Cadaques. This area is still relatively unknown to many British holidaymakers and there are almost no noisy nightclubs and lager louts, only beautiful scenery and peaceful sandy bays and coves. For those interested in watersports, this area has excellent windsurfing at the resorts of Roses, Estartit and Platja d'Aro and snorkelling at Aigua Blava. Proximity to the Pyrenees offers the possibilities of hiking in the summer and skiing in the winter.

Property remains comparatively expensive on the Costa Brava, partly due to the Spanish and French love affair with the region. Prices have also been pushed up by the Catalonian government's recent clampdown on coastal building.

## The Costa Dorada

The 'Golden Coast', running south of Barcelona to the Delta de L'ebre, is less wild than the Costa Brava. There are fewer coastal centres of population along this coast, with most development around Vilanova in La Geltrú and Torredembarra, and the terrain become less attractive and flat as you head south towards Tarragona. Sitges, a fashionable resort since the late 19th century, is the star of this stretch of coast, but because of its status property is much more expensive than elsewhere and apartments, in town especially, can be very hard to find.

Although the Costa Dorada does not have the density of foreign residents of other parts of Spain, the number of foreign visitors to the area means that there is access to English-language newspapers and magazines. Supermarkets stock certain foods from 'back home' and pubs and restaurants cater for those after non-Spanish cuisine. However, many of the resorts along this stretch of coastline become ghost towns during the winter.

| Some specialities of Catalonia | |
| --- | --- |
| amanida | salad of cured meat, cheese and fish |
| bacallá a la llauna | salted cod with beans |
| bacallá amb mel | salted cod with honey |

| | |
|---|---|
| *butifarra* | white cooked sausage |
| *canalons* | rolled pasta with meat, fish or vegetable filling |
| *crema Catalana* | custard glazed with caramelised sugar |
| *empedrat* | cod and bean salad |
| *escalivada* | grilled peppers, tomato, eggplant and onion |
| *esqueixada* | cod with peppers, tomato and onion |
| *faves a la Catalana* | fava beans with mint |
| *formatge llenguat* | strong cows' milk cheese |
| *fricandó amb moixarnons* | veal stew with wild mushrooms |
| *fuet* | salami |
| *llagosta amb pollastre* | lobster with chicken |
| *mel i mató* | honey and cheese |
| *múrgules farcides* | stuffed morels |
| *oca amb peres* | gosling with pears |
| *sarsuela* | mixed seafood stew |

#  THE PYRENEAN REGIONS

## Aragón

**Provinces:** Huesca, Teruel and Zaragoza.
**Main city:** Zaragoza.
**Airport:** Zaragoza.
**Regional tourist office website:** www.turismodearagon.com.

The northern part of Aragón incorporates a section of the Pyrenees while the south slopes toward the Ebro valley and rises again in Teruel. The Aragonese provinces comprise 9.5% of Spain but, like Extremadura, are heavily underpopulated with a total of only around 1.2 million inhabitants. The historical kingdom of Aragón was created by Sancho the Great of Navarre who reigned from 1000 to 1035. Later, in the 15th century, Aragón and Castile became one kingdom under the joint rule of Ferdinand and Isabella. Places of interest include the magnificent castle of Loarre about 25 miles/40km from Huesca, which was built by Sancho the Great as part of his forward defences against the Arabs. Pyrenean Aragón is fast becoming popular with hikers, particularly in the Ordesa National Park. There are also several ski resorts of which the most chic is Benasque. The town of Jaca, the capital in former times, was also on the pilgrim route to Santiago de Compostela.

Zaragoza is a lively city with some interesting Moorish architecture, notably the Ajaferiá Palace.

Geographically, the province of Teruel reaches out to the south rather than the Pyrenees and is one of the most unexplored areas with few inhabitants and poor roads. Property for sale in Aragón is scarce.

## Navarra (Navarre)

**Main town:** Pamplona.
**Regional tourist office website:** www.turismo.navarra.es/eng/home.

Navarre is one of the smaller regions of Spain, comprising 2.06% of the country's area and home to 1.35% of the population. A stretch of the Pyrenees fills the north-eastern part of the province and includes the historic pass of Roncesvalles on the route taken by mediaeval pilgrims to Santiago. The south of Navarre is on the north-eastern edge of the *meseta* and is a region of vineyards and other agriculture. The main city of the region is Pamplona, whose bull-running festival, Fiestaof San Fermín, takes place in July and attracts capacity crowds from all over Spain and beyond.

The origins of the kingdom of Navarre lie in a ninth century battle between the Basques and the Franks. The latter, in the process of retreating after an unsuccessful campaign against the Moors, were ambushed by some early Basque separatists who, having routed the Franks in the valley of Roncesvalles, declared the area around Pamplona independent. The event is immortalised in the *Chanson de Roland,* which, erroneously, claims the attackers were really Moors not Basques. During the 11th century, the kingdom of Navarre included Basque territory on both sides of the Pyrenees, which links its history with that of France as well as Spain. Navarre remained an independent kingdom, playing its own part in European power politics, until 1512, when the aforementioned King Ferdinand of Aragón and Castile annexed it to give his armies a safe corridor to attack the French on the other side of the Pyrenees.

Once this had been accomplished he allowed the Navarrese their autonomy, which they have retained almost uninterruptedly ever since. It is probably largely due to this continued independence that Navarre never became incorporated into the Basque country, in spite of its foundation by Basques and close links with this region.

The region has a strong north/south divide. While the north is mostly Basque-speaking and in certain areas very nationalist, the south is Spanish-speaking and resistant to Basque demands.

## Northern cuisine

The north is a wet verdant region renowned for its meat and fish dishes. The Basque Country has local specialities such as *marmitako* (potatoes with bonito) and *txangurro* (clams and spider crab) and the city of San Sebastián has a tremendous concentration of five-fork restaurants serving some of the finest food in Europe. Asturias has a similar cuisine, with its own local dishes such as the *fabada* (haricot bean and pork stew), regional cheeses and cider. Cantabria, meanwhile offers beef, anchovies and dairy products and Galicia has the *pote* (a soup made with ham, haricot beans and turnips), *caldeiradas* (bouillabaisse, followed by the fish), *pulpo* (octopus), a wide variety of fresh shellfish – including scallops and mussels – dairy products and pastries as well as the famed Albariño and Ribeiro wines.

The fertile valleys across Aragón, La Rioja and Navarre produce fruit and vegetables – asparagus, peppers, borage, cardoon, peaches and pears, potatoes, and cabbage hearts. Specialities include meat marinades (*chilindrones*) and confits. Desserts include cheeses, milk puddings and fruit (fresh, chocolate-coated or preserved in syrup).

| Some specialities of Navarre | |
|---|---|
| bacalao al ajo arriero | cod with pimento and tomato |
| canutillos | custard-filled pastry rolls |
| cochofrito | lamb stew with garlic and lemon |
| pichón a la Cazadora | pigeon in wine sauce |
| queso del roncal | cured sheep milk cheese |
| trucha a la Navarra | trout with cured ham |

# ◼ THE BAY OF BISCAY AND ATLANTIC COAST (THE GREEN COAST)

## País Vasco (the Basque Country)

**Provinces:** Alava, Guipuzcoa, Vizcaya (Biscay).
**Main city:** Bilbao (Vizcaya).
**Airports:** San Sebastián.
**Regional tourist office website:** www.paisvascoturismo.net.

The Basque Country (*Euskadi*) is one of the more heavily populated regions of Spain representing about 1.5% of the surface area and 6% of the population. Most Basques see themselves as an ethnic or national minority within Spain and in common with Catalans seek greater autonomy, or independence. It also has the most determined separatist movement, and a terrorist organisation, *Euskadi ta Azkatasuna* (ETA) which came into being as a direct result of the repression of the Basques, their culture and language (euskera), and their national aspirations, by the Franco regime. Its campaign continues today, although there have been no successful terrorist attacks since the Madrid airport bomb of 30 December 2006.

It is now widely accepted that the Basques are descended from the original aboriginal inhabitants of Europe, who lived in the region before the farmers and settlers arrived from the Middle East 10,000 years ago. There may be some connection with the now-extinct Picts in Scotland. Early skeletal remains featuring a distinctive elongated head which is characteristic of Basque people have been unearthed in the region, although many subsequent invasions have left their mark on the Basque Country, and other Europeans have been shown to be descended from a range of migrating peoples as well.

The claim that the Basques managed to resist domination by the Romans has been disproved by historians, who have ascertained that these invaders did, in fact, subdue the province to the extent of building roads and settlements there. After the Romans left, the so-called barbarians (the Franks and the Visigoths) who settled in much of the rest of Spain never managed more than a partial conquest of the indigenous population, who clearly outfought the barbarians during their dogged resistance. This was also one of the last corners of Europe to adopt Christianity and to build towns; the Basques habitually ambushed pilgrims on the route to Santiago. Nominally ruled by the dynasties of Castile and Navarre, they managed to keep a large measure of autonomy through the grassroots governorship of their own nobles and chieftains.

Through their long association with the Castilian crown, they also prospered, providing administrators for the Hapsburgs, and producing such notable historical figures as Ignatius Loyola, St Francis Xavier and the explorer Lope de Aguirre.

The strident nationalism associated with the region was unknown until the 19th century, and arose in response to the spread of centralist government, and ultimately as a reaction to the French Revolution. During the so-called Carlist Wars, the Basque provinces were split into the urbanised supporters of Madrid and the rural peasantry, who sided with Don Carlos (who made an unsuccessful attempt to usurp his brother's throne). As punishment, Basque areas had their autonomy rescinded, which upset the loyalists who had sided with Madrid and caused festering discontent. In the early 20th century, Basque industry, based around rich natural resources such as iron ore and timber, made the area around Biscay a hub of wealth, industry and banking. The Basque Nationalist Party, the PNV, was founded in 1910 with support broadly based in the liberal middle stratum of society. The Civil War of 1936 reopened the old gulf between the peasantry and the middle classes: the coastal provinces of Guipúzcoa and Vizcaya sided with the republicans who rewarded them with autonomy, while the inland province Alava sided with the government.

In 1936 the Basque Country was the scene of the most appalling brutality when the small but historic town of Guernica was bombed and over a thousand of its inhabitants massacred as they fled. It took four hours to reduce the town centre to rubble; the bombardment was carried out by the German airforce, a premonition perhaps of the greater conflict which was to follow. Miraculously perhaps, the ancient Guernikako Arbola (Tree of Guernica) under which the Basque Parliament used to meet survived the attack.

Franco's attempt to bludgeon the Basques into submission has become immortalised in the Picasso painting depicting nightmarish scenes juxtaposed with modern technology representing the horror of war and the artist's reaction to it. The huge canvas was only brought to Spain after the dictator's death – as Picasso had requested – and now hangs in the Prado museum.

1959 was the year that ETA (*Euskadi Ta Askatasuna*) came into existence and began the fight against the centralist state, receiving wide support throughout Spain during Franco's final years. In 1973 they were responsible for the assassination of Luis Carrero Blanco, Franco's proposed heir. Since 1959, their campaign of terrorism has continued, save for a handful of short-lived ceasefires. ETA's worst single attack came in 1987, when 21 shoppers were killed in a Barcelona supermarket. Then-Prime Minister José María Aznar himself was targeted by the group in 1995, perhaps the reason that he became so intolerant towards nationalist movements. In 2003 new terrorist laws introduced by Aznar's government following 9/11 were used to ban Batasuna, ETA's political wing. However, the simultaneous ETA bombings in seven different cities on Spain's Constitution Day in December 2004, attest to the fact that the nationalist troubles are far from over, and the ceasefire that was declared in May 2006 lasted for only seven months.

With high unemployment and its reputation for terrorism, the Basque country may not seem an attractive prospect for living and working. However, there are some possibilities: away from the main industrial areas around Bilbao there

**FACT**

■ Franco's attempt to bludgeon the Basques into submission has become immortalised in the Picasso painting depicting nightmarish scenes juxtaposed with modern technology representing the horror of war and the artist's reaction to it.

are rural areas characterised by a greenness reminiscent of the Emerald Isle, while traditional Basque farmhouses (*caerios*) resembling Swiss chalets may appeal to some.

Because of the cooler sea temperatures and the amount of annual rainfall, most Europeans choose not to live in the area and you will be something of an oddity if you do. The greatest drawback to living in this part of Spain would probably lie in mastering the Basque language, which bears no resemblance to other European languages, and would prove more difficult than learning Spanish. Unless you speak the language you may find life here rather isolating, as there is virtually no access to English-language media and foreigners are few and far between, even in the tourist season.

The Basque country is famous for its cuisine.

| Some specialities of the Basque Country | |
| --- | --- |
| *angulas a la Bilbaína* | baby eels in garlic sauce |
| *bacalao a la Vizcaína* | salted cod in red pepper sauce |
| *bacalao al pil-pil* | salted cod in garlic sauce |
| *kokotxas a la Donostiarra* | hake cheeks in green sauce |
| *leche frita* | fried custard |
| *marmitako* | bonito and tomato soup |
| *merluza Loskera* | hake in green sauce |
| *pochas* | broad bean stew |
| *queso de idiazábal* | smoked sheep milk cheese |
| *txangurro* | stuffed spider crab |

## Cantabria and Asturias

**Main towns:** Santander, Oviedo.
**Airport:** Avilés.
**Regional tourist office websites:** www.turismocantabria.net; www.infoasturias. com.

The spectacularly mountainous regions of Cantabria and neighbouring Asturias were considered too remote and inhospitable by the eighth century Moslem invaders, who left the area unconquered. The result was that Christians and the remnants of the Visigoths fleeing the Moors found it a useful place of refuge. Protected from the south by the natural barrier of the Cantabrian Cordillera, one of Spain's highest mountain ranges, the Christian northerners were slowly able, by a combination of violent sorties and general creeping encroachment, to push back the frontier of Moslem Spain.

In 718, there was a notable Asturian victory at Covadonga under Pelayo, who founded a small Asturian kingdom. From these modest beginnings the kingdom of Asturias spread out westwards and southwards until it reached León on the *meseta*. Eventually expansion reached the point where it allowed the Christian north to make a determined push against the Arabs and complete the reconquest of most of Spain in the eleventh century.

In the 19th century, Asturias became a centre for mining and steel production; today the main industrial town of Avilés has become the worst source of airborne pollutants in Spain.

Asturias was fiercely republican during the civil war, and produced one of its greatest heroes, the communist *La Pasionaria* (the Passionflower), an Asturian miner's wife, Dolores Ibarruri, who incited the housewives of Asturia to defend their homes with boiling oil. A legendary orator in her lifetime, she returned to Spain from exile on Franco's death. On the falangist side, Franco sent Spanish legionnaires and north African troops with a reputation for barbarity to subdue the region, an irony which was not lost on the Asturians, who prided themselves on their historical resistance to the Moors.

Another range of mountains, the Picos de Europa, form a natural barrier between Asturias and Cantabria to the east. The small region of Cantabria, of similar area and population size to La Rioja, is centred on the port of Santander. Once patronised by royalty, Santander is an elegant resort, popular with Spaniards from the capital. There are many smaller resorts east of Santander including Laredo, which is to the French what Benidorm is to the British, (and where the summer population increases the off-season population by a factor of ten).

Both the coastline and the interior of these regions are capable of stunning the visitor and there are some of the least spoilt parts of Spain's coastline here. However, the coastline is not known as la Costa Verde (the green coast) for nothing and the rainfall and cool temperatures here may have put off some prospective househunters. These regions are heavily agricultural and are far from developed – especially inland where lines of communication are hampered by the mountainous terrain and national parks.

Finding a home in Cantabria and Asturías will involve spending time in the area, preferably with someone who speaks Spanish fluently. Although property is available in these regions, those that buy are mainly Spaniards, so estate agents will not be as accustomed to dealing with foreigners as their colleagues on the coast. Property is a lot cheaper than that found on the Mediterranean coastline and there are many properties for restoration available to those with the ambition and money to take on such a project in this traditional area of Spain. The main places to look are Santander, Gijón, Cudillero, Laredo, Comillas, Castro Urdiales, Llanes, Noja and San Vicente de la Barquera. Most summer clientele to these towns and resorts are Spanish and French. Santander hosts an international music and cultural festival throughout August every year.

## Galicia's dictators

Is there something in the soil of Galicia that produces dictators? Certainly, two of Galicia's most famous sons are such: Fidel Castro in Cuba was the product of Galician emigrants and General Francisco Franco was a native Galician.

| Some specialities of Cantabria and Asturias | |
| --- | --- |
| *almejas a la marinera* | clams in wine sauce |
| *anchoa en cazuela* | braised anchovies and onions |
| *cocido montañés* | mountain chickpea soup |
| *marmite* | fish stew |
| *truchas a la montañesa* | trout in onion and wine sauce |
| *quesada pasiega* | cheese tart |
| *queso picón* | blue cheese |
| *arroz con leche* | rice pudding |
| *entrecote con queso cabrales* | steak with blue cheese sauce |
| *fabada asturiana* | bean stew |
| *fabes con almejas* | clam and bean stew |
| *merluza a la sidra* | hake in cider sauce |
| *pulpo con patatines* | stewed octopus and potatoes |
| *queso cabrales* | Asturian blue cheese |
| *sardinas asadas* | grilled sardines |

# Galicia

**Provinces and main towns:** A Coruña, Lugo, Orense, Pontevedra.
**Airport:** Labacolla (13km east of Santiago de Compostella).
**Regional tourist office website:** www.turgalicia.es.

It is hardly surprising that Galicia rates as one of the least developed and poorest regions of Spain. Its inland provinces of Lugo and Orense have a reputation as among the most backward in the country. Galicia sits in the northwest corner of the peninsula, geographically isolated and with poor communications with the other regions. Its sizeable, mainly rural population of three million people has steadily diminished through emigration, while those who remain survive at subsistence level on agriculture and fishing. Galicia has a Celtic past of which traces survive, including the bagpipes (*gaita*), and the Galician language, *galégo* (which also gave rise to Portuguese) – a separate language from Spanish spoken by about 80% of the inhabitants, in a variety of dialects. This region is often compared to Ireland because of a shared Celtic heritage, similar climate and a west coast shaped by the Atlantic into deep inlets. Other similarities include a past in which famines led to emigration in Spain and abroad. Cornered by the Atlantic to the north and west and Portugal to the south, the emigrants were forced southwards into Léon, Castile and Portugal, or to Latin America, to seek their fortunes.

In contrast to the countryside, the coastal cities of Coruña, Pontevedra, Vigo and Santiago are relatively prosperous; and tend to be Castilian-speaking.

Before history made Galicia such an isolated backwater, it had been the focal point of Christian nationalism in Spain by virtue of a miracle which took place on its soil: a shepherd was supposedly led by a guiding star to discover the remains of St James the Apostle, who, legend has it, preached there. From that moment, the Christians gained a holy patron *Santiago matamoros* (St James the moorkiller) in whose name they waged battles against the infidel. Near the site of the miracle a city, Santiago de Compostela (St James of the Field of the Star) grew up; the saintly relics were housed first in a church and then in a great cathedral. The latter became a famous place of pilgrimage throughout Europe in mediaeval times (even Chaucer's Wife of Bath had been there), and this cathedral remains – along with the city surrounding it – one of Spain's premier tourist attractions.

Although in 1936 Galicia voted for home rule in a regional referendum, the Civil War interrupted its implementation. There is virtually no heavy industry in the area and, without the radicalism that organised labour and industrialisation can produce, the politics of the region have remained largely conservative.

In contrast to the countryside, the coastal cities of La Coruña, Pontevedra, Vigo and Santiago de Compostela are relatively prosperous, and tend to be Castilian-speaking. Galicia has charm with its mixture of the traditional and the modern. Increasingly, new highways are making it easy to discover the beautiful Atlantic coast, which has some of the best beaches in Spain. Madrid is three hours away from La Coruña by road.

Property prices in Galicia can still be among the lowest in Spain, but as investors, tourists and emigrants discover the region they are rising at surprisingly rapid rates; 2006 saw a 19.3% increase across the region as a whole, on of the highest in the country, and Lugo was the star performer, with prices rising by a staggering 37.6% in just 12 months.

| some specialities of galicia | |
|---|---|
| caldo Gallego | beans, greens and potato soup |
| empanadas | savoury meat or fish pies |
| filloas | pancakes |
| lacón con grelos | boiled ham hocks, potatoes and vegetables |
| merluza a la Gallega | hake with potatoes and paprika |
| pimientos de padrón | fried green peppers |
| pulpo a feira | octopus with oil and paprika |
| queso de San Simón | smoked cow milk cheese |
| vieiras con jamón | baked scallops with cured ham |

# ■ INLAND SPAIN

## Castilla Y León (Old Castile)

**Provinces:** Avila, Burgos, León, Palencia, Salamanca, Segovia, Soria, Valladolid, Zamora.
**Main city:** Valladolid.
**Airport:** León.
**Regional tourist office website:** www.jcyl.es/turismo.

The nine provinces of the region of Castilla-León make it the largest region of Spain, covering almost a fifth of the country's surface area; but it has less than half the population of the next largest region, Andalucía. Modern Spain grew from the old kingdom of Castile (which was an independent country ruled by its founder Count Fernán Gonzalez in the 10th century), and a kingdom ruled by King Ferdinand in the 11th century. The new kingdom quickly swallowed up León, becoming the combined kingdom of Castile and León on and off until the 13th century. In the 14th century, by the marriage of King Ferdinand of Aragon and Isabella of Castile, the three kingdoms of Portugal and Aragon-Castile were united. Castille/Léon is frequently referred to as Old Castile while the region of Castile/La Mancha to the south is New Castile. Aragón-Castile became known as Spain in the wider world.

The great river Douro flows right across the *meseta* of Castille/León and on through Portugal to Oporto at its mouth. The *meseta* is characterised by its huge prairies, given over largely to cereals, and by its lack of inhabitants.

Some of the most beautiful cities in Spain are to be found here: Salamanca, León, and the walled city of Avila. The most scenic province is probably Soria which is full of the fine castles *(castillos)* which give rise to the region's name. Burgos, the city as opposed to the province, was the former capital of Old Castile, although its significance nowadays derives from its position as a main garrison of the military.

The people of Castilla-León are known as fairly conservative and formal, although people from the vibrant cosmopolitan city of Salamanca are the exception to this rule. The food served in Castilla-León is based on vegetables, haricot beans (*la bañeza* and *el barco*), chickpeas (*fuentesaúco*) and lentils (*la armuña*). Pork (raised on acorns and chestnuts) is flavoursome, and game is used in *botillo* (mountain sausage from León), savoury *morcilla* from Burgos and the red Segovian sausage known as *cantimpalo*. Other local dishes are based around roasted baby lamb, kid and sucking pig, trout and cod, and there are plenty of local cheeses made from goat's, ewe's and cow's milk. Sweets and pastries such as *yemas* and *hojaldres* (puff pastry) are the remnants of Moorish cuisine.

### Some specialities of Castilla-León

| | |
|---|---|
| *chuletitas de cordero* | lamb chops |
| *cochinillo asado* | roast piglet |
| *cocido* | chickpea stew |
| *cordero asado* | roast lamb |
| *judías con chorizo* | bean stew with chorizo |
| *queso de burgos* | sheep milk cheese |
| *sopa Castellana* | garlic soup |

## La Rioja

**Main city:** Logroño.
**Regional tourist office website:** www.lariojaturismo.com.

Rioja to most Britons means wine. La Rioja is the smallest of the Spanish regions, occupying just 1% of its surface area and home to a mere 0.67% of the population,

Rioja, famous for its vineyards

or just over 300,000 souls. Historically part of the medieval Castilian kingdom, La Rioja has so far chosen to remain independent. This single-province region takes its name from the Rió Oja, a minor tributary of the great Ebro river, which provides the water for the famous vineyards of the region. The main city of Logroño, replete with fine architecture, is on the pilgrim way to Santiago, and is the next main stop on the route after Pamplona in Navarre.

Guidebooks tend to gloss over La Rioja. There isn't a great deal to the province unless you are interested in wine and looking to buy a vineyard. Most of the vineyards are owned by large commercial concerns, though there are still a few family-owned bodegas. The most prestigious of these are centred around Haro in the northwest.

## Madrid

**Airports:** Madrid-Barajas, Madrid-Cuatro Vientos, Madrid-Torrejón.
**Regional tourist office website:** www.turismomadrid.es.

It is not by chance that the capital looks like a bull's eye on the map of Spain: located on a high plateau with impossible extremes of climate, the town had little else going for it other than its strategically central and easily defended position, until the capital was moved here in the 17th century. Madrid is 2200 feet/670 metres above sea level. All distances in Spain are measured from Puerta del Sol in the city centre. It is the seat of the Spanish parliament and famed for the Prado museum as well as its dizzy nightlife, which lasts from dusk till dawn.

Madrid and the surrounding area together form the autonomous community of Madrid, which is the most densely populated region of Spain, with about 600 inhabitants to the square kilometre. Madrid city, as opposed to the region, has a population of over three million inhabitants – referred to as *Madrileños*. Unfortunately, in common with other giant metropolises, Madrid has its fair share of eyesore high-rise suburbs. And, to its chagrin, it is considered by some as runner-up to trendy Barcelona as a place to live and work.

However, living in the capital has many advantages for those not wedded to the sun, sea and sand lifestyle offered by the Mediterranean coast: limited heavy industry and strict pollution controls, and a programme of tree-planting which has transformed the cityscape, have quite literally given Madrid a better atmosphere; there are scores of English language schools and various UK and American companies operating here, as well as all the job opportunities provided by any capital city, with a wide range of commercial and business activities.

Last but not least, some of Spain's most stunning sights are within easy visiting distance of the capital, notably the cities of Segovia, Avila and Toledo.

Madrid is the hub of all lines of communication in Spain and is served by Barajas Airport, which lies 16km east of the city and can be reached by metro from the city centre. There are a large number of foreigners living and working in Madrid (around 100,000) and because of this there are the facilities available to cater for their needs. There are social clubs, Anglican churches, English-speaking doctors and dentists and international schools. There are also two English-Language free sheets (*The Broadsheet* and *Guidepost*), which are published monthly.

The price of property here is the highest in Spain and mainly consists of apartments and flats. A two-bedroom apartment can fetch anything from €250,000–€600,000 or more. While Madrid is one of the cheapest capital cities in Europe, it is one of the most expensive places to live in Spain.

| Some specialities of Madrid | |
| --- | --- |
| *callos a la Madrileña* | tripe and chorizo stew |
| *caracoles a la Madrileña* | snails and chorizo in paprika sauce |
| *churros* | fritters |
| *cocido Madrileño* | chickpea soup |
| *cordero asado* | roast lamb |
| *leche merengada* | cinnamon-scented iced milk |
| *soldaditos de pavía* | batter-fried cod |
| *sopa de ajo* | garlic soup |
| *tortijas* | battered toast |
| *buñuelos de viento* | doughnuts |

# Extremadura and Castilla-La Mancha (New Castile)

**Provinces:** Badajoz and Cáceres (Extremadura), Albacete, Ciudad Real, Cuenca, Guadalajara, Toledo (Castilla-La Mancha).
**Main cities:** Badajoz (Extremadura); Albacete (Castilla-La Mancha).
**Regional tourist office websites:** www.turismoextremadura.com; www.castillalamancha.es.

Extremadura and Castilla-La Mancha are two of the regions of the *meseta* (the central tableland), which together comprise about a quarter of Spain's surface area but contain just over a sixth of its population. Extremadura is dominated by ranges of mountains and reservoirs. There are plans to enhance the agricultural prospects of this little known and bleak region, which is passed through by travellers between Madrid and Portugal, but otherwise virtually ignored by outsiders. Cáceres, the main town, was originally built with spoils from the activities of the local nobles in the New World. There is a famous six-arched Roman bridge at Alcántara near the Portugese border and further extensive Roman remains at Mérida. The climate here swings between the extremes of boiling summers to freezing winters, and perhaps as a result, this is the part of Spain that has least been affected by mass tourism.

The plain of La Mancha is probably best known for its windmills, and Cervantes' mournful Don Quixote who tilted at them and brought the word 'quixotic' into the English language. Nowadays, the plain is highly cultivated; and agriculture an important part of the local economy as in much of Spain.

Castilla-La Mancha contains what is probably one of the most beautiful towns in Spain, Cuenca, perched precariously on the side of a cliff. It also has one of the most famous, the medieval capital of Spain, Toledo, which sits on a craggy rock in a loop of the Tajo River. Toledo was once synonymous with crafted steel, especially sword blades; but its fame rests also on other achievements including scholarship, architecture, building, and the paintings of El Greco. This city also has connections with El Cid, who captured it in the 11th century. Although redolent with history, Toledo's importance declined in the 16th century when the capital was moved to nearby Madrid.

Few foreigners live in the region and estate agents are not used to dealing with them. As with many areas of inland Spain, the prospective house buyer will need to spend some time in the region, ideally accompanied by a Spanish speaker.

**FACT**

■ Castilla-La Mancha contains what is probably one of the most beautiful towns in Spain, Cuenca, perched precariously on the side of a cliff. It also has one of the most famous, the medieval capital of Spain, Toledo, which sits on a craggy rock in a loop of the Tajo River.

| Some specialities of Extremadura and Castilla-La Mancha | |
| --- | --- |
| caldereta de Cordero | lamb stew |
| faisán al modo de Alcántara | pheasant with truffles and foie gras |
| frite | potted lamb with paprika and garlic |
| gazpacho Extremeño | white gazpacho |
| queso de los ibores | aged goat milk cheese |
| queso torta del casar | semi-soft sheep milk cheese |
| ajo arriero | dried cod and potatoes |
| flores Manchegas | fried pastries with honey |
| mojete | dried cod and tomato salad |
| morteruelo | meat and bread paté |
| perdiz estofada | stewed partridge |
| pisto Manchega | vegetable stew |
| queso Manchego | sheep milk cheese |

# ISLAS CANARIAS (THE CANARY ISLANDS)

**Principal islands and resorts:** Gran Canaria: Las Palmas; Lanzarote: Arrecife; La **Palma:** Santa Cruz; Tenerife: Santa Cruz.
**Airports:** Gran Canaria, La Palma, Tenerife South, Tenerife North, Fuerteventura, Lanzarote.
**Regional tourist office website:** www.turismodecanarias.com.

The Canary Islands became Spanish territory as long ago as the 15th century. The best known of the Canary Islands are also the largest: Gran Canaria, Lanzarote and Tenerife. There are seven islands altogether, located about 70 miles off the Moroccan Western Sahara coast. The smaller islands are Fuerteventura, Hierro, Gomera and La Palma. With the exception of Lanzarote, which is comparatively flat, all these islands are characterised by high central mountains, and the consequent change of climate and spectacular scenery, a legacy of their volcanic origins. The climate is surprisingly mild considering their location, with the North-East Trade Winds bringing moisture-laden air – the 'horizontal rain' that supports much of the islands' vegetation. Ferries and jetfoils run by Transmediterranea and Fred Olsen link each of the islands, and communications with the rest of Europe are good.

The central island, Gran Canaria, is described as a 'miniature continent', with a range of climates from dry and desert-like around the periphery; lush and sub-tropical; to a more temperate climate as you climb the central mountains. The mountains are volcanic, like the islands themselves, which emerged from the Atlantic some 40 million years ago. There are legends woven around the islands, enmeshed in their history, like Homer's Garden of the Hesperides, or Atlantis (which we can report did not sink into the sea around here). Both the ancient Greeks and Phoenicians knew of the Canary Islands and there were originally aboriginal inhabitants, probably related to the Berbers of nearby North Africa, whose fate when the Spanish arrived is not recorded in the guidebooks. Gran Canaria has a Columbus Museum in the atmospheric Governor's Residence in its bustling main town (and port), Las Palmas, which records the visit of the explorer who discovered America. Colonists from the Canary Islands also went on to settle in North and South America.

The atmosphere of Gran Canaria today is surprisingly cosmopolitan, with an important fishing industry, import-export companies taking advantage of the islands' favourable tax regime and tourists from continental Europe as well as Britain thronging its beaches, notably in the tourist developments around the Playa del Inglés and Maspalomas in the south.

Gran Canaria is not a backwater. Ikea and Benetton have stores there, as does El Corte Inglés, the ubiquitous Spanish chain store. The capital, Las Palmas, has all the facilities of any large Spanish city and its own beach – a centre for sunbathing and socialising – while the coastline further to the southwest has Puerto de Mogan, which retains its old-fashioned charm and is a favoured stopping-off point for yachts. The north is less developed and has strong local traditions. Getting away from it all would mean living inland, near the town of Teror with its famous annual fiesta. The facilities make Gran Canaria an excellent place to live and work, especially away from some of the overcrowded resorts.

The Canaries have greater autonomy from central government than other regions of Spain and the two provinces they form are regulated from Las Palmas-

Gran Canaria and Santa Cruz-Tenerife. The three main islands have long been popular with tourists from all over the world and in recent years they have also become increasingly popular with timeshare and villa owners, many of whom have holidayed in the islands before settling there. The year-round warm climate is a great attraction that outweighs the inconvenience of travelling to the islands.

Apart from the scenery and the wildlife there is much of interest culturally and historically, and if you are interested in sailing and ships this is a good place to be. Other points of interest are the mysterious inhabitants, and the (almost) unique whistled language that used to be 'spoken' by shepherds on the island of Gomera.

In past times, the Canaries were a useful last-stop for ships bound across the Atlantic. Today, the Japanese tuna fishing fleet and many cargo vessels still stop off here and every November the ARC transatlantic yacht race takes off from Las Palmas.

The most popular places for foreign residents are also the tourist centres: in the Orotava Valley of Tenerife, and the south of Gran Canaria where there are several tourist developments including the Playa del Inglés and San Agustin. Apart from the three main islands there are also smaller foreign communities in Fuerteventura, Lanzarote and La Palma.

Hierro and Gomera are less visited and further from the convenience of facilities and services that many expats expect. Gomera is only a few miles away from Tenerife but completely different in its culture and the cost of property. Ferries travel to Gomera from Los Cristianos on Tenerife five times a day costing around £35 return. A population of 40,000 – mainly involved in farming and fishing – is now down to around 19,000 as the young have left, over-fishing has closed the tuna factories and cheaper produce has been discovered elsewhere. What this means for househunters is that there are plenty of properties on offer. The catch is that many properties have not being formally registered yet, or even put on the map.

Property prices have levelled out dramatically in the Canary Islands over the past few years, with 2007 even seeing modest price drops on all the islands except for Tenerife, which maintains a healthy 8.5% growth rate. Perhaps this is because of its popularity with the British, with many retirees relocating to the main towns like Playa San Juan or the resorts along the Costa Adeje. Property on the northern coast of Tenerife is still cheaper than that in the south as it rains more. Prices in Lanzarote and Fuerteventura are slightly cheaper (by 10%–15%) than on Tenerife. Germans seem to abound in Gran Canaria, and to a lesser extent are buying up properties in the smaller off the track islands of Gomera, La Palma and Hierro. The local tax in the Canary Islands on new homes is 5% compared to the 7.5% on the mainland. Tax on building plots remains 5% compared to the 16% on the mainland, which is an incentive for those who are prepared to tackle the bureaucracy involved in self-build.

## Some specialities of the Canary Islands

| | |
|---|---|
| *mojo* | potatoes and fish in sauce |
| *patatas arrugadas* | 'wrinkled' potatoes |
| *potaje de berros/zaramago* | watercress/mustard green soup |
| *puchero Canario* | chick-pea soup |
| *quesadilla* | cheesecake |
| *sancocho Canario* | salted fish, sweet potatoes, spicy sauce |

# Appendices

# ■ USEFUL BOOKS

## Guides

**The Blevins Franks Guide to Living in Spain** (Blevins Franks, 2003). Useful financial guide to Spain by international financial advisors, Blevins Franks.

**Buying a House in Spain**, Dan Boothby (Vacation Work Publications, 2003). Comprehensive guide to buying property in Spain.

**Doing Business With Spain**, Nadine Kettaneh (Kogan Page, 2001). Aims to help international companies take advantage of the Spanish market. Needs updating.

**Guide to Labour and Social Affairs** (Ministry of Labour and Social Affairs, 2005). A list of all of the employment and social security regulations, published in English.

**Lonely Planet Spain** (Lonely Planet, 2007). See also *Barcelona* (Lonely Planet Encounter) (2007), *Lonely Planet Andalucía* (2007), *Lonely Planet Madrid* (2006), *Walking in Spain* (2003).

**Retiring to Spain: Everything You Need to Know,** Cyril Holbrook (Age Concern, 2004).

**Rough Guide to Spain**, Mark Ellingham (Rough Guides, 2007). One of the best handbooks to Spain. See also: *Costa Brava, Rough Guide Directions*, Chris Lloyd (2005), *Rough Guide to Andalucía*, Geoff Garvey (2005), *Madrid, Rough Guide Directions*, Simon Baskett (2005), *Barcelona, Rough Guide Directions*, Jules Brown (2006).

**Spain** (*Alastair Sawday's Special Places to Stay*), Alastair Sawday and Jose Navarro (Alastair Sawday Publishing, 2007).

**Starting a Business in Spain**, Guy Hobbs (Vacation Work Publications, 2004). The definitive guide to setting up or buying a business in Spain.

**You and the Law in Spain**, David Searl (Santana Books, 2007). Revised edition of the very helpful and readable guide to Spanish law for foreigners.

## General background and history

**The British on the Costa del Sol**, Karen O'Reilly (Routledge, 2000). A sociological study of the phenomenon of mass British culture in Spain, detailing the day to day realities of expatriate life.

**Culture Smart: Spain**, Marian Meaney (Kuperard, 2003). Essential information on attitudes, beliefs and behaviour in Spain.

**España Britannia: A Bittersweet Relationship**, Alistair Ward (Shepheard-Walwyn, 2004). Historical overview of the intertwined strands of British and Spanish history.

**A History of Spain**, Simon Barton (Palgrave Macmillan, 2003). Up-to-date analysis of the historical development of Spain.

**Rough Guide History of Spain**, Justin Wintle (Rough Guides, 2003). Simple and accessible overview charting the major historical events from 750,000BC to 2003AD.

**The New Spaniards, John Hooper** (Penguin, 2006). A fully revised and updated edition of one of the seminal works on contemporary Spain.

**Spanish Civil War**, Hugh Thomas (Penguin, 2003). Objective analysis of the Spanish Civil War.

**Traveller's History of Spain**, Juan Lalaguna (Orion, 2006). Revised edition of this interesting study of Spanish places and mores.

**The Xenophobe's Guide to the Spanish** (Oval Books, 2002). An irreverent look at the beliefs and foibles of the Spanish.

## Literature associated with Spain

**As I Walked out one Midsummer's Morning**, Laurie Lee (Penguin, 1971). Autobiographical account of the author's journey to Spain on the eve of the civil war. Beautifully written coming-of-age story.

**Death in the Afternoon**, Ernest Hemingway (Arrow Books, 1994). An achingly spare account of bullfighting in sultry Seville.

**Duende:** A Journey in Search of Flamenco, Jason Webster (Black Swan, 2004). Frantic and passionate account of a journey fuelled by obsession and flamenco.

**Driving Over Lemons: an Optimist in Andalucía**, Chris Stewart (Sort of Books, 1999). Autobiographical account of an English couple who make the move to Andalucía to live a simple rural life among the villagers.

**Factory of Light, Tales from My Andalucían Village**, Michael Jacobs (John Murray, 2004).

**Foreign Affair, Two Innocents Abroad in Spain**, Shaun Briley (Ebury Press, 2003). A tale of how not to settle in a foreign land.

**Gatherings from Spain**, Richard Ford (Pallas Athene Publishers, 2000). Condensed version of the two-volume classic 'A Handbook for Travellers in Spain' first published in 1846.

**Homage to Catalonia**, George Orwell (Penguin Modern Classics, 2003). Vivid chronicle of Orwell's often brutal experiences fighting in the Spanish Civil War.

**No Going Back: Journey to Mother's Garden**, Martin Kirby (Time Warner Paperbacks, 2003). Comic account of a family moving to a small mountain farm in Catalonia and turning it into a viable smallholding business.

**A Parrot in the Pepper Tree**, Chris Stewart (Sort of Books, 2002). Part sequel and part prequel to Driving over Lemons.

**A Romantic in Spain**, Theophile Gautier (Interlink, 2001). Classic travelogue of the French novelist's journey to and around Spain, first published in 1845 as Voyage en Espagne.

**Snowball Oranges, One Mallorcan Winter**, Peter Kerr (Summersdale Publishers, 2000). A Scottish family give up sanity and security to go and grow oranges for a living in a secluded valley in the mountains of Mallorca.

**South From Granada**, Gerald Brennan (Penguin, 1992). Describes the essence of the Alpujarras region in the 1920s.

**Stranger in Spain**, HV Morton (Methuen, 1983). Witty travelogue of a Spain unspoilt by tourism.

# ◼ USEFUL WEBSITES

The web is awash with information about the various aspects of daily life in Spain for tourists and expatriates, although not all of it is correct, well-researched or up-to-date. The following is a list of the more helpful and informative sites relating to Spain to help you sort the wheat from the chaff. In addition to the regional sites each local tourist authority has its own website, all of which are listed in the *Regional Guide* in the *Overview*.

### About the country and general expat advice:

*www.andalucia.com*
*www.expatica.com*
*www.idealspain.com*
*www.spainexpat.com*
*www.spanishforum.org*
*www.spainexpat.com*
*www.tourspain.co.uk*
*www.tuspain.com*
*www.typicallyspanish.com*

### Other useful sites:

*www.dwp.gov.uk* - UK Department of Work and Pensions
*www.hmrc.gov.uk* - UK taxation and customs advice
*www.inem.es* - Spanish government-funded national recruitment database
*www.insalud.es* - Spanish health service
*www.interes.org* - guide to investing in Spain
*www.mae.es* - homepage of Spanish embassies abroad
*www.mcx.es* - Spanish office for commerce and tourism
*www.mir.es* - Spanish interior ministry
*www.monster.es* - comprehensive job search site
*www.mtas.es* - work and social security office
*www.spanishchamber.co.uk* - Spanish chamber of commerce in the UK
*www.naric.es* - information about transferring qualifications to Spain
*www.paginasamarillas.com* - Spanish Yellow Pages
*www.uktrakeinvest.gov.uk* - advice on doing business in Spain

# ◼ CONVERSIONS

## Weights and measurements: metric conversion chart

Spain uses the metric system of measurement in all respects. Those who are used to thinking in the imperial system will find that in the long run it is much easier to learn and think in metric rather than to always try to convert from metric to imperial. To facilitate this process a metric conversion table is given below.

### Conversion chart

**Length (12 inches = 1 foot, 10 mm = 1 cm, 100 cm = 1 metre)**

| inches | 1 | 2 | 3 | 4 | 5 | 6 | 9 | 12 | | |
|---|---|---|---|---|---|---|---|---|---|---|
| cm | 2.5 | 5 | 7.5 | 10 | 12.5 | 15.2 | 23 | 30 | | |
| cm | 1 | 2 | 3 | 5 | 10 | 20 | 25 | 50 | 75 | 100 |
| inches | 0.4 | 0.8 | 1.2 | 2 | 4 | 8 | 10 | 20 | 30 | 39 |

**Weight (14lb = 1 stone, 2,240 lb = 1 ton, 1,000 kg = 1 metric tonne)**

| lb | 1 | 2 | 3 | 5 | 10 | 14 | 44 | 100 | 2246 |
|---|---|---|---|---|---|---|---|---|---|
| kg | 0.45 | 0.9 | 1.4 | 2.3 | 4.5 | 6.4 | 20 | 45 | 1016 |
| kg | 1 | 2 | 3 | 5 | 10 | 25 | 50 | 100 | 1000 |
| lb | 2.2 | 4.4 | 6.6 | 11 | 22 | 55 | 110 | 220 | 2204 |

### Distance

| mile | 1 | 5 | 10 | 20 | 30 | 40 | 50 | 75 | 100 | 150 |
|---|---|---|---|---|---|---|---|---|---|---|
| km | 1.6 | 8 | 16 | 32 | 48 | 64 | 80 | 120 | 161 | 241 |
| km | 1 | 5 | 10 | 20 | 30 | 40 | 50 | 100 | 150 | 200 |
| mile | 0.6 | 3.1 | 6.2 | 12 | 19 | 25 | 31 | 62 | 93 | 124 |

### Volume

| 1 litre | 0.2 UK gallons | 1 UK gallon | = 4.5 litres |
|---|---|---|---|
| 1 litre | 0.26 US gallons | 1 US gallon | = 3.8 litres |

### Clothes

| UK | 8 | 10 | 12 | 14 | 16 | 18 | 20 |
|---|---|---|---|---|---|---|---|
| Europe | 36 | 38 | 40 | 42 | 44 | 46 | 48 |
| USA | 6 | 8 | 10 | 12 | 14 | 18 | |

### Shoes

| UK | 3 | 4 | 5 | 6 | 7 | 8 | 9 | 10 | 11 |
|---|---|---|---|---|---|---|---|---|---|
| Europe | 36 | 37 | 38 | 39 | 40 | 41/42 | 43 | 44 | 45 |
| USA | 2.5 | 3.3 | 4.5 | 5.5 | 6.5 | 7.5 | 8.5 | 9.5 | 10.5 |

# ■ EMBASSIES AND CONSULATES

## Spanish embassies and consulates in the UK and the Republic of Ireland

**Spanish Embassy:** 39 Chesham Place, London SW1X 8SB; 020 7235 5555; email embespuk@mail.mae.es.

**Spanish Consulate General:** 20 Draycott Place, London SW3 2RZ; 020 7589 8989; visa information line 09065 508 970 (costs £1 per minute from a UK landline); email conspalon@mail.mae.es.

**Spanish Consulate General:** Suite 1A, Brooke House, 70 Spring Gardens, Manchester M2 2BQ; 0161 236 1262; email conspmanchester@mail.es.

**Spanish Consulate General:** 63 North Castle Street, Edinburgh EH2 3LJ; 0131 220 1843; email cog.edimburgo@mail.mae.es.

**Consular Section:** Spanish Embassy, 17 Merlyng Park, Ballsbridge, Dublin 4, Ireland; +353 1 269 1640/2597; email emb.dublin.inf@mail.mae.es.

## British embassies and consulates in Spain

**British Embassy:** C/ Fernando el Santo 16, 28010 Madrid; 917 008200; email presslibrary@ukinspain.com; www.ukinspain.com.

**British Consulate-General:** Paseo de Recoletos 7/9, 28004 Madrid; 915 249700; email madridconsulate@ukinspain.com.

**British Consulate:** Plaza Calvo Sotelo 1, 2°, Apdo. De Correos 564, 03001 Alicante; 965 216022; email enquiries.alicante@fco.gov.uk.

**British Consulate-General:** Avda Diagonal 477, 13°, 08036 Barcelona; 933 666200; email barcelonaconsulate@fco.gov.uk.

**British Honorary Vice-Consul Benidorm:** to be contacted through Alicante.

**British Consulate-General:** Alameda de Urquijo 2, 8°, 48008 Bilbao; 944 157600/711/722; email bilbaoconsulate@fco.gov.uk.

**Honorary Consular Agent:** Granada; 669 895 053.

**British Vice-Consulate:** Avenida de Isidoro Macabich 45 1°, 07800 Ibiza; 971 301818/303816.

**British Consulate:** Edificio Eurocom, Bloque Sur, C/ Mauricio Moro Pareto, 2, 2°, 29006 Málaga; (Postal address: Apartado Correos 360, 29080 Málaga); 952 352300; email Málaga@fco.gov.uk.

**British Consulate:** Plaza Mayor 3, D, 07002 Palma de Mallorca; 971 712445/716048; email consulate@palma.mail.fco.gov.uk.

**British Vice-Consulate:** Sa Casa Nova, Cami de Biniatap 30, Es Castell, 07720 Menorca; 971 363373.

**British Consulate:** Edificio Cataluña, C/ Luis Morote 6, 3°, 35007 Las Palmas de Gran Canaria; 928 262508/658; email lapal-consular@fco.gov.uk.

**British Vice-Consulate:** Plaza Weyler 8, 1°, 38003 Santa Cruz de Tenerife; 922 286863; email tenerife.enquiries@fco.gov.uk.

**Honorary British Consulate:** Apartado de Correos/PO. Box 143, 41940 Tomares (Sevilla).
**Honorary British Consulate:** Plaza de Compostela 23–6° (Aptdo 49), 36201 Vigo; 986 437133.

# Other embassies and consulates

**Spanish Embassy (USA):** 2375 Pennsylvania Avenue, NW, Washington DC 20037; 202 452 01 00; 202 728 23 40. There are Consulates in Boston, Chicago, Houston, Los Angeles, Miami, New Orleans, New York (212 355 4090), Puerto Rico and San Franciso.
**Spanish Embassy (Canada):** 74, Stanley Avenue, Ottawa, Ontario K1M 1P4, Canada; 613 747 2252/7293; email cgspain.toronto@mail.mae.es. Consulates in Edmonton, Halifax, Montréal, Québec, Toronto, Vancouver and Winnipeg.
**United States Embassy:** C/ Serrano 75, 28006 Madrid; 915 872200; www.embusa.es.
**Canadian Embassy:** Edificio Goya, Calle Núñez de Balboa 35, 28001 Madrid; 914 233250; www.canada-es.org; email mdrid@international.gc.ca.
**Republic of Ireland Embassy:** Ireland House, Paseo de la Castellana 46, 4°, 28046 Madrid; 914 364093; email embajada@irlanda.es.
**Australian Embassy:** Plaza del Descubridor Diego de Ordas 3, 28003 Madrid; 913 536600; www.spain.embassy.gov.au.
**New Zealand Embassy:** Plaza de la Lealtad 2, 3°, 28014 Madrid; 915 230226; email embnuevazelanda@telefonica.net.

# Photo Credit List

| Page number | Photo description & number | Photographer | Credit line- for acknowledgments |
|---|---|---|---|
| 2 | Casa Battlo – Barcelona | Federica Gentile | Federica Gentile |
| 5 | Celebrating couple Seville | Guille el Frandaluz | Guille el Frandaluz |
| 5 | Ciudad de la Artes Valencia | Turespaña | Turespaña |
| 6 | Lavapies | Israel Cuchillo | Israel Cuchillo; www.israelcuchillo.es |
| 7 | Playa de Las Americas | Turespaña | Turespaña |
| 8 | Playa de Noja-1 Cantabria | Turespaña | Turespaña |
| 11 | Spanish cuisine | www.photos-madrid.com | www.photos-madrid.com |
| 28 | Ambiente en Ibiza | Turespaña | Turespaña |
| 35 | Barajas airport Madrid | Coralie Mercier | Coralie Mercier |
| 38 | Cathedral interior | Vicenç Feliu | Vicenç Feliu |
| 46 | Euros | Steve Noseworthy | Steve Noseworthy |
| 40 | fruit and nut market | Antonio Pavón | Antonio Pavón; www.flickr.com/Stoper |
| 39 | girls shopping | www.istock.com | - |
| 51 | Las Alpujarras pots | Ted Bowling | Ted Bowling; www.tedbowling.smugmug.com; tedbowling@gmail.com |
| 57 | La Sagrada Familia | Kingsley Dennis | Kingsley Dennis |
| 68 | Seville street | Heleina Postings | Heleina Postings |
| 71 | Raval apartments | Andy Delahunty | Avinash Bhat |
| 74 | L'Eixample | Steve Lambuth | Steve Lambuth; http://kaneokupono.com |
| 75 | Madrid archway | Ted Bowling | Ted Bowling; www.tedbowling.smugmug.com; tedbowling@gmail.com |
| 76 | Latina district | Israel Cuchillo | Israel Cuchillo; www.israelcuchillo.es |
| 77 | Recycling boxes | Marc Herman | Marc Herman; www.marcherman.net |
| 79 | Retiro park Madrid | Turespaña | Turespaña |
| 80 | Ciutat Vella, Barcelona | Ted Bowling | Ted Bowling; www.tedbowling.smugmug.com; tedbowling@gmail.com |
| 81 | Gran Via, Madrid | Ed Latawiec | Ed Latawiec; http://www.flickr.com/photos/ed-latawiec/ |
| 82 | Barcelona district | Avinash Bhat | Avinash Bhat |
| 83 | El Raval, Barcelona | Stefano Carlo Ascione | Stefano Carlo Ascione; stefanoascione@hotmail.com; http://www.flickr.com/photos/stefanoascione/ |
| 84 | Seville district | Heleina Postings | Heleina Postings |
| 85 TOP | Urban street corner | Jen Joaquin | Jen Joaquin; www.flickr.com/photos/jenjoaquin |
| 85 BOTTOM | Sitges for Barcelona where to live | Turespaña | Turespaña |
| 86??? | El Raval, Barcelona | James Borod | James Borod |
| 87 TOP | La Rambla | Avinash Bhat | Avinash Bhat |
| 87 BOTTOM | Salamanca district Madrid | Turespaña | Turespaña |
| 88 | Retiro Park, Madrid | Turespaña | Turespaña |
| 89 | Barcelona apartments | Avinash Bhat | Avinash Bhat |
| 90 | Seville centro | Heleina Postings | Heleina Postings |
| 54 | Spain dog for pets sections | Ted Bowling | Ted Bowling; www.tedbowling.smugmug.com; tedbowling@gmail.com |
| 158 | Tapas lined up | Ted Bowling | Ted Bowling; www.tedbowling.smugmug.com; tedbowling@gmail.com |
| 111 | Beachside apartments | Ted Bowling | Ted Bowling; www.tedbowling.smugmug.com; tedbowling@gmail.com |
| 117 | Cobble stone street Majorca | www.istock.com | |
| 118 | for sale on wall | Emanuele Pasin | Emanuele Pasin; www.flickr.com/photos/fudo82 |
| 125 | Hacienda Andalusia | www.istock.com | - |
| 130 | Hillside villa | Ted Bowling | Ted Bowling; www.tedbowling.smugmug.com; tedbowling@gmail.com |
| 135 | Mogrovejo in Cantabri | www.istock.com | |
| 135 | Pink house | David Burton | David Burton |
| 137 | Rural house | Ted Bowling | Ted Bowling; www.tedbowling.smugmug.com; tedbowling@gmail.com |
| 150 | Spanish street | David Burton | David Burton |
| 158 | Villa with pool | Actual Properties, Tenerife | Actual Properties; Tenerife; www.actualproperties.com |
| 162 | church Segovia | Ron Philips | Ron Philips |
| 163 | Jamon | Alexey Antonov | Alexey Antonov |
| 164 | craftsman | Ana Alas | Ana Alas; http://www.flickr.com/photos/anaalas/ |
| 165 | Paella | www.istock.com | - |
| 167 | pet Spain | Vegard Iglebæk | Vegard Iglebæk; www.flickr.com/photos/vegard |
| 168 | Trotters | Sarah Franklin | Sarah Franklin; www.eyeshoot.co.uk |
| 169 | Rastro fleamarket in La Latina, Madrid | Turespaña | Turespaña |
| 169 | Food shop window | Nuno Nunes | Nuno Nunes; http://nunonunes.org/ |
| 170 | meat stall | Jessica Spengler | Jessica Spengler |
| 172 | fruit market | Avinash Bhat | Avinash Bhat |
| 173 | Newspaper | Javier Micora | Javier Micora |
| 174 | ¡Hola! magazine | Jennifer Woodward Maderazo | Jennifer Woodward Maderazo |
| 178 | Spanish shopping street white | www.istock.com | - |
| 179 | phone booth | www.madrid-uno.com | www.madrid-uno.com |

| Page number | Photo description & number | Photographer | Credit line- for acknowledgments |
|---|---|---|---|
| 183 | shopping street | www.istock.com | - |
| 185 | Rural goatherd | Ted Bowling | Ted Bowling; www.tedbowling.smugmug.com; tedbowling@gmail.com |
| 190 | Schoolchildren | Pierre Caron | Pierre Caron |
| 202 | police van | Denis Desmond | Denis Desmond; www.flickr.com/southerncalifornian |
| 204 | Spanish policemen | Denis Desmond | Denis Desmond; www.flickr.com/southerncalifornian |
| 207 | city bike hire | David Burton | David Burton |
| 209 | Motorway at night | Israel Cuchillo | Israel Cuchillo; www.israelcuchillo.es |
| 211 | Metro | Avinash Bhat | Avinash Bhat |
| 212 | Metro station Madrid | Israel Cuchillo | Israel Cuchillo; www.israelcuchillo.es |
| 399 | Shopping street | Toby Eglesfield | Toby Eglesfield |
| 226 | Siesta | Rachel Carpenter | Rachel Carpenter |
| 233 | Agbar tower, Barcelona | Klaus Dolle | Klaus Dolle |
| 234 | Alacazar, Seville | Turespaña | Turespaña |
| 239 | Man and donkey | Johan Auster | Johan Auster; johanauster@gmail.com |
| 242 | Marbella playa Fontanilla | Turespaña | Turespaña |
| 249 | Market stall | Maria Diaz | Maria Diaz |
| 251 | Vineyard | Christopher Lamb | Christopher Lamb |
| 256 | Moncloa | Valérie Simard | Valérie Simard |
| 259 | Office Barcelona | Aldas Kirvaitis | Aldas Kirvaitis |
| 265 | Spain under construction | Pablo Saludes Rodil | Pablo Saludes Rodil |
| 277 | Wind farm | Israel Cuchillo | Israel Cuchillo; www.israelcuchillo.es |
| 298 | Bar | www.istock.com | - |
| 302 | construction | www.istock.com | - |
| 307 | Food in café | Xavier Poy | Xavier Poy |
| 310 | Cow farm | Rebeca González | Rebeca González |
| 315 | Lettuces | www.istock.com | - |
| 319 | Restaurante El Chuchi Madrid | Turespaña | Turespaña |
| 329 | Sherry barrels | Ella Ryan | Ella Ryan |
| 348 | Rural bar | Ted Bowling | Ted Bowling; www.tedbowling.smugmug.com; tedbowling@gmail.com |
| 353 | Bar | Avinash Bhat | Avinash Bhat |
| 367 | Tapas | Rogelio García Alonso | Rogelio García Alonso; http://www.flickr.com/photos/rogalonso/ |
| 372 | old couple on beach | Carlos Urena Plus Flickr | Carlos Ureña; www.flickr.com/photos/carlos-u |
| 382 | retired couple by mountain | Steven van Varenbergh | Steven Van Vaerenbergh |
| 383 | Spanish elderly people talking | Ted Bowling | Ted Bowling; www.tedbowling.smugmug.com; tedbowling@gmail.com |
| 384 | Street with old lady | www.istock.com | - |
| 390 | La Tomatina, Buñol, Valencia | Turespaña | Turespaña |
| 395 | Benicassim music festival | Óscar Romero Blaya | Óscar Romero Blaya; www.oscaromero.tk |
| 396 | Festival of San Fermin | Turespaña | Turespaña |
| 397 | Paseo del prado cesar | Cesar Tardaguila | Cesar Tardaguila; http://www.design-nation.net/incandescencias; http://www.design-nation.net/inthesink |
| 398 | drinks in bar | David Oliver | David Oliver |
| 401 | Barcelona Olympic stadium | Hanan Smart | Hanan Smart |
| 401 | Barcelona Park | Steve Lambuth | Steve Lambuth; http://kaneokupono.com |
| 402 | Fishing on beach | Ted Bowling | Ted Bowling; www.tedbowling.smugmug.com;tedbowling@gmail.com |
| 403 | Bulll fighter | Ed Latawiec | Ed Latawiec; http://www.flickr.com/photos/ed latawiec/ |
| 404 | Barcelona art museum | Steven Poon | |
| 405 | Chueca, Madrid | Pablo Twose Valls | Pablo Twose Valls |
| 408 | Aragon landscape | Turespaña | Turespaña |
| 411 | Roman ruins Extremadura | Turespaña | Turespaña |
| 415 | Bajamar beach | Saul Granda | Saúl Granda |
| 420 | woman making crochet | Ana Isabel López Martínez | Ana Isabel López Martínez; www.flickr.com/photos/anabelmoratalla/ |
| 422 | carpets in Andalusia | www.istock.com | - |
| 424 | Accordian player in park | Stephen Lau | Stephen Lau |
| 425 | Priests in mass | Jonathan Shock | Jonathan Shock; http://www.flickr.com/photos/jonstraveladventures/ |
| 428 | Andalucía landscape Huelva | Turespaña | Turespaña |
| 429 | Extremadura town | Turespaña | Turespaña |
| 431 | Ski town Sierra Nevada | Turespaña | Turespaña |
| 437 | Religious procession | Istock | - |
| 440 | Port Vell | Avinash Bhat | Avinash Bhat |
| 441 | Religious procession Holy week | Israel Cuchillo | Israel Cuchillo; www.israelcuchillo.es |
| 452 | Rioja landscape | Ted Bowling | Ted Bowling; tedbowling.smugmug.com; tedbowling@gmail.com |
| 458 | Extremadura town | Turespaña | Turespaña |

# ■ INDEX

# Index

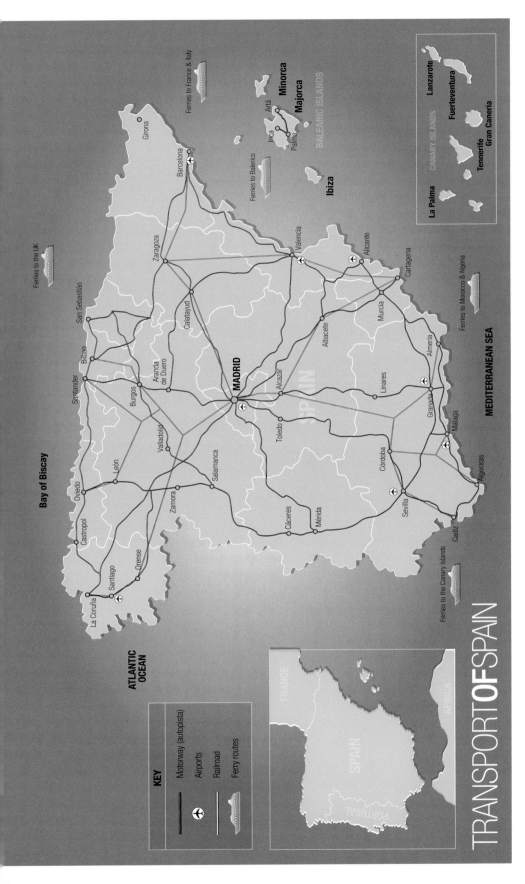

# TRANSPORT**OF**SPAIN

**KEY**

Motorway (autopista)

✈ Airports

Railroad

Ferry routes

ATLANTIC
OCEAN

Bay of Biscay

MEDITERRANEAN SEA

Ferries to the UK

Ferries to France & Italy

Ferries to Balerics

Ferries to Morocco & Algeria

Ferries to the Canary Islands

**BALEARIC ISLANDS**

**Minorca**

**Majorca**

**Ibiza**

Artá

Inca

Palma

**CANARY ISLANDS**

**Lanzarote**

**Fuerteventura**

Tennerife

**Gran Canaria**

**La Palma**

La Coruña

Santiago

Orense

Castropol

Oviedo

León

Zamora

Santander

Bilbao

San Sebastián

Girona

Barcelona

Zaragoza

Calatayud

Aranda
de Duero

Burgos

Valladolid

Salamanca

Cáceres

Mérida

**MADRID**

Toledo

Alcazar

Valencia

Alicante

Cartagena

Murcia

Albacete

Linares

Almería

Granada

Málaga

Córdoba

Sevilla

Algeciras

Cadiz

SPAIN

FRANCE

AFRICA

SPAIN

PORTUGAL

## Emergency services

| | |
|---|---|
| Fire service | **080** |
| Police | **091** |
| Ambulance | **061** |
| Civil Guard | **062** |
| Catalan Police | **088** |
| European emergency number | **112** |

## Hospitals

| | |
|---|---|
| Madrid: Hospital Clinico Universitario San Carlos | **91 330 3000** |
| Barcelona: Hospital General de la Vall d'Hebron | **93 274 6100** |
| Seville: Hospital Universitario Virgen del Rocio | **955 012 000** |

## Phone information

| | |
|---|---|
| Directory enquiries (international) | **025** |
| Directory enquiries (national) | **1003** |
| Operator | **1008** |
| International access Code | **0034** |
| Telephone fault line | **1002** |

## Travel

| | |
|---|---|
| Madrid Airport | **913 936 000** |
| Barcelona Airport | **902 404 704** |
| Seville Airport | **954 449 000** |

## Other information

| | |
|---|---|
| Weather report | **365** |

## Credit Card theft

| | |
|---|---|
| American Express | **917 437 000** |
| Master Card | **900 971 231** |

## Gas

| | |
|---|---|
| Gas Andalucia | **900 75 07 50** |
| Respol Gas | **901 100 100** |
| Respol faults | **901 121 212** |

## Embassies

| | |
|---|---|
| Australia | **91 353 6690** |
| Canada | **91 423 3250** |
| India | **91 309 88 83** |
| Ireland | **91 43 64 093** |
| New Zealand | **915 230 226** |
| South Africa | **91 43 63 780** |
| United Kingdom | **91 700 82 00** |
| United States | **91 587 22 00** |